Merthyr Tydfil

A Valley Community

Endpaper aerial views by kind permission of H. Tempest Ltd., St. Ives, Cornwall

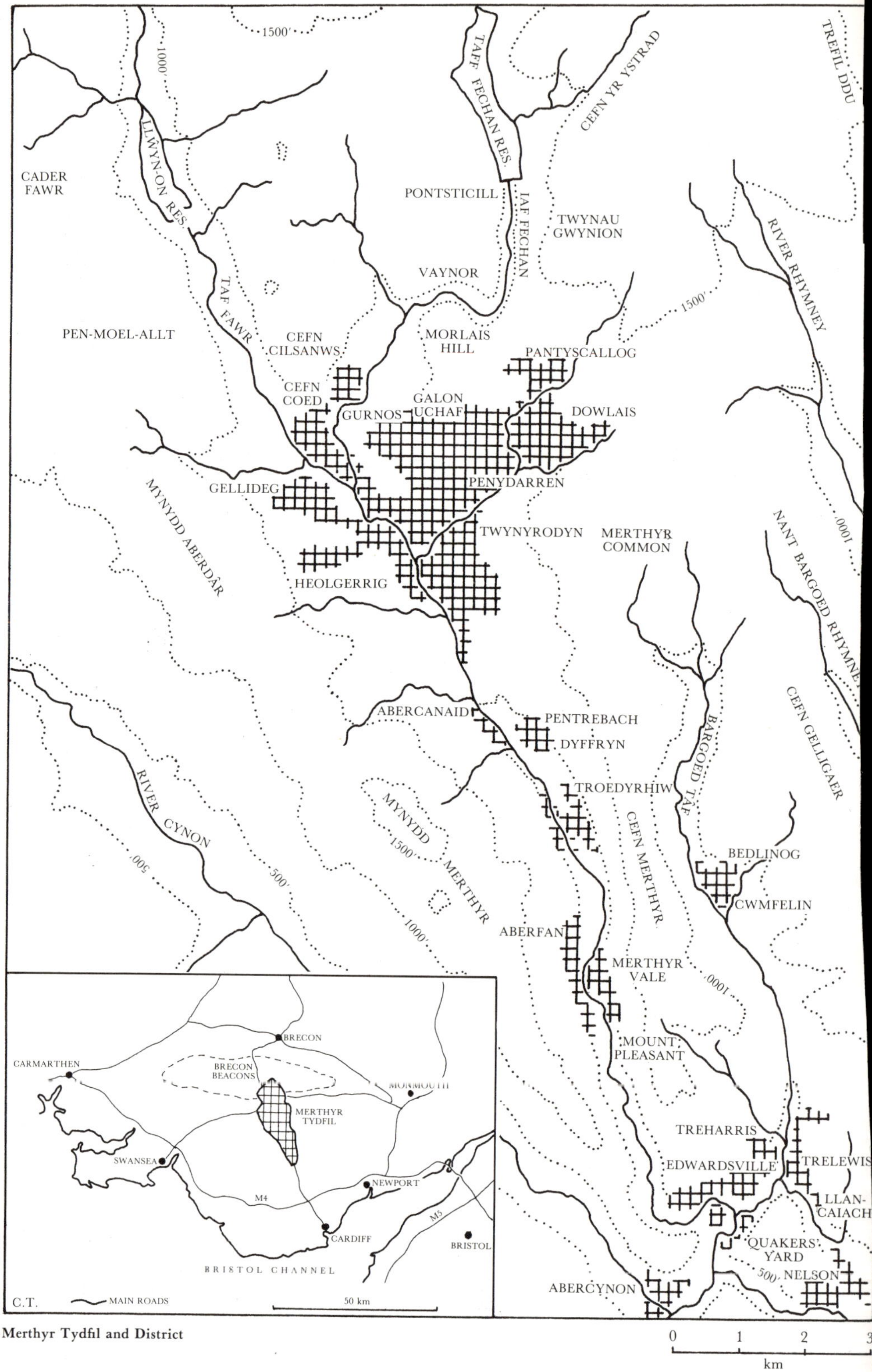

Merthyr Tydfil and District

0 1 2 3
km

Merthyr Tydfil

A Valley Community

Merthyr Teachers Centre Group

Published by The Merthyr Teachers Centre Group
in association with
D. Brown & Sons Limited Cowbridge

ISBN 0 905928 15 6

DESIGNED AND PRINTED IN WALES
by D. Brown & Sons Ltd., Bridgend, Mid Glamorgan

Contents

III. EARNING A LIVING

IV. SOCIAL AND CULTURAL HISTORY

V. APPENDIX

Foreword

This is the story of Merthyr Tydfil—the town of Tydfil the Martyr. In a few square miles of Welsh valley, possibly the most probed, prodded, mapped, mined and exploited acreage in the world, the breadth of human experience has run a course of wild variety. It is a story of defeat and victory, religion and riot, prosperity and black poverty; of ravages by plague and predator, and the creation of fine art and great invention; a valley that sent its children to all parts of the world, and accepted to itself the economic and political refugees of other towns and nations. St. Tydfil, surveying the history of the town to which she gave her name fifteen centuries ago, might claim like St. Paul that she, too, was a citizen of no mean city.

The last comprehensive history of Merthyr Tydfil was published by the Merthyr National Union of Teachers in 1932. Since then, while a number of pieces of individual research have shed further light on the locality, many features of the Borough, both geographical and social, which were commonplace forty-five years ago, have now themselves passed into history. Anyone today wishing to buy a complete book on the town's story would find it dauntingly difficult: the 1932 volume has long been out of print, and the copies that survive are the treasured possessions of their owners. For these reasons, and with a consciousness of the profound changes that have occurred in the Valley in the last fifty years, the need for a new book was recognised. It is the sincere wish of the authors that their work will be accepted as a worthy successor to the 1932 book, to which the present volume owes much, not least in inspiration. This complete exposition will be an invaluable and interesting volume for students, inhabitants (permanent and transitory), and anyone who asks the question 'Why Merthyr Tydfil?'

A feasibility study group was set up by the Merthyr Tydfil Teachers' Centre to discuss the updating of the 1932 book 'The Story of Merthyr Tydfil'. The group, having decided that the work was necessary and viable, was charged with carrying out the task. They invited main subject coordinators to form a Joint Editorial Board. The members were Jack Evans, Ron Gethin, Robert Evans, Clive Thomas, Fred Vaughan and Gareth

Hopkins. The Secretary, Bill Lawrence, and the District Education Officer Edwin Roberts together with the Chairman, Victor Jones, completed the group (which started work in mid 1975).

These section co-ordinators then invited specialists to contribute parts for each section. In this way they hoped to spread the work among teachers and other generous contributors. This presents a work of varied character, but the Editorial Board believe that the symposium approach will add to, not detract from, a volume of real value.

The Editorial Board wishes to record its gratitude to the contributing authors who so willingly gave of their scholarship, research, and many months of their spare time to a labour of love, and also to the members of the Merthyr Borough Council for their constant encouragement and support without which the project would not have been possible.

October 1981

Victor Jones
John O'Driscoll

The Physical Background

I

Introduction

by D. EMLYN EVANS, B.A.

Former Assistant Keeper of the Department of Geology, National Musuem of Wales, Cardiff

Most parts of the earth's surface have had a long and complicated history and the Merthyr area is no exception. On numerous times in the past it has been submerged beneath open seas and occasionally occupied either by estuarine lagoons, forest swamps, desert wastes or polar ice sheets. Each of these episodes has influenced profoundly, though indirectly, the activities of man in the locality. The occurrence of ironstone, limestone or coal, of good soil or bad soil and of high or low ground, are considerations closely connected with the geological past.

The story of this distant past, in Merthyr as elsewhere, is revealed by a study of the rocks which occur at or near the surface. The rocks in our area are of the sedimentary kind: most were formed from either gravel, sand or mud, and produced by the weathering of preexistent rocks; some were made up largely of decomposed vegetation and others as limy sea-floor deposits often incorporating scattered shells or sketetal remains of creatures that lived in ancient seas.

Such sedimentary deposits, after varying periods of time, have been converted into solid rocks. These, in turn, have been subjected to great pressures brought about by the movement of large continental land masses, sometimes towards and sometimes away from each other. In the former situation, sea-floor rocks between the continents have been compressed into giant folds which were often elevated above sea level to be subjected immediately to wear and tear, either by rain, running water or other agents of erosion. When continents moved away from each other, their peripheral areas tended to sag allowing for the formation of so-called 'shelf seas'.

Such a sequence of events is invariably recorded in the rocks of the locality. The eroded land surface excavated in the elevated rocks was probably

Era	*Age in millions of years*	*Periods of time or Systems of rocks*		*Some features and products of the periods with special reference to Wales*
QUATERNARY	$\frac{1}{100}$ - present	Recent or Holocene		Recent deposits of alluvium, peat, etc. Finishing touches to surface features and drainage.
	2 - $\frac{1}{100}$	Pleistocene		The so-called Ice Age during which our region experienced possibly more than one glaciation. Unconsolidated rock debris left by the melting ice.
CAINOZOIC or TERTIARY	7 - 2	*Pliocene*	*Neogene*	An era of prolonged but staggered uplift of land and the denudation of this emerging area by rivers and by the sea. Evidence of slight igneous activity in the Eocene of North Wales.
	26 - 7	*Miocene*		
	38 - 26	*Oligocene*	*Palaeogene*	
	54 - 38	*Eocene*		
	65 - 54	*Palaeocene*		
MESOZOIC or SECONDARY	136 - 65	*Cretaceous*		An age of partial submergence at least, beneath the chalk sea, but chalk only preserved on the bed of the Celtic Sea.
	195 - 136	*Jurassic*		A marine period possibly for the whole of Wales, but Lower Lias limestones and shales of Glamorgan were certainly deposited under marine conditions.
	225 - 195	*Triassic*		A desert period with salt lakes. Marls and sandstones deposited.

Era	*Age in millions of years*	*Periods of time or Systems of rocks*	*Some features and products of the periods with special reference to Wales*
PALAEOZOIC or PRIMARY	280 - 225	*Permian*	Largely a period of mountain building.
	345 - 280	Carboniferous	In the upper part a period of successive forest growths destroyed by continued subsidence giving rise to coal seams in the Coal Measures.
			In the middle an estuarine period in which the Millstone Grit was deposited.
			At the base a marine period in which the Carboniferous Limestone was deposited.
	395 - 345	Devonian	A period of uplift and denudation in North Wales and of deposition in South Wales of rocks collectively known as the Old Red Sandstone.
	440 - 395	*Silurian*	A marine period named after the ancient tribe of Silures. Rocks deposited include shales, sandstones, grits and limestones.
	500 - 440	*Ordovician*	A marine period named after the ancient tribe of Ordovices. Some of the rocks deposited provide evidence of vulcanicity in this period.
	570 - 500	*Cambrian*	A marine period so named because the rocks, which include shales, sandstones, and grits, were first studied in Wales.
EOZOIC or PRE-CAMBRIAN	4600 - 570	*Pre-Cambrian*	A series of periods over 4,000 million years in duration, characterised by frequent change from marine to land conditions.

* *Systems in italics not represented in rocks exposed at the surface in the Merthyr area.*

Fig. 1: The Stratigraphical Table

covered, after subsequent subsidence, either by sea-floor or land-based sediments and, if exposed at the present time, can be readily traced along the interface which separates the worn edges of the older rock layers from the usually differently inclined layers of the newer rocks. This feature is known as an unconformity. In areas of compression, the folded rocks have often failed to accommodate the pressures exerted and, accordingly have been broken along extensive fracture planes known as faults. Rocks under tension, in regions being slowly torn apart, are also traversed by similar fractures. Numerous examples of faults occur in our area where the dislocated rock layers are convincingly revealed.

In order to outline the geological history of an area it is usual to divide and subdivide geological time into major and minor divisions. The table (Fig 1) shows the general rock succession as it applies to the earth as a whole, representing in absolute terms a time of some 4,600 million years of earth history. The oldest rocks exposed at the surface in our area are those belonging to the Devonian System and collectively known as the Old Red Sandstone, so that for our purpose the story need only be traced from early Devonian times up to the present.

Comparatively recent investigations suggest that our area in Devonian times lay some twenty degrees south of the equator near the edge of a continent separated by a wide ocean from a neighbouring continent away to the south-east. The Merthyr area at that time was a small part of an extensive series of plains on which the Old Red Sandstone rocks were largely deposited either as gravels, sands or clays.

In mid Devonian times the area was uplifted and subjected to great erosion, with the result that no rocks belonging to the Middle Devonian period occur. The Upper Devonian period, however, saw a return to deposition of sands and gravels. At the end of the period both the continents mentioned above had moved nearer to the equator and to each other. The continental drift involved in the comparatively small South Wales area produced a subsidence which resulted in another flooding by a shallow sea in which great thicknesses of limestone and other calcareous rocks were formed. These are grouped together and are known as the Carboniferous Limestone series; the lowest of the three main divisions of the succeeding Carboniferous System.

Major earth movements persisted in our area as the movement of the continents continued. Elevation of land caused part of the Carboniferous Limestone to be raised above sea level and worn away. Renewed subsidence converted the South Wales area into an extensive coastal region in which the so-called Millstone Grit rocks were laid down, largely as river delta deposits or as coastal sands and muds.

As the earth movements continued, the muddy coastal conditions of Millstone Grit times were replaced by riverine to estuarine conditions in which the rocks of the Coal Measures series were deposited. Throughout Coal Measures times the oscillatory earth movements continued with

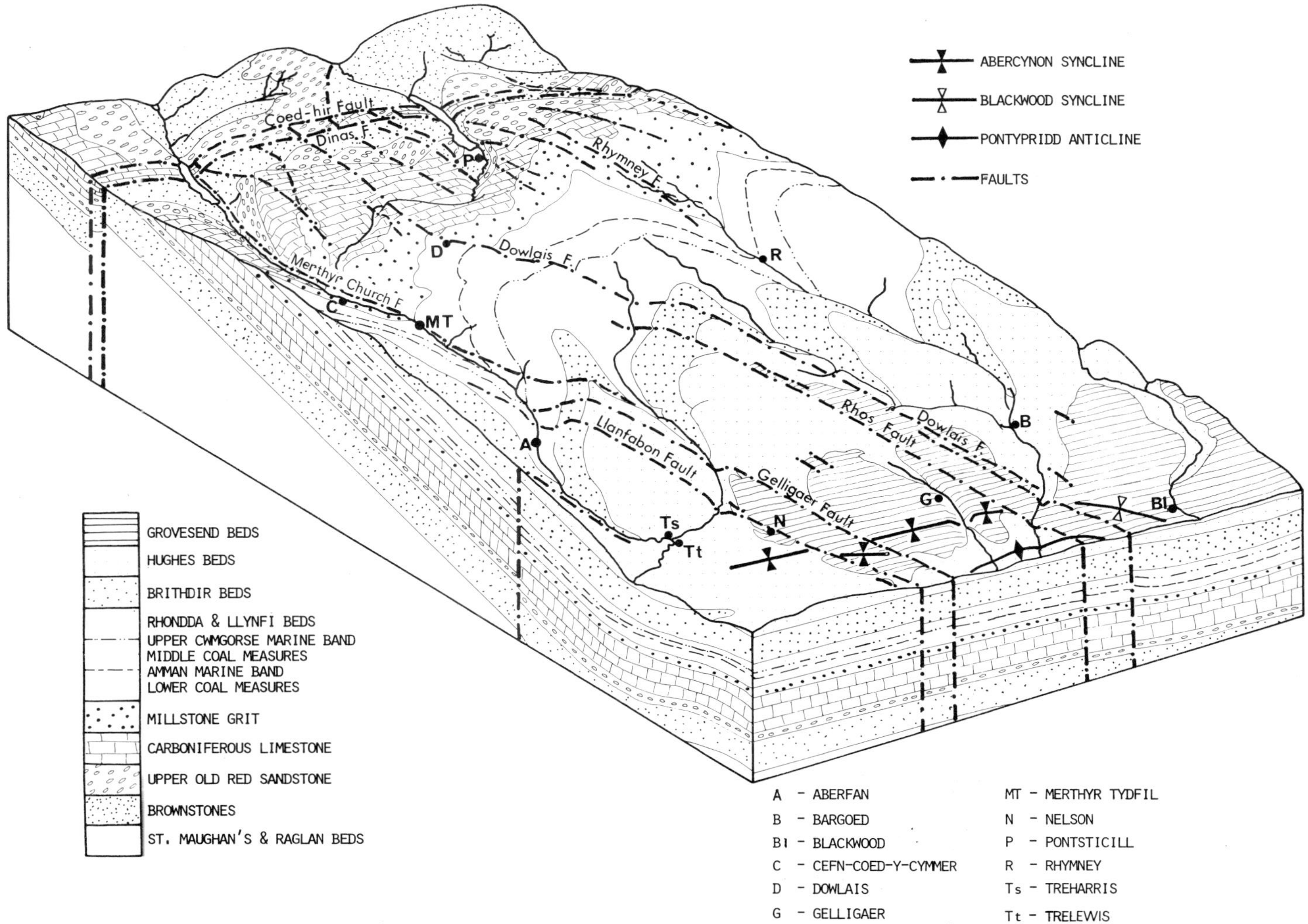

Fig. 2: A simplified block-diagram to illustrate the geology of the Merthyr area

System	*Series*	*Sub-Division*	*Character*	*Thickness*
WESTPHALIAN	COAL MEASURES	Successive Lower, Middle and Upper Coal Measures	Shales, Mudstones, Sandstones, Coal-Seams, Ironstones	3,900′ 1,190m
		Farewell Rock	Sandstones, Shales, Thin Coals	
		G. subcrenatum	Marine Band, Shales	
NAMURIAN	MILLSTONE GRIT	Shale Group	Variable Group of Shales, Mudstones, Thin Coals, Marine Goniatite Bands	150-200′ 46-61m
		Basal Grit	Quartzite and Conglomerate	120′ 37m
		~~ u/c ~~~~~~		
DINANTIAN	CARBONIFEROUS LIMESTONE	Llandyfan Limestone	Light Oolite Honeycomb Sandstone	40′ 12m
		Cil Yr Ychen Limestone	Dark Blue-Grey Limestones and Oolites	350′ 107m
		~~ u/c ~~~~~~		
		Llanelly Formation	Calcite Mudstone	30′ 9m
		~~ u/c ~~~~~~		
		Abercriban Oolite	Oolites, Dolomites and Calcite Mudstones	80′ 24m
		Lower Limestone Shales	Dark-Grey Shales and Thin Limestones, Dolomite	70′ 21m
DEVONIAN	OLD RED SANDSTONE — Upper	Grey Grits	Grey-Green Quartzitic Sandstone	100-250′ 30-76m
		~~ u/c ~~~~~~		
		Plateau Beds	Red Sandstones and Conglomerates	
		~~ u/c ~~~~~~		
	OLD RED SANDSTONE — Lower	Brownstones	Red and Brown Sandstones, Grits and Marls	1,300′ 396m

G = Gastrioceras, a Fossil Goniatite. u/c = Unconformity.

Fig. 3: The Geological Succession in the Merthyr Area
(*Not to Scale*)

increasing severity. At intervals the area was covered by extensive forests, each forest period being terminated by regional flooding usually by fresh water but occasionally by sea water as a result of local subsidence. The submerged and decaying forest vegetation gave rise to peat which, in turn, was buried by river-borne muds and sands, to be converted eventually into coal. This cyclic process was repeated about fifty times in South Wales, producing some fifty coal seams in one of the greatest periods of total land subsidence in the whole of our earth history.

At the end of Coal Measures times the two continents slowly collided and all the sediments in the shelf seas between were compressed to form the so-called Armorican mountains consisting of major folds — synclines and anticlines. It was at this time that the regional southward dip of the rocks of our area originated as part of the northern limb of the large downfolded structure of the South Wales coalfield. (Fig 2)

With this collision and ultimate welding of the continents, the distribution of air pressure and the related wind pattern changed, and the climate of our area during the succeeding Triassic period became desertic. It was under these conditions that the folded Carboniferous rocks were extensively eroded.

The Welsh area was eventually largely inundated by the Jurassic sea. It was during this period that the dominantly-limestone rocks of the Vale of Glamorgan coast and the Cotswold Hills were deposited. After minor earth movements came a major subsidence of parts of least of the Welsh area beneath the Cretaceous sea in which the well-known chalk was deposited.

The 180 million years which elapsed between the deposition of the lowest Jurassic rocks and the beginning of the Pleistocene period are not represented by any deposits in South Wales and so any attempt to reconstruct the geological history of this span of time must be largely speculative. It is usually assumed, however, that it was at the end of Cretaceous times, some 65 million years ago, that the Welsh area with its already consolidated, folded and faulted rocks, began to be slowly elevated thereby forming a land surface upon which the present cycle of erosion was originated. With the exception, within the last million years or so, of periods of extensive erosion by ice, the major agents of erosion moulding our landscape since Cretaceous times have been rain, running water and the sea.

The geological succession in the Merthyr area is summarised in Fig 3. The distribution of local geological measures is indicated in the block-diagram Fig 2, and in the maps Figs 4, 5, 6.

There is little relationship between the present river pattern in Wales and the distribution of the different groups of rock exposed at the surface. Furthermore, many of the older sections of our river valleys seem to indicate an original radial pattern centred on a land surface that once lay thousands of feet above Snowdon. The rivers of the eastern part of the South Wales coalfield, for example, flow towards the south-south-east and therefore directly across the structure of the region.

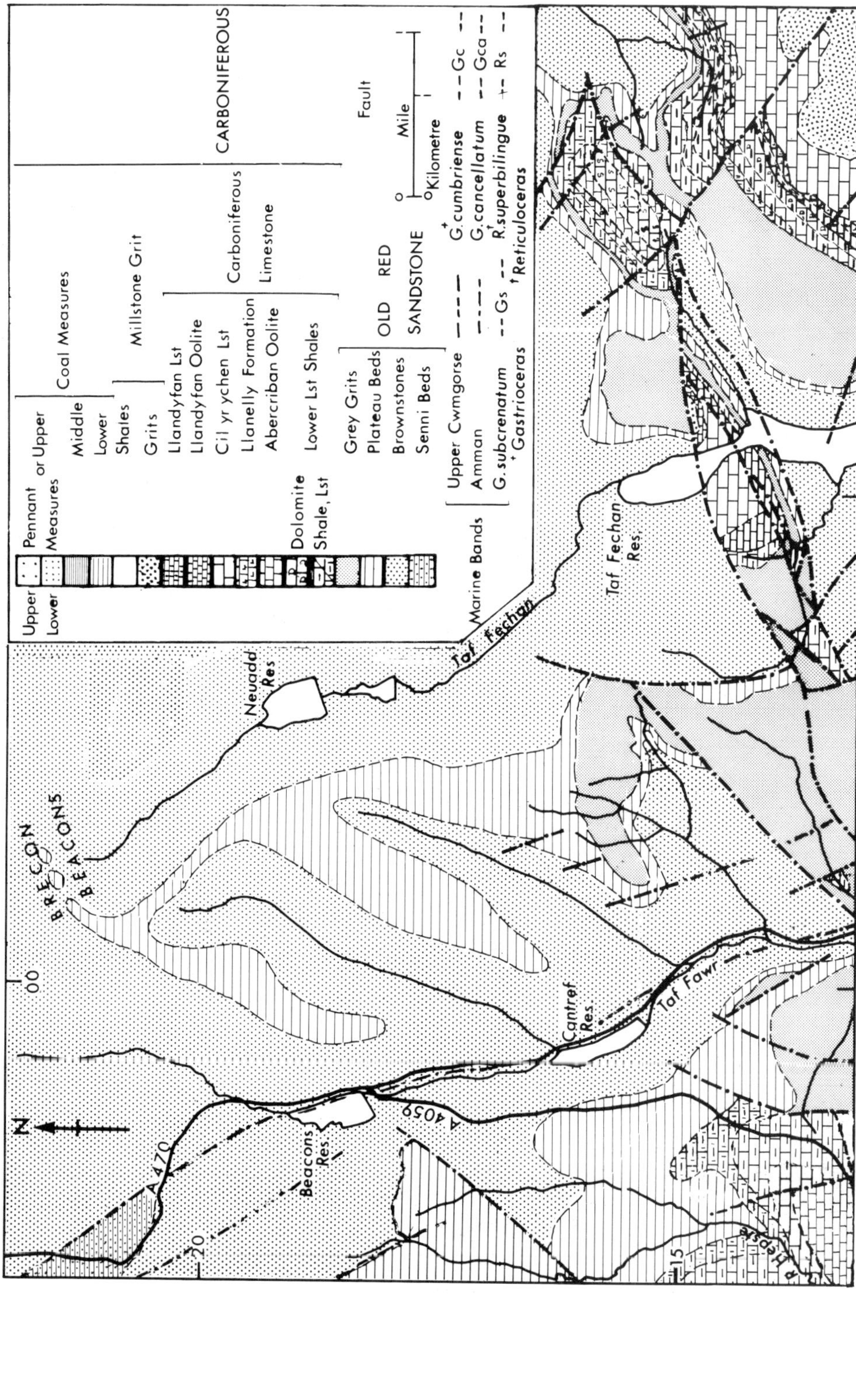

Fig. 4: Simplified Geology of the Merthyr District, Northern Section (Based on maps of the Institute of Geological Sciences)

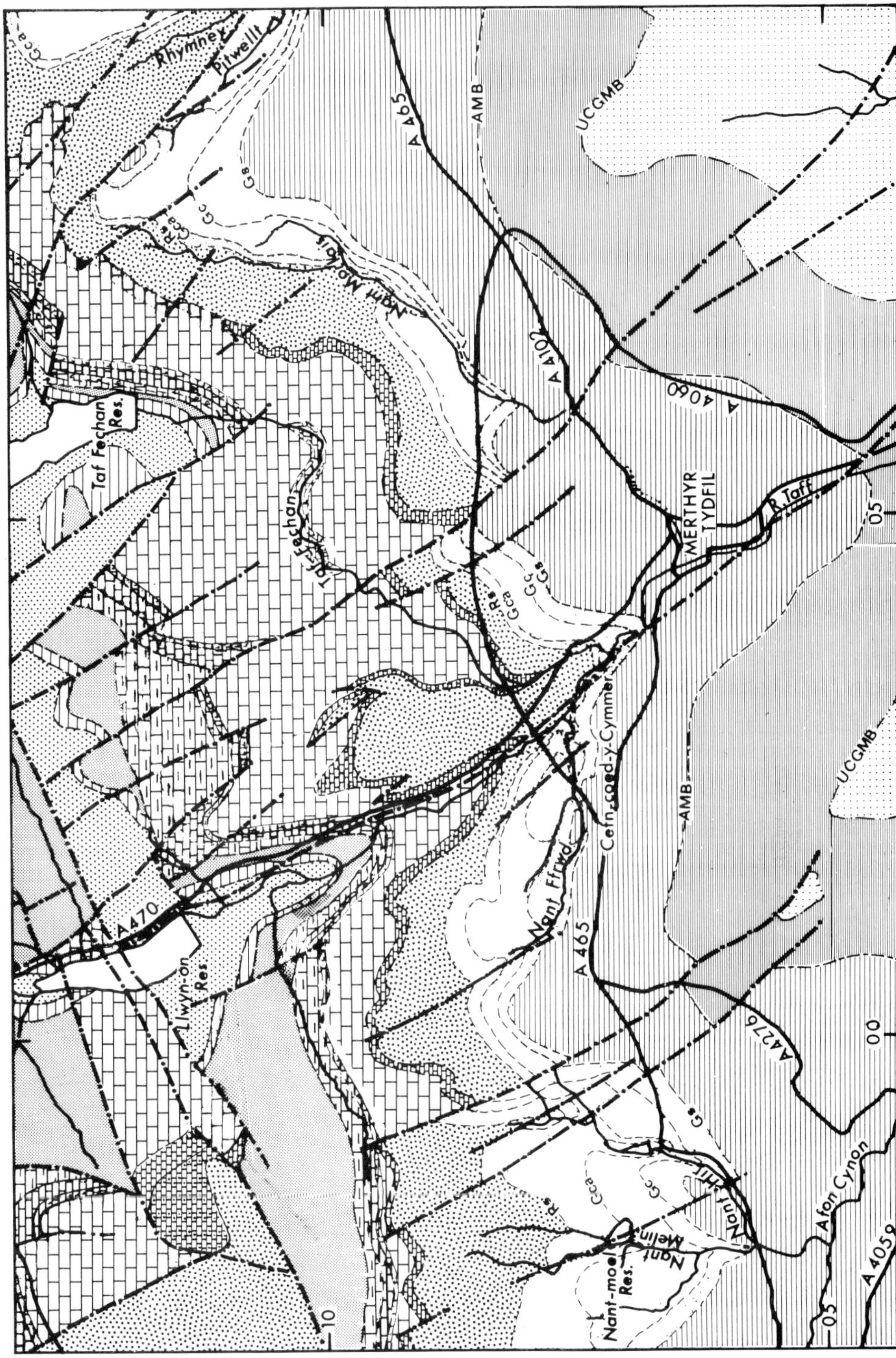

Fig. 5: Simplified Geology of the Merthyr District, Central Section
(Based on maps of the Institute of Geological Sciences)

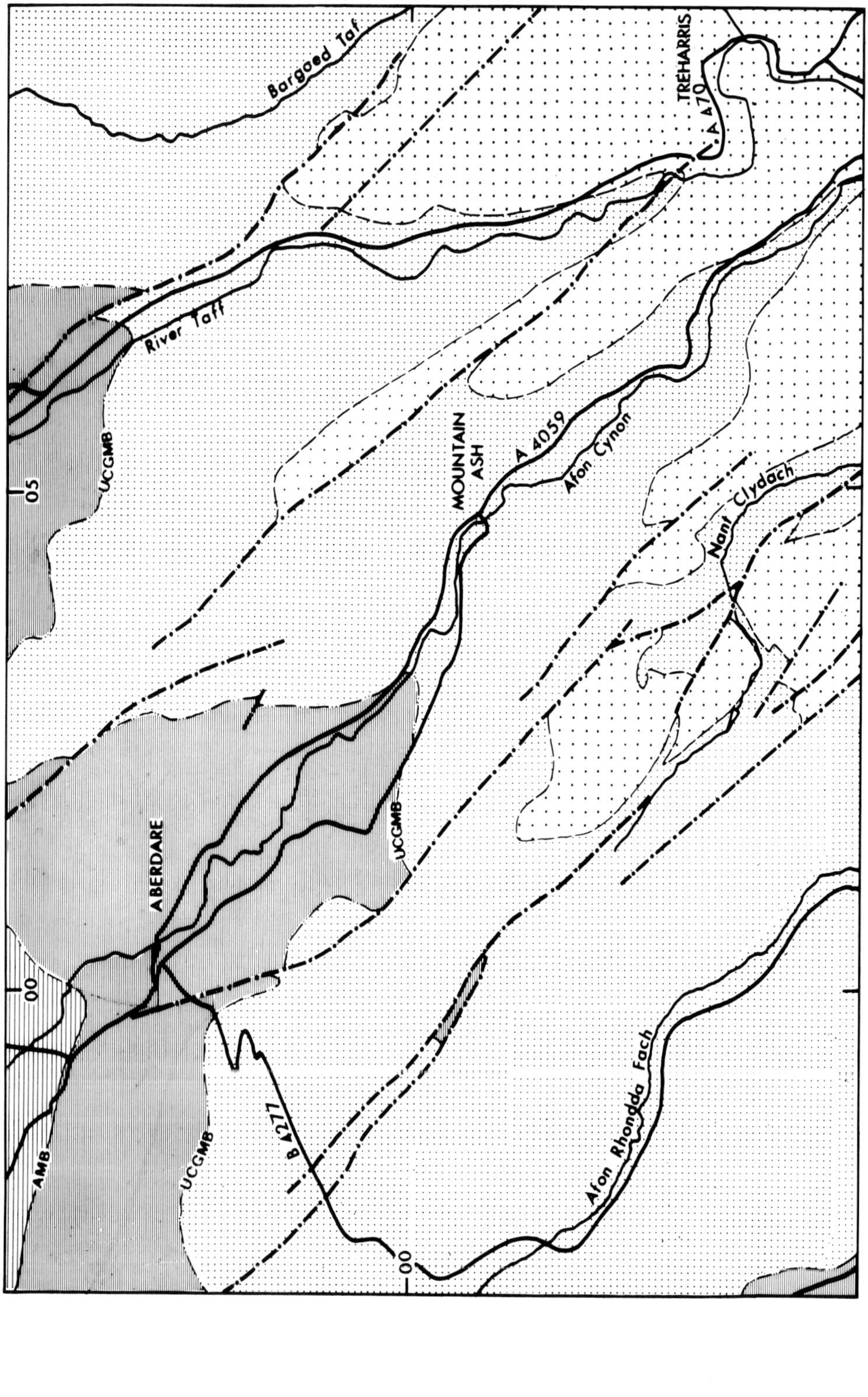

Fig. 6: Simplified Geology of the Merthyr District, Southern Section
(Based on maps of the Institute of Geological Sciences)

One of the earliest explanations offered to account for this discordance was that our land, having been submerged beneath the Cretaceous sea, had been covered by chalk or some contemporaneous deposit, and that during uplift and emergence of the area this rock cover, together with the differently aligned and folded rocks below, were warped and domed to produce a surface on which the radial drainage developed.

These rivers, it is claimed, were able to completely erode the newer covering and were eventually lowered, without any change of direction, on to the rocks beneath with their entirely different geological grain. The drainage system in this second stage of its evolution is described as having been superimposed on to the older rocks.

An alternative explanation is one which suggests that as the area of emerging land, probably in the area of Snowdonia, increased slowly with elevation, the courses of the radially disposed rivers were lengthened as they had to extend their lower reaches to flow into the continually receding sea. It is claimed, therefore, that is is not necessary to postulate the existence of a Cretaceous rock cover.

There is a third major feature of relief in Wales. It is generally accepted that there exist numerous plateau-like surfaces which extend across large areas of our hinterland. The highest and innermost, or 'High' plateau, varies in height from 1,700 to 1,900 ft. rising to 2,000 ft around the highest hills; the second, or 'Middle' plateau, from 1,200 to 1,600 ft.; and the 'Low' plateau ranging from 700 to 1,000 ft. A further series of at least four platforms occurs along the coast at heights of 600, 400, 300 and 200 ft.

These coastal platforms are generally interpreted as wave-cut benches formed when sea level, in relation to the land, was at the appropriately higher positions (Fig 24). In connection with the three highest eroded platforms, howeer, some authorities regard them as river-worn peneplains, but others prefer to think of them as sea-worn surfaces. Both schools of thought regard them as having been eroded at various periods of still-stand in a generally staggered uplift of the Welsh area in Tertiary times (Fig 1).

During this long period of uplift, regions of soft rock, together with areas that had been weakened by faulting or folding, were readily worn away by sea and/or river erosion. Some rivers flowing over such regions were able to deepen their valleys more quickly than others and were able accordingly to divert, into their own channels, sections of neighbouring rivers, (Fig 25). This process, known as 'river capture', has given rise, amongst other features, to the existence of old river valley sections which contain no streams; abrupt changes of river flow directions are also frequent relics of the same process. As time proceeded, the drainage pattern began to reflect more and more the geological grain of the underlying rock; this adaptation is well illustrated in our area and examples will be given in a later section.

Some two million years ago there commenced an alternating sequence of colder and warmer climates. This Pleistocene period, popularly known as the 'Ice Age', is now considered to have terminated about 10,000 years ago.

In Britain extensive glaciation occurred only in the Middle and Upper Pleistocene during which time there must have been major ice advances from the northern upland area down through the South Wales valleys including the Taf Fawr and Taf Fechan.

Towards the end of the Pleistocene period, climatic conditions were still sufficiently cold for the precipitation of appreciable winter snow. It was under these so-called periglacial conditions that many snow-formed cwms originated.

The end of the glacial episode saw the initiation of the present river drainage pattern. In general it followed the preglacial plan, with most areas, including Merthyr, showing little, if any, appreciable change.

The Old Red Sandstone

by RONALD T. GETHIN, B.A.

Former Head of the Geography and Geology Department, Merthyr County Grammar and Penydre High Schools

The Old Red Sandstone rocks of Devonian age may be identified readily by their prevalent red coloration. Soils developed on these rocks display the rich red tints so characteristic of the fields of southern Powys.

Towards the end of the Silurian period, about 400 million years ago, a great part of what is now Britain was affected by powerful earth-movements which resulted in the folding of mountain chains and the uplift of areas that had been accumulating marine sediments for all or most of 200 million years. This was the Caledonian orogeny, so-called because Scotland is the largest British area to show its effects.

In Wales, uplift brought into existence an upland area, which has been called 'St George's Land', extending from the English Midlands through mid-Wales and further westward into Ireland. To the south of this upland the sea covered much of present-day Devon and Cornwall. Between the upland and the Devon Sea the South Wales area became an extensive deltaic region built up with sediments washed down by rivers from the upland to the north, these sediments consolidating into the rocks of the Lower Old Sandstone.

Some time later renewed earth movement caused the uplift of the South Wales area, thus terminating sedimentation. During this period of uplift sediments were being laid down in other parts of Britain to become the rocks of the Middle Old Red Sandstone, and which are absent in South Wales.

A subsequent subsidence of the South Wales area resulted in renewed deposition of deltaic deposits, to form the rocks of the Upper Old Red Sandstone. The rocks of the Upper Old Red Sandstone are therefore separated from those of the Lower Old Red Sandstone by a discontinuity or unconformity.

By and large the rocks of the Lower and Upper Old Red Sandstone are conglomerates, sandstones, siltstones and mudstones, formed from the gravels, sands, silts and muds washed down by rivers to accumulate on flood-plains and deltas. These rocks are therefore of 'continental' origin, in contrast to the sediments which were laid down, contemporaneously, on the floor of the Devon sea further south. Nevertheless there were times when the Devon Sea spread into South Wales resulting in the deposition of marine beds similar to those of the same age in North Devon, thus enabling a correlation between the Devonian-age rocks of North Devon and those of South Wales.

It should be noted that 'Devonian' is a time-term indicating a period in geological history. The Devonian rocks of the Devon-Cornwall area are styled 'Marine Devonian'. Those of the South Wales area are termed 'Continental Devonian', or, more usually, 'Old Red Sandstone'.

The Lower Old Red Sandstone

The Lower Old Red Sandstone has been subdivided into three divisions, which are, in order of age, the Downton, Ditton and Brecon Series. Only the Breconian appears in our local area, and this, in turn, is subdivided into the older Senni Beds and the younger Brownstones.

The *Senni Beds* are about 1000 ft (305m) thick, and form the surface at the foot of the north-facing escarpment of the Beacons. The dominant beds are green, fine-grained sandstones. Mica flakes are frequently present on bedding planes, and predispose the rocks to split readily into flat sheets or 'flags' which have long been used for roofing and paving. There are also green conglomerates including the lime-rich 'cornstones', which were probably the evaporation-products of drying lakes. Siltstones, mudstones (often referred to as marls) and shales also occur, and suncracks in these finer-grained rocks provide further evidence of desiccation-periods. Not all beds are green, some being dull-red. The green colour has been ascribed by some writers to the reduction or solution of the ferric oxide, which gives colour to the red beds, by some organic agency deriving from a vegetative cover,[1, 2] but Robertson[3] refers to the presence of the dark-green mineral chlorite in the green rocks.

The Senni Beds contain the first evidence of plant life in the South Wales area. A notable locality is the old roadside quarry on the west side of the A470(T) three-quarters of a mile north-west of the Storey Arms outdoor centre, very near the RAC telephone box at SN 971 208. The first investigation was by F. and N. Gossling, and the site was subsequently described by A. Heard.[4] The most prolific band is a green, fissile siltstone, a few inches thick, which outcrops on the front part of a prominent ledge at the rear of the quarry, and yields stems of Gosslingia breconensis. Other plant fossils found in the quarry include Nematothallus, Protaxites, Zosterophyllum, Dawsonites and Pachytheca.[2]

The Brownstones. This was the name given to the formation by the Rev. W.S. Symonds.[5] The Brownstones are more than 1,300 ft (396 m) thick in the Beacons, where they form the magnificent north-facing escarpments overlooking the Usk valley. Rock-types resemble those of the Senni Beds, except that red, brown and purple colours predominate due to the presence of hematite. The Brownstones rest conformably on the Senni Beds without any sign of a break in deposition. Many of the sandstones are fine to medium grained. Some are thin-bedded or 'flaggy' and have been used for roofing and paving. The interbedded siltstones, mudstones and shales are also red, and sometimes merge into lime-rich 'cornstones', which, with suncracks in some of the finer-grained rocks, afford evidence of desiccation-cycles. Fossils are practically non-existent, evidence of plants being no more than oxidised indefinite impressions.

The alternation of harder sandstones with softer beds often gives rise to small waterfalls, examples occurring along the road A470(T) between the Storey Arms and the quarry in the Senni Beds at SN 971 208.

The Upper Old Red Sandstone

The Upper Red Sandstone belongs to the Farlow Series of the Old Red Sandstone, Farlow being a village in the Clee Hills area of Shropshire (Salop). The two local formations of the Upper Old Red Sandstone are the Plateau Beds and the Grey Grits. Robertson[3] in 1932 included the Plateau Beds at the top of the Brownstones in the Lower Old Red Sandstone, but he also stated that an impersistent quartz-conglomerate at the base of the Plateau Beds might represent an unconformity separating them from the Brownstones, since a conglomerate is sometimes evidence of a stratigraphical break or unconformity. Robertson[3] also tentatively included the Grey Grits in the Lower Old Red Sandstone but stated that there was a case for including the Grey Grits in the Carboniferous, on the evidence of a cessation of red coloration and the absence of a break in deposition between the top of the Grits and the bottom of the succeeding Carboniferous Limestone, eg. at Abercriban Quarry SO 063 127 (Plate 1).

At a subsequent date an angular unconformity between the Plateau Beds and the underlying Brownstones was observed by Dr Gwyn Thomas of Imperial College on an inaccessible east-facing rock-wall extending for 2 miles (3.2 Km) from Fan Hir SN 833 198 to Fan Foel SN 822 225 in the Black Mountain. In the Beacons area this unconformity is not apparent.

In addition, the occurrence of the brachiopod Cyrtospirifer verneuli in the Plateau Beds of the upper Tawe Valley, and the fish Holoptychius and Bothriolepis at other Plateau Bed locations in South Wales, establish the Upper Old Red Sandstone age of the Plateau Beds. There is therefore a marked gap between the Plateau Beds and the Brownstones, this gap corresponding with the period of Middle Old Red Sandstone deposition in other parts of Britain.

Plate 1: ABERCRIBAN QUARRY, PONTSTICILL, SO 063 127
Quarry face in Grey Grit of the Old Red Sandstone. Darker outcrop of Carboniferous Limestone Lower Limestone Shales above

The stratigraphic relationship between the Plateau Beds and the Grey Grits has also been controversial. In some exposures Grey Grits are observed overlying Plateau Beds, but in others the Grits are seen to rest directly on Brownstones, and both formations have been seen to pass upwards into Carboniferous Limestone. Hall, Taylor and Thomas[6] of the Geological Survey have suggested that either the Plateau Beds and Grey Grits were deposited contemporaneously as different 'facies' or rock types, with a later phase of Grey Grit deposition covering both, or that there was uplift and denudation of the Plateau Beds prior to the deposition of the Grits. J.R.L. Allen[7, 8] of Reading University makes a strong case for a substantial time-gap between the two formations, his arguments being based on the different colours of the two formations, and on the fact that the Plateau Beds possess several marine horizons, whereas the Grey Grits are largely river-borne deposits of continental origin. Recent discovery of marine fossils in the Grey Grits is referred to later. Like other writers, he points out there is no angular unconformity between the Plateau Beds and Grey Grits, any contact-zone showing no noticeable difference in the dips of the beds of the two formations.

The Plateau Beds are so-named because they form the table-top summits of the Brecon Beacons. They have a total thickness of only 20-80 ft (6-24.4m).

Generally speaking they possess bright red colours, and are tough, gritty sandstones, with occasional quartz pebbles. Towards the base are the impersistent conglomerates that inspired Robertson to suggest a possible unconformity between the Plateau Beds and the Brownstones below.

There are some exposures along the tributaries of the Taf Fawr and Taf Fechan, where Plateau Beds may be distinguished from the overlying Grey Grits by the typical grey-green of the Grits, and from the Brownstones below by the contrast between the interbedded purple sandstones and mudstones of the Brownstones and the redder coloration and more massive appearance of the Plateau Beds, which in some localities display pebbly bands towards the base.

In the Taf Fawr valley they attain a thickness of 15 ft (4.6 m) in Nant Llysiog SO 0246 1541, the base marked by a mudstone with grit granules. In Garw Nant Fawr, SO 0019 1306, they reach a thickness of 50 ft (15.2 m) with a purple tinge. South of the Llywn On reservoir the Plateau Beds are not represented, the Grey Grits resting directly on the Brownstones.

In the Taf Fechan valley the Plateau Beds are exposed in a gorge below a waterfall on Nant Car Fach at SO 0450 1389. The lowest visible unit is a massive purple sandstone 13 ft (4 m) thick, succeeded by purple-grey mudstone, purple-grey quartzitic sandstone and purple siltstone to a total thickness of 28 ft (8.5 m). The lip of the waterfall is in Grey Grit. On the eastern side of the Pontsticill reservoir, along Cwm Criban SO 065 129, some 50 ft (15.2) of Brownstones, with their purple siltstones and purple, cross-bedded micaceous sandstones, are overlain by 32 ft (9.8 m) of Plateau Beds which are mainly red sandstones and siltstones. In turn the Plateau Beds are followed by 30 ft (9.1 m) of grey-green Grey Grits.

On the High Plateau of the Beacons the Plateau Beds may be seen at an outcrop near the source of the Caerfanell at SO 0505 1920. The total thickness is about 20 ft (6.1 m), the base being a red siltstone with quartz granules, overlain by a quartz conglomerate containing fish-fragments, this horizon being 10-15 ft (3-4.6 m) above the base of the exposure.

The Grey Grits cover a large area locally. To the east of the Taf Fechan they form the surface of Pen y Gaer and Waun Rydd. Between the Taf Fechan and Taf Fawr they occupy much of Waun Llysiog, Cefn Car and Garn Ddu. West of the Taf Fawr they form the lower slopes leading up to the limestone of Cader Fawr SN 977 122, and also the ridge to the south of Cwm Cadlan and west-south-west of Pentwyn Isaf SO 009 107.

The predominant beds are grey, yellow, greenish-grey and olive-coloured, fine to medium-grained quartzitic sandstones. These colours are in contrast with the reds and purples of the Plateau Beds and Brownstones. The Grits have a thickness up to 200 ft (61 m) in places, but are usually much thinner.

An excellent exposure is the Abercriban Grit Quarry, SO 063 127 (Plate 1), which provided the stone for the dam of Pontsticill reservoir. The location shows the junction between the Grits and the overlying Carboniferous Limestone, there being no trace of any unconformity between the two formations. Below the 12 ft (3.7 m) of limestone is a band of pebbly quartz-conglomerate 4 ft (1.2 m) thick at the north end, and 1½ ft (0.46 m) at the south end. Below the conglomerate is an olive-coloured shale-band which tapers from 3 ft (0.91 m) at the north end to nothing at the south end. Below

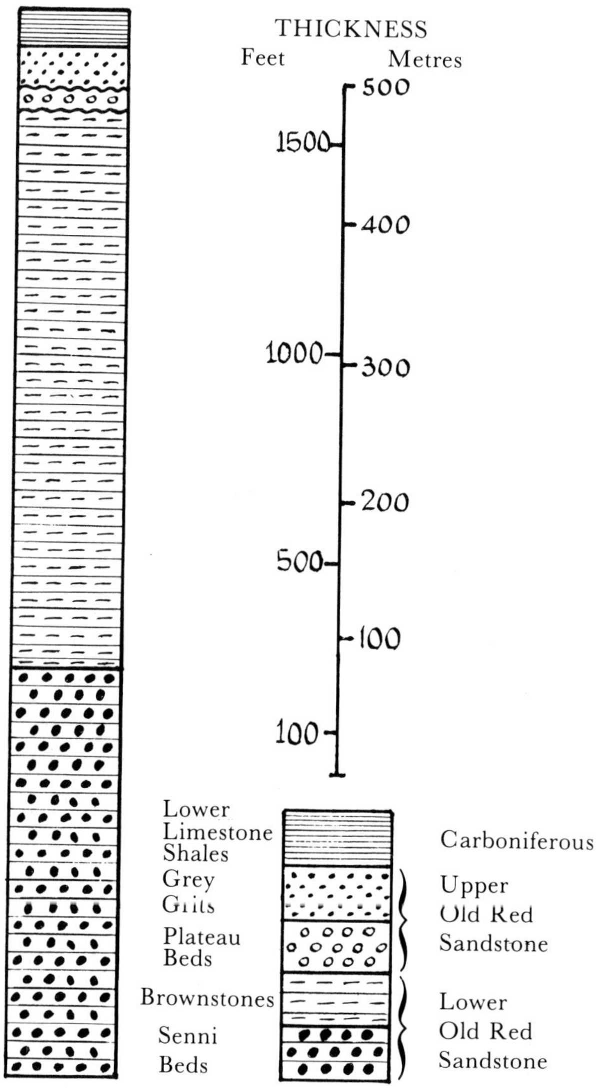

Fig. 7 The Old Red Sandstone Succession in the Brecon Beacons (From 'British Regional Geology, South Wales'. H.M.S.O.)

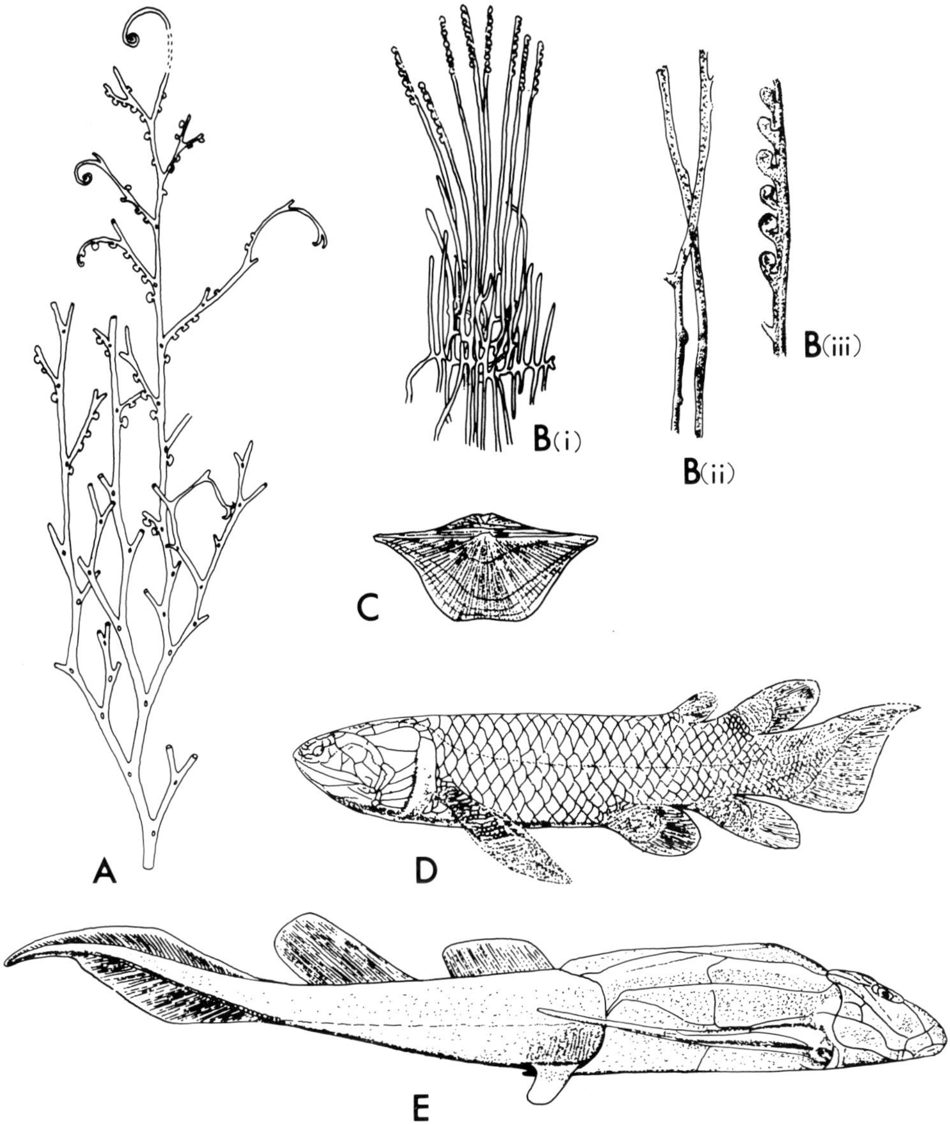

Fig. 8 A Section of Old Red Sandstone Fossils

A. Reconstruction of the aerial parts of the plant *Gosslingia breconensis* Heard, from the Senni Beds of the Lower Old Red Sandstone (× ½); B(i). Reconstruction of the aerial parts of the plant *Zosterophyllum* (× 1/6); B(ii) axes (× ⅔) and B(iii) (× ⅔) sporangia of *Zosterophyllum llanoveranum* Croft & Lang from the Senni Beds; C. The brachiopod *Cyrtospirifer verneuili* (Murchison) (× ⅔) from the Upper Plateau Beds of the Upper Old Red Sandstone; D. Reconstruction of the fish *Holoptychius* from the Plateau Beds (× 1/6); E. Reconstruction of the fish *Bothriolepis* from the Plateau Beds (× ⅓).

the shale are 35 ft (10.7 m) of olive-coloured, hard, quartzitic sandstone, showing feather-fracture.[9] The beds have a slight northerly dip, this deviation from the regional southerly dip of 5°-7° being probably associated with the nearby Neath Disturbance. Thin sandstones bordering an old tramroad on the floor of the quarry show good examples of mud-cracks. Red siltstones on the floor of the southern end of the quarry have yielded fish fragments, the siltstones probably being members of the Plateau Beds.

At Garw Nant Fawr SO 0019 1306 Grey Grits rest on Plateau Beds (referred to earlier). The base of the Grits is a white quartzite 2 ft (0.6 m) thick, succeeded by 5 ft (1.5 m) of mottled plant-bearing mudstone, 7-10 ft (2.1-3.0 m) of cross-bedded sandstone, a thin red-brown mudstone with lingulid brachiopods, and 55 ft (16.8 m) of greyish-green sandstone.

In the Taf Fechan valley Grey Grits are exposed in Nant Car Fach, above Plateau Beds in the water-fall, referred to earlier, at SO 0450 1389. Grey Grits form the lip of the fall. Plant fragments occur in a mudstone immediately below a 2 in (0.05 m) band of green-grey sandstone. This is followed upwards by a greenish-grey, hard, quartzitic sandstone with interbedded purple mudstones containing rootlets. Fish fragments, including Bothriolepis, have been found in a conglomerate 2 ft (0.6 m) above the base of the sandstone. On the eastern side of the Taf Fechan valley in Cwm Criban 30 ft (9.1 m) of Grey Grits lie above red Plateau Beds at the location referred to earlier, SO 065 129. A conglomerate at the base of the grits has yielded brachiopods and fish-fragments.

The finding of brachiopods in the Grey Grits is evidence of marine deposition. Robertson, as far back as 1932, hinted that the Grits might be placed in the Carboniferous on the grounds of an unbroken passage upwards into the Carboniferous, as shown at Abercriban quarry, the cessation of red coloration and the resemblance of Grey Grit conglomerates to those found at the base of the Millstone Grit. The presence of brachiopods gives further support to considering the Grey Grits as the sandy base of the Carboniferous.

In this description of the Old Red Sandstone greater attention has been given to the Upper Old Red Sandstone because of its relative nearness to the Merthyr area. Much of the recent information on the Upper Old Red Sandstone is the work of the Geological Survey geologists Hall, Taylor and Thomas.[6]

The Old Red Sandstone geological succession in the Brecon Beacons is summarised in Fig 7, and a selection of Old Red Sandstone fossils is shown in Fig 8.

References

1 J. Pringle and T.N. George., *British Regional Geology. South Wales. Second edition (1948).*

2 Summer 1964. Field Meetings in South Wales. *Proceedings of the Geological Association,* Vol 76, Part 4 (1965).

[3] T. Robertson., *The Geology of the South Wales Coalfield,* Part V, the Country Around Merthyr Tydfil. Second edition (1932).
[4] *Quarterly Journal of the Geological Society,* Vol 83 (1927).
[5] *Records of the Rocks,* 1872.
[6] I.H.S. Hall, K. Taylor and L.P. Thomas., *Stratigraphy of the Upper Old Red Sandstone in South Breconshire,* in *Bulletin of the Geological Survey of Great Britain* No 44, (1973).
[7] J.R.L. Allen., The Pre-Pickwell Down Age of the Plateau Beds in South Wales in *Nature,* Vol 204, No 4956. 24 October (1964).
[8] J.R.L. Allen., The Devonian Rocks of Wales and the Welsh Borderline in *The Upper Palaeozoic and Post Palaeozoic rocks of Wales* edited by T.R. Owen (1974).
[9] J.C. Roberts., Feather-Fracture and Mechanics of Rock-Jointing in *American Journal of Science,* Vol 2599 (1961).

The Carboniferous System

In view of its economic significance the Carboniferous System must be regarded as one of the most important of all the geological systems. It is so-called because of the occurrence of carbon, in the form of coal, in the rocks of this system. Within the system it has become traditional to recognise three lithological or rock-type, units, which are, in order of age, the Carboniferous Limestone, the Millstone Grit and the Coal Measures.

In Britain the rocks of the Carboniferous Limestone are mainly of marine origin, those of the Millstone Grit are essentially deltaic deposits, and the Coal Measures were formed in low-lying, swampy lagoons. These lithological units are by no means constant in their lithology or rock-type. Thus at the same time that Carboniferous limestones were being laid down in warm seas which covered much of Britain, shales and coals were being formed in marsh-lagoon environments in North-East England and Central Scotland. Consequently it has become necessary to sub-divide the Carboniferous System into time-divisions based on fossil content. The major time-divisions are, youngest first:

Upper Carboniferous:	Westphalian, corresponding roughly with the Coal Measures.
	Namurian, corresponding roughly with the Millstone Grit.
Lower Carboniferous:	Dinantian, corresponding roughly with the Carboniferous Limestone.

Geological Survey 1979	*Lithology*	*Vaughan Zones*	*Geological Society 1976*	
			Formation	*Stage*
Llandyfan Limestone	Light Oolites Honeycomb Sandstone	D_1	Penderyn Oolite	Asbian
Cil Yr Ychen Limestone	Light Grey Pisolites Dark Grey Oolites Sandy Base in Places	S_2	Dowlais Limestone	Holkerian
~ ~ ~ ~	~ ~ ~ ~ ~ ~	~ u/c ~	~ ~ ~ ~ ~ ~	~ ~ ~ ~
Llanelly Formation	Calcite Mudstones. Algal Limestones.	S_1	Llanelly Formation	
	~ ~ ~ ~ ~ ~	~ u/c ~	~ ~ ~ ~ ~ ~	Chadian ~
Abercriban Oolite	Oolites Dolomites	Z	Gilwern Oolite Clydach Beds	
			Blaen Onnen Oolite Pwll y Cwm Oolite	Courceyan
Lower Limestone Shales	Shales and Thin Limestones, Dolomite.	K	Lower Limestone Shales	

Fig. 9: Correlation of the Classifications Relating to the Local Carboniferous Limestones
(Not to vertical scale)

(a) The Carboniferous Limestone or Dinantian Series

by RONALD T. GETHIN

The local rocks of this series are the familiar grey limestones of the Cefn Cilsanws, Pontsarn, Morlais Castle, Pontsticill and Twynau Gwynion areas, where there are large exposures resulting from quarrying (Plate 2).

The term Dinantian derives from Dinant in Belgium, where these rocks have been studied. The term Avonian has also been applied to the Lower Carboniferous, these rocks having been studied by Vaughan in the Avon Gorge,[1] but the lowest limit of Vaughan's Avonian does not coincide with the lowest limit of the Dinantian as adopted at the Carboniferous Conference at Heerlen, Holland, in 1935. In its Special Report Number Seven of 1976[2] the Geological Society of London recommends that the term Avonian should be abandoned as a time division. It is important to realise that the term Dinantian relates to a time-division, whereas the more familiar term Carboniferous Limestone relates to lithology or rock-type.

In contrast with the rocks of the Old Red Sandstone, which, in our area, were largely of continental origin, the Carboniferous Limestones were laid down in seas which covered much of what is now Britain, the marine

Plate 2: TWYNAU GWYNION LIMESTONE QUARRIES
Mainly Cil yr Ychen or Dowlais Limestone

invasion of what is now South Wales having commenced in the Upper Devonian period. The limestones vary according to age and location, but there is a general absence of constituents other than calcium carbonate, suggesting that the rocks were formed in a sea lapping a lowland land-area, over which rivers flowed so slowly that little sediment was carried far into the sea. Another possibility is that the bordering land-area was a desert, with few or no rivers to carry sediment. The sea was warm, as indicated by the nature of the preserved fossils, notably the corals. Some of the calcium carbonate was precipitated chemically, this being another indication of a warm sea, but there was also a considerable contribution of fragments of lime-rich skeletons of plants and animals. There is therefore a wealth of fossil-content, the shallow, warm sea being a favourable environment for marine life. Brachiopods are numerous and so are corals, and there are also crinoids, gastropods, lamellibranchs and bryozoans. Examples of representative fossils are shown in Figure 10. Further details of fossil content may be obtained from a Palaeontology book.[3] The limestones show local variations, and these will be described, but a limestone may be distinguished from all other rock-types by the fact that it effervesces on the application of cold, dilute hydrochloric acid.

Divisons of the Dinantian

The study of the Carboniferous Limestone has become complicated by the existence of four classifications with their attendant variety of nomenclature.

In South Wales the original sub-division of the Carboniferous Limestone was based on lithology, i.e. on consideration of obvious rock-characters based on composition and texture. The oldest and lowest formation is the Lower Limestone Shales, consisting of shales with sandy or muddy limestones. This is succeeded by the Main Limestones with massive beds of limestone and little else. The youngest and uppermost formation is the Upper Limestone Shales, with muddy limestones and shales, but this formation is not represented in our area, Millstone Grit deposition having commenced on the north crop of the South Wales basin while the Upper Limestone Shales were being laid down in southern areas.

These lithological divisions are still referred to by geologists but were supplanted by a sub-division into time-units called zones, each zone being characterised by a typical fossil-assemblage. The zonal scheme was devised by Vaughan following his work in the Avon Gorge in 1905.[2] Each zone is named after one fossil, the so-called 'zone-fossil', but in the field a zone is recognised by its overall fossil-content, the zone-fossil even being absent in some locations. It has become customary to use the initials of the zone-fossils to designate the zone. In order of age Vaughan's zones were K, Z, C, S, D. K stands for Cleistopora, a coral; Z stands for Zaphrentis, a coral; C stands for Caninia, a coral; S stands for Seminula, a brachiopod; D stands for Dibunophyllum, a coral. With the exception of Dibunophyllum these zone-fossils have been re-named.

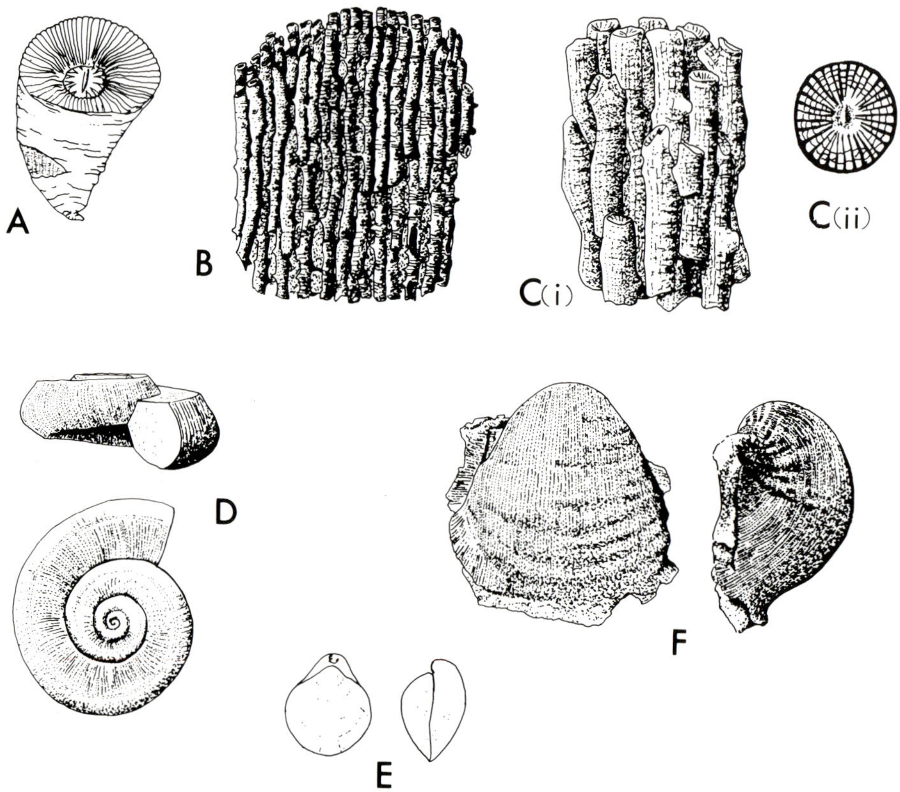

Fig. 10 A Selection of Carboniferous Limestone Fossils

A. The coral *Dibunophyllum bipartitum* (McCoy) (× ⅚); B. The coral *Syringopora geniculata* Phillips (× ⅔); C(i). The coral *Lithostrotion martini* Edwards & Haime (× ⅔); C(ii). A transverse section of a single corallite (× 2⅔); D. The gastropod *Straparollus* [*Euomphalus*] *pentagonalis* (J. Sowerby) (× ⅔); E. The brachiopod *Composita* [*Seminula*] *ficoidea* (Vaughan) (× ⅔); F. The brachiopod *Linoprotonia* [*Productus*] *corrugatus* (McCoy) (× ½); G. The coral *Hapsiphyllum* [*Zaphrentis*] *konincki*

At a later date the scheme was revised into K, Z, C_1 (Lower Caninia), C_2 S_1 (Upper Caninia), S_2 (Seminula) and D. The K zone is equivalent to the Lower Limestone Shales. The Z, C_1, C_2 S_1, and S_2 zones and the D_1 and D_2 sub-zones correspond to the Main Limestones. The D_3 sub-zone is equivalent to the Upper Limestone Shales. The zones represented in our local area are K, Z, S_1 (the upper part of C_2 S_1), S_2, D_1 and D_2. Absent are C_1 (Lower Caninia) and D_3 (the Upper Limestone Shales).

In 1976 a new classification, applicable to the British Isles, was recommended by the Geological Society of London in its Special Report Number 7. The report referred to the chaotic state into which the use of

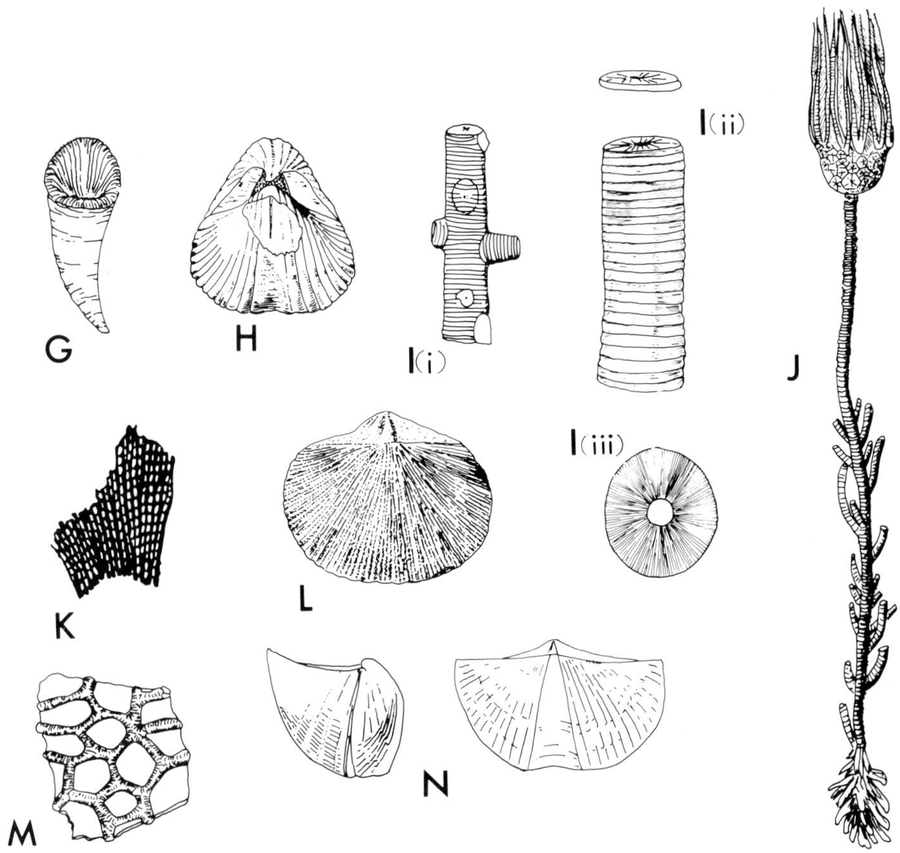

(Edwards & Haime) (× ⅔); H. The brachiopod *Davidsonina* [*Cyrtina*] *carbonaria* (McCoy) (× ⅔); I(i-iii). Some of the various forms of crinoid columnals or ossicles from the Carboniferous Limestone (× ⅔); J. Reconstruction of a complete crinoid *Actinocrinus* (× 2/9); K. The bryozoan *Fenestella plebeia* McCoy (× 1⅓); L. The brachiopod *Schellwienella crenistria* (Phillips) (× ⅔); M. The coral *Vaughania* [*Cleistopora*] *vetus* Smyth (× 5/6); N. The brachiopod *Syringothyris cuspidata* (J. Sowerby) mut. *cyrtorhyncha* North (× ⅔).

Vaughan's zonal scheme had fallen. In addition to the many redefinitions of zonal boundaries there were examples of inconsistent usages, especially between northern and southern Britain. For these reasons, and in view of recently-founded microfossil divisions, the Geological Society drew up a new classification for the Carboniferous Limestone. The Dinantian has been divided into a new series of time-units called 'stages', the stages being named after locations in which they were studied. The oldest stage is the Courceyan, after the barony of Courceys in County Cork. It includes the uppermost Old Red Sandstone and the K, Z and the lower part of C_1 Vaughan zones. Then comes the Chadian, investigated at Chatburn, a

Lancashire village named after St. Chad. Chadian includes the upper part of C_1 and the lower part of C_2 S_1 Vaughan zones. This is followed by the Arundian stage, studied at Hobbyhorse Bay, South Pembrokeshire, and getting its name from 'arundo', which is Latin for hobbyhorse. Arundian corresponds to the upper part of Vaughan's C_2 S_1 zone. It is not represented locally. The next stage is the Holkerian, studied in the sea-cliffs in the grounds of Holker Hall in Cumbria, and approximating to Vaughan's S_2 zone. Then comes the Asbian stage, named after the type-location at Little Asby Scar in Cumbria. It corresponds to the D_1 sub-zone of Vaughan. The youngest stage is the Brigantian, studied at Kirby Stephen, Cumbria, in the old homeland of the Celtic tribe, the Brigantes. It is roughly equivalent to Vaughan's D_2 and D_3 sub-zones. The Geological Society also recognises locally-named lithological formations within the time-framework of its stages.

The fourth classification is that drawn up by the Institute of Geological Sciences, a Government body responsible for the Geological Survey of Great Britain. This classification is used in the Geological Survey's Merthyr Tydfil Map, Sheet number 231, published in 1979. The subdivisions are lithological i.e. based on rock-characters deriving from composition and texture.

The table (Fig 9) provides a general correlation for the various classifications as applied to the local limestones. It will be noticed that the Geological Survey's lithological divisions correspond very closely to Vaughan's zones. This is not surprising, as Vaughan's zones possess distinctive lithological features which are of assistance in identifying field-occurrences of the zones. The table also indicates the lithological units proposed by the Geological Society, which correspond fairly closely to those of the Geological Survey, except for differences in nomenclature and in the recognition of four formations equivalent to the Abercriban Oolite. It would be interesting to know which classification and nomenclature will find most favour with geologists in the future.

With regard to the names of the lithological formations, the type-locations of Pwll y Cwm, Clydach, Llanelly and Gilwern are in the Clydach gorge area between Brynmawr and Gilwern. Blaen Onnen (more correctly Blaen Onneu) is a quarry 2 miles (3.2 km.) south of Llangynidr. Llandyfan and Cil yr Ychen are near Llandybie. Penwyllt is near Craig y Nos in the upper Tawe valley. Dowlais, Abercriban and Penderyn are in or near Merthyr

Features of Deposition in the Merthyr Area

The Carboniferous Limestone is absent in Mid-Wales, which must have remained above sea-level when the limestones were being laid down in North and South Wales. It is probable that the shoreline of the southern Dinantian Sea was never far north of the present northern limits of the limestone outcrop in our area.

In South Wales, limestone-formation was more continuous in the deeper waters which covered the Vale of Glamorgan, Gower and South Pembrokeshire. In our area, nearer the ancient shoreline, the sea was shallower, this partly explaining the thinning of limestone formations towards the north. There was also a greater tendency towards the development of sandy beds. Oolites formed in wide, shallow lagoons where there was much evaporation. Very fine-grained calcite mudstones, made up largely of algal (seaweed) remains were also deposited in shallow-water, lagoonal environments.

Another feature of North Crop limestone formation was fluctuation of sea-level. Occasional uplift to dry-land conditions resulted in the cessation of sedimentation, and its replacement by denudation. This caused unconformities or breaks in the rock-succession.

Thus, in the local area, bordering the northern rim of the South Wales coalfield, as the result of reduced sedimentation in shallower water and non-deposition during dry-land conditions, the total thickness of the Carboniferous Limestone is no more than 600 feet (183 metres) compared with over 4,000 feet (1,219 metres) in Gower and South Pembrokeshire.

Carboniferous Limestones in the Merthyr Area

The main outcrop runs roughly west-south-west to east-north-east through Cefn Cilsanws, Pontsarn, Morlais Castle, Pontsticill and Twynau Gwynion, varying between three-quarters and two miles in width. Further north another limestone outcrop forms the surface in the Dolygaer-Bryniau Gleision area, having been preserved as a fault-outlier between the Coed Hir and Dinas faults of the Neath Disturbance referred to in the section on Earth Movements[4].

Most of the constituents of limestone are removed by ground-water, so that soils are thin, bare rock often breaking through the vegetative cover. Extensive quarrying for furnace-flux, roadstone and lime-burning has provided excellent exposures. Typical limestone-features such as dry river-beds, underground streams, caves, stalagmites and stalactites may be observed, especially along the valley of the Glais, which joins the Taf Fechan near the Aberglais Inn at SO 043 097. A well-known Glais cave is Ogof Rhyd-sych, perhaps better known as 'Beaver's Cave' at SO 042 102. At the same location is an interesting 'fossil' waterfall, the Glais having formerly flowed over this fall prior to its finding an underground channel further upstream. Swallow-holes are present, the best examples being in the thin Millstone Grit covering-layer on Cefn Cilsanws, Twynau Gwynion and on either side of the Cwm Cadlan road from Llwyn-on reservoir to Penderyn. (Plate 3)

In the following description of the local limestones the sections will be headed by the names of the formations recognised by the Geological Survey, but it is intended to show correlation with the other classifications.

Plate 3: SWALLOW HOLE IN MILLSTONE GRIT OVERLYING CARBONIFEROUS LIMESTONE
Twynau Gwynion SO 068 099

The Lower Limestone Shales

This formation is similarly named by the Geological Society of London, which includes it in the lower Courceyan Stage. It corresponds to Vaughan's K zone.

Typically the formation consists of alternating bands of dark limestones and shales, but in the outcrop surmounting the Old Red Sandstone Grey Grits at the Abercriban Grit Quarry, SO 063 127 (Plate 1) it is a tough, dark grey crinoidal limestone about 12 feet (3.7 metres) thick. Much of it has been dolomitised, some of the calcium carbonate having been replaced by magnesium carbonate. Dolomite is pale grey on a fresh surface but weathers to yellow and brown. It may be distinguished from ordinary limestone by the fact that it does not effervesce on the application of cold, dilute hydrochloric acid. Most dolomites contain few or no fossils, which may have been obliterated during the dolomistisation process. It is probable that most dolomites were originally limestones which were changed by magnesium derived from sea-water and introduced into the limestones by solutions passing through them. In the Abercriban exposure the dolomitised limestone is brown, with parallel bedding-laminations showing groove and ridge patterns on weathered surfaces. Fossils in the un-dolomitised limestone include crinoids, the brachiopod Spirifer and thc bryozoan Fenestella.

An exposure with greater shale development may be observed in a small quarry on the south bank of Nant Car Fawr some 40 yards (36.6 metres) east of the A 470(T) Merthyr to Brecon road at SO 009 124, with alternate bands of limestone and shale to a thickness of 10 feet (3 metres).

Other outcrops may be seen along a stream tributary of the Callan at Dolygaer, SO 063 147, and on the scarps of Daren Fawr, SO 081 162, and Daren Fach SO 091 162 on Bryniau Gleision.

The total thickness of the Lower Limestone Shales locally is 60 to 70 feet (18.3 to 21.4 metres).

The Abercriban Oolite

This formation is made up largely of oolitic limestones, which show increasing dolomitisation in their lower horizons. It corresponds to the Z zone of Vaughan's classification.

Oolitic limestone, or oolite, has a texture resembling the roe of a fish. (Greek 'oon' – egg.) It is made up of rounded grains formed by the deposition of successive coats of calcium carbonate around a nucleus such as a grain of sand or a piece of shell. The particles grow in size by being rolled in limy, warm sea-water, subject to much evaporation which increases the lime-content of the water. Shallow, tidal water promotes the necessary rolling motion of the grains. The rounded particles are called ooliths, which may be up to 1 mm. in diameter. Larger ooliths are called pisoliths, the associated rock being a pisolitic limestone or pisolite.

The Abercriban Oolite is exposed in the New Tylerybont Quarry, Pontsticill, SO 065 116, better-known locally as the Baltic Quarry. It is located about 300 yards (273 metres) south of the dam of Pontsticill reservoir. The quarry is divided into two vertical sections by a ledge about 70 feet (21.4 metres) above the quarry floor.

Above the ledge, and towards its eastern end is a distinctive boulder-bed, (Plate 4) which is a very coarse conglomerate with limestone boulders up to 2 feet (0.6 metres) in diameter. The Abercriban Oolite lies below this bed.

Immediately beneath the boulder-bed is a coarse crinoidal limestone 6 to 8 feet (1.8 to 2.4 metres) thick, with a development of 'beef' calcite at its base. It contains fossil crinoids and was called the Coral Bed by T.N. George[4], because it is the bed which has provided rare findings of the zone-fossil Zaphrentis (re-named Hapsiphyllum konincki). Below the crinoidal limestone, and forming the lip of the south-facing ledge, is a fine-grained calcite mudstone, often showing algal markings, 6 to 8 feet (1.8 to 2.4 metres) thick. The Coral Bed, together with the underlying calcite mudstone, were referred to by George as easily identifiable 'Marker Beds'.

Below the calcite mudstone ledge the south-facing quarry-wall is in coarsely oolitic limestone to a thickness of about 35 feet (10.7 metres) and yielding the fossil brachiopods Camarotoechia and Schellwienella. Underneath the limestone is a bed of shale-mudstone 2½ feet (0.76 metres)

Plate 4: BALTIC QUARRY, PONTSTICILL, SO 065 116
Llanelly Formation (above) separated from Abercriban Oolite (below) by the 'Boulder Bed' of the Intra-Avonian Unconformity

thick. The upper beds of the limestone are light-grey in colour, but darken downwards, with rusty-brown dolomitised horizons at inconsistent levels. Dolomitisation is most widespread and complete immediately above the shale band.

Below the shale band is dark-grey oolitic limestone about 20 feet (6.1 metres) thick, and below this formation is another shale-mudstone band about 1½ feet (.46 metres) thick.- This limestone also has rusty-brown surfaces indicating various degrees of dolomitisation, which again is most complete immediately above the shale band.

Below the lower shale bed is a very dark limestone, extensively dolomitised, the prevailing colour of the formation being brown. The Geological Survey interprets this limestone as part of the Lower Limestone Shales. The ridge and furrow pattern on the weathered dolomite surfaces, and the frequent occurrence of the brachiopods Spirifer recall the Lower Limestone Shales exposure capping the Abercriban Grit Quarry (Plate 1).

In its Special Report Number 7 the Geological Society admits to uncertainty in the allocation of the local Oolite Group to the proposed classification. Included in the report is a cross-section which would seem to indicate that the Abercriban Oolite or Z zone is represented locally, in downward order, by the Gilwern Oolite and the Clydach Beds of the

Chadian stage, and the Blaen Onnen Oolite and Pwll y Cwm Oolite of the Courceyan stage. In the Baltic Quarry the uppermost Abercriban or Z beds are the crinoidal limestone and calcite mudstone beneath the boulder bed. These beds were identified as the Marker Beds by T.N. George in his 1954 publication[5], and the Marker Beds are re-named the Clydach Beds in the Geological Society's classification. It is therefore doubtful if the Gilwern Oolite formation is represented locally. It may be noted that George – a part-author of Special Report Number 7 – did not record Gilwern Oolite in our area in his 1954 paper.

With regard to the beds below the ledge of the quarry, the upper, light-grey, less dolomitised oolites could correspond to the Blaen Onnen Oolite, and the lower, darker, more dolomitised oolites to the Pwll y Cwm Oolite.

Another exposure of the Abercriban Oolite formation may be observed at the Abercriban Limestone Quarry, SO 066 125, about 700 yards (640 metres) north of the Baltic Quarry.

The Llanelly Formation

This formation is similarly named in the Geological Society's classification. It is the S_1 zone of the Vaughan classification. It may be observed in the Baltic Quarry, where the base of the formation is the boulder-bed referred to in the preceding section on the Abercriban Oolite (Plate 4). T.N. George has interpreted this bed as a surface of Clydach or Marker Beds, weathered and eroded under dry-land conditions preceding the deposition, under marine conditions, of the overlying limestones. The boulder-bed marks an unconformity, or break in the geological succession, and is sometimes referred to as the Intra-Avonian Unconformity. It denotes the absence of that part of the lower Chadian stage, corresponding to Vaughan's Lower Caninia or C_1 zone, which was being laid down in seas further south at a time when our area was dry land. On the west-facing wall of the quarry the boulder-bed thins out into dark shales.

Above the boulder-bed are some 25 feet (7.6 metres) of limestones which are mainly light grey, calcite mudstones. The formation is very precipitous, but there are a large number of fallen blocks which may be examined on the quarry floor. The limestones have a very fine-grained texture described as porcellanous, (resembling porcelain) and with a conchoidal fracture like that of flint. They are rich in algal (seaweed) material, most of it microscopic, but there are also rounded algal structures up to 1 inch (2.54 cm.) in diameter. The calcite mudstones are thought to have formed in shallow lagoons with restricted communication with the open sea, nearly all the calcite mud being of organic, algal origin. Apart from algal structures the formation locally is not rich in fossils, but in consideration of its general fossil content the Llanelly Formation is placed in the Society's Chadian stage.

The formation is 12 feet to 40 feet (3.6 metres to 12.2 metres) locally. Its upper part is probably not present, a sandy limestone outcropping on the hillside above the Baltic Quarry being regarded as a stratigraphical break or unconformity, indicating the non-deposition of upper Llanelly Formation beds and also all beds belonging to the succeeding Arundian stage of the Geology Society's classification. The sandy bed is considered the base of the Cil yr Ychen Limestone.

The Cil yr Ychen Limestone

This formation is equivalent to Vaughan's S_2 zone and also the Dowlais Limestone of the Geological Society's Holkerian stage. It is well-exposed in a number of disused quarries, which include the old Rhymney Ironworks quarries on Twynau Gwynion, SO 06 10, the Tylahaidd quarry on the east side of the Pant – Pontsticill road, SO 062 103, the old Penydarren and Dowlais Ironworks quarries around Morlais Castle, SO 049 096, and the old Cyfarthfa Ironworks quarry at Y Graig, near Cefn Coed, SO 035 083. It is also exposed in the large, currently-worked Vaynor Quarry near Pontsarn, SO 037 075, and on the west face of Cefn Cilsanws overlooking Cwmtaf, SO 02 09.

The basal, thin, sandy layer, referred to in the previous section, is also seen on Bryniau Gleision, a light-yellow sandstone being crossed by the old Roman Road between SO 076 154 and SO 083 157, and also appearing in nearby swallow-holes, the location being shown on page 34 of Robertson, 'Geology of the South Wales Coalfield, Part V, Merthyr Tydfil'[6].

Apart from this thin sandy layer, the Cil yr Ychen Limestone is made up very largely of massive beds of dark-grey, coarse oolite, but with pisolitic, algal and calcite mudstones in the upper strata. Shallow-water deposition is indicated by the presence of oolites, pisolites, algal limestones and cross-bedding. Fossils are concentrated in bands rather than being evenly distributed. Coral bands are more typical of the lower part of the formation, one particular band at the top of the steep bank, above the Taf Fechan, at the foot of Morlais quarry, and overlooking Vaynor, SO 047 100, seeming to consist entirely of the coral Lithostrotion. Another fossil coral in the lower part of the formation is Syringopora. The lower part of the formation is well exposed in the Tylahaidd quarry. In the upper part of the formation, in the higher parts of Morlais Castle quarries and in the Rhymney Ironworks quarries on Twynau Gwynion there are shelly bands made up largely of the zone-fossil, the brachiopod Seminula (re-named Composita ficoides). Of the local Vaughan zones only the S_2 is well-represented by the zone-fossil. Other fossils include the brachiopod Productus and the flattened gastropod Euomphalus, often mistaken for an ammonite.

Bands of chert up to 2 inches (5 cm.) thick occur in some of the quarries, the fragments being found on the quarry floors. Chert is a very hard, dense, siliceous rock, often very dark in colour and closely akin to flint, probably formed from solutions which had acquired silica from the siliceous skeletons of sponges. In contrast with limestone, chert is too hard to be scratched by a knife, and does not react to hydrochloric acid.

The Cil yr Ychen or Dowlais limestone is by far the thickest local limestone formation being 350 to 400 feet (107 to 122 metres) in thickness. It was also the most-quarried of the local limestones. (Plate 2)

The Llandyfan Limestone

This formation includes the D_1 sub-zone of Vaughan's classification, and the Penderyn Oolite of the Asbian stage of the Geological Society's classification. It may be examined in a thin exposure between the top of the dark-grey Cil yr Ychen limestone on Twynau Gwynion and the tumbled Basal Grit boulders of Millstone Grit on the Twynau summit, SO 066 107. (Plate 5.) It also surfaces on the higher parts of Morlais Castle golf course, a prominent outcrop north of Castle Farm, SO 055 094, having yielded a small number of trilobite fossils.

The limestone is a very coarse oolite, almost white on weathered surfaces, and is often referred to as the Light Oolite. It is characterised by a close-set joint pattern, and nowhere is it thicker than 30 to 40 feet (9.1 to 12.2 metres). Locally it does not contain the zone fossil, the coral Dibunophyllum, almost the only fossil being the large brachiopod, Productus hemisphericus.

Plate 5: LLANDYFAN LIMESTONE (FOREGROUND) CAPPED BY MILLSTONE GRIT
Twynau Gwynion, SO 066 107

Plate 6: HONEYCOMBED SANDSTONE BOULDERS
Morlais Castle Golf Course, SO 052 094

Near the base of the formation is a thin, brown, calcareous sandstone, weathered into a honeycomb structure, and known as the Honeycombed Sandstone. It is easily recognised, (Plate 6) and is a useful marker for the base of the formation.

Also included in the Llandyfan Limestone is the D_2 sub-zone of Vaughan. This is exposed on Cader Fach, on the west side of the Taf Fawr valley, to the north of the Cwm Cadlan road, at SN 985 115. It is a dark-grey oolitic limestone, with nodules of chert, and containing the fossil brachiopod Productus. It is about 40 feet (12.2 metres) thick, and is the Penwyllt Limestone of the Geological Society's classification, being included in the Brigantian stage.

A selection of Carboniferous Limestone fossils is shown in Fig 10.

References

[1] A. Vaughan, 'The palaeontological sequence in the Carboniferous Limestone of the Bristol area', *Quarterly Journal of the Geological Society,* Vol. 61, (1905) 181-307.

[2] Geological Society of London, *Special Report* No.7 (1976).

[3] A recommended Palaeontology book is *British Palaeozoic Fossils* published by the British Museum (Natural History).

[4] T.R. Owen, 'The structure of the Neath disturbance between Bryniau Gleision and Glynneath', *Quarterly Journal of the Geological Society*, Vol. 109, (1954) 333-359.
[5] T.N. George, 'Pre-Seminulan Main Limestone of the Avonian Series in Breconshire', *Quarterly Journal of the Geological Society,* Vol. 110, (1954) 283-322.
[6] T. Robertson, *The Geology of the South Wales Coalfield* Part 5, Merthyr Tydfil, Second Edition, HMSO (1932). This publication is invaluable for detailed descriptions of many exposures of the Carboniferous Limestone.

(b) The Millstone Grit or Namurian Series

by D. EMLYN EVANS

The Namurian rocks in South Wales display numerous features which provide clear evidence regarding the palaeogeographical conditions which existed in the area in Namurian times. A consideration of total thicknesses at different outcrops shows that there is a maximum of nearly 2,300 ft. in Gower and a minimum of some 100 ft. near Risca and Brynmawr. To the north of Brynamman it is 1,100 ft., in St. Brides Bay 500 ft. and near Merthyr 245 ft. This points to the existence of a comparatively small sedimentary basin.

Around its edges the lower sections of the Namurian sediments consist largely of sandy rocks of different kinds usually grouped together as the Basal Grit, and distinguished from the overlying Shale Group in which mudstones and shales predominate.

The lowest member of the Basal Grit along parts of the northern edge of the South Wales coalfield is a sandy rock having a varying pebble content. When traced from west to east it is found to lie directly upon beds of limestone which, from fossil evidence, can be shown to become progressively older eastwards. This feature has been interpreted (Dixey and Sibly 1919, Robertson and George 1929, Pringle and George 1937) as an unconformity with the pebbly sandstone or conglomerate being considered to be of Namurian age. In the Merthyr area at Pwll Taf (S0 027 081), in the cutting of the Heads of the Valleys road at Cefn Coed (S0 031 081), and near the old silica-stone hopper on Twynau Gwynion (S0 068 102) pebbly sandstones overlie unconformably a weathered rock platform of Carboniferous Limestone.

In these and similar localities around the north-eastern edge of the coalfield, caves of various dimensions occur in the limestone immediately below the conglomerate. A good example can be seen at Pwll Taf. (Plate 7) This is obviously the result of solutional weathering by ground water at some comparatively recent time in the 325 million years that have elapsed since the

Plate 7: PWLL TAF ON THE TAF FAWR, SO 027 081
Cave at junction of Carboniferous Limestone (below) and Millstone Grit

beginning of Namurian times. It is the collapse of the pebbly sandstone, as it becomes unsupported, that gives rise to the so-called swallow holes that are scattered over the present land surface occupied by the Millstone Grit. Good examples are to be seen above the Twynau Gwynion limestone quarries. (Plate 3)

Detailed examination, involving comparisons with modern sediments, of the pebbly sandstones and of the various other consolidated sandy, silty and muddy Namurian sediments by George (1970) and Oguike (1969), has provided striking evidence regarding the geography of Namurian times in the South Wales area. From this, and more global and varied evidence that has been accumulated in comparatively recent times, the picture that emerges is one of a distinct marine embayment situated near, if not upon, the Equator and into which some five major rivers deposited sediment forming extensive deltas. Throughout the fifteen million years or so of Namurian time the detailed geographical pattern changed continuously. Oscillatory uplift of land to the north and along the Usk anticline in the east, changes of sea level, and possibly slight alterations of climate produced changes in the kinds of sediment deposited in any one locality as well as the amount of plant or animal remains included. It follows that sediments deposited under such changing conditions will change in character laterally as well as vertically (see Fig 11).

Geologically, the most important strata are the bands of dark mudstones which contain marine fossils. These are readily recognised and provide so-called 'marker' bands which help to clarify the stratigraphy of Millstone Grit areas. Some of these fossils could only survive, it seems, in truly open sea conditions. The most distinctive of these were the goniatites, sea-creatures that lived in flat spirally coiled shells and which fortunately evolved fairly quickly through time, and, being free-swimming, were able, during marine incursions, to enter the South Wales embayment with every advance of the sea.

Although most of the very fine-grained or argillaceous rocks were laid down under conditions that could loosely be described as marine, the term 'marine band' in Millstone Grit stratigraphy is usually confined to the shales or muds containing, ideally, fossil goniatite shells (see Fig 12) or other fossil forms indicating the most marine parts of a marine sequence. In this connection Archer (1968) has shown that along the northern edge of the coalfield an incoming sea is indicated by a sequence in the muddy sediments which, starting with no fossil animal forms, is followed by a phase showing marine worm burrows—*Planolites*—then a phase represented by a brackish-water brachiopod known as *Lingula*, then a marine shellfish spawn or Spat phase, then a bivalve sea-shell or lamellibranch phase, then a thin-shelled goniatite phase—the *Anthracoceras* or *Dimorphoceras* phase, then a thick-shelled goniatite phase and lastly the brachiopod phase. As the sea receded the above phases ideally would be reversed in the overlying sediments.

The present classification of the British Millstone Grit is based on its sequence of goniatite fossils and this scheme should eventually replace the traditional one based upon rock types. Credit for the use of goniatites as the zonal fossils in the Namurian must go to Bisat (1924, 1928) who worked in northern England. The subdivisions, in descending order, are as follows:

YEADONIAN STAGE or Lower *Gastrioceras*, (G_1), in which the *G. cumbriense* and *G. cancellatum* marine bands occur.

MARSDENIAN STAGE or Upper *Reticuloceras*, (R_2), in which the *R. superbilingue, R. bilingue* and *R. gracile* marine bands occur.

KINDERSCOUTIAN STAGE or Lower *Reticuloceras*, (R_1), in which the *R. reticulatum* s.s., *R. nodosum* and *R. circumplicatile* marine bands occur.

ALPORTIAN STAGE or Upper *Homoceras*, (H_2), in which the *Homoceratoides prereticulatus, Homoceras undulatum* and *Hudsonoceras proteus* marine bands occur.

CHOKIERIAN STAGE or Lower *Homoceras*, (H_1), in which the *Homoceras beyrichianum* and *H. subglobosum* marine bands occur.

ARNSBERGIAN STAGE or Upper *Eumorphoceras*, (E_2).

PENDLEIAN STAGE or Lower *Eumorphoceras*, (E_1).

Details of the Namurian rock sequences exposed in various localities in the Merthyr area are shown diagrammatically in Fig 11. Also included are the basal portions of the overlying Coal Measures which extend down to the base of the *Gastrioceras subcrenatum* Marine Band. It had been usual for the

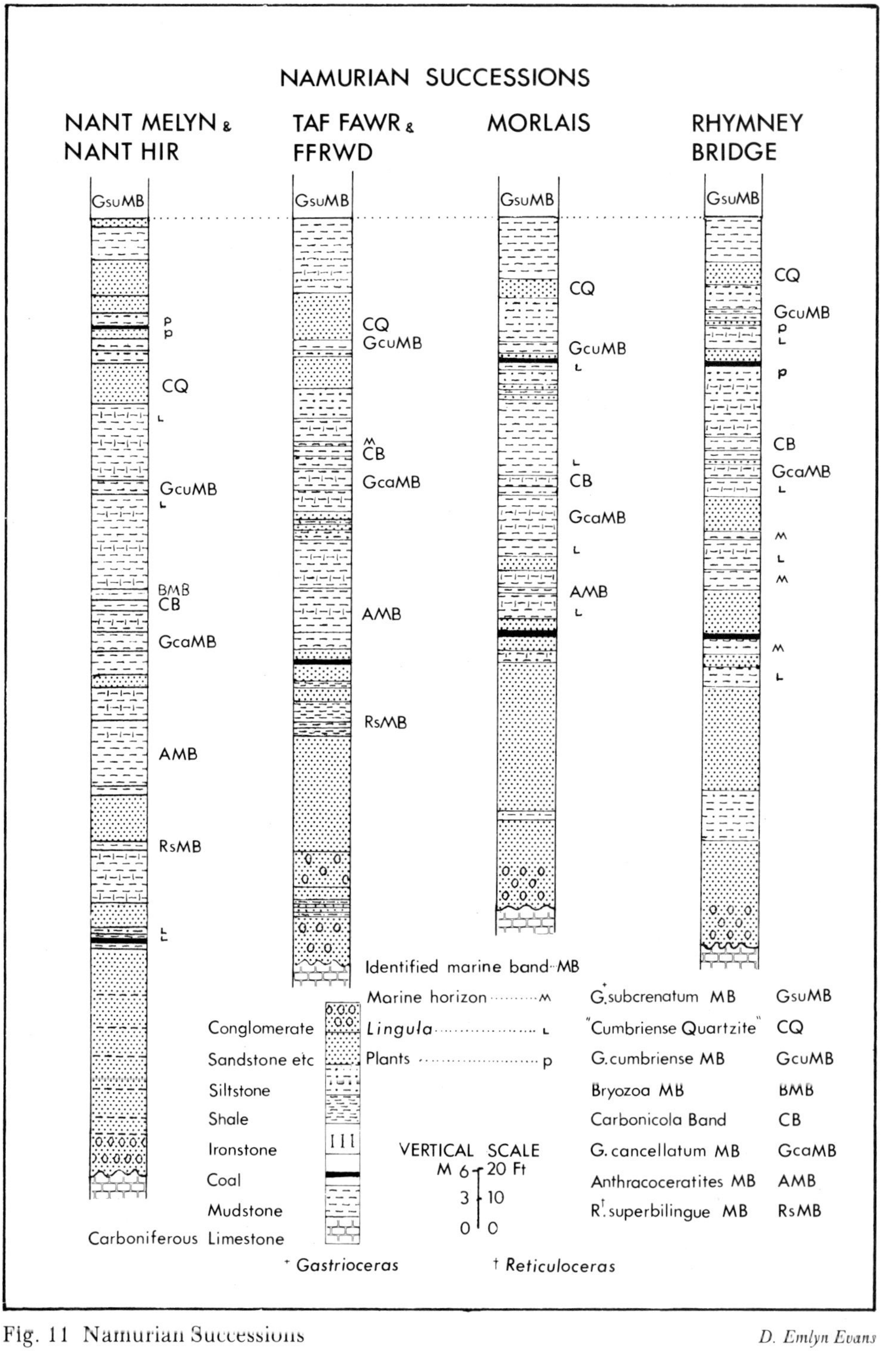

Fig. 11 Namurian Successions — D. Emlyn Evans

division between the Coal Measures and the Millstone Grit, previous to 1957, (Woodland, Evans and Stephens) to be drawn at the top of the so-called Farewell Rock – the uppermost member of a group of sandstones which apparently lay below the lowest workable coal seams in various places around the edges of the coalfield. Originally the Farewell Rock sandstone group was included in the Millstone Grit Series, but is now classified as part of the Coal Measures, since it lies above the *G. subcrenatum band.*

The Basal Grit Group forms well-marked ridges on the inter-valley uplands. It is fairly well exposed on the summit-region of Cefn Cilsanws, in the Taf Fawr section south of Pwll Taf, in various localities in Cefn Coed y Cymmer, on the hill slopes above Lakeside Gardens, in the old Bryniau silica quarries, on the Twynau Gwynion summit-area and in the Pitwellt and Rhymney River near Rhymney Bridge. The lower sections have little if any shale bands and no identifiable marine bands, so that the dating of these beds is not possible. However, from regional patterns of marine band distribution, it is considered that no sediments representing E and H stages were deposited in the area, which at that time was land standing well above sea level.

The Group includes various rock types. At the base are the pebble beds or conglomerates already mentioned. Above are particularly hard, thickly bedded sandstones or quartzites which made excavation for the Heads of the Valleys road difficult in Cefn Coed. They were formerly quarried to provide silica for furnace lining (Plate 8). These sandstones are separated by prominent hummocky surfaces (due to erosion) between which occurs oblique

Plate 8: DISUSED SILICA QUARRY IN MILLSTONE GRIT
The Bryniau, SO 056 091

layering (cross stratification) as opposed to parallel stratification, often with plant remains. These represent thick river channel sands of R_1 and early and middle R_2 age. Included in the sandstones of upper R_2 age (see Fig 11) is a thin band of sandy shale, once exposed in the Old Ganister Quarry 400 yards south-west of the road junction near Pant Cemetery as well as in the western bank of the Taf opposite the Cefn Coed sewerage works and in the Pitwellt stream north of Rhymney Bridge. A few feet above, in the two latter localities and also in the Upper Morlais stream bed, a thin seam of coal occurs. These occurrences point to slight submergences of land which introduced deltaic conditions, and as the delta moved southwards river channel sands were again deposited and built up to produce swamps occupied by appropriate vegetation and probably enclosed between river channels. Subsidence produced burial of the plant remains and introduced brackish water (with *Lingula* shells) at least as far east as the Nant Hir area. The overlying sandstone belonging to the upper part of R_2 becomes coarser when traced upwards and seems to have been deposited by the waves of a receding sea. The division between the old subdivisions of the Basal Grit Group and the Shale Group is usually drawn at the top of this sandstone.

The Shale group, with its included marine bands and other readily recognised strata, is very well exposed in the Ffrwd valley, the main Taf River banks south of Cefn Coed, the Upper Morlais stream bed and in the Pitwellt and Rhymney River beds north of Rhymney Bridge.

The mudstones near the base of the Shale Group, with the included *Reticuloceras superbilingue* Marine Band, provide clear evidence of a marine advance and of its subsequent retreat. The succeeding sandstone seems to have been deposited as a coastal sheet of sand by the waves of a receding sea.

In early G_1 times came the marine advance associated with the Anthracoceras Marine Band, and with the Gastrioceras cancellatum Marine Band, the latter being well-exposed at either end of the culvert carrying the Nant Morlais under the former railway line near Caeracca, SO 071 091. The ensuing deposition of muds was mostly in bays between the delta river channels. At one stage these bays were isolated from the open sea, forming brackish lagoons and freshwater lakes in which mussels flourished. This event is well indicated by the prominent band of mudstone containing numerous shells of the freshwater lamellibranch *Carbonicola.* Middle G_1 times saw a change to deltaic conditions with the deposition of mudstones, silt-stones and ironstones. The thin coal, the rootlet bed and the seat earth (fossil soil) below are evidence for the emergence of the delta-top region.

A further marine incursion produced the deposition of the *Gastrioceras cumbriense* Marine Band. The succeeding sandstone, known as the Cumbriense Quartzite has great aereal extent along the north-eastern edge of the coalfield. It forms the west bank of Pwll Wat, on the Taf, near the British Road Services depot in the old Cyfarthfa works, SO 038 071, and also outcrops along the western boundary of Prince Charles Hospital car park. It varies in thickness and consists of river-sand infillings of channels usually

Plate 9: MERTHYR CHURCH FAULT AT PWLL WAT ON RIVER TAF, SO 083 071
Foreground left bank in Cumbriense Shales. Right bank (downthrow) in Cumbriense Quartzite. Distant left bank: beds dipping steeply into river

cut into underlying mudstones and silts. In the eastern parts of the Merthyr area it is of some 6-7ft. in thickness and separated from the marine band below by some 6-8ft. in thickness of mudstones and siltstones, but west of the Dowlais Fault it becomes 15ft. thick and overlies the *Gastrioceras cumbriense* Marine Band. It might be that this fault was already in existence at the time of the deposition of this sandstone. The Gastrioceras cumbriense Marine Band, consisting mainly of shales, forms the eastern bank of Pwll Wat, on the upthrow side of the Merthyr Church Fault, which is well displayed in this location. (Plate 9).

The uppermost Namurian section commences with mudstones which were originally clayey river-flood-plain sediments. This phase was interrupted by a major advance by the sea which led to the formation of the widespread *Gastrioceras subcrenatum* Marine Band which is well exposed in the upper Ffrwd valley in a small tributary stream section (SO 0185 0740) and in the upper Morlais valley in an unnamed stream section (SO 073 091). This marine band is classified as the base of the overlying Coal Measures.

The outcrops of the goniatite marine bands are shown in the Geology maps of the local area. These bands yield other marine fossils, including brachiopods and lamellibranchs.

A selection of Millstone Grit fossils is shown in Fig 12.

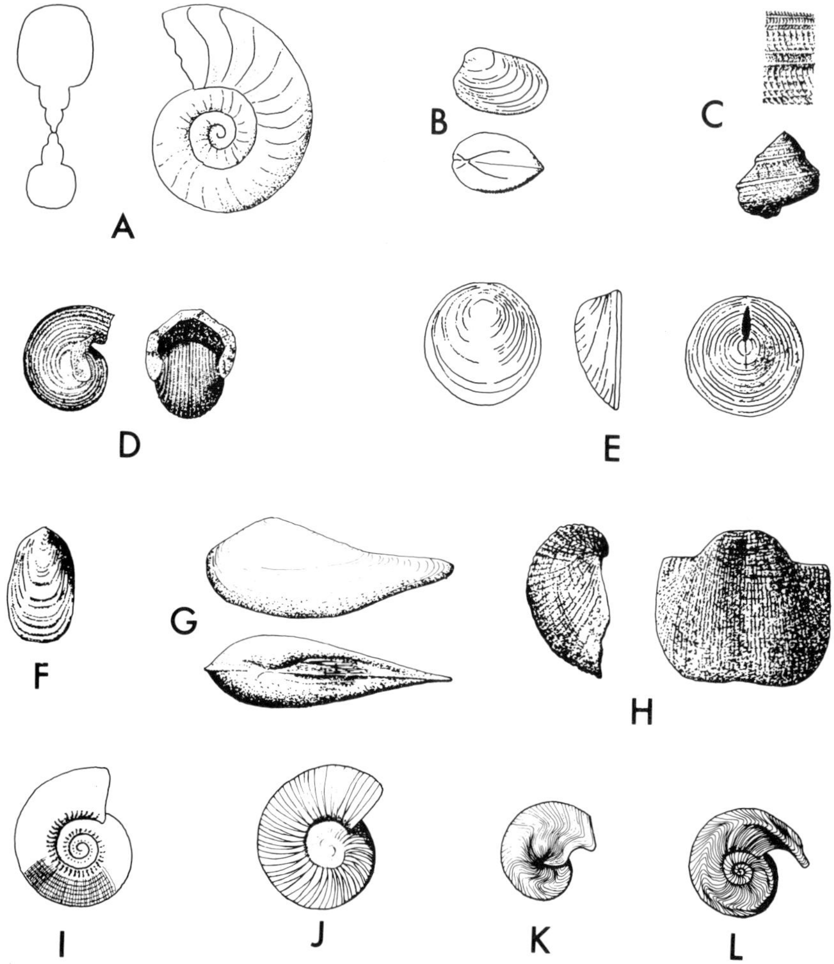

Fig. 12 A Selection of Namurian (Millstone Grit) Fossils

A. The cephalopod *Metacoceras falcatum* (J. Sowerby) (× ⅔); B. The bivalve *Nuculopsis gibbosa* (Fleming) (× 1); C. The gastropod *Glabrocingulum armstrongi* Thomas (× 1⅓); D The monoplacophoran (a gastropod-like primitive mollusc) *Euphemites urii* (Fleming) (× 1⅓); E. The brachiopod *Orbiculoidea nitida* (Phillips) (× 1⅓); F. The brachiopod *Lingula mytiloides* J. Sowerby (× 1⅓); G. The bivalve *Polidevcia Nuculana attenuata* (Fleming) (× 2); H. The brachiopod *Dictyoclostus Productus semireticulatus* (Martin) (× ⅔); I. The goniatite *Gastrioceras cancellatum* Bisat (× ⅔); J. The goniatite *Gastrioceras cumbriense* Bisat (× 1⅓); K. The goniatite *Anthracoceras arcuatilobum* Lugwig (× 1⅓); L. the goniatite *Reticuloceras superbilingue* Bisat (×⅚).

References

A.A. Archer, 'The Upper Carboniferous and later formations of the Gwendraeth valley and adjoining areas', *Mem. geol. Surv. U.K.*, i-xi, (1968) 1-216.

W.S. Bisat, 'The Carboniferous goniatites of the north of England and their zones', *Proc. Yorks. geol. Soc.*, **20**, (1924) 40-124.

W.S. Bisat, 'The Carboniferous goniatite zones of England and their continental equivalents', *C.r. Congr. Av. Et. Strat. Géol. Carb.*, Heerlen 1927, (1928) 117-133.

F. Dixey and T.F. Sibly, 'The Carboniferous Limestone series on the south-eastern margin of the South Wales coalfield', *Q. Jl geol. Soc. Lond.*, **73** (for 1917), (1918) 111-164.

T. N. George, *British Regional Geology: South Wales,* 3rd edn. (H.M.S.O., London, 1970), xii, (1970) 152.

G. Kelling, 'Upper Carboniferous sedimentation in South Wales', 185-224 *in* Owen, T.R. (ed.), *The Upper Palaeozoic and post-Palaeozoic rocks of Wales . . .* (University of Wales Press, Cardiff, 1974).

R.O. Oguike, *Sedimentation of the Middle Shales (Upper Namurian) of the South Wales coalfield,* Ph.D. thesis (unpubl.), (University of Wales, 1969).

J. Pringle and T.N. George, *British Regional Geology: South Wales,* (H.M.S.O.,-London, 1937), vi, 115

T. Robertson, 'The country around Merthyr Tydfil', 2nd ed., *Mem. geol. Surv. U.K.*, (1932) i-xiv, 1-283, xv-xx.

T. Robertson and T.N. George, 'The Carboniferous Limestone of the North Crop of the South Wales coalfield', *Proc. Geol. Ass.*, **40**, (1929) 18-40.

K. Taylor and L.P. Thomas, 'Geological Survey boreholes in south Brecknockshire and their bearing on the stratigraphy of the Upper Old Red Sandstone and the Carboniferous-Old Red Sandstone boundary east of the Afon Hepste, with an appendix on the invertebrate fossils by D.E. Butler', *Bull. geol. Surv. Gt. Br.*, **54**, (1975) 1-39.

A.W. Woodland and W.B. Evans, 'The country around Pontypridd and Maesteg', *Mem. geol. Surv. U.K.*, i-xiv, (1964) 1-391.

A.W. Woodland, W.B. Evans and J.V. Stephens, 'Classification of the Coal Measures of South Wales with special reference to the Upper Coal Measures', *Bull. geol. Surv. Gt. Br.*, **13**, (1957) 6-13.

(c) The Coal Measures

by MALCOLM BLANDFORD, M.Sc., F.G.S.

Geologist, National Coal Board Geological Services

1 *Introduction and Lithological Outline*

From Heolgerrig, Dowlais Top and Bedlinog to its southern extremities, the District Borough of Merthyr Tydfil is situated on Coal Measures. The Coal Measures were laid down some 290 million years ago, during the Upper Carboniferous Westphalian Period. In Western Europe the base of the Coal

Measures is taken as the Gastrioceras subcrenatum marine band which outcrops along the northern fringe of the Borough. The coalbearing strata above this marine band are the Coal Measures (T.N. George 1970[11]).

In South Wales the Coal Measures fall readily into three lithological groups i.e. groups differentiated by the composition and texture of their rock content. The lowest group, the Main Productive Group, formerly called the Lower Coal Series, contains most of the thick, workable coal seams and the more important ironstone bands. The group comprises the thicker coal seams and their associated seatearths (the structureless rocks beneath the coal-seams, containing the roots of ancient vegetation, and which are sometimes used as fireclays), separated by blocky, silty, grey mudstones which contain many thin clay-ironstone bands. These mudstones are often finer-grained, darker and carbonaceous immediately above the coal-seams. Note that true shales which are fissile mudstones, are almost totally absent from the Coal Measures in South Wales. Sandstones are present in the form of quartz-cemented quartzites, but are usually thin and impersistent. Marine bands are found, tending to occur just above coalseams, often sitting immediately on top of the coal. The rocks of the Main Productive group outcrop along the Heads of the Valleys road, and along the bottoms of the Taf and parallel valleys. They are some 640 metres thick in the Merthyr area.

The second lithological group is the Pennant Series, its base being the Number 2 Rhondda seam in this area. This group contains very few thick coal-seams, but there are several thin and largely unworked coal-seams and their seatearths, the latter often very sandy. Thin developments of silty mudstones may be present above coal-seams. Otherwise the group consists almost entirely of sandstones, grits and thin conglomerates. National Coal Board deep boreholes in the Trelewis area show the sandstones and grits to be largely cross-bedded, with subordinate channel deposits, together with some massive sandstone deposits devoid of any obvious bedding. The Pennant Series form the high plateau-ridges between the valleys, their steep sides being due to the predominance of hard sandstones in the sequence.

The third and topmost group, formerly called the Upper Coal Series, has the thick Mynyddislwyn seam (1.60 metres) as its base. This group is by far the thinnest, and the nearest outcrop is around Gelligaer. Sandstones are less important in this group, silty mudstones predominating. Some of the mudstones are shaly, and split into thin sheets because of the dense packing of fossil mussel shells, but in general the mudstones are blocky. Apart from the Mynyddislwyn seam, seams are thin and unworked. A map of the local Coal Measures is shown in Figure 13.

2 *Deposition and Formation of the Coal Measures*

So much for the appearance of the Coal Measures around Merthyr, but how did they get there? The Coal Measures are not a random heap of sedimentary rocks. The different rock-types occur in a regularly repeated cycle called

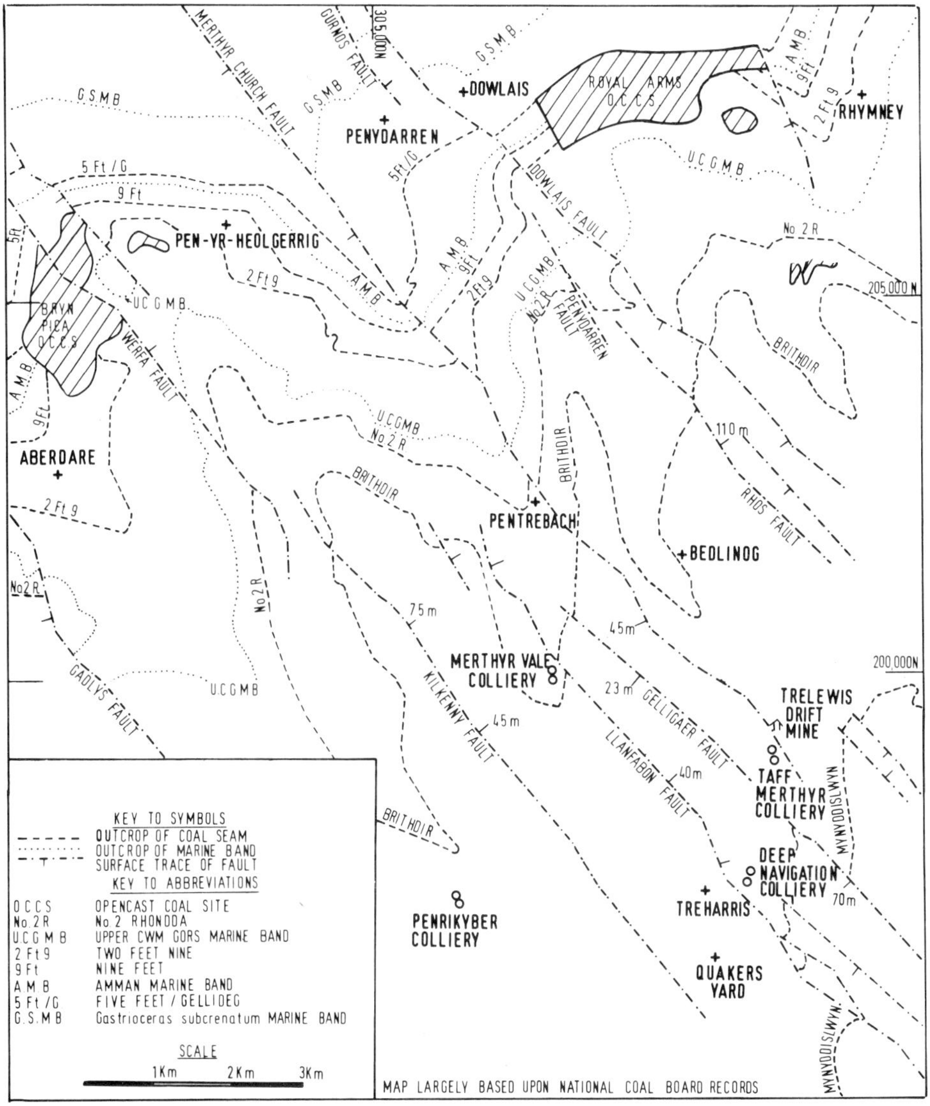

Fig. 13: Simplified Map of the Coal Measures in the Merthyr Area

a cyclothem (Pettijohn 1957[9]). Cyclothems are not all the same size, nor is every cyclothem complete. Also the individual rock-types may vary in importance from one cyclothem to the next (Figure 14).

The Coal Measures were laid down at a time when Britain was situated very near the Equator. They were laid down in an unstable basin of deposition, this instability accounting for the cyclic pattern of sedimentation.

A dense sub-tropical forest grew on low areas of swampland, which were just below sea-level. The forest debris accumulated in the swamp-water,

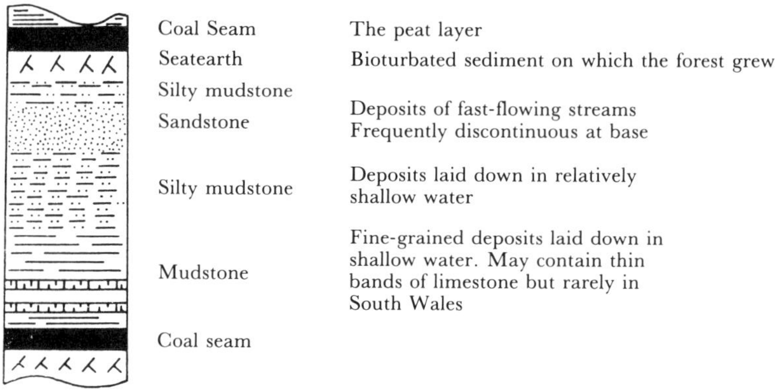

Fig. 14: The Cyclothem Pattern

where they partly decomposed and oxidised to form extensive peat deposits (Francis 1954[5]; Raistrick and Marshall 1946[12]). Periodically the area would subside to provide a brackish sea in which mud and silt accumulated in the quiet, low-energy environment, to cover the peat. Occasionally coastal spits and bars would accumulate in the turbulent high-energy environment near the coast, and these would be built out over the muds and silts as irregular sandy deposits.

Following the subsidence there would be a period of stability in which non-marine muds would accumulate slowly. As the basin of deposition filled up to approach sea-level, a new sub-tropical forest would establish itself, so beginning a new cycle (see Figure 15).

Occasionally the basin would subside sufficiently for truly marine, open, saline seas to exist. In the mudstones which accumulated in these seas marine fossils (crinoids, brachiopods, corals, etc) have been preserved. These mudstones are the marine bands which have proved invaluable in the classification and correlation of the Coral Measures.

Superimposed upon this cyclic pattern of sedimentation are the effects of the seasons. Rainy seasons swelled the streams which then carried down coarser sediments into the deposition area, but in the drier periods finer sediments were carried down by the impoverished streams. As a result the Coal Measures are made up of very thin laminations of coarser and finer material, e.g. coarser grits alternating with sandstones, and silty mudstones alternating with finer mudstones. Only in the very finest mudstones is this banding absent, a very slow settling process probably having removed the effects of seasonal change in river-flow.

Throughout the period in which the Main Productive Group was being laid down, the streams supplying the sediments flowed mostly from the north and east, providing mainly muds and silts. Sometimes these streams would cut right through the peat, to deposit sand or mud in the channels. Such channel fill deposits which partially or completely remove coal seams are called washouts (Figure 16).

Conditions changed dramatically with the laying down of the Pennant Series. Deposition did not begin at the same time everywhere, a condition described as diachronous. In the Merthyr area the Pennant base is the No 2 Rhondda seam. It is thought that the coarse, sandy material came largely from the South (Bluck and Kelling 1963[6]), and was deposited by rapid streams. Many of the sandstones and grits are cross-bedded, or are channel-fill deposits. The large number of angular iron-pyrite grains in the sandstones indicates that the deposits were eroded, transported and deposited

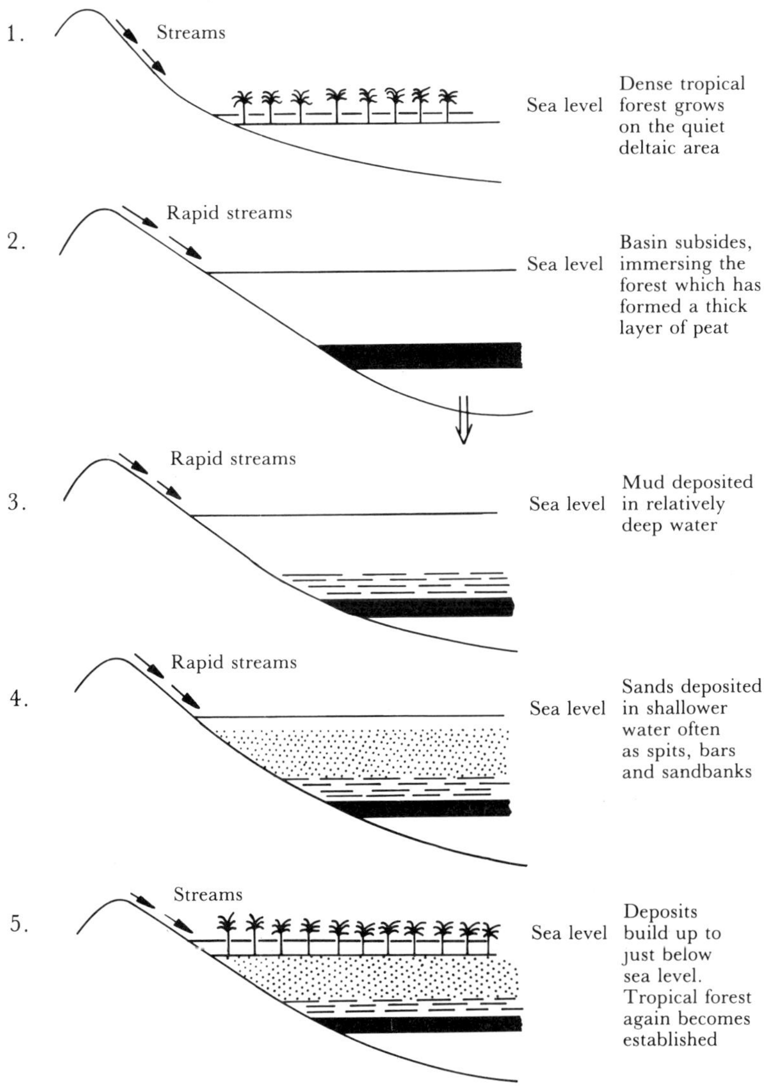

Fig. 15: The Deposition of Coal Measure Deposits

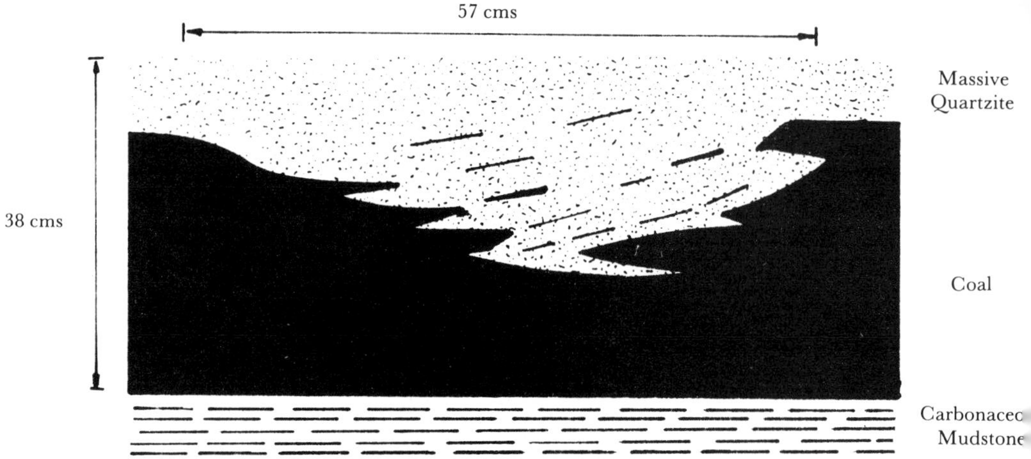

Fig. 16: Base of a washout channel cutting into the roof of the seven-feet seam at Penrikyber Colliery

Note that peat fragments have been churned up by the stream to form coal streaks in the channel deposits *(By courtesy of the National Coal Board)*

rapidly, as pyrite not only decays quickly when exposed to the air but also becomes rounded rapidly during transportation. The sandstones contain many coal and ironstone particles, indicating the erosion, transport and deposition of Coal Measures which had already lithified. The sandstones of the channel-fill deposits contain fragments of silty mudstone which were rolled, squeezed, gently eroded and infilled with sand-grains during transportation. Such fragments were noted in the deep boreholes of the National Coal Board in the Trelewis area (Figure 17). It would appear that such fragments were transported in a stiff clay state.

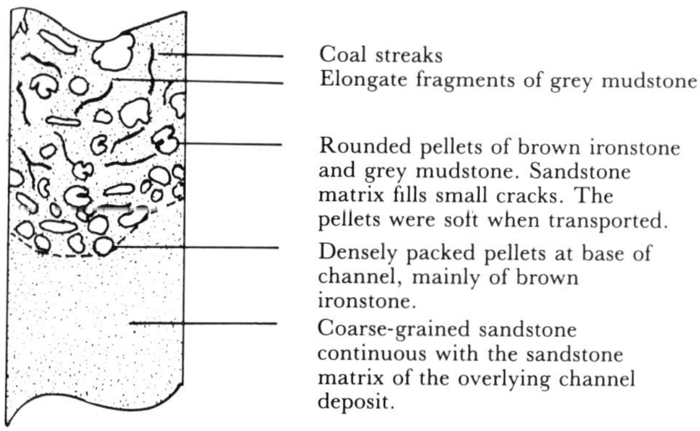

Fig. 17: Penecontemporaneous channel deposits from a deep surface borehole near Trelewis *(By courtesy of the National Coal Board)*

Streams became less vigorous at the close of deposition of the Pennant Series. Thus in the strata above the Mynyddislwyn seam sandstones became less important, with mudstones predominating.

The cylothemic deposition of the Coal Measures was finally brought to an end by the Armorican earth-movements. Crustal pressures pushing northwards from areas south of Britain caused buckling of the earth's crust in South Wales. The low-lying swamp areas were raised above sea-level, and deposition of the Coal Measures came to an end. These movements created the structural basin of the South Wales Coalfield, and resulted in the unconformity which occurs at the base of the overlying Mesozoic rocks.

The subsequent pressure of overlying sediments squeezed out pore-water, and compressed this vast thickness of sediment into rock. Grains were cemented together with quartz, calcite and clay cements, with low-temperature, low-grade metamorphism completing the lithification process from sediment to rock.

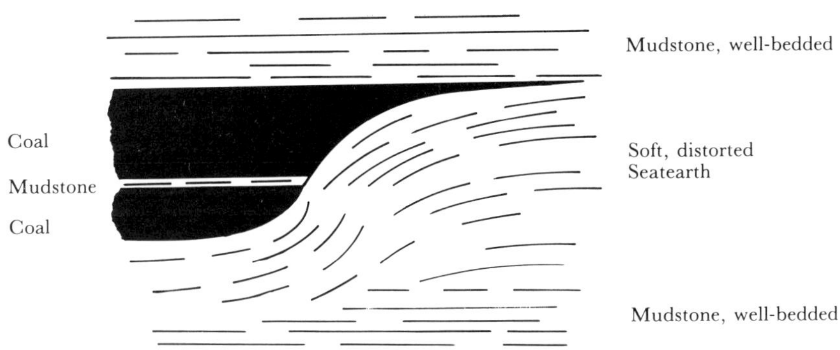

Fig. 18: Squash-out structure in the seven-feet seam at Penrikyber Colliery *(By courtesy of the National Coal Board)*

Coal-seam completely removed by a 'squash-out' structure. In this case the roof is unaffected. The seam is 116 cms thick.

3 *Classification and Correlation of the Coal Measures*

Geologists attempt to devise a classification of a geological system whereby satisfactory correlation is possible, correlation being the recognition of rock-formations of similar age in widely distributed localities. Detailed correlation is difficult in the Coal Measures because, in the main, the sediments are not open-sea sediments, and therefore do not contain a wealth of fossils of widely-spread, free-swimming organisms such as are generally used as time-indicators in classification.

The three-fold lithological division, i.e. a classification based on rock-types, and described in the introduction, is useful for preliminary field work, as the different rock types have a marked effect on topography, this making them easy to recognise in the field. Nevertheless this classification cannot be used for detailed work because beds are sometimes diachronous i.e. of different age in different locations. A classification based on lithology cannot be extended to cover all British coalfields.

Plant remains are the most common Coal Measures fossils, but plant-associations are delicately adjusted to their environments, and often tend to be very localised in habitat. Work on plants by Dix (1934[4]), Moore and Cox (1943[9]), Moore (1943[7] and 1948[8]) and Blundell (1951[1]) has failed to yield a satisfactory classification. Use has also been made of plant microspores in coal seams. They would seem of greater use than the parent plants because the spores were widely distributed by winds, water and insects, and are more often preserved intact. It is unfortunate that the examination of spores requires specialist laboratory equipment not normally carried by field geologists, a factor limiting the usefulness of plant spores.

Non-marine lamellibranchs (bi-valve shells of the mussel family) have been used as time-indicators, notably by Davies and Trueman (1927[3]) but identification of time-zones is not easy as many species are difficult to identify accurately in hand-specimens, and many are found through considerable thicknesses of strata.

The accepted method of classifying the Coal Measures is based on the occurrence of certain marine bands, i.e. rock-layers formed of sediments laid down in the open sea. These bands contain fossils of widely-distributed free-swimming organisms, which enable the bands to be identified wherever they occur. The Coal Measures are now universally classified using marine bands. The classification of the Coal Measures of this area (Woodland, Evans and Stephens 1957[14]) is shown diagrammatically in Figure 19.

3.1 The Lower Coal Measures

The base of the Lower Coal Measures in Western Europe is the Gastrioceras subcrenatum* marine band, and they extend upwards, in South Wales, to the base of the Amman marine band. These Measures are mainly grey, silty mudstones, with minor developments of sandstones, the most notable of the sandstones being the so-called 'Farewell Rock', below which there are no workable coals in the Merthyr area. The Lower Coal Measures also contain many of the worked ironstone deposits, which are bands of ironstone nodules, often closely associated with coal seams. Coal seams are generally less than 60 cm thick up to the Garw seam. All the worked seams are above the Garw. At the present time the Five Feet/Gellideg seam is extensively worked at Merthyr Vale colliery, and the Seven Feet seam is actively being exploited at the Merthyr Vale, Deep Navigation and Taff Merthyr collieries. The Measures include several marine bands, all occurring above thin coals below the Garw seam. The Amman marine band forms the roof of the Amman seam, which is a thin coal some 20 metres above the Seven Feet seam.

* a goniatite fossil.

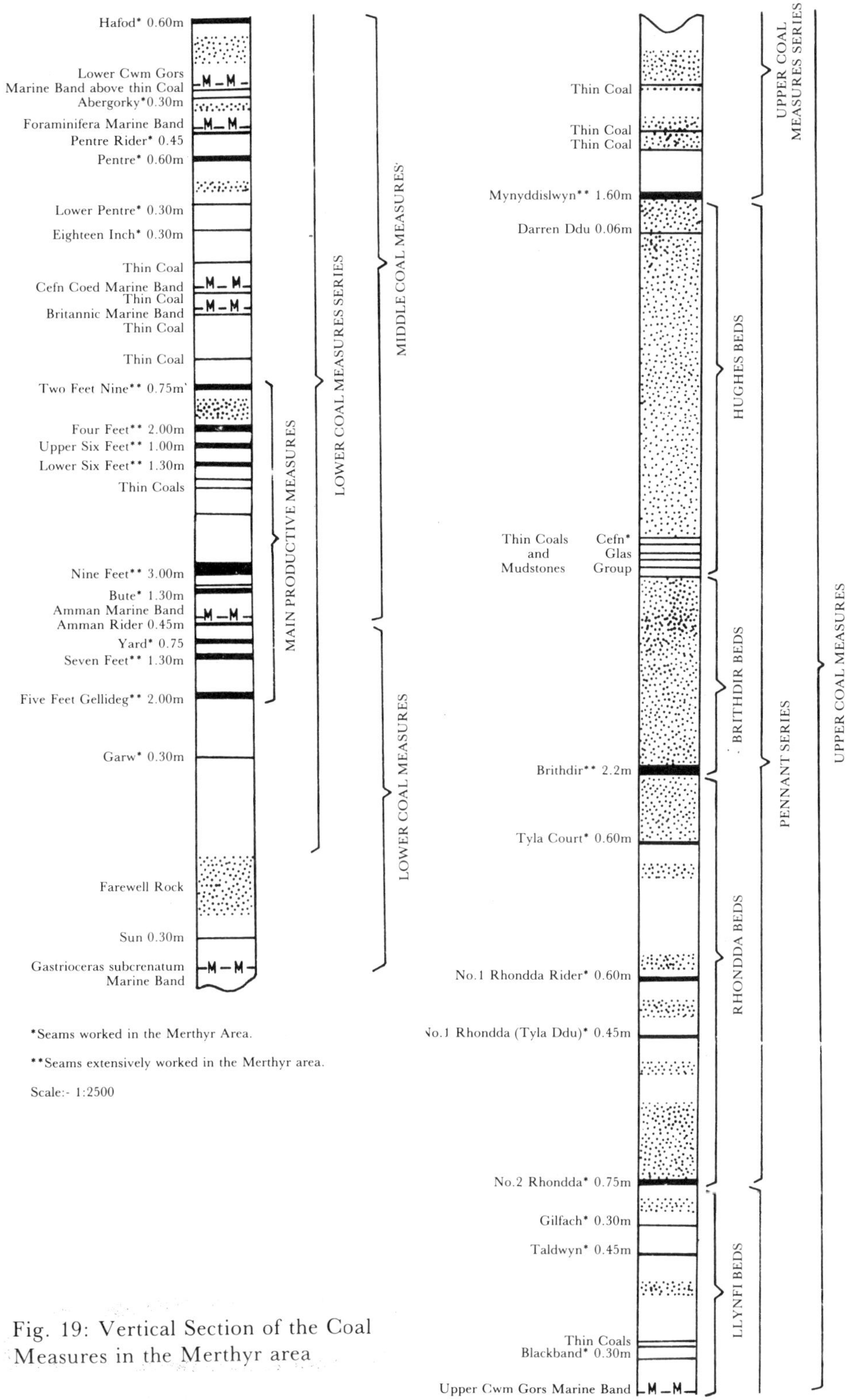

*Seams worked in the Merthyr Area.

**Seams extensively worked in the Merthyr area.

Scale:- 1:2500

Fig. 19: Vertical Section of the Coal Measures in the Merthyr area

3.2 The Middle Coal Measures

The Middle Coal Measures extend from the base of the Amman marine band to the top of the Upper Cwm Gors marine band. This group is also lacking in major sandstone bands, although sandstones begin to become important above the Two Feet Nine seam. The Measures are very similar to the Lower Coal Measures, being mainly silty mudstones, with subordinate thin sandstones. The silty mudstones become fine-grained downwards as the roofs of coal seams are approached. Thick coal seams are common. Although most seams have been exploited at one time and another, the seams that have been extensively worked around Merthyr are the Nine Feet seam, the Six Feet seam, and Four Feet seam, and the Two Feet Nine seam. There are several marine bands within this division.

The Lower and Middle Coal Measures together contain most of the thick coal seams, and the old Main Productive Measures division spans these two divisions.

3.3 The Upper Coal Measures

The Upper Coal Measures extend upwards from the top of the Upper Cwm Gors Marine band, and contain the Pennant Series and Upper Coal Measures described in the Introduction. They are a predominantly sandstone sequence, the most prominent exception being the Cefn Glas Group made up of some 20 metres of mudstones, thin coals and seatearths. The sandstones are variously cross-bedded, massive, and channel-fill deposits. Most coal-seams are thin, although many have been worked on a small scale. The only two thick seams extensively worked locally are the Brithdir seam (220 cm) worked in the Merthyr and Bedlinog valleys and currently being worked in the highly successful Trelewis Drift Mine; and the Mynyddislwyn seam (160 cm) which has been worked almost to exhaustion around Gelligaer.

4 *Structural Behaviour of the Coal Measures*

It is interesting to note the response of the Coal Measures to tectonic pressures in South Wales, and to observe the very different behaviour of the thick sandstones of the 'Pennant Series' from that of the weaker mudstones, coals and seatearths of the 'Main Productive Group'.

In general the Coal Measures in the Merthyr area dip just west of south, with an average dip of 4°, or 1 in 14, and are disrupted by large faults running from NW to SE.

The fault-pattern in the Pennant Series tends to be simple, the majority of the minor faults being parallel to the major ones, and with a smaller number of faults running from NE to SW. Most faults are single-plane faults i.e. with a single fault-face, often with a smash-zone of fault-gouge (a zone in which the rocks were pulverised by the dislocation process). Many faults are '*en echelon*', one fault taking up the throw as an associated fault dies out, e.g.

the Werfa Fault replaced by the Kilkenny Fault, and the Penydarren Fault replaced by the Rhos Fault (Figure 13). Faults tend to be persistent in length and in depth, even small faults with a throw of only a few feet extending over a mile in length, and affecting strata to depths of hundred of feet.

The fault pattern in the weaker, or less competent 'Main Productive Measures' is very different. Single-plane faults traced downwards from the overlying 'Pennant Series' are replaced by zones of several faults arranged '*en echelon*' both longitudinally and vertically. Fault patterns change rapidly, and adjacent seams only 50 feet apart, may have quite different fault patterns. In general, as one passes downward through the Main Productive Measures the number of faults increases to a maximum in the Nine Feet seam, and then decreases down to the lowest extensively-worked seam, the Five Feet/Gellideg seam. So-called 'Squash-out' structures are sometimes seen (Figure 18), the pressures due to faulting, having squeezed the coal towards zones of lower pressure, these features occurring in the Main Productive Group but not in the Pennant Series.

5 *Economic Exploitation*

The history of Merthyr Tydfil has been profoundly influenced by the Coal Measures. The presence of coal and ironstone in close proximity led to Merthyr becoming an early iron-making centre, and at the present time the Coal Measures continue to provide raw materials for industry.

The most obvious product is coal. At some time or other almost every seam has been worked to some extent. Today highly mechanised collieries at Merthyr Vale, Deep Navigation (Treharris), Taff Merthyr (Trelewis) and Trelewis Drift produce over one million tonnes of coal per annum, and employ over 2,000 men. The coal is used for the manufacture of smokeless fuel, and for electricity generation. There is also the Royal Arms Opencast site at Dowlais, first commissioned in 1958, and currently working seams from the Five Feet/Gellideg up to the Soap, the coal being destined for coking plants and electricity generation (Plate 10).

Underneath the coal-seams are the 'seat-earths', which are the 'fossil-soils' in which the swamp-forests grew. The seat-earths show an absence or scarcity of the alkalis sodium and potassium, which had been taken up by the forests. As a result they have a high melting point and can be used as fireclays for furnace-linings. Opencast sites around Merthyr have provided seat-earths for fireclays.

The Pennant sandstones were used extensively for building-stone in the past, especially in the southern part of the Borough. An old Pennant quarry may be seen on the east side of the main road at Merthyr Vale. A small quarry on Gelligaer Common still produces Pennant sandstone, rough or dressed, and its use as an attractive building-stone may be seen at the Castle Hotel Merthyr.

Plate 10: ROYAL ARMS OPENCAST SITE, DOWLAIS TOP, SO 080 082
For an idea of the enormity of these workings, see the Asda Superstore top left
(By permission of the National Coal Board and Taylor Woodrow Ltd. Photograph supplied by Taylor Woodrow Ltd.)

The Coal Measures have always provided much fill for road and rail construction. Pennant sandstone is still widely used as a fill-material. Burnt, red shale from coal tips has also been used for this purpose, and recent research by the National Coal Board has shown that the unburnt, black tip-material is even better-suited as fill-material. At present, local collieries are not finding a ready market for their waste but much of the fill for M4 motorway near Carmarthen was obtained from the tips of Brynlliw Colliery, near Llanelli.

Disused spoil-tips in Heolgerrig have provided the raw materials for a local brick factory for some years. Silty mudstones worked from local open-cast sites provide most of the remainder of the raw material supplied to the brickworks.

Thus after a very long period of exploitation, coal, and the rocks associated with it, still provide raw materials for several industries in the Merthyr area, and coal-mining is still the second largest employer in the Borough, a situation likely to continue into the next century.

A selection of Coal Measure fossils is shown in Fig 20.

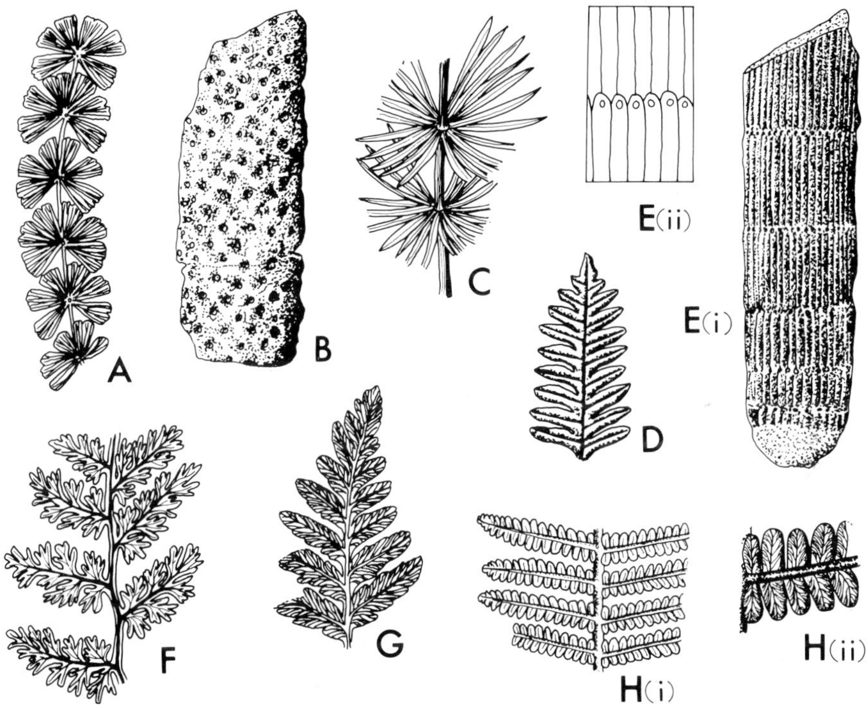

Fig. 20: A Selection of Coal Measures Fossils

Flora. A. The climbing plant *Sphenophyllum emarginatum* Brongniart (× ⅔); B. The tree root *Stigmaria ficoides* Brongniart (× ⅓); C. Foliage of *Calamites* trees, *Annularia stellata* Schlotheim) (× ⅔); D. The fern-like *Alethopteris serli* Brongniart (× ⅓); E(i). The pith cast of a tree branch *Calamites suckowi* Brongniart (× ⅓); E(ii). Ornamentation enlarged; F. The fern-like *Sphenopteris alata* Brongniart (× ⅔); G. The fern-like *Mariopteris nervosa* (Brongniart) (× ⅔); H(i). The true fern *Pecopteris polymorpha* Brongniart (× ⅔); H(ii). Part of frond enlarged (× 2);

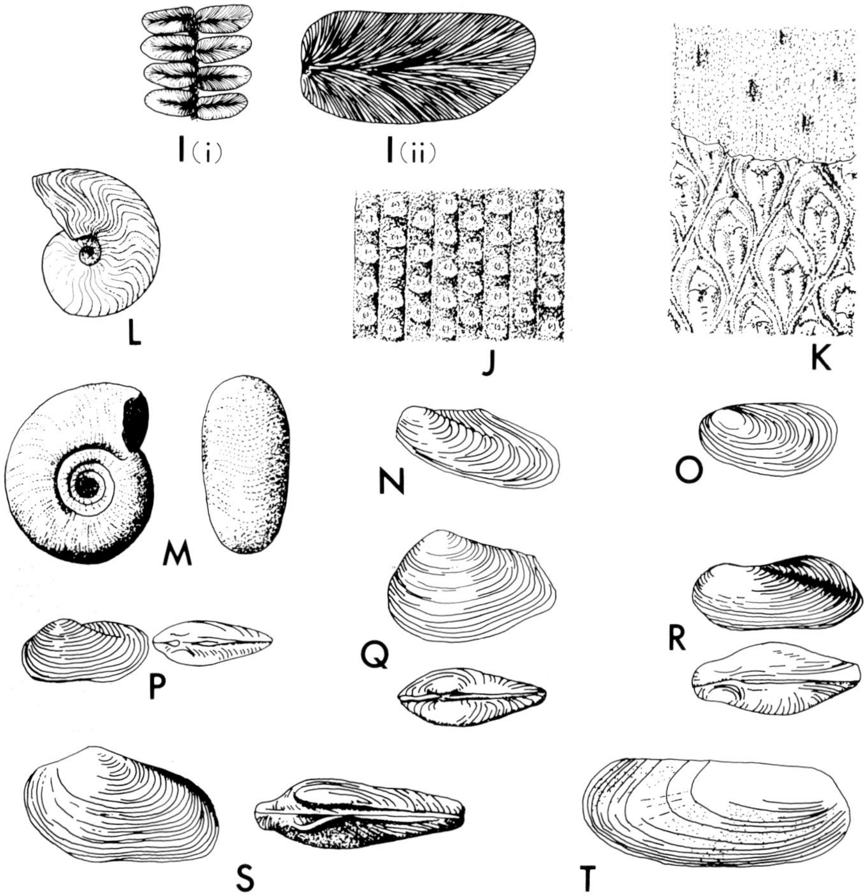

I(i). The fern-like *Neuropteris gigantea* Sternberg (× ⅓); I(ii). A pinnule enlarged (× 1⅔); J. Branch or stem of a tree, *Sigillaria mamillaris* Brongniart (× ⅓); K. Branch or stem of a tree, *Lepidodendron aculeatum* Sternberg (× ½).

Fauna. L. The goniatite *Anthracoceras cambriense* Bisat (× 1⅙); M. The goniatite *Gastrioceras subcrenatum* (Frech) (× ⅔). N. *Anthraconauta tenuis* Davies & Trueman (× ⅔); O. *Anthraconauta phillipsi* (Williamson (× ⅔); P. *Anthraconaia pulchra* Hind (× ⅔); Q. *Anthracosia similis* (Brown) (× ⅔); R. *Anthraconaia modiolaris* (J. de C. Sowerby) (× ⅔); S. *Carbonicola communis* Davies & Trueman (× ⅔); T. *Anthraconaia lenisulcata* (Trueman) (× 1).

Acknowledgement: The author wishes to thank the National Coal Board for permission to use and publish information from its extensive records.

References

[1] C.R.K. Blundell, 'The Succession and Structure of the North East Area of the South Wales Coalfield', *Quart Journ. Geol. Soc.*, Lond. 107, (1951) pp. 301-303.

[2] M.A. Butterworth & J. Millot, 'Microspore Distribution in the Coalfields of Britain', *Int. Committee for Coal Petrol* 3, Oh. (1960) pp. 157-163.

[3] J.H. Davies & A.E. Trueman, 'A Revision of the Non-marine Lamellibranchs of the Coal Measures, and a Discussion of their Zonal Sequence', *Quart. Journ. Geol. Soc.*, Lond. 83, (1927), pp. 210-259.

[4] E. Dix, 'The Sequence of Floras in the Upper Carboniferous with Special Reference to South Wales', *Trans. Roy. Soc.*, Edinb. 57, (1934) pp. 789-838.

[5] W. Francis, *Coal: its Formation and Composition,* Edward Arnold, London, (1954).

[6] B.J. Bluck & G. Kellings; 'Channels in the Upper Carboniferous Coal Measures of South Wales, *Sedimentology* 2, (1963) pp. 29-53.

[7] L.R. Moore, 'The Geological Sequence of the South Wales Coalfield: the 'South Crop', and Caerphilly Basin and their correlation with the Taff Valley Sequence', *Proc. S. Wales Inst. Engrs.* 60, (1943) pp.1 141-227, 228-242, 243-252.

[8] L.R. Moore, 'The Sequence of Structure of the Southern Portion of the South East Crop of the South Wales Coalfield', *Quart. Journ. Geol. Soc. London,* 103 (1948) pp. 261-300.

[9] L.R. Moore & A.H. Cox, 'The Coal Measure Sequence in the Taff Valley, Glamorgan, and its Correlation with the Rhondda Valley Sequence', *Proc. S. Wales Inst. Engrs,* 59, (1943) pp. 189-286.

[10] F.J. Pettijohn, *Sedimentary Rocks* (2nd Edit.), Harper and Row, New York, (1957) pp. 490-497.

[11] T.N. George, *British Regional Geology, South Wales* (3rd Edit.), (1970) H.M.S.O.

[12] Raistrick & Marshall, *The Nature and Origin of Coal and Coal Seams* (2nd Edit.).

[13] A.H.V. Smith & M.A. Butterworth, 'Miospores in the Coal Seams of Carboniferous of Great Britain', London (1967): The Palaeontological Association *Spec. Paper Palaeontology* No. 1.

[14] A.W. Woodland, W.B. Evans & J.V. Stephens, 'The Classification of the Coal Measures of South Wales with Special Reference to the Upper Measures', *Bull. Geol. Surv. Gt. Brit.* No. 3, (1957) pp. 6-13.

Bibliography

Adams, H.F., 'Seam Structure and Thickness in the South Wales Coalfield', *Trans. Inst. Min. Engrs.*, Lond., 115 (1955-56), 839-861. *Proc. S. Wales Engrs.* (1956) 71, 96-113, 114-115, 116-118.

Adams, H.F., 'The Coal Seams of South Wales', *Coke Oven Managers Assoc.*, Southern Section, March 1960.

Adams, H.F., 'The Seams of the South Wales Coalfield', London, *Inst. of Mining Engrs.*, (1967).

Bisat, W.S., 'On the Goniatite and Nautiloid Fauna of the Middle Coal Measures of England and Wales', *Summ. Progr. Geol. Surv.*, Lond., for 1929, Pt. III, 75-89 (1930).

Dunbar, C.O. & Rogers, J., *Principles of Stratigraphy,* John Wiley and Sons, London (1957).

Evans, D.E., 'The Classification of the Coal Measures of South Wales with Special Reference to Coal Seam Correlation', *Glam. Coll. Tech. Mining Soc. Magazine,* 1968-69 Session.

Hind, W., 'Carbonicola, Anthracomya and Naiadites', *Pal. Soc.*, Monograph (1894-1896).

Holmes, A., *Principles of Physical Geology* (2nd Edit.), Nelson, London (1965).

Hudson, R.G.S., 'The Goniatite Zones of the Namurian', *Geol. Mag.*, Lond., 82, 1-9 (1945).

Jeffrey, E.C., 'The Mode of Origin of Coal', *Journ. Geol.,* vol. 23, 218-230 (1915).

Moore, R.C., Lalicker, C.G. & Fisher, A.G., *Invertebrate Fossils,* McGraw Hill, New York, (1952).

National Coal Board, South Western Division, Production Dept., 'List of Standard Seam Namings and Equivalent Local Seam Namings for Collieries Working Seams Below the Two Feet Nine', *N.C.B. Report,* (1956).

National Coal Board, South Western Division, Production Dept., 'Seam Maps', London N.C.B. (1959).

Pettijohn, F.J., *Sedimentary Rocks* (2nd Edition), Harper & Row, New York (1957).

Read, H.H. & Watson, J., *Introduction to Geology,* Macmillan & Co. Ltd., London (1962).

Robertson, T., 'The Geology of the South Wales Coalfield, Part V: The Country Around Merthyr Tydfil' (2nd Edit.), *Mem. Geol. Surv. U.K.,* H.M.S.O. (1932).

Trueman, A. (Ed.), *The Coalfields of Great Britain*, Arnold, London (1954).

Weller, J.M., 'Cyclical Sedimentation of the Pennsylvanian Period, and its Significance' *Journ. Geol.* vol. 38, 97-135 (1930).

Wells, A.K. & Kirkaldy, J.F., *Outline of Historical Geology (5th Edit.), Chapt. 12, 248-273, Thomas Murby, London (1966).*

White, D. & Thiessen, R., 'The Origin of Coal', *U.S. Bur. Mines, Bull.* 38 (1913).

Woods, H., *Palaeontology, Invertebrate* (8th Edit.), Camb. Univ. Press (1963).

Earth Movements in the Area

by Professor T. R. OWEN

Department of Geology, University College of Wales, Swansea

The borough of Merthyr Tydfil is situated on the northern flanks of the major downfolded structural basin which has preserved the Coal Measures in the second largest coalfield of the British Isles. This downfold has a major E – W trend but is complicated by a number of minor folds within it. Minor upfolds occur for example at Pontypridd and near Swansea whilst minor downfolds or synclines are particularly well-marked in the Gorseinon, Pengam and Caerphilly districts. The Merthyr area however is essentially part of the straightforward, southward-tilted, northern limb of the main basin, the regional dips of the strata therefore being towards the south. These dips are generally low, in the order of 5 to 10 degrees, as typified by, for example, the tilt of the Carboniferous Limestone on the Morlais Castle Hill or the Pennant Sandstone on the high hill tops between the Taff and its neighbouring valleys. The tilts of these strata, as in fact most of the folds and faults in the Merthyr region, were produced by the strong N – S compressive earth-forces which operated late in the Carboniferous Period and which culminated in the Hercynian (Variscan or Armorican) Orogeny at the end of Carboniferous times.

As the compression began to be applied during the growing phases of the orogeny, the strata began to develop cracked joint systems and some of these minor fractures were later to assume far greater prominence by developing into major fractures or 'faults' in response to increasing compressive forces and increasing confining pressures. The majority of these fractures or faults in the Merthyr area trend almost NW – SE (Fig 21), a fault direction typical of this eastern quadrant of the South Wales Coalfield (Plate 11). Three major NW – SE fault systems can be picked out. These are (a) the Dowlais Trough, (b) the Merthyr Church Fault and (c) the Werfa Ridge. The fractures are characteristically arranged '*en echelon*'. The throws range from 30

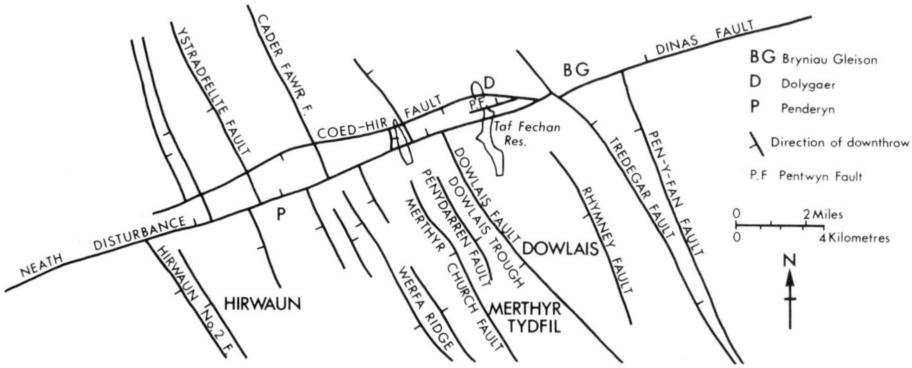

Fig. 21: Main Fault-Fractures in the Merthyr Area *T. R. Owen*

up to as much as 280 feet (the latter maximum occurring along the Werfa Fault on the west flank of Aberdare Mountain).

The Dowlais Trough is made up of the Dowlais Fault (downthrowing west) and the Penydarren Fault (downthrowing east). The throw of the former reaches 190 feet in the working of the Nine Feet seam. On Morlais Hill its throw is over 150 feet but it then rapidly dies out northwards. The Penydarren fracture has a stepped charcter with a *net* effective throw of about 120 feet (in the Seven Feet Coal, for example). The Merthyr Church Fault dislocates the Pennant escarpment southeast of Troedyrhiw and then runs up the Taff valley. It may well have determined the site of the valley in the Merthyr area. This fracture system again has a stepped character as was proved in the workings of the Hills Plymouth and Dyffryn pits. The maximum effective (westerly) downthrow is about 100 feet. The fault can be seen at Pwll Wat in the marked river bend near the old Cyfarthfa ironworks SO 083 071, (Plate 9), and near an old limestone quarry at the south end of the cemetery at Cefn Coed.

The Werfa 'Ridge' (actually a structural *horst*) changes its essential character from trough to horst along its length. The main elevated strip is about 1000 feet in width. The eastern bounding fracture is the Werfa Fault itself which achieves its greatest easterly downthrow (280 feet) where it accompanies a trough of the northern end of the disturbance.

The block-faulted character of the three NW – SE fracture belts just described, together with (i) the echelon pattern of the contributing fractures and (ii) the step-faulting, strongly suggest that they suffered a regional tension (E – W?) during some later stages of their development. Maybe (as in the case of the many NNW – SSE fracture belts in the western segments of the South Wales Coalfield) some of the faults were initiated as shear fractures during the main compression but were later used to facilitate stretching during the tensional relief that followed. It is possible that these later (vertical or gravity) movements occurred anywhere between Permo-Triassic and

Tertiary times. Local minor earthquake shakes at the beginning of this century (notably in 1906) may represent recent settling. The peat-covered moorland on Cefn Pennar shows some signs of very recent (but small) vertical movements.

The most important fault system, however, in the Merthyr district is the Neath Disturbance. This narrow, but extremely complex, belt of folding and fracturing is one of the major belts of disturbance in South and East-Central Wales. It is now known to extend from the vicinity of Neath as far northeast as the Welsh Borderland (in the vicinity of the Abberley Hills). At least a branch of it may extend from Neath westwards into Pembrokeshire, with another extending out from Neath past Mumbles Head into the Bristol Channel. In the Merthyr region it dominates the geological structure along a belt up to 1 mile wide extending in a NE – SW direction from Bryniau Gleision through Dolygaer to Abercar and thence across the high ground of Cader Fach and Cefn Cadlan to Penderyn Foel, where its effects are very clearly seen.

On Bryniau Gleision the main structural effects of the Neath Disturbance are the broad synclinal downfold preserving the Carboniferous Limestone outlier, and the Dinas Fault (the main NE – SW fracture of the Disturbance) on the southern flank. The Dinas Fault appears to dislocate the course of the Tredegar Fault. At Dolygaer, the Dinas Fault determines the floor of Cwm

Plate 11: MINOR N.N.W.-S.S.E. FAULT, HEADS OF VALLEYS ROAD, NEAR CEFN COED, SO 037 082
Millstone Grit (on right) downfaulted against Carboniferous Limestone

Callan, the Brownstones being extremely disturbed there. A subsidiary fracture (the Pentwyn Fault) courses through the old Dolygaer railway station and caused considerable trouble by leakage when the dam of the Pentwyn Reservoir was erected. At the Dolygaer Limestone outlier, however, the most important fracture (from the point of view of total downthrow) is the Coed-Hir Fault. This fracture can be seen (in a gulley north of Dolygaer Station) to throw the Millstone Grit conglomerate, on the south, against the Grey Grits on the north, thus faulting out the whole of the Carboniferous Limestone – a southerly downthrow of over 600 feet. (Fig 22).

Both the Coed-Hir and the Dinas fractures then continue westwards to the Taf Fawr valley (preserving even more small limestone outliers in otherwise Old Red Sandstone country) where they cross beneath the waters of the Llwyn-on Reservoir at Abercar. From here on it is the southern fracture – the Dinas Fault – that becomes dominant, with a downthrow north of over 700 feet on Cefn Cadlan. Many minor flexures occur (parallel to the trend of the main faults) in this region.

The author has demonstrated that the Dinas Fault is a major wrench (or 'tear') fault with a net sinistral shift (i.e. the northern side moving southwestwards) of about ¾ mile in the Merthyr and Penderyn districts. A similar movement was detected by the Geological Survey in the Coal Measures of the Vale of Neath. The tear movement and the parallel folds were due to the underlying influence of an ancient NE – SW fracture belt in the Precambrian basement, beneath the cover of Devonian and Carboniferous strata. The main Hercynian N – S compressive force was modified and resolved over the site of this old foundational structure. Faults such as the Coed-Hir fracture may well have been initiated later, as a result of tensional, gravity, movements (perhaps as late as Tertiary times).

Mention of Tertiary earth movements reminds one that substantial net uplift of the Merthyr area (as part of a larger Welsh region) must have taken place in late Tertiary times with the resultant levelling of platforms that now stand at heights such as 800, 1000, 1400 and 1800 feet above sea level. The

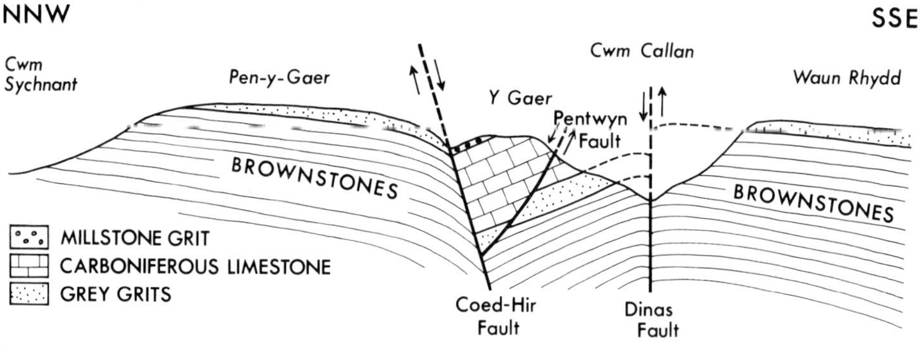

Fig. 22: The Neath Disturbance at Dolygaer *T. R. Owen*

Taff and other rivers have cut deeply into these platform relics. Whether the high level platforms were themselves the results of subaerial or marine erosive agents is a matter of controversy but the ultimate result in terms of a substantial rise above sea level, is the same. Lesser oscillations of the land, were of course to occur again in the Pleistocene, as ice sheets and glaciers came and went.

The most recent earth-movements to have occurred in the Merthyr region are landslips and tip-waste slides. Tragically, of course, Merthyr will always be associated with such phenomena because of the terrible Aberfan disaster on October 21st, 1966. The tragic slide which occurred then was from Tip No. 7 which had reached a height of 220 feet. The tip, mostly above the 800 feet contour was of spoil from the Merthyr Vale Colliery of the valley floor below. A flow-slide of 140,000 cubic yards travelled at up to 20 mph to reach the village. To quote from the recent book by Professor Anderson and Dr. Trigg (1975), 'The disaster which followed stunned the people of the Welsh Valleys and its chilling horror reverberated around the British Isles and beyond. The colliery waste engulfed the local junior school and dwelling houses, killing 116 small children and 28 adults.'

The Aberfan tips were situated on Pennant sandstones overlain by boulder clay and other drift deposits. The sandstones were jointed and fissured, the fissures being aggravated by the presence of a nearby fault zone and the effects of mining subsidence. These fissures (to quote again Anderson and Trigg) 'allow the infiltration of rainwater which, with some seepage delay, discharges downslope as springs.'

Anderson and Trigg (1975, pages 189-190) have summarised the Technical Reports submitted to the Aberfan Tribunal. These showed (again quoting Anderson and Trigg) that 'Factors contributing to the (tip) failure were summarised as follows:

(a) Water issuing beneath the tip caused back-sapping, defined as removal of material from the toe by an issue of water or a spring, the removal of this material leading to intermittent slips of progressively increasing size.

(b) Water under pressure acting in the tip material and in the limited area of the foundation where the slip surface was adjacent to the natural ground, reduced the effective stresses in the fill and initiated a shear displacement.

(c) Saturation conditions in the loose fill comprising the tip and covering the area of the mountainside below, made it susceptible to a catastrophic flow slide, since a shear displacement or shock wave could result in the transfer of most of the load on to the relatively incompressible water in the voids, thus reducing the frictional strength to a very low value.

(d) Water released by the slip and consequent flow slide subsequently caused a mud-run of tip rubbish, some of the natural ground having been torn away from the mountainside permitting the release of a quantity of water under pressure in the fissured sandstone.'

Signs of more ancient landslides occur elsewhere in the Taff valley, especially where the Pennant Sandstone outcrops on the valley sides. The best example is at Troedyrhiw (near the disused swimming pool SO 077 020) on the east side of the valley (Plate 12). An appreciable segment of the Pennant has slid down from its scar here. The landslip closely resembles several in the Rhondda valleys. These are believed to date back to the end of the Pleistocene glaciation (some 12,000 years ago), to a time when ice and snow were melting and when the water table was much higher. The Troedyrhiw slip could also date back to that phase. Another ancient landslip has occurred on the eastern side of Twyn Brynbychan near Perthygleision. This slip covers an area ½ mile across and occurred at the base of the Upper Pennant Measures (the horizon of the Cefn Glâs Coal).

Plate 12: LANDSLIP IN PENNANT SANDSTONE, TROEDYRHIW, SO 077 020
Landslip traversed by Merthyr Church Fault

Bibliography

J.G.C. Anderson, and C.F. Trigg, *Case Histories in Engineering Geology* (Elek Press, 1975).

T.R. Owen, 'The structure of the Neath Disturbance between Bryniau Gleision and Glynneath', *Quart. J. Geol. Soc.* Lond. Vol. 109, (1954), 333-365.

T.R. Robertson, 'The Country around Merthyr Tydfil' 2nd edition, *Mem. Geol. Surv. G. Britain.* (1932).

Landforms of the Area

by D. EMLYN EVANS

Before outlining briefly the probable sequence of events in the evolution of our landforms in the Merthyr district, it might be advisable to refer to some of the more obvious scenic features and to remind readers of the fact that all the hypotheses that have been suggested to account for them depend ultimately on individual interpretations.

The very occurrence of river valleys, and in particular the spacing between those in juxtaposition in regions such as ours, where rain and running water are the chief agents of erosion, are facts usually accepted without being fully understood even by geomorphologists. However, the general direction of the local valleys is now considered to be the direct consequence of events connected to elevation of land in the geological past. It was thought once that faults which occurred during the Armorican mountain building movement were the main control, but these are now considered to be limited in their effect.

A popularly accepted hypothesis is that which claims that erosion is more readily achieved in regions of soft rocks than in those of hard rocks. Those of our valley sections that are excavated in Pennant Sandstones, for example, are much narrower or gorge-like than those which consist predominantly of Coal Measures Shales; thus the Taf Valley between Pentrebach and Edwardsville is appreciably narrower than it is in the Merthyr area. There is one complication, however. The Carboniferous Limestone is seemingly a soft rock, but because of its peculiar properties of being soluble in most water that flows across limestone country, and of being traversed by innumerable joints or cracks, the rock is characterised by caves with their well known stalactites and stalagmites, by underground streams, by narrow gorge-like valleys, by surface swallow holes and by bare rocky pavements protruding through the generally thin soils. All these features can be seen in the comparatively narrow limestone outcrop that extends across the district.

Before going into greater detail it is well to remember that the geomorphology of the Merthyr area has not been studied in any detail as yet. However, it is possible to offer in general terms an outline of the events which have produced the present-day scenery.

A comparatively recent and seemingly popular view proposed by George (1974) is that the Welsh area in the last 30 million years or so has been subjected to staggered uplift of over 3,000 ft. and that the elevated land massif is bounded by major faults such as the recently discovered Llanbedr fault zone which runs north to south off the coast at Harlech. During the periods of little, if any, uplift, or still-stand, the sea during Neogene times was able to planate large tracts of the land surface which, with the subsequent elevation, were revealed as plateau-like surfaces sloping gently towards the receding sea and away from the central highlands. Brown (1960) has claimed to be able to identify seven major planation surfaces although he suggested that the three highest were river-worn and not sea-worn. The map (Fig. 23) shows the distribution of the three highest plateau-remnants in our area, viz. the High, Middle and Low Plateaux between heights of 1,700 and 2,000ft., 1,200 and 1,600ft. and 700 and 1,100ft., respectively. The highest will obviously be the oldest and furthest away from the present coastline.

The areas above 2,100ft., and described by Brown as the Monadnock Group, are the remnants of a land area surrounded by sea when the High Plateau was being eroded by marine action. It is conjectural whether or not this land was continued northward to join the land that existed in the Plynlimon and Snowdonia areas. However, it seems very probable that the headwaters of the Taf Fawr and Taf Fechan (and probably the Mellte to the west) were in existence as flowing off or through the Brecon Beacons highland at this period. With uplift of land the river courses were extended across a wave-worn platform to join the sea further south. During the following period of still-stand the sea was able to erode a second submarine platform as well as to encroach into part of the High Plateau land by cliff erosion. This kind of process was repeated on numerous occasions to produce, between our area and the present-day coast, the Low Plateau, the 600 ft., the 400 ft., the 300 ft. and 200 ft. Platforms, the preservation of which shows a marked deterioration with age, the best preserved being the lowest and newest. The process is shown in Fig. 24.

This sequence of events would account for the manner in which our South Wales rivers flow across the geological 'grain' of the region. With softer rocks being worn away with greater ease than harder kinds it follows that the downfolded or synclinal structure of the South Wales coalfield, which was produced in early Permian times, is now reflected in the present-day relief by escarpments running generally west to east. In the northern part of the area under discussion comes the north-facing Beacons escarpment of the Upper Devonian grits and conglomerates; further south come the similarly disposed escarpments of the Carboniferous Limestone, the Basal Grit, the Farewell Rock and finally the Pennant Sandstone. These features are best developed in the hill-top areas between the main rivers (see Fig. 2).

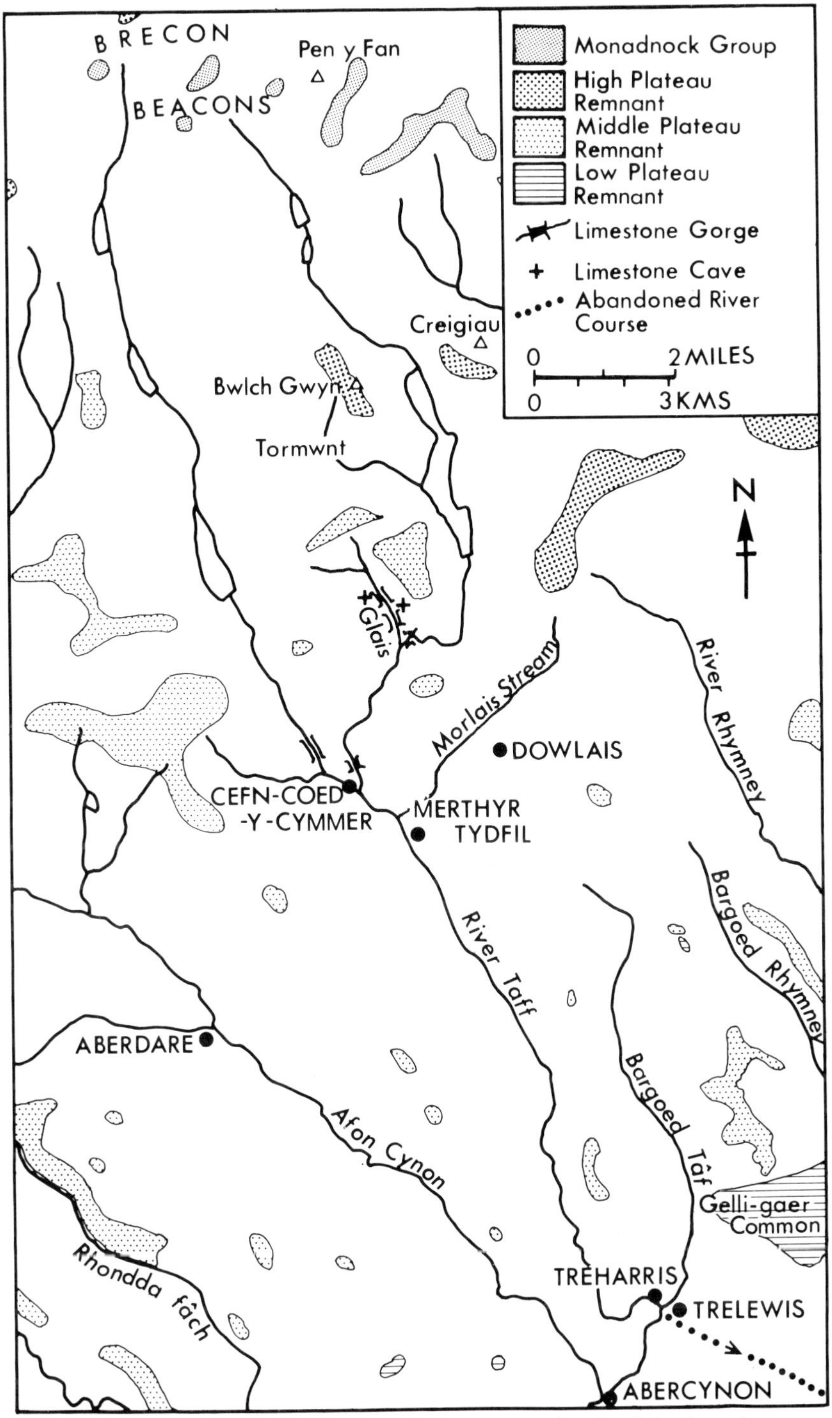

Fig. 23: The Main Geomorphological Features in the Merthyr Area (after Brown 1960)

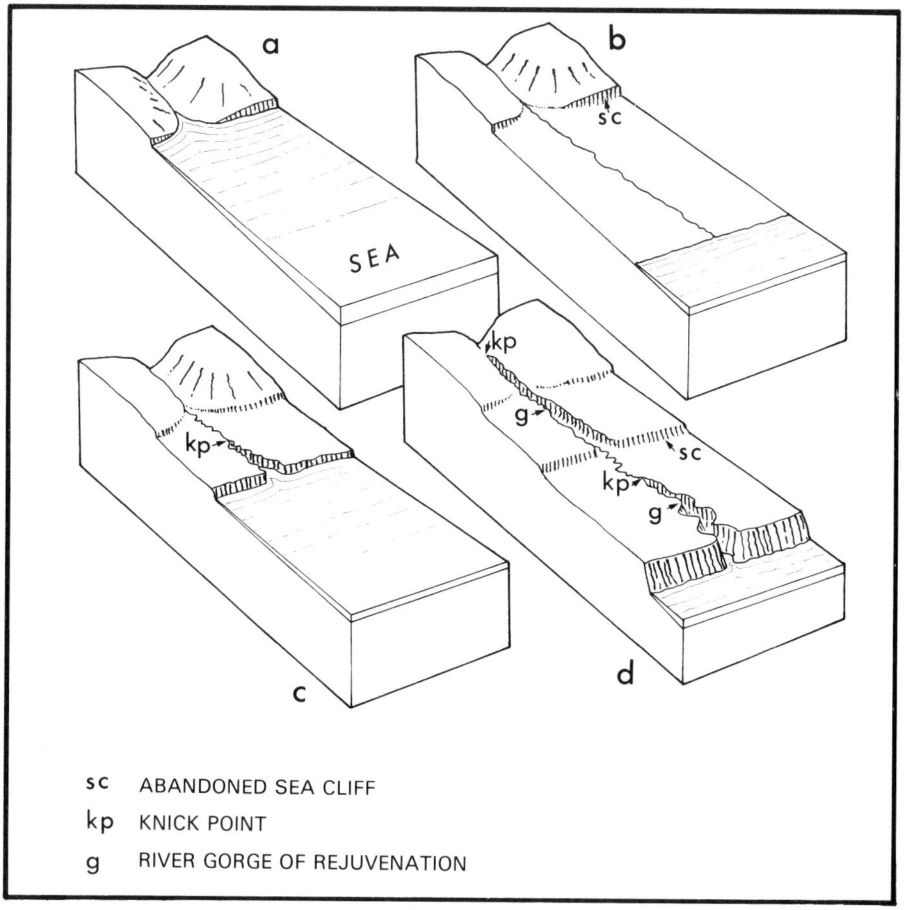

Fig. 24: Block-diagrams illustrating the formation of marine-planation surfaces

(a) Submarine wave-worn platform created by marine erosion.
(b) Uplift of platform to form coastal plateau.
(c) Coastal plateau partly eroded by sea. Rejuvenation-processes active.
(d) Second uplift and further rejuvenation.

The general hypothesis proposed by George would account also for the occurrence, at certain localities, of minor valley forms being excavated in the floors of older major valleys. The block diagram (Fig. 24) attempts to show how the formation of each wave-worn surface or plateau causes a minor river gorge to proceed upstream through the older valleys. The locations where streams flow via rapids, or even waterfalls, into the lower reaches, are known as knick points. By careful research it is sometimes possible to relate well-preserved knick points to their appropriate marine platforms. Some of the waterfalls in the upper reaches of both the Taf Fawr and Taf Fechan rivers might have originated as knick points, although it must be remembered that the more recent passage downstream of valley glaciers must have obliterated the original points but not necessarily the changes of slope in the valley floor. These could well have been re-asserted by more recent river erosion.

Related to the occurrence of this valley-within-valley form (or stream rejuvenation) due to uplift of land, is the process known as river-capture. A good example is provided by the headwaters of the Neath River. The headwaters of the River Neath, the Mellte and Little Neath, were originally tributaries of the Cynon, even after the formation of the 400 ft. platform. But the Neath, (see Fig. 25 a,b.) by exploiting a weakened fault zone, extended its headwaters along the faults in an east-north-easterly direction until eventually it was able to divert the Cynon tributaries into its own valley. It is interesting to observe that, following upon such capture, another kind of valley-within-valley form develops and proceeds upstream along the course of the captured river from the point of original diversion (Fig. 25c).

Another example of river capture occurs in the Treharris-Trelewis area. In this case the Bargoed Taf River probably flowed through Nelson and via the Tredomen Gap into the Rhymney River at Ystrad Mynach. Evidence for this is best seen in the small tributary valleys, especially between

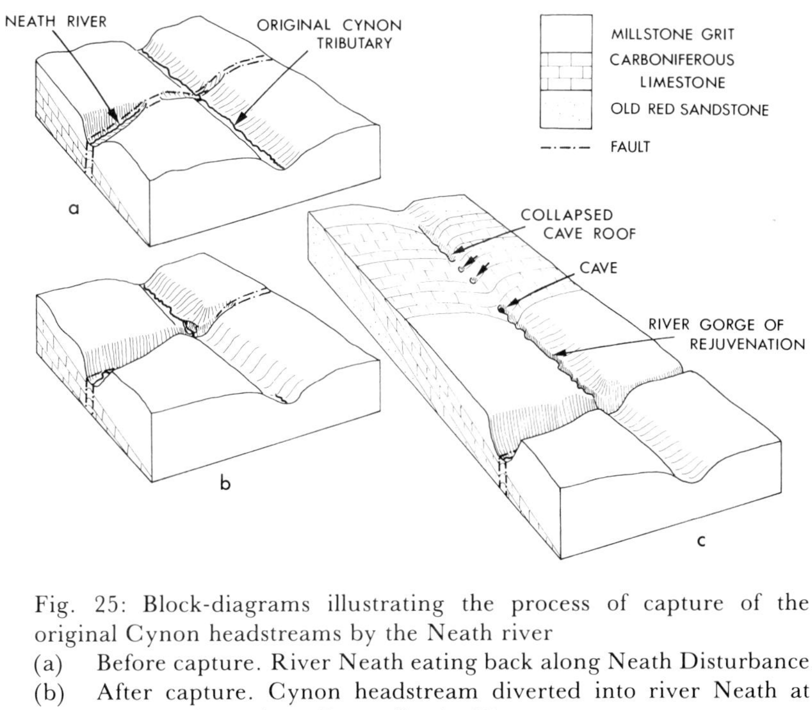

Fig. 25: Block-diagrams illustrating the process of capture of the original Cynon headstreams by the Neath river

(a) Before capture. River Neath eating back along Neath Disturbance.

(b) After capture. Cynon headstream diverted into river Neath at Pontneathvaughan. Dry valley in Hirwaun area.

(c) Rejuvenation-features upstream from point of capture.

Trelewis and Bedlinog, which carried little ice during glaciation and where, accordingly, good features of rejuvenation are to be seen. Due to extensive glacial erosion in the main valley such evidence is appreciably modified although traces are still discernible. It might be that the Taf Fawr itself flowed through this gap exploiting the fault zone which includes the Gelligaer and Llanfabon faults. A tributary of the Cynon extending its course in a north-easterly direction could have captured both the Taf Fawr and its tributary the Bargoed Taf following the uplift involved with the 400 ft. platform. This would account for the rejuvenated gorges which are so well displayed in the vicinity in the Upper Coal Measures Sandstones of the area. Taking this possibility further, it might be that the rejuvenation gorge which might have proceeded up the Taf Fawr valley has been practically preserved in the remarkable Ffrwd Gorge where the resistant Cumbriense Quartzite of some 15 ft. thickness has retarded its progress upstream.

When a gorge of rejuvenation, formed either by river capture or by uplift of land, proceeds upstream and encounters a band of outcropping limestone, the stream is often found to flow through the rock in a pipe-like cave (Fig. 25c). It has obviously been able to sink down through cracks or joints until it arrives at a more stable level where it eventually dissolves a linear cavern beneath the surface. This feature occurs in all three streams captured by the Neath.

Two small limestone caves occur in the Glais Stream, a tributary which enters the Taf Fechan at Pontsarn. They are Ogof Rhyd-sŷch, SO 042 102, better known locally as 'Beaver's Cave', and Ogof y ci, SO 040 105. Rejuvenation by uplift possibly associated with the 600 ft. platform, could be responsible for these features. A similar process possibly associated with this and a later platform could have occurred in the areas where the Taf Fawr and Taf Fechan streams cross the limestone outcrops, although there are no major caves there at the present time. The comparatively recent valley glaciers could have passed over such caves, leaving the roofs thinner but still intact, so that surface water in post-glacial times was able by solutional weathering to bring about cave-roof collapse to produce the narrow gorges seen at the present time, e.g. in the Blue Pool section of the Taf Fechan, SO 045 097 (Plate 13).

One further feature needs to be mentioned. The occurrence of major faults has affected in some measure the shape of the modern land surface. The Taf Fawr River, as it cut its course vertically downwards from above High Plateau levels to its present position, was able to exploit the weakened rocks along the Merthyr Church Fault zone, which incidentally consists of three, or even more, closely spaced and parallel faults. The Glais stream is aligned, in a similar manner, along the Dowlais fault.

The last major phase in the geomorphological evolution of the area is that known as the Ice Age. Contrary to popular concept this involved a complicated sequence of events. In the last 2,100,000 years the Northern Hemisphere experienced twenty-one periods of ice formation (Bowen 1977). A

Plate 13: LIMESTONE GORGE, BLUE POOL, PONTSARN,
SO 045 097

study of deep-ocean sediments, and their microscopic fossil forms, provides convincing evidence for these glaciations. First signs of really intense cold in Europe did not occur until 700,000 years ago, but not until about 450,000 years ago is there similar British evidence. This earliest British glaciation, known as the Anglian, was followed by an interglacial period of temperate climate – the Hoxnian. Then came the Wolstonian Glaciation, followed by the Ilfordean Interglacial. The Middle Pleistocene period could have terminated in a comparatively short cold, if not glacial, period but better evidence is available for the Upper Pleistocene period which commenced some 128,000 years ago. This period opened with the Ipswichean Interglacial which was followed by a cold period which extended through early and middle Devensian time and developed into the last major glaciation (of late Devensian time) commencing some 26,000 years ago and reaching a maximum stage some 18,000 years ago.

As yet no evidence has been found in our area for the earlier Lower and Middle Pleistocene glaciations but it is obvious that ice in great quantity accumulated on the high ground in the Beacons during the last glacial episode. The Taff valley was completely filled because the hills on either side, such as Cefn yr Ystrad (1,866 ft.), Cefn Cil Sanws (1,516 ft.) and On Llŵyn (1,376 ft.) are glaciated to their summits. Striated and polished rock surfaces over which the ice moved, indicate clearly, when such features are preserved, the direction of the ice-flow. It seems that at their maximum the ice-flows in the upper regions consisted of lobes of an icesheet that rode over all minor obstacles. There was, however, one major obstacle – the high sandstone escarpment of Craig-y-Llyn, at the head of the Rhondda valleys, which caused the Brecknock ice-flow to split, one part following the Cynon and Taff valleys, the other going down the Vale of Neath.

In the upper part of the Taf Fawr a lobe of ice seems to have branched off into the headwaters of the Hepste River. A similar branching of the ice from the Upper Taf Fechan seems to have moved down into the Glyn Collwn valley through the Torpantau Gap. Branch ice from the main Taf and Bargoed Taf valleys in the Trelewis-Treharris area undoubtedly flowed through the Nelson area via the Tredomen Gap into the Rhymney Valley at Ystrad Mynach.

Indications of the direction of the movement of glaciers or ice sheets are provided by striated rock surfaces which show scratching and polishing produced by the ice. A good example is to be seen at a location a few yards west of the old railway track south of Twynau Gwynion (SO 0685 0985). Numerous similar occurrences are to be found in our area.

The rock debris or 'drift' created by the glacial erosion provides further important evidence. In the upper regions this took the form of a clayey material enclosing usually rounded fragments of the different rock types over which the ice travelled. Fragments of Old Red Sandstone, Carboniferous Limestone and Millstone Grit rocks found in this so-called boulder-clay, testify to the northern source of the ice. In the lower parts of the valleys the glacial deposits, or drift, include layered sands and gravels laid down by water issuing from the melting ice.

Some of the more spectacular results of glaciation are the deep hollows or cwms sometimes enclosing tarn-lakes and carved out by ice usually on the northward facing flanks of the highest hills. These can be partially enclosed by drift in forms known as moraines. Good examples are those of Llyn Cwm Llwch near Pen-y-Fan on the north face of the Beacons escarpment and those of Llyn Fawr and Llyn Fach beneath Craig-y-Llyn. Other erosional landforms are the typically glaciated valleys of the Taf Fawr and Taf Fechan. The original river-worn V-shaped cross-sections of the valleys have been converted into U-shaped forms. This process produced near-vertical valley sides, a condition which sometimes gave rise to further developments.

During the very cold periglacial conditions which existed at the end of the glacial period proper, surface water and ground water were subjected to almost continuous freezing and thawing, processes which penetrated deeply into the great natural cracks or joints in the rocks of the area, producing in certain areas major instabilities. One of the best examples is the large landslide near Troedyrhiw near the disused swimming pool at SO 077 020 (Plate 11) where the very steep eastern side of the valley consisted of well-jointed Pennant Sandstone overlying soft shales. Similar slides occur on the west side of the Taf Fawr at Perthygleision south of Aberfan and in the Bargoed Taf valley above Bedlinog. In the Old Red Sandstone country where the rock beds dip into the valley, similar displacements occur. A small landslide occurs on the western side of the Taf Fawr above Storey Arms. Others occur in the upper Glyn Collwn valley, one below the crag of Cwâr y Gigfran SO 06 19 and another located some one-and-a-half miles to the south-east above the site of the former chapel (SO 078 182).

Another product of the period of periglacial climate was the production by thawing and freezing of a layer of stone-laden soil which slid slowly down the valley sides. This so-called 'head' consists of angular rock fragments derived from bedrock on the upper slopes and embedded in a fine-grained or even clayey matrix. It is accordingly very different from boulder-clay in the general shape of its stone content as well as in the lack of variety of rock types displayed. With the exception of the sandstone crags and the higher rises of the plateau, the deposit covers the entire surface of the district to a depth of several feet. It lies above the glacial drift, and in certain hollows and on lower slopes it may reach a depth of as much as twenty to thirty feet.

More recent deposits are the peat and alluvium. The former is due obviously to the high rainfall on the mainly acid soil of the area, either as blanket peats draped over the long gentle slopes and ridges or as basin peat found in hollows where drainage is poor. Such peats are often found in valley floors upstream from mounds of boulder-clay left by the glaciers, and which impound temporary glacial lakes.

The most recent deposit is the alluvium which our streams are depositing in the valley floors, and which usually lies upon 'head' or glacial drift.

Bibliography

D.Q. Bowen, 'Hot and cold climates in prehistoric Britain', *Geog. Mag.*, **49.** (1977) 685-698.

E.H. Brown, *The relief and drainage of Wales: a study in geomorphological development,* University of Wales Press, Cardiff (1960), xii, 186pp.

T.N. George, 'The Cenozoic evolution of Wales', in Owen, T.R. (ed.), *The Upper Palaeozoic and post-Palaeozoic rocks of Wales . . .* (University of Wales Press, Cardiff, 1974), 341-371.

D.G. Jones and T.R. Owen, 'The rock succession and geological structure of the Pyrddin, Sychryd and Upper Cynon valleys, South Wales', *Proc. Geol. Ass.,* **37,** (1956) 232-250.

Glossary of Geological Terms used in the Text

by RONALD T. GETHIN

Algae The algae are seaweeds.

Anticline A structural upfold whereby rock layers are in an arch-like formation.

Argillaceous The argillaceous sedimentary rocks are the fine-grained clays, shales, mudstones, siltstones and marls.

Armorican The Armorican orogeny, or mountain-building period which followed the Carboniferous period. It affected western Europe. In central and eastern Europe the same orogeny is referred to as Hercynian.

Bedding-plane A surface parallel to the surface of deposition of a bed of rock.

Bedding-surface The surface of deposition of a rock - layer.

Brachiopod A marine bivalve creature, the two valves being nearly always unequal in size. The presence of brachiopod fossils is an unfailing indication that the rocks containing them were laid down in the sea.

Brackish Describes water partly fresh, partly salt.

Bryozoa Marine colonial organisms often in the form of a closely-meshed grid. Like the corals, bryozoa are reef-builders.

Carbonaceous Containing carbon in the form of coal.

Carboniferous The Carboniferous system includes the Carboniferous Limestone (Dinantian), Millstone Grit (Namurian) and Coal Measures (Westphalian). So called because of the occurrence of carbon, in the form of coal, in the rocks of this system.

Channel deposits Deposits laid down on the bed of a stream.

Competent Describes a rock-layer which does not show much internal deformation when subjected to the stress of folding.

Conchoidal fracture Fracture of a mineral or rock in which the fracture – surface shows concentric ridges. Thick bottle-glass often shows this fracture.

Conglomerate A coarse-grained sedimentary rock made up of pebbles rounded by movement in water. Pebble-accumulations on beaches and river flood-plains become conglomerates when cemented.

Crinoid A fossil marine creature consisting of cup or calyx which was usually anchored to the sea-bed by a stem made up of jointed segments which constitute the usual fossil remains.

Cross-bedding A bed of sedimentary rock is often made up of very thin layers called laminae. The laminae are often parallel to the top and bottom of the rock-layer, but in some sandstones and oolites the laminae are inclined obliquely with regard to the top and bottom of the rock layer. Cross-bedding is the result of sediments being 'tipped' by wind or water in the same manner as materials on a waste-tip. Cross-bedding is also termed false-bedding. In water-laid deposits it is often called current-bedding. Current-bedding is typical of shallow-water deposits.

Dextral If one looks across a dextral tear-fault the rocks on the other side appear to have moved to one's right.

Diachronous A diachronous bed of rock appears to be a continuous unit, but was laid down at different times in different places. With the gradual rise of the Welsh Heartland, after the Carboniferous Limestone period, the Merthyr-Dowlais area began to receive deltaic deposits at an earlier date than the Pontneathvaughan area to the south-west. Thus the lowest Millstone Grit rocks of the Merthyr-Dowlais are older than those of the Pontneathvaughan area, although the rocks are broadly similar.

Dolomite The mineral dolomite is Calcium-magnesium carbonate. A limestone is made up largely of calcium carbonate, but should there be more than 15% of magnesium carbonate present the rock is called a dolomitised limestone or, simply, dolomite. Weathered dolomites are often brown or yellow and do not contain many fossils.

En echelon En echelon faults are parallel and have the same direction of downthrow, but the fault terminations are 'staggered', so that on a geological map the fault-outcrops have the appearance of a side-view of the treads of a flight of stairs, e.g. the relation between the Werfa and Kilkenny faults in Fig. 13 (Coal Measures).

Energy-environment A high-energy sedimentation environment would be one with rapidly flowing currents of water, e.g. coastal waters. A low energy sedimentation environment would be one with quiet waters, e.g. a lagoon.

Escarpment A land-form with a laterally-extended steep face inclined in a direction opposite to that of the dip of the rocks e.g. the north face of the Brecon Beacons.

Facies The general aspect of a sedimentary rock-unit. The term 'facies' is usually preceded by a term relating to the outstanding features of the environment in which the rock was formed, e.g. a shelly facies would indicate a sediment with a rich content of fossil shells.

Fault A fracture in a rock layer or layers whereby a bed or beds are displaced.

Fault-breccia Rocks in a fault-zone are commonly broken. If the rocks are hard the fragments are large and angular, and are called fault-breccia.

Fault gouge If the broken rocks in a fault-zone are soft the fragments are fine enough to be called 'rock flour', which is another term for fault gouge.

Feather-fracture Feather-like markings on a rock face, and which are due to stress. These markings are also called chevrons.

Fissile A fissile rock has the property of parting into very thin sheets parallel to the bedding of the rock e.g. shale.

Gastrioceras A member of the goniatite family.

Gastropod A member of the snail family, with a single coiled shell usually rising like a cone, but occasionally flat like an ammonite e.g. Euomphalus.

Goniatite A cephalopod (octopus family) with a plane-spiral shell like a Catherine-wheel, and with a resemblance to the related and better-known ammonite. Goniatites are important zone-fossils in the Millstone Grit.

Granule A rock-particle with a diameter between 2mm. and 4mm.

Gravel The precise geological definition is the same as that of granule, but the term is also used loosely with regard to unconsolidated coarse sediments such as river gravels and glacial gravels, in which case there is no reference to particle size.

Grit A sandstone in which the particle-shape is angular.

Hematite An oxide of iron, ferric oxide, Fe_20_3. A rock containing a large concentration of hematite would be an important iron ore. There are no local hematite ores.

Hercynian A period of mountain - building (see Armorican).

Horst An upthrown area between two parallel faults.

Interface The surface at which a lower system of rocks meets an upper system of rocks.

Knick point or nick point The change of slope at the meeting-place of the older, upstream, gentler long-profile of a river-valley with the younger, downstream, steeper long-profile resulting from rejuvenation.

Lithification The processes whereby loose sediments are formed into rock.

Lithological Relating to the general characteristics of a rock, and more especially its composition and texture. The lithology of a region would be a description of the rock-types present.

Marl A mudstone containing calcium carbonate.

Massive Most sedimentary rocks are made up of very thin layers called laminae. Strata that show no internal lamination exhibit massive bedding.

Metamorphism The process whereby rocks are changed from their original state by heat, pressure and chemically active fluids and gases.

Monadnock An isolated hill, standing above the level of the surrounding country. Monadnocks are the elevated, isolated remnants of a surface otherwise lowered by prolonged denudation.

Moraine An accumulation of material transported and deposited by ice.

Mudstone A very fine-grained rock made up of consolidated clay, in which the size of the grains is less than 1/256 mm in diameter. It has many similarities with shale, but lacks the fissility of shale.

Namurian A stratigraphic unit which corresponds roughly with the Millstone Grit series of the Carboniferous system. The term derives from Namur in Belgium, where these rocks have been studied in detail.

Neogene A name given to the Miocene and Pliocene periods of the Tertiary (see Fig. 1).

Orogeny A period of mountain-building. Orogenesis is the process of mountain-building.

Oscillatory Relates to short-term alternation in land and sea level, typical of Coal Measures deposition.

Outlier An area of younger rock surrounded or nearly surrounded, on the surface, by older rock. A fault outlier is the result of fault action.

Palaeogeography A reconstruction of the presumed geographical position of land and water at a particular time in the past.

Peneplain Literally 'almost a plain'. It is the form a land surface takes after prolonged exposure to the work of weather and rivers in a humid climate.

Periglacial Relates to conditions in a region adjacent to an ice-sheet.

Pyrite Iron sulphide, brassy-yellow, and commonly known as 'Fool's Gold'.

Quartz The crystalline form of silica. It is glassy in appearance, and very hard.

Quartzite A very hard sandstone with silica grains from 1/16 mm to 2 mm in diameter. The silica grains are cemented by silica. Local examples occur in the Grey Grits of the Old Red Sandstone, and in the Basal Grit and Cumbriense Quartzite of the Millstone Grit.

Rejuvenation Takes place with the relative uplift of land with regard to sea level. On the coast this produces raised beaches. Inland, rivers, endowed with renewed energy, cut new valleys within the old ones to create river terraces, which are the remnants of former flood-plains, and waterfalls at the knick-point junctions of old and new valley profiles.

Siltstone A fine-grained rock made of silt particles 1/256 to 1/16 mm in diameter.

Sinistral If one looks across a sinistral tear-fault the beds on the other side appear to have moved to one's left e.g. the Dinas Fault of the Neath Disturbance.

Spores Reproductive structures of non-flowering plants such as mosses, ferns and fungi.

Step-faulting A parallel series of faults, all down-throwing in the same direction.

Tear-fault A fault in which movement of the disturbed strata is lateral rather than vertical. Also termed a wrench fault. Example: the Dinas Fault of the Neath Disturbance.

Tectonic Relates to structural processes of rock-deformation e.g. the effects of folding and faulting.

Trough A downthrown area between two parallel faults. Also termed a graben.

Unconformity An interruption in the accumulation of sediments. When sedimentation is renewed, part of the rock-succession is therefore missing. The newer, upper strata are often inclined at a different angle to the lower beds below the unconformity, in which case it is an angular unconformity.

Washout A channel cut into sediment, and filled by later material. There are many examples in the coalfields, streams having cut channels in the rotting vegetation, the channels being subsequently filled with sand, to the exclusion of coal.

Westphalian A stratigraphic unit corresponding roughly with the Coal Measures. Westphalia is in West Germany.

Acknowledgements

The editorial board is very grateful for the ready response from the three authors invited to assist with the Geology section. All three have close local connections, Professor T.R. Owen being an ex-Cyfarthfa student from Pentrebach, Mr. Malcolm Blandford a former County School pupil from Dowlais, and Mr. Emlyn Evans hailing originally from Fochriw.

A major contribution was that of Dr. Michael Bassett, Keeper of the Geology Department of the National Museum of Wales, Cardiff, who was pleased to give us access to the considerable resources of his department. We are particularly indebted to the former Assistant Keeper, Mr. D. Emlyn Evans whose help went far beyond the writing of his own special sections. The fossil drawings, the block-diagram of the local area and some other diagrams are the work of Mrs. Gaye Evans, a former member of the department.

Use was made of the facilities put at our disposal by Mr. W. Lawrence, warden of the Merthyr Teachers' Centre, where Mrs. Joan Hammett readily assisted with manuscripts and diagrams.

Assistance with the processing of the photographic plates was given by Mr. Tony Hyde and Mr. Elwyn Morgan of the Merthyr Camera Club.

Weather and Climate

by GARETH HOPKINS, M.A., M.Litt.

Adviser in Geography, Mid Glamorgan County Council Education Department

Reservoirs in the Beacons signify the depressing aspect of Merthyr Tydfil's climate; it is wet. In the north the rainfall ranges from 60″ per year at Pontsticill to over 72″ near Dolygaer. The lowest totals in the District occur in Dowlais which receives 52·7″ of rain a year; Treharris is only a little wetter with 54·1″.

This distributional pattern can be explained largely by variations in relief, for rainfall generally increases with altitude; hence the high falls in the Beacons. Similarly the shallow and wide depression occupied by central Merthyr Tydfil has relatively low totals. However, the valley bottoms in the south, although lower, are also narrow and it is possible that air streams moving eastward across the valley are little affected by relief in this area. Consequently rainfall totals decrease generally in a south and east direction with the decline in altitude of the intervening mountain ridges.

The rainfall map (Fig. 26) represents the average annual amounts for the period from 1941 to 1970 as it is for this period that the statistical data is available in published form. However, rainfall records for some weather stations in the catchment area of the old Taf Fechan Water Board go back to at least the 1880's. It is possible, therefore, in the case of some stations to consider extreme values. The Pentwyn gauge, which is located near Dolygaer and which has the more complete records, received its lowest annual total of 44·06″ as early as 1889 and its highest fall of 93·45″ in 1954. So much for average values.

Clearly rainfall varies in time as well as space and so it is interesting to look at monthly totals. It is obvious that the winter months receive considerably more rain than any other. In fact the wettest month has twice as much as the driest; June on average is the driest and December the wettest. The cause of this disparity is the more frequent occurrence of depressions in the

Plate 14: EDWARDSVILLE DESTRUCTION CAUSED BY A TORNADO, 1913

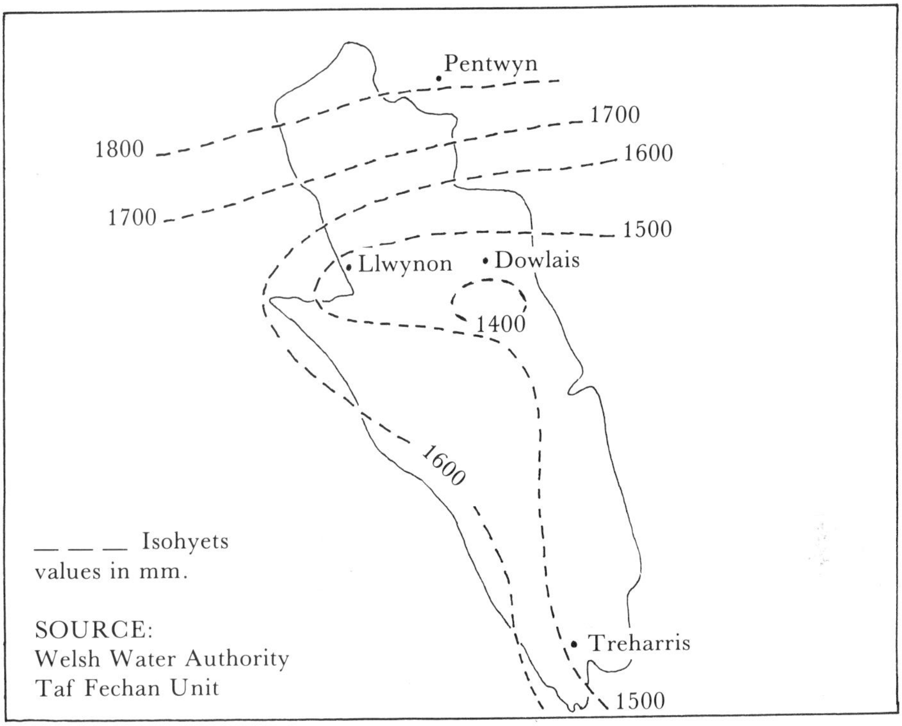

Fig. 26: Annual Rainfall

winter period, for these storms are the main rain makers in Britain. Often, however, climatologists consider seasonal patterns rather than monthly figures, particularly when comparing exceptional years. Such a year was 1976.

A low rainfall in the early months repeated, in fact, the pattern of the preceding winter. Few experts would have forecast what was to follow in high summer. Soaring temperatures, cloudless skies and little rain not only produced the finest of summers in living memory but caused a season of rainfall figures that emphasized the consequent drought which created inconvenience if not havoc. In the months of June, July and August, the rainfall at Pentwyn was a mere 5·66″, the lowest total since 1913 (see Fig. 27). Water levels in the Beacons reservoirs fell so much that the original valley appeared almost as it was before it was drowned to secure water supplies. Only the faithless need have feared, for no Indian Summer occurred in 1976. The rains returned in September with the intensity almost of a monsoon; autumnal totals were a third or more above normal. On the floor of the reservoirs the cracked, brown mud, baked hard by the summer sun, disappeared once more beneath flood waters as the mountain streams turned into swift torrents and drowned again the lower levels of the valleys. The exceptional drought of 1976 was brought about by the extension of the Azores high pressure system (anticyclone) across the British Isles and its extraordinary persistence for a number of months.

Rainfall, of course, is a major element in our weather; another is temperature. Now, if rainfall figures are almost readily available in Merthyr Tydfil, temperature statistics are few. There are but three places in or near the District with long standing records of temperature. These are the home of Mr. Glyn Bevan, Bronygarth, Gwaelodygarth Lane, the Taf Fechan Unit of the Welsh National Water Development Authority at Pontsticill and the Cwmbargoed site of Mr. J. Powell. Mr. Bevan's records extend over a forty year period from 1937, those for Pontsticill exist from 1941 and Mr. Powell's from 1967.

Average monthly statistics for these stations are quite close, the small variations resulting largely from the differences in height of the places. Gwaelodygarth Lane is about 770′ above sea level, Pontsticill 1,033′ and Cwmbargoed 1,220′. However, other factors such as aspect and exposure also have an influence so that the differences from one month to another are not regular. The influence of altitude is more evident when the temperatures at Merthyr Tydfil are compared with those of Cardiff. The latter, 203′ above sea-level, has mean monthly temperatures 2°F. to 5°F. higher. Yet the differences are smaller in summer than in winter, so that another factor

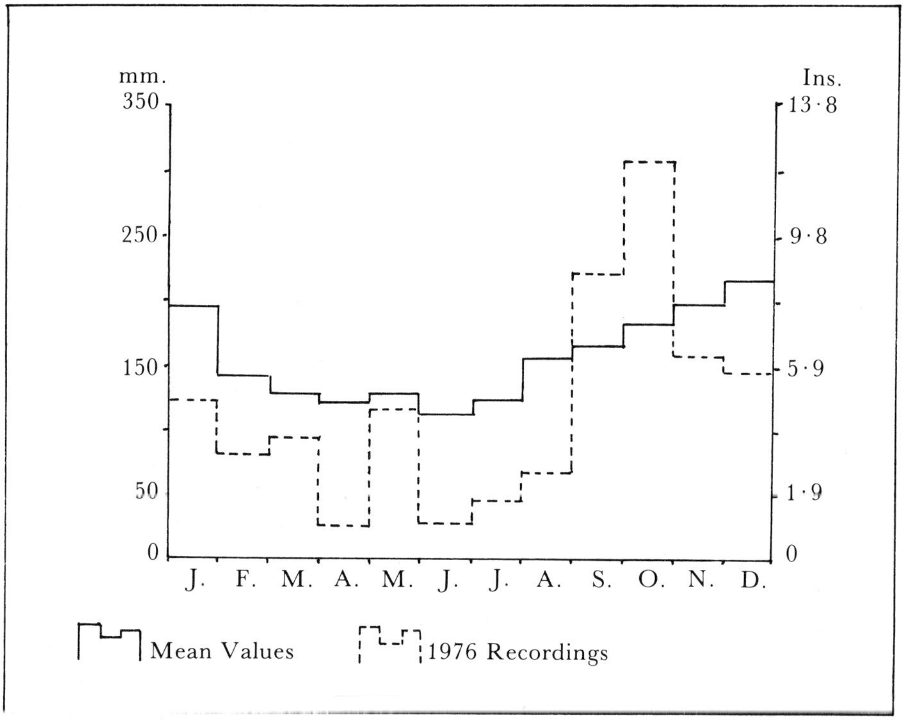

Fig. 27: Mean Monthly Rainfall—Pentwyn No. 15 Gauge

is at work besides variation in altitude, namely the relative proximity of Merthyr Tydfil and Cardiff to the sea. Large areas of water serve to moderate temperatures so that seaside towns on the western side of Britain have higher temperatures in winter than do places inland, other things being equal. In this way the effect of inland location exaggerates the winter differences due to the higher altitude of Merthyr Tydfil. Equally, the summer temperatures of coastal towns are lower than those of inland areas so that differences caused by altitude are this time offset to some degree.

The graph indicates the annual pattern of temperatures as revealed by the mean monthly figures. Such figures merely add substance to what people ought to know about the weather. Rarely does Merthyr Tydfil experience extremes of heat or cold, and when the thermometer does stray far from average figures, people feel uncomfortably hot or miserably cold. Merthyr Tydfil, nestling in the hills of southwestern Britain, enjoys on average a mild climate with cool to warm summers and cool but seldom cold winters. The annual range of temperature, defined as the difference between the mean temperature for the warmest month and that for the coldest month, is thus characteristically small. At Pontsticill it is 23°F. and at Bronygarth 22·1°F. (Fig. 28)

However, mean monthly temperatures give only a crude picture of the climate. They do not indicate how high temperatures may climb during hot summer days nor how far the mercury in the thermometer may contract on cold winter nights. Thus it is preferable to look at maximum and minimum temperatures, although, again, because of the need to generalize, mean figures have to be used. It is clear that such figures give a more realistic idea of actual conditions during the day. Obviously, the mean of the lowest temperatures hovers around freezing point in January and February while summer maxima lie in the mid 60°F. There is nothing in these figures to suggest a severe climate.

The difference between the highest and lowest temperatures in the day is called the daily range of temperature. Now daily ranges vary from month to month and those in winter are about half of the values in summer, roughly 8°F. compared with 15°F. Day temperatures are high, obviously, because the heat received from the Sun (insolation) is then highest but night temperatures are lower because some of the heat received during the day is lost by radiation from the Earth. One major factor influencing the levels of both insolation and radiation is the amount of cloud covering the sky. When conditions are cloudy both insolation and radiation tend to be low, as clouds act as an insulating blanket around the Earth. Cloud amounts are less in Spring and Summer than in Autumn and Winter, which helps to explain the higher daily temperature ranges in the summer.

Average temperatures, even those for maximum and minimum values, give only a general picture of conditions so that some actual values prove illuminating. Those for exceptional days arouse more interest than figures approaching the mean. The highest temperature recorded at Merthyr Tydfil

Fig. 28: Pontsticill—Temperatures

Mean Monthly Maximum and Minimum Values

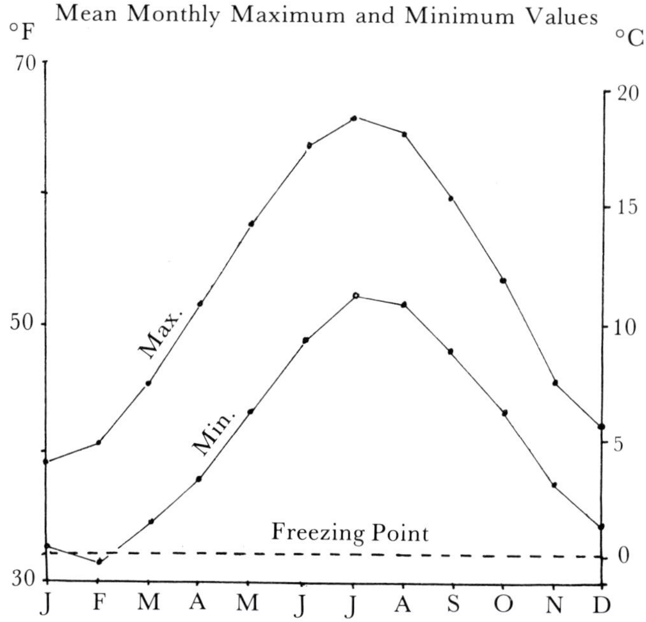

Fig. 29: Pontsticill and Cardiff Mean Monthly Temperatures

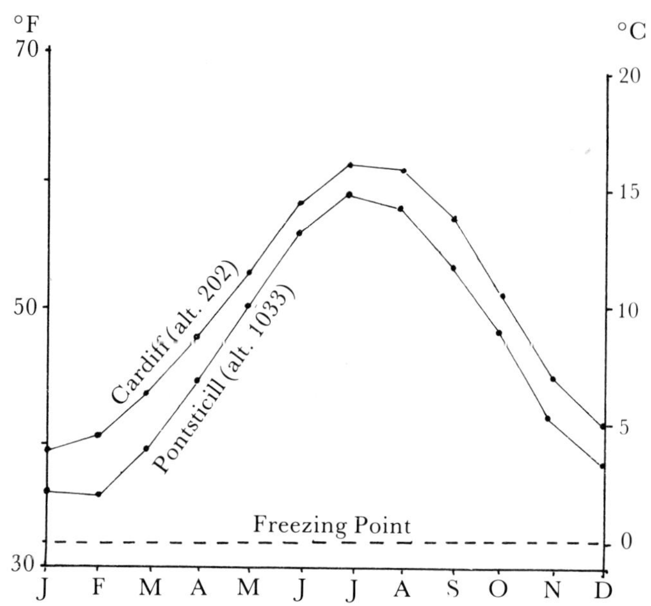

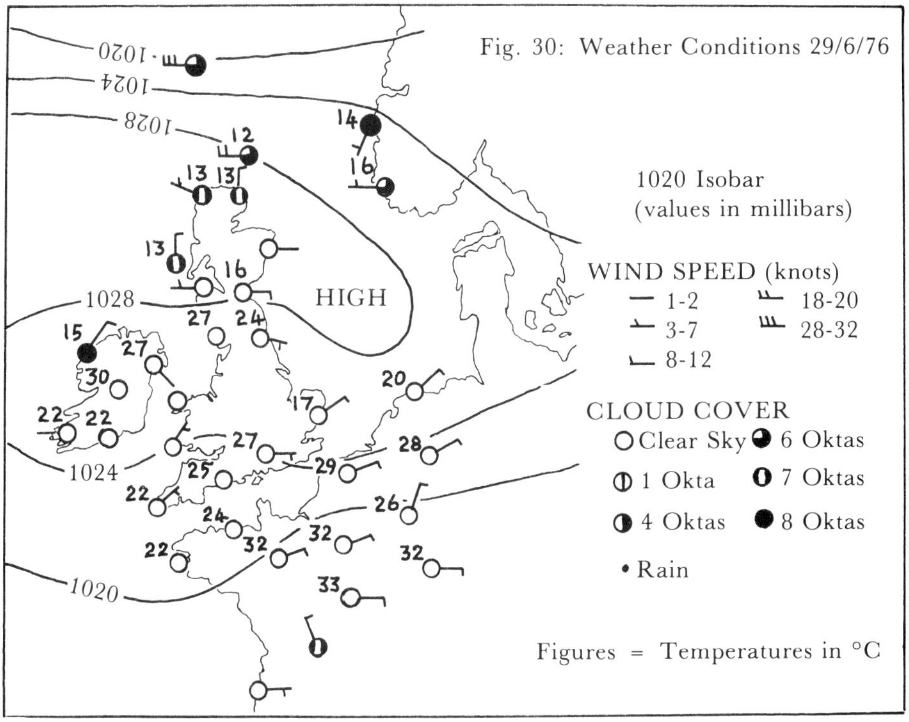

Fig. 30: Weather Conditions 29/6/76

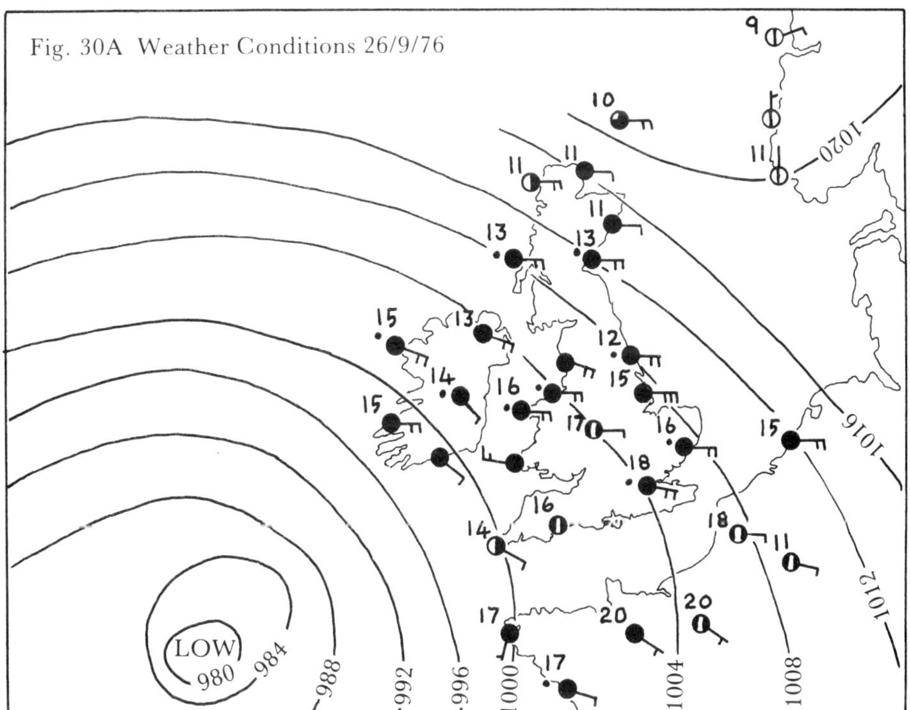

Fig. 30A Weather Conditions 26/9/76

over the last forty years is 94°F., reached on July 12th, 1949 at Bronygarth and on July 4th, 1976 at Pontsticill. The lowest value of 4°F. was recorded at Bronygarth while at Pontsticill the thermometer fell to 5°F. on Feb. 27th, 1945. Isolated days with extreme figures such as these rarely impinge on the memory. What impresses more is a prolonged period of low or high temperatures.

Notable for cold spells were the winters of 1955/1956 and 1962/1963. In the first of these at Pontsticill there were 100 days between October and April when the temperature fell to 32°F. or less, and on thirteen of these the thermometer dropped to 20°F., or less. In the second example, when blizzard conditions piled up snow drifts, the days with temperatures below freezing point numbered 97, 23 of which recorded temperatures below 20°F. Other years with severe but not so prolonged winters were 1939/1940 and 1946/1947. For those too young to have experienced them and for those with fading memories, the Merthyr Express provides permanent records of the prevailing conditions. In January 1940, the paper describes the frozen state of the lake at Cyfarthfa Park and, in February, the fifteen inches of ice on the Neuadd Reservoirs. Seven years later in February 1947, arctic conditions returned to Merthyr Tydfil with a vengeance. At Galon Uchaf, drifting snow reached the bedroom windows of some houses while a train at Penywern became snow bound for several days. Above Dowlais a drift, 22 feet deep, extended for half a mile.

Records of snowfall in Merthyr Tydfil are not plentiful. At Bronygarth the average number of days per year with snow is 18, but at Cwmbargoed the figure rises to 29. Cwmbargoed's greater altitude results in a higher precipitation and lower temperatures in winter and, consequently, in a greater incidence of snow.

Merthyr Tydfil, like Wales, in general, is not well blessed with summers of a mediterranean nature. Glorious summers are therefore something to be remembered. That of 1949 was one to have experienced for between June and September the Sun's rays pushed temperatures over the 70°F. mark on 62 days and twenty four of these occurred in July alone; on eight days the mercury climbed into the 80°'sF. Enjoyable but briefer summers occurred also in 1955 and 1975 but none could compare with that of 1976. The persistent high pressure of that summer not only kept the rain away but it held back the clouds and thereby let in the sunshine. Seventy degrees fahrenheit was reached on 65 days between June and September, 80°F. on 24 days and 90°F. on 5 days. Such heat and the absence of rain produced a landscape of Savanna appearance as the grass ceased to grow, turning yellow and brown in the process. Such summers are of rare occurrence.

Perhaps more than any other factor, atmospheric pressure influences the type of weather that occurs and yet, except on high mountains, our bodies are not sufficiently sensitive to detect changes in air pressure. However, variations in pressure over the Earth's surface produce air movement which is felt as wind. Now the direction from which the wind blows determines the

Fig. 31: Wind Direction—Cwmbargoed

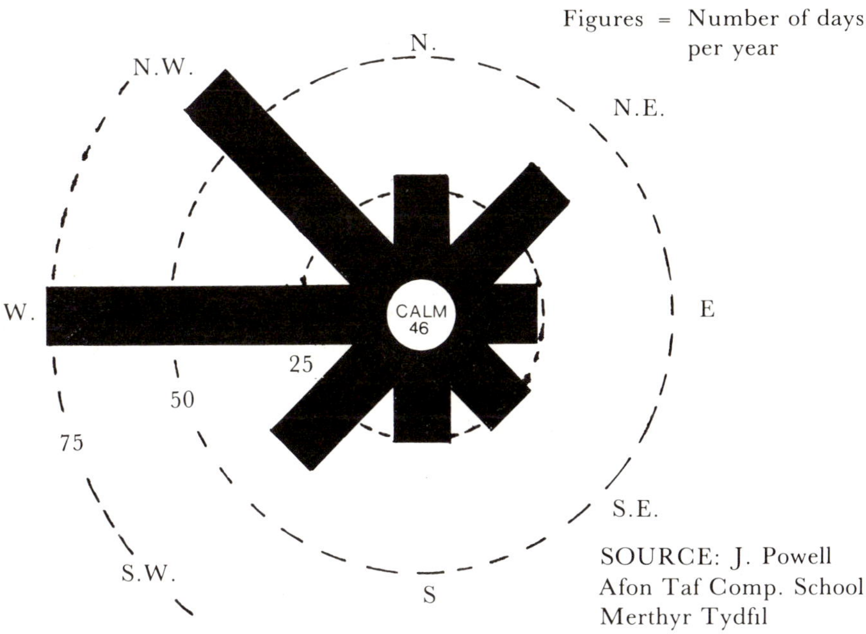

weather, for wind transfers to an area a mass of air different to that already existing over that area. In Britain southwesterly winds are associated usually with mild moist air; easterly winds bring often dry spells, hot in summer and cold in winter. In Merthyr Tydfil the wind-rose shows that the prevailing wind is from a westerly point. It is not surprising then that Merthyr Tydfil tends to be cloudy as well as wet; on average 60% of the sky is covered with cloud. Wind is more keenly experienced when it blows strongly. When depressions move swiftly across Britain, wind speeds rise, felling trees and blowing down wooden fences, but seldom is damage extensive or serious. Exceptions, however, occur and these are associated with severe storms which produce wind speeds of hurricane force. Edwardsville in 1913 was the scene of such a storm.

October 27th of that year brought terror to the inhabitants of the village, for the wind speed reached levels higher than anyone in Merthyr Tydfil had experienced before. The tornado, so described by the Meteorological Office, had swept north from Exeter across the Bristol Channel and just before 6 p.m. reached Edwardsville where it attained its maximum intensity. Dan Williams of Treharris was reported as having seen 'a dark cloud extending from the sky to earth like a huge waterspout'. This twisting column of rotating air carved out a three hundred yard wide path of destruction. In the churchyard, most of the tombstones were blown down and the cemetery chapel was wrecked as was the English Congregational Chapel. The roof tops of the houses in Nantddu Street were extensively damaged while slates blown from them were found buried to a depth of 1½" in the trunks of trees. One victim was claimed by this storm when Mr. C. Woodford of the Ton Pentre Football Club was killed after being blown against a wall. Repairs of the damage cost £40,000, a large sum in those days.

Tornadoes are even rarer than torrid summers so that the chances of Merthyr Tydfil experiencing another are slim. However, the events of autumn 1913 and summer 1976 help to remind us that although the climate of Merthyr Tydfil is moderate, averages are often made up of exceptional and extreme conditions.

Bibliography

Glamorgan Historian, Vol. XI, Meurig Evans, 'A South Wales Tornado' (1975), 212-227.

Taf Fechan Unit, Welsh Water Authority, Nelson, Mid. Glamorgan, *Rainfall and temperature data for Merthyr Tydfil.*

J. Powell, Afon Taf Comprehensive School, *Weather data for Cwmbargoed.*

Meteorological Office. *Averages of temperatures for Great Britain and Northern Ireland.* H.M.S.O.

Natural History of the Coalfield and Millstone Grit Uplands

by MARY E. GILLHAM, Ph.D.

A – History of the Vegetation

Although much of the built-up area of Merthyr Tydfil is no more than five hundred feet above sea level, the countryside is mostly of upland type, characterised by bleak rolling moorlands of grasses and rushes, with the oaklands, bracken and heather quite localised. It was not always so. Initially, most of the now barren hills were covered with woodland.

The destruction of trees probably started with the Mesolithic hunters of pre-history who used fire to open out clearings. The Pre-Neolithic forests established here in the mid-Boreal climatic period were of oak with hazel, which requires a richer soil than the oak-birchwoods of today's leached, eroded and otherwise impoverished hills. Progressive opening out of the forest canopy by burning, felling and grazing allowed heather and bracken to invade and peat formation during wet periods had buried and preserved some of the tree remains under an acid, heather-clad blanket peat by Medieval times.

Much remained, however, until the birth of the great Iron Industry in the eighteenth century. As iron smelting needed more and more fuel the trees were progressively felled and made into charcoal to feed the furnaces. Now, apart from Cwm Woods West of Abercanaid, the oakwoods are mostly relegated to narrow strips along the streams and rivers where the slopes were too steep for convenient tree felling or for subsequent agricultural use. Hill farming flourished on the denuded grassy acres, but this is now declining and the 'new look' is of coniferous plantations scattered across old grazing lands which are fast deteriorating into unkept mountainside.

Fortunately for the iron industry, the nineteenth century which saw the virtual end of the standing oak forests, also saw the opening up of the ancient

Fig. 32: FOUR COMMON MOORLAND GRASSES
Sheep's fescue (*Festuca ovina*), common bent (*Agrostis tenuis*), heath grass (*Sieglingia decumbens*), mat grass (*Nardus stricta*)

swamp forests of Carboniferous Age, which were preserved underground as coal; so organic fuel continued to flow to the furnaces, converted from living trees by time and pressure in the absence of free oxygen.

Merthyr's strategic position at the junction of the Coalfield which supplied the furnaces with fuel and the limestone hills which supplied them with flux, puts her between two very different types of landscape. To the South the Coalfield hills are acid and infertile, bearing tussocky grass moor and sessile oakwood. To the North the Limestone hills are more alkaline, bearing a smoother grass heath with rocky-floored ashwoods. Between the two are the Millstone Grits, which support an even poorer vegetation than the Pennant Sandstones (most unyielding of the Coalfield rocks).

Natural communities are not neatly aligned (square blocks of conifers and straight-edged fields are man-made) but neither are they haphazard. Animal life is largely dependent on plant life and plant life is controlled by the underlying geology, the rainfall, sunshine, wind and the animals themselves, particularly the sheep, cattle and ponies which can convert woodland to grassland and maintain it as such by nipping off all the young trees which should replace the old.

B – Moorland vegetation in relation to climate and soil

The moorland swards may be underlain by soils from several sources, but all are acid and infertile. Harder rocks – Pennant Sandstones from the Coal Measures and grits from the Millstone Grit series – weather slowly and yield a poor shallow soil: the shales are softer and give deeper, more amenable soils. Ice-transported tills or boulder clays have a high clay content, which makes them impermeable to standing water and gives rise to wetland communities. Peats form, because of the cold, wet climate, which is itself dependent on altitude rather than latitude. The soil organisms responsible for the breakdown of dead plant material and its reintegration into the

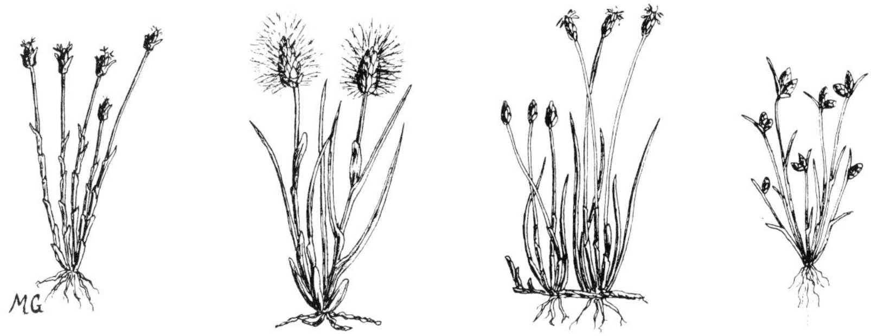

Fig. 33: FOUR COMMON MOORLAND SEDGES
Deer sedge (*Trichophorum caespitosum*), Hare's tail cotton-grass (*Eriophorum vaginatum*), common spike-rush (*Eleocharis palustris*), bristle club-rush (*Scirpus setaceus*)

soil for use by future generations function best in warm dry conditions where the medium is well aerated. Standing water inhibits them, excluding soil air, so that the residues accumulate, preserving sufficient recognisable remains for scientists to be able to piece together the history of plant succession over the centuries. The peats, too, become waterlogged in parts to form bogs, but are drying out, cracking and eroding in others to leave upstanding peat hags.

The continuous 'blanket peats' of the plateau overlie 'gley' soils which are poorly aerated and stained greyish by iron in the ferrous state. They are mostly covered by purple moor grass (*Molinia caerulea*), which is purple only when the wispy flower heads are produced in summer. During the long months of winter the leaves are bleached white over hundreds of acres, relieved by bronzy-red patches of cotton grass (*Eriophorum angustifolium* and *E vaginatum*) in water-filled depressions, the silky cotton heads of summer blown away or drowned. Grass leaves get detached and blown into snow hollows or piled against fences before the new leaves push through the dead mat in late spring. This moor grass forms a coarse but fairly level sward in the uplands, but grows in great tussocks, often with standing water between, where the soil water table fluctuates markedly from season to season, allowing air into the soil. Mat grass (*Nardus stricta*) is commonly present with smaller amounts of deer grass (*Trichophorum caespitosum*) and heath rush (*Juncus squarrosus*).

Much shallower brown earths, well aerated and stained reddish by iron in the ferric state, have built up on the steep valleysides since these were scoured free of loose material by moving ice. Little peat has been able to cling to their freely draining faces. Vegetation here is mainly bent/fescue grassland (*Agrostis/Festuca*) with a wider range of flowers typified by heath bedstraw (*Galium saxatile*), heath milkwort (*Polygala serpyllifolia*) and tormentil (*Pontentilla erecta*). With sufficient soil depth, shelter from wind and freedom from waterlogging, bracken (*Pteridium aquilinum)* occurs, growing to an

1

2

3

4

Plate 15: WETLAND PLANTS
Meadowsweet (1) and Angelica (4) grow in almost any type of wet habitat. Common Cotton Grass (2) is found in acid bogs. Mimulus or Monkey Flower (3) by riversides, as in Merthyr town itself

Photographs by Mary Gillham

elevation approximating to the former tree line in areas where trees were excluded from the summits by exposure. Given opportunity birch and oak will push up through this bracken, as on the East side of the A470 North of Edwardsville, but unfortunately this extremely attractive woodland was underplanted with conifers in the early seventies. Sometimes the plateau falls away in a line of cliffs along which heather (*Calluna vulgaris*), fine-leaved heath (*Erica cinerea*), sapling trees and ferns can be found.

Peat layers from a few inches to two feet deep accumulate on the peaty gley soils of valleys and hillsides terraces. These, too, are occupied mainly by purple moor grass but more species can grow with it because the soil is slightly enriched by nutrients washed from above. Wavy hair grass (*Deschampsia flexuosa*), sheep's fescue (*Festuca ovina*), red fescue (*F rubra*) and bilberry (*Vaccinium myrtilus*) grow in drier areas. Most noticeable, however, is the hybrid between the soft and conglomerate rushes (*Juncus effusus x J conglomeratus*) which marks the streams and seepages as gingery brown networks in winter and a darker green in summer.

On the better grazing lands soils are more uniformly loamy and the quality of the sward is enhanced by white clover (*Trifolium repens*) and other legumes able to capture atmospheric nitrogen and transfer it to the rooting medium. These herb-rich grasslands contain ribwort plantain (*Plantago lanceolata*), common sorrel (*Rumex acetosa*), self heal (*Prunella vulgaris*), creeping buttercup (*Ranunculus repens*) and field daisy (*Bellis perennis*). Grasslands ploughed and resown with perennial ryegrass (*Lolium perenne*) will be progressively re-invaded by the displaced natural grasses – bents, fescues, sweet vernal (*Anthoxanthum odoratum*), crested dogstail (*Cynosurus cristatus*) and Yorkshire fog (*Holcus lanatus*).

The Millstone Grit moorlands near Dowlais and North of Cefn Coed are bleak in the extreme and pitted by swallow holes – great cavities dissolved by water in the underlying limestone and into which the covering of grit has subsided. Swallow holes may show heather, western gorse (*Ulex gallii*) and woolly fringe moss (*Rhacomitrium lanuginosum*) on their craggy sides and bracken or rushes on their sheltered floors. The moorlands are of moor grass and mat grass, deer sedge and bog cotton, like those of the Coalfield, with glistening red insect-catching leaves of round-leaved sundew (*Drosera rotundifolia*) on the wetter patches of bog moss. Not many more than thirty species of flowering plants occur on the mosaic of ice-scratched grits and pockets of peat littered with 'erratics' brought from the North by moving ice.

C – *Fire, grazing and standing water on the hills*

Most of the hill vegetation is greatly modified by fires which sweep across the slopes in January, February and March when the dead grass and bracken can be quite inflammable. Some fires are accidental or acts of vandalism; others are part of the land management practised by hill farmers to destroy the mat of dead foliage and enable tender young grass shoots to push

Fig. 34: FOUR MORE COMMON MOORLAND SEDGES
Common yellow sedge (*Carex demissa*), carnation sedge (*C. panicea*), flea sedge (*C. pulicaris*), star sedge (*C. echinata*)

through. It is illegal to burn after 30 March, when plants and animals could be seriously harmed.

Burning, although giving a temporary flush of green, is a reprehensible practice because in the long term it encourages just those plants which it seeks to destroy. The tough moor grass and mat grass have their perennating buds well down in the fibrous 'stools' where they escape flames which can completely annihilate more valuable tender grasses. The great '*Molinia* deserts' of the plateau, where little but the *Molinia* survives, are thus a direct outcome of the repeated burning and, paradoxically, while the *Molinia* remains, the farmers will go on burning to rid themselves of its waste trash and so prolong the agony of having to tolerate it. That is, unless they plough and re-seed, when they could generate the alternative problem of a 'plough pan' impeding drainage and leading to a sea of rushes.

It is the same with bracken, whose fronds arise from underground stems which remain untouched by the fiercest of fires and spread at the expense of the shallow-rooted grasses and herbs which are more vulnerable. Peat fires which smoulder for weeks, like those in the Dowlais and Cil Sanws areas in the long hot summer of 1976, can do untold damage in destroying the organic 'body' of the ground surface and leading to soil erosion. Displaced soil may lodge against walls further down the hill where there is already sufficient for good growth, while the upper slopes become progressively more unproductive.

Sheep graze selectively, nibbling off the softer plants and leaving the harder ones. Wiry mat grass tufts are usually avoided, those tweaked out in error being discarded. This unpalatable species and the purple moor grass, which is relished only when young, are helped in their domination of overgrazed hill pasture by the systematic removal of their natural competitors.

Store cattle and ponies will bite off coarser plants and leave a more uniformly edible sward, but no livestock will take bracken, which romps away as the competing grasses are eaten back. Taller plants whose growing buds are not protected close to the soil surface get relegated to inaccessible crags and it is here that all the larger plants of golden rod (*Solidago virgaurea*), hemp agrimony (*Eupatorium cannabinum*), heather, bilberry, downy birch (*Betula pubescens*) and rowan (*Sorbus aucuparia*) are found. It is often only on the crags that ferns and oaks can survive the relentless browsing and grow to full size, inhospitable though the vertical faces seem in other respects.

The wetter peats or true bogs of both Coalfield and Grits are characterised by pale absorbent carpets of bog moss (*Sphagnum spp*) and dark green feathery domes of common hair moss (*Polytrichum commune*). Attractive flowers include cross-leaved heath (*Erica tetralix*), bog pimpernel (*Anagallis tenella*), lousewort (*Pedicularis sylvatica*) and bog asphodel (*Narthecium ossifragum*). Rarer ones are slender St John's wort (*Hypericum pulchrum*), cranberry (*Oxycoccus palustris*), lesser skullcap (*Scutellaria minor*), ivy-leaved bell-flower (*Wahlenbergia hederacea*) and sneezewort (*Achillea ptarmica*).

Small bog pools dot the uplands, some of them a legacy from the industrial era when streams were dammed to form reservoirs. Rhaslas Pond on Dowlais Top, with its extensive stands of shoreweed (*Littorella uniflora*) which draw the sheep like a magnet when the water recedes, lies just outside the district boundary, but its other species are shared by the smaller pools to westward. These include water starwort (*Callitriche spp*), water blinks (*Montia fontana*), water purslane (*Lythrum portula*), marsh willow herb (*Epilobium palustre*), marsh pennywort (*Hydrocotyle vulgaris*) and marsh cudweed (*Gnaphalium uliginosum*). Very acid pools have growths of bog cotton and bog moss, bog violet (*Viola palustris*) and bog asphodel and are often covered by the bronzed floating leaves of bog pondweed (*Potamogeton polygonifolius*). Jointed, sharp-flowered and bulbous rushes (*Juncus articulatus, J acutiflorus, J bulbosus* and *J kochiii*) are common, the last two often sprouting little tufts of fine leaves from the inflorescences. Lenormand's water crowfoot (*Ranunculus omiophyllus*) flowers almost throughout the year and the invasive New Zealand will herb (*Epilobium nerterioides*) is everywhere.

Field ponds of the tamer uplands show a wider range of water plants with creeping buttercup, lesser spearwort (*Ranunculus flammula*), cuckoo flower (*Cardamine pratensis*), bog stitchwort (*Stellaria alsine*) and brooklime (*Veronica beccabunga*). Taller marginal growths are of willow herbs, meadowsweet (*Filipendula ulmaria*), hemlock water dropwort (*Oenanthe crocata*), angelica (*Angelica sylvestris*) and greater bur-reed (*Sparganium erectum*). Rush-bordered ponds in the Treharris area are partly filled with broad pondweed (*Potamogeton natans*), greater pond sedge (*Carex riparia*) and flote grass (*Glyceria fluitans*). Other 'aquatics' here are water milfoil (*Myriophyllum alterniflorum*), lesser duckweed (*Lemna minor*), greater bird's foot trefoil (*Lotus uliginosus*), water pepper (*Polygonum hydropiper*), marsh St John's wort (*Hypericum elodes*) and water mint (*Mentha aquatica*).

D – Moorland Animals

Most abundant mammals of the moors are probably the short-tailed field voles which tunnel through the matted sward, their highways marked by withered ribbons of vegetation severed from their water supply. Life changes little in their restricted world when the moors are blanketed with snow, except that they enjoy a relative freedom from predation. Shrews fare less well, as their invertebrate food becomes scarce in winter. Hares and rabbits compete successfully with the sheep in parts, but are seldom numerous.

Stoats and weasels prey on the smaller herbivores and polecats have been increasing over the last fifty years from the mid-1930s. These are now found in many parts of the borough and one turned up in a trap at Gurnos Farm just North of Merthyr in 1975. Feral or gone-wild ferrets get mistaken for polecats on occasion. Foxes range freely over the whole area. These, too, have increased during recent years, possibly because of the spread of coniferous plantations, which offer extra cover. They feed on carrion as often as fresh meat and on invertebrates or vegetable matter when nothing more substantial offers. Stillborn lambs are an important food item seasonally.

Ravens and carrion crows also exploit this type of carrion and may be almost the only birds to be seen on the uplands in winter. Even the hardy skylarks and meadow pipits are partial migrants and tend to move down from the tops in severe weather. In summer these are joined by wheatears, particularly where screes or old walls supply nesting crevices. Cuckoos appear later to lay their eggs in the pipits' nests. The few heather moors have their quota of red grouse and thick hedges thrusting up through the abandoned mountain pastures may harbour redstarts, wrens and blackbirds.

Whinchats come to breed in summer where the bleakness is ameliorated by gorse and other scrub. The closely related stonechats of similar habitats would suffer in the Merthyr winters, so are much scarcer in the borough and the few residents move down to the coast in winter. Magpies are increasing in the uplands, but these will be based on farmland where there are tall hedges to contain their big domed nests. Also common to moorland and farmland are the few curlew which nest among the tussocks and the

Fig. 35: FOUR BIRDS OF THE MOORLAND
Carrion crow, magpie, curlew, lapwing

Plate 16: MOORLAND BIRDS
The Willow Warbler (1) builds a roofed nest among coarse grasses. The Whinchat (2) likes rough grass moor dotted with gorse, hawthorn or bramble *Photographs by Keri Williams*

diminishing lapwings. Both move away in the colder months and the wintering linnets and thrushes which replace them stay mainly on the richer feeding of the hill farms where weed seeds and haws in the unkempt hedges are the chief attraction. The visiting thrushes are mainly fieldfares, redwing being more abundant in southern Glamorgan. Buzzards and kestrels are almost always around. Snipe nest quite commonly in the quagmires, making off at the last possible moment with characteristic zig-zag flight; jack snipe are infrequent, though seen every year.

On warm days common lizards bask in the sun and scuttle among the grass bases, while upturned stones may yield a cluster of bronze slow worms. Adders have decreased of late, but grass snakes are still quite plentiful. These are often unable to escape from moorland fires and may prove to have diminished during the 1976 conflagrations. Frogs, toads and newts breed prolifically in the wetlands, the palmate the commonest of the three newt species. Small brown trout, loach and miller's thumbs inhabit many of the moorland streams and there may also be eels, minnows and three-spined sticklebacks. Trout and minnows occur in the upper of the old mine ponds at Penywern – carp, bream and minnows in the lower.

J.O. Evans has found a wealth of animal life in a moorland pool at the junction of the Millstone Grit and Vaynor limestone on the southern flank of Cil Sanws Mountain. As well as sticklebacks and frogs, the common, palmate and great crested or warty newts are all present, this being remarkable for so small a pool. No less than seven species of dragonfly and damselfly pass their nymphal stages in the water and fly out over moor. These are the blue-bodied southern aeschna *(A cyanea)*, which is a hawker dragonfly, three darter dragonflies: the red common sympetrum *(S striolatum)*, the blue-green broad-bodied libellula *(L depressa)* and the stout, buff-bodied four-spotted libellula *(L quadrimaculata)* and three damselflies, the large red *(Pyrrhosoma nymphula)*, the blue-tailed common ischnura *(I elegans)* and the blue common coenagrion *(C puella)*.

Larvae of the caddis fly *(Limnephilus flavicornis)* construct cases from chopped lengths of rush. These are quite common; much rarer is *L xanthodes* which makes its case from fragments of leaf. Larvae of the alder fly *(Sialis)* resemble quite closely those of whirligig beetles *(Gyrinus)*, adults of which scud around on top of the water like silver drops of mercury. Supported with them on the surface film are pond skaters *(Gerris)* and water measurers *(Hydrometra stagnorum)*. Other flat-bodied water bugs are water boatmen *(Notonecta)*, lesser water boatmen *(Corixa)* and water scorpions *(Nepa cinerea)*.

Great diving beetles *(Dytiscus marginalis)* are fearsome predators in both the larval and adult phases, feeding on almost everything else, even to small fish and tadpoles. With them are striped water beetles *(Acilius sulcatus)* whose adult females, like theirs, have grooved wing cases. Small yellow-brown beetles *(Deronectes)* are quite common. Freshwater shrimps *(Gammarus pulex)* co-habit with water hog lice *(Asellus aquaticus)* and tiny copepods *(Cyclops)*.

Swarming in the mud of the pool floor with the larvae of craneflies *(Tipulidae)* are the larvae of non-biting midges *(Chironomus)*. These crimson 'bloodworms' have haemoglobin in their blood, as do humans. Adult males gyrate in swarms on summer evenings to entice the females up to mate, and are known as 'dance gnats'. Water snails include dwarf pond snails *(Lymnaea truncatula)*, wandering snails *(L pereger)* and round-spined trumpet snails or button ramshorns *(Planorbis spirorbis)*.

Small heath butterflies are commonest of the moorland species, but meadow browns and graylings can be abundant in season, while red admirals ascend to the windiest tops and persist till late November some years. A succession of common heath moths *(Ematurga atomaria)* is disturbed by the feet of mountain walkers in May and June and sometimes in August. Papery, cigar-shaped larval cases of rush moths or sac moths *(Coleophora)* abound on the flowering and fruiting heads of heath rush and soft rush and mottled grey marbled beauty moths *(Cryphia domestica)* lay their eggs on similar coloured patches of lichen *(Lecidea)* on ancient moorland walls. Woolly bear caterpillars of fast-flying fox moths *(Macrothylacia rubi)* and handsome green and black striped caterpillars of emperor moths *(Saturnia pavonia)* can be found among heather, bilberry and bramble.

Dor beetles *(Geotrupes stercorarius)*, minotaur dung beetles *(Typhaeus typhoeus)*, violet ground beetles *(Carabus violaceus)* and bronzy-green ground beetles *(C nemoralis)* blunder among the grass tufts. Seven-spot ladybirds *(Coccinella 7-punctata)* were particularly abundant in 1975 and 1976 and two-spot ladybirds *(Adalia bipunctata)* and ten-spot *(A 10-punctata)* are also to be found, the latter more often where there are bushes. Sexton beetles *(Necrophorus vespillo)* and carrion beetles *(Phosphuga atrata)* help to dispose of carcases.

Large black slugs *(Arion ater)*, which are more usually woodland species, are everywhere in wet weather, the high rainfall compensating for the humidity which they normally find under trees. Big red slugs *(A rufus)* are present in smaller numbers, but snails are uncommon, because of a shortage of lime for their shells.

Natural History of the Coalfield Woodlands, Man-Made Habitats and Rivers

by Dr. MARY E. GILLHAM

A – Woodland Plants

Oak woodland, whether self regenerated on the steeper slopes among bracken or planted on land not wanted for agriculture, is usually sheep-dominated and floored with moss, grass or bracken. A browse line on the lower branches indicates the height to which sheep, cattle or ponies can reach and the shrub layer is poorly developed with few viable saplings. The dominant trees are mostly sessile or durmast oak *(Quercus petraea)* with acorns borne directly on the woody twigs instead of on slender green stalks as in the common or pedunculate oak *(Q robur)* of the Vale of Glamorgan.

Downy birch is the chief associated tree in Cwm Woods, Abercanaid, growing in quite damp areas with grey and goat sallows *(Salix cinerea* and *S caprea)*, but alder *(Alnus glutinosa)* dominates the wettest parts. Rowan and blackthorn *(Prunus spinosa)* become draped with ivy *(Hedera helix)*, honeysuckle *(Lonicera periclymenum)* and bramble *(Rubus fruticosus agg)*. Birches regenerate most readily and spill out into tall bracken with foxgloves *(Digitalis purpurea)* beyond the woodland edge. This marginal terrain was once farmed, but the old hedgelines are now little more than rows of isolated hawthorns *(Crataegus monogyna)* and hazels *(Corylus avellana)* with standard trees growing from horizontal axes where the original trunks were 'pleached' or laid into the fabric of the hedge.

Ground flora in Cwm Woods consists largely of wood soft grass *(Holcus mollis)* and wavy hair grass, with bents, fescues and small bilberry plants. Flowers are sparse, with common dog violet *(Viola riviniana)*, red campion *(Silene dioica)*, pignut *(Conopodium majus)*, hogweed *(Heracleum sphondylium)*,

Fig. 36: FOUR FLOWERS OF THE COALFIELD WOODLANDS
Golden saxifrage, woodland loosestrife, enchanter's nightshade, wood avens

yellow pimpernel *(Lysimachia nemorun)*, wood sorrel *(Oxalis acetosella)* and bluebell *(Endymion nonscriptus)* the most frequent. There is a rich fungus flora, one of the two most important members being the birch bracket or razor strop *(Piptoporus betulinus)*, which parasitises and kills birch trees, continuing to live on the dead timber. The second is the honey fungus *(Armillaria mellea)*, which is also a tree killer, its warted yellow toadstools strung together with black, bootlace-like strands of fungal threads.

Durmast oakwoods on the steep sides of the still beautiful Taff-Bargoed Valley North of Bedlinog show crabapple *(Malus sylvestris)* and ash *(Fraxinus excelsior)* with false brome *(Brachypodium sylvaticum)* and tufted hair grass *(Deschampsia caespitosa)* important. The latter is often indicative of water-logging, the rock here being full of aquifers, with water emerging to give sodden patches rich in lady fern *(Athyrium filix-femina)*, male fern *(Dryopteris filix-mas)* and broad buckler *(D dilatata)*. The local Pennant Sandstone is unstable, with numerous chasms in the plateau above and landslides on the slopes. A fine beechwood *(Fagus sylvatica)* has developed on the stony yellow rubble spilling down from a little mine on the western flank of the valley.

Non-indigenous coniferous plantations are taking over more and more land, with Sitka spruce on the more exposed summits, Norway spruce on less exposed ones, lodgepole pine on steep unstable slopes and Japanese and hybrid larch on the deeper 'brown earths'. Fencing of the young trees against livestock leads to an increase in the associated flowers at first, but the dense shade cast by mature conifers and the ground carpet of fallen needles, relegates most of the ground flora later to the rides, margins and firebreaks.

B – Woodland Animals

Grey squirrels are widely distributed in both deciduous and coniferous woodland, seeming now to have completely replaced the native red squirrels. The last records of reds are of a pair sighted just North of Cefn

Plate 17: The GREY HERON, largest of the woodland birds, nests in conifers at the head of Llwyn On Reservoir *(Photograph by Keri Williams)*

Coed in 1970 and of one in Cyfarthfa Park in 1971. Bank voles and long-tailed field mice or wood mice are busy wherever there is cover, leaving little caches of hazel nut shells, acorns and haw, sloe and holly stones from which the kernels have been extracted through neatly nibbled holes. Live-trapping during the mid-seventies has failed to reveal any yellow-necked mice, although these occur not far away at Heol Senni and near the Ty'n-y-Cae Youth Hostel. (None have yet been recorded in the three counties of Glamorgan.)

The hedgehog's defence mechanism of rolling itself into a prickly ball is too often ineffective in these days of fast traffic and there are many road casualties. Badger setts are scattered through the woods and spill out onto the open hillside in caves or in easily weathered strata where burrowing is facilitated. Even more foxes den up in the woods than on the moors and stoats and weasels are frequent.

Woodlands may support twenty to thirty resident species of bird in summer as against the three to four carried by an equivalent area of moorland and they attract sizable flocks of tits, goldcrests and chaffinches in winter. This is the direct outcome of the multiplicity of feeding habitats and wide range of food, both plant and animal.

Hatching of the chicks of blue and great tits is usually synchronised with the appearance of the green looper caterpillars of the winter moths *(Operophtera brumata)*, which might otherwise defoliate more of the oaks and associated trees than they do. Tits take them mostly from the leaves. More aerial feeders, like willow warblers, wood warblers, redstarts and pied flycatchers snap them up as they dangle at the ends of long silken strands. These and the rarer spotted flycatchers take flying prey. Even the normally seed-eating chaffinches (probably commonest of the woodland birds both winter and summer along with the blackbird) will take St Mark's flies *(Bibio marci)* in flight. House sparrows, too, will chase butterflies, usually ineffectually, but have learned to hover and snap up flower-feeding insects.

Greater spotted woodpeckers, tree creepers and nuthatches tweak beetle larvae, centipedes and woodlice from under the bark of trees. Starlings are the chief rooters out of wireworms and leatherjackets from below the soil, where ground-feeding dunnocks seek smaller prey. Woodcock and pheasant are also ground feeders. Green woodpeckers probe in the mounds thrown up by yellow ants *(Lasius flavus)* while blackbirds overturn the litter of the woodland floor, exposing earthworms and millipedes. Wrens poke into crevices for spiders; song thrushes search for snails, whose shells they break on some improvised anvil. Robins follow sheep around, snapping up whatever is disturbed by their passing, and join other insect-eaters at the wild fruit harvest in autumn.

Goldcrests, which are increasing, take invisible minutae from twigs and bark and siskins and redpolls tour the mature stands of conifers and the wetter broad-leaved woods in winter, foraging for the small seeds of birch and alder. Jays go for larger objects, relishing acorns and beech nuts in mast years, and wood pigeons will take almost any vegetable matter. Magpies and carrion crows prey on the eggs of other birds, sparrow hawks, which are not uncommon, on the birds themselves. Tawny owls prefer small mammals, as can be seen by dissection of the pellets which they cough up after meals: little owls take beetles and other large insects, ejecting pellets shining with the indigestible black wing cases.

Willow warblers are much the most abundant of the warblers, formerly with the common whitethroat, but these latter almost disappeared in the early seventies, due to drought in their wintering quarters in the Sahel zone of the Sahara, and are only now recovering their numbers. Blackcaps and garden warblers are around, and even the occasional lesser whitethroat. Chiff-chaffs are more localised and in the South, around Quaker's Yard.

Grasshopper warblers appear during the early growth phases of coniferous plantations, although less abundantly than willow warblers, whilst birds

Fig. 37: FOUR CONSPICUOUS MOTHS
Emperor moth, small elephant hawk moth, large yellow underwing moth, garden tiger moth

of the moorland fringes, such as whinchat and tree pipit, are quite characteristic. Others at this stage are blackbird, song thrush, robin, dunnock, wren, whitethroat and chaffinch. More mature coniferous stands attract principally goldcrests and coal tits, but the various Corvids, owls, kestrels and buzzards will nest in conifers as well as deciduous trees.

The speckled wood, most characteristic of the woodland butterflies in the rest of Glamorgan, is seldom seen around Merthyr and is recorded mainly for the Quaker's Yard region in the South. Holly blues and green hairstreaks are also rare, as was the silver-washed fritillary (first recorded in the Taf Fechan Gorge woodland in 1950) until 1976 when it was not uncommon. Small pearl-bordered fritillaries are commoner, mostly on woodland edges and the open flyways afforded by streams.

Such tree-sheltered but partially open habitats are much frequented by moths as well as butterflies, two typical species being the ghost moth and the white ermine. The handsome yellow swallow tail moth is another frequenter of this type of situation, as are the abundant lesser yellow underwing and the common yellow underwing.

Both the common magpie moth *(Abraxas grossulariata)* and the clouded magpie *(A sylvata)* are abundant in woods and by streams, along with the heavily built goat moth *(Cossus cossus)*. Buff tips frequent the oaks and birches whose twigs they so resemble when their wings are closely folded, and December moths *(Poecilocampa populi)* occur wherever there are trees.

Black-tipped soldier beetles *(Rhagonycha fulva)* are often to be seen on angelica and hogweed flowers; red-brown skipjacks *(Athous haemorrhoidalis)* on bracken. Larvae of the slender black and yellow wasp beetle *(Clytus arietis)* bore into dead tree trunks and the adults mimic the more dangerous wasp in their jerky movements as well as their colouring. A long-snouted weevil likely to be found is the mottled yellow and grey *Dorytomus longimanus*.

C – *Plants and Animals of Industrial Waste*

Old coal tips can become scarred by gully erosion or too unstable because of underlying springs. The natural plant succession is from annual 'weeds', through grass turf to birch and sallow scrub and so to oakwood, but the ubiquitous free-range sheep seldom allow this to proceed full term. More often the tips are held at an early successional phase of sparse sheep's fescue and sheep's sorrel *(Rumex acetosella)* with two tiny mosses *(Polytrichum juniperinum* and *P piliferum)* and grey, cup-bearing lichens *(Cladonia)*.

In the early phases plants which demand a high base status in the soil may appear: great mullein *(Verbscum thapsus)*, viper's bugloss *(Echium vulgare)*, carline thistle *(Carlina vulgaris)* and ploughman's spikenard *(Inula conyza)*. Later, as minerals are washed out of the friable slag by rain, the community changes to the opposite extreme of undemanding, acid-tolerant plants such as heather. North American pearly everlasting *(Anaphalis margaritacea)* has spread sheets of white everlasting flowers over many tips, as well as along railway lines and roadsides.

Conifers are useful stabilisers of tips and perennial ryegrass is often sown on them after application of chicguano (poultry manure). This grows greener than any of the mountain grasses and attracts the sheep from miles around, but makes good initial coverage if grazing is kept in check, as on the Troedyrhiw Tips and Dix's Field in 1976.

Meadow pipits congregate on the open tips with starlings, wheatears, pied and grey wagtails and woodlarks. Scrub-grown tips become colonised by the usual scrub birds – tits, wrens, robins, dunnocks, blackbirds, etc. The dry warmth of tip material makes admirable basking for reptiles.

The plants appearing on other types of industrial waste depend very much on where this is sited. Local iron waste is less toxic than the non-ferrous heavy metal waste of the Swansea region, but clinkery masses on Dowlais Top show little more than the five types of grazed coal tips, the sheep's fescue probably a special ecotype able to cope with the harsh conditions, as can the associated brown bent *(Agrostis canina)*. Showy plants like rose-bay willow herb *(Epilobium angustifolium)* and evening primrose *(Oenothera erythrosepala)* turn up on valley wastelands, where there may be a succession of yellows from the February coltsfoot *(Tussilago farfara)* through bird's foot trefoil *(Lotus corniculatus)* to ragwort *(Senecio jacobaea)* in late summer, this last often defoliated by the tiger-striped caterpillars of the red and black cinnabar moth. Spread of the earlier flowering Oxford ragwort *(S squalidus)* West and North along railway lines from Oxford to Aberfan and Merthyr has been closely chronicled. Sticky groundsel *(S viscosus)* is locally common, with weld *(Reseda luteola)* and a host of others.

Toadflaxes are particularly characteristic of railway lines, the yellow *Linaria vulgaris*, mauve *L repens* and dwarf *Chaenorhinum minus*. Blown dust lodging in wall crevices makes life possible for ivy-leaved toadflax (*Cymbalaria muralis)*, the mortar for lime lovers such as biting stonecrop *(Sedum acre)* and the high rainfall for the elder and rowan domiciled on chimneys. Such a wealth of flowers inevitably brings a wealth of dependent insects. Nectar feeders come in droves to the showy pink flowers of soapwort *(Saponaria officinalis)*, hemp agrimony and red valerian *(Centranthus ruber)* which is a

Fig. 38: FOUR COLOURFUL BUTTERFLIES
Red admiral, small tortoiseshell, painted lady, peacock

particular favourite of silver Y moths and humming bird hawks in warm years such as 1975 and 1976, when these reach Britain from the continent.

It says much for the lack of smokiness in so industrial an area that only the 'rural' speckled form of the peppered moth has been found. The black specimens which exemplify the 'industrial melanism' theory of only dark moths surviving bird predation on smoky urban backgrounds, are rare, if, indeed, present at all. Mottled moths are beginning to replace the black ones again in the mid-seventies in newly designated 'smokeless zones' throughout the country.

The most prolific nectar is supplied by the alien *Buddleja davidii,* which springs up everywhere among the industrial ruins and is aptly named the butterfly bush. Its purple flower spikes supply hosts of small tortoiseshells, red admirals, peacocks, hedge browns, meadow browns, small coppers, brimstones, orange-tips and the various skippers and whites. Other feeders on nectar and pollen include thick-legged flower beetles *(Oedemara nobilis)*, bees, wasps, hover flies, drone flies and, of course, moths.

The seed harvest which follows is cropped by birds, not least the familiar house sparrow. Goldfinches flock to thistle and evening primrose seeds and greenfinches are becoming more urban in their feeding habits. Linnet, chaffinch and, more rarely, bullfinch and yellowhammer, are also attracted.

D – Plants and Animals of Buildings, Mines and Old Canals

Black headed, lesser black backed and herring gulls feed on rubbish tips and river effluents. Those from the North of the district go to roost at night on the Pontsticill Reservoir, those from the South fly down river to the Taff Ely Sea Basin, while others may join the new hillside roosts. The communal nesting of gulls on Merthyr factory roofs is nationally famous. It was in 1905 that the normally shore-dwelling gulls started to come inland on a national scale; in the late 1920s that they arrived in Merthyr and in the mid-1940s that they set up breeding colonies on a Cyfarthfa factory roof only a year or so after this was constructed in 1944. By 1958 there were fifty to sixty nests, in the ratio of about four lesser black-backed gulls' nests to three herring gulls'. These were removed by factory personnel in 1959 and the one hundred and fifty resident gulls finally driven away. By 1963 the colony had restarted on factory roofs at Hirwaun.

The town jackdaw colonies have been the subject of a special study by John Griffiths, who has compiled much valuable data on the birds of the Merthyr district. He has observed up to five thousand jackdaws converging on the night roosts, flying higher and later and with more displaying on fine nights than on rainy ones. They nest colonially in two cliff sites and on groups of buildings which are also used as breeding sites by starlings, house sparrows, pied wagtails, swifts, swallows and, more locally, house martins. Sand martins nest in drainpipes opening into the town section of the River Taff and into Cyfarthfa Park Lake. Rooks no longer live in tall trees on the urban fringes as they used, but dippers, which are normally birds of remote mountain streams, can be seen shooting down partially culverted waterways among houses South of the College of Further Education. Collared doves became established towards Hirwaun by 1970.

The colonisation of Merthyr's man-made habitats by animals of one sort and another could make a book in itself, but one group deserves special mention here – the animals of deep mines. G.T. Jefferson who has studied these, draws attention to the quantities of organic material introduced into mines by men and ponies as a source of energy denied true cave animals. The 'white beetles' or 'queens' reported by miners are usually newly moulted American cockroaches *(Periplaneta americana)* which have not yet hardened and darkened their cuticles. One pit shows a rare mutant form of white-eyed cockroach which has remained stable over eleven years as five per cent of the total population. Scavenging beetles are present too: *Blap mucronata*, the big black churchyard beetle, favours dark places and is also known as the cellar beetle. *Harpalus affinis*, with metallic sheen and red legs is nocturnal anyway, so darkness does not worry it. There are plenty of wood borers tunnelling into the pit props, sometimes introduced with foreign timber but able to survive because of the uniform conditions of warmth and dampness.

The vast numbers of springtails include one blind species, *Sinella coeca,* whilst a small thysanuran insect, *Nicoletia,* in 'Deep Navigation' at Treharris, is not only a new British record, but is represented by females only, these reproducing parthenogenetically. Woodlice occur, particularly *Androniscus dentiger*, several annelid worm species and occasional swarms of fungus gnats bred in the fungi growing on timber, faecal material and other debris. Preying on the detritus and fungus feeders are centipedes, common house spiders *(Tegenaria)* and, again in 'Deep Navigation' and another pit further West, a very rare spider, *Zelotes rusticus*. There are also the inevitable mice and rats, occasional bats and even some dozens of pied wagtails reported roosting in an air shaft at Cwm Pit. As many as three to four hundred pied wagtails habitually roost above the drying ovens of the paint plant at Hoovers Limited in Merthyr, luxuriating in the rising warmth. Their long tails help them to balance on wires, pipes and girders and they enter and leave via the ventilation louvres. The occasional one or two drop off dead when the machines start up again after the weekend break, but they seem oblivious to the continuous noise.

Back at Cwm Pit a few score pied wagtails have roosted in the reedmace *(Typha latifolia)* of an old colliery pond which was the feeder reservoir for the older Cyfarthfa Canal from about 1780 to 1805. In good condition still, this embanked pond supports nesting moorhens, frogs, minnows, marsh fritillary butterflies, whirligig beetles, caddis larvae and three damsel flies, the common blue *(Enallagma cyathigerum)*, the banded agrion *(Agrion splendens)* and demoiselle agrion *(A virgo)*. The adjacent bog is of particular value in being the only known site for the lesser spike rush *(Eleocharis uniglumis)*, which is recorded inland in Britain in only four counties and these in Eastern England. Also here is the rarer variety of early marsh orchid *(Dactylorhiza incarnata* ssp *strictifolia)* with the common and heath spotted orchids *(D fuchsii* and *D ericetorum)*, bog pimpernel and lesser skullcap with marginal sheep's bit *(Jasione montana)* and wild thyme *(Thymus drucei)*. This area warrants conservation, but its future is insecure due to the threat of open cast mining.

The old course of the Glamorgan Canal down through Abercanaid features in one of the Glamorgan Naturalists' Trust's booklets: 'Three Walks in the Coalfield' and is another example of a rich natural community established in a man-made habitat. The briskly flowing stream leading the drainage waters alongside the green walkway of the disused canal and towpath contains a wealth of water plants with water horsetail *(Equisetum fluviatile)*, yellow flag *(Iris pseudacorus)*, two bur reeds *(Sparganium emersum* and *S erectum)*, greater water plantain *(Alisma plantago-aquatica)* and several score more sheltering the massed frogspawn of spring. Animals include sticklebacks and minnows, water boatmen, water crickets, pond skaters, great diving and whirligig beetles, four different kinds of tube-dwelling caddis larvae, stoneflies, dragonflies and damsel flies, five inch long horse

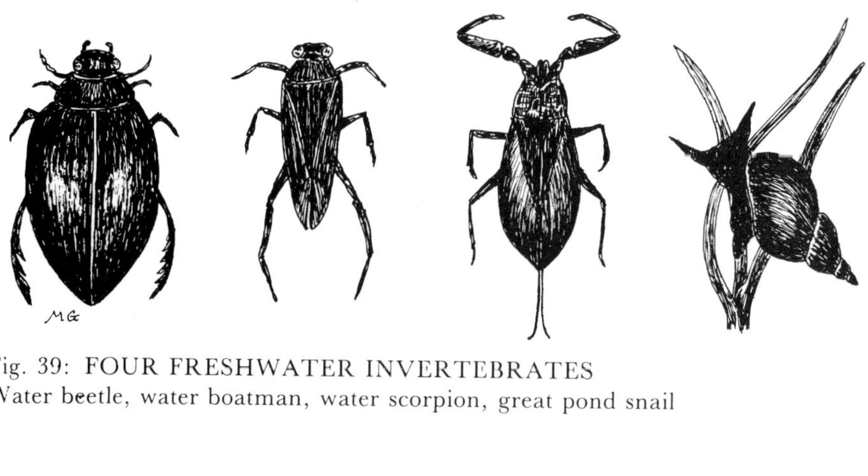

Fig. 39: FOUR FRESHWATER INVERTEBRATES
Water beetle, water boatman, water scorpion, great pond snail

leeches and massed water snails feeding on the stonewort *(Nitella flexilis)*. Other man-made freshwater habitats are the upper lake at Bryn Cae Owen, Cyfarthfa, holding perch, roach, carp, bream, tench and minnows, and the lower lake with brown trout, three-spined sticklebacks and minnows. The local big hawker dragonfly is the common aeshna *(Aeshna juncea)*.

E – Plants and Animals of the River Taff

The saga of Merthyr's river and its wildlife over the past two centuries is worthy of more space than can be given here. The best and worst are passed: the otters have gone, but so have the main sewage outfalls. Today's uneasy partnership between man and nature has been sealed by a conscious clean-up of the town section of the river banks and a spontaneous regeneration of the natural communities on the southern reaches.

The rural valley southwards from Mount Pleasant to the wooded gorge above the confluence with the Taf-Bargoed at Quaker's Yard has escaped urbanisation and is probably less frequented now than when Trevithick's steam engine chugged down the Penydarren line alongside. The tramway still exists – a verdant reminder of a great past – as is the ivy-draped stone bridge at Pont y Gwaith, where a busy ironworks flourished in the last quarter of the sixteenth century. Downstream from this 'Bridge of the Works' in the last quarter of the twentieth century great cohorts of swifts zoom through the narrow air corridor between overarching trees, sieving midges from the legions bred in the sultry flood below.

Wood warblers still pipe from riverside alders along this southern stretch; dippers patrol the deep-cut sections shaded by mighty beeches and grey wagtails forage on pebble banks among sheets of flowering yellow cress *(Rorippa islandica)*. But there have been changes. Winter heliotrope *(Petasites fragrans)*, whose pale pink flowers scent the river banks in February and March, was introduced from Southern Europe only in 1806. Japanese knotweed *(Polygonum cuspidatum)*, commonest now of all the riverside undershrubs, arrived in 1825 to effect a rapid change from a prized garden plant to a pernicious invader. *Buddleja*, from the same part of the world, got here in 1896. The Himalayan or Indian balsam *(Impatiens glandulifera)* is one of the most striking colonists along the lower Taff, where it arrived in the early part of this century after reaching Britain in 1839. The explosive seed distribution has enabled it to work its way upstream well into the Merthyr district, but it is much less exuberant here than in the lowlands. Monkey flower *(Mimulus guttatus)*, which brightens the town stretches of the river, arrived from North America in 1812; its compatriot snowberry (*Symphoricarpus rivularis*) reached the area in 1817.

The most obvious change in the bird life is epitomised by the strident clamour of gulls squabbling over flood-borne debris between short flights upstream to regain lost ground. Kingfishers have returned to the river since their virtual disappearance following the 1962/63 freeze-up, but they have

Fig. 40: FOUR BIRDS OF THE WATERSIDE
Common sandpiper, snipe, water rail, moorhen

difficulty in detecting their prey in the murky waters and are more likely to fish elsewhere.

The noxious appearance of the river water is due to non-toxic coal dust, but the invisible bacterial pollution is a lot more lethal. Coal dust in suspension inhibits the growth of plants on the river bed by cutting down the light which they need for photosynthesis, so that non-fungal vegetable life is practically restricted to unicellular diatoms. Pulverised coal also coats the gills of fish and may be the prime factor limiting the distribution of trout and bullheads, the latter not being found where the average suspended solids exceed a concentration of 20 milligrammes per litre. Trout, abundant in the Taff headwaters, decline on the Merthyr stretch, but are more abundant now than in the dirtier Taff of a decade or so ago. Oxygen intake by invertebrates, too, is impeded by the blanketing of their respiratory organs, but some survive under stones, the sludge tending to settle out on upturned surfaces. Net-spinning caddis larvae are at a grave disadvantage because their food-catching nets get silted up.

Pollution with domestic sewage is less serious since the recent installation of a trunk sewer. The most damaging effect of this type of organic effluent is to deplete the water of the oxygen needed by animals, this vital element being used by the multitudes of fungi, bacteria and protozoa which are employed in its decomposition. The greyish wefts of 'sewage fungi' at sewer outfalls include bacteria and rotifers as well as fungi. Filaments of *Sphaerotilus natans* predominate where water flow is brisk; bacterial cells of *Zooglea* embedded in a jelly matrix where it is more stagnant.

The first larger animals to put in an appearance below the ingress of contaminants are tubificids (Oligochaete worms which reach out from a forest of vertical mud tubes). Next come blood worms (Chironomid or midge larvae which live in rather similar tubes), then water hog lice *(Asellus aquaticus)* before the appearance of a more normal clean water fauna heralded by freshwater shrimps *(Gammarus pulex)*.

Deoxygenation is worst in the still water impounded behind weirs, where bubbles of methane gas can sometimes be seen rising from the decomposing sludge. Most of the dissolved oxygen of this water is in the surface layer which slides away over the weir, but oxygen becomes re-incorporated as it tumbles into the froth below. Conditions are thus better under the weir on this count, but may be more opaque from the general stirring up of sediments. Tributary streams fed by acid waters from mines sometimes bring in heavy deposits of orange ferric hydroxide and bacteria, which blanket out the algae and most of the small animal life where they enter the river. Chemical effluents include oil from garages and road surfaces.

A detailed biological survey was carried out by a team from University College, Cardiff and the University of Wales Institute of Science and Technology in 1969 and 1970 as part of the local authority's Taff Valley Project. Findings then reflect a more polluted state than exists now but the general trends of plant and animal distribution still apply.

Animals found only upstream from Merthyr at that time included two stoneflies (*Leuctra geniculata* and *L fusca*), two mayflies (*Ephemerella ignita* and *Ecdyonurus dispar*), water cricket (*Velia*), five species of caddis (excluding one member of the Hydroptilidae which was found just above Edwardsville) and one water beetle belonging to the Dytiscidae.

Other mayflies *(Baetis rhodani* and *B scambus)* turned up more frequently downstream from Merthyr, but Chironomid midge larvae were the main downstream animals, being more than ten times as abundant as they were upstream, where they were still the most numerous. Others with a markedly downstream distribution were worms *(Chaetogaster, Nais barbata, N elinguis, N variabilis, Pristina foreli, Lumbricillus nivalis* and *Lumbriculus variegatus*). Leeches *(Trocheta subviridis)*, wandering snails, river limpets *(Ancylastrum fluviatilis)* and water hog lice were also more characteristic of the polluted waters.

Dragonflies winging along the Taff and Taf-Bargoed at Quaker's Yard may have hatched in smaller, purer bodies of water. Those likely to be seen are the brown aeshna *(Aeshna grandis)*, the common sympetrum *(Sympetrum striolatum)* and the large red damsel fly *(Pyrrhosoma nymphula)*.

Fish found between Merthyr and Quaker's Yard were brown trout, bullheads, stone loach, minnows and three-spined sticklebacks, all feeding almost exclusively on midge larvae, although mayflies are taken in cleaner waters. Remarkably few young trout or bullheads were found, suggesting that the nurseries may be elsewhere and only grown fish come into the more polluted waters. Roach and eels were found only below the confluence with the Taf-Bargoed.

The Taff is notoriously subject to flash floods, the whole system changing when water races down in spate from the Beacons, flushing out the pollutants and stirring up the silt to leave little beaches of almost pure coal dust high on the banks.

Much less affected by urbanisation are the Millstone Grit rivers, notably the Nant Ffrwdd which enters the Taf Fawr after careering down two sizable waterfalls in the narrow gorge which it has carved into the hard grits West of

Merthyr. There is a fine hanging valley tributary and tufaceous deposits where lime-rich waters seep from between rock layers, throwing some of the lime out of solution to nurture unexpected flowers like tutsan *(Hypericum androsaemum)*, wild garlic *(Allium ursinum)* and sweet woodruff *(Asperula odorata)*, along with several special rarities which equate this attractive river with the headwaters of the Neath a little to the West along this same rock outcrop.

Natural History of the Mountain Limestone and Old Red Sandstone

by Dr. MARY E. GILLHAM

A – Plants of the Limestone Grasslands

Biologically the area reaching up to the Brecon Beacons National Park North of Merthyr is much richer than that to the South and boasts four nature reserves, the Taf Fechan Reserve managed jointly by the local authority and the Glamorgan Naturalists' Trust, the Glais Reserve by the Glamorgan Naturalists' Trust, the Cil Sanws-Darren Fawr Reserve by the Brecon Naturalists' Trust, and the Darren Fach Reserve by the Merthyr and District Naturalists' Society. This latter Reserve has also been designated as a site of special scientific interest (SSSI) by the Nature Conservancy Council and a Forest Nature Reserve occurs at Penmoelallt just across the valley on the opposite side.

The limestone hills North of Cefn Coed appear greener than the rough grazings of the Beacons to the North and the Coalfield to the South, their swards richer in number of species and in food value. Fertile limey soils contain a lot of earthworms which ensure a self-maintaining system of manuring and tillage by dragging organic matter down from the surface and throwing up paler mineral matter as worm casts. The resulting mixture can become impoverished by nutrients leaching out or enriched by nutrients flushing in. Limestone communities which arise under a regime of heavy sheep grazing are well exemplified on Morlais Hill, where the rock weathers down to an alkaline rendzina soil with a pH of 7.0-8.0.

The natural hill grazings are dominated by common bent grass and carnation grass *(Carex flacca)* with flat meadow grass *(Poa compressa)* and a few very rare species like mountain melick *(Melica nutans)* and mountain everlasting *(Antennaria dioica)*. The sward is mostly of perennials, mat formers

Fig. 41: FOUR FLOWERS OF THE LIMESTONE SCREES AND GRASSLANDS
Common thyme, meadow rue, mossy saxifrage, salad burnet

and rosette plants, which cling so tenaciously to their little patch that annuals cannot find room to germinate. Special limestone plants are rock rose *(Helianthemum nummularium)*, salad burnet *(Poterium sanguisorba)*, eyebright *(Euphrasia nemoralis)* and common milkwort *(Polygala vulgaris)*, whose flowers may be blue, mauve, pink or white. Others which are very characteristic are bulbous buttercup *(Ranunculus bulbosus)*, barren strawberry *(Potentilla sterilis)*, crosswort *(Galium cruciata)*, lady's bedstraw *(G verum)*, small heath bedstraw *(G sterneri)* at what is probably its southern-most site in Britain, harebell *(Campanula rotundifolia)* and carline thistle. Morlais Hill has yielded no less than 109 species of moss.

Few of the plants grow to more than a few inches high and they survive only because more vigorous growers cannot find the necessities of life. Given artificial fertilisers, coupled with alleviation from grazing, most would disappear under a thick mat of grasses which, in their turn, would be succeeded by shrubs and these by trees.

This does sometimes happen. Sheep farming went into a steep decline between 1914 and 1920, when shepherds failed to return to the land from the armed forces. Hawthorns sprang up and passed through their vulnerable seedling and sapling phases so that they could withstand later inroads by sheep. One field below Vaynor Quarry is full of well grown thorns which survive into the eighties despite the broken down walls, but are not being replaced so the area may revert to turf as they die.

Haws nibbled right back throw out new shoots each year but these get nipped off so that thirty year old bushes may be only six inches high but have massive trunks at ground level. It is impossible to age these accurately by cutting through the base and counting the annual rings, as with a normal tree, because a sheep cropping all the leaves in spring will initiate the production of a second crop in June, so that there will be two rings produced that summer, with a circle of smaller vessels marking the unproductive months between. Hawthorns which have 'got away' produce mini-woodland communities giving scattered shade to woodland flowers like lesser celandine *(Ranunculus ficaria)*, dog's mercury *(Mercurialis perennis)*, lords and ladies *(Arum maculatum)*, twayblade *(Listera ovata)* and early purple orchid *(Orchis mascula)*.

Where glacial till has sludged down Morlais Hill towards the road, soil depth changes from a few inches to a few feet, soil pH from 8.0 to 5.0 and soil texture from friable to clayey. Lime-lovers disappear and the plant community becomes dominated by bracken with an understorey of moorland plants.

Rain water readily disappears underground in these porous limestone soils – an advantage in a high rainfall area. Where the underlying strata enable a spring to bubble up the water emerges charged with lime, which precipitates out as a crusty deposit of tufa. Such springs sometimes support a special association of plants including the rare marsh arrow grass *(Triglochin palustre)* with marginal stemless thistle *(Cirsium acaulon)*, hard rush *(Juncus inflexus)* and hairy sedge *(Carex hirta)*.

B – *Plants of Cliff, Scree and Woodland*

The crevice plants of natural and quarried rock faces survive with very little soil and are typified by mossy saxifrage *(Saxifraga hypnoides)*, rock cress *(Arabis hirsuta)*, knapweeds *(Centaurea spp)* and hawkweeds *(Hieracium spp)*. Three plants which lose less water by remaining tiny are rue-leaved saxifrage *(Saxifraga tridactylites)*, spring whitlow grass *(Erophila verna)* and hairy bitter cress *(Cardamine hirsuta)*. Biting stonecrop has succulent leaves: wall rue *(Asplenium ruta-muraria)* and maidenhair spleenwort *(A trichomanes)* obtain extra moisture by growing in absorbent moss cushions. Thyme and yellow trefoil *(Trifolium dubium)* form their own moisture retaining curtains. Bird's foot trefoil and hairy hawkbit *(Leontodon hispidus)* root deeply into crevices, along with seedling hawthorn, sycamore, ash and goat sallow which escape being eaten only by growing on unscalable rock faces.

Grasses come into their own where soil accumulates on inaccessible ledges – grasses which would dominate the level areas too, crowding out most of the smaller limestone flowers, if it were not for the sheep. Among them are cocksfoot *(Dactylis glomerata)*, hairy oat *(Helictotrichon pubescens)*, yellow oat *(Trisetum flavescens)*, soft brome *(Bromus mollis)*, quaking grass *(Briza media)* and the two mountain fescues.

Rock slabs of the old Morlais Quarry floor wear a thin skin of rendzina, black with humus and often sodden with rain, but curling away from the rock face during dry spells. There is insufficient depth to support any but the tiniest of plants among the velvety moss covering and the two saxifrages are as large as any. Minute associates include parsley piert *(Aphanes arvensis)*, two sandworts *(Arenaria serpyllifolia* and *A leptoclados)*, field speedwell *(Veronica arvensis)*, field madder *(Sherardia arvensis)*, fairy flax *(Linum catharticum)* and early hair grass *(Aira praecox)*. These are all annuals, completing their life

1

2

3

4

5

Plate 18: WOODLAND PLANTS
Creeping Jenny (1) and Black Bryony (3) will grow in most sorts of woodland. Turkey Oak (2) and Bird's Nest Orchid (5) are special plants of the Taf Fechan Gorge Nature Reserve. Japanese Larch (4) is a more successful species than European larch *Photographs by Mary Gillham*

cycle during the early months of the year so that only the drought resistant seeds are left by the time the soil skin shrivels in summer. Field daisy, common dog violet, pearlwort *(Sagina procumbens)*, dovesfoot cranesbill *(Geranium molle)*, centaury *(Centaurium erythraea)* and yellow wort *(Blackstonia perfoliata)* survive as mini-versions of their normal selves.

Where the Darren Fach cliff face is protected by woodland shining cranes-bill *(Geranium lucidum)*, marjoram *(Origanum vulgare)*, basil *(Clinopodium vulgare)*, greater woodrush *(Luzula sylvatica)* and brittle bladder fern *(Cystopteris fragilis)* grow. The cliffs of Darren Fawr above the open scree to the South are unshaded – a saxifrage type habitat as at Morlais – with vigorous *Cotoneaster* at the North end.

The true mountain scree above the tree line supports great drifts of rare limestone polypody fern *(Thelypteris robertiana)*, the equally rare green spleen-wort *(Asplenium viride)* and six other fern species. The very local meadow rue *(Thalictrum minus)* gets bitten off as it tops the stones but reaches eighteen inches high on inaccessible rock faces.

The edges of these limestone outcrops are often quite sharply demarcated, as where convex tongues of acid soil have spilled down gullies between them in the Cil Sanws area by sollifluction from the Millstone Grit above. Sheep relish the green herbage of the limestone shoulders but avoid the browner, tussocky moorland plants of the humped but much wetter bulges between, unless food is very short. Sheep's fescue is the only plant species common to both.

Worms throw up a top dressing of fine soil on the old Morlais Quarry spoil tips, making them a more amenable habitat than the natural limestone screes where soil remains deeply buried. Rock rose, herb Robert *(Geranium robertianum)*, wild strawberry *(Fragaria vesca)*, and mouse-ear hawkweed *(Hieracium pilosella)* are typical plants, but there is a wealth of others, neatly cropped to a smooth sward.

Some of the scree slopes below Darren Fach on the eastern flank of the Taf Fawr, where the rare mountain sedge *(Carex montana)* grows in profusion, have become fully scrub covered. Hawthorns predominate with blackthorn, rowan, hazel, dogwood *(Cornus sanguineus)* and the ash which will dominate the woodland-to-be if the plant succession is allowed to proceed to its logical conclusion. These establish better on scree than on grassland because their tender young growth takes place secretly in high humidity and immune from grazing among the tumble of boulders. Sheep, as well as men, find these rugged slopes more difficult to clear of trees than are the valleys or the plateaux.

Special shrubs of the scree woodland are purging buckthorn *(Rhamnus catharticus)* and two rare whitebeams *(Sorbus porrigentiformis* and *S Leyana)*, the latter known in Britain only here and in the nearby Penmoelallt Reserve, the other not much commoner. Rarities among the herbs are narrow-leaved bitter cress *(Cardamine impatiens)*, false cleavers *(Galium spurium)* and adder's tongue fern *(Ophioglossum vulgatum)*.

Fig. 42: FOUR SHRUBS OF THE LIMESTONE CLIFFS, SCREES AND WOODLANDS
Purging buckthorn, the two rare whitebeams (*Sorbus leyana* (left) and *S. porrigentiformis*), yew

Bouldery ashwoods occur on both sides of the Taf Fawr North of Cefn Coed, grading into oakwood as soils deepen and acidify towards the Millstone Grit on the West side and into sycamores where they deepen and acidify towards the Old Red Sandstone on the East side. Small-leaved lime *(Tilia cordata)*, wych elm *(Ulmus glabra)*, holly *(Ilex aquifolia)* and yew *(Taxus baccata)* are common. Parts of the woodland floor are white with flowering garlic in spring, followed by wood sanicle *(Sanicula europaea)*, three-nerved sandwort *(Moehringia trinervia)*, lady's mantle *(Alchemilla glabra)*, yellow archangel *(Lamiastrum galeobdolon)* and a host of others.

Ash woodland with maple *(Acer campestre))* and sycamore prominent in its two southern blocks and beech *(Fagus sylvatica)* in its northern part has grown up on limestone pavement near Vaynor. The land is flatter here and the limestone has fragmented into clints or blocks separated by grikes or crevices which may be three to four feet deep while only a few inches across. Trees are rooted mostly in the grikes and past freedom from grazing enabled them to overtop the blocky surface and grow away. Their contorted roots embrace the rock faces, sometimes prising them loose by insinuating themselves beneath. Solution-pitted clints have been cleared from hard-won agricultural land and stood in line on their edges as weirdly shaped walling stones.

There are rich assemblages of mosses forming continuous mats over the clints in the moist shade of the trees. These dried out completely during the 1976 drought (when the shallow-rooted beeches and birches lost their leaves prematurely) but were restored to their normal lushness after only three weeks of heavy rain. This is the most southerly limestone pavement in Wales - apart from a scrap at Porthcawl – and one which has progressed full term, to the final successional phase. Better known is the one at Ystradfellte, which is held at an open country phase by sheep grazing.

C – Animals of the Limestone Hills

There have been several reliable sightings of pine martens in recent years in the North of the borough and it seems that these handsome Mustelids, formerly the prerogative of Scotland, are moving South through Wales with the spread of conifers. Badgers, stoats and weasels live in the scree woodlands. Foxes were so numerous by 1976 that the local farmers were meeting every winter week-end and killing two or three per shoot in the Taf Fawr and Taf Fechan Valleys, sometimes sighting as many as seven in a day. Grey squirrels roam the bouldery woods, hares the wilder uplands and rabbits the tamer ones. Lifted logs reveal an abundance of vole tunnels and an abundance of moles inevitably follows the abundance of earthworms, which are their chief food.

Merlins quarter the hills in pursuit of lark, pipit or linnet, buzzards sail out from the cliffs over the Brecon Road and kestrels hunt the entire region. Sparrow hawks are in most of the woods, their short rounded wings giving them manoevrability among the trees and slight vantage points such as fallen logs providing convenient plucking stations. They build their nests in April, then go away for a month, returning sometimes to find a buzzard in occupation, so that they have to build another. Short-eared owls hunt across the area by day from the Hirwaun Moors and long-eared owls forage by night from the refuge of the On Llwyn Woods. Tawny and little owls hole up in old woodland trees, rock outcrops, cliffs and swallow holes, barn owls in old stone barns. The grubs of a small moth usually appear in owl pellets a few days after these have been coughed up, and other exploiters of the owls secrete themselves in crevices beside the nests.

Big flocks of jackdaws nest and roost on the Darren Fawr and Darren Fach cliffs, which are also a haunt of raven and carrion crow. The warm, dry soils of Morlais Hill favour winter survival of the rare stonechat and yellowhammer. Tree pipits frequent the 'open savanna' type of grassland dotted with thorn trees which supply the elevated song posts from which they can launch their swooping courtship flights. Woodcock crouch among fallen leaves and even blackbirds will nest on the ground among rushes.

Holes in the gnarled rowan, ash and birch trees are much in demand – their diameter dictating what is likely to be nesting in them, with the

Fig. 43: FOUR BIRDS OF PREY
Merlin, kestrel, buzzard, sparrow hawk

exception of the nuthatch, which plasters any sort of hole up to a suitable size with mud. Greater spotted woodpeckers may be ousted by starlings. Green woodpeckers buzz like a hole full of humming bees when disturbed at the nest and the coal tit's warning hiss is disconcertingly like that of a snake. Tree creepers, which potter mouse-like up moss-grown trunks, rear their young in crevices behind loose bark.

Hole-nesting pied flycatchers and redstarts take the same sort of food so cannot share the same feeding range without being in serious competition. The same applies to ground-nesting wood warblers and willow warblers. The latter return to the nesting sites a week or a fortnight earlier in spring than the wood warblers, so get first choice of territory, but the latecomers are more aggressive and can push their competitors' boundaries back or oust them altogether. Wood warblers prefer the steeper habitats. Missel thrushes are among the earliest of the woodland nesters, wheatears of the moorland nesters (excluding ravens). Nesting crevices of wheatears among stones become very foul by the time the brood is ready to leave. Beetles, maggots, mites, ticks, fleas and flat-flies can be found among the 'dandruff' of quill flakes peeled from the fledglings' growing feathers.

All the common moorland invertebrates, parasites and predators, plant feeders and scavengers, are to be found on the limestone hills, plus many extra ones. Shiny bloody nosed beetles *(Timarcha tenebricosa)* simulate a nose-bleed to deter predators. Oil beetles *(Meloe proscarabeus)* produce an evil smelling yellowish fluid when handled and employ bees to bring up their young, which behave like cuckoos in ejecting the rightful recipient of their food. The rather similar devil's coach horse beetle or cock tail *(Staphylinus olens)* adopts a threatening attitude by elevating the segmented abdomen (which is only partly covered by the short wing cases) and opening its jaws wide. The yellow-spotted green tiger beetle *(Cicindela campestris)* scuttling over the short grass can be fiercely predatory. Wingless coal black weevils *(Otiorrhynchus clavipes)* of the limestone hills are more characteristic of southern chalkhills. Brilliant velvety red earth mites *(Trombidium holocericeum)* congregate in rocky alcoves where sheep shelter from mountain winds.

The open grasslands can be alive with grasshoppers and butterflies in high summer, the flower-starred turf supplying the necessary food plants. Common blue, silver studded blue and the related brown argus are typical, though also found in the Treharris area of the South. Small coppers and small skippers abound in season, with the inevitable small heaths, meadow browns and Vanessids. Wall browns and graylings sun themselves on rock faces, hedge browns on brambles. Green hairstreaks are rare but inhabit favoured clearings in some of the upland woods. Marsh fritillaries, too, are quite local, preferring water shaded by trees, both here and in the Coalfield at Cwm Pit and Cyfarthfa Lakes. Commas, relative newcomers to the district, were around at Vaynor as late as November in 1976. This long hot summer was good for migrants, painted ladies being among those which

1 

 2

3 

 4

5 

 6

Plate 19: BEETLES AND WASPS' NEST
Soldier Beetle with red thorax and red thighs (1). Wasp Beetle, black with yellow stripes (2). Bloody-nosed Beetle which exudes red fluid from snout (3). Oil Beetle with short wing cases (4). Thick-legged Flower Beetle on hawkbit (5). Tree Wasps' Nest on hawthorn (6)

Photograph 5 by Mary Gillham, others J. O. Evans

flew in from the South. Clouded yellows came to some parts of Glamorgan during this summer but the last known large scale invasion of these to Merthyr was around 1944.

Brown plume moths *(Emmeline monodactyla)* and plain golden Y moths inhabit hawthorn scrub. Only yellow and black striped caterpillars of the broom moth *(Ceramica pisi)* have been seen, not the green form. Blue-striped lackey moth caterpillars *(Malacosoma neustria)* spin communal webs on haw, sloe and bramble at the woodland edges. The irritant hairy pelts of the big woolly bear caterpillars of northern oak egger moths *(Lasiocampa quercus* var. *callunae)* and fox moths *(Macrothylacia rubi)* repel most birds, but the mountain cuckoos relish them. Another woolly bear caterpillar is that of the wood tiger moth *(Parasemia plantaginis)* which frequents bosky hollows on the open hillsides and spins some of the larval hairs into the silk cocoon when it pupates.

J.O. Evans has attracted a number of moths to a mercury vapour lamp on the northern slopes of the Taf Fechan Valley at Cefn Coed and these are listed alphabetically at the end of the chapter. Moths congregated above the lamp will suddenly drop to earth when a pipistrelle or long-eared bat flies into their midst, locating the laggards with its inbuilt radar system and snapping them up. Snails find abundant lime in their food for shell building and the little wrinkled snail *(Helicella caperata)* feeds extensively on the feathery leaves of yarrow *(Achillea millefolium)*. Of the familiar grove snails the larger brown-lipped *Cepaea nemoralis* is commoner than the more delicate-shelled white-lipped *C hortensis*.

Great crested newts have been present for many years in the Bryniau Ponds near Morlais Castle where a local beauty is the golden ringlet dragonfly *(Cordulegaster boltoni)*. The Quarry Pond here contains roach, perch and minnows, the Dog Pond roach, perch, minnows and tench.

D – River Valleys of the Limestone Karst Country

The River Taf Fawr passes from Old Red Sandstone to Carboniferous Limestone just South of Llwyn On reservoir, but no change in flora is apparent because its former course is infilled with transported fluvio-glacial material to give a flat flood plain between precipitous slopes. Only below Cefn Cemetery is it actively carving into the limestone to form the Taf Fawr Gorge. A deep pool occupying a sink here was found by F.S. Baguley in the 1976 drought to lie astride the junction of the limestone and the Millstone Grit.

Limestone Gorge features are better developed on the River Taf Fechan which flows along the North Border Ridge for over two miles instead of cutting across it and is joined en route by the still better example of the River Glais. Both are deservedly Nature Reserves; the Glais also an SSSI – on geological grounds, but it merits this status on botanical grounds too and the

Plate 20: BIRDS OF SHRUBBY LAKESIDE AND RIVERSIDE
Long-tailed Tit's (1) spherical nest in a gorse bush. Common Sandpiper (2) on nest among waterside mint and coltsfoot

Photographs by Keri Williams

fauna may well prove as rich. Both reserves are described elsewhere: only the briefest reference is possible here.

The valleys carry mixed oak-ash-beech wood with small-leaved lime and turkey oak *(Quercus cerris)*, dogwood and bird cherry *(Prunus padus)* which is near the South of its geographical range here. Roots of hazel and wych elm are parasitised by toothwoot *(Lathraea squamaria)* and another equally devoid of green colouring is bird's nest orchid *(Neottia nidus-avis)* which lives on decaying humus. Other orchids found occasionally are broad helleborine *(Epipactis helleborine)*, fragrant orchid *(Gymnadenia conopsea)*, lesser butterfly orchid *(Platanthera bifolia)*, early purple and common spotted orchids and twayblade.

Meadow saxifrage *(Saxifraga granulata)* shares muddy banks with primroses *(Primula vulgaris)*, false oxlips (the primrose x cowslip hybrid) and sweet woodruff *(Asperula odorata)*. Unusual flowers include herb Paris *(Paris quadrifolia)*, wild columbine *(Aquilegia vulgaris)*, water avens *(Geum rivale)*, snakeroot *(Polygonum bistorta)* and marsh valerian *(Valeriana dioica)*. Watercress *(Nasturtium officinale)* drapes the walls of collapsed caverns, tussock sedge *(Carex paniculata)* forms imposing stools at the river edges and insectivorous butterwort *(Pinguicula vulgaris)* grows on raw tufa instead of peat, with an uncommon yellow sedge *(Carex lepidocarpa)* and giant horsetail *(Equisetum telmateia)*.

Mosses and liveworts abound. Roy Perry identified 99 mosses and 23 liverworts on one side of the river only in the Taf Fechan Reserve in a single visit in February 1976. Several of these expedite tufa formation by actively extracting carbon dioxide from the dissolved calcium bicarbonate in the water trickling over them. The calcium carbonate thrown out of solution sometimes takes on the filigree pattern of the moss which it entombs, 'petrified' *Cratoneuron commutatum* being particularly attractive in little grottoes. Cushion mosses *(Gymnostomum calcareum* and *Eucladium verticillatum)* form great tufa bosses several feet thick on cliff faces. Liverworts *(Conocephalum conicum* and *Pellia endiviaefolia)* appear as though sculpted in the rock itself. Active in the formation of less shapely tufa deposits are green and blue-green algae.

Fungi are as numerous as mosses and include interesting forms like the edible morel *(Morchella esculenta)*, bolete *(Boletus scabrum)*, wood hedgehog *(Hydnum repandum)*, orange fairy clubs *(Clavaria)*, puffballs *(Lycoperdon)* and scarlet *Cordyceps militaris* growing from buried moth pupae. The big, gelatinous coral-red *Tremiscus helvelloides*, discovered in 1973 as a 'first' for Wales and a 'third' for Britain, grows on old quarry tramroads just East of the Taf Fechan between Pontsticill Reservoir and the reserve. One of the few red algae found in fresh water, *Lemania fluviatilis*, grows in the crystal clear torrents with branched green *Cladophora* and aquatic mosses.

Potholes left above flood level as the river cuts deeper into its bed receive a lot of frogspawn in Spring. Wandering snails and river limpets browse on blue-green algae and diatoms among sand grain tubes of *Agapetus* caddis

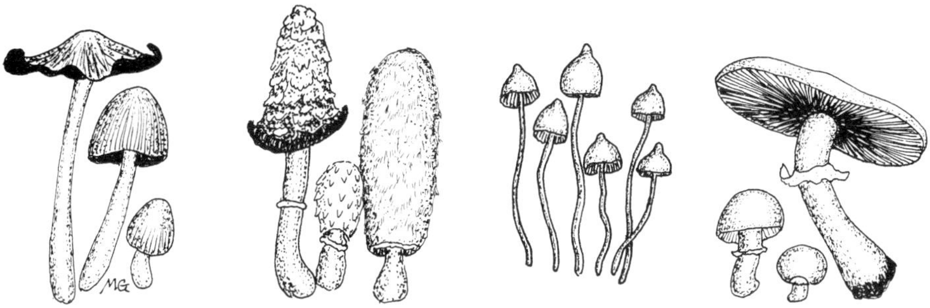

Fig. 44: FOUR COMMON FUNGI
Ink cap, shaggy cap or lawyer's wig, liberty cap, common mushroom

larvae and detritus-feeding freshwater shrimps. Other caddis spending their youth in the Taf Fechan stream complex before taking to the air on gold-spangled wings are *Diplectrona felix* and *Wormaldia*. Stonefly larvae *(Nemoura cambrica, N erratica, Protonemoura meyeri* and *Leuctra nigra)* feed on blue-greens, diatoms, fungal threads, animal scraps and other detritus. Helodid beetle larvae enjoy a similar diet, as do the young stages of various flies *(Thaumalea,* soldier flies *(Stratiomyids)* and blackflies or buffalo gnats *(Simuliids)*). Pond skaters and water crickets are surface feeders.

Many of these contribute to the diet of the special white trout which inhabit Ogof y Ci Cave on the Glais. These fish have become depigmented in their dark habitat but retain the power of sight and move out of the underground labyrinth for breeding. More unique in Ogof y Ci are the blind, creamy-white spiders *(Porrhomma rosenhaureri)* known elsewhere at only one site in Ireland. All members of this species live underground, as do those of the cave shrimp, *Niphargus fontanus*, water louse, *Proasellus cavaticus* and two springtails, *Onychiurus schoetti* and *O dunarius*. Thirty species of animals have been found in this cave, some drifted in by chance, others spending their entire lives here although many of their kind live in daylight.

Ogof Rhyd Sych further downstream harbours the lesser horseshoe bat and there is a fine moist luminescence on the surface of some of the fluted, iron-stained calcite curtains which drape the walls. This is probably due to bacteria – Streptomycetes – but may be 'moon milk', a micro-cystalline form of calcite with the consistency of toothpaste, which is deposited under the catalysing influence of other micro-organisms.

Otters, once common on the headwaters of the Taff, have declined over the past twenty years, but there is still the occasional sighting, as on the Taf Fechan below the reservoirs in 1973. Water voles tunnel in the banks and the more elusive water shrews are sometimes seen. Roach, stone loach and minnows occur as well as trout, on both the Taf Fawr and the Taf Fechan.

Bird life in these steep, wooded valleys is rich, from the dippers and grey wagtails nesting in spray-washed crevices to the buzzards of the treetops. Tawny owls in the neighbouring parish of Penderyn catch both trout and bullheads to feed to their young and may possibly do so here. Swifts, swallows, house martins and sand martins hawk flies over the water but are not waterside nesters. Some of the sand martins may be ones breeding in the furnace wall of the old Cyfarthfa steelworks downstream.

Butterflies, like other insects, are common – brimstones, orange-tips, green-veined whites, silver-washed fritillaries, ringlets, painted ladies, etc, and there are many moths – brimstones again, drinkers, garden tigers, large and small elephant hawks, silver ground carpets *(Xanthorhoë montanata)* and common white waves *(Cabera pursaria)*. Bird cherries sometimes get completely defoliated by the net-spinning small ermine moth *(Yponomeuta padella)*, (a Microlepidopteron) which is so specific as to be named after its host plant. Gall-forming insects include the meadowsweet gall midge *(Dasyneura ulmariaea)* and alder gall mite *(Eriophyes laevis inangulis)*. A study of leaf hoppers is being carried out in the Taf Fechan reserve during 1976-77 under the direction of M Claridge of UCC. Rather more than forty species have been found, some quite unusual and almost all new for Wales, as this complex group has been studied very little.

E – Mountain Streams of the Old Red Sandstone

The Devonian rocks which form the bulk of the Brecon Beacons National Park, extend well into the parish of Vaynor as a moorland plateau dissected by streams such as those forming Merthyr's northern boundary. The Nant Llysiog-Nant Wern Ddu system flows West to the Taf Fawr North of Llwyn On Reservoir and the Nant Rhyddau East through Blaen Car to the Taf Fechan at Pontsticill Reservoir.

The iron-impregnated waters of the spring at Ffynon Llysiog were formerly used medicinally, but lie two rugged miles above the Brecon road, so the ailing who availed themselves of them were no weaklings. This and other sources of the western stream system rise in a quaking bog where the *Sphagnum* raft sways alarmingly underfoot. High moss-grown waterfalls intercept the flow about the 1500 foot contour, with bilberries on their craggy sides, and deep trout pools are held back by resistant sills of the hard sandstone which alternate with layers of softer marl to give a noble series of stepped waterfalls in the lower valley.

Sludging of peat in wet weather can release impounded bog water as flash floods which have carried away curved stone dams constructed to regulate the flow and check the amount of rock debris carried down to reservoir level. Ivy-leaved bellflower and New Zealand willow herb (often affected by the mildew, *Erisyphe*) colonise shingle banks where foxgloves sometime survive into their second year to flower. Few free-swimming creatures can maintain position in the turbulent stretches. Stoneflies shelter under stones; mayflies make good the ground lost during the aquatic phase by flying back upstream before laying their eggs; river limpets and Jenkin's spire shells *(Pomatopyrgus*

Fig. 45: FOUR COMMON RUSHES
Toad rush (*Juncus bufonius*), bulbous rush (*J. bulbosus*), heath rush (*squarrosus*), field woodrush (*Luzula campestris*)

jenkinsi) cling tightly to rocks; river pea shells *(Pisidium)* bury themselves in sand banks.

In the still waters of the occasional ox-bow by-passed during spates life is less precarious. The spawn and tadpoles of frogs and toads, palmate and great-crested newts can be found and several kinds of water beetle able to trap a silvery air bubble under their wing cases for underwater breathing. Water boatmen, large and small, use the surface film as a ceiling, turning upside down to walk on it. Their paths cross those of pond skaters walking on the same nebulous skin the other way up – their worlds poles apart in substance but contiguous in space. Swarms of midges rise like puffs of smoke in sultry summer air, the females homing in on the jostling males to produce yet more midges. The resulting larvae wriggle endlessly, like miniature eels, among freshwater shrimps and caddis of various types.

The valley becomes gorge-like as it leaves the rolling moorland to plunge down to the level of Cwm Taf, between alders, birches and rowans. Butterwort and greater woodrush cling to vertical, water-washed slabs; golden saxifrage, water forget-me-not and ragged robin *(Lychnis floscuculi)* inhabit marginal quagmires. The Nant Car valley which enters Llwyn On a little further South is wooded throughout its lower reaches. It is rich in wildlife and is a haunt of large and small pearl bordered fritillaries, comma and green-veined white butterflies and the demoiselle agrion *(Agrion virgo)* with irridescent purple wings and emerald body. Polypody ferns *(Polypodium vulgare)* and the lichens *Usnea* and *Parmelia* clothe the branches and wood sanicle and *Cotoneaster* pinpoint the unexpected 'islands' of limestone caused by downthrow faulting.

Nant Rhyddau rises East of the watershed at about 1,670 feet and joins with other springs bubbling from rushy hollows to cut through the scanty peat to a clear bed of pebbles. Not confined to the Old Red Sandstone, it passes across the limestone outlier which surfaces between the Pentwyn Fault and the Dinas Fault. Crisp mats of liverwort *(Pellia)* and dwarf fool's watercress *(Apium nodiflorum)* alternate with stretches of streambed peppered with stony *Agapetus* caddis tubes and scudding shrimps. Many insects living among the bog pimpernel and star sedge *(Carex echinata)* alongside come to grief in the insectivorous butterwort rosettes.

Blaen Car is deeply recessed into orange-red cliffs over which streams tumble in silver cascades of some 15 to 30 feet. The two pools which receive them harbour some fine trout and smaller fry which attract herons, dippers and grey wagtails. They mark the transition from the open moorland of the plateau to the steep wooded valley of rock outcrops and scree leading down to Pontsticill Reservoir. Emergent stoneflies take wing very little, adult caddis fly mainly at dusk, but dancing flocks of mayflies can fill the entire air on summer evenings from ground to treetops, like a scintillating cloud of stardust, with the toy aeroplanes of predatory dragonflies zooming through their midst.

F – The Mountain Reservoirs

The East shore and headwater marsh of Llwyn On Reservoir lie within the Merthyr district, as does the South West quarter of Pontsticill Reservoir. Both are typical mountain lakes, oligotrophic or poor in nutrients, with clear water and steep stony sides.

Llwyn On, built in 1926, covers 144 acres at an elevation of 854 feet in a 63 inch rainfall area and is 73 feet deep at its deepest. The water is soft, but only slightly acid (pH 6.9) and nutrient levels are much lower than in eutrophic reservoirs as at Lisvane in Cardiff. Thus total hardness, which fluctuates little, is only 33 parts per million (ppm) – made up of 22 parts calcium and 11 parts magnesium – as opposed to 193 ppm – 136 Ca and 57 Mg – at Lisvane. Comparative phosphate levels are 0.05 and 0.16 ppm respectively, nitrate levels 0.1 and 1.4 ppm both varying seasonally. Such low concentrations, particularly of phosphate, are limiting to plant growth and hence to total productivity, this affecting the number of water fowl which come to feed.

Free-floating algae are inhibited by low temperatures; shoreline vegetation by exposure. Waves beating on the leeward (Merthyr) shore scour some parts bare and hold much of the rest at an early successional phase of shoreweed *(Littorella)*. The constant turnover of water prevents stratification in summer so that there is no warm surface layer to stimulate the growth of plankton – and subsequent sinking of some of this to nourish cold water organisms on the bottom. (Talybont shows good stratification and more water fowl; Pentwyn is shallow and warms through completely in summer (unless dry, as in 1976) so both show a higher productivity although their nutrient levels are almost the same.) Steepness of shoreline is also important, gently shelving shores, which are well developed only on the headwater marsh, giving a richer vegetation and better feeding for dabbling ducks.

Plate 21: The RING OUZEL or mountain blackbird is a rare bird of the high crags *Photograph by Keri Williams*

The phenomenal drop in water level in 1976 provided unrivalled opportunity for observing the zonation of vegetation which is usually submerged. By early July, when the drought had still nearly two months to run, the buttressed stone bridge between the underwater confluences with Taf Fawr of Nant Gwineu (dry) and Nant Car (still flowing) had emerged above water level and the drowned village of Ynys y Felin with its road undulating over projecting spurs of glacial drift, saw the light of day on the East shore towards the dam.

Drying sediments covering the North part of the lake bed were liberally sprinkled with the shells of desiccated wandering snails and patterned with the footprints of wagtail and sandpiper. Larger footprints provided moist pockets for the aquatic liverwort, *Riccia crystallina.* Residual moisture in the open community of marsh yellow cress was exploited by a dense sward of seedlings, mostly of land plants which moved downshore as space became available. The fast maturing marsh cudweed grew as parallel belts from the upshore fruiting specimens through flowering and vegetating ones to those just germinating on mud recently vacated by the shrinking waters. Greater plantain *(Plantago major)*, knot grass *(Polygonum aviculare)* and coltsfoot are opportunist land plants which follow the water down.

Aquatics have various ways of surviving these invasions to take over again at re-submergence. Water crowfoot and water starwort produce tiny leaves on short shoots among flopped water shoots up to twenty times as long; marsh yellow cress and water horsetail withdraw into their underground stem system; water purslane and water blinks pass the drought as seeds. Marsh foxtail *(Alopecurus geniculatus)* and oval sedge *(Carex ovalis)* are well able to survive drying out in summer.

Eight vegetation belts occupied the shelving shoreline by the drowned village to a depth of 15 feet. The uppermost belt was of long grass and marsh thistle *(Cirsium palustre)* spilling from the marginal sprucewood; zone 2 of soft rush with meadowsweet and lesser stitchwort *(Stellaria graminea)*. Zone 3 was of common spike rush *(Eleocharis palustris)* with lesser spearwort and marsh bedstraw; zone 4 of corn mint *(Mentha arvensis)* and a tight rosette form of shoreweed with water mint and fiorin grass *(Agrostis stolonifera)*. Zone 5 was an almost pure sward of bright green, 2 inch high shoreweed at the peak of flowering, the water pepper of the causeway margins grading downwards to water bistort *(Polygonum amphibium)*. Zone 6 was a shoreweed sward of very different appearance, pale with the big dying leaves of the aquatic phase not yet succeeded by the small green ones of the terrestrial phase. Massed water crowfoot seedlings occupied bare patches between old stems of yellow cress. Zone 7 was of water milfoil, the sturdily abbreviated land form upshore and flaccid water form below (and locally preserved as such upshore by permanent springs). Zone 8 was of stonewort *(Nitella)* with milfoil and intermediate starwort.

Silt deposited by the Taf Fawr as it enters the lake nurtures some further species of flowering plants with bottle sedge *(Carex rostrata)*, reed canary grass *(Phalaris arundinacea)* and rushes brightened by kingcups *(Caltha palustris)*, golden saxifrage and valerian *(Valeriana officinalis)*. Voles build tennis ball sized nests on the skirted sides of tussock sedge stools *(Carex paniculata)* which shelter big populations of spiders, copse snails *(Arianta arbustorum)* and blue leaf hoppers (*Cicadella viridis)*. Newts occur and quantities of frogspawn get stranded as the water recedes whilst toads mate both in and out of the water.

Fig. 46: FOUR BIRDS WHICH HAWK FLIES
Swift, sand martin, house martin, swallow

Coot and moorhen skulk here and on the central sallow-clad peninsula, coot numbers building up to 200 or so in winter, but the whistling of the two resident pairs of common sandpipers is more often heard on rocky shores. Waders which drop in occasionally are greenshank, green sandpiper, wood sandpiper and oyster catcher. Cormorant and shelduck sometimes fly up from the sea and stay to feed, common gulls flock in from the North.

Dabbling ducks – mallard, teal and wigeon – find little food on steep shores. Mallard are the most abundant, with 100 or so present in winter and about 10 in summer, but they are usually seen resting, the implication being that they go elsewhere at night to feed. Tufted duck and pochard are the most abundant of the diving duck with winter flocks of 50-80. Goldeneye are characteristically present, but in dispersed groups of five or so. They are the most efficient divers, feeding in rougher and deeper water (to 32 feet) on shrimps, water snails, water bugs and caddis and midge larvae and travelling up to 50 yards during underwater spells of 46 seconds.

Goosander come occasionally to fish (the stocks being of brown and rainbow trout and minnows) and there are a few scaup, pintail and long-tailed duck. Both Bewick and whooper swans visit in winter, overlapping with the courting ceremonies of great crested grebes (four birds in 1976). Little grebes are less regular, Slavonian grebes and great northern divers as rare as the odd Canada geese and ospreys on passage. Kingfishers and dippers breed, while swifts, swallows and martins come in multitudes.

The old established heronry in Sitka and Norway spruces at the head of the lake was one of only three or four in the three counties of Glamorgan, but was destroyed by the piecemeal felling of the trees in the late 1970s. It had contained twenty to thirty nests most years and fresh eggshells could be found beneath the squawking nestlings from March to July – among the softer 'eggs' of stinkhorn fungus *(Phallus impudicus)*, which is unusually plentiful here. The heron trees were shared by goldcrests, coal tits, tree creepers, wood pigeons and owls, whose pellets were packed with the skulls and bones of local mice, voles and shrews.

Pontsticill Reservoir, together with Pentwyn, is 2½ miles long and occupies 349 acres in a 70 inch rainfall catchment of 6,339 acres. The Merthyr quarter, immediately above the 107 feet high dam, is deep and almost vertical sided. When water level dropped in July 1976 the South West margin was seen to consist of restricted shallows falling away in precipitous stony slopes veined with vertical rock faces (ORS) and becoming flatter and more silted about 20 feet below normal water level. When submerged this slope is unstable and bare – very different from the water crowfoot and yellow cress swards of the silted shallows nearer the lake head.

New Zealand willow herb had colonised the former shallows below the vertical wavecut earth bank in 1976, water pepper the steep slopes below with a sprinkling of marsh cudweed germinating 20 feet down. A 14 pound trout, the Welsh record, was caught in Pontsticill in 1973. Both brown and rainbow trout are present, with pike, roach, perch, stone loach, minnows and sticklebacks. Water fowl and the great flocks of roosting gulls favour the shallower North end of the reservoir and cannot be claimed as part of Merthyr's wildlife.

* * * * *

I wish to acknowledge my debt to Mr J.O. Evans who has given freely of the knowledge acquired during a lifetime's study of natural history in the Merthyr area and has made lists and specimens available: also to Mr Keri Williams, for the superb bird and mammal photographs. These two, Dr. M. Claridge and Dr. J. Etherington have checked through the script. Additional information has come from Miss Jenny Rees, Dr. G.T. Jefferson and Mr. D.N. Johnson.

APPENDIX I

List of Butterflies

Argus, brown *Aricia agestis*
Blue, common *Polyommatus icarus*
holly *Celastrina argiolus*
silver-studded *Plebejus argus*
Brimstone *Gonepteryx rhamni*
Brown, hedge *Pyronia tithonus*
meadow *Maniola jurtina*
wall *Lasiommata megera*
Clouded yellow *Colias croceus*
Comma *Polygonia c-album*
Copper, small *Lycaena phlaeas*
Fritillary, marsh *Euphydryas aurinia*
pearl bordered *Boloria euphrosyne*
small pearl bordered *B selene*
silver washed *A paphia*
Grayling *Hipparchia semele*
Hair streak, green *Callophrys rubi*
Heath, small *Coenonympha pamphilus*
Orange tip *Anthocharis cardamines*
Painted lady *Cynthia cardui*
Peacock *Inachis io*
Red admiral *Vanessa atalanta*
Ringlet *Aphantopus hyperanthus*
Skipper, small *Thymelicus sylvestris*
Speckled wood *Pararge aegeria*
Tortoiseshell, small *Aglais urticae*
White, green veined *Pieris napi*
large *P brassicae*
small *P rapae*

APPENDIX II

List of Moths

Attracted to a light trap on the north flank of the Taf Fechan at Cefn Coed

Other species are mentioned in the text. Nomenclature is according to Kloet G S and Hincks W D. Check List of British Insects, 2nd edition (revised), Part 2. Lepidoptera. *R. Entom Soc.* London, 1972.

Angleshades,
common *Phlogophora meticulosa*
small *Euplexia lucipara*
Antler *Cerapteryx graminis*
Arches, buff *Habrosyne hyritoides*
dark *Apamea monoglypha*
green *Anaplectoides prasina*
light *Apamea lithoxylea*
Bordered beauty *Epione repandaria*
Bright line
brown eye *Lacanobia oleracea*
Brimstone *Opisthograptis luteolata*
Brocade, dark *Blepharita adusta*
dusky *Apamea remissa*
Buff tip *Phalera bucephala*
Burnished brass *Diachrysia chrysitis*

Cabbage moth *Mamestra brassicae*
Chevron *Eulithis testata*
Cinnabar *Tyria jacobaea*
Clay, purple *Diarsia brunner*
 triple-spotted *Xestia ditrapezium*
Cloud bordered brindle *Apamea crenata*
Dark spectacle *Abrostola triplasia*
Dart, shuttle-shaped *Agrotis puta*
 white-line *Euxoa tritici*
Dot *Melanchra persicariae*
Drinker *Philudoria potatoria*
Elephant hawk, large *Deilophila elpenor*
 small *D porcellus*
Emerald, large *Geometra papilionaria*
Emperor *Saturnia pavonia*
Ermine, buff *Spilosoma luteum*
 white *S lubricipeda*
Flounced rustic *Luperina testacea*
Footman, common *Eilema lurideola*
 dingy *E griseola*
Ghost moth *Hepialus humuli*
Golden Y,
 beautiful *Autographa pulchrina*
 plain *A iota*
Gold spangle *A bractea*
Gold spot *Plusia festucae*
Gold tail *Euproctis similis*
Heart and dart *Agrotis exclamationis*
Heath, common *Ematurga atomaria*
Humming bird hawk *Macroglossum stellatarum*
Lime hawk *Mimas tiliae*
Mother Shipton *Callistege mi*
Muslin moth *Diaphora mendica*
Old lady *Mormo maura*
Peppered *Biston betalaria*
Poplar hawk *Laothoe populi*
Prominent,
 cockscomb *Ptilodon capucina*
 iron *Notodonta dromedarius*
 swallow *Pheosia tremula*
Rosy rustic *Hydroecia micacea*
Scalloped, oak *Crocallis elinguaria*
Silver Y, common *Autographa gamma*
 scarce *Syngrapha interrogationis*
Swallow tail *Ourapteryx sambucaria*
Thorn, early *Selenia demtaria*
 purple *S tetralunaria*
Tiger, garden *Arctia caja*
 scarlet *Callimorpha dominula*
True lovers' knot *Lycophota porphyrea*
Wainscot, large *Rhizedra lutosa*
 smoky *Mythimna impura*
Yellow underwing,
 common *Noctua pronuba*
 least *N interjecta*
 lesser *N comes*

Bibliography: Chapters IV, V and VI

J.M. and M.A. Edington, Spatial patterns of habitat partition in the breeding birds of an upland wood. J Animal Ecol. 41, 331-357. (1972)

R.W. Edward, K. Benson-Evans, M.A. Learner, P. Williams and R. Williams *A Biological Survey of the River Taff.* Unpublished typescript.

J.R. Etherington, *Environment and Plant Ecology.* London. (1975)

J.O. Evans, The vegetation of Penmoelallt Woodland, Breconshire. *Nature in Wales.* (Autumn No) 79-84. (1960)

J.O. Evans, *Lists of moths, beetles and freshwater animals collected in the Merthyr Area.* Unpublished. (1976)

M.E. Gillham, Taf Fechan Gorge: Proposed Nature Reserve North East of Merthyr Tydfil. *Glam Nats. Trust Bull. 9.* 27-29. (1969)

M.E. Gillham, a New Acquisitions by the triple county of Glamorgan *Glam Nats Trust Bull. 13.* 7-9. (1974)

M.E. Gillham, b *Tremiscus helvelloides,* a colourful fungus new to Wales. *Glam Nats Trust Bull. 13.* 17-19. (1974)

M.E. Gillham, a Taf Fechan Gorge Nature Reserve. *Glam Nats Trust Bull. 14.* 29-31. (1976)

M.E. Gillham, b The Glais Nature Reserve. *Glam Nats Trust Bull. 14.* 25-27. (1976)

Glamorgan Naturalists' Trust *Three Walks in the Coalfield.* Cowbridge. (1975)

J. Griffiths and G. Griffiths, The roosting of jackdaws in Merthyr Tydfil. *Nature in Wales. 8.* 22-24. (1962)

J. Griffiths, *The birds of Merthyr Tydfil and District.* Unpublished typescript. (c1963).

J. Griffiths and G. Griffiths, Urban depopulation of rooks in Merthyr Tydfil. Nature in Wales. *9.1.* 14-16. (1964)

J. Griffiths, Bird life in an industrial valley in South Wales. *Nature in Wales. 8. 4.* 179-183. (1964)

A. Heathcote, D. Griffin and H. Morrey Salmon *The Birds of Glamorgan.* Cowbridge. (1967)

G.T. Jefferson, A white-eyed mutant form of the American cockroach *(Periplaneta americana). Nature. 182.* 892.

G.T. Jefferson, The Fauna of Caves and Mines. *The Cardiff Region Zoology.* Survey prepared for Brit Ass meeting at Cardiff.

D.N. Johnson, *The feeding habits of overwintering wildfowl on the freshwater lakes of South East Wales.* Unpublished thesis in Zoology Department Univ. Coll., Cardiff. (1974)

R.S. Smith and J. Edington. Broadleaved woodlands in South Wales and their conservation. *Nature in Wales. 13.* 146-154. (1969)

R.S. Smith. *An ecological basis for land use decisions in the South Wales Coalfield.* Unpublished PhD Thesis. Univ. Wales, Cardiff.

History

II

The Prehistory

by ANDREW ROBERTSON

The several thousand years of man's occupation of Britain prior to the Roman Conquest are known as 'British Prehistory' and yield no form of written documentation apart from a few sparse commentaries by some classical writers towards the end of the period. Our knowledge of British Prehistory is, therefore, inferred entirely from archaeological research. To simplify matters prehistory has been divided into five periods.

1. The Palaeolithic

The word 'Palaeolithic' is derived from the Greek and means 'old stone age', or that part of prehistory which we associate with cave men dressed in animal skins. For the palaeolithic in Britain we have relatively little information, despite the vast expanse of time covered. This unsatisfactory state of affairs results from a combination of factors.

The most important of these was the presence of huge masses of ice in the form of glaciers which spread southwards across Britain, advancing and receding, in four major glaciations during the period between 800,000B.C. and 8,000B.C. This series of glaciations would have had two important results. Firstly it would have made most of Britain too inhospitable to support human life during much of the period and secondly the scouring action of the ice sheets would have removed much evidence of occupation by palaeolithic groups in the periods of milder interglacial weather that preceded each advance of the ice sheet. The palaeolithic population of Britain as a whole would have been extremely small, so it is correspondingly more difficult to recover archaeological material relating to it.

Material does exist, however, mostly from the south east of Britain where the obliterating effects of the ice were absent.

The majority of these southern sites belong to the 'upper palaeolithic' or the later part of the period. There are, however, a few fairly well

Key to sites shown on Fig. 47 (Opposite)

1.–2.	Cairns on Nant Madden
3.	Buarth y Caerau cairn
4.–7.	Cairns on Cefn yr Ystrad
8.–9.	Cairns on Cefn Cilsanws
10.–11.	Cairns on Lech Sychryd
12.	Iron Age open settlement of Buarth Maen
13.	Garn Las cairn
14.–20.	Cairns on Merthyr Common
21.–24.	Cairns on Gelli Gaer Common
25.	Cairn on Cefn y Brithdir
26.–34.	Cairns on Cefn Merthyr
35.	Y Gaer, Iron Age Hill-fort
36.	Castell Morlais, Iron Age Hill-fort covered by Medieval castle
37.	Gwersyll, Iron Age hill-fort
38.	Camp on Gelli Gaer Common

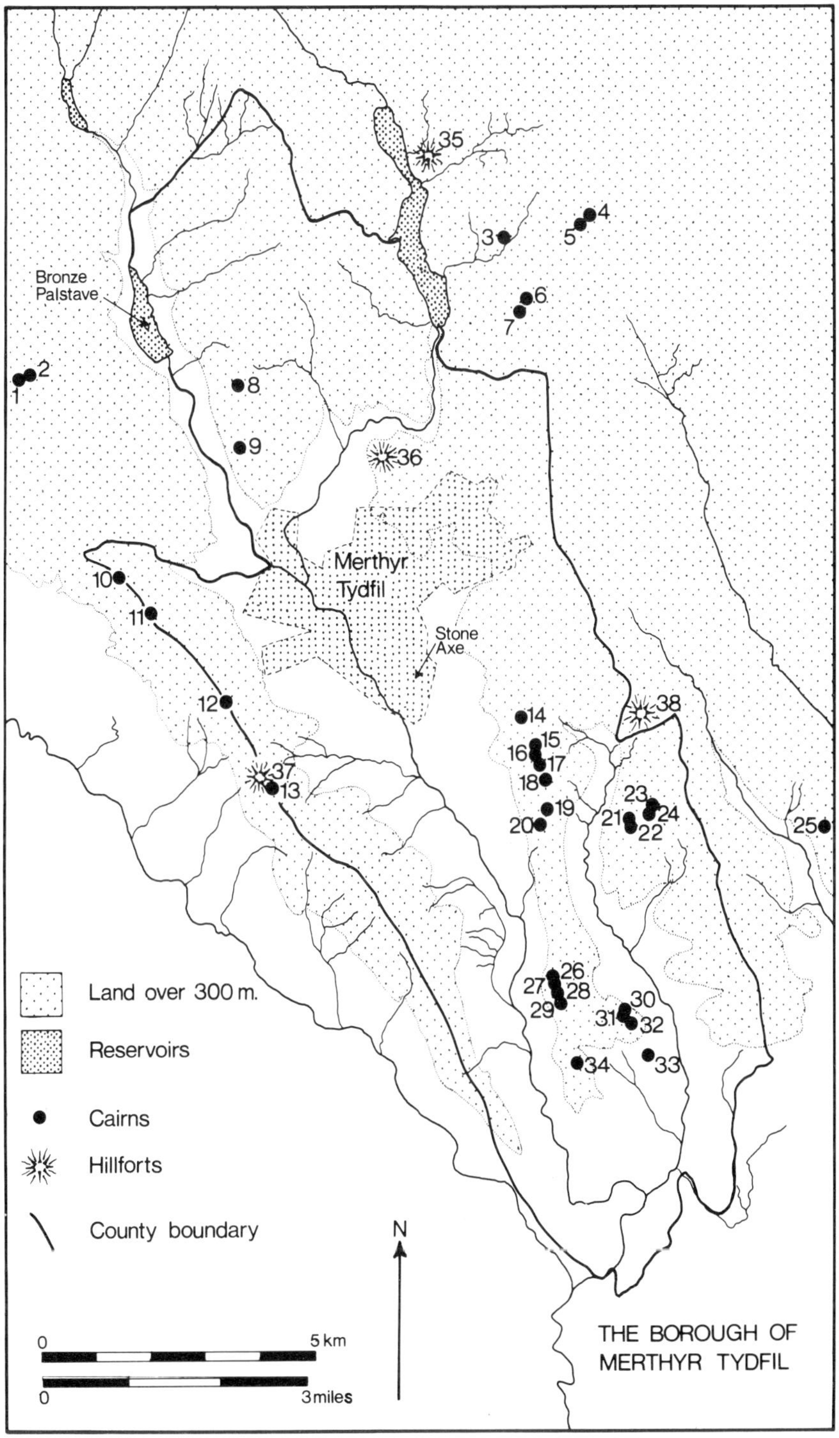

Bronze Palstave
Merthyr Tydfil
Stone Axe
1
2
3
4
5
6
7
8
9
10
11
12
13
14
15
16
17
18
19
20
21
22
23
24
25
26
27
28
29
30
31
32
33
34
35
36
37
38
Land over 300 m.
Reservoirs
Cairns
Hillforts
County boundary
N
0
5 km
0
3 miles
THE BOROUGH OF MERTHYR TYDFIL

documented sites belonging to the earlier phase or 'lower palaeolithic', the most famous of these being at Swanscombe in Kent. There are two Middle palaeolithic sites in Wales, both, cave sites. One is at Coygan in Carmarthenshire and the other at Pontnewydd in Denbighshire. Because no lower palaeolithic material has been recovered from the region of Merthyr Tydfil, we cannot assume that no lower palaeolithic settlers existed in our area, though we cannot know where they may have camped or how they may have lived. What we may infer from other sites in Britain is a quite credible picture of small, nomadic groups, probably no larger than a family or two, fashioning tools and implements for hunting from suitable stone such as flint or chert, or from bone or wood. These earliest 'Britons' would certainly have known and exploited fire for warmth and protection during the nights in a landscape that they shared with a host of predatory animals including wolves, lions and bears. Their existence depended on their ability to hunt because agriculture was unknown at this time. From the evidence of animal bones that have survived on lower palaeolithic sites in Britain it is apparent that a wide variety of species were hunted including wild oxen, horses, deer, and even elephants and rhinoceroses. Any vegetable matter that they ate to supplement their predominantly carnivorous diet would have to be gathered from wild sources – berries and nuts, roots and, in all probability, a wide range of herbs.

For long periods of time, however, Merthyr would have been covered by a sheet of ice and it is unlikely that during these spells of glaciation, which lasted for thousands of years, any human communities could have braved the extreme climate.

At some time during the last of these major ice advances, probably about 40,000 years ago, a new type of man arrived in the landscape. This was Cro-Magnon man (modern man), indistinguishable either physically or in brain capacity to ourselves. His arrival in Britain would have been facilitated by the existence at that time of a land bridge linking the east of England with mainland Europe. The advent of Cro-Magnon man heralds the beginning of the upper palaeolithic, and for Britain as a whole we have far more information about this period.

For the first time radio-carbon dating may be satisfactorily applied to sites on which organic material is found. Radio-carbon dating is the dating of organic material by measuring the amount of decay in the radio active isotope of carbon, C 14, which is incorporated in all organic material during its life. Such material as bone or carbonised wood is ideal for use in this process.

Again there is no definite evidence for upper palaeolithic groups in the Merthyr area but there is a considerable body of evidence for their presence elsewhere in South Wales. The most important of the South Wales sites include Paviland caves on the Gower peninsula and the cave site at Hoyle's Mouth in Pembrokeshire. Of these, the most important is that at Paviland where the skeleton of a young man, erroneously known as the 'Red Lady', was found in 1823. This was the deliberate interment of an upper palaeolithic youth over whose body a quantity of red ochre had been sprinkled. The bones of this body were recently dated by the radio-carbon technique and produced a date of about 16,000 years B.C.

We know from sites in this country and abroad that these upper palaeolithic people were very dependent on hunting for their livelihood and it is in this area of their culture that we find the most plausible explanation of the extraordinary cave art that they produced at such famous sites as Lascaux in France. However there is no evidence to suggest that the upper palaeolithic groups in South Wales achieved the cultural heights reached by their European counterparts. Whether any of these early groups had permanent or migratory habitations around Merthyr is open to speculation but it is more likely than not.

2. *The Mesolithic*

The word 'Mesolithic' is again Greek and means 'middle stone age'. It is the period of time between the end of the last Ice Age and the arrival in Britain of the first settled farming communities. During this time the environment changed quite considerably, the more open tundra of the late upper palaeolithic giving way to dense forests, principally of birch trees, on the hills and valleys of Merthyr Tydfil. Naturally such a dramatic change in the environment of our area would have brought about an equally dramatic change in the life style of its early inhabitants. No longer would hunting have entailed following the huge herds of deer associated with tundra zones. Prey would now have been more difficult to track down and the drastic reductions in the size of herds would have made hunting more difficult in the newly formed post-glacial forests. Perhaps it is partly for this reason that the majority of mesolithic sites in Britain are either near rivers, on flood plains or on coastal sites. In these locations food obtained by hunting could be easily supplemented with supplies of fish and shell-fish. It is also likely that vegetable matter, especially roots, became an increasingly more substantial part of our ancestors' diets.

Mesolithic flint industries are characterised by the widespread use of very small flint flakes that were manufactured for making composite implements. These tiny flakes are called microliths by archaeologists and in the Merthyr area examples have been found in Pant Sychbant, at Penrhiwceiber near Llyn Fawr, and on the bed of the Upper Neuadd reservoir during the drought of 1976. Unfortunately these local sites do not provide us with very much information and it has therefore been necessary to use the evidence from other sites in South Wales and England to produce this sketchy outline of mesolithic life in our area. The major Welsh sites are Daylight Rook and Nab Head, Pembrokeshire, Aberystwyth in Cardiganshire and Trwyn Du, Rhuddlan and Prestatyn in North Wales. In England the most informative site so far excavated is at Star Carr in Yorkshire.

It is now thought that it was during the mesolithic (around 6,500B.C.) that Britain finally became an island separated from mainland Europe by the rise in sea level that resulted from the melting of the glacial ice sheets.

3. The Neolithic

The Neolithic, next in the sequence, means 'new stone age' and is characterised by a number of innovations that were imported, presumably by new settlers, from Europe. The most important of these innovations was the introduction of the technology of agriculture, both the cultivation of the land for growing a wide range of crops including wheat and other cereals and the husbandry of domestic animals, the principal species being sheep, goats, pigs and oxen. The tremendous significance of this advance cannot be overstated. No longer were men quite so dependent on the fickle whims of nature but were instead able to assert far more control over their environment.

Agriculture made permanent settlement possible, a reliable source of food and, if modern parallels are a reliable indicator, a considerable increase in population. The environment of Merthyr would have been drastically altered by the activities of these early farmers. The forests of oak, elm, hazel and lime that covered the surrounding slopes would have been gradually cleared, to be replaced by grazing pasture and small areas of cultivated land. How this clearance was effected we are not sure. From the careful analysis of residual pollen grains in soils that were in the process of forming about 3,000 years B.C. it is clear that there was a considerable reduction in the elm forest of Britain at this time. Until recently this elm decline was thought to be a result of the activities of neolithic farmers, but in the light of the recent epidemic of Dutch Elm disease, it must be considered as a possibility that the disappearance of this particular species of tree may have been the result of a similar epidemic.

There are several ways in which the first of these farming settlers could have cleared the forests from their newly acquired land; the most obvious method would be what is known as 'slash and burn'. In this the trees were first cut down and left lying on the ground until they were sufficiently dry to burn. Once burnt the ground between the stumps would be cultivated either with digging sticks or a rudimentary plough called an ard. Burning the trees would have two beneficial results. Firstly, potash, important for healthy plant growth, would have been produced and, secondly, any undergrowth that had existed between the trees would have been destroyed.

For the initial felling of the trees polished stone axes, would have been used. These axes are diagnostic of the neolithic period and we are lucky enough to have a fine example from the Merthyr area. This is the Twyn-yr-odyn axe (Fig. 48) which was found in a ditch just outside Merthyr Tydfil.

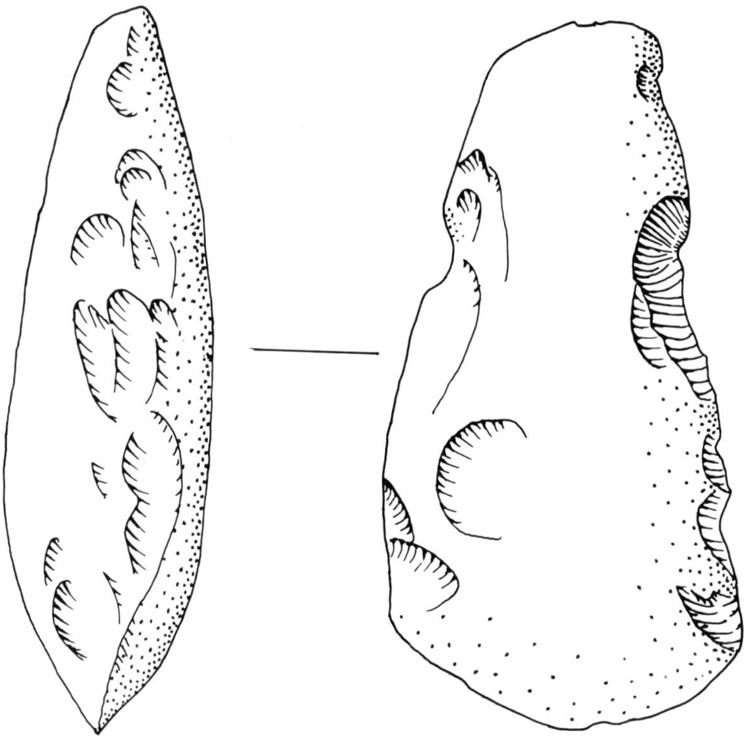

Fig. 48: The Twyn-yr-odyn polished stone axe

These axes, made variously of flint, chert, suitable igneous rock or, as in the case of the Twyn-yr-odyn axe, felsite, have been demonstrated in experimental field tests to be surprisingly efficient. It is also clear that they were considered so important by neolithic communities that in some cases good sources of suitable stone which could be quarried or mined, may have often dictated the siting of a settlement. By careful laboratory analysis of the type of stone used for the manufacture of these axes it has become possible to suggest the sites of various axe factories. In Wales there are five of these so called 'factories' of which those at Ramsey Island and an undiscovered site in the Prescelly Mountains are the nearest to Merthyr.

In what type of houses neolithic farmers in the Merthyr area lived we cannot be sure; indeed very little is known of neolithic houses in Britain as a whole. Whereas in Europe at this time most of the new settlers were building long communal houses, from the evidence of excavated sites this was not the case in Britain.

A cairn excavated by Derek Webley in 1956 and 1957 on Cefn Cilsanws in Vaynor (O.S. ref SO/250099) was found to have a complex pattern of stake holes immediately adjacent to it and partially covered by it. This stake structure was interpreted by the excavator to be the remains of a small beehive shaped hut. He assigned the structure to the neolithic period on the basis of two fragments of neolithic pottery, one of which was a rim sherd decorated by repeatedly impressing the clay fabric with a small bird bone prior to firing. The present writer cannot agree with this interpretation and considers it far more likely that the stakeholes represent a ritual structure belonging to the early bronze age and probably associated with the bronze age cairn that partially covered it. The very small amount of pottery used to date the site could very easily be intrusive and its therefore of very doubtful reliability.

A far more credible neolithic settlement site, and indeed one of the best examples of this type of site ever excavated in Britain, is that at Mount Pleasant in the parish of Newton Nottage, near Porthcawl. This house site consisted of a rectangular structure 5.5m long by 2.5m wide. The walls were of sandstone slabs laid dry and surviving to a height of four to six courses. According to the excavator, Mr. H. N. Savory, the post holes indicated a gabled roof and in addition there was some evidence to suggest a verandah on the south side of the house. The only reason that this particular site had survived was that it had been covered by the construction of a bronze age round cairn which had protected it from the ravages of modern ploughing. This remarkable good fortune cannot be expected on many sites and taking into consideration the slight construction of the house it is not surprising that so few sites of this type have been recovered by archaeologists.

When trying to visualise neolithic Merthyr we may imagine a landscape that became gradually more and more open with time as the woodland of the late mesolithic was slowly cleared by the determined efforts of these earliest farmers. On the recently cleared ground we can imagine the new farmsteads being built, probably on the higher land, where the soil would be lighter and therefore more easily cultivated. We know from the work carried out by environmental archaeologists that the climate at this time was getting much warmer and by the middle of the period temperatures, on average, would have been higher that they are today, making areas that we consider uncomfortably inhospitable quite suitable for settlement and for growing healthy crops of wheat and other cereals. The fields in which these and other crops were grown would be small, so that they could be easily managed and can be visualised as laid out in a patchwork around small houses with straw or reed thatched roofs. The fields would probably have been protected from the domestic stock and from the wild animals of the surrounding forests by hurdle fences or thorn hedges. Domestic stock would have been allowed to graze beyond the limits of cultivation and even in the surrounding woodland where their browsing on the bountiful supply of leaf fodder and, in the case of pigs, on the roots of trees, would have greatly aided the clearance of new land. To prevent the stock straying there would have been a herdsman, probably accompanied by one or more dogs. We are fairly certain that dogs were among the first animals to be domesticated, possibly as early as the upper palaeolithic.

Amongst the crafts that would have been practised on the settlement were the manufacture of pottery, basket making, the carving of bones into tools and dress pins, flaking flint into arrow heads, scraping and cutting tools, tanning and working leather, and, in all probability, the weaving of woollen fabrics used to make clothing. Evidence for these activities is scarce in Merthyr but we do have the material, already mentioned, from the Cefn Cilsanws cairn which is at present on display in the National Museum of Wales, as well as other scattered finds of pottery and flints.

Until recently the evidence that we had suggested that neolithic poeple formed a peace loving society. There were, for instance, no obviously offensive weapons being manufactured during this period and the settlement sites that we know of in Britain do not appear to have been strongly defended by walls, palisades or ditches. Recent interpretations of evidence from sites like Crickley Hill in Gloucs and Carn Brae in Cornwall now suggest that there may have been some localised conflicts during this period, the principal weapon in use being the bow and arrow. It seems likely that neolithic society, which became highly organised with time, channelled much of its energy into the construction of massive religious monuments and large communal tombs. It is during this period that the magnificent ritual complexes of Avebury and Stonehenge were first conceived in southern England. The absence of known sites like these in the Merthyr area does not mean that the neolithic people of south Wales did not construct similar monuments. The sites on Mynydd Eppynt-Trecastle Mountain, Nant Tarw and Cerrig Duon – in Brecknockshire, were built in the later stages of the neolithic or the early bronze age and probably drew on a wide area, possibly including Merthyr, for manpower to build them and to provide a 'congregation'. Possibly other sites existed nearer to our area, but have been destroyed by agricultural or industrial activity.

The best known sepulchral monuments of the neolithic are collective chambered tombs. These normally consist of a stone built burial chamber covered by a long cairn of earth or rubble. They were not the tombs of individuals but were apparently communal in function. From the evidence of excavation it also seems likely that they remained open and in use for quite considerable periods of time. The nearest known examples to Merthyr are to be found on the coastal plain of South Wales. Among these are Tinkinswood and St Lythans near Cardiff and Cleppa Park, Heston Brake and Gaerllwyd in Monmouthshire.

4. The Bronze Age

About 2000 B.C. a new group of settlers arrived in the British Isles. Through the very distinctive pottery that these people buried with their dead they have become known to us as the Beaker folk. Traces of three Beaker burials have been found in the Merthyr area. On the Penderyn to Brecon road a finely made reddish/buff beaker was discovered together with a

One Inch

Plate 22: HANDLED BEAKER FROM A CAIRN AT PEN GLOCH-Y-PIBWR, CWM-DU, BRECKNOCKSHIRE
(Courtesy, National Museum of Wales)

spindle whorl (used in the manufacture of yarn for weaving). Unfortunately this was a chance find and we have no record of either a burial or of a cairn. A better recorded site is that on Cwm Cor Farm, Dolygaer, Llandetty, Brecknockshire. Here a well made, brick red beaker was found in a small cist (a cist is a grave lined with stone slabs) with a cremated body and a typically bronze age barbed and tanged arrow head made of flint, unfortunately now lost. The third example is from a cairn at Pen Gloch y-pibwr, Cwm-du, (Plate 22) again in Brecknockshire. The beaker has a handle and is rather badly made of dark grey ware with a grey buff surface; it was found with an inhumation burial.

Although no bronze objects were found in any of the above mentioned sites it is to the Beaker folk that archaeologists credit the introduction of the technology of metal working to western Europe. It is, therefore, with the arrival of these people that the first part of the bronze age, the early bronze age, begins.

The early bronze age is marked by a relative scarcity of metal and by primitive methods of making bronze objects. The principal material used in the manufacture of tools was still flint. The most commonly found bronze implements from this period are flat axes and small triangular dagger blades which were made in simple open moulds. A very fine example of one of these daggers (Fig. 49) was found in a cairn on Cefn Cilsanws in 1908 together with human remains and was subsequently deposited in the Cyfarthfa Castle Museum in Merthyr. This particular specimen is very similar to examples found in the Wessex area, belonging to what has become known as the Wessex culture, and by comparison with these may be dated with a fair degree of certainty to circa 1600 B.C. Another cairn on Cefn Cilsanws, already mentioned in connection with the neolithic finds made during its excavation, produced no bronze age finds at all. This was rather surprising as round cairns are generally accepted as being diagnostic of the early bronze age. The method of burial that seems to have been favoured at the start of the early bronze age was inhumation, thereby continuing a neolithic tradition. As time progressed, there was apparently a move towards cremation burials in which the ashes of the deceased were normally placed in some form of pottery vessel being covered by a barrow or cairn. Good examples of such vessels have been found in our area at Abercar farm in Cwm Taf Fawr. Two pots were found on this site, the larger of which was the cinerary urn which was inverted over the cremated remains of the body, the other being a small pot known as a 'pigmy cup'. The latter was found to contain a small quantity of burnt oak and birch and this probably represents some form of ritual incense that would have been used during the burial ceremony. These finds were made in 1859 by a local farmer and the pots are now in the museum of the Royal Institution of South Wales, in Swansea.

Fragments of a cinerary urn were found by Derek Webley during his excavations of a burial mound in Cwm Cadlan near Penderyn. This site,for which there is no published report to date, is unusual in a number of

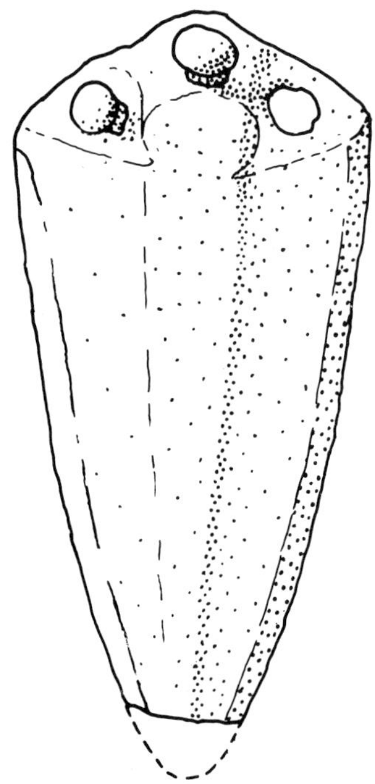

Fig. 49: The bronze dagger from an early bronze age round cairn on Cefn Cilsanws

respects. The whole mound was surrounded by a ring of large boulders and embedded into the top of the mound was a large standing stone. These features appear to be of a later date than the original cairn. The original burial was not found but near the periphery of the mound the fragments of pottery mentioned above were found together with cremated bone and human teeth and it is reasonable to assume that these finds indicate a secondary burial.

The available evidence suggests that the commencement of the bronze age saw a dramatic change in the structure of society. It is apparent from an appraisal of the type of grave goods mentioned above and the adoption of the practice of burying individuals that the picture of egalitarianism that pervades the neolithic gives way to one of a more clearly defined, class structured society in which the warrior aristocracy resided on the topmost tier. Farming communities probably carried on a way of life unaltered since neolithic times except that they were now subject to the chieftains whose burial mounds remain along the crests of our hills to this day as memorials of their power.

In summing up the early bronze age it is important to stress that it is an extremely complicated period, during which there was a great deal of change, both social and technological, with a great many influences arriving in our area from other parts of Britain and Europe.

One of the great mysteries of British prehistory occurred some time around 1400 B.C. All the traditions of metal working, of pottery styles and of burial ritual and religious monument building appear to have come to a sudden end, to be replaced by new cultural traits and institutions. Why this happened or even what such changes entailed for those who lived through it, are questions that remain unanswered. This transition theory that has been put forward to explain this phenomenon centres around the apparent changes in the climate that we know were well under way by 1100 B.C., but which probably began some time before this date. As already mentioned the climate was rapidly becoming warmer when the first neolithic settlers appeared in Britain. This trend is thought to have continued throughout the early bronze age, giving rise to what is called a climatic optimum, a period during which agriculture would have prospered around Merthyr even on the relatively high ground, resulting in a dense settlement pattern and a relatively high population. Even a minor deterioration in the general climate is likely to have brought about a devastating effect on farming communities over a surprisingly short period. Highland settlement, the type in fact that would, for obvious reasons, have predominated around Merthyr, would have become impractical and this would have led to depopulation. The pressures that the ensuing movements of people would have put on the ownership of the land that remained suitable for agriculture probably gave rise to the building of defences around previously open settlements, a feature characteristic of the later stages of the bronze age which endured to become diagnostic of the iron age.

One of the most universally apparent changes that occur at this 'transition' is the wholesale abandonment of the religious and sepulchral practices that had, apparently, remained largely unaltered from the neolithic. The new religion is water orientated, replacing the celestial centred cults that are represented at sites like those already mentioned on Mynydd Eppynt, in Brecknockshire. Large quantities of what must have been very valuable bronzes belonging to this period are found deliberately thrown into rivers and bogs, reflecting a tradition that was to continue throughout the late bronze age and the iron age. It is possible that the curiously inscribed stones referred to as 'cup marked stones' that are known from several locations around Merthyr and indeed throughout Britain, belong to this period and are possibly of some religious significance. The beautiful looped palstave axe (Fig. 50), dated to circa 1000 B.C., found during the construction of the Llwyn On reservoir, is likely to be an example of the type of water offering mentioned above. This axe, now in the National Museum, represents the only middle bronze age find from the Merthyr area. This, however, does not do justice to the amount of bronze work that was being produced at this time in Britain as a whole. The vast increase in the output of metalwork during this period is one of its most interesting

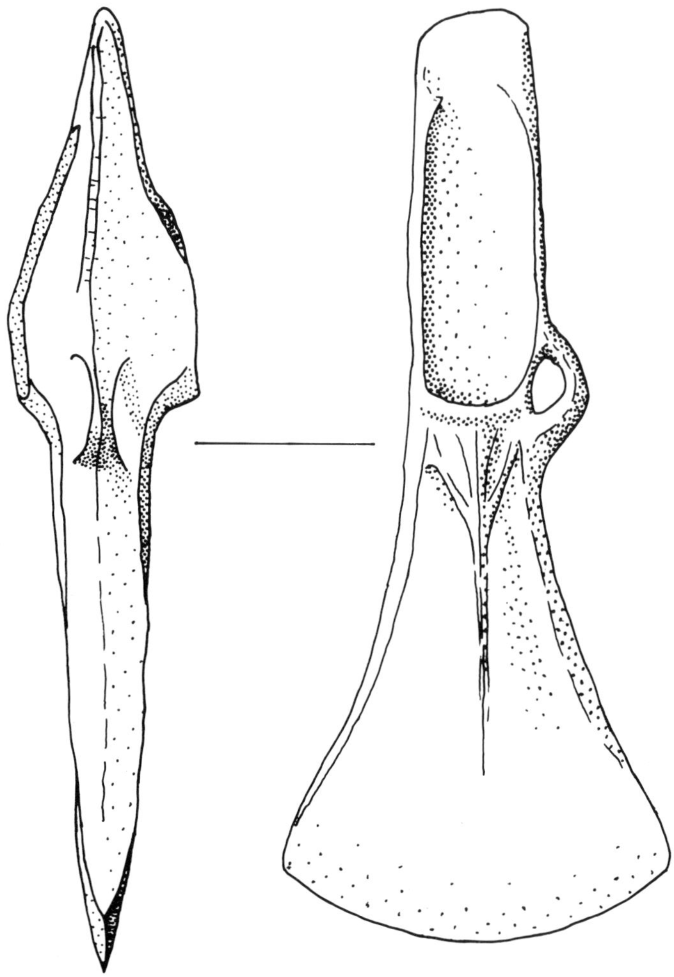

Fig. 50: The bronze palstave axe of middle bronze age date found during the construction of the Llwyn On reservoir

features and this, together with a much wider selection of tool and weapon types, must represent great advances in the technology of metallurgy. The introduction of two piece moulds made the casting of more complicated forms, including socketed, possible for the first time. It is instructive to compare the quantity of weapons, as opposed to tools, which were being produced during this period. Warfare had obviously become one of the major preoccupations of society.

The late bronze age is represented by a continued proliferation of bronze weapon and tool types and more advances in the techniques of casting. Items of personal adornment of distinctive style – bracelets, pins and finger rings – appear in Britain in large quantities, probably as a result of influences from Europe which were to increase as the period progressed. There are no finds that may be assigned to the late bronze age from the borough of Merthyr itself, but about eight miles to the west lies the site of one of the most important finds of this period from the whole of Britain. This is Llyn Fawr, at the head of the Rhondda Fawr Valley. The finds from this site are predominantly bronze and are all late bronze age in character, as one would expect. Among them, however, were found three objects, a sickle, a spear head and the hilt and part of the blade of a sword, that were made of iron. The site, which is dated to the period between 650 and 600 B.C., marks, as closely as any is ever likely to, the point at which the iron age starts in Britain. It must be pointed out, however, that to regard the term 'iron age' as anything but one of convenience would be misleading. The iron age, during its early phases at least, should be regarded merely as a continuation of the late bronze age.

5. *The Iron Age*

The iron age is generally regarded as that period in which Britain became colonised by a predominantly Celtic people arriving in large numbers from the Continent in a series of waves from the 7th century onwards. This theory is based on very meagre and dubious reports by classical commentators of whom Julius Caesar is the best known. It is true that as the iron age progressed art styles became increasingly uniform all over Europe and this has been used in the past to support the theory of the Celtic colonisation of Britain. The presence of art forms in areas adjacent to their conception does not, however, always represent invasion but is equally likely to result from trade, copying and adoption. An overwhelming body of evidence suggests that, apart from areas of eastern England at an early stage of the iron age, and southern Britain during a later phase, there was very little ethnic change in the population of the British Isles during this period. Rather than envisaging Merthyr, or any other part of Wales, being subjected to massive incursions of Celts, a more accurate and believable picture would be one of ethnic continuity throughout the iron age, over which is veneered a Western European art style.

The best known type of site belonging to the iron age is the hill-fort consisting of man made defences enhancing a naturally strong position. Such a site is to be found at Castell Morlais, just north of Merthyr. Unfortunately the iron age site is confused by the presence of a medieval castle built on top of the defences. A more easily interpreted site lies just beyond the western boundary of our area at Gwersyll on Mynydd Merthyr. The semi-circular rampart here (Plate 23) probably represents an incomplete site. Why it should have been abandoned is unknown but this not uncommonly happened during this period. Very little is known about these two forts but much can be inferred. The people who built them, as we

Plate 23: THE HILL-FORT OF GWERSYLL, ON MYNYDD MERTHYR, photographed from the air
(Courtesy, Prof. St. Joseph)

have already seen, were probably descended from late bronze age stock and indeed, on the evidence of some of the more recent excavations of similar sites in Britain, the forts themselves may well have had their origins in this earlier period.

The economy practised by iron age people would still have been strictly agricultural, and predominantly pastoral. When the climate of this period is taken into account it seems unlikely that such exposed locations as Gwersyll and Castell Morlais could have been inhabited during the winter months and seasonal occupation seems more feasible, summers being spent on the high ground and winters in the more sheltered valleys where any evidence of encampments are likely to have been destroyed long ago by agriculture and industry. Another type of upland settlement that probably belongs to some phase of the iron age is the unenclosed hut group of which the site on Buarth Maen is a good example. This site which is situated above the Afon Cynon, almost on the ridge of Mynydd Aberdar, consists of a group of hut circles which are connected by lengths of low dry stone walling. Whether or not these open settlements were occupied at the same time as the hill-forts or by the same tribe is not known.

The existence of querns (simple grinding stones for milling grain) on upland iron age sites must indicate that either there was some arable farming practised in these areas or that grain was imported from lowland sites. The former suggestion is the more likely. Clothing would be of well woven woollen cloth and it is probable that each household produced its own requirements on simple looms. Whether people around Merthyr indulged in the flamboyant tartans that are known to have been worn by other iron age groups in Britain, is impossible to say, but the fashion for trousers, that the Romans thought so distasteful amongst barbarian groups, is almost certain to have been favoured by the men in our area, if only to keep out the worst of the weather.

The more basic requirements of each community – pottery vessels, baskets, wooden utensils and the more mundane metal work – would have been produced locally, but there is a great deal of evidence to suggest that some industries were highly specialised during this period. The finer forms of pottery were produced in centres like Glastonbury, in Somerset, and traded over considerable distances. Glastonbury ware, as it is known, has been found on a number of sites in South Wales, though whether it was some luxury item in the pots that was being traded or the pots themselves remains a mystery.

Ornate metalwork, with the beautiful curvilinear decoration which is so characteristic of the iron age, must surely be the work of very skilled and highly trained craftsmen, though it is likely that the equipment with which they made these masterpieces was very basic. Large quantities of this metalwork has been found in Wales, some of the more impressive sites being those at Llyn Cerrig Bach in Anglesey, Tal-y-llyn in Merioneth, and, closer to our area, the hoard from Seven Sisters in Glamorgan. The majority of the material from these sites may be seen in the National Museum.

Politically, the iron age communities around Merthyr would probably have belonged to the tribe that the Romans were to record as the Silures. Unlike the Belgic dominated tribes of southern and eastern Britain, the Silurian tribe was likely to have been a loosely combined confederacy of smaller groups that united under a chosen war leader in times of trouble, in the way that they united under Caractacus to face the Roman legions.

In iron age Britain, including the Merthyr area, religion seems to have centred around the worship of very localised deities associated with natural features like springs, rivers and woods. The high Priesthood that presided over religious ceremonies were the druids, and their cult is known to have been centred on Britain. The evidence of the classical writers suggests that in Wales the cult was particularly strong, the seat of their power possibly being on the island of Anglesey, which was known as Mona to the Romans.

With the Roman invasion of 43 A.D. British prehistory ends, though the Welsh tribes continued to be independent, resisting the might of the legions, for some time after this. Probably the traditions and culture that we have traced through this chapter did not die immediately, or completely, with the arrival of the Romans, but the effects of Roman occupation would have had profound implications for the future of Merthyr Tydfil.

Bibliography

G. C. Boon & J. M. Lewis Eds., *Welsh Antiquity,* National Museum of Wales, Cardiff. (1976)

R. Bradley, *The Prehistoric Settlement of Britain,* London. (1978)

C. Burgess & F. Lynch, *Prehistoric Man in Wales and the West,* (1972)

B. Cunliffe, *Iron Age Communities in Britain,* London. (1974)

P. W. Dixon, *Excavations at Crickley Hill, 1969-70,* Gloucestershire Coll. of Arts. (1970)

C. Houlder, *Wales: An Archaeological Guide,* London. (1974)

Royal Commission on Ancient and Historic Monuments in Wales, *Glamorgan Volume I, Part 1 and 2,* H.M.S.O. (1976)

C. Renfrew Ed., *British Prehistory,* London (1974)

H. N. Savory, *The Excavation of a Neolithic Dwelling and a Bronze Age Cairn at Mount Pleasant Farm, Nottage, Glamorgan,* National Museum of Wales, Cardiff. (1955)

'A corpus of Welsh Bronze Age pottery, Part II — Food Vessels and Enlarged Food Vessels' *B.B.C.S. XVII,* 1957, 196-233. (1957)

'Prehistoric Brecknock', *Brycheiniog XV,* 1970, 3-22. (1971)

Guide Catalogue of the Early Iron Age Collections, National Museum of Wales, Cardiff. (1976)

D. Webley, 'The Bronze Knife-dagger from Cefn Cilsanws (Breck.)', *B.B.C.S. XVIII,* 1957, 195-6. (1957)

'A cairn cemetery and secondary neolithic dwelling on Cefn Cilsanws, Vaynor, Breck.', *B.B.C.S. XVIII,* 1958, 79-88. (1958)

55 B.C. – 1485 A.D.

by H. WATKINS
Afon Taf High School

The 55 B.C. Roman Invasion

Throughout the afternoon and into the evening of August 25th 55 B.C., nearly ten thousand men had been on the beaches of Boulogne, and systematically embarking in the eighty transports drawn up in the surf. A little before midnight, with a fair wind from the south, they cast off and sailed for the shores of Kent. For the first time Roman legions were to land on this island, which was to become in time, a small but not unimportant part of a huge powerful empire.

Their commander was Caius Julius Caesar. He came not only to warn the British not to interfere on the continent, namely Gaul but to conquer the whole island. In spite of his two campaigns of 55 and 54 B.C., Julius Caesar had had no time to bring Britain into the Roman Empire, it was left to the emperor Claudius 100 years later to complete this task in 43 A.D.

The invasion force that Claudius sent into Britain was not very large, a little over 40,000 men, four legions, the second Augusta, the Ninth Hispana, the Fourteenth Gemina and the Twentieth Valeria. Claudius sent an able General Aulus Plautius to subdue Britain. By A.D. 47 he had conquered all South-East Britain and defeated Caratacus at the Battle of the Medway Crossing. Caratacus then fled to the West to the land of the Silures.

The Silures

Merthyr Tydfil in the days of the Romans was part of the Kingdom of Siluria, the people dwelt in crude roughly square timbered, wattle and daub huts, tending their flocks and tilling small plots of land on the treeless tops of the surrounding hills. The South-East of Wales down to the Bristol Channel was occupied by the Silures. Their tribal centre was Venta Silurum

(Caerwent). South and Central Wales was known as the Republica Civitatis Silurum the self-governing administrative area of the Silures. The strength of this tribe lay in their untameable, resolute spirit and the rugged character of the country they occupied. In the spring of A.D. 50, Ostorius Scapula advanced into Silurian country in South Wales. Naval squadrons operated in the Bristol Channel to support him. Somewhere in Central Wales he defeated Caratacus (CARADOC). It was a famous victory. Caratacus's wife and daughter were captured and his brothers surrendered. Caratacus sought refuge with Cartimandua, Queen of the Brigantes. But there is no escape for the defeated; he was put in chains and handed over to the Romans and taken to Rome. He was pardoned by Claudius and while walking round the city after his release was gazing on its splendour and size. 'Why on earth', he said 'when you have all this, do you want our miserable tents?'

In Silurian territory the fighting never stopped. Guerrilla warfare in the forests and marsh country was the order of the day; battles were fought by chance, or followed courageous planning, for revenge and for booty with orders and without.

Although Ostorius Scapula established camps to operate against the Silures, he did not meet with success always in this area. On one occasion he lost not only nine of his senior officers and many men but also two auxiliary cohorts. The obstinacy of the Silures was extraordinary. They heard a remark of the Roman General to the effect that they must be completely wiped out and this roused them to fury. They began to urge other tribes to join the revolt giving them presents and plunder and prisoners. Ostorius Scapula died exhausted by the weight of his responsibilities. The Britons were overjoyed that such a famous general had been killed by the strain of war, even if not in battle. It was left to a later successor Julius Frontinus to finally subdue the unconquered Silures.

He built auxiliary cohort forts well applied, well sited and virtually invincible. From these watch was kept, in winter over what he had won in the Summer.

Coastal forts, which could be provisioned by land and sea arose at Carmarthen, Neath and Cardiff.

Such an assault the Silures, for all their bitter fighting could not endure. At last they sued for peace. They were allowed to build a tribal centre – VENTA SILURUM, the modern CAERWENT, but it always remained one of the smallest tribal capitals; the Romans had long memories. The conquest of the whole of Wales was left to the greatest of Britain's governors, Julius Agricola.

The Roman Fort at Penydarren

Roman occupation on the site of Penydarren Park was noted first during the construction of Penydarren House in 1786 for the ironmaster Samuel Homfray.

In the year, 1867, Mr Charles Wilkins in his History of Merthyr, records the fact that when Penydarren House was built, the workmen found a great many Roman bricks and tesselated pavement in digging the foundations. It was not identified as a fort until the excavations of 1902-1904. The fort stood on a steep-sided spur 213 metres (700′) above sea-level commanding a wide view of the valleys to the east, south and north-west and forming a link in the line of the road from the coastal fort at Cardiff to Brecon (Y GAER).

This Roman road crossed the summit of the Fochriw Mountain running from the GELLIGAER fort almost direct north to a point on the existing parish road near TWYNYWAUN, north-east of DOWLAIS. To the north-west, the nearest point shown on the Ordnance Map of the existence of the Roman road lies close to the western corner of CYFARTHFA CASTLE; then it takes its course north-west to the GURNOS FARM and then to PONTSARN (SARN is the Welsh word for a paved road or causeway. PONTSARN the bridge by the causeway. SARN HELEN — Helen is probably a corruption of 'Y lleng' the Welsh for 'the legion' so SARN HELEN is the causeway of the legion).

From PONTSARN the road proceeded across the river TAFF FECHAN up the valley, across the eastern spur of the BEACONS along the crest of the ridge called NANT CALCH which forms the eastern boundary of the GLYN VALLEY. It then descends to MAES MAWR near TALYBONT, BRECONSHIRE, fords the river USK, and pursues its course to LLANSANTFFRAID at which point it apparently disappeared, but about one-third of a mile, in a north-easterly direction, it joins the Roman road leading from Abergavenny (GOBANNIUM) then to BRECON to the Roman fort Y GAER.

The size of the fort will remain obscure since the bulk of it was removed in 1904 to make way for a football ground, the remainder is now occupied by a housing estate.

The fort was sited so that the garrison could have a convenient and ample water supply from the river Taff, an adequate provision of firewood, fodder and pasture; it was also in an area likely to attract a native population. It was conveniently spaced linking the forts from CARDIFF – to GELLIGAER – to BRECON. The average distance between forts linked by roads is of the order of 20 km. The length of a normal day's march would appear to have been about 20 km; but greater distances could certainly be covered in a forced march.

The shape of the auxiliary fort or 'castellum' at Penydarren conformed to the normal 'playing card' shape i.e. a square or oblong enclosure with rounded corners, an area of about 5 acres. Four gates, breaking the four sides and joined by roads that centred on the H.Q. building (principia); the commanding-officer's house (praetorium) next to it, the barracks; latrines, the granaries near the gates; the bath houses, cemeteries, outside (Plate 24 and 25).

The Garrison

The garrison consisted of auxiliary troops. These men were not usually Roman citizens and were conscripted from the provinces of the Empire. Men from Germany, Spain, Gaul, Syria and even Parthia served on this island. They formed three kinds of fighting units. First, and most important, was the cavalry; mounted on small, tough horses, they wore the same helmets and breast plates as the legions. Second the auxilia was grouped in cohorts of 500 or 1,000 men. Therefore, Penydarren must have been garrisoned by 1,000 infantry or 500 cavalry or a part mounted battalion; a cohort – cohors quingenaria equitata – nominally 500 strong consisting of 6 centuries of 60 men each and 4 turmae (cavalry) of 30 men each giving a full strength of 360 infantry and 120 cavalry. The centuries and turmae were commanded by centurions and decurions respectively. The commanding officer at Penydarren being a prefect (Plate 26). Third the infantry consisting of archers with composite bows of steel and bone, slingers, able to fire roundshot, with speed and accuracy and swimmers trained to swim across rivers guiding their horses, and holding their weapons clear of the water. Ideal troops for fighting in the terrain of South Wales.

The Fort

The defences of the fort included a ditch in an inner rampart footing (paved causeway) 6ft. 4inches wide. The principal discoveries made within the fort were a stone-lined well 4ft. in diameter and 15 feet deep probably belonging to the head-quarters building (principia) and part of a well-built granary (horreum) of stone 65 ft. long by 35 feet broad (overall) with externally buttressed walls, 3 feet wide. The interior was divided by transverse sleeper-walls set from 3 ft. to 6 ft. apart presumably to support a floor of timber. There were usually two granaries to a fort, designed to hold a year's supply of corn for the whole garrison. They were long narrow structures with massive walls stengthened with external buttresses. The function of these may have been to take the thrust of the corn stacked high inside; to take the weight of the heavy tiled roof – or to enable the roof to be carried out well beyond the side walls, so that damp would not trickle down them and spoil the corn inside (Plates 27 and 28).

The floors of the building were commonly raised well above the ground and ventilation was provided by inserting air-vents in the side walls below floor level.

The Barrack blocks were arranged in pairs. Each section of eight men shared two rooms, the inner one about 15 ft. square for sleeping and the outer about 15 ft. by 12 ft. square for sleeping and the outer about 15 ft. by 12 ft. for their equipment. Beyond this, running the full length of the block was a verandah. Latrines were small rectangular buildings furnished with wooden seating, a flushing system and paved floors with water channels (for washing sponges which the Romans used instead of toilet-paper).

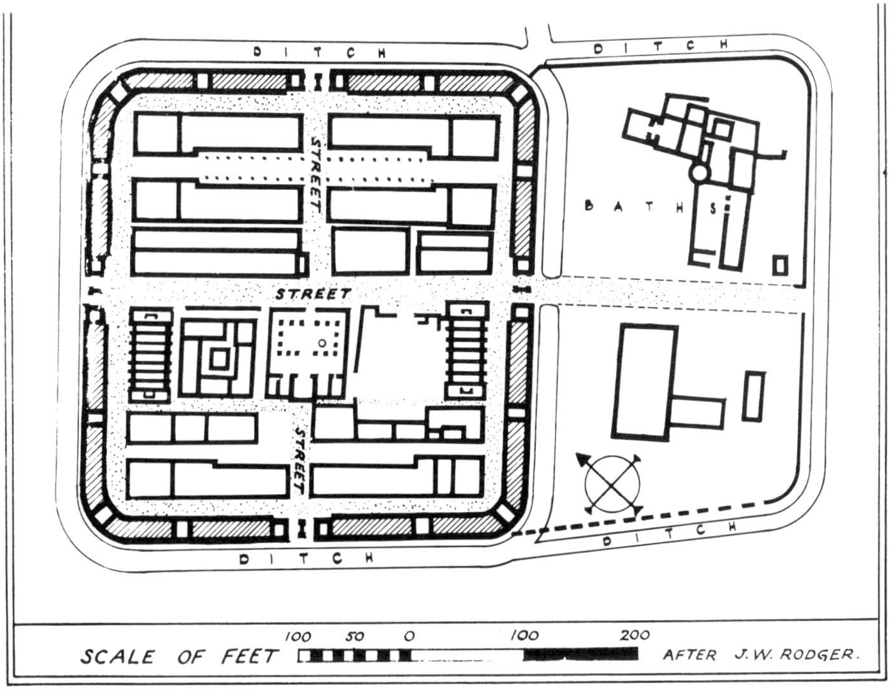

Plate 24: PLAN OF AUXILIARY ROMAN FORT OR 'CASTELLUM' PENYDARREN PARK
(By permission of National Museum of Wales)

Plate 25: MODEL OF AUXILIARY ROMAN FORT
What the fort at Penydarren must have looked like
(By permission of National Museum of Wales)

Plate 26: TYPICAL AUXILIARY SOLDIER
Part of the garrison at Penydarren Park. Conscripted from the Provinces of the Empire
(By permission of National Museum of Wales)

The regular pay of the soldiers 300,denarii per annum,was an inducement to traders to settle as close as possible to a fort and in the same place would be found the dwellings of camp followers of all sorts. The bath-house, parade-ground and cemeteries would be outside the fort.

The excavations of 1902-1904 revealed three large hypocausted rooms (one apsidal) at least one furnace chamber and part of a stone culvert.

The baths at Penydarren, dimensions of the rooms were (9.1 × 6.7m) = 30 × 22ft. and 15.2 × 4.6m = 50 × 15ft. The bath-house was an orderly row of rooms of graduated temperature extending in all to 90 feet. Opening off the enclosed yard with its long fuel store we find the combined undressing

Plate 27: ROMAN FORT, PENYDARREN PARK; RUINS OF GRANARY *(By permission of Cambrian Archaeological Association)*

Plate 28: ROMAN WELL AT PENYDARREN PARK, MERTHYR TYDFIL

(By permission of Cambrian Archaeological Association)

room (APODYTERIUM), as the Romans called it and cold bathroom (FRIGIDARIUM). There was also a latrine with wooden seating arranged over the main outfall drain. The heated rooms were originally two in number, the circular room being an addition; the heating was by the hypocaust method whereby heat from a wood fired furnace fired from outside circulated under the heavy concrete floors which were supported on columns of tiles (PILAE). The requisite draft was supplied by very small chimneys, made of box-tiles, in the walls here and there.

The process of bathing was to proceed by easy stages into the hot moist room and there to scrape off the accumulated dirt and sweat with a strigil before finishing with a cold plunge which sufficed to close the pores against the Glamorgan winter chill.

Scrupulous attention was paid to the seemly burial of the dead so that their spirits were content. Until the 3rd Century the rite was cremation in urns with or without grave-offerings, tombstones, and shrines. Soldiers subscribed to a burial fund (ad signal) and private burial clubs existed.

Further excavations revealed an accumulation of roofing – tiles, floor tiles, flue-tiles, painted wall plasters, tufa voussoirs and charcoal. Much pottery was found black and the traditional red SAMIAN ware FLAVIAN, (1st Century) TRAJANIC AND HADRIANIC pottery of the 2nd Century. A very rare mottled ware made on the Continent. Coins found were a Republican denarius of c.150 B.C. and a bronze coin of VESPASIAN (A.D. 69-79 or TITUS (79-81)). These finds are now preserved in the Cyfarthfa Castle Museum. The Roman fort at Penydarren was occupied for a fairly short period from c.A.D. 74 to c. 120 or thereabouts and then abandoned during the early years of HADRIAN'S reign. It may have been superseded by a new and smaller stone fort at GELLIGAER.

The Story of Tydfil

In the 5th Century A.D. Roman occupation of Britain ended when the legions were recalled to fight Barbarian attacks on Rome.

Confusion followed the withdrawal of the Romans. However one important influence to emerge in the post Roman period was Christianity. Many Christians came to South Wales. Many were refugees from Roman Britain, others were Gallo-Roman Christians spreading from the west; also Christians with Irish connections came to the area. Many famous Christians emerged in this area, most notable were St. Illtud, founder of the monastery at Llantwit Major and Brychan Brycheiniog.

Brychan Brycheiniog is important because of his connections with Tydfil who gave her name to the town.

The origins of the story of TYDFIL can be traced back to TEWDRIG the son of TEITHFALLT who became King of South Wales including BRECONSHIRE (which was never conquered and retained its independence from the fifth to the tenth Century) Monmouthshire and part of Herefordshire somewhere around 440 A.D. and up to 470 A.D. It appears that TEWDRIG, according to a twelfth century manuscript, sent his daughter MARCHELL (the mother of Brychan Brycheiniog) to Ireland to avoid the plague that was ravaging Wales 'I am very uneasy lest your health should suffer from the pestilential disorder which at present ravages our country'. In Ireland MARCHELL married AULACH MACGORMUC the son of CORINEOG OR CORMACH MACEURBE one of the rulers of Ireland, King of WEXFORD. Sons born to this marriage were TEILO and BRYCHAN. Brychan was brought back to Wales by his parents when he was four years old, who took up their residence at SENNI (the GAER upon the banks of the river ISGAER near BRECKNOCK). Brychan was educated by a chieftain called DRICHAN, spending his youth in military exercises, he succeeded his father as ruler about the year 400 A.D. Brychan supposedly had four wives: PRAWST ; RIBRAUST, PROISTRI and CWRDDIL, daughter of PEBIAN, King of ERGING (the WYE VALLEY).

According to three ancient Welsh Manuscripts:

1. DE SITU BRECHENIAUC a Latin manuscript of about the year 1200 A.D.
2. A Latin manuscript COGNACIO BRYCHAN dated 1650.
3. A Welsh manuscript called ACH KYNAWC,

Brychan had many children, twenty-five names are given, by some sources others fifty. Later writers reduce the number within narrower bounds by considering several of his grandchildren to be included in the lists. Nearly all of them embraced a religious life and were founders of numerous churches in Wales, in local place names in the SENNI and MERTHYR TYDFIL areas.

SONS/GRANDSONS

CYNOG, CLEDWYN, DINGAD, ARTHEN, CYVLEVYR, RHAIN, DYVNAN, GERWYN, CADOG, MATHAIARN, PASGEN, NEFAI, PABIALI, LLECHAU, CYNBRYD, CYNVRAN, HYCHAN, DYVRIG CYNIN, DOGVAN, RHAWIN, RHUN, CLEDOG, CAIAN.

DAUGHTERS/GRAND-DAUGHTERS

GWLADUS, ARIANWEN, TANGLWYSTL, MECHELL, NEVYN, GWAWR, GWRGON, ELERI, LLEIAN, NEVYDD, RHIEINGAR, GOLEUDDYDD, GWENDDYDD, TYDIA, ELINED, CEINDRYCH, GWEN, CENEDLON, CYMORTH, CLYDAI, DWYNWEN, TUDVYL, ENVAIL, HAWYSTYL, TYBIAU, SANOS.

Galon Uchaf could possibly be named after Tydfil's brother, HYCHAN. ('Hychan's Heart). Tanglwys and Sanos, were her sisters and from them we get HAFOD TANGLWYST and KILSONOS (CILSANWS), the summer residence of Tanglwyst, and also the place of Sanos Church (Kil is a word of Irish origin such as Kilkenny and is witness to the considerable Irish settlement in this area).

Probably Brychan may have founded sometime in the 5th Century after the break-up of the Roman Empire a small principality in South Wales and many of the missionaries who evangelised South Wales, Cornwall and Brittany sprang from the royal house of Brecon. The legend of King Brychan as a father of saints appealed to the imagination of later writers who made him the actual father not only of nearly all the saints who founded parishes in Brecknock and other districts of South Wales but also of many saints who probably had no connection at all with Brecon.

The Martyrdom of Tudvyl

The story relating to the martyrdom is as follows. In the month of August c. 450 A.D. or 480 A.D. Brychan Brycheiniog, his sons and daughters journeyed from his home in Brecon to the Taff Valley to stay with his third daughter TANGLWYSTL at her residence HAFOD TANGLWYST near YNYSYGORED in the now village of ABERFAN. At this time the raids of the Irish Picts had been severe and the chieftain and his family gathered to talk over troubled times. Here in this valley, Brychan and his family lingered before returning to Breconshire. Between Aberfan and Troedyrhiw, the party was supposed to have been massacred by the GWYDDIL FFICHTI or Irish Picts. Rhun with others escaped for a while but were pursued and while defending the bridge over the Taff at Troedyrhiw was killed. While they plundered the valley, NEFYDD, a son of Rhun's arrived with Brychan's retainers and avenged his family's deaths by putting the pagans to the sword. Where TUDVYL died no one is sure. TUDVYL was supposed to have been well known for her religious works and legend tells that she knelt and prayed which gives the appearance of martyrdom. Many believe that the martyrdom of TUDVYL occurred on the site of the old church. It would seem that it was the general custom to bury where the martyrdom took place. With respect to the name MERTHYR TYDFIL, it is important that we examine the authenticity of the tradition that TUDVYL was a saint and of her supposed martyrdom. The Welsh word 'merthyr' meaning 'martyr' is derived from the Latin 'martyrem' but Merthyr's place name is derived from the Latin 'martyrium', which originally meant a saint's burial place or church consecrated to his bones. In a place name then, 'merthyr' is associated with the worship of a tomb and means much the same as 'llan' a burial place or church dedicated to a saint. Accordingly, MERTHYR TYDFIL marks the spot dedicated to ST. TYDFIL commemorated on August 23rd. Similarly, MERTHYR DYFAN, near BARRY, MERTHYR CYNON in Breconshire and MERTHYR MAWR near Bridgend are dedicated to S.S. DYFAN, CYNON and MAWR. There is no evidence that TUDVYL was martyred;

Merthyr Tydfil means the grave (or the church) of TUDVYL and not TUDVYL the martyr.

The Church of St. Tydfil

St Tydfil's Parish Church at the lower end of the High Street keeps holy the spot first sanctified by the life and death of the Martyr Tydfil. The present stone building was erected in 1808. The Celtic memorial set by the otherwise unknown ARTBEU and now preserved in the north aisle of the church, shows that the site was kept holy by others after her. The first church was probably constructed of wattle and daub, followed later by a more substantial wooden building until the first stone structure was erected in the 14th Century. Set against the north wall in the aisle of the church are two stone pillars. These have provided a constant source of legend and curiosity. The small pillar originates from the beginning of the 19th Century. In pulling down the Norman Church in 1807 a curious stone coffin was found and in it a skeleton of great length. What was more remarkable was that the coffin formed part of the foundation of the Church. The inscription found over the coffin has excited the curiosity of many people, the letters being cut out in red sandstone. The right hand pillar has as much mystery surrounding its origins as the smaller, reminding us that the building was used for Christian worship even in the eighth century. (Plate 29)

Plate 29: ST. TYDFIL'S CHURCH
(Photograph by Robert Haines)

Merthyr Tydfil in Saxon and Norman times

Little is known of what happened in Glamorgan or Merthyr Tydfil for centuries after the Romans left the district. During the immediate post-Roman period the principality was involved in a series of dynastic quarrels as well as being engaged in a perennial struggle with the Anglo-Saxon invaders.

There is plenty of evidence that the West Saxons penetrated well into the east of Glamorgan burning and plundering wherever they went, as they did in 831 A.D. ravaging Caerphilly and Cardiff and returning over the Severn with a great quantity of spoil.

The Kingdom of Morgannwg

Morgannwg which included the Merthyr district was first incorporated into the Kingdom of GLYWYSING. The land of GLYWYS was an area extending from the TAWE to the USK.

MORGAN AB ATHRWYS an 8th Century, King of Glywysing, also of GWENT probably gave his name to MORGANNWG (GWLAD MORGAN – the land of Morgan).

The Vikings came to South Wales in the 10th Century ravaging the coastal area. Many Vikings established trade links with South Wales. There is no direct link between the Vikings and Merthyr nor does Merthyr seem to have been directly involved in the struggles for control of Glamorgan between rival chieftains in the 10th and 11th Centuries.

The Norman Conquest

On Saturday, October 14th 1066 there was fought the decisive Battle of Hastings resulting in the death of Harold and the winning of the English throne by William, Duke of Normandy. The Norman attack on Wales was not led by the Conqueror himself, but by three of his most powerful and trusted lords - WILLIAM FITZOSBERN, earl of Hereford, Roger of Montgomery, earl of Shrewsbury and Hugh of AVRANCHES, earl of Chester. To secure peace, William allowed the Welsh Kingdoms of Morgannwg, Gwynllwg and Brycheiniog to retain their independence. They were to act as buffer states. However they formed instead a vacuum. They offered a tempting avenue for expansion especially for the border barons.

It was William FITZOSBERN, earl of Hereford, who made the first move to invade South Wales. His army of mounted Knights and archers quickly overran ARCHENFIELD (S.W. Hereford), Southern Gwent as far as Caerleon. However this invasion was halted by the death of WILLIAM FITZOSBERN in FLANDERS in 1071.

Glamorgan at this time was reputed to be a land of seven cantrefs GORFYNYDD; PENYCHEN; Y CANTREF BREINIOL (The Privileged

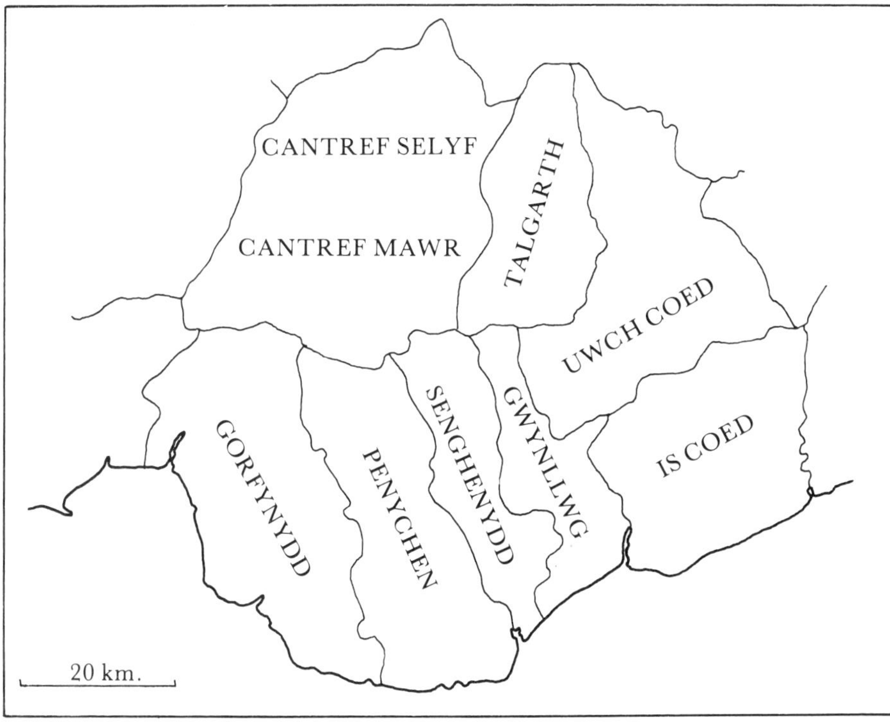

Fig. 51: S.E. Wales Pre-Norman Administrative Divisions

Cantref), GWYNLLWG; GWENT ISCOED and GWENT UCHCOED (Below and Above the Wood), the two regions of ERGING (ARCHENFIELD and EWAIS). (Fig. 51)

The Taff and the Rhymni flowing south from the mountains of BRYCHEINIOG in parallel valleys but a few miles apart were the western and eastern boundaries of CANTREF BREINIOL.

MERTHYR TYDFIL was part of the CANTREF BREINIOL, the ancient title appears to have been SENGHENYDD a term limited in later times to that part of the CANTREF which lay north of the Cefn Onn ridge. The district contained no important church or ecclesiastical manor but must have been the chief seat of civil power in MORGANNWG.

Prior to the Norman Conquest, Senghenydd was one of the cantrefi or sublordships of Morgannwg. It occupied a long but narrow stretch of land between the rivers TAFF and RHYMNEY and extending northwards from the sea at CARDIFF to the border of BRECKNOCK.

It was divided into three commotes:—
SENGHENYDD UWCH CAIACH; SENGHENYDD IS CAIACH; and CIBWR (Today the districts of Merthyr Tydfil and Gelligaer; Caerphilly and Whitchurch). (Fig. 52)

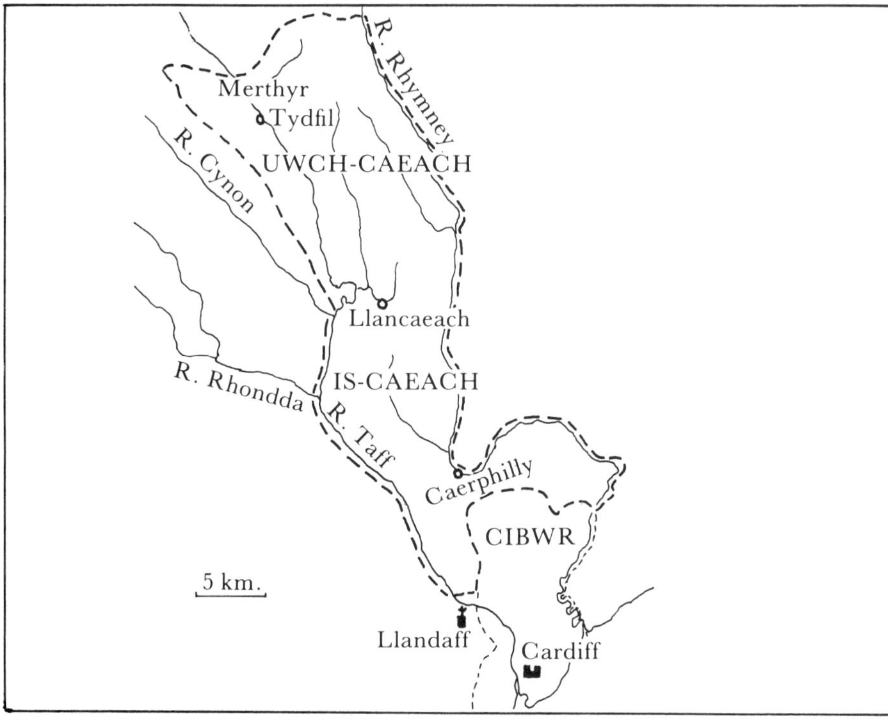

Fig. 52: Lordship of Senghenydd *(By kind permission of the late Dr. W. Rees)*

The conquest of Morgannwg and the mountainous realm of Gwynllwg was left to the powerful baron, ROBERT FITZHAMON, earl of Gloucester, a close confidant and supporter of WILLIAM RUFUS.

In 1090, Robert Fitzhamon, earl of Gloucester, Dorset and Devon launched his attack against the Welsh Chieftain IESTYN Ap GWRGANT, across the Severn Estuary. He advanced through lowland Morgannwg as far west as the river OGMORE – but no further. Powerful as he may have been, not even FITZHAMON could allow his supply lines along the coast to become too long when the more mountainous areas of MORGANNWG, GLYN RHONDDA, MEISGYN and SENGHENYDD, remained in Welsh hands and from which a counter attack could be easily made. (Fig. 53)

FITZHAMON left these three mountainous highland areas in the hands of native Welsh chieftains, he made no effort to extend any direct Norman authority there. Senghenydd, of which Merthyr was a part, was granted to EINION ap CYDIFOR. Welsh life and customs remained undisturbed in this region for many years.

In 1094 a Norman force led by Fitzhamon attacked Northern Morgannwg but was routed at Gelligaer. The tide of Norman conquest had washed up to

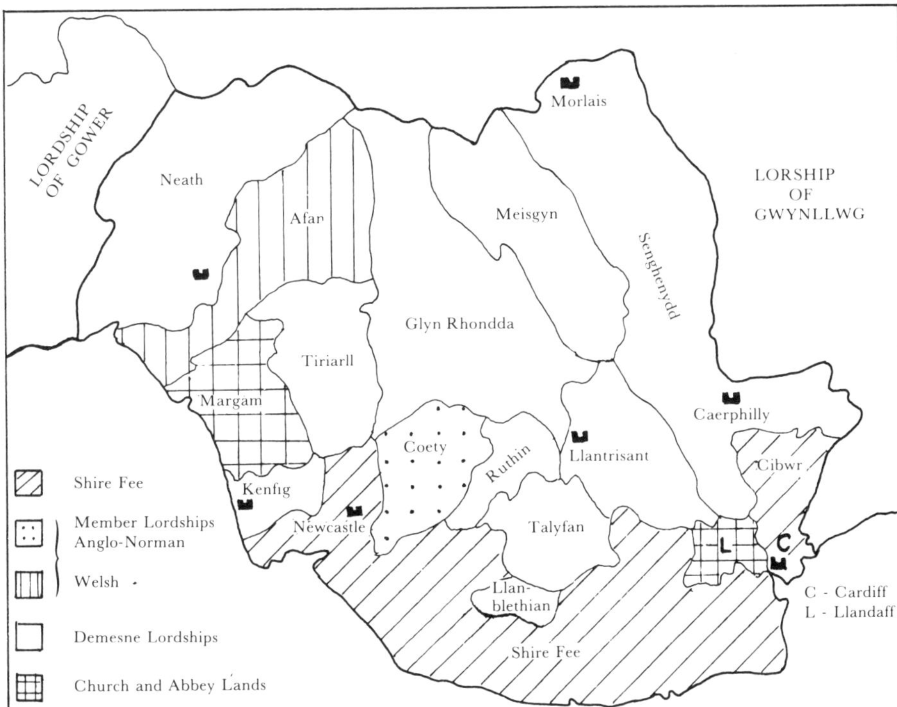

Fig. 53: Marcher Lordship of Glamorgan

the six hundred foot contour line and had come to a halt. The Normans with their mounted Knights and manors had failed to establish themselves in the highland moors.

Ivor Bach

Border skirmishing and plundering raids between the Normans and the natives of Upper Senghenydd were continuing features for many years.

The Norman Lord of Glamorgan was WILLIAM FITZCOUNT, Earl of Gloucester, and Cardiff was the principal castle of his lordship. About ten miles away in the hills above CAERPHILLY a Welsh Chieftain, IVOR ap MEURIG, or Ivor Bach in 1158 ruled over a wild tract of woody mountainous country from his stronghold at Senghenydd.

William Fitzcount, Earl of Gloucester had broken his agreement with Ifor and had deprived him of the use of woods and mountains, territory he had already seized and refused to return.

News was spread abroad by wandering priests and bards going on their rounds among the people, calling the Welshmen of the hills to assemble, for an attack on Cardiff Castle.

Ivor Bach with the men of Senghenydd managed to creep stealthily up to the castle at dead of night. No doubt they brought roughly made scaling ladders and ropes with them. Swiftly and silently in the darkness they climbed the walls, overpowered the sentries and stole along the corridors. They captured the Earl, the Countess HAWISE and their only son ROBERT and carried the three down the walls and away to the safety of Ifor's stronghold which according to tradition was situated where CASTELL COCH now stands.

The prisoners were held as hostages until the Earl agreed to return to Ifor all the land he had seized together with some additional territory as compensation for the wrong he had done.

Very little is known of Ifor Bach after this episode.

Various place names record Ifor Bach's memory around VAYNOR and DOWLAIS namely PANT-CAD-IFOR and CADAIR IFOR.

As a result of Ifor Bach's attack in the 12th Century the wooden keep of CARDIFF CASTLE was replaced by a stone one.

After the death of Henry I in 1135, Welsh resistance increased and some lands were reconquered by the Welsh. One of the most important Welsh uprisings of the period was the attempt of Llywellyn ap Iorwerth – Llywellyn the Great, Lord of Gwynedd, to construct something approximating to a Welsh Kingdom which made the position of Senghenydd of some importance.

When Llywellyn raided South Wales in 1231 he was helped by Rhys ap Gruffydd of Senghenydd. In 1238, Llywellyn summoned all the princes and chieftains of Wales to STRATA FLORIDA to pay homage and swear fealty to David as his heir.

The English Crown forbade Rhys ap Gruffydd and other tenants in chief in Glamorgan to comply. But soon after 'Rhys son of Gruffydd, Heol, son of Meredith and G. de Tuberville, were at war with each other, and disturbed the peace in Glamorgan, Mischin and Seynhinith', and in 1245, Rhys and others were reprimanded by the crown for their disorder and support of David. In 1256, Rhys ap Gruffydd died and was succeeded by his son Gruffydd.

The Revolt of Llewellyn II

The powerful Richard de Clare, Earl of Gloucester and Glamorgan (1240-1262) was consolidating his control over the upland districts of Meisgyn and Glynrhondda. In 1262, the two commotes of UWCH-CAIACH and IS-CAIACH were in the possession of the new lord of SENGHENYDD – Gruffydd ap Rhys.

In 1267, open conflict erupted between Gilbert de Clare and Llywellyn ap Gruffydd, prince of Gwynedd. The object of the dispute was the strategic cantref of Senghenydd.

In January 1267, Earl Gilbert staged a rapid foray into Senghenydd and captured Gruffydd ap Rhys and imprisoned him.

Earl Gilbert now began to turn the commote of IS-CAIACH into a castellany by constructing a new castle at CAERPHILLY on the 11th April 1268 to guard the Rhymney Valley and the approach to CARDIFF.

Llywellyn protested claiming Gruffydd as his vassel and the commote as subject to his own authority.

By September 1268, Llywellyn had gained control of UWCH-CAIACH of which the parish of MERTHYR TYDFIL was a part. Attempts at settlement pressed by HENRY III failed and on October 13th 1270, Llywellyn attacked and destroyed the newly constructed castle at Caerphilly.

Gilbert reacted by seizing Machen, Edlogan and Llebenydd but was dissuaded from attacking Senghenydd and Meisgyn by Henry III.

Gilbert was probably not prepared to engage in full-time warfare at this time and it is possible that he wished to appear as the aggrieved party. He offered to surrender Caerphilly into royal custody. In late October the King sent the bishops of Coventry and Lichfield and Worcester to take control of the castle and secure the withdrawal of Llywellyn's forces.

Arrangements were completed at the beginning of November, Gilbert, however, seems merely to have been playing for time. By a simple ruse he regained control of the castle. Gilbert was now able to gain control of the MERTHYR TYDFIL area, UWCH CAIACH and NORTHERN MEISGYN. Llywellyn was finally defeated and came to an abrupt and frightening end on December 12th 1282 at CILMERI on the banks of the River IRFON near BUILTH when he was ambushed and killed by a Knight, Stephen de Frankton. This marked the end of the Norman Conquest of Wales and the extinction of Welsh independence.

The Story of Morlais Castle

Authentic records of Morlais Castle are scanty and it is difficult to obtain a complete history of the Castle. Morlais Castle is situated some two miles north of Merthyr Tydfil on an exposed limestone ridge 1,252 feet high which commands extensive views of the upper Taff valley and the south slopes of the Brecon Beacons to the north. (Plate 30)

It stood about 470 feet above the Taf Fechan which marked the boundary of the 'ancient district of Brecheiniog and Morgannwg'

Today the castle is very badly ruined, consisting of mounds of debris and grass-covered banks with only occasional traces of wall face visible. The castle appears to occupy the site of an Iron-Age hill fort becoming later a defensive post of the stronghold of the native lord of Senghenydd. During the years 1254 to 1282 Llewellyn ap Gruffydd tried to unite Wales under his leadership. Faced with this threat the Marcher lords had to take counter-measures.

Plate 30: BUCK'S VIEW OF MORLAIS CASTLE 1741

(By permission of The National Library of Wales)

Gilbert de Clare, Earl of Gloucester and Lord of Glamorgan erected castles at suitable places in order to protect his lands.

By 1270 he had completed CAERPHILLY CASTLE. He probably built MORLAIS CASTLE as an outpost to give warning of any attack coming from the north (1270). It is doubtful if the Castle was ever completed, but enough of it was completed for de Clare's men to live there. It is possible to judge, even from the few ruins that remain today, that the Castle was strongly built. The Castle was roughly oval shaped, enclosed within an embattled wall with five or six circular towers. It was defended on three sides by a moat and on the west side by a steep escarpment.

The Castle was divided into two courts or 'baileys' by a wall. The 'Inner Bailey' contained Kitchens and an oven. The larger 'Outer Bailey' contained barracks, a forge, water tanks and a well (Fig. 54).

At the forge appliances were made using charcoal.

Even in Norman times the uses of iron were known and a supply was obtained near the site of the former Goitre Pond, now filled in and part of a modern housing estate.

Cinders from Morlais Castle shows that the uses of coal and charcoal were known. The tanks were used for the collection of rain water.

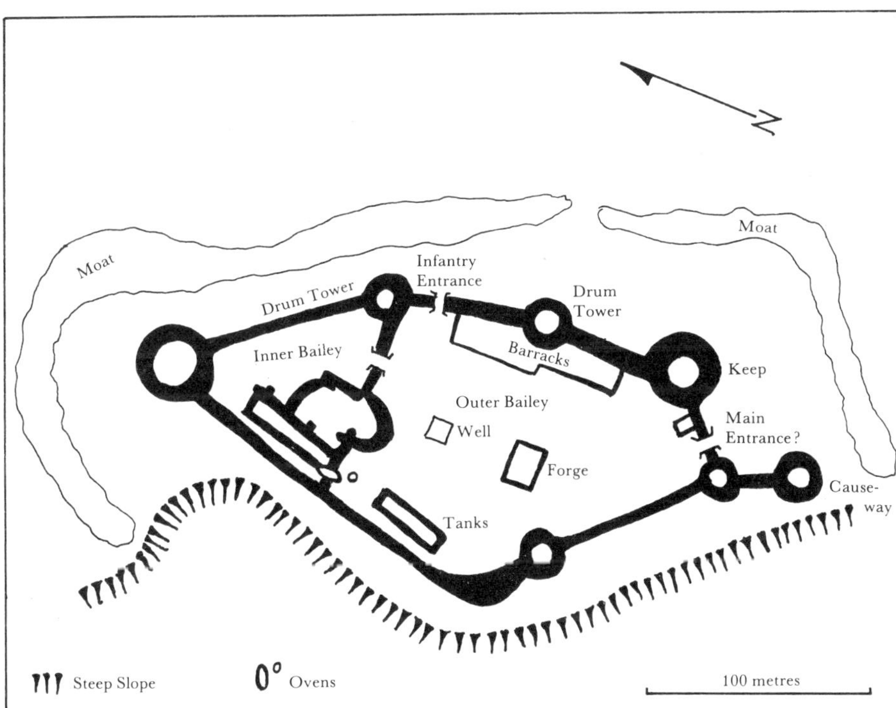

Fig. 54: Morlais Castle

The well was a deep hole cut out of the limestone rock. Originally it was much deeper than it is today, as the pit has been partially filled over the centuries by people throwin in stones.

However it is doubtful if any water was obtained here as no water could have been obtained at a depth of less than 400 feet and it is extremely doubtful if such a depth was ever reached.

The crypt was once at the bottom of the main tower with living rooms above. The crypt is a fine example of 13th Century architecture and it gives proof of how carefully and soundly the Castle was built. The room is approached by descending a flight of steps and entering by an arched doorway.

A central pillar supports a grained roof of twelve arches. (Plate 31)

The Castle was partially excavated in 1833 by Lady Charlotte Guest. Coins from the reign of Edward I and some Scottish coins have been found there. Carving chisels, hammers, nails, even a pole-axe have been found among the ruins.

When Edward I completed his tour of the new principality of Wales in 1284, he visited Glamorgan and the Red Earl received him with the greatest honour. The Edwardian conquest and settlement of Wales brought to light a matter of the greatest importance that is the relationship between the crown and the Marcher Lords. The lords of the March had inherited and for two centuries successfully maintained powers and privileges not enjoyed by the other members of the feudal aristocracy, the chief feature being the right to wage private war.

It was this privilege which Edward I was not prepared to tolerate and which led to the most spectacular incident of the first half of his reign, and which resulted in the trial and disgrace of two of the greatest magnates of the realm. HUMPHREY DE BOHUN, earl of Hereford and lord of Brecon, and Gilbert de Clare, earl of Gloucester and lord of Glamorgan. Trouble had been brewing between the two men for some time.

There was a financial dispute. When Humphrey de Bohun came of age in 1270 he obtained possession of the lordship of Brecon.

His mother EVE DE BREOS, wife of Humphrey the Good, had owned the Manor of Vaynor by right of heirship, and he purchased from his guardian, Earl Gilbert freedom to arrange his own marriage for £1,000 a sum the latter claimed had not yet been paid in full by 1290.

Moreoever, Humphrey resented the fact that Gilbert had been in charge of operations in Brecon in the Welsh campaign against Rhys ap Moredudd of Ystrad Tywi in 1289.

The chief cause of the quarrel was almost certainly the building of MORLAIS CASTLE on a tributary of the Taff in the ill-defined border area between Brecon and Uwch Caiach. Gilbert undoubtedly intended Morlais to secure his power in the region between Brecon and Caerphilly. De Bohun, however, claimed the castle was being constructed within his boundaries, and protested to the King.

Plate 31: THE CRYPT AT MORLAIS CASTLE

Efforts at mediation undertaken by Queen Eleanor, John Pecham, archbishop of Canterbury and the King's cousin, Edmund, earl of Cornwall, met with no avail.

The matter could only be handled by the King himself. Edward issued a proclamation forbidding private warfare in the March. Gilbert's response was defiant. On February 3rd, 1290, Gilbert's men displaying his banner entered the fertile lands of Brecon, killed some of Humphrey's men and carried off livestock and other chattels back to MORLAIS.

Another raid occurred in early June and a third in November. The soldiers of de Clare laid waste the land, killed several people and stole 1,070 head of cattle, 50 horses and large numbers of sheep, goats and pigs. A pitched battle was reputed to have taken place between the two Earls the site of which is called MAES-Y-FAENOR. Apparently de Bohun gathered his forces, including the men of Vaynor and men from all over Breconshire who were billeted in farms, barns, stables and even in the small wooden church. The battle raged throughout the day. An old Welsh poem stated:

> 'Ban wyr Bohun a oru
> Gwaed Fel Mor Bros Faenor Fu'
>
> ('The battle was won by the men of Bohun
> And blood like an ocean in Vaynor was seen')

Some of the dead were buried at the lower end of Vaynor Churchyard, but some years later this ground was swept away by the flooded river. In a field at the side of a footpath leading to Vaynor Church, there stands a mound which is supposed to be the grave of some of the men who fell in this battle.

Edward was determined to demonstrate the supremacy of the monarchy and reduce the power of the Marcher Lords. In 1291 he set up a royal commission to hear the case in Brecon itself. A jury of 24 men was assembled. Gilbert was clearly guilty and his failure to appear at Brecon added to his defiance of the King.

Edward ordered the Earls to appear before him at Abergavenny in October. Neither party dared absent himself this time.

At Abergavenny Edward struck hard. Bohun was clearly the injured party in 1290 but his retaliatory raids into Glamorgan while the royal commission sat at Brecon brought him under suspicion. He was committed to jail and his lordship seized into the King's hands.

The King then turned to Gilbert, who dropped his show of defiance and attempted to evade his responsibility by raising technical objections. Earl Gilbert's contumacious behaviour since 1290 was clearly beyond a doubt, the Court dismissed his appeal, he was also imprisoned and his lordship confiscated.

Both earls appeared at Westminster in January 1292 for final sentencing. Glamorgan and Brecon were declared forfeited for life, and the earls returned to jail. Edward had fully vindicated his position and he soon relented. The earls were allowed to redeem their bodies, Gilbert for a fine of 10,000 marks, Humphrey whose offence was deemed less serious for 1,000 marks. On May 7, Gilbert recovered Glamorgan, while Humphrey resumed control of Brecon only on July 15. The drama was completed. The dignity of the crown had been fully asserted at the expense of the mightiest lords of the March.

Edward's policy however created a feeling of deep resentment among the magnates and led to a major baronial opposition to the King in the last year of his reign and to foreshadow the troubled reign of Edward II.

Earl Gilbert's own difficulties were by no means over. In 1294, a new revolt broke out in Wales led by Madog ap Llewellyn.

It quickly spread to Glamorgan, where it was led by MORGAN ap MAREDUDD, the son of Maredudd ap Gruffydd, the former lord of Machen, Edlogan and Llebenydd whom the Red Earl had disposessed in 1270.

Morgan's rising commanded the support of all the Welsh in the lordship. The rebellion broke out in October 1294, the Welsh capturing a number of strongholds including MORLAIS and expelling the earl from his domain. In April 1295 Gilbert counter-attacked. By the middle of May he was in control of Cardiff and the surrounding territory but was unable to subdue Morgan and his allies. By June the revolt subsided.

King Edward again travelled through Wales attending to details of pacification. Morgan claimed to be fighting only the earl and professed his loyalty to the King (Fig. 55). By June 7th 1295 he was received into the King's peace 'against the earl's wishes', and his allies quickly followed suit.

Edward once again took Glamorgan into his own hands. Certain parts of Morlais Castle were pulled down to prevent it being used as a fortress in the future. After this, it was probably allowed to fall into decay.

On October 20, 1296, Edward once again restored Glamorgan to Gilbert. Six weeks later the Red Earl was dead. Humphrey de Bohun died in 1298.

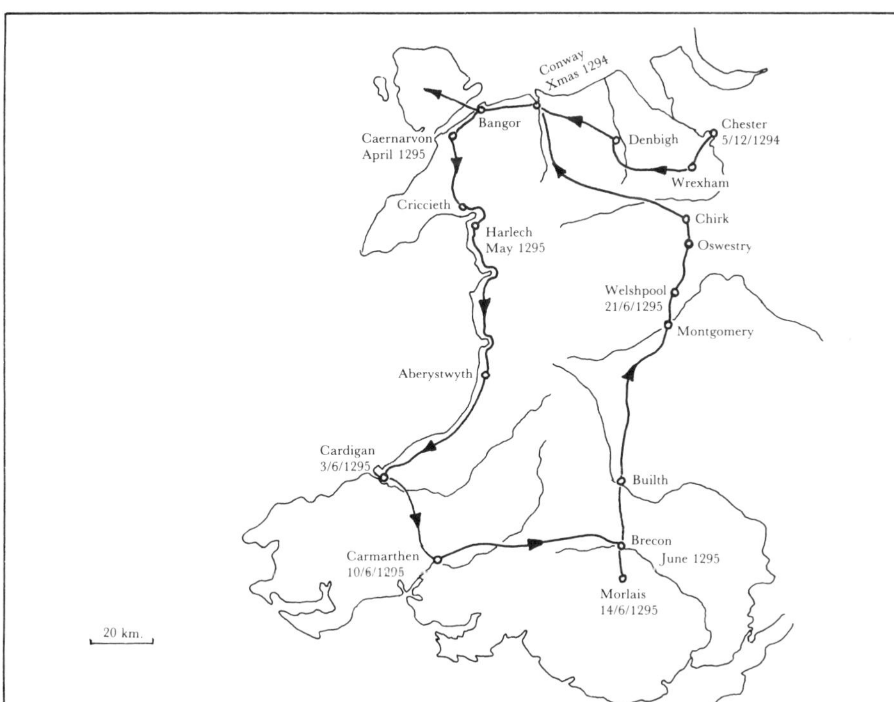

Fig. 55: Edward I retakes Morlais Castle

The Revolt of Llywelyn Bren

Early in 1314, the Welsh community of the lordship of Glamorgan including the men of Merthyr Tydfil rose in rebellion. During the course of a brief campaign the Welsh rebels led by LLYWELYN AP GRUFFYDD or LLYWELYN BREN caused widespread destruction before the forces arrayed against them broke their resistance.

Llywelyn Bren was a man of great influence and possessions in the county and he held high office under GILBERT DE CLARE, the Norman Lord of Glamorgan and the last earl of Gloucester and Hertford. On the death of his patron at BANNOCKBURN in 1314, Edward II took over his possessions, Llywelyn was deprived of his offices, Edward II appointed stewards for the area on behalf of the crown. INGERAL BERENGER, BARTHOLOMEW DE BADLESMERE and PAYN DE TURBERVILLE, Lord of Coity. From July to September these lands were convulsed by rebellion.

Llywelyn complained that the new officials had undermined many of the ancient customs and privileges of the men of Morgannwg particularly the right to collect timber and firewood from the forest.

Llywelyn was a man of some standing, literate and cultured, possessing extensive estates in Senghenydd, Eglwyswladus (Gelligaer) and Merthyr, a small castle and a mill at Whitchurch an annual grant of £5. 6s. 8d. and a great number of cows, bulls, oxen, sheep and pigs.

In the winter of 1315-16 the plight of this community may well have been exceptionally difficult.

The people of the upland areas of Glamorgan at this time of adversity were exposed to a ruthless administration which had only a short term interest in the lordship and which was determined to extract the greatest possible amount of revenue. Llywelyn made representations to Edward II against the abuses of the royal officers and the first open breach came when he was ousted from his office by PAYN DE TURBERVILLE, the newly appointed Keeper of Glamorgan and Lord of Coity.

Very resentfully, he was heard to utter a threat against Payn 'The day will come when I will put an end to the insolence of Payn and give him as good as he gives me'.

Llywelyn went to London to the King's Court to answer a charge of sedition. However, Edward II spurned him, swearing and maintaining that he should die if the crime charged against him was proved. Treated with contempt, Llywelyn was ordered to come before the King at the parliament which was to assemble at LINCOLN, on January 27th, 1316. But Llywelyn returned to his own land and his own people.

On the day of parliament's assembly, Llywelyn raised rebellion in Glamorgan. Edward II anticipating trouble had instructed PAYN DE TURBERVILLE to provision and garrison CARDIFF CASTLE and other castles in the lordship. Early in 1316, Llywelyn Bren appeared before CAERPHILLY CASTLE.

The castle was damaged, the bridge being burned and the outer ward destroyed. The insurgents carried war across the whole extent of the lordship, men from all over Blaenau Morgannwg actively participated in the rising.

Llywelyn who was said to have had an army of 10,000 men from the Uplands descended on the low country, killing, burning and plundering. English officials and sympathisers were killed, captured or forced to flee. The accounts show that a number of mills, including fulling mills, were destroyed in Senghenydd, Meisgyn, Glynrhondda and Neath.

Edward II took counter-measures, a royal army numbering 150 men-at-arms and 2,000 footmen was gathered. It left Cardiff on March 12th, advanced towards CAERPHILLY CASTLE relieving it after a nine-week siege, then attacked the Welsh entrenchments on the ridge formed by Cefn Carnau and Cefn Onn inflicting heavy losses on the defenders. Confronted with the forces arrayed against them Llywelyn and his men withdrew into the highland interior around Merthyr Tydfil. Being pursued, Llywelyn offered peace and compensation only to be met with refusal.

To avoid further suffering among his own people, Llewelyn accompanied by two of his sons surrendered to Earl Humphrey de Bohun.

On March 26th Llywelyn, along with his family, was removed to the Tower of London. The King's Officers took possession of Llywelyn's livestock. By August many former rebels had their lands returned to them on payment of ransom.

In 1317, HUGH Le DESPENSER was granted Glamorgan. Confiscation in Senghenydd was harsh, over 1,000 cattle and 500 sheep were confiscated. Heavy fines were levied as a punishment for participation in the rising.

Hugh le Despenser had Llywelyn Bren brought to CARDIFF, where he was hanged, beheaded and quartered. It was a mutilated body which was laid to rest at GREYFRIARS.

With the death of Llywelyn outbreaks of resistance were crushed for a century.

The Despensers and Glamorgan

The reign of Edward II also saw, for the time being, the end of trouble between King and Marcher Lords. The Earl of Gloucester had died in 1314 and his estates passed to the husbands of the Earl's three daughters in 1316; Hugh Despenser the Younger who had married Eleanor, Hugh Audley husband of Margaret and Roger Damory husband of Elizabeth.

Hugh Despenser the Younger became Edward II's favourite but so misused his position at court as to incur the emnity of the barons by threatening their privileges and even their lands. They urged the King to dismiss him in 1321 and when this failed they resorted to force.

Once again Merthyr and South Wales was caught up in the enmity between the Despensers, the King and the Marcher Lords.

The Marcher Lords, Bohun, Mortimer and others joined by the family of Llywelyn Bren ravaged the lordship of Glamorgan took Newport and Cardiff, seized Caerphilly Castle and sacked other castles and manors doing damage estimated at £14,000 in medieval money. The King was forced to submit and the Despensers were banished.

Soon however, Edward had reorganised his forces and occupied the MARCHES, Roger Mortimer was captured and thrown into the Tower, the Earl of Lancaster was defeated at the Battle of Boroughbridge in Yorkshire in 1322 and beheaded.

The Despensers were able to return and the Younger renewed his attempt to establish his power by securing from the King the grant of the lordships forfeited by the treasonable earls. Soon, Despenser was in control of all South Wales from the River Wye to the Swansea river and hoped that in the event of the King's overthrow he might be able to construct there a small principality for himself.

In 1326, Edward II fled to Wales, pursued by his wife Matilda, Roger Mortimer who had escaped from the Tower and the sons of Llywelyn Bren. The King remained at CARDIFF for two days while attempting to levy men from Despenser's lands in South Wales. Eventually Edward and Despenser were captured and executed.

Merthyr Tydfil in the Middle Ages

The inhabitants in Norman times, as in the Early Ages still lived high up on the moorlands and dwelt on the same old rectangular platform sites of early British times. Excavations by Lady Eileen Fox on the eastern side of Gelligaer mountain, above and opposite Ogilvie Colliery revealed a settlement of five or six long homesteads. These houses were 61 feet long by 20′ and 54′ by 18′ built lengthways into the hillside on rectangular platforms.

This type of dwelling must also have existed in the Merthyr area. The walls were made of stone slabs or slab and turf and were on average a little over 3 feet thick while the mainstay of the roof was a ridge pole, supported by two posts, itself sustaining some sort of thatch covering. The fireplace was in the middle of the house and the smoke escaped if at all through an opening in the roof.

A drainage ditch existed to dispose of internal seepage from the hillside itself and this was also apparently used as a repository for household refuse and sewage, the lower end was paved and much cleaner, thus the house seems to have been divided into a 'clean' and a 'dirty end'. A great part of the area was still marshy and wooded especially in the valley bottoms. The houses of the freemen, large or small were scattered over the slopes of the hills, avoiding both the bare, exposed hill-crests and the marshy valley bottoms. They all lived within the same great clearing in the woods; they formed in this way a free tref or village and together paid their dues to the chieftain or King. Merthyr Tydfil was just a hamlet with a wattle and daub church, a mill and scattered farmsteads. The food and clothing of the people were of the plainest and provided very largely by their herds and flocks. Dairy produce – milk, cheese, butter, eggs with only a little meat and dark bread was their regular diet and homespun woollen garments their dress. The farmers of the parish also cultivated small plots of land on which their chief crop oats was grown also clover, barley, alfalfa, broccoli, beet etc. The Welsh slopes and uplands were not suitable for the cultivation of wheat, and wheat was the basis of Anglo-Norman Society. The Anglo-Norman manor could not sustain itself without a year crop of wheat so manors were restricted to the Vale. In summer time the animals were driven to the higher parts of the hills. The more well to do natives kept two farms one as a summer and the other as a winter residence. The summer residence which was built nearer the hill-top was known as the hafod. We learn from the records of Llewelyn's Bren's Rebellion that sheep were not very plentiful in those days. These were chiefly kept to provide a coarse woollen cloth for making clothes and blankets, the shearing taking place twice a year. The flour of the district was ground at the mill which belonged to the great de Clare family and which stood near the Chapel of St Tydfil.

In addition the people were bound to do certain work for the lord. Many of the men from the district were called upon to cut down trees and haul timber to make the stalls for the TWYNYWAUN FAIR.

The Waun Fair was reputed to be one of the oldest fairs in the country and was held at a spot roughly between FOCHRIW and DOWLAIS TOP near the present-day village of PANTYWAUN. Its fame was widespread for as well as being a centre where the people of the region bartered for their requisites, many travelled from afar to trade there. The men of the Vale of Glamorgan brought their superior corn and root products exchanging them for the sturdy animals bred in the mountains, and so important was it considered that IESTYN Ap GWRGANT, Lord of Glamorgan granted the fair his charter in the year 1140.

The district also had its carpenters and wood-turners making wooden vessels such as cups, bowls, dishes and buckets. We learn from official accounts that these wooden disci were made in the woods between the TAFF and the CYNON, that is, on the slopes of the Aberdare Mountain.

Two places near the PARISH CHURCH were known as the 'FRIARY' and the 'ISLE OF WHITE' having some connection with the CISTERCIAN Monks who visited the parish from Neath or Margam to conduct church services at St Tydfil's Church.

Of all the monastic orders introduced into South Wales none had made a greater impact on the landscape than the CISTERCIANS – the WHITE MONKS – whose abbeys were TINTERN founded in 1147, MARGAM and NEATH in 1147, and STRATA FLORIDA in 1164. The Cistercian monks were the best farmers in the Middle Ages; their income derived primarily from sheep rearing. The creed of their order compelled them to seek out and to develop the wasteland and wilderness. They therefore crossed the 600 ft contour-line and established themselves firmly in the barren Welsh uplands.

Gerald of Wales gives us a vivid picture of the Welsh of the Middle Ages, their love of part-singing and instrumental music, the musical instruments favoured by them being the harp, pipe and crwth; their touchiness and family pride, ready wit in speech and skill in story-telling, religious devotion, frugality in food and dress are also noted. They were not addicted to gluttony or drunkenness.

Accustomed to fast from morning to evening, they dedicate the whole day to business, and in the evening partake of a moderate meal. They consider hospitality and liberality among the first virtues. Travellers on entering a house, only deliver up their arms. Water was then offered to them. If they suffer their feet to be washed, they were treated as guests. If they refuse, they only wish for refreshments, and not a night's lodging. A thin bread made from oats (bara-ceirch) was eaten, and bread baked on a griddle known as cakebread or bara planc. The latter was baked every day. Sometimes the meat was chopped and made into broth.

The beds were made from rushes covered with a coarse cloth (brychen). The fire was never allowed to go out. Guests would usually be seated in threes. The foods to be eaten were probably brought in on large wooden platters and placed in front of the diners on the rushes and fresh grass spread over the floor. Each mess, or group of three would eat off the same platter.

During the meal the family would always wait on their guests; in fact the host and hostess would stand up all the time in order to be able to pay full attention to the needs of everyone present. They would take nothing to eat themselves until all the company had been satisfied.

Gerald of Wales even recorded details like fussiness about teeth, the fashion of moustaches and shaven chins among men and of 'page-boy' hair styles in both sexes.

By 1300 definite if comparatively slow changes had occurred in the Welsh way of life that Gerald the Welshman knew, plague, revolt and war were to accelerate these changes enormously in the 14th and 15th Centuries. The tribal system in Upland Wales was clearly breaking down. The practice became current of actually dividing out the land hitherto held in common by the tribe and so making an individual holding permanent.

The idea was growing that a man should be taxed according to the tribe to which he belonged. Thus the reference in 1316 'to two beadles above and below the Caiach collecting and levying rents, advowries, farms, please and pre-requisites of the courts of the patria de Senghenyth'.

It thus became possible to mark out the limits of the tax areas. This gave rise to a great many of our present day parish boundaries. All these features were greatly speeded up in the 14th Century as a result of the BLACK DEATH at its middle and the revolt of OWAIN GLYNDWR at its end.

The idea too was growing that the land should be worked for profit and not merely in order to provide a living for the members of the manor or tribe.

At Merthyr there was in 1307, 15 acres of arable and 15 acres of meadow land. In 1288-89, the reeve of the Manor of Merthyr was one HYWEL Ap GRONW. The revenues derived from the pasturing of pigs, the dairy produce of a herd of cattle, and the sale of stock, hides and corn. Expenditure included sums spent upon the materials for a plough and the labour for its making; maintenance work was undertaken upon the mill and a stable, and agricultural tasks were done as pieceworks.

Before the end of the century a grandson of Llywelyn ap Rhys had secured an extensive estate in UWCH CAEACH which was to be the nucleus of that of his son EDWARD LEWIS.

The poet Rhys Brychan describes the hospitality provided at the neuadd (hall) at the Manor of Merthyr by one who was clearly a person of consequence in the northern parts of Senghenydd, Lewis ap Richard.

Y min wyth olud i mae'n y thilyn
a bailch a divailch y sy'n dovyn;
aniaithr diaithr a dynn yw nauadd.
o daw i'r nauadd e dyrr i newyn.
ofnog yw aliwns ar vin gelyn
a ry garw Merthyr a grym wrthym;
Lewis o waed Rys, rosyn y dalaith
uchel yw ailwaith ach lywelyn.

The emergence of a dominant family in Senghenydd can be established by record evidence. The comparative affluence of Lewis ap Richard Constable of Caerphilly in the later years of his life is conveyed by his Will of 1521.

'Lewis ap Richard, esquire, bequethed a sum of £20 for the repair of the bells of Merthyr Tydfil Church and a further bequest was made for the regilding of the image of St TYDFIL.' His feoffees were to convey his lands to his son Edward ap Lewis.

In 1540 Edward Lewis possessed at Merthyr a concentration of holdings, which included TIR CWRT (COURTHOUSE) assessed at the substantial sum of 27s. 10d. This was probably a long-established seat of the family. It was by then in the occupation of a tenant for Edward Lewis had by then taken up residence at Y FAN a house built in close proximity to the castle of CAERPHILLY in ISCAEACH.

The End of the Middle Ages

The Hundred Years War between England and France broke out about 1340. Recruiting agents toured Wales raising troops, most likely men from the Merthyr district joined the ranks and would have fought at Crecy in 1346.

The Revolt of Owain Glyndwr

In 1400, Owain Glyndwr's rebellion broke out in North Wales calling upon all Welshmen to fight for their independence. Owain Glyndwr appeared in Gwent and Glamorgan, where the Welsh of the hills rose up in sympathy with the rebels. His forces attacked the English towns of Abergavenny, Usk, Caerleon, Newport and in 1404, Cardiff. He was defeated in 1405 and died in 1417.

There is no evidence that OWAIN GLYNDWR passed through MERTHYR but local place names like YNYSOWEN and BRYN CAE OWEN record his memory.

In 1403, men from the district around MERTHYR did march under Glyndwr's banner to attack CAERPHILLY CASTLE which fell to their onslaught. By 1408, Edward, Duke of York, the King's cousin acquired control of the whole lordship of Glamorgan.

Resistance in Glamorgan had ceased by June 1407 when King Henry IV pardoned those of the inhabitants who had already submitted and agreed to pay fines.

On February 28th 1415, Richard Beauchamp inherited the lordship of Glamorgan whose father was lord of Abergavenny.

His rule as Lord of Glamorgan lasted only seven years, Glamorgan then fell into the hands of RICHARD NEVILLE afterwards Earl of SALISBURY and WARWICK.

The Wars of the Roses

During the Wars of the Roses, Merthyr Tydfil like the rest of South Wales became a recruiting ground. The Welsh Marches and Glamorgan followed the fortunes of the House of York, the rest of the Principality remained true to Lancaster.

In 1478, Glamorgan passed into the hands of RICHARD, DUKE OF GLOUCESTER who in 1483, became King RICHARD III.

Bosworth

On 7th August, 1485, Henry Tudor with his uncle Jasper Tudor landed at MILFORD HAVEN after years of exile. Hundreds of Welshmen flocked to the red dragon of Cadwaladr on a white and green background including men from Merthyr led by WALTER HERBERT. Henry was the long-awaited hero, the true successor of CADWALADR and ARTHUR of LLYWELYN and GLYNDWR.

On August 22nd the Yorkists under RICHARD III and the Lancastrians under Henry met at BOSWORTH. It was a bloody battle resulting in the death of RICHARD III and the proclamation of HENRY TUDOR as HENRY VII.

To the Welshmen crying 'HIR OES I HARRI' it meant the triumph at last of the race and freedom from bondage. In their efforts the people of the small parish of Merthyr Tydfil like the rest of Wales had become a nation with a language, and a literature an outlook and a destiny all of its own.

LIST OF DATES

1. 55-54 BC. Julius Caesar's Invasions of Britain.
2. 43 AD. The Claudian Invasion of Britain.
3. 50 AD. Ostorius Scapula invaded Siluria.
4. 74 AD. Roman Fort built at Penydarren by Julius Frontinus.
5. c 120 AD. Roman Fort Abandoned.
6. 410 AD. End of Roman Britain.
7. c 450 AD. Death of Tydfil the Martyr.
8. 14th October 1066. Battle of Hastings. Death of Harold.
9. 25th December 1066. Coronation of William I.
10. 1067. William Fitzosbern invades S. Wales.
11. 1090. Robert Fitzhamon conquers S. Wales.
12. 1094. Normans defeated at Gelligaer.
13. 1158. Ifor Bach's successful attack on Cardiff Castle.
14. 1211 Cadwallion ab Ifor Bach ravages The Vale of Glamorgan.
15. 1231. Llywellyn ab Iorwerth Llywellyn The Great invades S. Wales.
16. 1270. Morlais Castle built.
17. 1270 completed restoration of Caerphilly Castle by Gilbert De Clare.
18. 1282. Llywellyn ap Gruffydd. Llywellyn the Last killed near Builth.
19. 1294. Morlais Castle captured by Morgan ap Maredydd.
20. 1295. Edward I ordered the demolition of Morlais Castle.
21. 1314. Revolt of Llywellyn Bren.
22. 1317. Llywellyn Bren executed at Cardiff.
23. 1326. Hugh Le Despenser executed at Hereford.
24. 1327. Edward II murdered at Berkeley Castle, Glos.
25. 1403. Owain Glyndwr attacks and captures Caerphilly Castle.
26. 1417. Death of Owain Glyndwr.
27. 1485. Battle of Bosworth. Henry Tudor proclaimed Henry VII.

Bibliography

Merthyr Tydfil in Roman Times

A. Richmond, *Roman Britain — I*, Pelican Books (1955)
V.E. Nash-Williams, *The Roman Frontier in Wales*, Univ. of Wales Press (1954)
D. Fraser, *The Invaders*, Univ. of Wales Press, Cardiff (1965)
G. Tingay, *From Caesar to the Saxons – The Story of Roman Britain*, Longman (1972)
N.U.T., *The Story of Merthyr Tydfil* (1932)
F. Haverfield, *Military Aspects of Roman Wales*, Transactions of the Honourable Society of Cymmrodorion.

Merthyr Tydfil and the Dark Ages

N. Chadwick and M. Dillon, *The Celtic Realms*, Cambridge Univ. Press (1967)
J.E. Lloyd, *A History of Wales*, **1**, (1912)
C. Thomas, *Britain and Ireland in early Christian Times AD 400-800*, Thomas and Hudson (1971)
E.G. Bowen, *Britain and the Western Seaways*, Thomas and Hudson (1972)
J.T. McNeill, *The Celtic Churches, A History AD 200-1200*, Univ. of Chicago Press (1974)
G.H. Doble, *S. Nectan, S. Keyne and the Children of Brychan in Cornwall*
R. Williams, *A Biographical Dictionary of Eminent Welshmen*
C. Wilkins, *The History of Merthyr Tydfil*, Merthyr Central Library
C. Wilkins, *Tales and Sketches of Wales*, Merthyr Central Library (1879)
T. Jones, *A History of Brecknockshire*, Merthyr Central Library

Merthyr Tydfil in Norman and Saxon Times

D. Fraser, *The Defenders*, Univ. of Wales Press, Cardiff (1967)
A. Clark, *The Story of Monmouthshire*, Christopher Davies (1962)
I.M. Davies, *Everyday Life in Wales*, Book III (1951)
Gelligaer Historical Society, *Gelligaer Story* (1969)
C.J.O. Evans, *Glamorgan – Its History and Topography*, (1938)
N.U.T., *The Story of Merthyr Tydfil*, (1932)
J. Williams Ab Ithel, *Brut y Twysogion* or *The Chronicle of the Princes of Wales*, Longman (1860)
A.G. Prys-Jones, *Gerald of Wales*, George G. Harrap (1955)
L.G. Nelson, *The Normans in South Wales, 1070-1171*, Univ. of Texas Press, London
Glamorgan County History, **III**, *The Middle Ages*, Univ. of Wales Press (1971)

The Story of Morlais Castle

N.U.T., *The Story of Merthyr Tydfil* (1932)
T.E. Clarke, *Medieval Military Architecture*
C. Wilkins, *History of Merthyr Tydfil*
T. Lewis, *Vaynor Gleanings*, Cefn Coed and Vaynor Local History Society
G.T. Clarke, *A Guide to Merthyr Tydfil* (1874)
Glamorgan County History, **III**, *The Middle Ages*, Univ. of Wales Press (1971)

Merthyr Tydfil Middle Ages
N.U.T., *The Story of Merthyr Tydfil* (1932)
A.H. Dood, *Life in Wales,* B.T. Batsford Ltd. (1972)
J.C. Davies, *The Despenser War in Glamorgan*
W. Rees, *South Wales and the March, 1284-1415*
W. Rees, *The Ancient Petitions of Wales,* Univ. of Wales Press
D. Fraser, *The Defenders,* Univ. of Wales Press, Cardiff (1967)
W. Rees, *Caerphilly Castle and its place in the annals of Glamorgan,* (1974)
M. Williams, *The South Wales Landscape,* Hodder and Stoughton (1974)

The Late Fifteenth and Sixteenth Centuries

by W. MANSEL RICHARDS

The late fifteenth and sixteenth centuries are sometimes referred to as the beginning of modern times. In Western Europe the boundaries of human experience were suddenly widened, and the spirit of man leaped upwards to pinnacles of achievement, hitherto unreached. This was to be the Age of the Renaissance of Learning and the Reformation of the Church, the period of the Spanish Armada and of great seamen like Drake and Raleigh, the era of Shakespeare and of strong Tudor monarchs who centralised political power around the throne and forged a strong nation-state. Outside Britain it was a time when Erasmus and Luther preached a reformed message, when Leonardo da Vinci and Michelangelo painted, when Columbus and Vasco da Gama explored new lands and the age when the printing press was used in Europe for the first time.

The villagers of rural Merthyr Tydfil and their neighbours in the ancient cantref of Senghennydd within the Lordship of Glamorgan lived in comparative isolation at the northern end of the well-wooded Taff Valley (see Fig. 52). They would have had little awareness of these new forces at work. An occasional traveller or passing tinker may have transmitted some fascinating glimpses of the changing outside world at market, fair or inn, but the communication of news and events, from the wider world outside their own locality, would have made little impact on the folk of this remote neighbourhood. The simplicity of life and the sylvan charm of the scenery, to be badly despoiled in later centuries, remained pure and unspoilt, as contemporary observers pointed out. John Leland, the King's wide-travelling antiquary, found in the late 1530's, during his journeys in North Glamorgan, 'many hills . . . and woods good plenty, but few villages or corn except in a few small valleys about the river sides'.[1] One such place he found at Vaynor which he described as 'The good valley for corn and grass'.[2] Forty years later, in the reign of Elizabeth I, one of Glamorgan's own sons, Rice Merrick, wrote of its 'many great hills and high mountains' though apt enough for 'great breeding of cattle, horses and sheep' and in 'nourishing and bringing up tall, mighty and active men'.[3] But the colour, pageantry and high drama of the Tudor era clearly made very little impact on sixteenth century North Glamorgan.

But let us turn back to August 22nd 1485 – a day of some significance for the subsequent history of Wales. By dusk on that day, Henry Tudor, a Welsh Lancastrian and founder of the Tudor Dynasty, had defeated the Yorkist King of England Richard III on the field of Bosworth, near Leicester. The Tudor saga had begun.

The first 50 years of Tudor rule 1485-1536 saw relatively little diminution of lawlessness, criminal disorder and violence in Wales and the Marches, which had been so prevalent during the late Middle Ages. Royal authority was imposed with greater urgency, but did not go completely unchallenged. Disturbances were common; men who could afford weapons went armed. Criminals moved from one Marcher lordship to another in order to avoid arrest. Many thieves and murderers were safe from the wrath of the King once they had crossed the River Taff in its upper reaches from Merthyr Tydfil into the Lordship of Brecknock. Neither life nor property was safe. On June 7th, 1472 Llewelyn Duy, a vagabond of Mynydd Islwyn was accused of abducting one Ieuan ap David ap Griffith ap Ichell, from Penarth and with keeping him prisoner at Merthyr Tydfil, until he paid a fine to secure his release.[4] Cattle stealing above all else, appears to have been the most common offence which all too often went unpunished. On April 20th, 1476 Meurig Benllwyd and Richard ap Jenkin, yeomen, were accused of stealing five cows at Rudry in the Lordship of Senghennydd, while the ancient and widely-known Waun Fair above Dowlais Top had 'an unsavoury reputation as a haunt of cattle thieves.'[5]

Determined to try to restore law and order in the 'Welsh Marches' Henry Tudor gave wide powers to the Council of Wales and the Marches, which was to administer to the needs of Wales, from the red-sandstone castle of Ludlow in Shropshire and other similar strong points, conveniently close to the Welsh border. But there does not seem to have been a great respect for its authority. The Sheriff of Glamorgan's steward even hanged a 16 year old boy whose father had dared to make a formal complaint to the Council at Ludlow.[6]

Under Henry Tudor, Wales was governed in a traditional and medieval manner. The great political and administrative changes for Wales were not to come until the next reign, that of his remarkable son, Henry VIII. This masterful 'Renaisance King' and Thomas Cromwell, his energetic and imaginative administrator, brought about the union of Wales with England in 1536. It was to have momentous consequences and has determined the course of Welsh history, to the present day, surviving even the Devolution referendum of 1979.

The real transformation began in the year 1534, when a new President of the Council of Wales and the Marches was appointed by King Henry VIII. This Bishop Rowland Lee was a tough, fearless and single-minded cleric and a warm admirer of Thomas Cromwell. He travelled extensively along the border country, repressing crime, enforcing the law, hanging thieves and cattle-rustlers and soon became the terror of the Welsh banditry. One writer of the time reported 'it is said that over 5000 men were hanged within the space of six years', – a gross exaggeration doubtless, but an indication of the profound impression Bishop Lee made on the Welsh people at this time.[7] Although he never entered the Lordship of Glamorgan, there can be little doubt that mention of his name put fear into the heart of many a local criminal.

To assist this brutal, but energetic and effectual royal agent in the Marches, the London Parliament passed several laws. Jurors giving a false verdict were to be punished; the passage over the River Severn was to be carefully watched for thieves; the justices of neighbouring English shires were empowered to try various offences committed within the Welsh Marches; and criminals who fled from one lordship to another in order to avoid arrest were to be handed back on command of the Council of Wales and the Marches. In 1535 the following year, a most important Act was passed – 'An Act for the making of justices of the peace in the existing counties of Wales'. Bishop Lee did not, however, think Welshmen were fit for the important local office of justice of the peace, stating
'There be very few Welshmen in Wales above Brecknock that may dispend ten pound a year in land, and to say truth, their descretion less than their lands'.[8]

These had been years when the dangers of the break from Rome had reached crisis proportions. A firm policy had been vital. Now Thomas Cromwell's clear legal mind and imaginative vision took over. A single uniform administrative machine and a sovereign united Kingdom were more than ever necessary; and accordingly the year 1536 saw the first Act of Union come into force whereby Wales was united to the realm of England. The marcher lordships were eliminated and the whole of Wales was divided into counties. The cantref of Senghennydd in which Merthyr Tydfil was located became part of the new shire of Glamorgan (Fig. 56). Henceforth Wales was to be ruled 'after no Welshe lawes', but according to 'the Lawes customes and statutes of this realme of Englande'. English became the official language, and customs which had governed the social life of the area for centuries were swept into the abyss of the past.[9]

One of the effects of the Acts of Union had been to assist the rise of important families in Wales by making it easier for them to transmit intact to their heirs, any landed estates which they had been able to build up and consolidate during their life times. Previously when a man died his possessions had been divided up between all his sons (according to the old Welsh custom of 'cyfrau'), but after the Acts of Union it was replaced by the

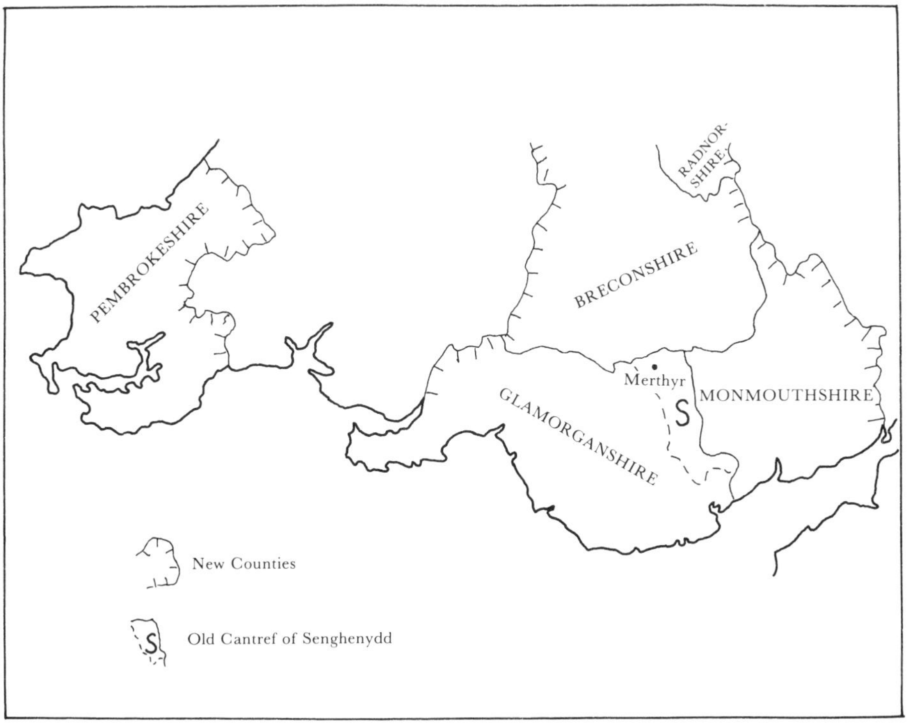

Fig. 56: New Administration Divisions—Act of Union 1536

law of 'primogeniture' as in England, whereby the estate became the sole inheritance of the eldest son. This was one of the factors that helped consolidate the estates of the wealthy Lewis and Pritchard families, the two most notable landowning families in the Merthyr Tydfil area. Edward Pritchard built a large and imposing residence at Llancaiach Farm near Nelson* (Plate 32), but it was Edward Lewis of the Court Estate who had the closer links with the village of Merthyr Tydfil.

By the year 1540, Edward Lewis (who claimed descent from the great twelfth-century Welsh leader, Ifor Bach) owned a considerable estate centred around the Court House of Merthyr Tydfil (on the site of the present Labour Club). Soon afterwards he was renting this residence together with his Troedyrhiw House to tenant-occupiers within the Lewis family, for Lewis himself had moved southwards to Y Fan, an impressive house built in close proximity to Caerphilly Castle. John Leland referred to it as 'a fair place called Vanne, where Mr. Edward Lewys dwellith'.[10]

* Llancaiach Fawr has remained unaltered in substance and is the most complete example of a stately Elizabethan mansion in this area. Welsh cultural traditions were well supported by the Pritchard family at this time and Dafydd Benwyn – a Bard who flourished between 1550 and 1600 composed a poem in praise of the splendour of Llancaiach, which is preserved in the Jesus College manuscripts at Oxford (*The Story of Gelligaer*, p.52).

Plate 32: LLANCAIACH HOUSE *(Photograph by Robert Haines)*

It appears that Edward Lewis' father, in common with other wealthy estate builders of the late fifteenth century, had been a pious churchman and patron of learning. A poem by Rhys Bychan has survived, which praises the warm hospitality provided by this elder Lewis in his neuadd or hall at Merthyr Tydfil.[11]

O daw ir nauadd e dyrr i newyn.
Ofnog yn aliwns ar vin Gelyn
A ry garw Merthyr a gryn wrthyn;
Lewys o wnaed Rys, Rosyn y Dalaith,
Uchel yw ailwaith ach Lywelyn.

Whoever comes to Neuadd (the Hall) will satisfy his hunger.
Fearful are strangers in the face of an enemy
When the powerful might of Merthyr is with us;
Lewys of the blood of Rhys, the Rose of the Territory,
Noble is he, like Llywelyn's line.

This local magnate was clearly a man of some social consequence in the northern part of Senghennydd; certainly his Will of 1529 showed him to be a man of affluence. A sum of £20 was given for the repair of the bells at

Merthyr Tydfil Church and a further bequest was made for the regilding of the image of St. Tydfil.[12] The younger Lewis in turn was to acquire large landed estates and considerable social prestige during the mid-Tudor years being appointed Sheriff of the County of Glamorgan in the years 1548 to 1555 and again in 1589. The estate-building by this North Glamorgan patriarch, Edward Lewis, owner of the impressive Court and Troedyrhiw houses, is a good example of one of the clear-cut trends in Welsh Tudor history, *viz* the growth of the landowning class of squire in sixteenth century Wales.

There can be no doubt that law and order in the Merthyr Tydfil area, as in other places within what had formerly been the Welsh marches, improved considerably as a result of the Acts of Union and their efficient machinery of justice. No longer could criminals escape to other Marcher lordships. A regular and uniform system of royal law courts now came into existence. The Crown appointed eight justices of the peace to each county from among the local landowners. These met four times a year in the Quarter Sessions. Each county, was in turn, divided into units called hundreds. Here the local J.P. held court where minor cases were tried and sentence passed. The twelve shires of Wales also, were divided into four circuits (Monmouthshire came under the London circuit). The resident judge presided over these important 'Great Sessions' twice a year. Merthyr Tydfil became part of Wales' south-east circuit, centred at Brecon.

Further to assist the establishment of law and order in Wales, the Council of Wales and the Marches was strengthened. Increasing recourse was also made by the people of Wales to the Courts of Law in London. Thus in 1558, at the opening of Elizabeth's reign a Chancery suit was instituted by a member of the important landowning Lewis family of Merthyr Tydfil – one Gabriel Lewis against Phe Thomas and Gabriel Griffiths. The object of this law-suit was to gain dwellings and certain lands in the Parish of Merthyr which had been bequeathed by will to Gabriel Lewis by Edward ap Richard of the Mardy Estate. There are no records to illustrate the outcome of this case but it does furnish a local example, of the increasing use made by the Welsh of the well-oiled Tudor machinery of justice, in the years following the Act of Union.

This Union not only dealt a heavy blow to crime and violence in Wales, but unfortunately to the language and culture of the nation. The 'language clause' of the Acts of Union made English the official language of law, justice and administration throughout Wales. It stipulated that no one could hold office in Wales, unless he had a knowledge of the English Language. Naturally, all those among the upper classes in Wales, who aspired to hold any official position of consequence under the Tudor Crown were obliged to take full cognizance of this legal provision, concerning the knowledge and use of the English language. Many of them already had some acquaintance with this language before the passing of the Act, but they were now more than ever encouraged to learn and use English, to adopt English attitudes, and to move away from their native cultural affinities. The process was a long and gradual one, spanning a number of generations, but its final outcome was an anglicised gentry separated from the Welsh speaking 'gwerin' (folk) by linguistic as well as social barriers.

Throughout the Middle Ages the Roman Catholic Church in Wales had been a great patron of learning and the arts. Following the disastrous effects of the Owain Glyndŵr Rebellion, a gradual economic recovery took place in Wales during the late fifteenth century. Not only could the wealthier abbeys of Neath and Margam afford once again to patronise poets and literature, but there is evidence that many ordinary clergy in Glamorgan were able to give financial encouragement to Welsh poets and bards. Even the humble parish priest of Merthyr Tydfil in the late fifteenth century was thus able to offer patronage to the brilliant Guto'r Glyn, one of the outstanding poets of the time. In return he received one of Guto's most outstanding eulogies.[14]

There was however, a supine and lack-lustre quality to the spiritual and organisational side of this late medieval Church in Wales. This has been illustrated most vividly by Professor Glanmor Williams, our own, distinguished, Dowlais born historian who has suggested that 'at its best religious life was pietistic and unmilitant. At the worst it was credulous and ignorant'.[15] Bishops appointed at this time to dioceses in Wales were absentee, their only interest in these bishoprics being as stepping-stones to more lucrative livings in England. This is well illustrated by the Spaniard-Athequa who was Confessor to the unfortunate Queen Catherine of Aragon and who became the unlikely Bishop of Llandaff. He never once visited his diocese and had probably never even heard of the obscure Glamorgan parish of Merthyr Tydfil. Similarly, the more efficient clergy were not attracted to the poor livings offered by the Church in Wales. Those who were, often remained non-resident, such as the Elizabethan Rector of Merthyr Tydfil, John Smith, who was also Arch-deacon of Llandaff, Chancellor of Exeter Cathedral, and possessed other, income producing livings within that Devon diocese in which he was a resident. Bishop Kitchen's Report for Llandaff at the opening of Elizabeth's reign referred to a similar case in the neighbouring Parish of Gelligaer 'John Herbert bying a laye Man, a scolar and a student at Oxon, Christe Church there, is a parson of Kellygayre (Gelligaer) in the said Diocese, not resydent'.[16] The lower clergy too were usually ill trained and unsuited to the responsibilities of their calling, a defect well illustrated locally in the appointment of Robert Jenys, to the living of Vaynor in 1488. Being an Englishman he could hardly have been held in the highest esteem by his Welsh-speaking parishioners. He was eventually replaced half a century later by Hugh ap Rhys who was to be the last of the Roman Catholic parsons in that lovely rural vale.[17] (Plate 33.)

In those distant days, people often made pilgrimages to some holy place, and it is not unlikely that the nearby Tydfil's Well and another at Rhydycar were sacred spots, to which they frequently resorted, to pay their respects to a holy place and to seek benefit from the reputedly healing qualities of the

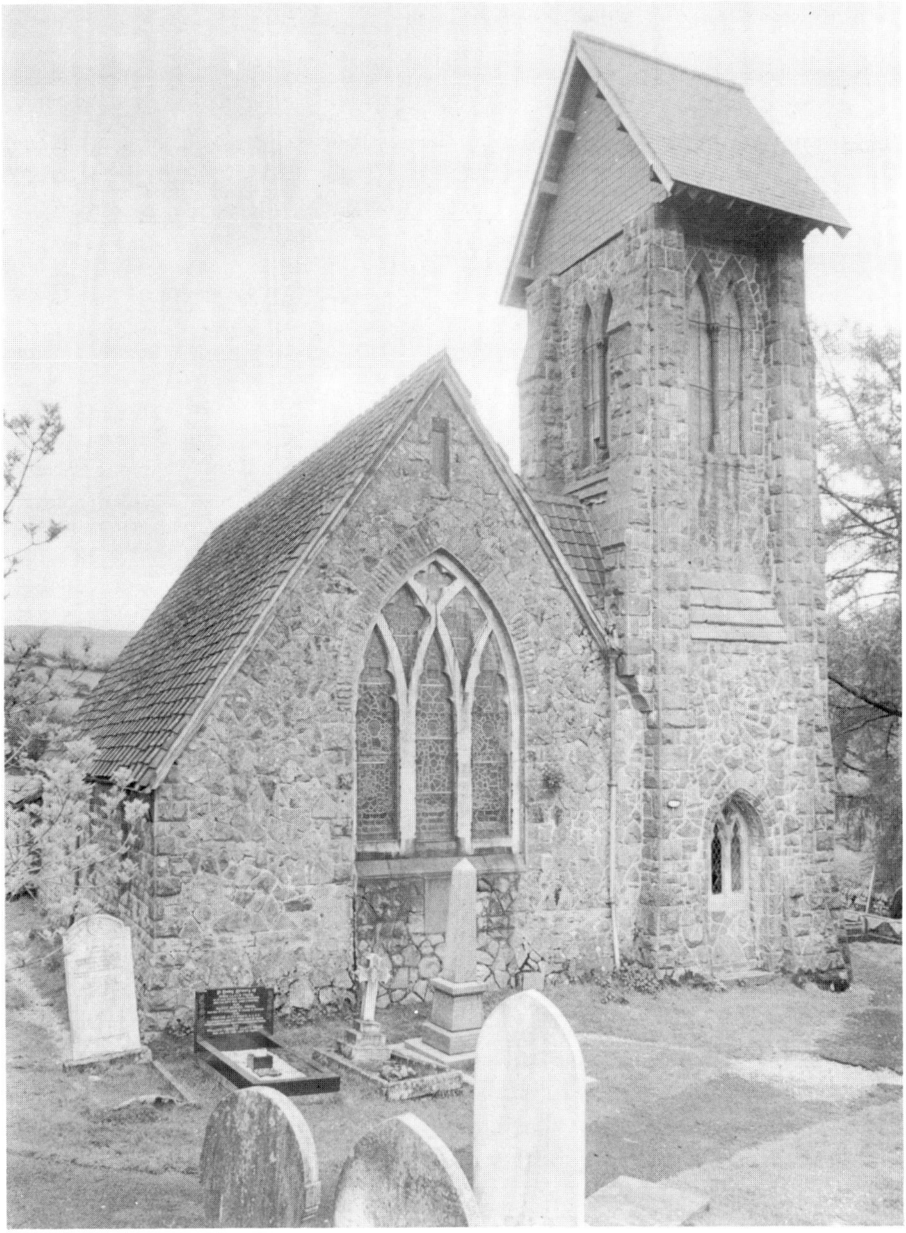

Plate 33: VAYNOR CHURCH (in 1980) *(Photograph by Robert Haines)*

well-water. Some Merthyr Tydfil folk must have left farm or cottage to travel along the muddy tracks of the Brecon Beacons in order to venerate the large holy cross in the nave of Brecon Priory.[18] The most celebrated shrine in Glamorgan itself was that of the Blessed Virgin Mary at Penrhys in the remote and thickly wooded Rhondda valley which attracted pilgrims from far and wide.[19]

King Henry VIII's 'Great Matter' had caused a profound crisis within the realm between the years 1527 and 1534. This fearsome monarch was determined to have his marriage to the prematurely ageing and wrinkled Catherine of Aragon 'annulled' so that he would be free to marry the raven-haired and flirtatious Anne Boleyn whom he was confident would bear him the eagerly anticipated male-heir to the throne. The consequences were to be the disgrace of Cardinal Wolsey, the elimination of the Pope's jurisdiction over the Church in England and Wales, and its replacement by the King's Supremacy over a 'National Church' based upon the authority of parliamentary statute. Thus began a process by which England and Wales were transformed gradually from Roman Catholic to Protestant countries. By the year 1540, all abbeys, friaries and convents had been closed, their property and wealth secularized by the Crown and their inmates scattered through the land.

The simple folk of Merthyr Tydfil could no longer travel to Brecon Priory (its dissolution led to the founding of Christ College Brecon in 1541) while Neath Abbey also closed its doors for the last time. Meanwhile, another step in the direction of reform was the campaign launched against holy shrines and religious images. Thomas Cromwell spearheaded their destruction and gave instructions that the Rhondda shrine of Penrhys should be moved 'as secretly as might be'.[20] This suggests that public opinion in Glamorgan, seemingly indifferent towards monastic destruction, was expected to react much more sharply towards the removal of the popular and revered shrines. The image of Rhondda's Virgin Mary was removed to London and with a number of others, burned publicly.

The mid-century reign of Mary Tudor witnessed a return to the Roman Catholic faith, and the martyrdom by public burning at Cardiff of Rawlins White a Protestant fisherman. In the year 1558 both the Virgin Mary and Queen Mary were replaced by the 'Virgin Queen', Elizabeth I. Following in the footsteps of her powerful father Henry VIII this last monarch of the Tudor line renounced the Pope, and introduced a compromise religious settlement which became acceptable to the majority of her subjects. The local clergy were forced to take an oath of loyalty to the new Queen as 'Supreme Governor of the Church', and statutes were issued compelling attendance by the people at local churches in which Protestant services were to be ministered. This would have applied to the Merthyr Tydfil Parish and Vaynor Churches and the new, small, roughly-built churches of Capel y Fforest,* on the hillside above Troedyrhiw and Capel Y Fan over-looking

* Writing three hundred years later, William Edmunds in 'A History of Merthyr Tydfil' (1864) commented 'There are the remains here of a dwelling house and a cemetery, snugly situated in a small glade between the Taff and Bargoed valleys, to the east of Troedyrhiw. A sum of money has been left to the church for its re-building. Churchmen have talked of starting this task, but nothing has been done.'

Aberfan[21]. Both these small Churches served the scattered population of farmers and iron workers south of the village of Merthyr Tydfil during the reign of Elizabeth when the Protestant faith was consolidating slowly in the valleys of South Wales.

There were those inevitably, whose consciences would not allow them to accept the doctrines and government of this new Elizabethan Church and who remained loyal to the old Roman Catholic faith. They avoided attendance at Church, celebrated Mass in secret and were called 'recusants'. The loyalty of many Glamorgan gentry in particular remained suspect. Edwards Lewis of the Van for example, is known to have concealed and given hospitality to 'recusant priests', despite his ostensibly Protestant appointment as a justice of the peace charged with the persecution of adherents of the Roman Catholic faith. He even employed one such priest as a tutor to his son.[22] Locally, the Edwards family of Taimawr Farm (off the Swansea Road) were Roman Catholics during the early seventeenth century while the nearby Pontycapel – the Chapel Bridge, is thought to be associated with the secret papist chapel at the Edwards' home—Taimawr.[23]

There were also men and women of an opposite persuasion whose consciences demanded a much purer simple reformed Church than that given them by Elizabeth. These 'Puritans' as they came to be called were to become a major force throughout the land in the succeeding years. One of the pioneers of this movement, John Penry of neighbouring Breconshire, was captured and executed in the year 1593 for his criticism of the Elizabethan Church. There is no evidence of his activity in the Merthyr Tydfil district, and it is unlikely that the nearby valley of Vaynor in southern Breconshire ever heard the force of his message. The young Elizabethan vicar of Vaynor, Josias Morgan nevertheless, had to withstand the onslaught of puritan criticism, from members of his flock in succeeding years.[24] One religious leader with local associations, who is thought to have had a more significant influence on the Puritans of North Glamorgan between the years 1580 and 1620 was the indefatigable Thomas Llewellyn of Rhigos. The translation of parts of Tyndale's Bible into Welsh has been ascribed to him; but though modern scholars throw doubt upon this tradition, they acknowledge him as one of the most influential authors of 'cwmdidau', the religious and moral verses so popular in Tudor Glamorgan. Certainly his verses have a strongly puritan tone to them. Undoubtedly the main religious achievement of Elizabethan Wales, however, was the translation of the Gospels into the Welsh language by the literary giants William Salesbury and Bishop Richard Davies, with Bishop William Morgan publishing the whole Bible in Welsh in the year of the Spanish Armada – 1588. This Welsh Bible gradually assisted the process of transforming the Welsh into a Protestant nation. The people of Wales came to identify themselves with Protestant services in the Welsh language, although an equally significant religious change for Wales came later in the eighteenth century with the arrival of the Methodist Revival.

The Upper Taff Valley meanwhile came to experience some industrialization on a limited scale. The wooded hillsides around the Tudor village of Merthyr Tydfil were to echo to the sound of iron making over two hundred years before the giant complexes of Cyfarthfa and Dowlais made the area world-renowned for the manufacture of iron. The second half of the sixteenth century brought a number of Sussex iron-masters to the Taff and other South Wales valleys. Legislation had been introduced by Parliament to prevent massive deforestation in the well-established iron-producing areas of England. Thus, the resourceful Anthony Morley, an iron master from Sussex and others, were soon establishing furnaces and forges, on nearby tree-clad slopes, long before the names of Crawshay, Guest or Homfray were heard of, in these parts.

The areas chosen were well-wooded, and possessed ample supplies of charcoal fuel; they were also well-endowed with rivers and streams which provided the water for driving the water wheels, which operated the crude bellows, which in turn, produced 'blast' for heating the fuel used in smelting the ores. Most important, iron-ore was easily worked from outcrops and shallow pits.[25] The dependence of this infant Tudor iron-making industry upon charcoal made it necessary to locate the works at considerable distances apart, and in well-wooded districts. Rice Merrick lamented that 'many forests and woods in the neighbourhood of these iron works which were spoiled and consumed'.[26]

During the reign of Elizabeth I, blast furnaces and forges appeared among the leafy, wooded glades of Pontygwaith (near Edwardsville), Pont y Rhun (Troedyrhiw), Duffryn (Pentrebach) and Blaencannaid (near Heolgerrig). The blast furnace of Blaencannaid whose Tudor owners are not known has been described as 'simple to a degree'.[27] It was located in a natural hollow on the Aberdare mountain slopes to make for easy charging or loading of the necessary raw materials. A stream flows into the hollow and forms a small waterfall behind the furnace which probably drove a water wheel.*

Traditionally, the furnace further down valley at Pontygwaith is thought to have survived until its partial demolition by Oliver Cromwell's troops in the mid-seventeenth century. There are no surface remains on the site, but a water colour, said to be a copy of this original surface is preserved in the Merthyr Tydfil Museum.**

Some superficial remains of the Pontyrhun furnace however, could be seen as recently as 1874.[29] Its outstanding relic is the remarkably beautiful old fire-back discovered by Anthony Hill, the nineteenth century iron-master, during the building of Pentrebach House, (near the Pentrebach

*An excavation of the site was undertaken in July 1965, by the Department of Archaeology of the University College of Cardiff, which revealed the existence of a sixteenth-century 'Charging Platform'.[28]

** The furnace at Pontygwaith is discussed by Mr. Clive Thomas in his chapter "Early Industrial Developments up to 1870"

roundabout). It carries the date 1553, and shows the motto of the Garter, 'Honi Soit Qui Mal y Pense' with the royal arms of France and England quarterly upon a shield occupying the centre space. This is surmounted by a crown with the initials E.R. probably those of the sickly boy-King Edward VI.* It is a superb piece of early iron craftmanship and suggests that an older house of Tudor origins existed on the site of the present mid-Victorian house.[30] But perhaps of even greater significance for the future industrial fame of the Merthyr Tydfil District, were the grants by this mid-Tudor boy monarch, Edward VI, to William Herbert, Lord President of Wales and the Marches and Earl of Pembroke of lands, manors and other property in the County of Glamorgan. This great sixteenth century Glamorgan landowner was the ancestor by marriage of Lord Windsor and the Marquis of Bute. They in turn, were to lease the mineral rights of their inherited lands to John Guest, from which emerged the mighty Dowlais Iron and Steel Works of the nineteenth century.

Iron-smelting was not the only industrial activity in the Merthyr Tydfil area during the Tudor period. Coal, too, was increasingly being used at this time for heating homes, and there were small coal workings at Hirwaun and the Waun near Dowlais.[31] It is these local iron furnaces, however, whose iron-masters developed an export trade from the port of Cardiff to Bristol, Ireland, the Midland Counties, and the Netherlands that provide us with our earlier glimpses of the first slow, faltering steps towards Merthyr Tydfil's development as the iron-manufacturing capital of the world in a later century.

Throughout the Tudor era Merthyr Tydfil and the neighbouring countryside remained attractively rural and 'very woody' according to Leland. The inhabitants of the village depended upon pastoral farming for their livelihoods, and there was a number of fairly substantial farms in or on the outskirts of the growing village. The Garth Farm behind the Pant Cad Ifor Inn at Pant, known in earlier maps as Madoc's Castle, would have been one of a number which included Blaencannaid, Tai Mawr and Nantygwenith by the end of Elizabeth's reign. Rice Merrick points out that there were a substantial number of freeholders in the parish of Merthyr Tydfil whose farms would have been prominent features on the local landscape. Cattle-breeding seems to have been of primary importance at this time. Upland Glamorgan said John Speed was 'replenished with cattle which is the best means unto wealth that this shire doth afford; upon whose hills you may behold whole herds of them feeding'.[32] One very big Merthyr Tydfil stock-breeder, Lewis William Lewis (died 1603), had owned 65 dairy cattle and 41 stores (beef cattle). He also had 360 sheep which showed the importance, too, of sheep-rearing.[33]

* We must remember that although this iron fire-back was found at the site of Pentrebach House, it does not necessarily prove that it was made at the Pontyrhun furnace or even in the vicinity of Merthyr Tydfil, although we may surmise that it was manufactured in our locality.

This emphasis on flocks and herds and on the local hills is reinforced by the tithe figures for Merthyr Tydfil extracted from the Valor Ecclesiasticus, a nation-wide survey of Church property and income compiled for King Henry VIII in 1535. The total annual tithe figure for the parish of Merthyr Tydfil was given as £20 11. 8d. of which the tithe on lambs amounted to £13. 13. 4d. and on calves and cheese £6. 15. 0d. Over half the parish priest's tithe income thus came from livestock and their products.

Horses were of lesser importance, though Leland singled out Hirwaun and Aberdare for having 'a great race and breadth of horses'. These were now beginning to be used instead of oxen as large draught farm animals, and also as pack animals, the need for which arose chiefly from the growth of the iron and coal industry in Upland Glamorgan.

The emphasis on pastoral, as opposed to agrarian farming in this area can be attributed to the handicap of climate and soil, under which the hill farmer laboured. In the parish of Merthyr Tydfil the tithe of corn amounted to only £4 6. 8d. The main crop was oats, which had a particular value as a source of winter fodder for animals as well as the making of oatmeal bread.

The later years of the sixteenth century however were to see increased attention being paid to corn growing. Merrick informs us that whereas in the 'elder time' they grew 'but small stores of corn', but 'now of late years there groweth more plenty of grain'. This new trend he attributed to 'good husbandry, toil and travail both in lining the ground and enclosing it'. Merrick did not altogether approve of it, finding now 'that the people do degenerate from their ancestors both in tallness of person and activity and lustiness.'[34]

The Merthyr Tydfil farmer did not have far to travel to market which was held in the village in the vicinity of the Church, every Monday between May and Christmas at which corn, oats, meat, general provisions and cloth were the chief products for sale.[35] Of much greater importance to the farming folk of Merthyr Tydfil and the surrounding countryside however, was the fair held outside the village on the Waun Hill above Dowlais Top. It remained throughout the sixteenth century one of the most famous livestock fairs in Wales.

Merthyr Tydfil during the Elizabethan Age, although small, was a rather more important village hamlet in the vale of the Taff than we have hitherto envisaged. Apart from the Church of Tydfil and the simple homes clustered about it, the lands of the village itself were divided about equally, between the Court and Mardy Estates, whose owners were a younger branch of the family of Edward Lewis of the Van.[36] Relatives of substantial yeoman stock occupied Troedyrhiw House. Other Elizabethan evidence informs us that a mill existed in the village. The ruins of Morlais Castle would have looked down on the fertile lands of Vaynor with its small ancient Church. Many local names testify to a region which was handsomely wooded and remained so until the late eighteenth century viz: Goetre (dwelling in the wood), Coed Cae (wooded field), Gwernllwyn (alder grove), and Gellideg (fair grove).[37]

The upper Taff region with 'its green fields, its corn lands, its merry sound of the harp at eventide, its simple recreations and uneventful life of the people'[38] must not obscure from us the fact that Merthyr Tydfil can provide glimpses of the much wider canvas of the history of Wales during the Tudor period. The lawless pattern of life in the Welsh 'Marches', the political and administrative changes brought about by the Union with England, the new opportunities afforded to the squire class, the increasing use of the Tudor law courts, the great religious drama and the new industrial scenario of these years were being staged in miniature along the Heads of the Valleys region. The Merthyr Tydfil district can claim a recognisable, if relatively small niche in the history of Wales, therefore, during the colourful age of the Tudor monarchs four centuries ago.

References

This chapter has leaned heavily upon Glamorgan County History Vol. III 'The Middle Ages' (1971) edited by T.B. Pugh, M.A., B.Litt., and Vol. IV 'Early Modern Glamorgan' (1974) edited by Glanmor Williams, M.A., D.Litt., and M. Fay Williams, M.A., and hereafter referred to as G.C.G. Vol. III or Vol. IV respectively.

1 Leland, 'Itinerary Wales', in G. Williams *GCH,* Vol. IV, p. 2.
2 Leland, 'Itinerary Wales', in the *Story of Merthyr Tydfil* (Merthyr Tydfil Teachers Association, 1923), p. 116.
3 Merrick, 'Glamorgan Antiquities', in G. Williams, *GCH,* Vol. IV, p. 2.
4 T. B. Pugh, *The Marcher Lordships of South Wales 1415-1536,* Selected documents. Univ. of Wales Press (1963) p. 25.
5 Merrick, 'Glamorgan Antiquities', in G. Williams, *GCH,* Vol. IV, Ch. I, p.44.
6 Penry Williams, "The Political and Administrative History of Glamorgan 1536-1642', *GCH,* Vol. IV, Ch. III, p.143.
7 Hugh Thomas, *A History of Wales 1485-1660* (Univ. of Wales, 1972) Ch. III, p.42.
8 Penry Williams, 'The Political and Administrative History of Glamorgan 1536-1642', *GCH,* Vol. IV, Ch. III, p.144.
9 *The Gelligaer Story*, Gelligaer U.D.C. (1959) Ch. VI, p. 49.
10 Leland, 'Itin. Wales', in J.B. Smith, *GCH,* Vol. III, Part II, Ch. VI, p. 33.
11 J.B. Smith, *GCH,* Vol. III, Ch. VI, p. 33O.
12 *Ibid.*
13 G. Williams, *GCH,* Vol. III, Part II, Ch. III, p. 152.
14 G. Williams, *Wales through the Ages,* Vol. II, (Christopher Davies 1965), p. 28.
15 G. Williams, *GCH,* Vol. IV, Ch. IV, p. 229.
16 *The Gelligaer Story,* (Gelligaer U.D.C. 1959), p. 51.

[17] C. Wilkins, *The History of Merthyr Tydfil* (Merthyr 1908), p. 89.
[18] *The Story of Merthyr Tydfil,* Merthyr Tydfil Teachers Assoc. (1932), p. 108.
[19] G. Williams, *GCH,* Vol. III, Part II, Ch. III, p. 164.
[20] G. Williams, *GCH,* Vol. IV, Part III, Ch. IV, p. 214.
[21] *The Story of Merthyr Tydfil,* Merthyr Tydfil Teachers' Assoc. (1932) p. 110.
[22] *The Gelligaer Story,* p. 58.
[23] C. Wilkins, *The History of Merthyr Tydfil* (Merthyr 1908), p. 146.
[24] *Ibid,* p. 89.
[25] D. M. Rees, *Mines, Mills and Furnaces,* Ch. IV, (H.M.S.O. 1969), p. 52.
[26] Merrick, 'Glamorgan Antiquities' in G. Williams *GCH,* Vol. IV, Ch. I, p. 5.
[27] C. Wilkins, *History of Iron, Steel and Tinplate Trades of Wales* (Merthyr Tydfil 1903), p. 14.
[28] D. M. Rees, *Mines, Mills and Furnaces,* Ch. IV, (H.M.S.O. 1969) p. 55.
[29] *Ibid,* p. 52.
[30] T. V. Davies, Letter to Merthyr Express – with reference to *Archaeologia Cambrensis* Third Series No. XXXIV, April 1863, also C. Wilkins, *History of Merthyr Tydfil,* pp. 159-160.
[31] G. Williams, *GCH,* Vol. IV, Ch. I, p. 50.
[32] Speed, 'Great Britaine' in G. Williams *GCH,* Vol. IV, Ch. I, p. 3.
[33] G. Williams, *GCH,* Vol. IV, Ch. I, p. 3.
[34] Merrick, 'Glamorgan Antiquities' in G. Williams *GCH,* p. 5.
[35] C. Wilkins, *The History of Merthyr Tydfil,* (Merthyr Tydfil 1908).
[36] *The Story of Merthyr Tydfil,* (Merthyr Tydfil Teachers' Assoc. 1932), pp. 361-367.
[37] C. Wilkins, *The History of Merthyr Tydfil.*

Acknowledgements

The author wishes to record his thanks to Professor Glanmor Williams of University College Swansea for his valuable suggestions and encouragement, to Mr. D. R. Gethin, deputy head of Cyfarthfa High School for his translation of Rhys Bychan's poem of the late fifteenth-century, and to Mr. D. Bowen, Head of the Art Department at Cyfarthfa High School for generously donating his unique drawings for inclusion in the book.

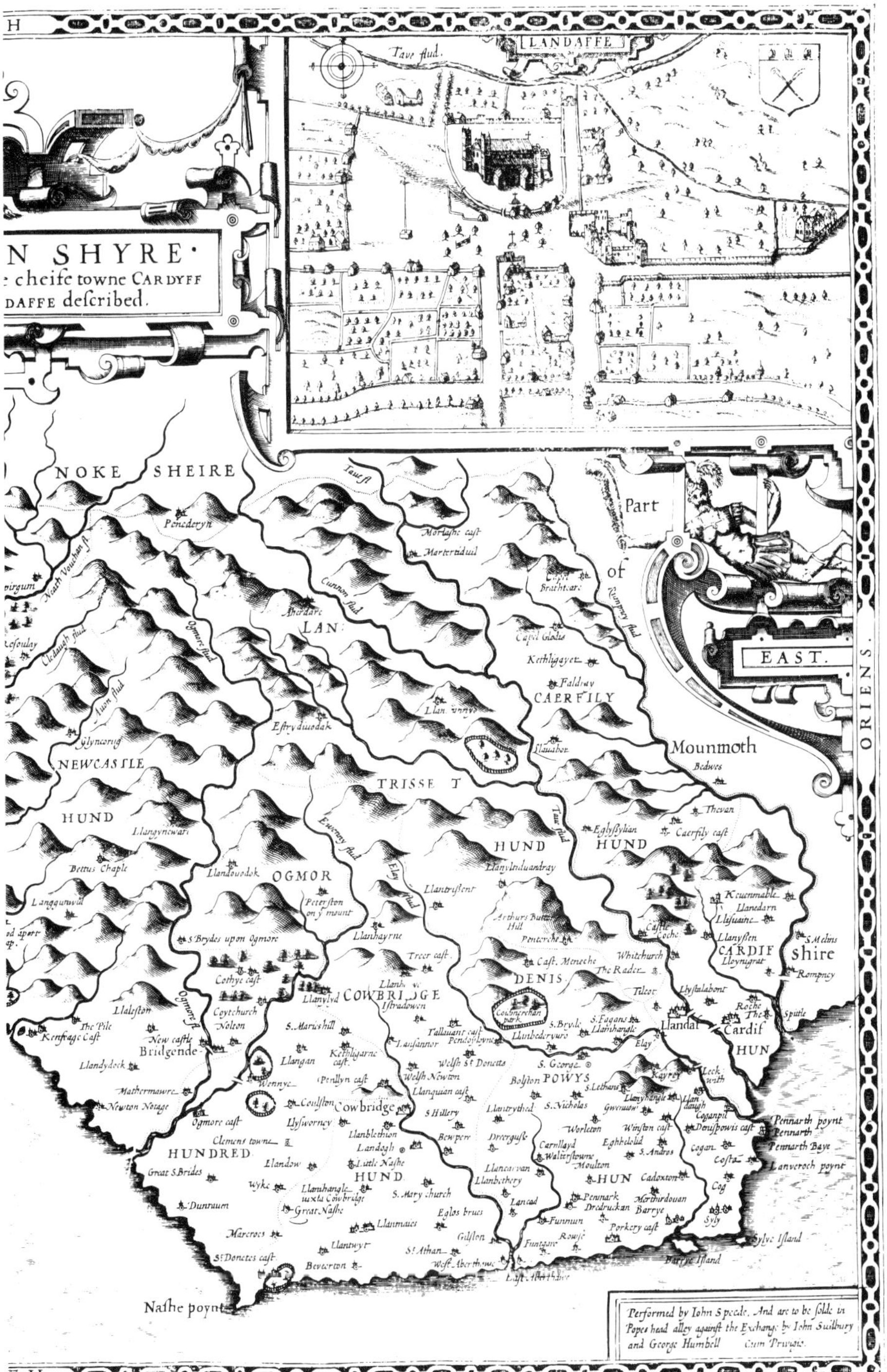

Fig. 57: From John Speed's Map of Glamorgan (1610)

The Seventeenth and Early Eighteenth Centuries

by W. MANSEL RICHARDS

A plain weather-worn, memorial stone, affixed to the west wall of Vaynor Church, nestling in the beautiful Taf-Fechan valley, north of Merthyr Tydfil, informs the visitor of the birth in the seventeenth century of the remarkable Catherine Morgan. Born in the year 1688, when the green, picturesque scenery of Vaynor, extended southward along the river valley, through the growing village of Merthyr Tydfil,—this very old lady died in 1794, aged one hundred and six years. At her death, Merthyr Tydfil was a sizeable, industrial town, on the threshold of its iron-making greatness with the largest concentration of people in Wales, living along the banks of a partially polluted River Taff*. The rustic loneliness and relative isolation of the pre-industrial Merthyr Tydfil village had disappeared, never to return.

This locally born lady[1] who was to live 'through seven monarchs' reigns' had been born into a century which was 'revolutionary' in character. A widening constitutional and religious chasm had developed between the Stuart Kings and Parliament which led to a bitterly fought Civil War in the middle years of the seventeenth century. Royalists and Anglican Church goers fought bitter campaigns against Parliamentary Round head troops and Puritans. In some instances, families became divided, sons taking opposite sides to fathers and brothers becoming each others' enemy in some of the major battles and lesser skirmishes of this Civil War. Cavalier and Royalist were defeated eventually by the troops of Parliament and the New Model Army; the doomed King Charles Stuart was beheaded at Whitehall, London in January 1649 and the Monarchy was replaced by a puritan republic soon to be dominated by Lord Protector Oliver Cromwell.

* The first census of 1801 gave Merthyr Tydfil 7,700 inhabitants.

The second half of the seventeenth century saw the 'Restoration' of the exiled House of Stuart and the return of the Anglican Church. Charles II, the colourful 'Merry Monarch', became king in 1660 to be followed by his Roman Catholic brother James II (1685-88). During these years, the deposed Puritans felt the chilling impact of persecution by fine, imprisonment and torture. But a notable landmark in the history of British 'liberty' was reached in 1688-9, the year when Catherine Morgan first saw the light in remote Vaynor. It was the year of the 'Glorious Revolution', when King James II was forced into exile and the sovereignty of Parliament over the Monarchy was confirmed. Of even more importance for the Merthyr district was the granting of religious toleration to all British subjects by the new Protestant monarchs, the Dutch-born William III (1689-1702) and his English born wife, Mary. Only one more of the House of Stuart - the childless Queen Anne (1702-14) - would there-after rule over Britain. From 1714 onwards the Stuarts were replaced by the Georges of Hanover (a north German branch of the Stuart family) who thereby ensured a Protestant succession to the British throne throughout the long life of Catherine Morgan and so, down to the present day.

Let us concentrate on local events however, during this extra-ordinary era. The opening years of the early seventeenth century saw the emergence of a strong Puritan-Dissenting faith, whose extreme Protestant message seems to have burned especially bright in the upland districts of South Wales. This was most marked along the borders of North Glamorgan and Southern Breconshire where the poor soils and damp climate presented a stiff challenge to the people. Their hard struggle for a bare existence bred a hardy, 'independent' spirit. Certainly, the Elizabethan poet-preacher Thomas Llewelyn of Rhigos may well have planted the seeds of his dissenting beliefs across this 'Blaenau' region during the later years of the sixteenth century. Isolated cottages and lonely hill-farms provided the scenes of many of these early Puritan services and some of Thomas Llewelyn's successors are thought to have held regular services at 'the lowly, white-washed farm house of Blaencannaid' on the wooded, western mountainside overlooking the village of Merthyr Tydfil.[2] Charles Wilkins, the celebrated Merthyr Tydfil historian gave 1620, as the year when these Puritans or Dissenters first met at this remote spot to hear the word of God.

Blaencannaid Farm was undoubtedly one of the very early Puritan meeting houses of Wales and as such, will always have an honoured place in the history of Welsh Puritanism.* Modern scholarship has, however, rejected the suggestion, for want of documented evidence, that there was any organised gathering of radical Protestant believers, existing as a separate Puritan Church in the Merthyr Tydfil area before the outbreak of

* Blaencannaid Farm was rebuilt in 1840. In July 1917, a filled-in doorway in the cellar of the house was opened out. A room was discovered measuring 10 ft by 8 ft.

the Civil War in 1642!* In this sense it is an exaggeration to refer to Blaencannaid as 'the birthplace of Welsh dissent'.[3] That distinction belongs to the Church of Llanfaches in the county of Gwent which was constituted as a separate Church in 1639. Nevertheless, there is little doubt that the secret Puritan services held at Blaencannaid Farm during the early years of the seventeenth century were among the first in Wales.

The villagers of Merthyr Tydfil however, in the main, seem to have been quite uninterested in this early Nonconformist movement being nurtured in the surrounding hills. Like many Welsh people during the first half of the seventeenth century, a number of them cherished the old medieval practices, more out of habit than conviction. A few were thus openly Roman Catholic in their loyalties, despite facing the possibilities of harsh punishment for their beliefs. A handful of 'recusants' (i.e. Roman Catholics who refused to attend their parish church) still existed in the Upper Taff Valley. As late as the year 1622, twenty seven persons in the county of Glamorgan were brought to court at Cardiff for refusal to attend the services of the Established Church of England.[4]

Many Roman Catholics, who at various times during the seventeenth century were persecuted as badly as the dissenting Puritans, also sought safety among the local hills. Local tradition thus claims that Pontycapel (the Chapel Bridge) at Cefn Coed y Cymmer derives its name from a secret Roman Catholic Chapel held at nearby Taimawr Farm, the home of the Edwards family at this time.

The deteriorating relationship between the supporters of King Charles I and Parliament led to the outbreak of Civil War in the year 1642. The Welsh people, in the main, remained loyal to the King's cause and Wales came to be regarded as 'the nursery of the King's infantry'.[5] By the summer of 1645 the Royalist fortunes were, however, on the wane following decisive defeats in the English battles of Marston Moor and Naseby. The King returned to South Wales at this time, in an effort to raise more men and extra revenue. At Llandaff he was met by one of his influential Glamorgan supporters, Colonel Edward Pritchard of Llancaiach Mansion (near Nelson) (see Plate 32) who, together with other prominent royalists had gathered together a force of over 4000 men. The King's reception however, was partly hostile. He received complaints concerning the appointment of Englishmen to command the King's troops in Wales, the insolent and high-handed demeanour of some of these Cavalier officers and the savage behaviour of the Royalist troops as they plundered their way across South Wales.

When the disappointed and ill fated King left Cardiff for the northward journey to Brecon, tradition has it that he was entertained, on August 4th, 1645, at Llancaiach Mansion (Plate 32) by Colonel Edward Pritchard. The

* The arguments in support of this viewpoint are to be found in *Merthyr Historian* Vol. 1, p.91 (Merthyr Tydfil Historical Society) - Glanmor Williams - 'Earliest Nonconformists of Merthyr Tydfil'.

King and his followers were then escorted over Gelligaer mountain. Silhouetted sphinx-like on the distant skyline, Penyfan, the highest peak in the Beacons, must have acted as a sign post to their destination, the town of Brecon.[6] Charles Stuart's heart must have been heavy, though a sad smile may have rewarded the loyalty of those folk who perhaps climbed the nearby hills, to see the King pass along the old Roman track, on the high moorland above Dowlais Top.

The King's mission in South Wales, upon which so much depended, had been a failure. Charles reached Brecon Priory on August 5th, where he was received by Sir Herbert Price, the Governor of the town and its castle. Here, he stayed the night and it is perhaps significant, that on that same night he wrote the well-known warning letter to his son - 'Charles, it is very fit for you to prepare for the worst. Wherefore my pleasure is, whensoever you find yourself in danger of falling into the rebels' hands, that you convey yourself to France and thence to be under your mother's care . . . This is all at this time from your loving father, Charles R.'[7]

The depressing tone of this letter was matched by events. In a battle at Brecon 700 Royalists were either killed or taken prisoner, and the town and county were taken for Parliament. Meanwhile, the county of Glamorgan passed to Parliament even more quickly, within a few days in fact of the King's departure from Llancaiach House. The King's recent host Colonel Pritchard, with a number of other former Royalists, went over to the Parliamentary cause and by September 1645 were in command of Cardiff Castle.

Large numbers of people in both counties nevertheless, remained firm for the King, despite the fact that they were watched by Parliamentary spies. Among the most ardent of these local Royalists were John Thomas Williams, a native of Merthyr Tydfil and the High Constable of Caerphilly, who in the year 1647 promised to provide the King with a band of fully armed men at his own expense. The important Lewis of the Van family who still owned extensive estates, in and around Merthyr Tydfil also remained staunch supporters of the Stuart monarchy. The troops of Oliver Cromwell are believed to have destroyed their ironworks at Pontygwaith (below Merthyr Vale) although the Lewises escaped capture.*

The arrival of these Roundhead troops in the neighbourhood had been occasioned by a Royalist rising in Glamorganshire in the year 1648. Colonel Horton, the commanding officer of Cromwell's force was despatched south from Brecon to put down this Royalist threat to Cardiff. Eight thousand men rallied to the King's cause, but were routed by Horton's professionally trained forces in the fields of St Fagans outside Cardiff. This Battle of St Fagans on May 5th 1648 was to be the most important single event of the

* One of Lewis' partners in the ownership of Pontygwaith iron-works was Thomas Cook, an Englishman, who married a local girl from Cefn Forest. Their farm near Treharris was thereafter to be named Ty Cook.

Civil War in South Wales. It is possible that men of Royalist sympathy from the Merthyr Tydfil area fell on those fertile, green fields that day.

There is a local tradition that while travelling towards Merthyr Tydfil from Brecon, Colonel Horton's soldiers caught sight of the solid ruins of the 13th century Morlais Castle and effected its complete destruction.* A few hours later, these same Puritan soldiers were stabling their horses a few miles down the valley inside the Parish Church of Merthyr Tydfil.[8]

These middle years of the seventeenth century (1640-1660), the era of the Civil War and the Puritan Commonwealth emboldened the Puritans living in the upper Taff Valley. They sought revenge for their earlier persecution and discovered a new assurance and confidence. This led to their open and increased activity in the Merthyr Tydfil district. Walter Cradock, one of the most well known zealots of these years, wrote of their extra ordinary ardour and energy:

> 'I have observed and seen in the mountains of Wales, the most glorious work that I ever saw in England. The Gospel is run over the mountains between Breconshire and Monmouthshire as fire in the thatch.'[9]

Further evidence of local Puritan activities during these same years comes from the parish records, written by the bitterly anti-Puritan Rector of Merthyr Tydfil, Nathan Jones. He clearly wished to see those fires extinguished as quickly as possible.

> 'We have in the parish of Merthyr Tydfil, a company of men and women combined, who have a long time been accustomed to have unlawful conventicles (meetings), wherein they have settled government as they please, contradictory to the statues and ordinances.'[10]

He informs us wretchedly that they refuse to pay tithes, removed the Bible from the pulpit of the Parish Church as he was about to preach, rang the Church bells to disturb the services and entered the Church from the nearby tavern to smoke their pipes.** One of their more physical members, Richard Jones, the Parish Clerk, even pulled this Rector from his pulpit on one occasion tearing his vestments in the process. They used the Parish Church for business purposes and were determined only to allow preachers of 'godly' Puritan persuasion to minister unhindered.[11]

Nathan Jones was not the only Anglican clergyman to suffer from Puritan fervour. The gentle breezes of the green Vaynor valley also felt the winter gusts and cold winds of this stormy era. The old and long serving vicar of Vaynor, Josias Morgan had his divine service rudely interrupted one

* This seems a very improbable tradition as it is difficult to appreciated why Colonel Horton and his troops should have found it necessary to embark on what would have been a costly, laborious and time-consuming operation.

** Wilkins informs us that a 17th century map shows the Parish Church and a tavern marked Penfynwent - Head of the Graveyard. It is possible that this Inn became the Three Salmons of a later date, and later, Eggafords Shoe Repairing Shop.

Sunday morning. At a given signal, several of his dissenting parishioners walked into the little Church during his sermon, dragged him from the pulpit and violently pushed him through the narrow doorway. A local miller of Puritan beliefs by the name of Reynallt Morgan then ascended the pulpit and preached doctrines more radical and vigorous than any member of the congregation had ever heard before.[12]

These puritan outrages became widespread. The bells of the Parish Churches of Merthyr Tydfil and Gelligaer were sold, the ancient monuments and carvings of Llandaff Catherdral were effaced and the organ broken to pieces. The font of Bedwas Church in neighbouring Monmouthshire was placed under a 'ewe-tree to water horses and cattle in'. Christ College, Brecon meanwhile was also seized by the Breconshire puritans who carried away its silver plate and ornaments and nearly pulled down the building itself. The small mountain Church at Cefn Forest, overlooking Troedyrhiw had ceased to exist as an effective place of Anglican worship for the farmers and ironworkers of the area, if we are to believe the Rector of Merthyr Tydfil, Nathan Jones. In 1650 he wrote, 'There is a hamlet in the parish 4 or 5 miles from the Church, which had a chapel and was duly served by the curate of the parish. It is now abolished and become a dwelling house. In this hamlet there are not more than three attending the services and there are about 50 householders who seldom come to Church and many with their families are in a sad condition'.[13]

During the late 1640's and 1650's when Oliver Cromwell's Puritan régime was supreme, an energetic and creative attempt was made to convert Wales wholly to Puritanism. This was done in two main ways: by the building of puritan schools and the appointment of puritan preachers to replace the Anglican clergy. In 1650 an Act for the better Propagation and Preaching of the Gospel in Wales (known as the Propagation Act) became law. One of its objectives was the establishment of state-sponsored schools to educate people away from Anglicanism to the puritan faith. Not for the last time in its history, Merthyr Tydfil was in the forefront of a pioneering educational development. One of these Puritan schools was set up in Merthyr Tyfil and the relatively high salary of its schoolmaster, William Walters, £20 in the year 1651, suggests it was one of the most important Puritan schools in Wales. Whether from lack of classroom discipline or by active encouragement on the part of Mr Walters, the Puritan schoolboys of Merthyr, according to Nathan Jones, endangered the Church steeple by removing its lead![14]

The other effect of the Propagation Act was to deprive the Anglican clergy of their livings. A body of seventy commissioners were appointed by Cromwell's Government to enquire into complaints against the clergy and to reject those whom they considered unfit. Surprisingly, the local Rector, Nathan Jones, survived, although about three hundred clergy in Wales were dismissed, including the old Vicar of Vaynor, Josias Morgan and the Rector of Gelligaer, Robert Covey.

It became necessary to find others to take their place and so a body of twenty-five 'Approvers' were empowered by this Act to select 'Godly and Painful men' to preach the gospel in Welsh. Among these Approvers were such Welsh Puritan stalwarts as Cradock, Morgan Llwyd and Vavasor Powell. The men appointed as preachers were to receive a state-stipend of £100 a year. But it was a difficult task as the number of Puritans in Wales was small. They found it necessary therefore, to establish a system of itinerant or travelling preachers.

In spite of the undoubted sincerity and 'godliness' of these preachers their work met with considerable criticism and hostility. They were not men of learning, even when we make allowances for the prejudice contained in Nathan Jones' description ... 'preach they cannot, unless they be sent; teach they cannot what they never learnt.'[15] Scorn and contempt were also poured upon them by one of the most notable Glamorgan poets of the seventeenth century, Edward Dafydd of Margam (1600-78). In his poem 'Cerdd y Ffanaticiaid' (Poem of the Fanatics) he cites Blaencannaid Farm as a conventicle (meeting place) and refers to Howel Lewis as a Baptist with 'a party of Highland Tribesmen about him'.[16]

Nevertheless, many of these itinerant preachers of this period were to lay the foundations of Welsh Nonconformity. Of those ministering in the Merthyr Tydfil area, the best known and most powerful were Jenkin Jones, Edward Jenkins, Henry Williams and, of course, Howel Lewis of Blaencannaid. Jenkin Jones had earned himself a respected reputation, fighting both in the Parliamentary armies and in the pulpits for the salvation of souls. Edward Jenkins and Henry Williams were more Independent in outlook, the latter remaining a powerful and influential dissenter in the Merthyr area for many years after 1660.[17]

Meanwhile, the Puritan or Dissenting faith was developing strongly elsewhere in the neighbourhood. Colonel Edward Pritchard of Llancaiach, the lapsed Royalist, recently converted to the Puritan cause and now imbued with great religious zeal, gathered groups of dissenters to his impressive Elizabethan home. Tradition has it that this small stately mansion gave birth to the very strong Baptist cause in the Gelligaer district of Glamorgan.[18] Other nonconformist pioneers were soon drinking deeply of the waters of dissent at nearby Berthlwyd Farm, overlooking Quakers Yard, which also holds a special place in the early history of the Baptist cause in the South Wales valleys.[19]

This southern area of the Merthyr Tydfil district is even better known however, for its associations with a unique group of Puritans, known as 'the Quakers'.

These were persecuted more bitterly than others, especially in the grimly retaliatory years following the Restoration of 1660. They came to be regarded by the authorities of the time as especially sinister extremists and zealots capable of undermining the established order in society and religion. They appear to have penetrated into the Merthyr Tydfil district by the year

1656 and worshipped at first with other Puritan groups at lonely Blaencannaid Farm. Elsewhere in South Wales however, other Puritans did not exude the same warmth and encouragement towards them. Thus Joshua Miller, the Puritan minister of St Andrew's Church, Cardiff showed his pique and anger towards local Quakers, whom he alleged, interrupted his services. 'I have never met with such railing, reviling, brawling spirit or heard the like . . . such words . . . I have had from them . . . that the Oyster women of Billingsgate would blush to name.'[20]

It was not long before ministers of Puritan sympathies were refusing even to bury Quakers within their churchyards. It became necessary therefore for them to consecrate their own burial yards. By 1665 these Merthyr Quakers had moved downvalley to the tiny hamlet of Rhydygrug (Ford of the Heather) where they built their own burial ground. A village, known as Quakers Yard was to grow and develop over the years.*

The Puritan faith clearly, had developed and prospered in the upper Taff Valley during the middle years of the seventeenth century when Britain was ruled as a Puritan Republic, under the firm and 'godly' control of Oliver Cromwell. This was greeted with not unexpected disgust by the anti-Puritan Rector, Nathan Jones. In condemnatory mood, he wrote:—

> 'I am sure we have 5000 men and women in the parish that received not the Lord's Supper these ten years and many children unbaptized.''[21]

This figure of five thousand is open to serious doubt, but it does suggest perhaps that the population of the Merthyr Tydfil district was rather more numerous than hitherto supposed in the century before the industrial revolution.

The relatively isolated village of Merthyr Tydfil meanwhile retained its country-like, agricultural appearance throughout the late seventeenth and early eighteenth centuries. Lying in the shadow of the Parish Church in the heart of the village were two inns, - the Penfynwent** or Head of the Church Yard (later The Three Salmons) and the Star. Not far from the simple, thatched dwellings scattered around the Church of St Tydfil was a Mill and the Parsonage with the green fields and hills of the Mardy and Court estates, centred on the nearby large, stone houses of those names. The wider Parish contained another stone house of substantial proportions at Troedyrhiw, all three of these houses belonging to the Lewis of the Van family until the early eighteenth century.[22] Among the 93 farms in existence at the close of the seventeenth century (according to Charles Wilkins) were Blaencannaid, Cwm y glo, Tai-mawr and Nanty-gwenith, while further down valley were located Hafod Tanglwys, Troedyrhiw, Ty Cook and Pen

* This burial ground measured 51 feet by 34 feet and was surrounded by a stone wall 6 feet high. The last burial took place in 1891. The Merthyr Tydfil Borough Council undertook a project in 1974 by which the burial ground was given a concrete surface.

** The site today of Eggafords Boot and Shoe repairing workshops.

Graig Fargoed (near Trelewis). These farms continued to graze cattle and sheep on the surrounding hillsides and corn crops wavered in the upland breezes. The farmer and his family lived simply on barley bread, pork and butter milk. He produced the shoes on his feet and the coat on his back. Small woollen mills appeared by the sides of streams at Gellifaelog, Melin-Caiach near Treharris, Melin Cannaid on the Cannaid stream and at Cefn Coed along the Taf Fechan river.

By the early eighteenth century, the sheep of the region far outnumbered cattle, although the major part of the farmers' capital was tied up in their cattle.[23] Professional drovers herded cattle, sheep and geese from the villages of North Glamorgan, along the old tracks to Hereford, Gloucester and London. These remarkable men were the messengers, bankers and news-vendors of those times. Some of the more eminent drovers of North Glamorgan, in the century before the industrial revolution, were Walter Edwards of the Parish of Ystradofodwy (Rhondda) and Thomas Richards who died in 1795 and is buried in Aberdare Parish Churchyard.[24]

Records of the time refer to the trades and professions of other people in North Glamorgan and its surrounding area, besides the agricultural population. We read of lawyers, doctors, weavers, smiths, cobblers, carpenters, saddlers, masons, inn-keepers, butchers, millers and tailors. But in this beautiful, handsomely-wooded but rather lonely valley in Upland Glamorgan, the bulk of the people remained poor, simple farmers throughout the seventeenth and early eighteenth centuries.

The century of the Stuarts saw a continuation of the earlier development in Tudor times of the small scale industrial activities along the western side of the upper Taff Valley. By the opening of the eighteenth century the small, iron furnaces, those 'fires of Vulcan', appear to have declined and disappeared at Pontygwaith, Pontrhun and Blaencannaid. Coal-mining on a limited scale had become of greater local significance. There were coal workings on the Waun near Dowlais, and at Hirwaun, but the smallness of local demand and the difficulties of transporting coal any distance precluded major developments during the seventeenth and early eighteenth centuries. In this respect, the Merthyr Tydfil district did not compare with the Neath and Swansea regions with its rich coal deposits and good port facilities for export. Nevertheless, thick coal seams were present, just a few feet below the surface soil on the hill slopes surrounding the village communities of Upland Glamorgan and Gwent. Local farmers and villagers would hardly miss the opportunity of winning this coal, especially in such places as Cwm y Glo where it could be easily mined by tunnels driven into the hillsides.[25]*

* Cwm y Glo means 'Valley of Coal', where there was a large number of outcropping seams. Wilkins mentions Cwm y Glo Farm as flourishing as early as 1600, many years before coal was worked for industrial purposes. We can assume therefore that the farmers of the early seventeenth century extracted its coal on a small scale, describing the source of their supply as 'Cwm y Glo' (F.J. Pedlar, *History of the Hamlet of Gellideg M. T.*, 1930, pp.38.39.

Quite early in the seventeenth century, we have documentary evidence of coal workings in the Cantref of Senghennydd, in the northern part of which Merthyr Tydfil was located. Thus on February 7th 1611, William, Earl of Pembroke granted to Philip Williams, 'the right to dig coal and quarry stone in all the common lands or forests in Senghennydd supra . . . for 21 years at the yearly rent of 10 shillings'. In another lease, dated September 21st 1619, similar rights were granted to William Lewis of Merthyr for 99 years . . . at the rent of 40s per annum.[26]

At about the same period, Sir John Stradling, one of the ablest of the well known family of St Donats and a member of Parliament and Sheriff of Glamorgan (died 1637) was writing a ballad on the mineral riches of Upland Glamorgan:[27]

'And in Glamorgan's hille parts
Cole greatly doth abounde.
For goodness and for plenty too
Its equal never was founde',

Apart from its value as a fuel, coal also became recognised during the seventeenth century as a valuable commercial commodity and, in consequence, a number of small capitalists emerged who were determined to exploit these coal deposits of the upper Taff region. We have no local entrepreneur to compare with Sir Humphrey Mackworth of Neath who estimated that his coal works in Neath had brought him a return of over £40,000 between the years 1695 and 1705. Nevertheless, a number of gentlemen farmers from south Glamorgan and some local peasant farmers directed their capital and energies into the hills of North Glamorgan. Thus the inventory of Edward Herbert of Cogan near Penarth, 'a gentleman farmer' shows that he held 'one grant under ye Earl of Pembroke of ye coalworks and lyme kilns within ye parish of Merthyr Didvill [sic] for 99 years'. William Edward meanwhile, yeoman farmer of Eglwysilan bequeathed to his wife 'all that coal-workes, pitts and veins of coal together with the lime kilns and quarries of stones . . . situated . . . in a place called Tule Dowlais . . . within the parish of Merthyr Tydfil'.[28]

From these, and other seventeenth century records, it is clear that coal from the Merthyr Tydfil district was well known as a fuel. Small mines and drifts supplied coal to the villages and farms of southern Breconshire, north Glamorgan and upland Gwent. It was carried in baskets and sacks, on the backs of mules and horses and lime was often brought back on the return journey. Certainly, small-scale coal mining ventures were probably more numerous than we have hitherto imagined in the upper Taff valley during the seventeenth and early eighteenth centuries.

On the other hand, the iron furnaces and forges along the western side of the Taff which had flourished under the Sussex ironmasters in the late Tudor period, were, in turn to decline during the century of the Stuarts. By the year 1625 the Pontrhun (Troedyrhiw) Works were in the possession of a Thomas Erbury. The Pontygwaith furnace, a little to the south, later possibly destroyed by Colonel Horton's Roundhead troops was owned by the wealthy Lewis of the Van family and their English partner, Cook.

A variety of factors probably contributed to the decline of Blaencannaid, Pontrhun and Pontygwaith furances. Severe competition from the Forest of Dean and other iron-making regions, the effect of the partial destruction of some of them by Roundhead troops, and the gradual reduction of charcoal fuel in their immediate vicinity due to the inevitable thinning of trees, would have made a damaging impact on these works in an area of very limited local demand.[29] Certainly, by the time the literary traveller, Daniel Defoe was passing through the area in the year 1723, no mention was being made of iron-making or the appearance of furnaces or forges. Instead, passing through the Merthyr Tydfil area in that year, Defoe described 'a most agreeable vale opening to the South, with a pleasant river running through it called the Taaffe'.[30]

These 'iron furnaces' had disappeared from the Taff Valley landscape, not to reappear until that lone furnace at Dowlais under the managership of Staffordshire's John Guest blazed forth a new and great iron-making tradition in the period of peak demand after 1759. Within forty years, the village of Merthyr Tydfil was to be transformed into the largest town in Wales.

Let us return however, to the religious history of the last half century of the Stuart era which can be divided into two distinct and recognisable phases. An era of renewed Puritan Persecution during the reigns of Kings Charles II and James II 1660-1685; and the Age of Religious Toleration under the rule of King William and Mary and Queen Anne 1689-1714.

On May 25th 1660, some twenty months after the death of Oliver Cromwell, Prince Charles, the handsome, exiled son of the executed Charles Stuart, landed at Dover. Later, he was crowned King Charles II with Cavalier pomp and splendour in Westminster Abbey. The Church of England was restored with the Stuart Monarchy. Bitterly anti-puritan in temper, that Church instituted an immediate Anglican backlash in harsh and intolerant reaction to the Puritan regime of the 1650's. There followed nearly thirty years of trouble and persecution for dissenters or non-conformists of all persuasions, who were not loyal to the Anglican Church.

These strict and repressive laws knowns as 'the Clarendon Code' were put into force almost immediately by the Cavalier Parliament of the early 1660's. The effect was to put the clock back twenty years. Local Puritans once again, were forced to worship in fear and trembling; to conceal themselves from the malice of spies and informers; to endure excommunication, fines, imprisonment and distraint of goods and property and to face the hostility of bishops, constables and churchwardens.

The dissenting Puritans in the Merthyr Tydfil district struggled on bravely during these years of post-Restoration oppression. In the year 1661 a number of local Quakers including Lewis Beck (carpenter) and John Harris were imprisoned in the County Gaol at Cardiff for attending a meeting in the Parish of Merthyr Tydfil.[31] By 1665 these and other Quakers had moved from the environs of Merthyr village and Blaencannaid Farm to Rhydygrug, as the later village of Quakers Yard was then named. Two years later, they built their own burial yards after leasing a small plot of land between the rivers Taff and Bargoed from Mary Chapman, a Monmouthshire widow. They were further encouraged by a visit from their famous founder, George Fox.[32] In his 'Journal' he could give the district no name; he refers to a journey from Pontypool to Swansea when he 'went over the hills'. One source, written many generations later, suggested that he dined with a group of Quakers at Cefn Forest. Some years after the visit of Fox, William Penn, another prominent Quaker and founder of Pennsylvania on the North American Continent, is alleged to have visited this tiny Taff hamlet. There is no documentary evidence to support his visit however and the tradition seems improbable.*

The Merthyr Puritans meanwhile, further up-valley were encouraged in their struggle for religious freedom by a visit in 1668 of one of the greatest Welsh Puritans, the lion-hearted Vavasor Powell. He preached bravely to large and eager congregations from an open-air pulpit, near the Parish Church of St Tydfil. But the new Rector, Gregory Jones who had succeeded old Nathan Jones, no doubt angry at such open defiance of the law and possibly jealous of the receptive open-air crowds, informed the justices at Cardiff. Soldiers later arrested Vavasor Powell at Merthyr Tydfil. Following a series of trials, he was placed in the Fleet Prison in London where he died in 1670, aged fifty three years. In this way, Vavasor Powell, one of the great Welsh figureheads of the seventeenth century, while preaching religious liberty had his own personal freedom taken from him while visiting the small village of Merthyr Tydfil in the year 1668. He may well have regarded this visit to Merthyr Tydfil as his own, personal experience of the Garden of Gethsemane.

Dissenters were compelled once again, to conduct their meetings in remote and secluded locations. The Rector, Gregory Jones, reported to the Bishop of Llandaff that hundreds of Puritans attended these meetings or 'conventicles' at the homes of such courageous local stalwarts as Howell Rees and Philip and Joan Morgan.[33] We have no records of where these were located. They may have been remote local farmsteads. There was an inevitable return of large numbers to lonely Blaencannaid Farm which soon proved inadequate for the increasing membership.

In the year 1669 the faithful transferred therefore along the mountainside to the even more secluded Cwm y Glo Farmhouse. To avoid suspicion, its barn was stored with hay during the weekdays and emptied for secret

* Fox Street, Penn Street and Fell Street in Treharris are reminders of the connection of the district with these famous Quakers over three centuries ago.

services on Sundays by the sympathetic owner.[34] This simple farm building was to remain the spiritual home of the Merthyr dissenters for a further twenty years, until 1689, when the coming of the 'Protestant monarchs', William and Mary, enabled the government of the day to introduce the Toleration Act, the effect of which was to give religious tolerance (but not equality) to all dissenters.

No longer was it necessary for these Nonconformists to hold their meetings in secret barns or in private houses. There commenced a programme of chapel-building in different parts of Wales. A new generation of preaching-ministers also underwent a more organised and improved method of training. They proved of considerable assistance to those wandering preachers who had served the widely-separated and isolated churches of Upland Glamorgan and who had fanned with such vigour 'the Fire in the Thatch'. One of these newly-trained ministers was David Richards who was ordained at Merthyr Tydfil in the year 1688.[35] (The year of Catherine Morgan's birth.)

Of greater significance locally, was the decision to erect a more permanent chapel at Cwm y Glo. It was no longer necessary to build in such a lonely, isolated mountain glen, but perhaps the spot had too many traditions and fond memories to be foresaken. It is possible too that the Cwm y Glo dissenters were not convinced that religious toleration was a permanent reality. Thus a sixty year lease was obtained from the landowner Captain David Morgan of Hensol and a stone chapel built in 1690. This replaced the nearby farm at Cwm y Glo where the dissenters had worshipped since 1669. The new, partially-hidden chapel at wooded Cwm y Glo (a building similar to Welsh barns of the time) was to remain the nerve centre of Nonconformity in north Glamorgan for a further 60 years.*

The years 1689-90 had been of major significance to the folk of the upper Taff valley and surrounding districts. It brought an end to the intense, if fluctuating persecution faced by dissenters, which had stretched back to the beginning of the seventeenth century and beyond. Both Quakerism and the old, indigenous Roman Catholic faith were spent forces, although a handful of adherents lingered on.[36] On the other hand, the clergy of the Established Church of England appear to have been relatively prosperous in the Merthyr Tydfil district by the end of the seventeenth century.

These Anglican clergy at Merthyr Tydfil, Vaynor and other surrounding parishes were able to claim their customary income from glebe (or church) lands, regular surplice fees for baptisms, marriages and burials together with service offerings on Sundays and Holy-days. A nation-wide Book of Valuations, published in the year 1680 illustrates that among the most financially desirable livings in the County of Glamorgan were those of

* Some of the tall, overhanging trees at Cwm y Glo were cut down in the year 1879. Deeply embedded in them were some iron-hooks, to which it is possible, the faithful had tethered their horses, while at worship. (F. J. Pedlar, *History of the Hamlet of Gellideg*, M.T. 1930).

Merthyr Tydfil and Gelligaer with annual values of £20 5s. 9d. and £20 7s. 9d. respectively.[37] An even more lucrative source of income came from 'tithes', a tenth of their produce paid annually by local farmers to the Parish Priest. One such fortunate clergyman was William Watkins, the Rector of Vaynor. On June 19th 1689, he signed a new, modified form of a more ancient agreement, which seems to have given him a regular and substantial income from the farming folk of the green Taf-Fechan valley[38] viz:

> June 19th 1689 – In the Reign of William and Mary. – It is covenented, concluded and agreed upon, by, and between the Freeholders and the rest of the Inhabitants of the same . . . to be kept and observed, according to the former custom, from henceforth in manner as followeth:—
>
> 1st Every owner of sheep to pay the tenth fleece of wool and half a fleece out of five for want of ten.
>
> 2nd Every owner of sheep to pay a lamb out of every ten and half a lamb out of every five.
>
> 3rd Calves to be tithed at Allhallowtide.
>
> 4th Corn, the tenth sheaf thereof.
>
> 5th Colts, a penny a male, and half-penny a female.
>
> 9th Offerings (at Easter) 3d every married couple to the parson, and 2d to the sexton; a widow or widower 1d and a half. Every single person above the age of sixteen one penny.
>
> 10th Fees for marrying, baptizing and burying-to the parson 6d; to the sexton 2d.
>
> 12th* Churchyard to be fenced by the Parishioners – For every person interred in the Chancel ten shillings to the Parson.

The year 1689 had been of national importance and of no little significance, it appears, to this parson of Vaynor. An earlier Rector, Josias Morgan had possessed only 'a very indifferent parsonage house and about 27 acres of glebe' in the year 1609.[39] By the year 1721 however, over a century later, Vaynor was valued at above £50 a year. Other livings in the County of Glamorgan were far less substantial however according to Thomas Price, the Rector of Merthyr Tydfil who wrote 'many poor clergymen are not able to purchase more than bare food and raiment for their families.'[40] These latter clergy, however, may well have been the unbeneficed curates, who had to depend very largely on whatever stipends their rector or vicar chose to allow them.

By the end of the Stuart Era (1714), the Merthyr Tydfil district was again the scene of some educational activity, due mainly to the efforts of an important society known as the Society for the Propagation of Christian Knowledge (S.P.C.K.), the charity of a couple of wealthy, local, christian gentlemen, and the initiative of Thomas Price, the Rector of Merthyr

* This latter clause suggests that only those Vaynor parishioners of means could expect to find a last resting place inside the Church. The majority were buried in simple graves within the surrounding Churchyard.

Tydfil. Only seven of the sixty schools established in Wales by the Puritan Commonwealth had survived the Stuart Monarchy's Restoration of 1660. These did not include the Merthyr Tydfil school, nor its well-paid Puritan schoolmaster, William Walters. By the year 1662, Hugh Lloyd, the Bishop of Llandaff was bewailing the absence of schools in his diocese 'Glamorgan . . . is utterly destitute of schools.'[41]

The Restoration Government and the Established Church who were now responsible for education, appear to have been quite indifferent to the instruction of the people. They seem to have preferred to persecute Puritan ministers, rather than provide parish schools for the nation's children. Thus upland Glamorgan had to await the formation of the important charitable movement – the S.P.C.K. in 1699.

This important Society received powerful support in South Wales from the rich Neath industrialist, Sir Humphrey Mackworth and from Thomas Price, the learned, early eighteenth century Rector of Merthyr Tydfil. To the latter must go the credit for the translation into Welsh of the Society's publication which were distributed among the prisons of Wales.[42] By 1716 however, 'the badness of the air obliged' Thomas Price 'to quit his residence at Merthyr Tedvil'.[43]

Another educational philanthropist with local connections was the unfortunate Thomas Lewis of the Van who founded three S.P.C.K. schools in Merthyr Tydfil during the years 1713-14. He was forced to abandon any further educational enterprises owing to the £10,000 fine imposed upon him for his Jacobite sympathies and support for the Old Pretender in 1715. This crippling punishment necessitated the sale of his Merthyr Tydfil property, the Court Estate, including the Court House (today's Labour Club), which had been in the possession of his family for centuries. In the same year, a charity was set up under the terms of a will belonging to another member of the Lewis family – Edward Lewis of Gilfach Fargoed in the nearby Parish of Gelligaer. This was to be the pre-cursor of the long-established Lewis School, Pengam.[44]

Popular education in Wales was to receive its major stimulus, a little later, from the Circulating Schools, initiated and organised by the remarkable Griffith Jones, Vicar of Llanddrwror in Dyfed. However, it must not be forgotten that a substantial number of schools, founded by charity movements and rich landowners, were already in existence in Upland Glamorgan between the years 1699 and 1735. Thus on January 21st 1713, the curate of Margam was informing the S.P.C.K. that 'there is hardly a parish in that part of the world where there is not a private school for teaching children to read'[45] One was most certainly situated at Merthyr Tydfil, which together with its three S.P.C.K. schools gave the district some educational tradition, long before the arrival of the Circulating Schools of the mid-eighteenth century.

By the opening years of the eighteenth century, the effect of the civil wars and religious upheavals of the seventeenth century, no longer troubled the rural calm of Upland Glamorgan. Nonconformist services at Cwm y Glo were subjected, no longer, to external interruption; Quakerism down the valley appeared a spent-force; open air services at its burial yard were discontinued, it seems, after one of the drunken revellers, who came to disrupt the proceedings, fell into the river and was drowned.[46] The Established Church at Merthyr Tydfil village and Vaynor co-existed sleepily with its lusty, dissenting neighbour at wooded Cwm y Glo, where the worshippers were, in the main, farmers, tradesmen, and craftsmen of some economic importance.[47] Among their number were Llewelyn Sion Llewelyn, the blacksmith-bard of Cefn Coed y Cymmer and Edward o'r Gurnos, a former sentinel on the nearby slopes during earlier years of persecution.* With others, they helped to sustain this lonely, stone built, mountain-side chapel as the Mother Church of Merthyr Dissent during the first half of the eighteenth century.

Peace and unity among the members however, did not prevail at Cwm y Glo during these later years. The atmosphere of fellowship and co-operation produced during the long years of persecution, unfortunately came to a bitter end. The Chapel's lease of sixty years, signed in 1689, was coming towards the expiry-date, while the membership had become divided over doctrinal interpretations and theological disputes.

The Calvinist group, who were inclined to Independency, led by the moderate and tolerant Reverend James Davies, soon found the new, younger co-Pastor Richard Rees possessed views not to their taste. Living on the opposite hill-slopes, on his lonely farm at Gwernllwyn Uchaf, Dowlais, the Reverend Richard Rees became the zealous leader of the Arminian faction at Cwm y Glo which broke away to set up a Church at nearby Cefn Coed y Cymmer. In 1747 this Unitarian-inspired Hen dŷ Crwdd opened its doors for the first time, while the Independents established themselves two years later at Ynysgau on the banks of the Taff on the edge of the Merthyr village.[48]**

Catherine Morgan of Vaynor had been born into the Merthyr Tydfil district in the late seventeenth century. Her girl-hood memories would have been the stories recounted of secret conventicles at Blaencannaid, Cwm y Glo and Berthlwyd Farms. The tale of a doomed King's lonely journey along a nearby mountain track and the threatening tramp of Roundhead boots passing through the district might well have impressed the youthful Catherine. The stories of Puritan outrages at Merthyr village and Vaynor would have been part of local lore. During her early years, Merthyr Tydfil was the dissenting stronghold of South Wales, centred on Cwm y Glo Chapel on the slopes of Aberdare Mountain. Here, the 'Fire in the Thatch'

* Edward o'r Gurnos was born at Cwm y Glo Farm in 1694 and died in 1800, aged 106. A tablet to his memory was placed at Ynysgau Chapel (demolished in 1966). It was removed to Soar-Ynysgau Chapel, Merthyr Tydfil.

** The Aberdare folk who worshipped at Cwm y Glo established their Unitarian 'Old Meeting House' in Mill Street, Aberdare in 1751.

burned fiercely! Life remained simple, based on agriculture, the main inhabitants of Merthyr, 'a village of about forty houses in 1696' being 'hedgers, ditchers, farm-labourers, a few craftsmen, a store-keeper, several publicans, the parson and the squire.'[49] The river and the streams teemed with fish, game abounded in the hillsides, the upland hills were covered with grass, bracken and peat, the lower slopes had a heavy growth of deciduous trees, among which were pastoral lands, hay and corn fields. The faithful attended church or mountain-side chapel on foot or on horse-back.

Long before her death in 1794, the old dissenters had opened their chapels at Hen dŷ Cwrdd and Ynysgau. Their numbers would soon be increased here and elsewhere. New religious energies were also being unleashed within the Anglican church in the wake of the great Welsh Methodist Revival. Howel Harris of Trevecca, the famous revivalist preached in Merthyr on several occasions. Meanwhile the extraordinary genius of Hywel Rhys, the remarkable stone-cutter and poet-philosopher, cast its influence over the green Vaynor valley and far beyond. The first furnace was operating at Dowlais where a number of farms had been converted into agents' houses and warehouses, while many others were 'tipped over' and 'so undermined the foundations of others by coal and iron-works that they eventually tumbled down'.[50] Cyfarthfa, with its first furnace erected in 1765 was especially ruthless and almost immediately twenty farms were engulfed by the growing Cyfarthfa Works and its neighbouring tips.

A new era of economic and social transformation was reaching along the Heads of the Valleys, centred on the Merthyr Tydfil district. Old Catherine Morgan had been a child of the late seventeenth century and early eighteenth century, when the last rulers of the Stuart dynasty and the first of the Hanover monarchs were to occupy the throne of England and Wales in the pre-industrial era. She lived long enough, however, to see the dawn of an industrial era which would transform a whole kingdom, and no part of it more than Merthyr Tydfil and the valleys of South Wales .

References

[1] J. E. Jenkins, *Vaynor, Its History and Guide* (Merthyr Tydfil 1897), p. 31.

[2] C. Wilkins, *The History of Merthyr Tydfil* (Merthyr Tydfil 1908), p. 169.

[3] *G. Williams, Merthyr Historian* (Merthyr Tydfil Historical Society 1976), Vol. 1, Ch. 10, p. 85.

[4] T. Richards, *The Religious Census of 1676* (London 1927), p. 82.

[5] J. G. Williams, *Wales and the Civil War – Wales Through the Ages,* Vol. 2, (Christopher Davies 1965), p. 62.

[6] *The Gelligaer Story* (Gelligaer U.D.C. 1959), p. 52.

[7] M. Owen, *The Story of Breconshire* (Cardiff 1911), p. 69.
[8] *The Story of Merthyr Tydfil* (Merthyr Tydfil Teachers' Association 1932), pp. 119-121.
[9] G. Williams, op. cit. p. 85.
[10] *Ibid,* p. 87.
[11] *The Story of Merthyr Tydfil,* op. cit. pp. 119-121.
[12] C. Wilkins, op. cit. pp.89-90.
[13] *Ibid,* pp. 167-168.
[14] *The Story of Merthyr Tydfil,* op. cit. pp. 119-121.
[15] Thomas Richards, *The Puritan Movement in Wales 1639-1653* (London 1920), Ch. 16, p. 155.
[16] R. I. Parry, *Notes on the Aberdare Valley* (Aberdare 1964), p. 18.
[17] Merthyr Historian, op. cit. p. 86.
[18] *The Gelligaer Story,* op. cit. p. 53.
[19] G. Davies, *An Historical Survey of Treharris and District* (Unpublished essay).
[20] M. F. Williams, *Glamorgan Quakers 1654-1900* (Morgannwg 1961), Vol. 5, p. 52.
[21] Merthyr Historian, op. cit. p. 87.
[22] C. Wilkins, op. cit. pp. 138-141.
[23] M. W. Williams, *Glamorgan County History,* Vol. IV (Univ. of Wales 1974), Ch. VII, p. 325.
[24] E. Greening, *A History of Aberdare* (1967), Ch. 6, p. 21.
[25] *Ibid,* p. 25.
[26] C. Wilkins, *A History of the Iron, Steel and Tinplate and Other Trades of Wales* (Merthyr Tydfil 1903), p. 19.
[27] E. Greening, op. cit. p. 24.
[28] *G.C.H.,* Vol. IV, op. cit. pp. 364-465.
[29] D. M. Rees, *Mines, Mills and Furnaces* (H.M.S.O. London 1969), p. 58.
[30] *The Story of Merthyr Tydfil,* op. cit. p. 143.
[31] G. Davies, op. cit.
[32] M. F. Williams, op. cit. p. 60.
[33] *The Story of Merthyr Tydfil,* op. cit. pp. 127-128.
[34] T. Lewis, *The History of the Hen Dŷ Cwrdd, Cefn Coed y Cymmer* (1947), p. 15.
[35] Merthyr Historian, op. cit. p. 91.
[36] *G.C.H.,* Vol. IV. Glanmor Williams, Ch. IX, p. 475.
[37] *G.C.H.,* Vol. IV. E.T. Davies, Ch. IX, p. 437.
[38] J.E. Jenkins, op. cit., p. 18-20.
[39] T.J. Harris, *Education in the Parish of Vaynor prior to 1870* (Cefn Coed and Vaynor Local History Society 1966), p. 1.
[40] E.T. Davies, op. cit., p. 438.
[41] *Ibid,* p. 449.
[42] *Ibid,* pp. 454-455.
[43] T.J. Harris, op. cit., p. 3.
[44] E.T. Davies, op. cit., p. 455.
[45] *Ibid,* p. 449.
[46] M. F. Williams, op. cit. p. 65.
[47] Merthyr Historian, op. cit. p. 94.
[48] J.S. Rees, *The History of Ynysgau Church, Merthyr Tydfil* (1954), pp. 7-8.
[49] *G.C.H.,* Vol. IX, op. cit., p. 372.
[50] *Ibid.*

Acknowledgements

I wish to express my thanks to Professor Glanmor Williams of the University College of Swansea for his invaluable advice and encouragement and to Mr. Dewi Bowen, Head of the Art Department, Cyfarthfa High School, for kindly providing his drawings.

Jacobitism

by ROBERT S. EVANS

On 10 June 1688 a son was born to Mary of Modena, the Queen of James II. James' pro-Roman Catholic policies had alarmed a great number of Englishmen who took solace from the fact that James would be succeeded by his Protestant daughter, Mary. The birth changed this, a line of Roman Catholic Kings seemed inevitable. To ensure that this did not happen several Englishmen sent a letter to William of Orange, Mary's husband, inviting him to come to England. This set in motion a train of events which culminated in the deposition of James and the offering of the crown to William and Mary. In the Bill of Rights which accompanied the offer it was laid down that no Roman Catholic could succeed to the English throne. James and his son were therefore excluded from the throne.

Many were, however, unwilling to accept this situation. Tories, in particular, who were characterised by their support of the church and the throne, refused to accept that Parliament had the power to depose a monarch. They remained true to James until his death in 1701 when they transferred their allegiance to his son, James Stuart, known to us as the 'Old Pretender'. Such supporters were known as 'Jacobites' (from the latin Jacobus - James).

Jacobitism was very strong in Wales. This is hardly surprising since the landed gentry, who dominated Welsh politics, were largely Tory. For example, in 1713, 23 of the 27 Welsh Members of Parliament were Tories. Loyalty to the Stuart cause in many cases dated back to the Civil War.

Two Jacobite Societies flourished in Wales. In North Wales, the 'Cycle of the White Rose' was founded on White Rose day (10 June) 1710. Its most influential member was Sir Watkin Williams Wynn of Wynnstay. In South Wales the Society of Sea-Sergeants was founded in 1725. It met annually at Tenby and other sea ports to drink the health of 'the King over the water'. Its most influential member was John Phillips of Picton Castle.

Jacobitism was not confined to the gentry. Many farmers were also Jacobites; locally Jacobite feeling was strong. William Llewelyn, a local antiquarian of the nineteenth century, tells the story of a local farmer living at Pen Craig Fargoed farm who was a devoted adherent of the Stuarts. He had borrowed a guinea from a friend, but on meeting him on a subsequent occasion could not pay the debt. He asked for an extension of the loan in the following terms:

> 'Three things I should like much to see:
> Longer loan of your guinea;
> See the Pretender gain the throne;
> And with French money pay your loan.'

This anecdote illustrates the strength of Jacobite feeling in the area. There were two prominent local Jacobites, Lewis of the Van, a landowner of some substance from Caerphilly, and David Morgan of Pengraig Taf.

In 1715, the Old Pretender made an unsuccessful bid to overthrow the Hanoverians. There was strong support for him in Wales. Riots took place in Wrexham and Pembrokeshire. Squires used clubs to break up loyalist meetings. Lewis of the Van's actions were less spectacular, he made several speeches in favour of the Pretender. For these indiscretions he was fined £10,000. To pay this fine he was forced to sell the Court Estate including the Court House (now Merthyr Labour Club).

David Morgan was born in 1693. His father was William Morgan of Coedygorres; on his mother's side he was descended from two illustrious local families, the Matthews of Gwaeth-voed and the Stradlings.

David was raised in the family home at Penygraig Taf, high on the mountainside near Pontygwaith. Little is known about his early life; the first event of which we have record is his matriculation at Christ Church College Oxford in 1711. He made the law his profession and was called to the Bar at the Middle Temple in 1721. He practised frequently at Westminster but undoubtedly found time to visit Penygraig which became an important meeting place for local Jacobites.

In 1745 Charles Edward Stuart, known as the 'Young Pretender' or Bonnie Prince Charlie and to David Morgan as the 'White Rose of Arno's Vale', made his attempt to restore the Stuarts. This is known as the 'Forty-Five'.

He left his exile in Italy and travelled to Nantes, avoiding the British Mediterranean fleet which, coincidentally, was commanded by Admiral Matthews, a cousin of David Morgan. From Nantes he sailed to Moidart where he landed on 25 July 1745.

David Morgan, who was well informed of Charles' movements, set out to join him. It is said that he stopped at the Llancaiach Smithy to have his horse shod. He is reported to have told the blacksmith, 'You are against me now, but when I return you will be all with me.'

He journeyed to Preston where he joined Charles' army on its march southward. He immediately impressed Charles by his enthusiasm and courage, something which seemed to be lacking in his Highland supporters. Morgan was offered the Colonelcy of a troop of Manchester men, which he refused, probably because he hoped to command a regiment of South Wales men whom he confidently expected to join the rebels in the near future. Morgan therefore had no commission, but he was active in raising arms and ammunition. He became a trusted friend and advisor of Charles and was often called 'the Young Pretender's Counsellor'.

Morgan must have cut an impressive figure for, as Charles Wilkins says, 'he wore a white cockade in his hat, a sword by his side and (was) mounted on a bay horse.'

Morgan's enthusiasm was not matched by other Jacobites. The number of English and Welshmen who joined the rebels was pitifully small. Gradually Charles began to turn his attention from men like Morgan who urged bold and decisive action to the Highland chiefs who advocated retreat. On 'Black Friday', 6 December 1745, the Jacobites reached Derby where Charles decided to retreat, a retreat which was to end disastrously at the Battle of Culloden in April 1746.

David Morgan was mortified by the decision. He refused to retreat; saying he would rather hang than starve. At Ashburn in Staffordshire he left the Pretender's army and made his way to Stone where he was arrested on suspicion of being a member of the Pretender's Army. He was imprisoned for eight months at Newgate.

His trial took place in July 1746 'for having been in Arms at Derby . . . and adhering to the King's enemies'. The evidence against him was overwhelming. He was found guilty and sentenced 'to be hanged by the neck, but not until death; to be cut down alive, bowels taken out and burned before the face; head severed from the body, and the body divided into four quarters, to remain at the King's disposal'. This gruesome penalty for treason was carried out a few days later at Kennington Common. In the intervening period his wife, of whom we know very little except that she married David Morgan when he was a law student, comforted him. She pleaded for mercy for him, but to no avail; he was as doomed as the cause he had courageously supported.

Bibliography

C. Wilkins, *History of Merthyr Tydfil* (1903).

NUT, *History of Merthyr Tydfil* (1932).

D. Williams, *History of Modern Wales*

P.D.G. Thomas, 'Eighteenth Century Welsh Politics', in *Wales through the Ages,* Vol. II, ed. Roderick.

New Cambridge, *Modern History*, Vols. V & VII.

Political History in the Nineteenth and Twentieth Centuries

by RICHARD MORGAN

Merthyr Tydfil in the nineteenth century was considered to be 'the most radical constituency in the whole of Great Britain'. The rural village of the eighteenth century had by the middle of the nineteenth century become one of the most important iron making centres in Great Britain and had experienced a massive increase in population. The origin of the radical tradition of the town goes back to the seventeenth century where meetings of Dissenters took place even before the outbreak of the Civil War. In the eighteenth century the radical attitudes of the inhabitants became apparent in their politics. By the beginning of the nineteenth century the dissenting congregations had moved towards unitarianism and chapels had been opened at Aberdare and Cefn Coed y Cymmer. They soon embraced the most militant and energetic element of the town drawing support from a close knit group of schoolteachers, farmers, craftsmen and small business men. It was these Unitarians who had been prominent in the Cyfarthfa Philosophical Society where support had been given to the revolutionary ideas of Republican France. These Unitarians were to play a significant role in the development of radical politics in Merthyr and their influence was to be felt throughout the century.

As Merthyr expanded into a major iron and coal centre during the nineteenth century, thousands of Welsh people flooded into the town. These immigrants or 'dynion dwad' poured into Merthyr from the surrounding countryside attracted by the higher wages and the greater opportunities of town life. They were drawn chiefly from Glamorgan itself with the remainder coming from West and North Wales. Merthyr almost overnight became the biggest town in Wales and a totally Welsh town at that.

This influx of population, particularly those from rural Wales, strengthened the non-conformist character of the town. To many of these people the chapel was a tangible reminder of the way of life which they had left behind. They became centres not only for religious worship but for social gatherings, and through the Sunday School movement did invaluable educational work. Many of the political issues of nineteenth century Wales were ecclesiastical issues which prompted a specific Non-Conformist reponse. This is undoubtedly one of the threads that run through Merthyr politics throughout the century.

To this Welsh radical Non-conformity was added another vital ingredient which was to shape the political character of the town – the deplorable living and working conditions of the overwhelming majority of the population. All the worst aspects of the Industrial Revolution were to be found in Merthyr – long hours of work, low wages, child labour, overcrowding, insanitary housing, disease and child mortality. Three-quarters of deaths were under the age of five. Life expectancy among the working class was about twenty-two years. The workers were completely at the mercy of economic factors beyond their control. There was little in the way of poor relief and the unfortunate soon became victims of the hated Court of Requests run by local shopkeepers with the purpose of confiscating goods from destitute workmen. Trade recessions usually meant unemployment, wage cuts and, inevitably, an increase in social tension.

Workers regarded their methods of payment as being unjust. Many ironmasters (although Crawshay was a notable exception) owned truck or Tommy shops. Workers received all, or part, of their wages in tokens which had to be spent in these shops where prices were generally 25-30% higher than other shops. Some firms also employed the Long Pay system, paying wages at monthly intervals or even longer. This inevitably meant workers ran up large debts.

There is little evidence of organised resistance among the working class during the early years of the 19th century, although from the earliest days there were spasmodic outbreaks of violence. In 1801 Aaron Williams, a labourer at Cyfarthfa and Samuel Hill, a collier, were hung for organising a revolt.

There were serious strikes in 1816 during the depression which followed the end of the Napoleonic wars. It was at this time that the notorious Scotch Cattle began their activities although they were confined chiefly to the Monmouthshire valleys.

In the years 1830-32, Britain was in the grip of the Reform Fever – the hated Tory Party who had held power for 60 years had at last been defeated and a Whig Government elected which was pledged to reform the corrupt and unfair political system. At the same time, Trade Unionism which had only been legalised in 1824 was being organised on a national level by Robert Owen, a native of Newtown. There was considerable interest in both these movements with the impetus for reform coming from Unitarians, but also from William Crawshay, the owner of the Cyfarthfa Iron Works who had been encouraging his workers to agitate for reform. Street marches and meetings were held and attacks were made on the homes of prominent Merthyr Tories. At the end of May 1831, William Twiss, a well known Trade Unionist, together with a Welsh interpreter, visited the town with the purpose of enlisting support for Robert Owens' National Association for the Protection of Labour. The Reform agitation and Trade Union activity coincided with an economic slump which resulted in unemployment and wage cuts causing considerable distress. Twiss addressed a meeting at Waun Hill where the agitation for reform and a National Union was soon lost in local grievances. Speakers began to attack the revenues of the Church of England but the subject which aroused the wrath of the crowd was the Debtors Court. Led by Lewis Lewis known as Lewsyn yr Heliwr, the crowd marched on the court, destroyed it and attacked its administrator, Joseph Coffin. Many of the confiscated possessions of the Workers were re-possessed and the middle class who had now lost control of the situation sought refuge in the Church. The Iron Masters meeting at the Castle Hotel sent for the troops.

The Argyll and Sutherland Highlanders arrived from Brecon and were followed to the Castle Hotel by an angry crowd. There is some confusion as to the events which led the military to open fire but it is likely that the crowd, who had been addressed by Lewis Lewis, attempted to disarm the soldiers and enter the Castle Hotel. The soldiers opened fire on the crowd of whom at least 20 were killed and scores more injured. Many of the soldiers were also hurt and they were obliged to retire in some disorder to Penydarren House where they awaited re-inforcements.

All roads into Merthyr were now besieged by the workers who began organising themselves along military lines. Several notable successes were achieved, particularly the disarming and dispersing of the Swansea Yeomanry. They approached from the West and were met at Clwydyfagwyr where they were relieved of their weapons and sent back in disgrace. An ammunition train was stopped at Cefn Coed and a force of 100 cavalry sent to clear a road was beaten back near Crew Pitch.

However, the failure to take Penydarren House was to prove disastrous for the workers. Troops were now pouring into Merthyr from all directions. A great meeting was held on Waun Hill on Monday June 6th at which the Iron Masters first pleaded with and then threatened the crowd with the consequences of their action. The Riot Act was read and the failure of the crowd to disperse led the military to prepare their weapons for firing. Faced with this massive military power, the people dispersed and the uprising petered out.

The sequel of these events were of greater importance than the uprising itself. The Whig Government and particularly, Lord Melbourne, the Home Secretary were anxious to prove that the Whigs were just as capable of maintaining law and order as their Tory opponents. A large number of people were tried and convicted at the Glamorgan Assizes, twelve including two women were convicted to be transported while two were condemned to death. One of these two was Lewis Lewis who had undoubtedly played a prominent part in the insurrection. He was however, reprieved in somewhat mysterious circumstances and transported to New South Wales.

Considerable controversy surrounds the role played by the only man who was executed – Richard Lewis, better known as Dic Penderyn who was born in Pyle near Aberavon and not in nearby Penderyn as the name might suggest. Merthyr Historians differ in their account of the part played by Dic Penderyn in the riots, Dic being presented by some as virtually an innocent bystander while by others, as second only to Lewis Lewis in importance. Lewis was accused of stabbing Private Donald Black in the affray outside the Castle Hotel. At the trial the only substantial evidence against him was the testimony of James Abbot the barber who had a long-standing feud with Dic. This evidence convicted him.

Despite a huge petition organised by Joseph Price, the Neath ironmaster and three letters from the Judge at the trial, Judge Bosanquet, the Home Secretary, stood firm believing that, unless the government took a firm stand, violence and trade unionism (which he regarded as synonymous) would sweep through South Wales. Dic Penderyn was executed at Cardiff at 8.00 a.m. on 13th August, 1831. Dic's last words 'O Arglwydd dyma gamwedd' – 'O Lord what an iniquity' – were not lost on the massed crowds who saw him executed and escorted his body to Aberavon, permission for burial at Merthyr having been refused.

An ironic postcript to Dic's execution was the confession to the crime by a Welsh emigrant to America on his deathbed some 40 years after the event.

Apart from the emotionalism which surrounded and still surrounds the execution of Dic Penderyn, the riots were undoubtedly of major significance in the history of Merthyr Tydfil and South Wales. The Trade Union movement began to make its presence felt and within a short time the employers retaliated by locking out workers at the Dowlais and Plymouth Works. The radical influence was strengthened rather than weakened in the town and the radicals exercised their power through their new M.P. Sir John Josiah Guest and by taking control of the Board of Guardians.

The bloody uprising of 1831 was instrumental in giving Merthyr its Parliamentary seat by the Reform Act of 1832. Sir John Josiah Guest, owner of the Dowlais Ironworks, was returned unopposed in 1832 having previously represented Honiton. Sir John Guest represented the constituency until his death in 1852 and there is little doubt that he belonged to the liberal wing of the Whig Party reflecting the radical views of his constituents. In a speech to his constituents in 1832 he spoke on the evils of the Tithes and Slavery and stressed the need for Free Trade and an extension of the educational system. His main business rival, William Crawshay, had little interest in politics and, with the exception of the 1837 Election, he supported Guest.

The Constituency which had been created in 1832 consisted not only of the town of Merthyr but the scattered villages down the valley, and Aberdare and its surrounding villages including Penderyn. Although the population of the Constituency was estimated in 1831 as being about 30,000 only about 500 or 2.4% of these were enfranchised almost all of the voters being drawn from the Middle Class 'Shopocracy'. Very few of the labouring multitude would *have lived* in premises where they paid £10 a year rent. Even in 1865, when the population of Merthyr and Aberdare and the surrounding villages was estimated at 70,000 there were only 1,387 registered voters, of whom only 126 were working class. The small number of voters and the existence of the Open Ballot suggests that Merthyr Tydfil may well have been a 'Pocket' borough – that is in the pocket of the local Ironmasters. This was certainly the case to some extent, contested elections being something of a rarity. However, it is only fair to point out that much of the population of a town so dependent on the Iron Works were satisfied that they should be represented by one of the 'iron' masters, particularly as both Guest and his successor H.A. Bruce reflected the radical views of their constituents and perhaps just as important, enjoyed the support of the other Iron Masters.

The passing of the Reform Act and the election of Sir J.J. Guest as M.P. brought little immediate improvement for the people of Merthyr Tydfil. Disillusionment with the limited nature of the Reform Act, the savage repression of Trade Unionism and the harsh administration of the 1834 Poor Law Amendment Act which introduced the Workhouse System, led to support for the Chartist Movement. This movement had originated in London in 1836 when a group of working class men led by William Lovett, founded the London Working Men's Association. In May 1838, this body published the 'People's Charter' from which the name of the movement was derived. The Charter made six demands – annual Parliaments, universal male suffrage, equal electoral districts, the end of property qualifications for M.P.'s, the payment of members and a Secret Ballot. Significantly, its aims were political rather than social and economic and its purpose was to change the existing constitution in such a way that the working classes, who formed the bulk of the population, should have a controlling influence over the government of the country.

The first meeting of the Chartists in Merthyr took place in October 1838 when a Working Men's Association was established with Morgan Williams, a weaver – proprietor – journalist of Penrheolgerrig as its first secretary. At first, Merthyr Chartists were dominated by the influence of the Carmarthen lawyer, Huw Williams, but within a short time, Merthyr had won the reputation of being a leading political centre in its own right. By the Autumn of 1839, there were several thriving Chartist Lodges in the Merthyr Area.

In the early 1840's Chartist Lodges met at Public Houses like the Cross Keys, at Bethel Chapel in Dowlais and the Unitarian Schoolroom of David Evans in Georgetown. The best known meeting place, however, was the 'Three Horse Shoes' a pub owned by Daniel Llewellyn of Georgetown. As the movement increased in popularity so also did the number of meeting places – at one time there were thirty in Georgetown alone. The large open public meetings usually took place at Caedraw, Dowlais and on the hill near Morgan Williams' home at Heolgerrig. At the height of Chartist activity in the Summer of 1842 weekend meetings were drawing crowds of up to 1,000. Heavy subscriptions were levied on the members and some of this was spent on the purchase of fire-arms, while much went to encourage the Chartist Movement in other ways, particularly in the distribution of information. Money was sent from Merthyr to help in the defence of Frost, William & Jones after the Newport uprising.

The most famous event in the history of Chartism in South Wales was the Triple advance on Newport led by John Frost, Zephaniah Williams and William Jones. The march, which culminated in an attack on the Westgate Hotel, Newport with considerable loss of life, was disorganised and disrupted by rain. Considerable argument centres around the non-appearance of the Merthyr Chartists on this march. The Merthyr Chartists tended at this time to be a moral rather than a physical force* and this may have been the crucial factor. Perhaps it was simply poor communication, while it has been suggested that the presence of troops at Dowlais may have prevented action. However, the years that followed saw Merthyr established as the centre of the Chartist Movement in Wales. The success of the movement was reflected by the signing of petitions, massive meetings and a flourishing press, of which 'The Advocate and Merthyr Free Press' and 'Udgorn Cymru' with a joint circulation at one time of 12-15,000 were the best known.

The Government became seriously alarmed at the strength of the Chartist movement in Merthyr and spies were sent in to report on Chartist Meetings. 1842 was a crucial year in Chartist History – a year of distress caused by wage cuts and unemployment, political agitation and industrial action and it was rumoured that armed men were being drilled on Merthyr mountain. In August 1842 the men of Staffordshire and Lancashire launched the first general strike in British history. Merthyr alone of the mining towns in South Wales joined the strike which was condemned by the Home Secretary, Sir James Graham, as being politically motivated. He said 'You have in Merthyr some dangerous men deeply involved in the Chartist conspiracy, which has given life and impulse to this insurrectionary movement'. The reaction of the Merthyr authorities to the strike was swift and severe; more troops were brought into the area; a proclamation was issued against future meetings and the Iron Masters of Cyfarthfa and Dowlais dismissed known Chartist leaders. Reports were sent to the Home Secretary by a spy known as William Griffiths who infiltrated Chartist Meetings at the 'Three Horse Shoes' in Georgetown.

The leaders of the Chartists in Merthyr were drawn from the middle and 'better' working classes. Most of them were not connected with the Iron

* Moral force Chartists believed that the strength of their arguments would win government support for the Charter, whereas the Physical force Chartists believed that violence should be used, if necessary, to secure the Charter's aims.

Works and a study of their occupations tends to confirm the view of Captain Napier, the Chief of Police, that 'every other tradesman in the town at heart cherishes Chartist principles'. In 1843 the Secretary of the Chartist Committee was David Morgan a shoemaker, while the Chairmen were Evan Williams, a butcher and Timothy Davies, a tailor. Undoubtedly, Chartism gave the opportunity to men such as these, as well as Trade Unionists, Ministers and others, to denounce the evils, political, social and economic which they saw around them. These men continued the radical tradition present at the end of the 18th century which had manifested itself during the Reform Crisis of 1830-32. Many of the issues upon which they turned their attention seem to have little direct relation to the six points of the Charter. The monarchy was a favourite target. David Ellis in a speech in October 1842 spoke with indignation when he said that 'he had just heard that the Queen was in the family way again and he supposed that the monkey was going to fill the country full of Idlers'. The corruption of the Bishops and the iniquities of tithes were also subjects guaranteed to enjoy popular support. Another issue on which the Chartists were particularly sensitive was the increase in the size of the professional police force which they considered had been done simply to 'put down the liberties of the people'.

The severe repression of late 1842 and the improvement in the economic situation during the 1840's, led to diminution in Chartist activity. There was a temporary revival in 1848 and meetings continued into the 1850's, but the radicalism of Merthyr inspired by events in Ireland, France and Germany was now channelled into a variety of Reform societies which continued to inject political ideas into the working class. The Reform League found particularly fertile soil in Merthyr and the basis was laid for the momentous election of 1868.

1868 stands as a landmark in the political history of both Merthyr and Wales. In Merthyr the defending member, the man who had held the seat since the death of Sir J.J. Guest in 1852, was Mr. H.A. Bruce later Lord Aberdare. Born in Duffryn Aberdare, he was called to the Bar in 1837 shortly afterwards taking a position of Stipendiary Magistrate at Merthyr Tydfil. He became one of the trustees of the Dowlais iron works and continued the tradition by which Merthyr was represented by the 'iron interests'. As the candidate of the ironmasters, at a time when the franchise was restricted, he was virtually invincible. However he was by no means complacent about his position and he played a full part in the government of the town and did much philanthropic work. On a National level he was also successful being appointed Secretary of State in the Home Department in 1862 and he was already being talked of as a future Home Secretary, a position which he achieved during Gladstone's first ministry 1868-72, after his defeat in Merthyr Tydfil and when he had become M.P. for Renfrewshire.

The election of 1868 saw three candidates contesting two seats, the Merthyr constituency having been granted an extra seat by the 1867 Reform

Act. The three candidates were the retiring member H.A. Bruce, Richard Fothergill, an ironmaster and coal owner with powerful interest in both Aberdare and Merthyr, and finally Henry Richard, a rank outsider in every respect, noted for his championing of the rather unpopular cause of international pacifism and his aggressive defence of Welsh nonconformity. The result, perhaps one of the biggest electoral upsets in the history of Wales, saw Richard top the poll with 11,683 votes to Fothergill's 7,139 and Bruce's 5,776.

Undoubtedly the obvious difference between this election and previous ones had been the increase in the number of voters resulting from the 1867 Reform Act. All male householders had been enfranchised and in the Merthyr constituency this had meant an increase in the number of voters from 1,300 to 14,000. Voting was still open and the voters were still theoretically subject to the same pressures as they had always been. However there had been signs during the fifties and sixties that the power of the iron interests in the constituency were in decline. Penydarren, Hirwaun and Aberaman had all closed in the ten years prior to the election and there were persistent rumours that Cyfarthfa and Plymouth were threatened. At the same time there had been an increase in the coal interests of the constituency particularly in the Aberdare area. One result of this was that the united front of the employers which had always been a feature of the constituency was now weakened – the interest of the iron masters and the coal owners frequently being in conflict.

More crucial perhaps was the increasing militancy of the working class of Merthyr and Aberdare. During the 1850's and 1860's there were a series of strikes by both iron-workers and colliers, the latter emerging as the most organised element of worker protest. The miners protested as much against the deplorable working conditions and the lack of any form of consultation and representation as they did against the cuts in wages which inevitably followed the fluctuation in the country's economic fortunes. A new antagonism had developed between employer and employee. Previously, despite times of stress, there had been a feeling of mutual interest – that the interests of the worker and the owner were inter-dependent. By 1868 a definite rift had appeared, a 'them and us' situation – 'Men now believe that the masters are oppressors, that they look upon the workers not as men of flesh and blood but rather as kinds of machines for the minting of money'.

The strike of 1867 reflected the changing attitude – anger at the cuts in wages, over the enforcement of the double shift system and a strong feeling of resentment over what the workers considered to be inhuman treatment: it was in this atmosphere that the 1868 election took place and the newly enfranchised workers of the constituency showed their political strength.

However, the man who topped the poll, Henry Richard, had not gained a reputation for championing the cause of the industrial worker. He represented another powerful element in the constituency – radical nonconformity. The fifties and sixties had seen Nonconformists of all shades united by the injustices under which they suffered and the feeling had grown that only political representation could improve the situation. This aggressive nonconformity present in the Riots and Chartism was rekindled by the crushing indictment of the Welsh people and particularly of Welsh nonconformity made by the 1847 Report on Education in Wales – a report which became known as 'Brad y Llyfrau Gleision' (The Treachery of the Blue Books). Henry Richard led the storm of indignation which swept the principality and which gave ammunition to the Liberationist Society – a society formed in 1842 to co-ordinate the fight for religious equality, Disestablishment and Reform. Dissent emerged as a powerful political force throughout Wales and nowhere more than in Merthyr Tydfil. Although noted more for its sin than its sanctity, Merthyr was strongly Nonconformist. The Chapel cut across class barriers, uniting the radical middle class with new-found unity and strength of the working class. Both gained in mutual respect and self confidence and readily adopted the radical doctrine of the Liberationist society. It is this interest which Henry Richard represented – he stood as a working class, Welsh nonconformist Liberal and it was the Welsh working class nonconformist which gave him his memorable victory. Significantly he was assisted throughout his campaign by many men who had been active in the Chartist movement two decades previously. The influence of the industrialists in the election can be seen in the success of Richard Fothergill who employed thousands of workers in the constituency. Bruce tended to get most of his support from the Dowlais and Penydarren area where iron interests were still strong.

Henry Richard and Richard Fothergill were re-elected in 1874 despite the intervention of a new candidate, Thomas Holliday, who appealed for support as 'the working man's representative'. Holliday collected 4,912 votes to Richard's 7,606 and Fothergill's 6,908. He undoubtedly lost some credibility because he was supported by the Marquis of Bute. By the time of the election of 1880, Richard Fothergill had fallen into financial difficulties and he decided not to seek re-election. The Liberals put forward Charles Herbert James to fill the vacant seat. James, from an old Merthyr family, had always been a staunch supporter of Henry Richard and nonconformist issues. Richard and James were opposed by the Conservative W.T. Lewis, later Lord Merthyr, who was also supported by the Marquis of Bute. It was the first time that an acknowledged Conservative had fought the constituency and there was considerable bitterness both during and after the contest. Richard and James campaigned on the by now familiar issues of religious equality, arbitration, extension of the franchise, and for reforms of the penal system, the Licensing Laws and the Land Laws. The results saw Richard top the polls with 8,035. James was also elected with 7,256 while Lewis trailed behind with 4,445; Richard and James were returned unopposed in the elections of 1885 and 1886 but the death of the former and the retirement of the latter in 1888 necessitated by-elections which saw the election of Liberals D.A. Thomas and W. Pritchard Morgan

The passing of Henry Richard in 1888 marks the beginning of the transition in Merthyr from the radical nonconformity of the nineteenth century to the election of Keir Hardie in 1900. Richard had personified issues and values which although still powerful were beginning to lose their grip on the industrial valleys of South Wales. Richard's contribution to his constituency, to Wales and to the cause of international peace stands second to none. Although he is better known for his stand on Nonconformist issues than for his interest in Welsh affairs, he was always conscious of his language and culture and in a speech to his constituents in 1881 he declared that he had always been mindful of three things:

'Not to forget the language of my country, not to forget the people and cause of my country and to neglect no opportunity of defending the character and promoting the interest of my country.'

Henry Richard combined the love for his country with the desire to work for international co-operation and conciliation.

The Merthyr constituency inherited by D.A. Thomas and W. Pritchard Morgan differed from that won by Richard twenty years earlier. The Ballot Act of 1872 had made voting secret and the number of voters had been increased yet again by the Reform Act of 1884-5. The character of the town was also changing. The iron works faced with stiff competition from Germany and the U.S.A. was now in definite decline and Merthyr, once the largest town in Wales, had slipped behind Cardiff and Swansea and was soon to be overtaken by neighbouring Aberdare.

Despite these changes Merthyr remained firmly Liberal and was considered one of the safest Liberal strongholds in the British Isles. Yet there was a danger for the Liberals in this strength. Complacency set in and Liberal organisations in the constituency went into decline. The troubles of the Liberal party in the Merthyr constituency stemmed from the conflict arising over the nomination of a successor to Henry Richard in 1888. The Liberal Association had promised to nominate a working man as candidate but had gone back on its pledge. They in fact supported Ffoulkes Griffiths a Baptist barrister from London who had been prominent in the 'Cymry Fydd' movement. Griffiths, although supported by the sitting member D.A. Thomas and by the Liberal estbalishment, was well beaten by W. Pritchard Morgan who also stood as a Liberal. Morgan's success was undoubtedly due to the fact that he was supported by the working class who felt let down by the official Liberal nomination of the middle class Ffoulkes Griffiths. Morgan, whose search for gold had taken him to Australia and Korea (he was referred to disparagingly by his opponents as 'Yr aelod dros China' – the member for China), canvassed enthusiastically as the working man's candidate. Pritchard Morgan's fiercest critic was his fellow Liberal M.P., D.A. Thomas, a man of an altogether different mould.

D.A. Thomas had been born at Ysguborwen, Aberdare. After getting a 2nd Class Honours in Maths at Caius College, Cambridge, he returned to the Merthyr area and soon became involved in local affairs. At the age of 31 he was returned as Liberal M.P. in place of Charles Herbert James. He soon dominated the constituency to such an extent that he virtually dispensed with the local Liberal associations, a move which was to have disastrous consequences for the future of the party in Merthyr. D.A. Thomas soon emerged as one of the most powerful figures in Welsh politics. He had inherited the Cambrian collieries in the Rhondda and Aberdare Valleys and he was active in Cardiff Chamber of Commerce, an organisation representing the new capitalist class of coal owners, shippers, exporters and insurance brokers. He established a reputation as one of the more promising radicals in Gladstone's Liberal party. He was an ardent advocate of Irish Home Rule, woman's suffrage, and reform of the House of Lords. He supported, if not with much enthusiasm, the stock Welsh programme of Disestablishment, free education, land reform and temperance.

He was however no supporter of devolution. He was opposed to a Secretary of State for Wales or an elected National Council – his chief objection was that he feared the domination of the industrial South East by the rural North and West. He was at odds with many of his fellow Liberals over a number of Welsh issues, the most important undoubtedly being Cymry Fydd. Cymry Fydd, drawing its support chiefly from the Liberal Party and its inspiration from the Young Ireland Movement, had originally been concerned with safeguarding the cultural and linguistic tradition of Wales. However, in the 1890's it advocated 'the necessity of declaring for self government'.

D.A. Thomas bitterly opposed Lloyd George on this issue and succeeded in destroying it after Lloyd George's humiliation at the famous Newport meeting in January 1896. Ironically, although Thomas was the victor here his influence and career went into steady decline – he appeared more and more at odds with his colleagues, bitterly disillusioned that he had been rejected for office and increasingly associated in South Wales with coal interests.

Nowhere were the contradictions in his personality and political attitudes seen more than in the election of 1900. Despite the fact that Pritchard Morgan and D.A. Thomas were returned with comfortable majorities in the elections of 1892 and 1895 the Merthyr Liberal movement had been in decline. Pritchard Morgan spent much of his time seeking his fortune in the Far East while D.A. Thomas seemed more preoccupied with national issues.

The 1890's had seen attempts to establish branches of the Independent Labour Party (I.L.P.) in Merthyr and Aberdare. At first they enjoyed only moderate success but the deterioration in the economy during the 1890's saw the movement in Wales gain popularity. Throughout the coalfield the paralyzing effect of the depression could be felt – a drop in demand leading almost inevitably to unemployment and wage cuts and to a deterioration in industrial relations, particularly between the colliers and the owners led by W.T. Lewis (later Lord Merthyr). The increasing bitterness of the situation led to the great strike of 1898 when over a hundred thousand men were thrown out of work in South Wales. Great hardship was experienced in the industrial valleys, particularly in Merthyr and Aberdare. The collapse of the strike after six months and the total defeat of the miners led to a hardening of attitudes. The South Wales Miners' Federation was formed to replace the many scattered mining unions and this gave the movement greater unity and coherence. The most important political effect of the strike was the growth in the popularity of the I.L.P. When the strike had started there had been no more than half a dozen branches of the I.L.P. in the whole of South Wales, when it was finished there were thirty-one, some of them with as many as two hundred members. In September 1898 a conference of all the I.L.P. branches in Merthyr, Dowlais and Troed-y-Rhiw was held in the Welcome Coffee Tavern, Merthyr. At this conference it was decided that a Socialist would fight the next General Election whenever it came. The strike had brought Keir Hardie to South Wales, where he had attacked the indifference of the miners' representatives in Parliament – he criticised the fact that no South Wales M.P. had protested against the presence of soldiers in South Wales and had made no use of their parliamentary time to speak on behalf of the miners.

The famous Khaki election of 1900 gave the newly formed Labour party its opportunity. The recently formed Merthyr and Aberdare Trades Council nominated Keir Hardie to fight in the forthcoming election. Hardie's nomination did not go unchallenged, William Brace, vice president of the S.W.M.F. and the militant Marxist, Tom Mann, attracted some support. That Keir Hardie rated his chances of nomination as slim can be seen in a letter he wrote to Llywellyn Francis, a Pen-y-Darren barber and an enthusiastic I.L.P. supporter.

> 'Dear Comrade – Many thanks for your letter. I have decided to accept Preston. It is not likely now that Merthyr will succeed in putting forward a Labour candidate. Your wisest policy would be to defeat Pritchard Morgan, and thus leave the way open for a good Labour man at the next election. He is one of the most dangerous types the House of Commons contains – Yours faithfully.
>
> J. Keir Hardie'

Despite these misgivings Hardie was nominated to fight the Merthyr constituency. He held out no high hopes of success and concentrated his main efforts on winning in Preston. The election was fought at a difficult time for Keir Hardie, but also for the Liberal Party. The outbreak of the Boer War in 1900 had seen widespread support for Imperialism throughout Wales. The Liberal Party at a national and local level was badly divided between those who supported and those who opposed the war. Pritchard Morgan spoke enthusiastically for the war effort and denounced his fellow Liberal M.P., D.A. Thomas, for being pro-Boer. Keir Hardie and the Labour Party could find little consolation in this. Hardie was known for his opposition to the war and local members of the I.L.P. were physically attacked because of their hostility to the war. It seemed a golden opportunity for the Conservatives but they had been for a long time unable to find a suitable candidate. Eventually one Arnott Reid 'The Times' correspondent in Singapore accepted the nomination, thinking that Merthyr was in the north of England. Arriving in Merthyr after the sea journey from Singapore he alarmed local Conservatives when in his election address he declared:

> 'I have lived, loved and married, owned children and houses, experienced the world, the flesh and the devil; made and lost; made and explored; mined; distilled; manufactured; built, lent and borrowed; bought and sold with Indians, Chinamen, Japanese, Malay, American, Negro, half caste, Hindoo, Buddhist, Jew and Christian.'

This was hardly the message which would appeal to the constituents of Merthyr Tydfil and Reid departed before the election. Hardie's two rivals were the Liberals D.A. Thomas and Pritchard Morgan. The animosity which existed between these two undoubtedly worked in Hardie's favour. D.A. Thomas had never made any attempt to conceal his dislike and contempt for Pritchard Morgan and during the campaign he joined with Labour supporters in attacking him. Keir Hardie arrived in Merthyr from Preston on the day prior to polling. He spoke only three times in the constituency, once in Mountain Ash, once in Aberdare and once in Merthyr. Amid scenes of great excitement and tension the votes were counted at the Drill Hall. The election figures were:

D.A. Thomas	8,745
J. Keir Hardie	5,745
W. Pritchard Morgan	4,004

Hardie later described the scene after the declaration of the result 'A great cheering crowd. A march to a wierd song while perched on the shoulders of some stalwart colliers, I trying vainly not to look undignified. A chair helped considerably. That night, from the hotel window, in response to cries loud and long continued, I witnessed a sight I had never hoped to see this side of the pearly gate. My wife was making a speech to the delighted crowd.'

By electing the first Labour member of Parliament for Great Britain (Keir Hardie had been elected for the I.L.P. for West Ham in 1893), Merthyr wrote itself into the history of the Labour Party. It continued its reputation as a radical constituency carrying on the tradition of the Chartists and of 1868. This however is not to suggest that Merthyr had swung completely to Labour. D.A. Thomas continued to top the poll until he moved to Cardiff in 1910. Undoubtedly Hardie had profited from the decline of the Liberal organisation and the rift between D.A. Thomas and Pritchard Morgan. Another factor which assisted Hardie was the concern shown over the recent

Taff Vale judgment which put the position of the unions into jeopardy. Possibly his anti-war stand helped to attract the strong Irish vote in Merthyr.

Hardie soon became involved in Welsh issues. In 1902 he opposed the Education Bill which was to cause so much resentment in the principality and which led to the 'Welsh Revolt'. He campaigned for Welsh disestablishment and also proposed a measure of Home Rule for Wales, but on socialist rather than nationalist grounds.

> 'the Nationalist Party I have in mind is this – the people of Wales fighting to recover possession of the land in Wales . . . that is the kind of Nationalism that will be emblazoned on the red flag of Socialism.'

Hardie's position was still precarious in Merthyr. After he was elected first chairman of the Parliamentary Labour Party he was obliged to spend much of his time outside his constituency attending Socialist gatherings in Europe and the United States. However Labour's position in Merthyr was strengthened with more and more Labour representatives elected to local bodies. In the 1906 election Hardie was opposed by D.A. Thomas and a newcomer Henry Radcliffe, a prominent Welsh Methodist. Hardie fought his campaign on a radical programme which included old age pensions, women's suffrage, nationalization of basic industries, abolition of the House of Lords and home rule all round with Ireland having priority. Hardie defeated Radcliffe but D.A. Thomas easily topped the poll. In 1910 D.A. Thomas left Merthyr to fight Cardiff for the Liberals. His place was taken by Edgar Jones who continued to top the poll in both elections of 1910. Hardie was not opposed by another Liberal but opposition did come from Pritchard Morgan who now stood as an Independent and who waged a vindictive campaign against Hardie, accusing him and the Labour Party of, amongst other things, atheism, assassination and the advocacy of free love. Hardie however increased his majority by over 3,000 votes and in the December 1910 election he had no trouble in defeating J.H. Watts, 'a Liberal unionist'. Much of Hardie's support in these elections came from Non-Conformist Ministers who began to see Socialism as practical Christianity.

Keir Hardie died in 1915. His last years were not happy ones. A new mood of militancy had spread through the Labour Movement. The period 1908-1914 is characterized by waves of violent strikes which led to riots in Ton-y-Pandy and disturbances in Merthyr and Aberdare. Syndicalism, anarchism and other ideas of direct action were making an impact in the Valleys. Hardie sympathised deeply with the men but his dilemma arose out of his belief that a socialist revolution must come through consent and not through the violence advocated by C.B. Stanton who was to succeed him in 1915. His other great difficulty arose out of the outbreak of the first World War in 1914. He denounced the war as an outrage, the product of capitalism and militarism. He was howled down by a mob in Aberdare and the Labour Party in Merthyr divided between those who supported the war and the pacifist supporters of Hardie and the I.L.P. Hardie was denounced in the House of Commons by his fellow M.P. Edgar Jones who accused him of stirring up sedition. On his death the Labour Party in Merthyr divided between James Winstone, representing the I.L.P. but not a pacifist, and C.B. Stanton who fought the by-election on a strong anti-German programme. Stanton representing the feelings of the time easily defeated Winstone by 4,000 votes.

The by-election of 1915 was the last one to be fought for Merthyr and Aberdare as a whole. Under the 1918 Representation of People's Act Merthyr and Aberdare now became two separate constituencies. The Coupon Election of late 1918 saw the Liberal, now Sir Edgar Jones, elected to represent Merthyr. However the war had proved a disaster for the Liberals much of their misfortune resulting from the bitter differences arising between Lloyd George and Asquith and their respective followers. Labour's position had unexpectedly improved during the war. The Trade Union movement had become far more powerful and militant, a militancy reflected in the bitter industrial strife of the period 1919-1921. The intense passions aroused by the Sankey report and 'Black Friday' led to an increase in support for the Labour Movement in the Merthyr area.

The '20's and '30's in Merthyr were to be a time of economic disaster. The Iron Works, the original reason for the existence of the town, had now gone into rapid decline. Merthyr in common with the other old industrial areas of Britain was soon, after the end of the war, to experience the physical and moral devastation of economic depression. Unemployment, at one time as high as 61.8%, gave Merthyr the doubtful distinction of being second only to Jarrow in the British 'Unemployment League'. Heavy industry had virtually disappeared from the town by 1939.

The political repercussions were inevitable. The Capitalist system, which at one time had brought prosperity of a kind to the town's inhabitants, was now discredited. The election of 1922 saw R.C. Wallhead of the I.L.P. defeat the Liberal, Sir R.C. Mathias, by 2,000 votes. The disintegration of the Liberal Party throughout the country during the '20's saw Labour emerge as the main opposition to the Conservatives. Wallhead had no difficulty in increasing his majority even during the controversies of 1931. He remained in the I.L.P. when it disaffiliated from the Labour Party in 1932. The by-election caused by his death in 1934 saw the Labour Party in Merthyr split for the first but not the last time. The Labour Party decided to put up a candidate against the I.L.P. The man they chose was S.O. Davies, the miners' agent for Dowlais. 'S.O.', as he became popularly known, had been born in Abercwmboi. He had started work in the mines at the age of twelve and had studied in his spare time to get a Bachelor of Arts Degree from the University of Wales. Since his arrival as miners' agent in Merthyr Tydfil in 1918 he had built up a reputation for militancy on behalf of the working men. Strongly religious, his political philosophy was derived from a mixture of Christianity and Socialism which, combined with his love for Wales, were to be the main features of his political life. In the by-election of 1934 he comfortably defeated his main opponent the Liberal J. Victor Evans by 18,000 votes to 10,000. Campbell Stephenson for the I.L.P. polled 3,508 while Wal Harrington the Communist polled 3,409. Significantly there was no Conservative. In the General Election of the following year S.O. Davies defeated his only opponent Mr. Claude Stanfield of Troed-y-rhiw by over 11,000 votes. From this point onwards S.O. had little trouble, his majority in the post-war elections rising to well over 20,000 against a variety of opponents which included Labour, Conservative, Liberal and Plaid Cymru.

S.O. Davies was a controversial figure throughout his political career, never fearing to become embroiled in the thorniest political problems, even if it meant attracting the displeasure of his own party. In 1948 he was expelled with twenty-one other Labour M.P.'s after signing a telegram of good wishes to the Communists in the Italian Parliamentary Elections. A few years later he attracted much criticism for his anti-American speeches during the Korean war. He was a strong supporter of devolution for Wales and unsuccessfully introduced a Home Rule Bill in 1955. At all times he strove valiantly and with some success to attract new industries to the Merthyr area and he never missed an opportunity to champion the cause of his constituency. Ironically, despite the fact that he represented his constituency conscientiously for over thirty years, his last years saw him involved in bitter acrimony with his local party.

The Labour Party in Merthyr Tydfil by the time of the election of 1970 felt that it was time for S.O. Davies who had represented the constituency for thirty-six years to stand aside. The official candidate put forward by the Labour Party was Tal Lloyd, a prominent local Trade Unionist. S.O. Davies however showed that he was not prepared to be jettisoned in this way and he decided to fight the campaign as an Independent Labour candidate. He was expelled from the Merthyr Labour Party but despite this he attracted considerable support in the constituency. There was a widespread sympathy for S.O. and the feeling that the local party were showing little gratitude to a man who had devoted his life to the town. In the election of 1970 S.O. Davies easily defeated Tal Lloyd (Independent Labour 16,701, Labour 9,234) and retained the seat until his death in early 1972.

This crisis within the ranks of Labour greatly embarrassed the Party in the town and saw bitter acrimony between the supporters of the official Labour and the Independent Labour candidates. The split in the party became more than ever dangerous because of a new challenge which emerged – this time from the forces of Nationalism. Plaid Cymru which had been formed in the 1920's, had made little progress in Merthyr, or indeed anywhere else in Wales, prior to the election of Mr. Gwynfor Evans in Carmarthen in 1966. In Merthyr the Plaid Cymru had first fought the seat in 1951 but had made little impression. However, in 1972 the divisions in the Merthyr Labour Party and the astonishing success of Plaid Cymru in a Caerphilly by-election a few years earlier seemed to give the party an opportunity to make inroads into this Labour stronghold. The candidate chosen by Plaid Cymru was Mr. Emrys Roberts and he was opposed for Labour by Mr. Ted Rowlands who had been defeated at Cardiff North in 1970. Despite the fact that the seat was also contested by C. Barr, Conservative, A. Jones, Communist and A. Donaldson, Liberal (the Communists and Liberals fought the seat for the first time in thirty-eight years), it was Plaid Cymru that set the pace throughout the campaign. The result saw Ted Rowlands retain the seat for Labour but with a vastly reduced majority (Labour 15,562, Plaid Cymru 11,852, the other three candidates lost their desposits). Undoubtedly the Nationalist Party were fortunate in contesting the seat after a period of some bitterness which had caused considerable disillusionment with the Labour Party. As expected, many people returned to their traditional loyalty in the election of of 1974 when Mr. Rowlands was returned with a five figure majority. However, his chief rival once again was the Nationalist Emrys Roberts who was determined to show that the success of his party in 1972 rested on a solid foundation support in the town. There seemed considerable justification for this view when in 1976 Merthyr became the first council in Wales to be controlled by Plaid Cymru.

However, this control was short-lived. In 1979 Labour regained control of the District Council and in the General Election of that year the Labour majority was increased.

The Development of Local Government

by R. S. EVANS

The rapid development of Merthyr Tydfil as an industrial centre and the accompanying rise in population created problems of sanitation, law and order with which the existing system of local government was unable to deal.

Since the Middle Ages local government had been administered by Justices of the Peace whose primary function was to maintain law and order and to ensure that the poor of the parish were adequately cared for. The only local 'council' (if we can call it that) was the Parish Vestry which was a mass meeting of the ratepayers whose main task was to carry out the terms of the 1601 Poor Law. This involved appointing overseers of the poor and arranging for the collection of a 'poor rate' to finance aid to the poor. This body was however totally inadequate to meet the needs of a rapidly expanding industrial district.

During the nineteenth century some attempts were made to improve facilities in the town. This involved the election of two important bodies.

The first of these was the Board of Guardians set up as the result of the Poor Law Amendment Act of 1834 which required the establishment of workhouses built and maintained by the Boards. These workhouses ('Bastilles') were to house the able bodied poor who were to be set to work in return for their keep. Typical tasks were stone breaking, cutting model or picking oakum; women and girls did the housework.[1]

To administer the Act locally various parishes were joined together to form a 'Union'. These were the parishes of Aberdare, Gelligaer, Llanfabon, Llanwono, Merthyr, Penderyn, Rhigos, Vaynor and Ystradyfodwg. In 1863, Llanfabon, Llanwono and Ystradyfodwg were removed from the Union.

The first Board of Guardians met in November 1836. It consisted of 23 members with J. Bruce Pryce as its first Chairman.[2] The Board was very lax in carrying out its duties; it was not until 1853 that a workhouse was opened. (It now forms part of St. Tydfil's hospital.) The Board found itself very busy, for example, in 1865 4,530 paupers were 'relieved'. One in twelve persons was in receipt of Parish aid.[3] In addition to providing poor relief the Board set up a Cottage home at Llwydcoed for poor children and orphans and an 'Infirmary' to deal with sick paupers.

The Board of Guardians existed until 1930 when its functions were taken over by the Public Assistance Committee of the Merthyr Borough Council.[4] A 'Relieving Officer' examined the cases of applicants who wished to 'go on the Parish'. In the light of his reports the Committee made its awards.

With the setting up of the Welfare State in 1948 poor relief was transferred to central government. Since 1966 the Department of Health and Social Security has been responsible for poor relief.

The second body to arise out of the needs of the town was the Board of Health. In 1849 a severe cholera epidemic struck Merthyr killing 1,432 people.[5] As a result a local Board of Health was established in 1850. It consisted of 14 members with Sir John Josiah Guest MP as its first Chairman[6] It was to remain in existence until 1894 during which time much valuable work was done, for example, streets were paved, lights erected, drainage schemes were implemented and reservoirs were constructed. Between 1859 and 1863 the Pentwyn reservoir was constructed at a cost of £82,000. In 1876 authorisation was obtained for the construction of the lower Neuadd reservoir; in 1895 similar authorisation was received for the construction of the Upper Neuadd reservoir.

The Board appointed Medical Officers of Health to report on sanitary conditions and suggest remedial measures. The most notable was Dr. T.J. Dyke (1816-1899).[7]

Despite the work of these two bodies Merthyr still needed an effective system of local government. The Municipal Corporations Act of 1835 seemed to provide the answer to the needs of Merthyr. The Act allowed towns to apply to the Privy Council to form a Corporation which would consist of a Mayor elected for one year; Aldermen elected for six years and Councillors elected for three years. The electors were to be ratepayers of three years standing.

On 7 April 1837 a public meeting was held to consider application to the Privy Council for a Charter of Incorporation. John Guest, the Member of Parliament for Merthyr, spoke in favour and at a subsequent meeting on 19 May it was decided to apply for a Charter. For unknown reasons the application was never made. The most likely explanation is that the other ironmasters feared that the creation of a municipality would endanger the dominant position they held in local administration.[8]

It was twenty years before the matter was raised again. The High Constable (an honorary official whose chief function was to take the lead in public affairs) was persuaded to convene a public meeting at the Temperance Hall (now Scala Cinema) on 23 September 1857. A resolution to apply for a Charter was overwhelmingly approved. With such notable supporters as Robert Crawshay, Thomas Stephens and William Menelaus it seemed likely that the move would succeed. However, the movement was dealt a severe blow when William Crawshay the 'Iron King' got to hear of the meeting. He hurried to Merthyr from Caversham and organised an opposition meeting which was packed with workers from Plymouth and Cyfarthfa. He was joined by G.T. Clark trustee of Dowlais Works and Anthony Hill of Plymouth who thought the proposed application 'unnecessary and improper.'[9]

The meeting proved to be a fiasco. The Temperance Hall had been booked for a concert on the same evening. The meeting was still going on at 7 pm when the concert party arrived. One of the artists turned off the gas and the meeting ended in chaos without formally passing its resolution. However 'this coalition of ironmasters defeated the presentation of any petition for another nineteen years.'[10]

In 1873 a further meeting was planned but was cancelled due to the threat that it would be obstructed by hostile workmen who would not give the promoters a fair hearing.[11] The opponents of incorporation led by Morgan Williams and Matthew John held a meeting on Market Square where resolutions against incorporation were passed.

In 1874 meetings in favour of incorporation were held in Abercanaid, Troedyrhiw, Georgetown and Penydarren.

On 30 October a meeting at the Bush Hotel decided to draw up a petition requesting Incorporation.

The petition, which contained 3,600 signatures, was presented in 1876 in unfavourable economic circumstances due to the financial collapse of the Plymouth and Aberdare Iron companies and the closure of Cyfarthfa due to an industrial dispute. Nevertheless the Privy Council decided to hold a public inquiry at the Bush Hotel in December with a Major Donelly in the chair.[12] It was fourteen months later that the Privy Council announced to the petitioners that 'their prayers' could not be answered 'for the present.'[13] Probably the closure of Plymouth and Cyfarthfa weighed against them.[14]

In 1880 another attempt was made, hoping that a new Liberal Government under Gladstone would be more amenable. However the Privy Council decided that the economic circumstances of the Parish could not have changed sufficiently for the case to be reconsidered.

1894 was an important year in the history of local government, Merthyr was granted the status of Urban District Council. There were six Wards, Dowlais, Penydarren, Cyfarthfa, Town, Plymouth and Merthyr Vale. Each Ward had three councillors. This council took over the functions of the Board of Health and the Burial Boards. In 1902 the provision of elementary education was transferred from the School Boards set up in 1870[15] to the council.

The industrial upturn of the 1880s and 1890s led to an increase in the population of the town; it also revived the incorporation movement. At a

Chamber of Trade meeting in November 1896, the High Constable, Frank T. James, raised the issue again.[16] The Chamber of Trade set up a committee to look into the issue. The Urban District Council were persuaded that incorporation would benefit the town. Petitions were drawn up, in favour and in opposition to incorporation, and presented to the Privy Council.

5 October 1897 C. Neve Cresswell arrived in the town to hear the case. The two Members of Parliament D.A. Thomas and W. Pritchard Morgan supported incorporation. Thomas suggested a referendum on the issue.[17] Cresswell felt that Merthyr needed wider powers of local government but the Privy Council rejected the idea probably because of the bulk of opposition to incorporation particularly in the lower end of the valley.

Perseverance seemed to be the strong point of the supporters of the incorporation movement. In 1901 a Committee headed by F. Sydney Simons[18] organised a petition. A new inquiry was arranged for 28 April 1903 to be chaired by the Honourable Everard Fielding. It lasted ten days 'far longer than . . . [I] . . . had anticipated any inquiry would last and longer than any inquiries had lasted previously.'[19] The main reason for the long duration of the inquiry was undoubtedly the strength of the opposition, namely, Glamorgan County Council, Breconshire County Council, GKN, Ocean Colliery Company, Nixon's Navigation Colliery Company and the various railway companies.

The Privy Council took some time to come to a conclusion mainly because of the question of whether or not Cefn Coed should be included in the Merthyr borough. Eventually they decided against Cefn's inclusion because of 'the intricate questions and difficulties which would be raised by having separate county authorities to deal with.'

Eventually, sixty-eight years after the first incorporation meeting, in May 1905 a Bill to constitute a 'Borough of Merthyr Tydfil' received royal assent.

The people of the new borough were delighted. Celebrations were planned for 10 July 1905. The Charter was exhibited throughout the Borough, a banquet was planned at the Drill Hall and, according to the official programme, 'a band will play at the recreation ground and a display of fireworks will take place.'[20]

In April 1908 Merthyr's local government status was enhanced when the town was made a 'County Borough'. New powers were added to the Borough's existing powers. In July 1908 the Borough was granted its own Commission of the Peace. In September Merthyr was allowed to have her own police force and chief constable. The Office of High Constable now became defunct; four mayors used the title before it eventually fell into disuse.[21] In 1910 the Borough was allowed to hold its own Court of Quarter Sessions and have its own Recorder.[22]

In 1920 the Council applied and obtained persmission to provide and run (but not manufacture) its own omnibus service. This service commenced in August 1924.[23]

Plate 34: TOWN HALL, MERTHYR TYDFIL *(Photograph by Robert Haines)*

The functions of the County Borough Council were full and varied touching on most aspects of local life. Education, town planning, housing, libraries, museums, public health, parks, public baths, police, fire brigade and omnibuses are merely a few of the council's powers. To provide these services the council was empowered to levy rates.

The council consisted of thirty-two members, one alderman and three councillors from each of the eight Wards, Dowlais, Penydarren, Park, Town, Cyfarthfa, Plymouth, Merthyr Vale and Treharris. The councillors held their seats for three years, one-third retiring annually. Aldermen were elected for six years.

The County Borough remained in existence until 31 March 1974 when as a result of local government reorganisation Merthyr was merged into a new county, Mid Glamorgan. The town still retained its Borough status and mayor. The Merthyr Tydfil District Council which replaced the old Borough Council has thirty-three members. The geography of the Borough has changed, the Vaynor district (Cefn Coed, Trefechan and Pontsticill) and the Bedlinog district (formerly under Gelligaer Urban District Council) have been added to the Borough (Figs. 58 & 59).

The District Council still has wide powers, for example, control of housing, slum clearance, public health and leisure services but many of its

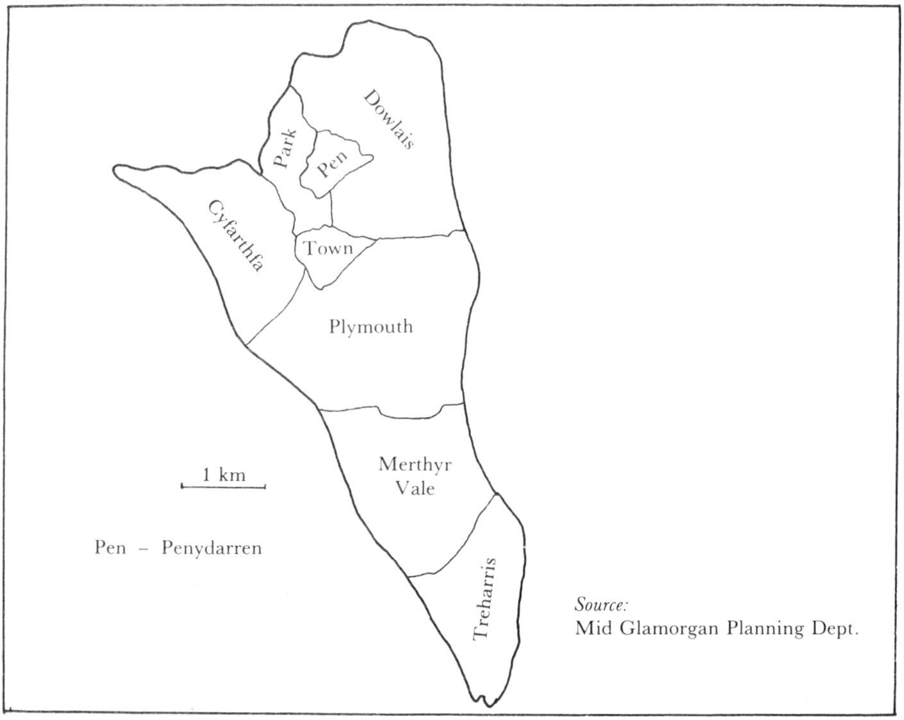

Fig. 58: County Borough Wards 1908-1974

functions have been lost, the most notable being education (now under control of Mid Glamorgan) and water (now the responsibility of the Welsh National Water Development Authority).

Since 1974 further changes have taken place. In March 1976 proposals were put forward by the Local Government Boundary Commission to further sub-divide the new district into 'Communities' with elected Community Councils. Indeed Vaynor and Bedlinog have councils consisting of fifteen and five councillors respectively. The plan proposes ten Community Councils, Vaynor, Pant, Dowlais, Penydarren, Heolgerrig (including Gellideg), Cyfarthfa, Troedyrhiw (including Pentrebach and Abercanaid), Aberfan (including Merthyr Vale), Treharris (including Edwardsville and Quakers' Yard) and Bedlinog.[25]

1976 was very significant in the development of local government for another reason also. In the district elections Labour control was overturned with Plaid Cymru taking control of the council. This was yet another 'first' for Merthyr in political history; Merthyr became the first district council in Wales with a Plaid Cymru majority.

This swing to Nationalism was, however, short lived. In the 1979 elections Plaid Cymru suffered a major set back when, despite an increase in

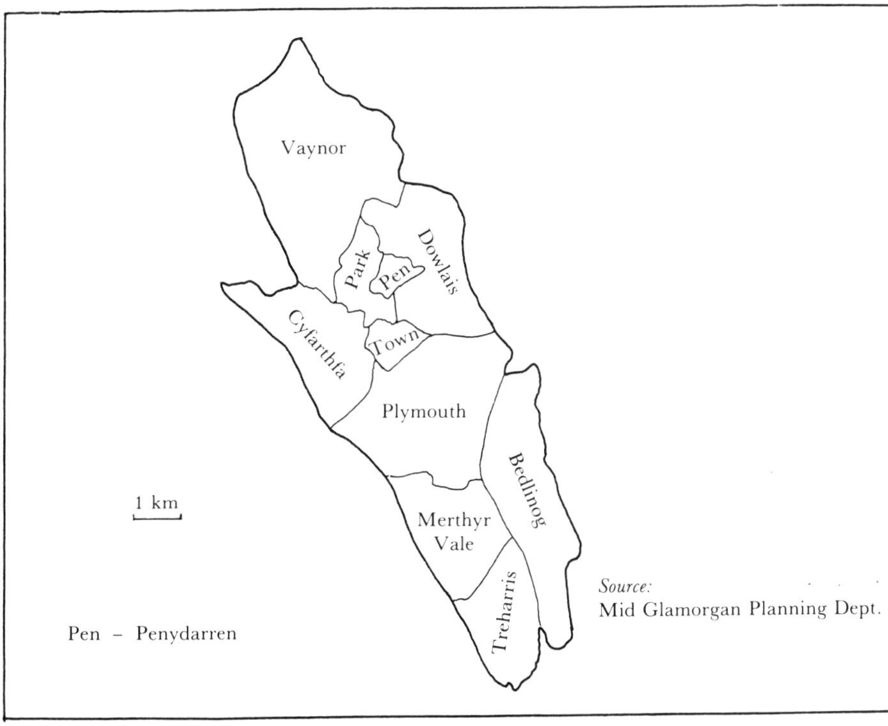

Fig. 59: Borough District Wards 1974-

the votes cast for many Plaid candidates, Labour was swept back into power with 27 seats. Plaid Cymru was reduced to a 'rump' of three members.

During the 1970's, following the publication of the Kilbrandon report, much discussion took place on the question of devolution. In Wales it was proposed to set up an Assembly at Cardiff. The last Labour government passed legislation to set up such an assembly provided that the people of Wales voted in favour of the proposals in a referendum.

The referendum produced a massive 'No' vote in Wales. Consequently, Local government in Wales will remain unchanged in the foreseeable future.

References

1 F. Vaughan, 'Poor Relief in Merthyr in Nineteenth Century' in *Merthyr Historian* (1976).
2 Wilkins, *History of Merthyr Tydfil* (1908) pp. 428-9.
3 Wilkins, op. cit., p. 429.
4 NUT, *Story of Merthyr Tydfil* (1932) p. 270.

[5] See section on Health.
[6] NUT, p. 264; 433 for list of members.
[7] See section on Health for Dyke's career.
[8] H.W. Southey, 'History of the Incorporation Movement' in Wilkins, op. cit., p. 537 ff.
[9] H.W. Southey, p. 540
[10] M.S. Taylor, *Fifty Years a Borough* (1955) p. 11.
[11] H.W. Southey, p. 541.
[12] H.W. Southey, p. 542.
[13] M.S. Taylor, p. 11.
[14] H.W. Southey, p. 544.
[15] See section on Education.
[16] H.W. Southey, p. 546.
[17] H.W. Southey, p. 551.
[18] H.W. Southey, p. 560.
[19] Everard Fielding at 1903 Inquiry.
[20] Extract from Official Programme.
[21] M.S. Taylor, p. 20.
[22] M.S. Taylor, p. 20.
[23] M.S. Taylor, p. 22.
[24] Local Government Boundary Commission Draft Proposals, p. 2.
[25] Further details contained in Draft Proposals op. cit. passim.

Earning a Living

III

Agriculture and Forestry

by T. S. JONES and M. GILLHAM, Ph.D.

Agriculture

'Happy the man whose wish and care
A few paternal acres bound
Content to breathe his native air
In his own ground.'

Pope

The farming systems now practised within the Borough of Merthyr Tydfil have evolved within the constraints of climate and topography but are partly in response to the economic and social pressures of a large urban community.

Looking to the left as you drive up the Taff Valley the tidy pattern of small enclosures on farms like Perthygleision and Ynysygored Farms appears almost static, but one is ever conscious of the large acreage of rugged rough grazing which surrounds them. There is in fact some 2½ acres of rough grazing for each acre of crops and grass in the Merthyr District. Additionally, we have large areas of common land. The character and social pressures of the coalfield are distinctly different from those which apply north of the town.

Merthyr District, which extends south to Quaker's Yard, illustrates this. If, instead of following the main road, you turn off at Treharris and climb steeply onto the high plateau, you will find a number of homesteads sited at easy distances on either side of the old Roman road. Shelter, access and water supply were all important to the siting of the farmhouse and buildings. This top land is relatively flat, shallow and free draining. Much of the area has been reclaimed from bracken and gorse during the post-war period. It is naturally acid and phosphate deficient, 3-5 tons of ground limestone and ½ ton basic slag per acre normally necessary to correct these deficiencies before

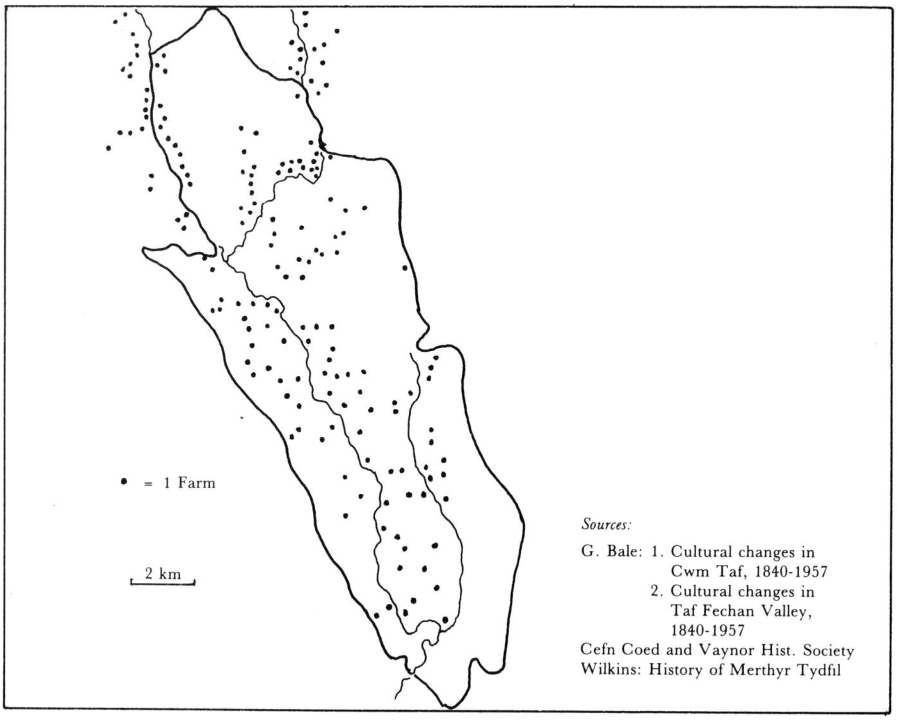

Fig. 60a: Location of farms in eighteenth and nineteenth centuries

reseeding to ryegrass/clover leys. When clearing some of the rougher areas, it is now general practice to build up fertility by first planting to a pioneer crop of rape which is fed off to fattening lambs.

The present husbandry systems have required the erection of miles of wire fencing now costing approximately £1 per yard to erect. In 1975 Messrs. Bowen Brothers (at The Forest) were the first in the area to adopt aerial spraying of bracken. Bracken clearance makes shepherding much easier and makes possible a considerable increase in grass production.

An easier vantage point may be attained by proceeding north along Heol Adam to a point on Gelligaer Common near Clawdd-Trawscae Farm. Looking westward you can here appreciate the relationship between clean land and rough grazings, and sense how important the common land can be as summer grazing for the adjacent farms. Nowhere is the craft of drystone walling better demonstrated than here.

Industrial settlement of the coalfield established large numbers of small holdings, but these numbers are being progressively reduced. There are still relatively few large economic units.

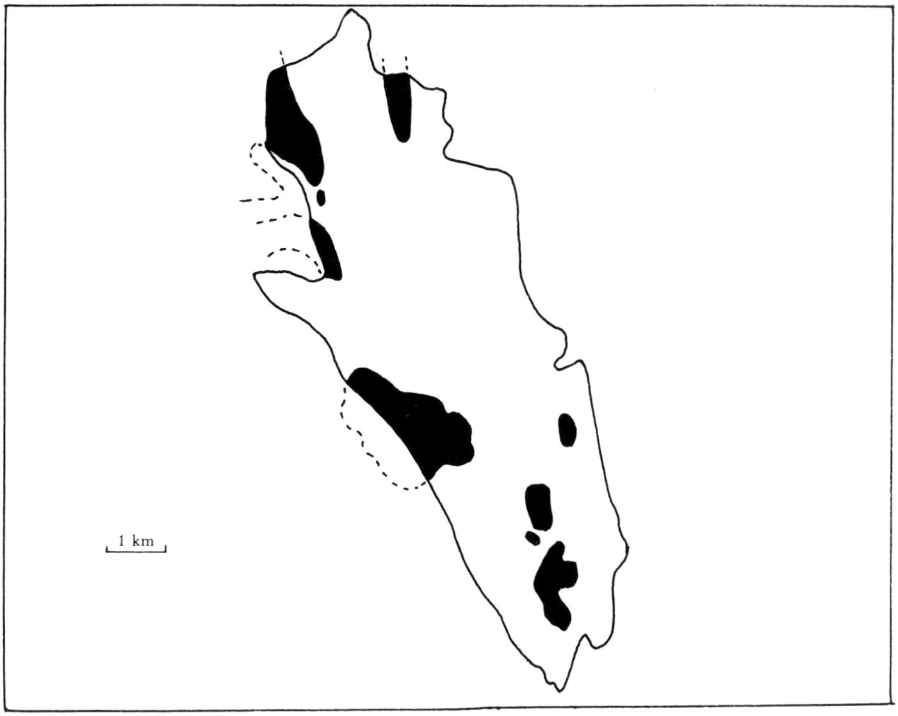

Fig. 60b: Forestry Commission areas, 1980

Table 1

Crops and Grass	*Number of Holdings (Merthyr Parish)*	
Acres	*1960*	*1970*
Under 29¾	49	21
30-99¾	27	23
Over 100	8	7

In the years of depression these small farms provided a good level of subsistence but little cash. Consequently, many farmers became interested in milk production. Cows were hand-milked and the milk often retailed with a pony and trap. This income provided for the family needs between the annual sales of store lambs and draft ewes. In 1950 there were 48 registered milk producers in Merthyr parish alone, but regulations were introduced requiring that milk be pasteurised or bottled under approved conditions. The smaller units could not justify the cost of modernising their dairies so that the number of milk producers decreased rapidly in the following quarter of a century.

The final exodus from milk production was precipitated by the Dairy Herd Conversion Scheme (E.E.C. sponsored 1973), but the changes to the drystock systems had been encouraged by the plans of the creameries to adopt bulk milk collection. The cost of improving access to a standard suited to large tankers proved impossible in many cases. At the same time subsidies for the maintenance of cows on hill grazings had been increased and the labour supply was both affecting and being affected by policy changes. Whereas in 1960 there were 34 full-time 'adult male workers' employed on farms in Merthyr parish, this number had been reduced to 8 by 1970. Surprisingly, the numbers of 'total cattle and total sheep' had remained almost unchanged (see Appendix 1).

Most of the beef cows are either Hereford/Friesian crosses or Welsh Blacks. On the larger farms they are run with a Hereford bull, but more often mated by AI on the smaller units. In most cases only one calf per cow is suckled. The more forward calves are weaned at 4-5½ cwts. for sale in the autumn through Nelson, Newport or Abergavenny Markets. Smaller calves are over-wintered for sale later as stores. Draft ewes (since 1967), the bulk of the store lambs and rams are sold through annual sales conducted by the Nelson Sheep Breeders' Association. This is a farmers' organisation co-operating with the auctioneers, Messrs. Seth Phillips and Sons. Some stock are sold at the Penderyn sales. Buyers are encouraged from further afield by the larger well organised sales which have replaced the numerous centres previously operating. Whereas fat lamb prices have improved greatly during 1976, the drought conditions have reduced the number of lowland farms which have sufficient autumn feed to fatten purchased store lambs. The store lamb and suckler calf enterprises remain vulnerable to market fluctuations (see Appendix 2). The growing of rape and reseeding has enabled an increased number of the lamb crop to be fattened off the hill.

Lambing is mainly in early April and it is now regular practice to in-winter ewe lambs for a short period in order to make them familiar with concentrated food. (Sheep which have not been so taught are often reluctant to go near the trough. Consequently, heavy losses can occur during periods of snow, or bad weather.) The level of supplementary feeding is normally relatively low, but more recently 'feed blocks' which have a high energy value but also contain Urea and minerals have been introduced as a convenient method of raising the standard of the ewes' winter diet. The application of lime during reclamation operations has tended to depress the availability of copper in the herbage. Farmers now regularly dose or inject the ewes during mid-pregnancy in order to avoid 'sway back' lambs.

The South Wales or Nelson type ewe has a high reputation for hardiness and is an excellent mother, suitable for crossing with Suffolk rams for the production of fat lambs on the lowlands. Most of the draft ewes sold for this purpose are 'full mouthed'—4-6 years old.

Sheep farming in the coalfield presents many problems. Death on the roads, dog worrying and foxes can, in some instances, account for some

Plate 35a: ABERCRIBAN FARM, NOW BENEATH PONTSTICILL RESERVOIR
(By permission of Clive Thomas)

Plate 35b: PENDDEUGAE-FACH FARM, TROEDYRHIW
(By permission of Clive Thomas)

20% of the lamb crop. It is only the more favoured farms that can expect to rear 100 lambs from 100 ewes. Trespassers create difficult problems by damaging walls and wire fences whilst mining subsidence has made stock management more difficult by robbing many areas of their natural water supply. Farms along the west slope as you drive up to Bedlinog are fully dependent upon the mains water supply which happens to run above them. Over the hill can be seen the derelict homesteads which have been left high and dry.

Apart from the lime and slag used at the time of reclamation, the level of fertiliser usage remains low, mainly as a complete fertiliser is applied to the hayfields. Any pastures which are not well managed quickly revert to bent and bracken. Few farms in the area are sufficiently large to justify full mechanisation. Hay baling and similar operations are undertaken by larger neighbours or specialist contractors. In spite of hill farming subsidies (now called compensatory payments), the majority of units in the area do not possess sufficient stock to generate a margin large enough to provide an adequate standard of living with a surplus for re-investment in the business. Amalgamation of farms now proceeds naturally, but it will be some time before the bulk of the area is farmed as viable units.

A number of small holdings have been purchased by non-farmers. These are partly responsible for the overgrazing of the commons by ponies. The Dowlais Top area, with its high rainfall and peat overlying Millstone Grit is difficult to improve, but it is at nearby Nantyffin that the Kinsey family have achieved so much in the field of grassland improvement. This is one of the few local farms where silage is made. Mr. Kinsey in-winters some of his ewe lambs, but others are sent away to 'tack at about £4 per head' (1977). More sheltered farms are able to avoid this cost. Much has been done to improve pastures, fences, roads and water supply but there has been little investment in buildings in the area, with the possible exception of sheep handling pens and dipping facilities.

Bovine tuberculosis was eradicated under the Attested Herd Scheme by 1960 and the area cleared of brucellosis by 1976.

North of the town we leave the coalfield for more kindly soils derived from limestone and red sandstones. These are more agreeable to stock, even at higher elevations. Here, in contrast with the coalfield, it is the dictates of water conservation and afforestation which have regulated the process of change in the character and balance of the rural society.

T. S. JONES
Agricultural Advisory Officer

Appendix 1—Cropping and Stocking of Merthyr Parish

	1960	*1965*	*1970*
Cereals	76 acres	38 acres	32 acres
Potatoes	30	14	4
Swedes, etc.	31	23	7
Mangolds	5	1	—
Rape	73	42	43
Kale	39	28	3
Temporary Leys	292	196	152
Permanent Grass	2,570	2,649	2,329
Rough Grazings	7,167	6,912	5,563
Dairy Cows	215	185	93
Beef Cows	159	171	247
Total Cattle and Calves	1,089	876	877
Sows	18	27	33
Breeding Ewes (+ 2 tooth)	11,438	10,613	9,917
Total Sheep	19,378	19,451	18,143
Fowl (over 6 months)	1,502	1,870	3,278

Source—MAFF

Appendix 2—Budget for 100 Ewe Flock 1976

HILL FLOCK—90% lambs reared
Selling 75% store lambs
25% fat lambs

	Per 100 Ewes £
OUTPUT	
34 lambs sold store 25 kg live wt at 44p/kg	374
11 lambs sold fat 14 kg dcw at 92p/kg	142
14 Surplus ewe lambs at £7.50 each	105
24 Draft ewes at £9 each	216
Wool: 127 fleeces × 1.6 kg at 62p/kg	126
Compensatory allowances 100 at £3.60	360
	1,323
Less	
Ram replacements—2 at £50—3 year life	33
Output	1,290

VARIABLE COSTS (excluding forage variable costs)	
Winter feeding at £1 per head	100
Tack and transport—31 lambs at £5	155
Shearing costs—127 head at 20p	25
Veterinary and other costs at 50p per ewe	50
Total Variable Costs	330
GROSS MARGIN	960
GROSS MARGIN PER EWE	£9.60

Source—ADAS

Forestry

The indigenous broad-leaved forests of several centuries ago have been progressively felled over the years, first for building timber and domestic fuel and to clear the land for farming, then for industrial uses—charcoal for iron smelting and pit props for coal mines, the clearance receiving impetus from the two world wars. From the middle of the eighteenth century the poorer upland soils, denied the protection of their former tree canopy, were washed down by surface drainage to colour the little streams, which carried them on to the rivers to join the tide-borne silts of the Bristol Channel.

What remained offered poor prospects to the farmer and was available for reafforestation, although often able to support only inferior timber trees. Careful selection of species is necessary to get the right tree for the right site and in the most exposed areas no forestry is possible. Even when grazing animals are excluded, the ancient cover of birch and pine seldom reappears on the barren plateau sites but the hillsides will become recolonised by the former woodland type of durmast oak, downy birch and alder. The trees, however, will be stunted and unsuitable for commercial purposes.

Alien conifers, which fit the landscape less well aesthetically and support a poorer wildlife, are less demanding of soil nutrients and can yield good timber crops on otherwise unproductive land. Except on slopes too steep for cultivation, good hardwoods can usually be grown only where agriculture can give greater profit and, as the poor hill farms become abandoned, more and more are being taken over for coniferous forests. Farm abandonment is often due to the imbalance of good bottom-lands on which stock summered on the hills can be overwintered, this having been taken over by building development or industry, so increasing urbanisation is largely responsible for the larger tracts of land becoming available for tree planting during the past few decades.

There is still a lower percentage of afforested land in the Merthyr District than in West Glamorgan, particularly around the Neath and Afan. The borough's Forestry Commission plantations are outliers of St. Gwynno's Forest to the south and Cwm Taff Forest to the north. Those south-west of the town, mainly at Abernant and on Mynydd Merthyr, are in the administrative area of St. Gwynno's, which is centred between Rhondda Fach and the Cynon Valley and occupies some 3,900 hectares or 9,630 acres. Those to the north of the town form part of Cwm Taff's total of 2,064 hectares or 5,098 acres, which lie mainly in the western valley of the Taff Fawr. Twenty one workers domiciled in the Merthyr District are currently employed in these forests.

Merthyr's first coniferous or softwood forestry blocks sprang up around the reservoirs under the management of the Cardiff Corporation Waterworks Department in Cwm Taff and the Taf Fechan Water Supply Board in the Eastern Valley. Farm livestock were excluded from the vicinity of the reservoirs so that their excrement should not pollute the water supply, so the adjacent land became available for tree planting. If the sides are at all steep, forest cover can prevent soil erosion, but this benefit is partly offset by the exposure of bare soil in drainage furrows and broad ditches along access roads. Tree leaves falling in the water can, themselves, act as a pollutant during their decomposition, as well as blocking outlet grids, but these problems are less with needle-leaved softwoods than broad-leaved hardwoods.

It was not until 1946 that the Forestry Commission leased its first land from the Water Board in Taf Fechan and in 1949 that the first lease was signed in Taf Fawr. More land was acquired by purchase on Aberdare Mountain just West of the town in the mid fifties and this was followed by a steady series of acquisitions during the sixties and seventies—bringing the present total in the Merthyr District to 1,420 hectares (3,505 acres). About 1,280 hectares (3,160 acres) of this land was planted by 1977.

Existing broad-leaved woodlands have been retained as such and are being managed by the Forestry Commission largely for their amenity value. The light-demanding grand firs planted under the deciduous trees East of the A470 road south of Aberfan are being allowed to die out. New plantings have been of softwoods, both because of restrictions of soil fertility, climate and altitude and because of the greater demand for and quicker growth of softwood timber.

The older forests north of Merthyr town have reached the productive stage and timber is being extracted. The crop is not fully mature until seventy years or more after planting, but thinning starts at twenty years, the trees removed being used mainly for pit props and fence posts. On average a mile of forestry road is required for every eighty to a hundred acres of forest, to facilitate routine management and get the timber out. These roads, augmented by picnic sites and carparks, have opened up new areas for walkers. A particularly attractive example, with an old farm building converted to a forestry museum and information centre, is sited just over the parish boundary in the forked valley of Garw Nant Fawr at the north-west corner of Llwyn On Reservoir.

Forests south of the town are in their early phases as yet, often with an understorey of purple moor grass (*Molinia*) which carries a tinder-dry cover of dead leaves for half the year. The reprehensible habit of 'burning the mountain' so prevalent among young South Walians has taken its toll. Fires usually occur in February and March but the most disastrous one to date was during the August drought of 1976 when 70 hectares (173 acres) of young hybrid larch and others were destroyed between Mount Pleasant and Edwardsville—causing closure of the A470 Cardiff to Merthyr road when at its height.

Strips left unplanted as firebreaks minimise the danger and forests are often separated from the surrounding moorland by a strip of open plough-land to keep flames at bay. These sheltered marginal areas and open ground alongside rides and under pylons can occupy ten to fifteen per cent of the total and offer a haven from grazing sheep and biting wind to a variety of wild flowers and the associated animal life.

The five species of conifer most commonly planted in the Merthyr area are Sitka spruce, Norway spruce, lodgepole pine, Japanese larch and hybrid larch. Four others used less often are Scots pine, grand fir, noble fir and Western hemlock.

SITKA SPRUCE (*Picea sitchensis*), the largest of the spruces, reaching to 300 feet, is a native of Western North America and takes its name from Sitka, the old Russian capital of Alaska. On the Alaskan island shores the trees grow trunk to trunk in saturated soil; on the Oregon headlands they withstand the full force of sea winds. Hence they are admirably suited to the wet acid boglands and windy heights around Merthyr, yielding reasonably well in the poorest and most exposed sites capable of supporting trees at all. The wood makes good paper pulp, chipboard, pit props and sawn timber.

NORWAY SPRUCE (*Picea abies*) is Europe's tallest native tree, growing to 200 feet in the northern and Alpine forests. It has less spiky foliage than Sitka and is thus suitable for Christmas trees. The name spruce derives from Prussia, where it is an important forest dominant. It was native to Britain before the Ice Ages but did not manage to get back by natural means after the ice receded and before the land bridge to Europe was severed, but was re-introduced about 1500. More tolerant of late Spring frosts than is Sitka, though less tolerant of acid soil and high wind, it is planted on the frosty bottomlands rather than the windy tops. Much timber is imported from Scandinavia, Russia and the Baltic, as deal or whitewood.

JAPANESE LARCH (*Larix kaempferi*) is a Japanese mountain representative of a circum-polar genus. It demands higher fertility than the spruces and is usually planted on the richer bracken-clad brown-earth soils of the hill slopes rather than the acid Molinia-clad blanket peats of the plateaux. It is deciduous, the leaves falling after yellowing in Autumn. This allows more

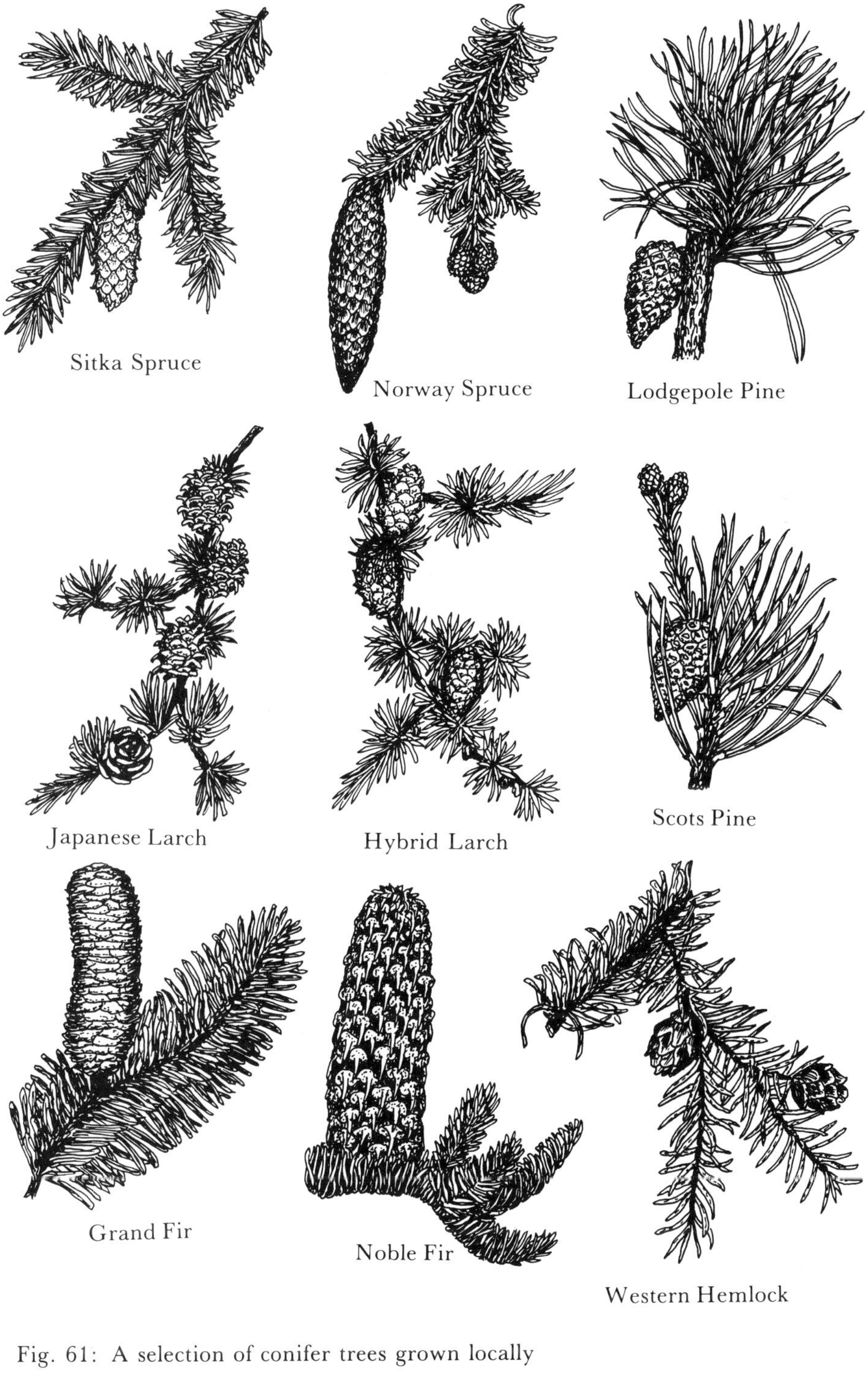

Fig. 61: A selection of conifer trees grown locally

light to penetrate and permits a good growth of understorey plants until the soft green leaf rosettes appear again in Spring.

HYBRID LARCH (*Larix eurolepis*). The European larch had been brought to Britain from the Alps in 1620 and became the most important plantation tree by the mid nineteenth century, after which a large proportion succumbed to aphid attack. The Japanese larch introduced in 1861 proved a better successor and by 1904 had crossed with the European larch to produce a hybrid which was better than either. This is a fast grower, producing close-grained wood and is more resistant to insect attack than the parents.

LODGEPOLE PINE (*Pinus contorta*) is the upland variety of the shore pine, growing at elevations of as much as 11,000 feet in its native Western North America. It earned its name as the Indian's choice of pole for supporting their wigwams. Hardy and adaptable, with dense foliage to smother out competitors, it is well suited to poor dry soils and exposed sites and is widely planted in the Merthyr district.

SCOTS PINE (*Pinus sylvestris*) is the only northern European pine to survive the Ice Ages. It is a true British native, recognisable by the brick red upper trunk and branches.

GRAND FIR (*Abies grandis*) is the largest of the firs, reaching to nearly 300 feet in the high rainfall area of its native Vancouver Island and thriving in wet soils around Merthyr.

NOBLE FIR (*Abies procera*) is native to the middle altitudes of the Canadian Sierras and has the largest cones of any, with short crowded needles.

WESTERN HEMLOCK (*Tsuga heterophylla*) is yet another from Western North America with drooping branches and foliage like an untidy version of our native yew. It needs constant moisture and shelter and thrives where mist is prevalent.

Industrial Development to 1918

by C. THOMAS, B.Ed.

A. Introduction

Prior to the Industrial Revolution the economies of both upland and lowland areas of the County of Glamorgan were wholly agricultural in character. In the south of the county the lowland farms enjoyed richer soils and better climate whilst those of the upland areas to the north endured a heavier rainfall and predominantly acid mountain pastures. The agriculture of the Bro, therefore was more varied and productive than that of the north which practised a form of subsistence agriculture based on the rearing of sheep. The larger valley farms such as Troedyrhiw were more fortunate than their hill counterparts in that they were able to utilise the rich river alluvium for the growing of grain crops and providing pasture for the rearing of cattle. Such farms were not the rule and the agriculture of our area was typified more by the smaller sheep orientated farms, the remains of which can still be seen on the valley sides and hill tops.

Generally speaking then, the difference between the Bro and Blaenau is perhaps characterised from an agricultural point of view by a comment made by Thomas Fuller in the middle of the seventeenth century, 'The north of this county is so full of mountains that almost nothing is to be had; the south is so fruitful a valley that nothing at all is wanting therein'.[1] The physical factors affecting agriculture in South Wales remained unaltered but the discovery of rich mineral reserves in the upland region changed within a very short period of time the whole character of the area. The discovery and exploitation of ironstone and coal was not only responsible for the despoilation of the landscape on a massive scale, but also for the creation of a new economic and social order.

However, that story is to come for the first 'industries' of the Merthyr Area grew out of its rural economy. Lime burning, corn grinding, tanning and the production of woollen goods were established to serve the needs and even supplement the income of some of the local inhabitants.

The use of lime enabled some of the poorer upland areas to be brought into cultivation. The limestone was quarried from the outcrops to the north of Merthyr and burned using coal as a fuel in small kilns. These kilns were usually owned by a farmer and served, with only seasonal use, to improve or manure the land. The running kiln which became popular in the late eighteenth century was a large stone built bowl about ten feet in diameter tapering to a grate at the bottom where the lime and ashes would be drawn out.[2]

The lime produced by these kilns served not only as a manure but formed a base for mortar, and was also used for whitewashing walls of farms and later on the cottages of industrial Merthyr. A study of nineteenth century Ordnance Survey maps of Merthyr shows that these kilns were not confined to the farming areas. One was sited alongside the Penydarren Limestone Tramroad near to the site of Gwaunfarren Baths, another was found to be in the centre of Caedraw and three built alongside the Gurnos Limestone Tramroad near Cefn Bridge can still be seen.

The corn produced by the local farmers would have been ground at one of the mills that were once found throughout the upper reaches of the Taff Vale. Unlike their more spectacular wind driven counterparts to be found in other areas of Britain, they were powered by water and as a result were sited on the banks of the Taff or one of its fast flowing tributaries. Nearly all of these early corn mills have now disappeared practically without trace and we have to rely therefore, on place names and old maps to remind us of their existence. Such mills were to be found at Y Garn (Ponsticill), Aberglais, Troedyrhiw and one which relied on the Morlais Brook for its driving force, was situated near Pontmorlais and survived until the late nineteenth century.

Lime burning and corn grinding might not, however, be strictly considered industries because they were a necessity rather than an economic extension of a rural community. Leather and woollen manufacture on the other hand grew out of the rural economy to provide by-employment and a degree of increased wealth.

Although not as prosperous as the industry carried on in the lowland areas of Glamorgan the tanning of leather was important to people locally. During pre-industrial times in towns like Cardiff and Swansea the leather workers constituted powerful vested interests while in Merthyr only the parish records and nineteenth century gravestones proclaim the passing of the cordwainer, shoemaker or cobbler.

The growth of the tanning industry throughout Glamorgan was encouraged with the arrival of the Sussex Ironmasters during the sixteenth and seventeenth centuries.[3] During this time great areas of oak woodland were felled for use in the forges and the bark of the oak tree was one of the pre-requisites of the tanning industry. The growth in population and the use of horses in ironworks and collieries after 1800, increased the demand for leather and so tanneries like those in Bridge Street, Caedraw and Dynevor Street, Georgetown continued to manufacture leather throughout the nineteenth century.

Plate 36a: OLD FULLING MILL ON BANKS OF TAFF-FECHAN NEAR CEFN COED
(By permission of Clive Thomas)

Mention has already been made of the water driven mills which were once to be found in the environs of Merthyr Tydfil. Other mills existed, however, which although an integral part of the agricultural community had nothing to do with the grinding of corn. These mills, called in Welsh Y Pandy, were fulling mills concerned with the manufacture of woollen cloth.

The fulling process dates back to Roman times when the woollen cloth was placed in a large trough of water and kneaded. This kneading was accomplished originally by the feet and has given us such surnames as Walker and Tucker. Up until the Middle Ages these mills were still described as 'walk mills', but during the thirteenth century fulling stocks operated by water were introduced from Italy. The mill carried out two separate processes; firstly after sorting, the raw wool was scoured by boiling in stale

Plate 36b: BANK OF OLD LIME KILNS NEAR CEFN BRIDGE
(By permission of Clive Thomas)

urine. It was then dried and sorted to remove thorns or twigs. The carding and spinning were done in the cottages of the district and the yarn then sent to the local weavers. After weaving it was returned to the fulling mill where the cloth was again soaked in urine, kneaded with Fuller's earth and soap, before being finally washed in clean water.[4]

There were a number of fulling mills in and around the Parish of Merthyr. The Pandy Farm at Cyfarthfa suggests the one-time existence of a mill nearby while others existed at Melin Canaid and Melin Caiach. The remains of one of these mills can be seen on the banks of the Taff Fechan near Cefn Coed. Two interesting points concerning this mill are that the urine used in the fulling process was collected by the mill owner from the houses of Cefn Coed, and there occurs near to the mill the flower soapwort (Saponaria Officinalis), a plant introduced into the area and used in the final washing of the cloth.

So far, mention has only been made of the fulling mills. In addition to these, factories existed where the woollen yarn was woven into cloth. Such mills were to be found in Caedraw, Treharris and Heolgerrig where reputedly red waistcoats were made for the followers of the Chartist cause in the 1830s.

A flannel factory was also to be found in the little hamlet of Ynys-y-felin which now lies beneath the waters of Llwyn-Onn reservoir. Here the farmers of the valley purchased cloth which would later be made up into suits by one of the itinerant tailors who visited their homes from time to time.

The growth of Merthyr Tydfil as a centre of the iron industry dates traditionally from the arrival of John Guest in the area in 1759. However, long before this date, the iron ore resources of the Parish had been worked on a very limited scale. This early period of iron manufacture is very poorly documented and many of the facts behind its development are unfortunately lost in the obscurity of those years.

During the sixteenth century certain restrictions were placed on the felling of timber for charcoal in the Weald of South-East England. These of course had an adverse effect on the industry of the region which used charcoal in the smelting of iron. As a result, a number of the Sussex ironmasters sought other areas in which they could establish their industry. The valleys of South Wales possessed many advantages for the successful development of such an industry failing only in the fact that they were far removed from the profitable London market. The valleys were well wooded, the area was rich in iron ore which could be easily worked from the outcrops or shallow pits and the swift flowing streams provided power for the water wheel which drove the bellows for the furnace.

A number of small ironworks and forges were established throughout Wales during the sixteenth century and some ironmasters inevitably found their way into the Vale of Taff. Unfortunately the physical remains of the small works these men founded have long fallen to the rigours of time with the result that we can only be certain of the exact site of one of these furnaces. We are told that works existed at Pontygwaith and Pontyrhun, but only at Blaencanaid are remains actually in evidence.

Much confusion surrounds the early development of the iron industry in the Taff Valley. The name Pontygwaith obviously implies the existence of a 'works' of some form. Wilkins in his *History of Merthyr Tydfil* writes of Anthony Morley who owned iron works in Merthyr and Llanwonno and says 'it is probable that the Merthyr Branch was at Pontygwaith'.[5] William Rees, however, in *Industry before the Industrial Revolution* indicates that Morley's furnace was at Pontygwaith on the banks of the Rhondda Fach.[6] To complicate matters further, Wood in *Rivers of Wales* written in 1813 says that 'several miles below Pontyrhun, at Pontygwaith, are the remains of another furnace, and near it in the river are the oak stakes which formed a weir called Wattle Weir, but not the slightest tradition has reached the present period relating to these works'. More definite, however, is the existence of a works at Pontyrhun which was owned by Thomas Erbury in 1625 and built on land belonging to Sir Edward Lewis.

Although it is not known who was responsible for the setting-up of a works at Blaencanaid and nothing is known of its subsequent history, the remains tell us quite a lot about these early ironworks.

The furnace was very small being about 12 feet in height and 4 feet in diameter. It was built into the hillside so that the materials needed for iron manufacture could be loaded easily from above. These materials, iron ore, charcoal and limestone would have been prepared on the charging platform the remains of which can still be seen to the rear of the furnace. When the furnace was ready for tapping the molten iron would have been run out onto the casting floor which was often given shelter by a simple roof. A few yards from the furnace is a small waterfall over which flows the Canaid Brook. The water of the Brook powered a small waterwheel which would in turn have worked the bellows, thus providing the furnace with a blast of air. Such furnaces were generally seasonal in their operation and amounts of pig-iron produced very small.

A visit to Blaencanaid is still a rewarding one for those interested in industrial history. It can be accomplished after gaining the permission of the farmer at Blaencanaid and a scramble through briar and bracken of a forestry plantation will bring you to the site. Even today its location is isolated and one is left wondering how much more so it must have been during the sixteenth and seventeenth centuries.[7] From the fact that these small ironmaking enterprises are so poorly recorded one can perhaps assume that they had very little effect on the lives of the people of the Taff Vale; different indeed from the developments which were to take place some two hundred years later.

By the beginning of the eighteenth century the traditional iron making areas of Britain were encountering serious difficulties. De-forestation which had continued apace despite attempts to curb it during Elizabeth's reign, was having dire effects on the prosperity of the iron industry throughout the country. Whole areas of woodland in many English counties completely disappeared and supplies of fuel for the furnaces became more and more scarce. But as the industry's ability to produce iron slowly diminished the demands for its product began to increase. Great changes in the textile industry as well as the increasing needs of the workshops of Birmingham and Sheffield made demands which the British iron industry was unable to meet.

Scarcity of timber sent up costs of production and as a result many companies concerned with the manufacture of iron goods were forced to import bar iron from Sweden.[8] Government protection from foreign competition was useless because home consumption was outstripping production.

The solution to this problem was in fact quite simple—coal. It had been used by many industries in Britain for centuries and was even used in the working of some metals, but at the beginning of the eighteenth century how it might be used in the smelting of iron ore remained a mystery.

In forging metals coal had more or less the same qualities as charcoal but this was not the case in the actual smelting of iron ore. When heated using coal the ore yielded only impure and brittle pig iron which was quite impossible to work.

The solution came eventually from an area not unlike our own.

In about the year 1709 a man by the name of Abraham Darby took over a small ironworks on the banks of the River Severn at Coalbrookdale, Shropshire. Over a period of years he and his son experimented using coke instead of coal to smelt the ore. This innovation was slow to be adopted throughout the country but it eventually made available the vast reserves of coal with which the country was endowed. From this period on ironworks gravitated towards the areas of Britain where ironstone occurred in coal bearing rocks, i.e. the coalfields of the Central Lowlands of Scotland, North East of England, Lancashire and South Wales. So, largely as a result of Abraham Darby's experiments with coke the hitherto 'upland wilderness' of South Wales was to be transformed within a very short period of years. The earth was to be torn apart, furnaces would be set up on the banks of the rivers and spoil heaps accumulated that nature would fail to hide in the next two hundred years.

Abraham Darby's work with coke in the smelting process solved only one of the problems the industry faced during the early part of the Industrial Revolution. The pig iron produced by the blast furnace was brittle and contained many impurities. Before it could be used in the production of iron goods it had to be rid of those impurities and made malleable. The process used for much of the eighteenth century enabled only small quantities of pig iron to be dealt with at a time, so despite the fact that output of pig iron increased rapidly as a result of Darby's invention the same could not be said for the production of malleable iron.

The process which overcame this was to be known as 'puddling' and was invented almost simultaneously by two men who worked many miles apart and were unaware of each other's existence. The one, Henry Cort working for the Admiralty at Portsmouth was to become famous for his invention, while the other Peter Onions of Merthyr lacked Cort's access to men of influence and would remain almost unknown. Onions' patent of 7 May, 1783[9] in fact predated that of Cort's by nine months but the latter was able to make his process known at once and undertake its commercial development.

The answer to the problem of producing large quantities of malleable iron centred around a furnace in which the coke and pig iron were kept separate. The iron was melted and then stirred by the puddler in order to aid the removal of carbon. After a while when the iron became a spongy mass it was removed from the furnace, hammered to get rid of the slag and finally passed through rollers.

The fruits of Onions' and Cort's labours were indeed revolutionary, puddling was adopted throughout the country and the production of bar iron at Cyfarthfa alone rose from ten to two hundred tons per week.

We will look at the individual enterprises which established themselves within the Merthyr area later but first let us consider some general physical and geographical factors which contributed to their prosperity.

The works begun at Dowlais, Cyfarthfa, Penydarren and Plymouth in the second half of the eighteenth century differed only in detail from those which

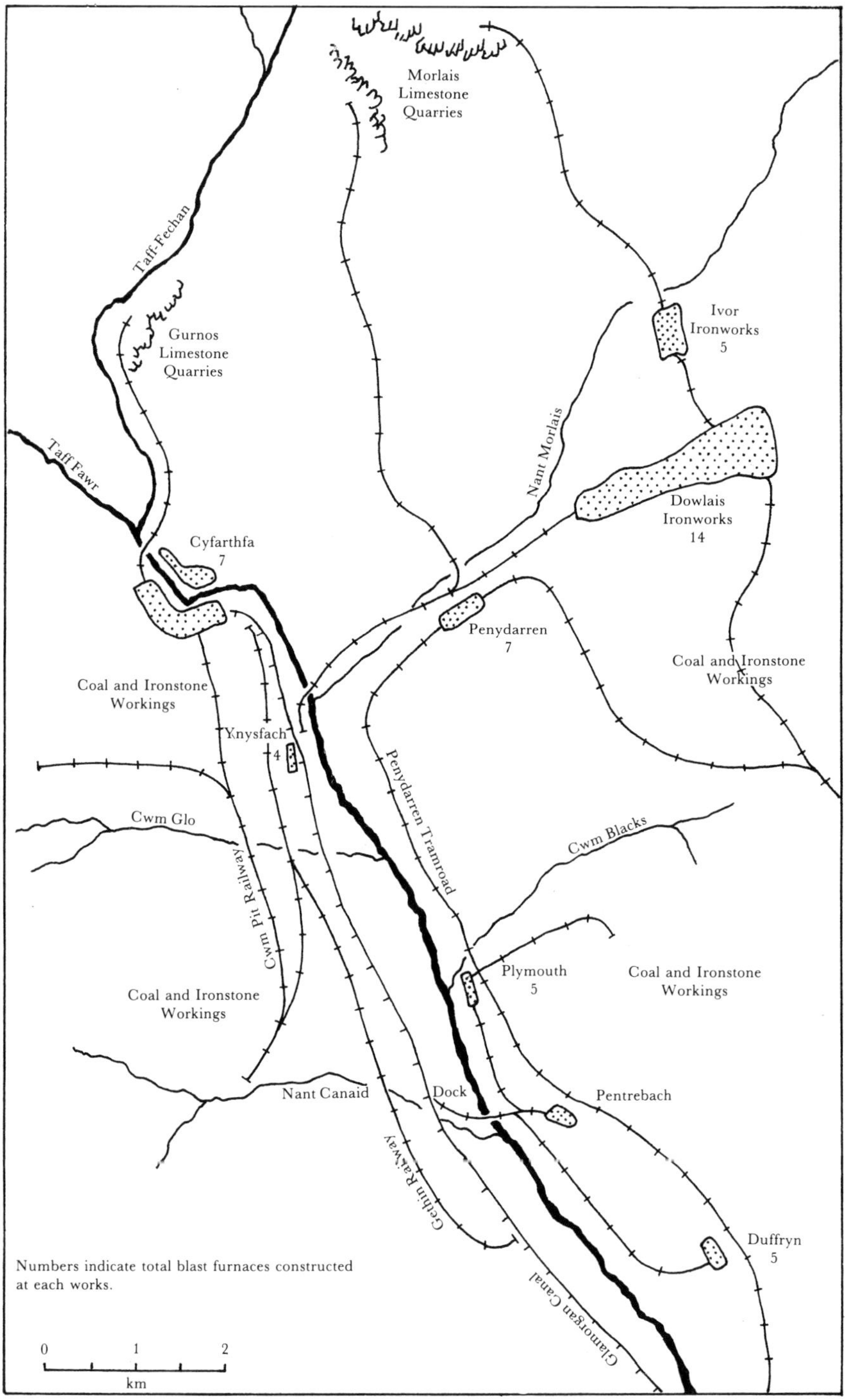

Fig. 62: Position of Merthyr ironworks and sources of raw materials

had existed in the Merthyr Valley two centuries previously. They were small, consisting generally of a blast furnace, cast house, kilns and a smithy. The charge for the furnace was loaded via the bridge house and the furnace relied on running water nearby to power its bellows. Over a period of years the furnaces became larger, the works' buildings became more numerous and more specialised in the operations they performed, and the power of steam eventually replaced that of water. All this however, took many years to accomplish before Cyfarthfa and later Dowlais were to be recognised as the world's greatest ironworks.

Before iron, Merthyr owes its existence to the River Taff. The Taff Fawr and Taff Fechan begin their journeys about a half a mile apart on the slopes of Pen-y-Fan and flow over the rocks of the Old Red Sandstone, Carboniferous Limestone and Millstone Grit Series before reaching the comparatively soft Coal Measure Rocks. The combined effort of Taff Fawr and Taff Fechan which have their confluence near the site of the Cyfarthfa Ironworks was responsible for the creation of a basin in which the village of Merthyr Tydfil was situated. To the south of Merthyr the rocks are again harder and as a result the Taff Valley once more becomes narrow and restricted. But around Merthyr itself the erosive force of the Taff and its many tributary streams exposed many seams of coal and veins of ironstone, materials which were eagerly sought after by the Guests and Crawshays. At

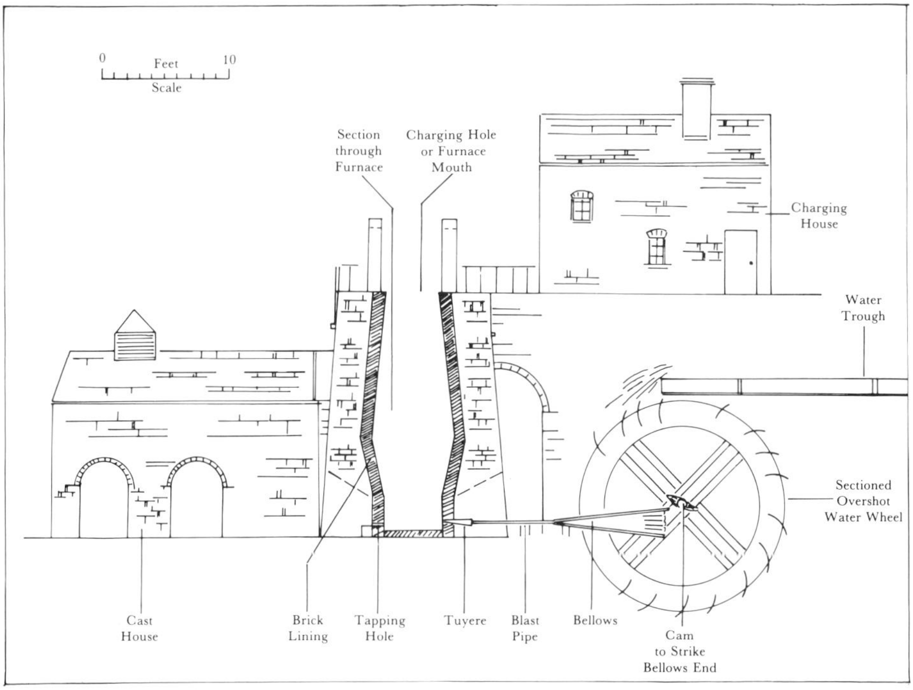

Fig. 63a: Composite early nineteenth century blast furnace

(Reproduced by kind permission of the National Museum of Wales)

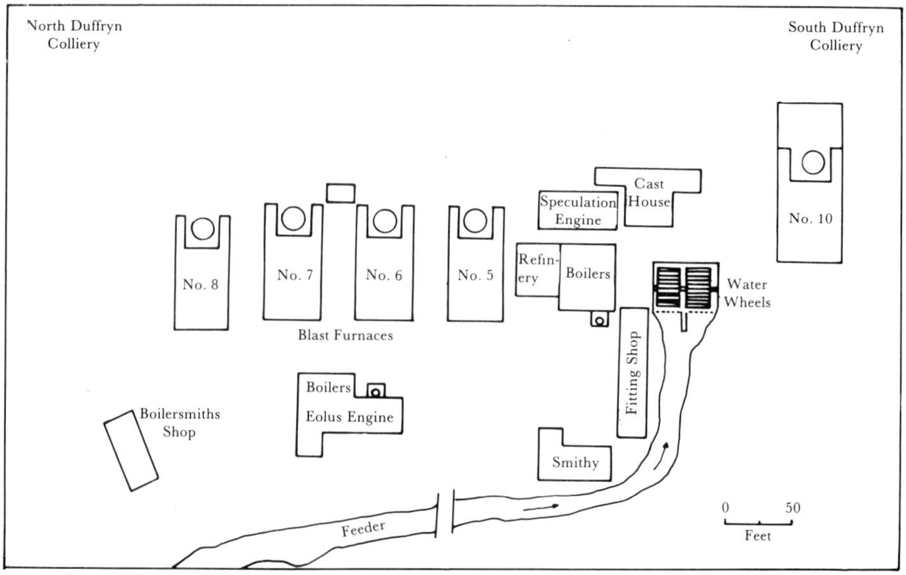

Fig. 63b: Plan of Duffryn Furnaces, 1861

first the ore was extracted by a process known as 'scouring'. A dam was made across a stream and when full the water was released, washing away soil, gravel and stones from the surrounding hillside and leaving behind the heavier iron ore. This method however, made available only surface deposits and did much to disfigure the area's landscape at a very early date. Later the ore which was found in balls or nodules was mined from patches, levels and shallow pits on the hillside overlooking Merthyr and Dowlais.

Besides coal and ore, limestone is an important raw materials in the iron making industry. It acts as a flux and helps separate impurities from the pig iron. This material was also to be found near at hand, the four ironworks quarrying their stone from the banks of the Taff Fechan near Cefn Coed and Pant.

Possessed as it was of all the physical attributes for the development of an iron industry the area lacked the skill and money to develop its resources. In addition the region was almost as remote and inaccessible as it was during the sixteenth century. The necessary skill was to come with the likes of the Guests and Crawshays, from many areas of Britain and much of the capital from the coffers of London and Bristol merchants.

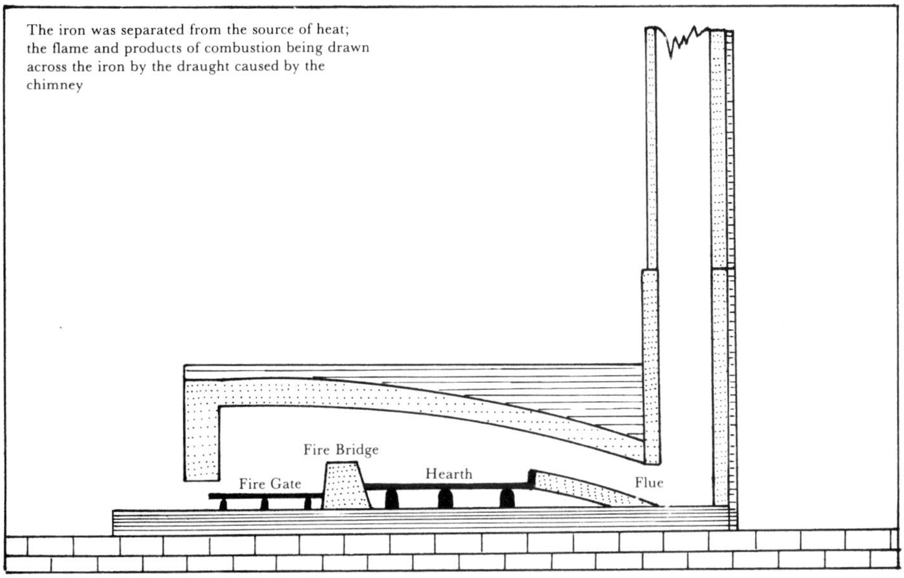

Fig. 64a: Section through a puddling furnace

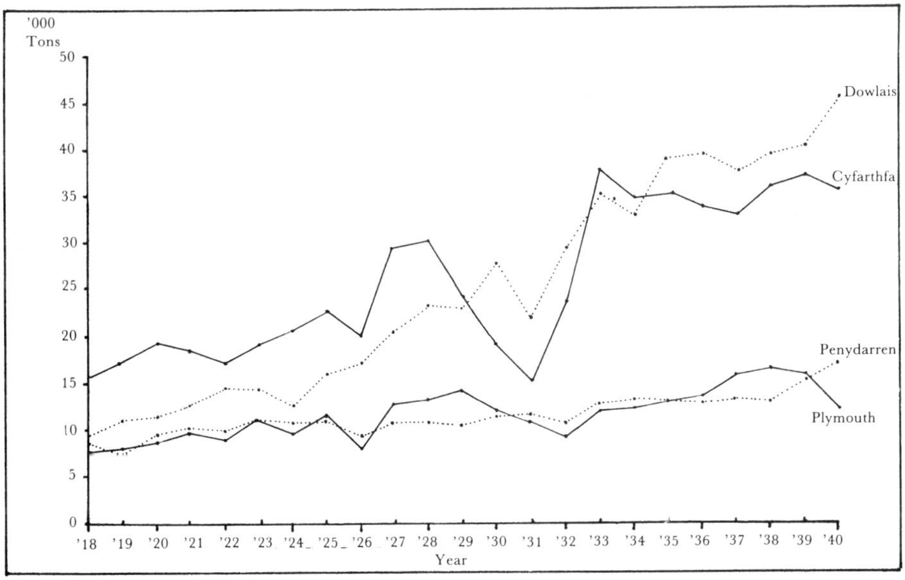

Fig. 64b: Iron carried by Glamorgan Canal for the four Merthyr Ironworks, 1818-1840

(Figures from Old South Wales Ironworks, *J. Lloyd)*

B. The Iron Industry

Dowlais

Of the four Merthyr Ironworks which grew and prospered during the eighteenth and nineteenth centuries the one at Dowlais was the most successful. It was the first to become established and developed into one of the largest and most important ironworks in Britain, at a time when this country led the world in iron production. It was well sited to utilise the raw materials of the area and was well blessed with masters and managers who were skilled in the organisation of labour and the production of iron. It was a works which began when the smelting of iron by coke was in its infancy and was one of only two works in South Wales which successfully made the change over to steel production during the second half of the nineteenth century.

The original Dowlais lease was granted in 1748 by Herbert, Lord Viscount Windsor to Thomas Morgan of Ruperra for 'buildings, advantages and privileges of Marchnad-y-Waun together with twenty acres of land in the Parish of Merthyr Tydfil, with power to work mines and veins of iron and coal, and all quarries of stone and tiles and full liberty to make and sink pits and erect lime kilns'. In 1757 this lease, together with others was granted to Thomas Lewis of Newhouse, Llanishen and two years later a company with nine partners and a joint capital of £4,000 was formed to build the 'Merthyr Furnace'.

This early furnace at Dowlais was very small and was built into the hillside on local ground near to the Dowlais Brook. By 1760 it was producing 500 tons of iron annually and was using 8 tons 1 cwt. of coal to smelt one ton of iron.

At this time the most prominent in the running of the works seem to have been Thomas Lewis and Isaac Wilkinson who came from Denbighshire. As yet nothing is heard of the Guest family, a name which was to become synonomous with that of Dowlais.

The first of that family to gain fame from their enterprise at Dowlais was John Guest who came into the district from Brosely in Shropshire. He was associated with Isaac Wilkinson in 1763 when they were granted a lease to erect a works on land belonging to the Earl of Plymouth. However, soon afterwards, he seems to have found his way to Dowlais and on the 30 April, 1767 was appointed manager of those works.

He built his house on the banks of the Morlais Brook at Gellifaelog quite near to the works and his first years at Dowlais were ones of consolidation rather than rapid growth. Skilled ironworkers came from Staffordshire to assist Guest in his venture and soon rows of cottages were seen on the hillside near the works.

By 1767 the amount of iron produced had increased to 15,000 tons but this improvement in output had its accompanying drawbacks.

Firstly, there were difficulties with establishing a consistent water supply to power the 'air engines' and inevitably the problems of transporting the iron to Cardiff were making themselves felt. The first was overcome in 1798 when Dowlais became the first works in Wales to install a Boulton and Watt Double Acting Steam Engine to supply air for the furnaces. The second, however, was not so easily overcome, for the problem of transport communication was one which was to hinder the works for much of its existence. Because of its remoteness and altitude it was not as conveniently situated as some of the other Merthyr Works.

In 1786 four years after becoming a full partner in the Dowlais concern John Guest retired from active control of the works. He died a year later, was followed in the management of the business by his son Thomas Guest and it is from that date that the real expansion of the works began. This expansion was encouraged by the opening of the Glamorgan Canal in 1790 but rivalry between Cyfarthfa and Dowlais over the operation of the Canal began almost at once. The original idea of constructing a branch canal from Merthyr to Dowlais was replaced by a tram road connecting the works with the canal at Ponty Storehouse, Georgetown.

By 1793 a third blast furnace had been built at the works and output was increasing to the extent that by 1796 Dowlais sold 2,000 tons of pig iron to Cyfarthfa at £5 5s. 0d. per ton. Towards the end of the century the animosity between Dowlais and Cyfarthfa over the Glamorgan Canal culminated in the construction of the Penydarren Tramroad to link with the Canal at Navigation (Abercynon). Dowlais, Penydarren and Plymouth combined in employing George Overton to engineer the tramroad which effectively by-passed the congested stretch of canal between the Basin and Terminus at Cyfarthfa.

The early years of the nineteenth century saw the construction of new forges and rolling mills at Dowlais but further expansion was somewhat hindered by the depressed state of trade throughout the country. Fluctuations in trade generally over the first two decades of the nineteenth century resulted in disturbances and strikes. The costs of household provisions for the ordinary people were high and wage rates were notoriously susceptible to changes in trading conditions.

In 1810 the Dowlais Works experienced its first strike when as a result of a reduction in wages from 12/- to 10/6 per week, the Puddlers struck work. But as so often happened with these early strikes the owners gained the upper hand and after five weeks the men drifted back to work. Here are some examples of wages paid to the different types of workmen at about this time:

Furnace Keepers	21/-	Colliers	15/-
Fitters	15/-	Smiths	15/-
Bridge Servers	15/-	Boys	3/- to 8/-

From 1807 when he took over the management of the works after his father's death, Dowlais was able to benefit from the ability and drive of

Josiah John Guest. Probably more than any other person he was responsible for the success story which was Dowlais and under his direction developments at Dowlais continued apace.

By 1830 the Company was beginning to benefit from the growth of the railways. In that year the Big Mill was built to cope with orders for rails which were arriving at the works. Before the decade was out orders for Dowlais rails would be received from many parts of the world. Here are just some examples:

1835	London and Southampton Railway Company
1836	Liverpool and Manchester Railway Company
1836	Berlin Leipzig Railway
1836	St. Petersburg-Pauloffsky Railway Company
1835	Baltimore and Sasquihanna Railway
1836	New Orleans and Nashville Railway Company

The so-called 'Railway Mania' certainly had an effect on Dowlais where a new works was put into production. The Ifor Works, named after Josiah John Guest's son, were begun in 1839 and were operational in time to take advantage of the boom years of the 1840s. These would be years in which the South Wales Iron Industry in general and Dowlais in particular would reach the height of its prosperity. Both works were operating to capacity by 1842 and in the two years which followed received orders from Russia for 86,000 tons of rails. By 1845 the works which employed 7,300 men, women and children and produced 88,400 tons of pig iron probably justified its claim to be the greatest in the World.

However, even with orders coming in from all parts of the World and output breaking all records it soon became evident that the years of prosperity would come to an end.

By 1848 the Dowlais lease was due for renewal and many attempts to frame terms for a new agreement had already failed. The rent paid to the Marquess of Bute remained at £100 per annum and the Dowlais Company received £10,000 alone as a result of sub-leasing coal rights to the Penydarren Company. It seemed that deadlock had been reached and the works would close. But in April 1848 a new yearly rent of £25,000 to £30,000 was agreed upon and once more the great works came to life. One can perhaps imagine the relief of the Dowlais people on hearing that the works would continue and understand the emotions, which lay behind the welcome Sir John and Lady Charlotte received on their return to Merthyr.

Despite a fall in orders, plans to modernise the works were drawn up following the renewal of the lease. From now on however, owing to illness, Sir John was to play a minor role in the running of the works and on his death in 1852 the works continued under the management of John Evans. The works, Sir John's vast wealth and large estates, were left to Lady Charlotte and the children, G. T. Clarke and H. A. Bruce being appointed Trustees.

In 1856 the works came under the management of that great engineer William Menelaus, a man who was to play an unrivalled part in the reconstruction of the works. That year marked not only another turning point in the fortunes of the Dowlais Ironworks but heralded radical changes in the iron industry as a whole. Dowlais made its greatest loss ever of £52,000 and took out a licence to use Sir Henry Bessemer's method of making malleable iron without the use of coal or charcoal. Many disappointments would follow before the commercial production of steel would become a viable proposition at Dowlais.

These were difficult years indeed at Dowlais, but under the direction of men like Menelaus the Works would continue a prosperous enterprise for many years to come.

June 1865 saw the first rolling of Bessemer produced steel at Dowlais, and the following two decades the conversion of the works, from one concerned with the manufacture of iron components, to one engaged in the production of steel rails and sections. By 1880, the year Sir Ifor Bertie Guest was created Baron Wimborne, steel was being produced at the works by both acid Bessemer converters and Siemens-Martin open hearth furnaces. The use of the acid bessemer process meant the local coal measure ore, rich in phosphorus and sulphur, was no longer suitable. Local ore production as a result declined rapidly and ceased altogether during the early 1870's. The company had to search for other sources which could supply the large tonnages of haematite necessary for large scale steelmaking. To satisfy this need the Dowlais Company began the opening of mines and quarries in northern Spain and it was the exploitation of iron-ore resources first near Bilbao and later at Obregon which began the immigration of Spanish workers to Dowlais towards the end of the nineteenth century. Although at this time the ironstone mines were being closed, more extensive coal mines were being sunk and through the 1870's Dowlais once again became a profitable concern.

In 1882, on the death of William Menelaus, E. P. Martin became general manager and continued the successful development of the works. So successful was Martin as manager in fact, that Lord Wimborne formed a limited liability company in 1899, two years prior to the merger with the Patent Nut and Bolt Company of Birmingham. In 1902 a further amalgamation with the largest producer of wood screws in the world, resulted in the formation of the firm of Guest, Keen and Nettlefold.

Developments at the works continued apace with the completion in 1909 of two new blast furnaces built to an American pattern with fully automatic charging equipment. These 'A' and 'B' 'Yankee' furnaces, which cost £2,500,000 to construct, accompanied modifications to the rolling mills.

In June 1912 the people of Merthyr and Dowlais gave a rousing welcome to King George V and Queen Mary. The Royal couple visited many of the departments of the Dowlais Works and saw the famous coal and steel arches which had been erected in honour of their visit.

Plate 37a: NEW BLAST FURNACE PLANT, DOWLAIS STEELWORKS, 1907
(By permission of John A. Owen)

Plate 37b: DOWLAIS IRONWORKS, 1870 *(By permission of John A. Owen)*

Although perhaps not planned as such their visit marked a fitting climax to the history of a great works. It remained prosperous until the First World War but no amount of capital, new plant or managerial skill thereafter could make it a viable, economic enterprise. The changing economics of iron and steel manufacture demanded large, integrated plants, with cheap, easy access to large reserves of ore and producing a diversity of steel products. Dowlais unfortunately failed these requirements and, like the three other Merthyr iron-making concerns, suffered the consequences.[10]

Cyfarthfa Ironworks

The word Cyfarthfa means 'the barking place' and refers to the fact that this part of Merthyr Tydfil was once the favourite haunt of the huntsman. This continued reminder of the area's long lost rurality gives no indication whatsoever of the activities carried on along the banks of this stretch of the Taff during the past two hundred years. When the word was still a true reflection of the surroundings the area must have been very different to what we see to-day. It is, I suppose, difficult to ignore the many industrial scars, the ruined masonry and spoil heaps, and picture the spot as Anthony Bacon would have seen it when he first came to the area in 1765. Today the site of the Cyfarthfa works is occupied by the buildings of such concerns as Thorns Triang, Star Brick and Hoover which obscure somewhat the last remains of that once great ironmaking concern.

The original founder of the works was Anthony Bacon a native of Whitehaven in Cumberland. Cyfarthfa it seems was not among his first enterprises for he had travelled widely in the 'Colonies' of North America, possessed fishing rights off the coast of Cumberland and coal mines on Cape Breton Isle. These and other interests were apparently set aside on him realising the tremendous economic potential of the Merthyr region.

Following his arrival in South Wales he proceeded to secure mineral rights over a tract of land of about 4,000 acres on the opposite side of the valley to that already leased to the Dowlais concern. The rent paid to Lord Talbot of Hensol and Michael Richards of Cardiff was set at £100 per annum, identical to that agreed at Dowlais almost twenty years earlier. The first small furnace was erected in 1765 probably somewhere near to the confluence of the Taff Fawr and Taff Fechan. By 1767 a second furnace had been built and Bacon played a leading part in organising the building of a road to Cardiff. The development of the works seemed to have been very slow however, production picking up with the outbreak of the American War of Independence in 1775. Bacon possessed a contract to furnish the Board of Ordnance with cannon and Cyfarthfa began these supplies in June 1776. This contract was later transferred to Francis Homfray who leased the foundry and forge at Cyfarthfa in 1783 and there seems to be no truth in the story that he lost the contract because he was suspected of supplying cannon to the Americans as well as the British Government.

On his death in June 1786 Bacon was the owner of furnaces at Plymouth and Hirwaun as well as Cyfarthfa. But, because his sons were still minors it was necessary that arrangements be made for the running of these works until such time as they achieved their majority. The Plymouth works was leased to Richard Hill, Hirwaun to Mr. Glover of Abercarn and Cyfarthfa to Richard Crawshay of Normanton, Yorkshire.

Many years later, in a speech at the Bush Hotel in Merthyr his grandson William gave an account of how his grandfather embarked on his career in the iron trade and started on the road which would eventually lead him to Cyfarthfa.

Richard Crawshay was the son of a Yorkshire farmer, who at the age of sixteen following a dispute with his father left home for London. There he sold the pony which had carried him from Normanton and found employment at an iron warehouse. By perseverance and hard work he made progress in his employment eventually gaining full charge of the business. In subsequent years Crawshay developed a business connection with Anthony Bacon, the firm of Bacon and Crawshay holding contracts to supply cannon to the East India Company and the King of Sardinia. In 1786, the year of Anthony Bacon's death Richard Crawshay came to Cyfarthfa to take over the lease of the works and under him the gradual and then rapid expansion of the works took place. The growth of the works after 1789 was due significantly to its nearness to the terminus of the Glamorgan Canal, an advantage much envied by the proprietors of the other Merthyr Ironworks.

Cyfarthfa attracted many visitors who were most impressed with what they saw. Benjamin Malkin for example visited the works on two occasions in 1803 and again three years later. Following his first visit he wrote: 'His (Richard Crawshay's) house is surrounded with fire, flame, smoke and ashes. The noise of the hammers, rolling mills, forges and bellows incessantly din and crash upon the ear. Bars and pigs of iron are continually thrown to the hugely accumulating heaps that threaten to choke up every avenue of access.

'The machinery of this establishment is gigantic; and that part of it, worked by water, among the most scientifically curious and mechanically powerful to which modern improvement has given birth. The most remarkable piece of mechanism in Merthyr Tydfil is the great waterwheel made by Watkin George. Its diameter is fifty feet, and it has the power of fifty horses. It has the advantage of water from above, on its centre, and beneath it; or in other words, it possesses all the forces of an overshot, breast and undershot wheel. I apprehend it to be the largest in the kingdom. Watkin George and William Aubrey, were the two principal engineers, and they are both natives of this country. Watkin George in particular, who planned and executed this immense undertaking, was a common village carpenter. Owing to his success in these mechanical inventions, he got forward by degrees and became at last so useful to Mr. Crawshay, as to obtain a share in his works. He has lately quitted the concern with from thirty to forty thousand pounds in his pocket.'

By 1806 the number of blast furnaces had increased to six, two rolling mills had been constructed and employed 1,500 men. Malkin now observed that 'Mr. Crawshay's ironworks of Cyfarthfa are now by far the largest in this kingdom; probably, indeed, the largest in Europe; and in that case, as far as we know, the largest in the world'.

The second Crawshay to control Cyfarthfa, William, had little time for Merthyr and preferred to run Cyfarthfa from the London Office at George Yard. As a result he appointed his son, also called William, as Manager of the works. The second William devoted a great deal of time and energy to making Cyfarthfa a most prosperous undertaking. He worked unstintingly but constantly quarrelled with his father who remained in overall control of the works. William was also somewhat wary of his brothers Richard and George, both of whom had other interests and cared little for involvement at Cyfarthfa. On numerous occasions William pressed his father for a partnership in the concern but he refused to relinquish control. Despite his constant complaints regarding his position at Cyfarthfa, William was able to establish himself as an 'Iron King'. He built Cyfarthfa Castle at a cost of £30,000 in 1825, a year later purchased Hensol Castle for £17,500 and when his father

Plate 38a: CYFARTHFA IRONWORKS about 1870
(By permission of Merthyr Borough Council)

died in 1834 he was left in control not only of Cyfarthfa but the works at Hirwaun as well.

As at Dowlais, the '30s and '40s saw the construction of new furnaces, forges and mills at Cyfarthfa and Ynysfach to keep pace with the demands of the new railway companies. In 1836 two new furnaces and a blast engine house were built at Ynysfach and in 1846 the New Mill was opened at Cyfarthfa. This mill contained twenty puddling furnaces and in March 1847 made 1,144 tons of railway iron in one week.

At its peak, the Cyfarthfa ironworks occupied a considerable area of land. Built into the hillside below the present site of the Thorns factory were the seven blast furnaces and near to these on the west bank of the Taff were the cast houses, forges, mills and refineries of the works. These continued in a southerly direction towards the terminus of the Glamorgan Canal. On the opposite bank of the river where the Triang factory now stands were other mills and forges. The site at Ynysfach, although smaller than that at Cyfarthfa is interesting in that it possesses the best remains of any local iron-works. Hidden now behind the College of Technology, it was linked by tramroad with the main works and nearby collieries. The upper parts of the four furnaces have been demolished and the lower parts altered as a result of the removal of the cast houses and the sealing off of the furnace bases. What one cannot fail to appreciate is the impressive engine house which stands beside the furnaces. This was one of two such structures at this site which housed huge beam engines which fed the furnaces with a blast of air. The architecture is typically Cyfarthfa, the ultimate seal being the use of dressed limestone around the quoins and archways. Grand as it is, a study of old photographs of the Cyfarthfa site will reveal buildings of similar style but even larger dimensions.

In 1845 the works had eleven furnaces and made 45,760 tons of iron. Two years later William retired to Caversham Park and left the works in the charge of a son by his second marriage, Robert Thompson Crawshay. William, however, continued to influence policy at Cyfarthfa largely as a result of his son's poor state of health. By 1850 Cyfarthfa was past its peak of prosperity and the ensuing years were ones of decline. Trade was unfavourable and Cyfarthfa lacked the organising ability of men such as Menelaus who helped Dowlais through these difficult years. Problems confronted the concern at an alarming rate.

By the 1850s Cyfarthfa was forced to import iron ore from Whitehaven, that from the 'miserable patch of argillaceous mine' at Cyfarthfa being no longer suitable for the making of iron. In 1864 the Cyfarthfa lease was renewed after almost thirty years of intermittent negotiations but to add to the difficulties, as a result of spasmodic production many of Cyfarthfa's best men began to leave. Robert Thompson was continually troubled by ill health and was unable to deal firmly with labour disputes. By 1867, the year of William's death, Cyfarthfa's supremacy in the iron trade had gone for ever and Robert was left to make the best of a sick enterprise.

Plate 38b: CYFARTHFA IRONWORKS in 1881
(By permission of Merthyr Borough Council)

In 1872 preliminary negotiations were begun for the sale of the works with valuations ranging from over £1 million to under £800,000. Offers were so low and indefinite that the idea was abandoned until 1874 when Robert Thompson Crawshay was prepared to reduce the asking price by a considerable amount.

Union activities at this time undoubtedly strengthened Robert's resolve to sell the works. He remained stubborn to the last in his opposition to trade union demands, lacking it seems the sensibility and foresight of his wife who recognised the fact that 'The time is fast passing away when one set of people could say to another, "You shall do all the work and we shall do all the play".'[11] Because of the workers refusal to consent to a wage reduction of 20% Crawshay issued dismissal notices and closed the works in April 1874. Although the strike ended in March 1875 the works was not to re-open before Robert Thompson Crawshay's death in May 1879.

On his death the works passed onto the joint ownership of his three sons, William Thompson, Robert Thompson and Richard Frederick Crawshay. Only William Thompson was to live at the Castle, Robert residing in London and Richard at Abergavenny, but under the auspices of Crawshay Brothers and Co. they were to play their part in the modification and refurbishing of the works. Re-vitalisation came with the construction of a £15,000 steel works capable of producing 50,000 tons of finished steel a year.

A Dowlais trained engineer was appointed consultant engineer to the project which approached completion in May 1884, with the lighting of two blast furnaces. In 1890, as a result of the great strain placed upon the finances of the Crawshay partners, a limited liability company was formed. By 1897 the works had reached its final form, employing 4,000 and producing annually 75,000 tons of steel. Five new blast furnaces replaced the old masonary ones, four Bessemer converters were installed as well as new rolling mills and a sleeper plant.

The resurrection of the Crawshay Empire was to be short lived however, for in 1902 when Guest, Keen and Nettlefold of Dowlais acquired the share capital of Cyfarthfa, the company effectively ended investment there and concentrated all future spending at Dowlais. Iron production ended in 1910 but in 1915 the works was re-commissioned as a result of grants from the Ministry of Munitions. Shell steel was produced for the First World War but on the 29 August, 1919 the last blast furnace was stopped.[12] Only the collieries like Cwm, Gethin and Castle, which had been opened in the 1850s and 1860s, were to remain productive for a few more years.[13]

Plymouth Ironworks

In 1974 the Merthyr Borough Council embarked upon two large land reclamation schemes which almost eradicated the not inconsiderable remains of the Plymouth ironworks. The levelling of massive coal tips at Cwm Blacks and Duffryn saw the end of buildings and watercourses which once formed a vital part of a works, which although eclipsed locally by the giants of Cyfarthfa and Dowlais, was nevertheless a quite extensive and important enterprise.

The works began in a similar fashion to those already established at Dowlais and Cyfarthfa, in fact Anthony Bacon and John Guest, the two men responsible for the initial developments at those sites were also concerned with the early history of the Plymouth Works.

In December 1763 the Earl of Plymouth leased land to John Guest and Isaac Wilkinson for the setting up of various buildings associated with the manufacture of iron. The land concerned lay to the south of Merthyr, to the east of the River Taff, the works itself probably being established on the banks of a small brook later to be known as Cwm Blacks. It is not known whether Guest and Wilkinson actually produced iron on this site for they very soon disposed of the rights to Anthony Bacon.

Following Bacon's death in 1786 the works was leased to his brother-in-law Richard Hill who already had experience of iron manufacture at Hirwaun and Cyfarthfa. Hill's lack of capital was aggravated further in 1799 when Thomas Bacon came of age and was able to negotiate new terms to the lease. Hill was forced to seek financial support for the venture and eventually managed to secure two wealthy partners. As a result in 1803 the Plymouth Forge Company was set up, new furnaces and forges were constructed and iron production was able to gain momentum.

The Plymouth ironworks was eventually comprised of the three quite separate sites of Plymouth, Pentrebach and Duffryn. The first, and probably the site of the original furnace, coincides with Baker's Garage, the second was about half a mile to the south and grew up near the mansion which Anthony Hill built for himself and the third at Duffryn, between Pentrebach and Troedyrhiw. It is somewhat difficult to explain the dispersal of the works in this manner but one of the reasons must surely have been the importance of an adequate supply of water for driving machinery. Water was diverted from the Taff by a weir built near to the present College of Technology, and then carried by open feeder to the Plymouth site where it powered machinery. It then continued by feeder to be used successively at Pentrebach and Duffryn before being returned to the River Taff at Troedyrhiw. Plymouth relied on water power long after many of its rivals had invested in steam. A bill of sale drawn up in 1834 states that a steam engine was being used at Duffryn and indicates that Anthony Hill had found it necessary to move with the times. In that year the Plymouth Company possessed 'seven well constructed blast furnaces capable of making 500 tons per week of pig iron'.

From 1826 Anthony Hill was the sole manager of the works, John having retired and Richard concerning himself with the selling side of the business. As 'Master' at Plymouth Anthony was well liked and respected but his energies were not directed wholeheartedly to the efficient running of the works. He experimented on a considerable scale and involved himself in the study of the sciences on which the manufacture of iron was founded. The works was renowned for its good quality iron and managed to secure the order for cables for Brunel's 'Great Eastern' in 1859.

The reasons why the works at Plymouth were never destined to enjoy the outstanding success and prosperity of its neighbours are difficult to fathom. The Company's mineral takings covered a large area and yielded in the early years ample supplies of iron ore and coal, in fact the Plymouth Collieries enjoyed the longest operational life of any iron company pit in the Borough. Capital to expand and improve the works remained a problem for the Hills and it might be said that Anthony Hill was not possessed of the same business acumen as that enjoyed by William Crawshay and Josiah Guest.

The works were put up for sale in 1834 but no buyer could be found. As a result Plymouth continued in the ownership of the Hill family up until Anthony's death in 1862. In that year it was sold to Messrs. Fothergill, Hankey and Bateman for £250,000. The coal mines at Graig, Duffryn and Abercanaid were probably the best part of the bargain for the blast furnaces at Plymouth and Duffryn and the forges and mills at Pentrebach were old, outmoded and conversion to steel production appeared out of the question.

Under the direction of Richard Fothergill efforts were made to revitalise the Plymouth Works. High quality cold blast pig iron production, at which Plymouth had excelled, was abondoned in favour of cheaper bulk produced hot blast iron. In making this transformation, however, the company was committing itself to competition with the likes of Dowlais and Cyfarthfa. They quite soon found that such competition would be fierce and that with declining local resources and limited capital the company would inevitably fail.

As a result of a creditors meeting in 1875 a committee of control was set up to run the Plymouth Works but five years later it was to be finally closed. Although advertised in 1882 the works was never to be sold, its buildings either falling into decay or utilised by the Hills Plymouth Colliery Company.[14]

Penydarren Ironworks

When Francis Homfray, the founder of the Penydarren ironworks, came to our district in 1782, the works at Dowlais, Cyfarthfa and Plymouth were already quite well established. They occupied the most convenient sites and had access to the richest mineral takings. It is not surprising therefore that of the four local ironworks, Penydarren was the last to start and the first to close down.

Before becoming established at Penydarren Homfray visited a number of the works in the area, leasing the cannon boring mill at Cyfarthfa in 1783. His stay there was a short one and in 1784 he helped his three sons, Jeremiah, Thomas and Samuel establish their own works on the banks of the Morlais Brook. The works' site was not ideal, confined as it was to the bottom of a narrow valley and the lease the Homfrays secured far from satisfactory. From the outset Penydarren experienced difficulty with its water supply. This resulted from the fact that the Dowlais works was sited nearby on higher ground and was able to control many local streams at will. In 1784 in return for Homfray granting certain rights of passage for waggons and horses John Guest allowed Penydarren to make alterations to a particular watercourse. The lease gave the Homfray family rights to mine iron ore but not coal, a handicap the works had to endure for the whole of its existence. The coal rights of Pwll yr Hwyaid had already been leased to the Dowlais Company so the Homfrays were forced to negotiate rights to mine coal from John Guest.

Despite all these difficulties the works gained and grew in reputation. Samuel Homfray was the first of the Merthyr ironmasters to use some of his wealth in the building of an impressive mansion. Penydarren House was built quite close to the works but was 'sufficiently removed from the town by the extent of the pleasure grounds, and contains all the conveniences and luxuries requisite for a family of wealth and importance'.

Of the three brothers who came to Merthyr, Samuel was to play the leading part in the running of the Penydarren Ironworks. He was on the one hand a somewhat arrogant and overbearing individual but on the other a respected and sympathetic employer. Jeremiah certainly found his brother difficult to work with for in 1789 he relinquished his role as part manager of

Plate 39a: THE PENYDARREN IRONWORKS DURING DEMOLITION, probably about 1880
(By permission of Merthyr Borough Council)

Plate 39b: THE REMAINS OF NO. 5 BLAST FURNACE AND OTHER BUILDINGS AT DUFFRYN IRONWORKS, 1966
(By permission of Clive Thomas)

the works to join with others in the building of furnaces at Ebbw Vale. In 1796 the works produced 2,000 tons of iron more than Dowlais and was soon employing a thousand men. In 1800 Samuel Homfray invited a Cornish engineer by the name of Richard Trevithick to Penydarren to construct a forge engine for use in the works. The two men, both similar in personality became close friends and when the engine had been completed Trevithick suggested the construction of an engine which could be used for moving waggons. Homfray made facilities available to Trevithick and aided by local workmen he set about his task of building a steam locomotive which would pre-date Stephenson's 'Rocket' by a quarter of a century.

By the end of the eighteenth century William Foreman, an ordnance agent at the Tower of London, had become a prominent partner in the enterprise. After Samuel Homfray left Penydarren in 1813 William Foreman came to Penydarren House to live and took charge of the ironworks.

But if the works was without the rich mineral reserves of the other local companies it was certainly not lacking men of influence capable of securing large and profitable contracts. William Thompson a London alderman and a man who twice became Lord Mayor of London became a partner soon after Foreman took up residence at Penydarren. The company enjoyed the years of boom and slump in the first half of the nineteenth century and during those years cables were made for the Menai Suspension Bridge and rails manufactured for the Liverpool and Manchester Railway. In all, seven blast furnaces were built into the hillside near the site of the Morlais Motors Garage and puddling furnaces and rolling mills occupied the site of present day Trevithick Street.

In 1854 William Thompson, the company's most influential partner, died and five years later the works closed for good. The Penydarren ironworks was purchased by Messrs. Fothergill and Hankey but gradually became derelict. Today only a few crumbling remains are barely discernable to remind us of its existence.[15]

Table 1

Estimated statement of the number of persons employed in the Ironworks and Collieries in the Parish of Merthyr Tydfil in 1841.

Dowlais	5,192
Cyfarthfa	3,000
Plymouth	2,400
Penydarren	1,909
Other Small Collieries	299

Source: Appendix to the First Report of the Child Employment Commissioners 1842.

Plate 40a: GRAVESTONE ILLUSTRATING IRONWORKS OCCUPATION *(By permission of Clive Thomas)*

Plate 40b: GRAVESTONE ILLUSTRATING IRONWORKS OCCUPATION *(By permission of Clive Thomas)*

For over a century ironmaking in Merthyr flourished, making the name of our town synonymous with iron manufacture. But by the end of the 1840s it became increasingly obvious that this prosperity could not last much longer. The local ore reserves were practically exhausted and the cost of importing iron ore made Merthyr produced iron, less competitive in World markets; in fact the locational factors which had first attracted the ironmasters to the area were becoming less relevant and the economic implications of Merthyr's geographic isolation were becoming more and more apparent.

First Penydarren and then Plymouth succumbed and only the giants of Cyfarthfa and Dowlais were able to continue. But eventually, even these two great companies, which had established world-wide reputations for quality of products, were forced to acknowledge the harsh realities of economic change. Although both manufactured iron and steel into the twentieth century and Dowlais in particular remained a formidable concern, the second half of the nineteenth century saw a marked change in emphasis as far as industry in the Merthyr District was concerned. Iron was no longer all important and the mining of coal began to grow in importance.

C. *The Coal Industry*

Man has been aware of the existence of coal in South Wales for perhaps more than 2,000 years, its exploitation for profit, however, is a fairly recent event. In 1670 Edward Herbert of Penarth 'a gentleman farmer' held 'one grant under ye Earl of Pembroke of ye coaleworks and lymekilns within ye Parish of Merthyr Didwill for 99 years' and in 1697 William Edward, a yeoman of Eglwselan, bequeathed to his wife 'all that coale-works, pitts and veins of coale, together with limekilns and quarries of stone situated in a place called Tule Dowlais'.[16]

For centuries however, the lack of demand locally and problems involved in transporting the coal hindered the growth of the industry in the Taff Valley. It was not until the beginning of the nineteenth century that the area's potential in terms of coal production began to be realised.

The early history of intensive coal mining in the Merthyr Valley differs considerably from an area like the Rhondda. There mining began in the 1850s and 1860s in response to a demand for high quality steam coal but in the Merthyr area mining began almost a hundred years earlier to supply the needs of the local ironworks. Up until the middle of the nineteenth century the levels and pits of the Taff and Taff Bargoed Valleys were owned almost entirely by the iron companies and existed to supply coal to their furnaces and forges. In the second half of the century however, deeper pits were sunk to tap the profitable steam coal seams and collieries owned by the ironworks originally, continued to mine coal for sale purposes long after the works themselves had closed.

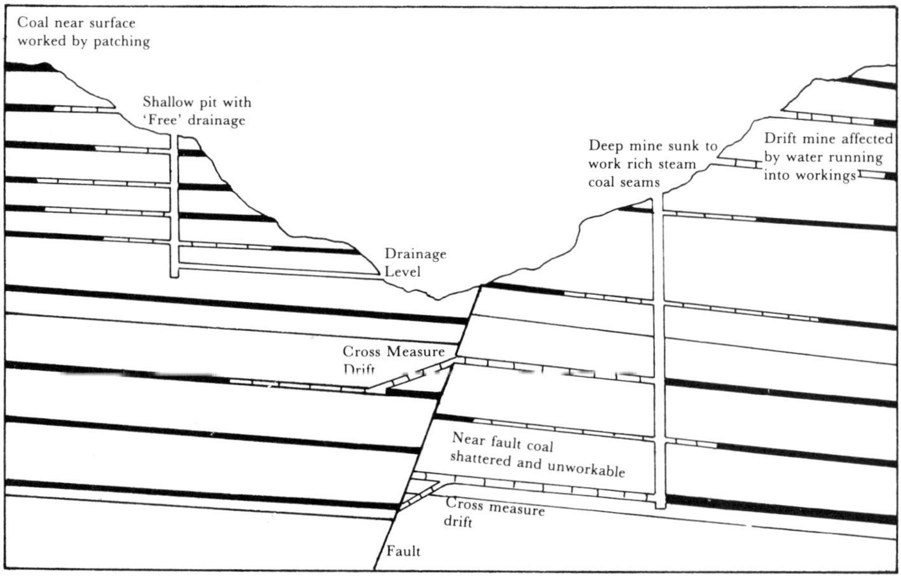

Fig. 65a: Simplified section across the Taff Valley to illustrate different methods of working coal

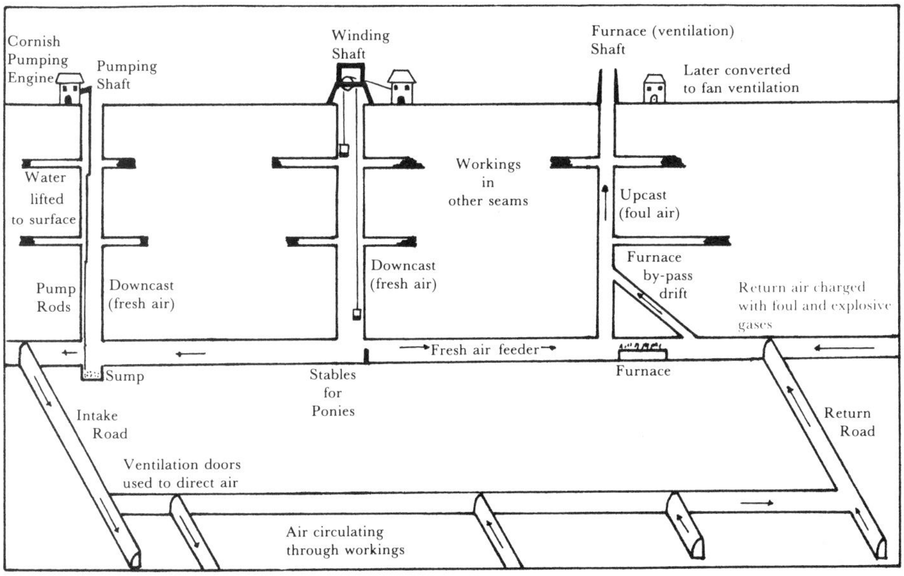

Fig. 65b: Simplified diagram of mid-nineteenth century colliery Merthyr colliery

The South Wales Coalfield is an elongated basin some ninety miles long and approximately sixteen miles wide with coal bearing rocks lying above a succession of Millstone Grit and Carboniferous Limestone rocks. Most of the coal mined in our area has come from the seams of the Lower Coal Measures for here were to be found rich reserves of good quality coal. A much smaller amount of coal was mined from the seams of the Pennant Series and remains of these workings can be seen on the valley sides particularly between Troedyrhiw and Pentrebach.

The seams of the Lower Coal Series outcrop around Merthyr and Dowlais and dip gently at a gradient of 1:13 to the south. Thus, a seam like the famous Merthyr Four Foot Seam which outcrops on the mountainside near Heolgerrig and Dowlais, was to be found sixteen yards beneath the surface at Upper Abercanaid Colliery, 225 yards at Castle Pit Troedyrhiw and 425 yards at Merthyr-Vale Colliery. The early workings can be found therefore, in the north of our area where the seams were quite easily accessible and could be worked by level, drift or shallow cut. In all something like twenty different seams have been mined in the Taff Valley, from the Cwmdu No. 1 which crops high on the valley sides above Troedyrhiw, to the Gellideg mined some 545 yards below the valley floor at Merthyr-Vale. Faults which trend north-east to south-west across the area also play a large part in determining the depth of a seam at a particular point. These faults are numerous but the two most significant are the Merthyr Church and the Dowlais Faults, the first giving a downthrow of 70 metres to the west at Pentrebach and the second a downthrow of 40 metres to the west at Cwmbargoed. Movement along these fault plains resulted in the shattering of the seams for many yards either side of the fault and this, together with such occurrences as 'rolls' and 'wash outs' have made mining in our area a difficult and dangerous task.

Table 2

Relative depths, in yards, of major steam coal seams in selected Merthyr collieries.

	Coal Seams			
	Four Feet	*Six Feet*	*Nine Feet*	*Gellideg*
Cwm Pit (Cyfarthfa I.C.)	13	34	90	126
No. 1 Pit Upper Abercanaid (Plymouth I.C.)	16	44	82	150
No. 1 Pit South Duffryn (Plymouth I.C.)	143	150	207	258
No. 1 Pit Penydarren (Penydarren I.C.)	218	235	294	—
Castle Pit (Cyfarthfa I.C.)	255	267	330	388
No. 1 Pit Bedlinog (Dowlais I.C.)	491	541	564	—
No. 1 Pit Merthyr Vale	425	444	481	539
No. 1 Pit Deep Navigation	691	717	742	—

The thickness and configuration of seams also varied from pit to pit and this was obviously a major factor in determining profitability. The Six Feet seam, known at Dowlais as the Big Coal for example, was not a single seam of coal. At South Duffryn Colliery the two three foot bands of coal were separated by almost twenty feet of fire clay, shale and rock whilst at Merthyr Vale only three feet of shale separated the coal.

Seams like the Saron, Gilfach, Taldwyn, Hafod, Abergorki and Gorllwyn were mined quite extensively by the levels and drifts of the Plymouth Iron Company between Troedyrhiw and Pentrebach but it was the deeper steam coal seams like the Four Feet, Six Feet, Nine Feet, Seven Feet and Gellideg which were much sought after by the steamship companies and navies of the world. Largely as a result of Four Feet coal exported from Robert Thomas' level at Waunwyllt the term 'Merthyr Coal' became a virtual passport to success and in attempts to capitalise on this success many companies from other parts of South Wales incorporated 'Merthyr' into their titles, for example, Graigola Merthyr (Swansea Area), Hood's Merthyr, Bute Merthyr (Rhondda).

The early history of coal working in the Merthyr area is somewhat poorly documented. The workings existed as a necessary adjunct of the iron industry, only a small amount of what was being mined being sold to the householders of the town. It was not until 1850 that an Act of Parliament was passed making the keeping of accurate colliery plans compulsory and by this time many pits and countless levels had been opened and worked to exhaustion by the four iron companies. These early workings were of necessity sited close to the ironworks and many pits mined both coal and iron stone.

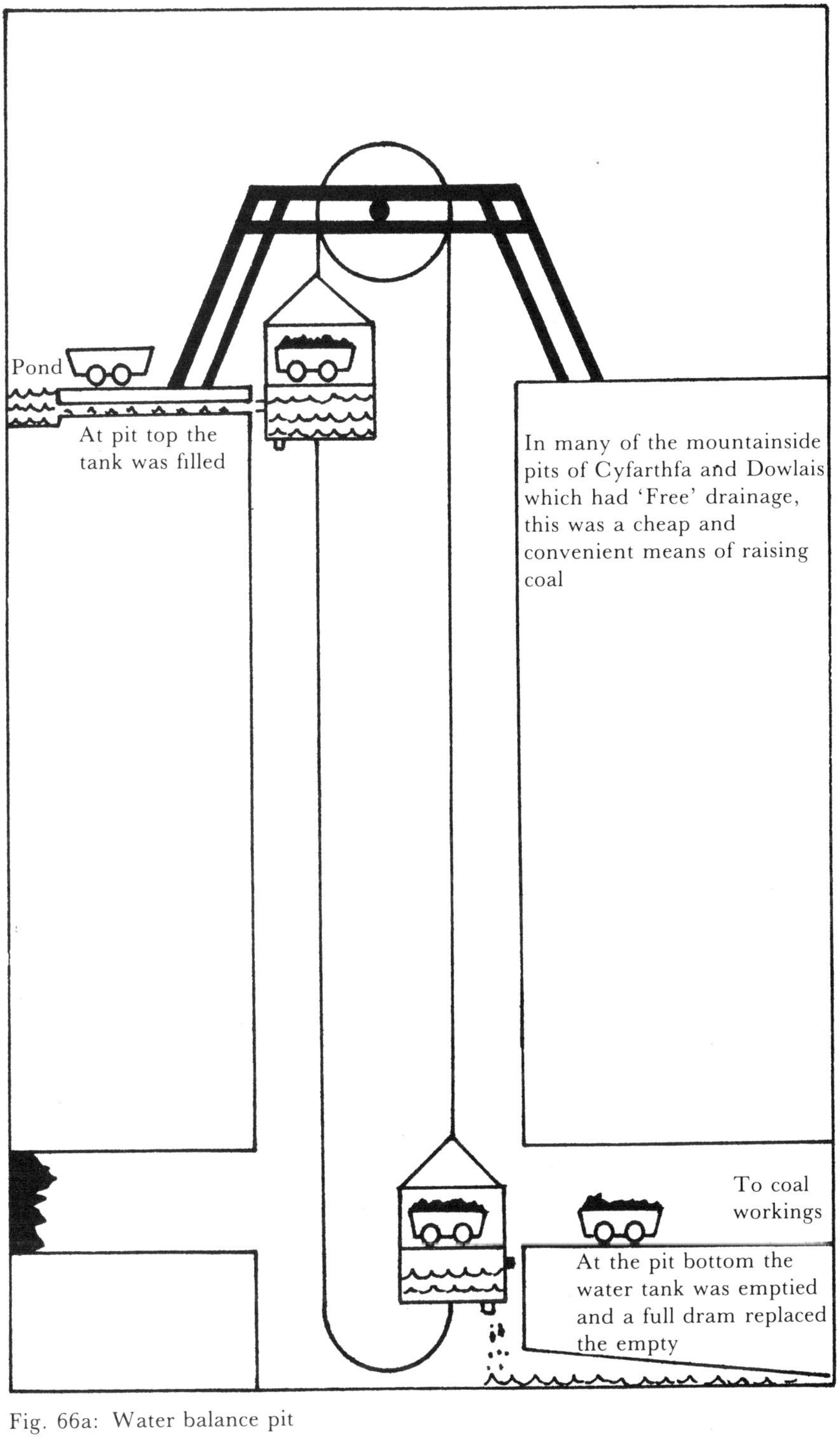

Fig. 66a: Water balance pit

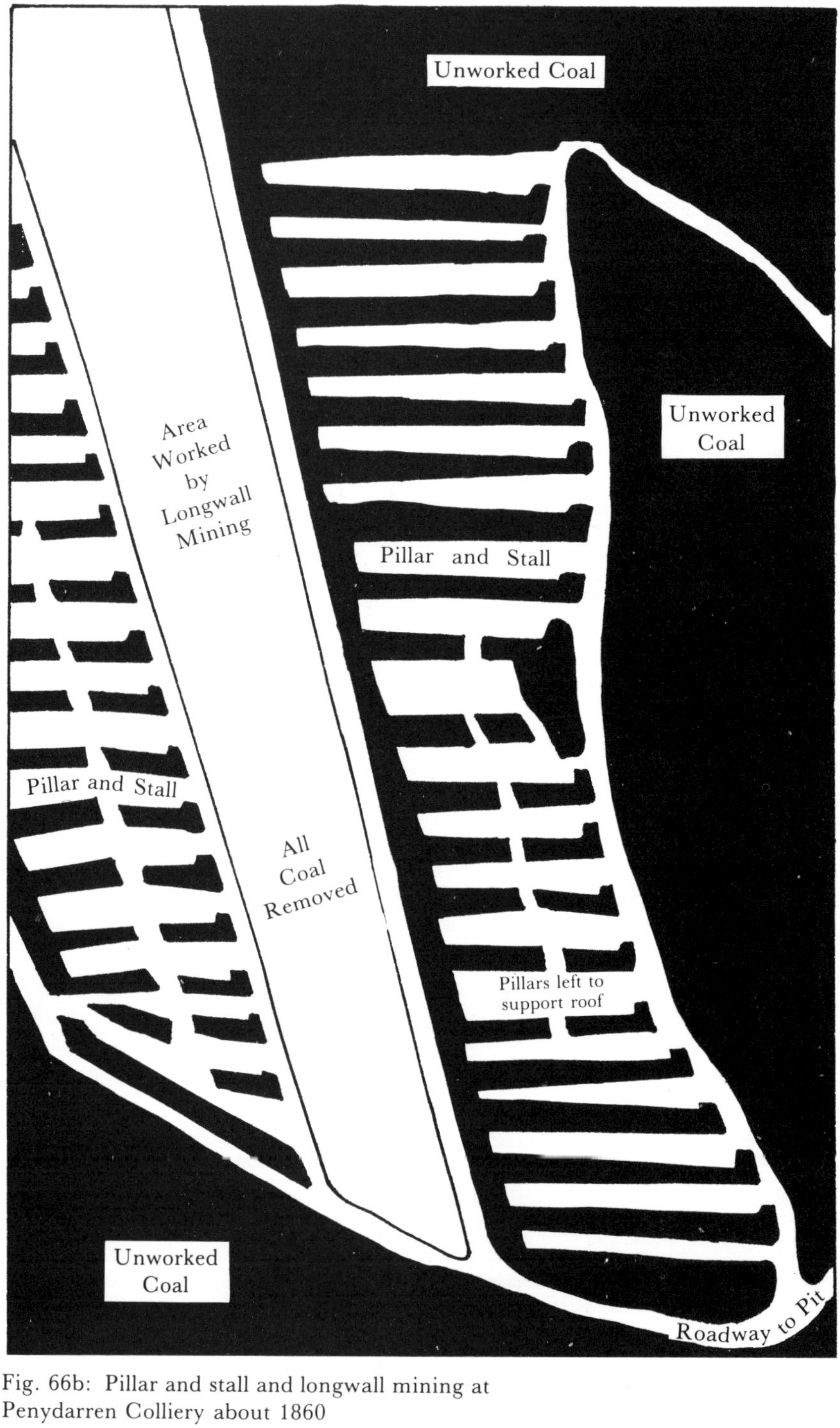

Fig. 66b: Pillar and stall and longwall mining at Penydarren Colliery about 1860

The techniques of mining were of course very primitive indeed. Where the coal was near the surface, such as at Heolgerrig and Dowlais, it was removed by 'patching', a method which was more like quarrying than mining but was still sufficiently effective to be in use at Tyle Dowlais up until the middle of the nineteenth century.[17] Patching however, resulted in a great deal of damage to the land surface and its effects are still in evidence locally. Where the seams were exposed on the valley sides the coal was won by levels or drifts. These were no more than tunnels into the hillside which were cheap and simple to open and maintain. They posed none of the problems of shaft working and scores were worked by the iron companies, during the nineteenth century. The early levels relied on natural ventilation, free drainage of water and haulage was carried out by humans and animals.

The first pits in the area were sunk during the 1820s and 1830s but it is difficult to say exactly how many were opened during these years of boom in the iron industry when collieries were forced to expand rapidly to keep pace with the demands of the works. Pwll y Mynydd at Winch Fawr, Heolgerrig was the first Cyfarthfa pit to be sunk in 1828,[18] and this like many other pits of this period was the responsibility of the Cyfarthfa mining engineer Henry Kirkhouse. In all, something like twenty pits were sunk on the Aberdare Mountain between Nant Ffrwd and Nant Canaid by the Cyfarthfa Company, while between 1837 and 1856 nineteen similar shafts were sunk by the Dowlais Iron Company. The Plymouth Iron Company was equally active opening pits at Pen cae bach, Clynmil and Cwmblacks to mine ironstone and extensive collieries at Upper Abercanaid, Graig and Duffryn.

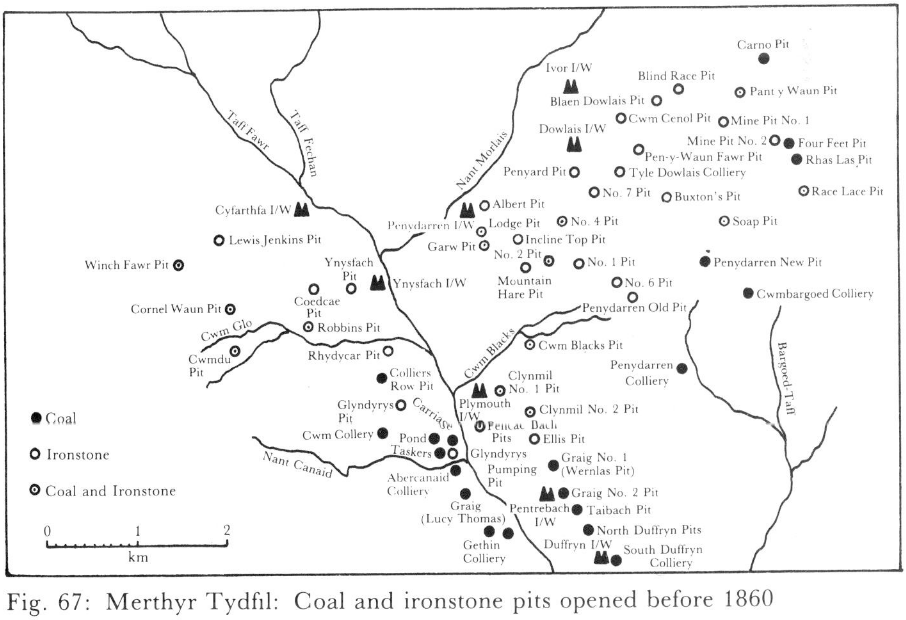

Fig. 67: Merthyr Tydfil: Coal and ironstone pits opened before 1860

Plate 41a: A BALANCE PIT BELONGING TO CYFARTHFA COLLIERIES (possibly Cornel Waun Pit)
(By permission of Merthyr Borough Council)

Irrespective of what company they belonged to the pits relied on the water balance system for bringing coal to the surface. By this method the carriages were suspended in the shaft by chains passing over a single sheave. Underneath each carriage which accommodated a single tram was a water tank capable of holding up to two tons of water. A tram containing coal was placed on the carriage at the pit bottom and an empty tram in the carriage at the top. The tank of the top carriage was then filled with water and allowed to fall to the pit bottom thus raising the carriage with coal to the pit top. Finally, a valve in the water tank of the carriage which had been lowered to the pit bottom was released and the water run out. The procedure could then be repeated. This method was cheap and functioned well in shallow pits with free drainage and moderate output, but was slow and inefficient in some of the deeper pits which were being opened. The problem of water supply was one which frequently hindered production. In 1852 John Evans of Dowlais wrote to Lady Charlotte Guest, 'We are getting very short of water. If we do

Plate 41b: PUMPING ENGINE HOUSE AT GETHIN NO. 1 PIT
(By permission of Clive Thomas)

Plate 41c: BALANCE HAULAGE ENGINE HOUSE AND WINDING ENGINE HOUSE IN BACKGROUND AT GETHIN NO. 2 PIT *(By permission of Clive Thomas)*

not get rain shortly our new coal pits will be obliged to stop' and as late as 1864 William Crawshay complained to his son, 'Engines will take the place of water balance pits if we have more such summers as this'.[19]

The mines of South Wales in general and Merthyr in particular lagged behind those of other coalfields in terms of technical innovation. True, South Wales did differ from other coalfields in that it possessed many 'geological peculiarities' but ideas and recommendations were slow to be accepted by managers and workers alike. In the Merthyr area coal continued to be worked by the wasteful pillar and stall method. John Nixon advocated the introduction of what was known as the Longwall system of working coal which was used in the North of England. He saw it as being more efficient as far as coal production was concerned, safer for the collier and less of a hindrance than the traditional method in the efficient ventilation of the colliery. Despite all his efforts, the Merthyr colliers clung doggedly to the traditional method long after the Longwall system had been introduced into South Wales.

Ventilation too was most inefficient in these mid-century mines and most, if not all, were worked by naked lights. An air flow was effected by a furnace which involved the use of either a single partitioned shaft or two separate pits. A large furnace was sited at the bottom of what was called the upcast shaft and this caused a column of hot air to rise through the shaft, drawing fresh air down the downcast shaft and causing a circulation throughout the mine workings. Not infrequently did air charged with methane ignite when it came in contact with the flames of the furnace. By the end of the 1850s Fochriw Colliery was still worked by a single shaft partitioned down the middle by bratticing. One side of the pit served as the upcast and the other as the downcast. The foolhardy nature of this practice was brought to note by a disaster at the Hartley Pit in the North of England in 1862 where a single shaft was blocked and 204 miners were entombed. Following this disaster an Act of Parliament made it compulsory for all but the smallest mines to have two shafts.

For almost the first hundred years of its history no legislation affected coal production in the Merthyr area. The Report of the Children's Employment Commission of 1842 did no more than publicise the incredibly harsh conditions and abuse suffered by the children who worked in the mines. Mary Davies, aged seven, of the Plymouth Collieries had already been at work for eighteen months when she was interviewed by Robert Franks who found her to be a 'very pretty little girl who was fast asleep under a piece of rock near the air door below ground.[20] Her lamp had gone out for want of oil; and, upon waking her, she said the rats, or someone, had run away with her bread and cheese, so she went to sleep.' Mary like many others of her age was employed to open and close the doors which directed the flow of air underground. Some children were employed by their fathers to fill drams while others like eleven year old Henrietta Frankland of Cyfarthfa pulled drams containing four to five hundredweight of coal in workings thirty to thirty-three inches high. The early age of their employment and long hours spent in an atmosphere impregnated with dust resulted in children having to endure disease, stunted growth and physical deformities. The Act of 1842 which followed the Report did little to improve conditions. As a result of the Act women and boys under ten were excluded from work underground but when the sole commissioner appointed to see that recommendations were implemented visited South Wales in 1845 he found that 'many provisions of the Act had not been generally attended to'.

The workers themselves could do nothing to improve their lot. Attempts were made to organise a union by William Twiss of the Friendly Society of Coalmining who set up his headquarters at the Miners Arms during the lockout of 1831. This attempt ended, however, with Twiss making off with what funds remained. In April 1834 Anthony Hill of Plymouth complained of the fact that his colliers were reluctant to work as a result of a 'combination among the men in the clubs'.[21] The position of the collier at this time was complicated by his dependence on conditions in the iron trade and where 'negotiations' did take place they were concerned with rates of pay rather than conditions of work.

Plate 42a: PIT PONIES AT MERTHYR VALE COLLIERY, 1965
(By permission of Trevor Steed)

Plate 42b: A 'BONDFUL' OF MERTHYR VALE COLLIERS about 1910 *(By permission of Clive Thomas)*

Things did begin to improve in the 1850s with the passing of two Acts which made provisions for such things as the reporting of accidents, keeping of accurate plans, adequate ventilation and safety in shafts. The Act of 1850 provided for the appointment of inspectors and it is from reports of men like H. F. Mackworth and T. E. Wales that one can learn a great deal of those early Merthyr Collieries. Initially, however, the task they had before them was a very difficult one. Mackworth had responsibility for the whole of the South West Area and it was not until the end of the 1850s that South Wales had an inspector of its own.

Safety and conditions of work left much to be desired as far as the Merthyr Area was concerned. In his report for 1854 Mackworth stated, 'It may create some surprise to know that the fatal accidents amongst the 850 colliers

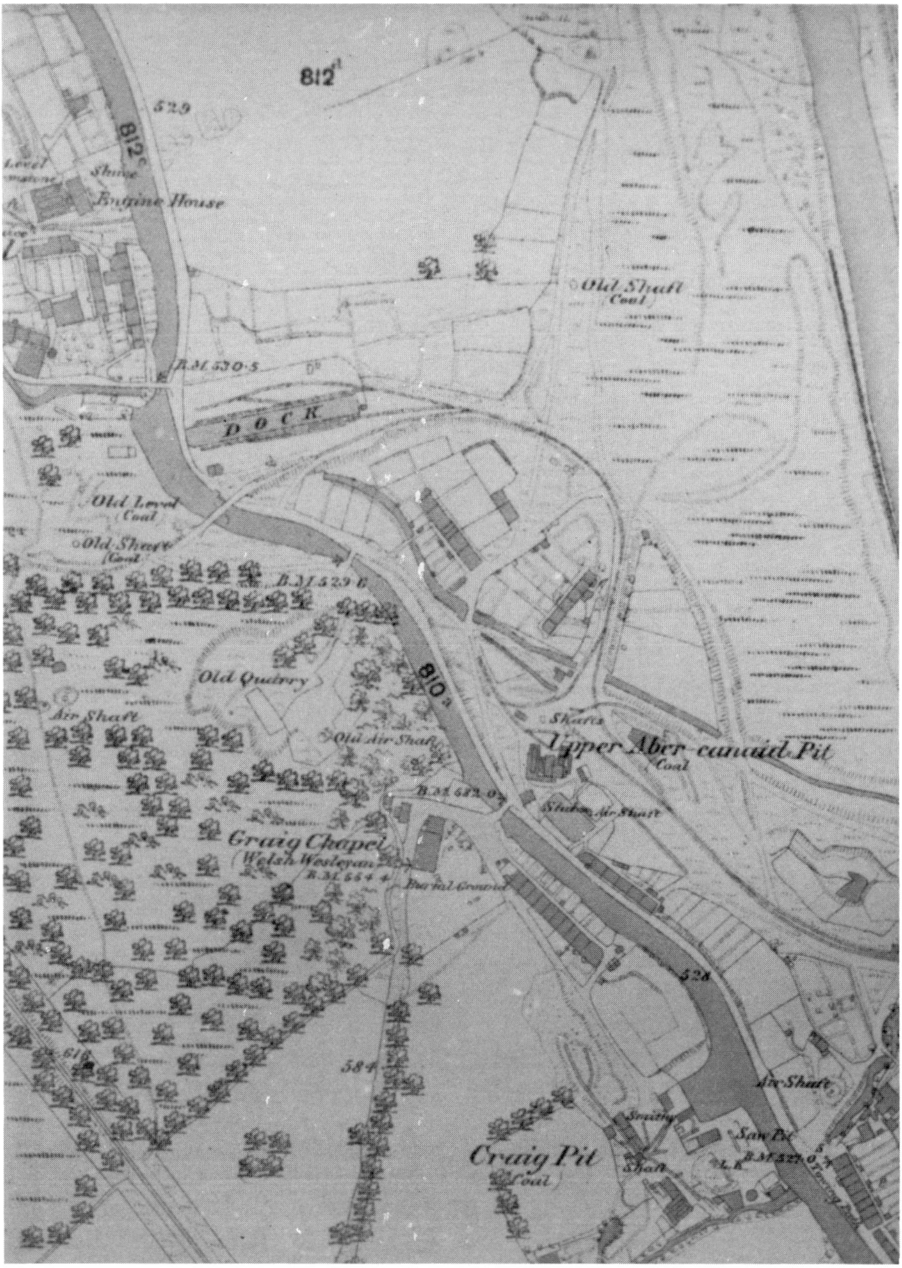

Plate 43: COPY OF 1875 O.S. MAP OF GLAMORGAN CANAL AT ABERCANAID. The surface workings of Hill's Plymouth's Upper Abercanaid Colliery, Lucy Thomas Graig Pit and the engine house of Glyndyrys Pumping Pit can be seen *(By permission of Ordnance Survey)*

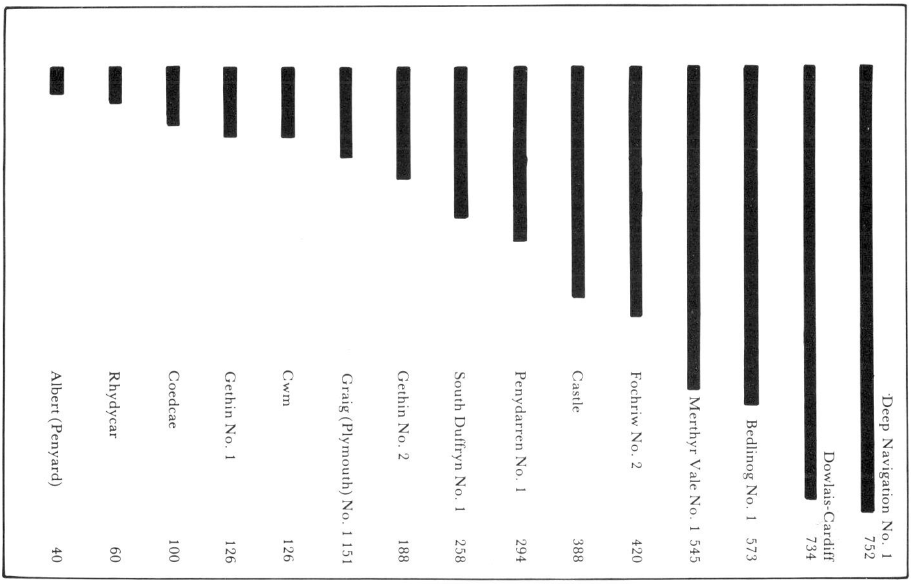

Fig. 68a: Diagram to show relative depths of some pits in the Merthyr Area (All depths in yards)

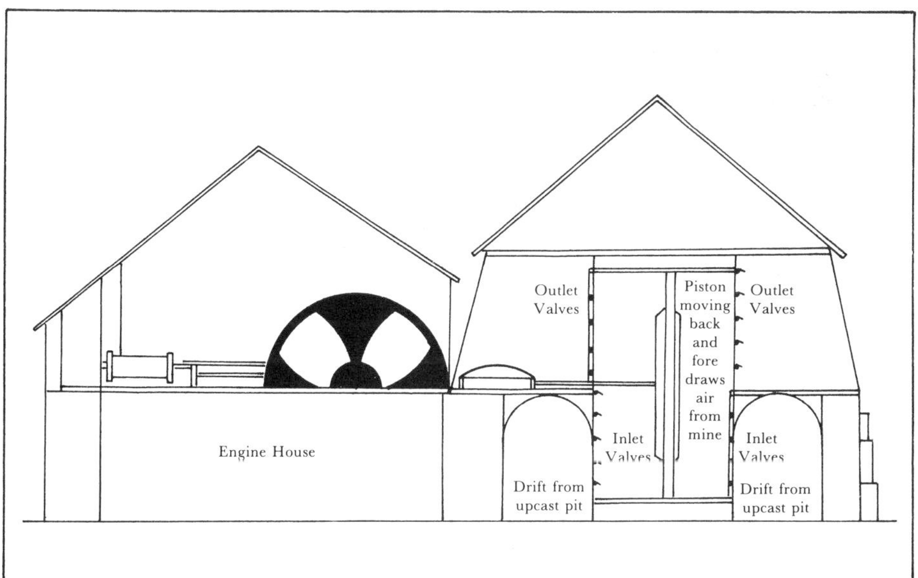

Fig. 68b: The Nixon Ventilator—a reciprocating air pump used at Merthyr Vale Colliery (not to scale)

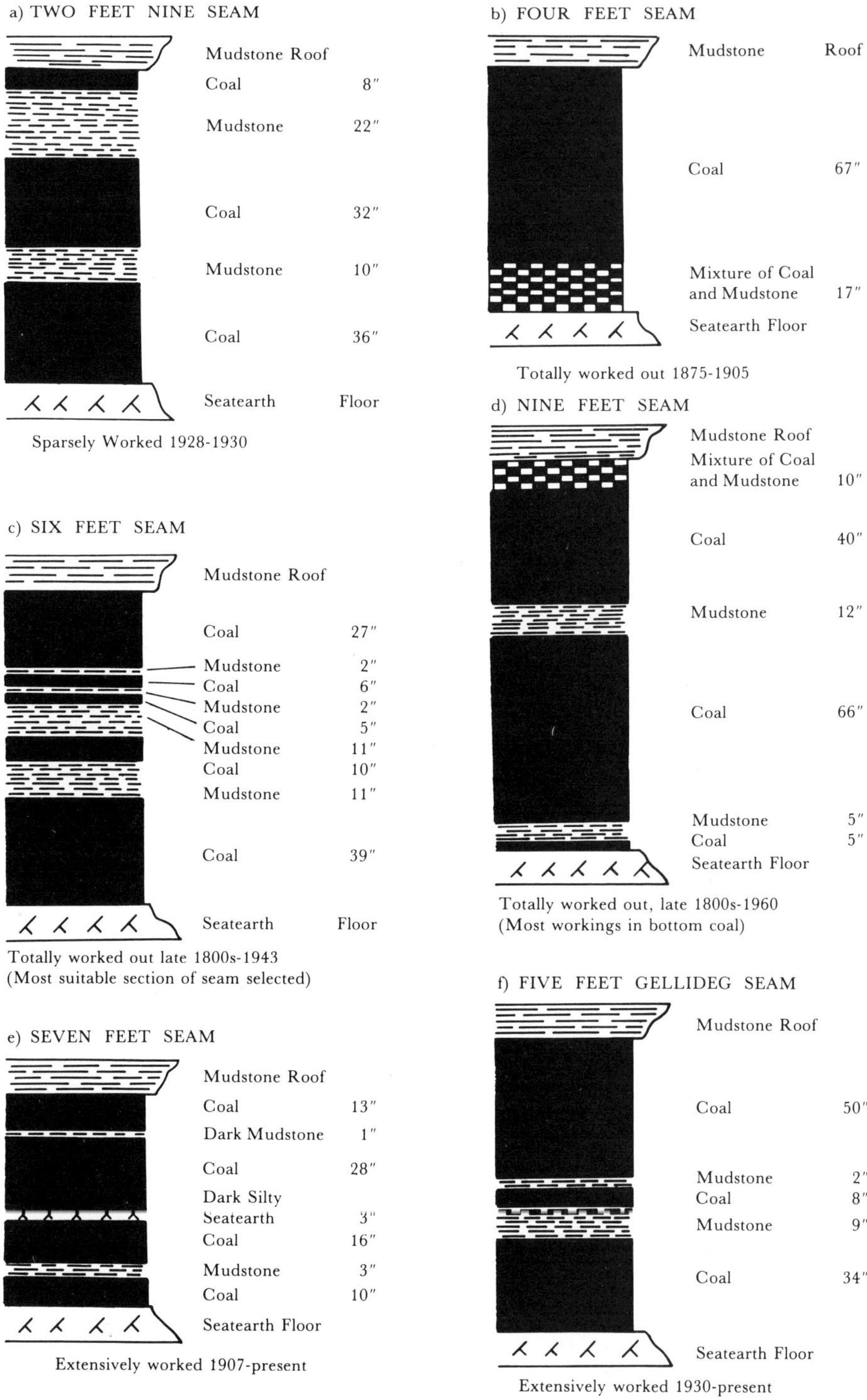

Fig. 69: Seam Sections at Merthyr Vale Colliery

Based upon information kindly supplied by National Coal Board

employed at Dowlais amount to more than double the average for great Britain'. Accidents occurred as a result of ignorance on the part of the worker and indifference on the part of management and the following is merely a very small selection involving young people.

> *Cardiff and Merthyr Guardian—Friday, 10 July, 1863*
>
> An inquest was held on Monday 6 instant, at the Miners Arms, Georgetown, before the Deputy Coroner, Thomas Williams, on the body of William Williams, aged eleven years. Deceased was a doorboy at Robblin's Pit, Cyfarthfa. On Thursday 2 instant, between two and three in the afternoon, while he was at work a journey of trams loaded with coal passed over his legs. He was taken home and attended by doctors but died on Saturday. The verdict was accidental death.
>
> *Cardiff and Merthyr Guardian—Friday, 14 October, 1864*
>
> Philip Samuel, a young fellow twelve years of age was working in a stall with his father in the Plymouth Iron Company's Abercanaid Collieries on Tuesday when a mass of coal fell on him from the roof and crushed him so seriously that he died an hour afterwards.
>
> *Cardiff and Merthyr Guardian—Saturday, 16 June, 1866*
>
> Fatal accident to a doorboy at Cwmbargoed Pits. On Tuesday last David Evans of Brecon Street, Dowlais, was killed in the Cwmbargoed Big Coal Pit. The poor little fellow who was only twelve years of age was riding on a tram when a stone fell from the roof and he was killed instantly.

Recommendations made by the inspectors to improve safety were sometimes implemented grudgingly but more often ignored. Following an accident at the Rhas Las Pit (Dowlais) when three men were killed, an inquiry reported that the deceased 'came by their deaths by the breaking of a guide chain, and the falling of the roof accompanied by rubbish and stones' and recommended that 'the advice and instructions of the Government Inspectors be followed in the future management of the Rhas Las Pit'. Two men were killed in a shaft accident at Fochriw in 1869 and on the 6 December Thomas Wales made a number of suggestions as to how the method of winding in the colliery could be improved. These recommendations went unheeded however, and before January 1870 was a week old a further five men had died in an identical accident.

Matters were certainly not helped by the poor relationship between mine manager and inspector. John Evans, Manager of the Dowlais Collieries dismissed inspection as 'mere burlesque' while Mackworth saw Evans as someone 'ignoring his responsibilities and the evils of the mines'.

One factor which substantially mitigated against improvement in conditions was that where prosecution did sometimes follow an accident it was not unusual for a mine owner or manager to sit as a magistrate in the case. After reading report after report of inquests into mine deaths one cannot help but

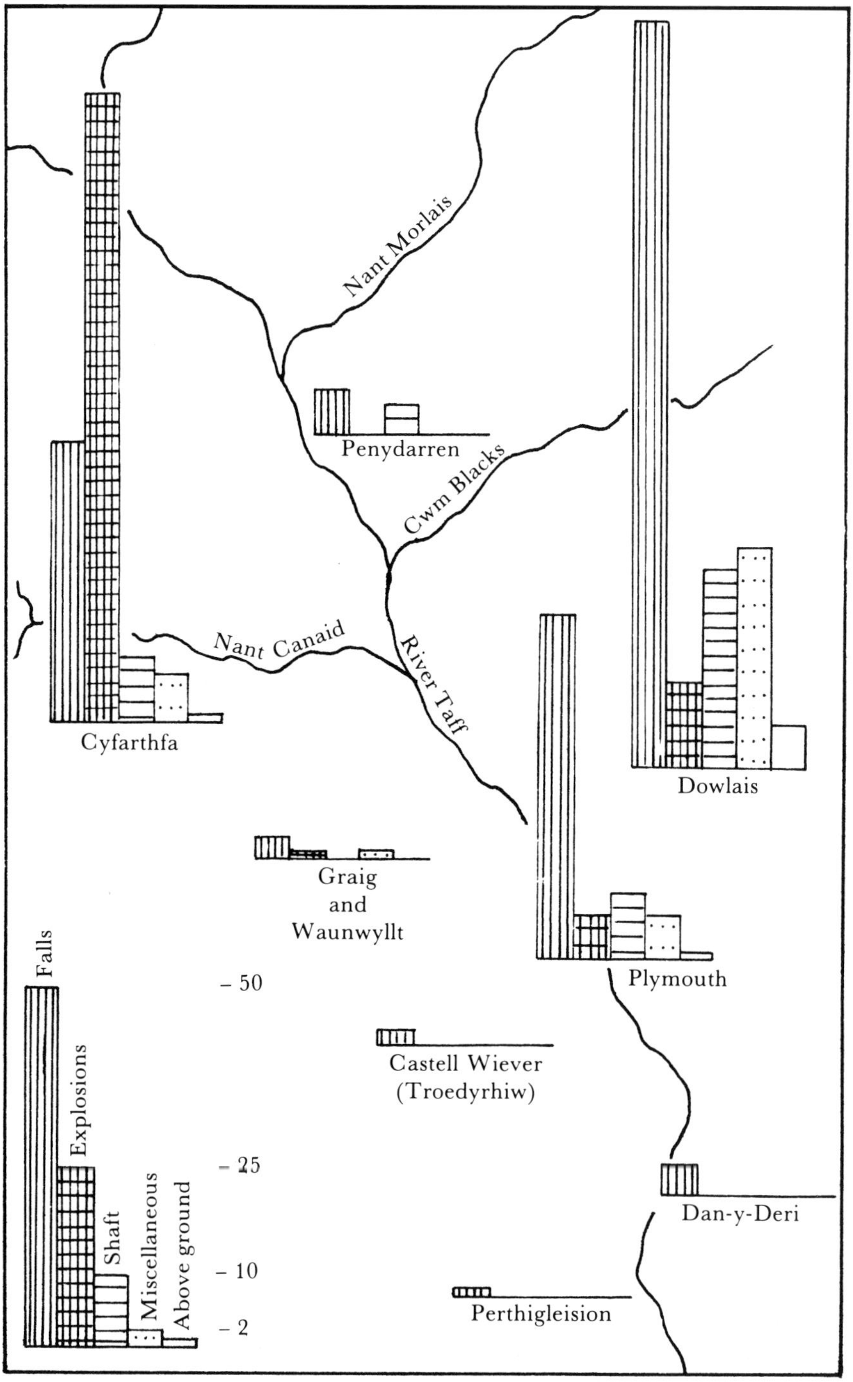

Fig. 70a: Fatal Accidents: Merthyr Collieries 1850-1870
(Figures for 1852 omitted)

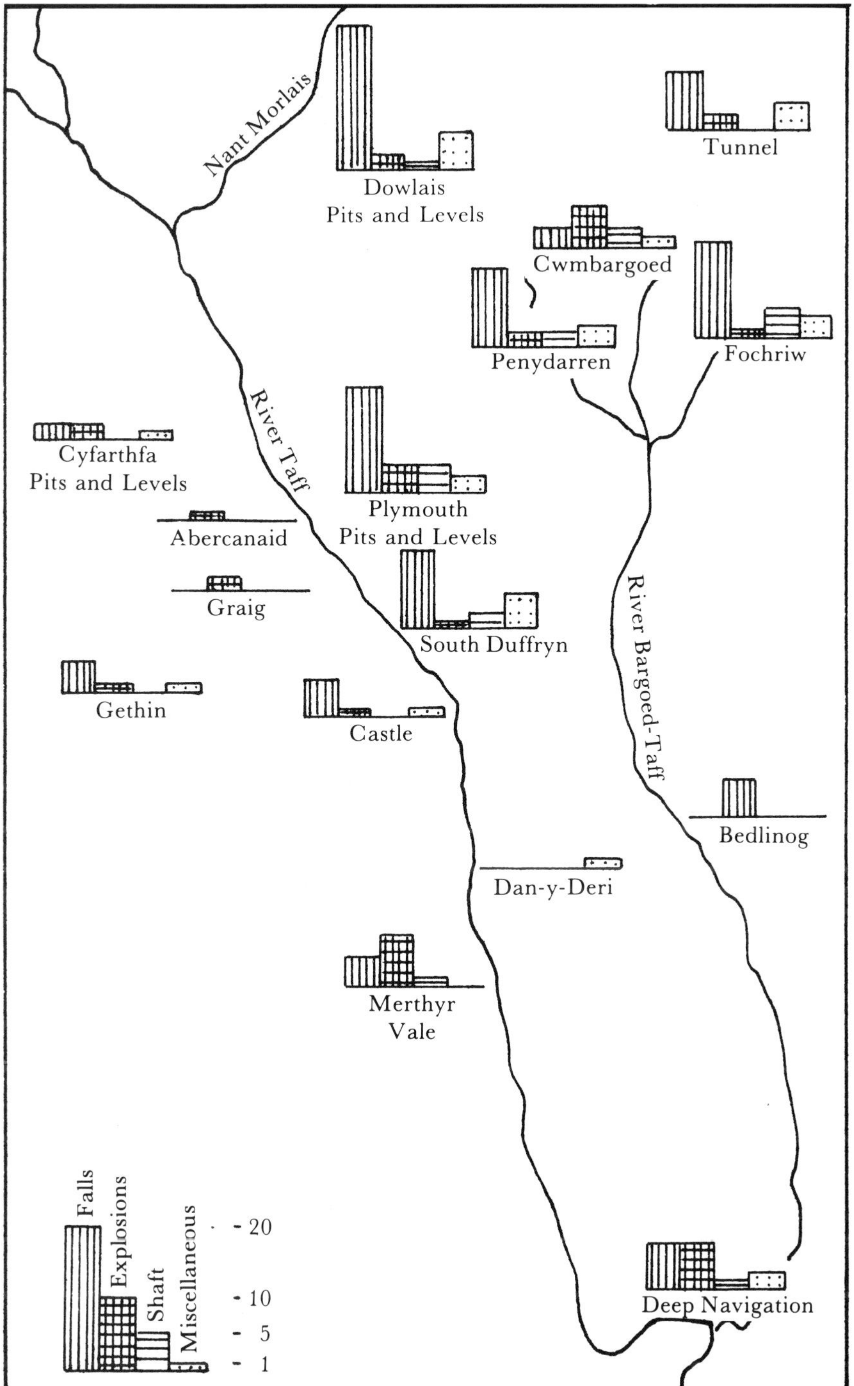

Fig. 70b: Fatal Accidents: Merthyr Collieries 1871-1882

treat the verdict of 'Accidental Death' with a certain amount of cynicism. How ineffective legislation and inspection was at this time is apparent from a case reported in the Cardiff and Merthyr Guardian on 3 September, 1865.

> At Merthyr Police Court on Monday, Mr. T. E. Wales the Government Inspector of Mines summoned Mr. Moody for allowing a boy named Thomas Lewis, under the age of twelve years to be employed in Gethin Colliery, who was shortly after killed by an accident on 21 July. Mr. Simons remarked extensively on the inefficiency of the present Act of Parliament for the prevention of such offences.
>
> The boy was proved to be not more than nine years of age, when he came to his death. A letter was read from Mr. Crawshay to Mr. Wales which stated that the cause of the boy being employed was owing to the misrepresentation of his age given on a certificate by his father.
>
> There was no penalty inflicted on Mr. Moody, but an order that he should pay costs. As regards the father of the boy, the amount of fine was left for the consideration of Mr. Fowler.

Ignitions of Fire Damp were frequent causes of death in the Merthyr mines of the 1850s and 1860s. With two exceptions the collieries of the Taff Valley never suffered the large scale disasters which occurred in many other valleys of South Wales but small explosions happened with alarming regularity. The inspectors found no difficulty in pinpointing the cause of these explosions for allied to generally inadequate ventilation was the common practice of using naked lights.

On 6 May, 1852 an explosion took place at Glyndyrys Pit, Cyfarthfa when William Evans a fifteen year old collier took a candle into old workings. Even as late as January 1885 following an accident at Fochriw No. 2 Pit Thomas Wales reported that, 'The colliery is worked with open lights, although the coals worked are the South Wales fiery steam coals, and lying at a depth of 400 yards from the surface. For several years past I have, as strongly as I could, impressed upon the Dowlais Iron Company the danger attending the working of these coals with open lights, but up to the present with no satisfactory result, nor do I think anything short of legislation will induce the Company to work with safety lamps which in my opinion ought to be insisted upon.' At Plymouth, it seems rules regarding the use of safety lamps were more stringently adhered to, for the *Cardiff and Merthyr Guardian* of 29 July, 1864 reports the case of Evan Evans. Evans who was convicted of working with an open safety lamp was fined 1/- as well as having to pay 11/9 costs.

From what has already been said it is apparent that conditions in the Merthyr pits generally were poor but it was the Gethin Colliery at Abercanaid which was to pay most dearly for its willingness to ignore the basic principles of safety. Here two explosions occurred within the space of four years, the first on 19 February, 1862 killing forty-seven and the second on 20 December, 1865 taking thirty-four men and boys.

The Gethin Colliery which belonged to the Cyfarthfa Iron Company was opened in the period 1848-52 and comprised two working shafts, a pumping shaft and a furnace ventilation pit. At the time of the first explosion 153 men were at work below ground and all but four of these used naked lights. Of the forty-seven that died twenty-one died of burns and twenty-six of suffocation by 'choke damp'. The inquest found that the ventilation of the pit was 'deficient in quantity, badly arranged and liable to interruption', and upheld a verdict of manslaughter against John Moody the Viewer of the Works. The second explosion occurred after many of the workmen has been aware of the presence of large quantities of gas for several days and recommendations made by Mr. Wales were strangely reminiscent of those made following the first.

The newspaper reports of these disasters provide us with harrowing accounts of the circumstances of the victims and their families.

> *Cardiff and Merthyr Guardian—Friday, 21 February, 1862*
>
> Yesterday afternoon (Wednesday) a report was spread that a fearful explosion of firedamp at No. 1 Pit, Lower Gethin Colliery, had taken place.
>
> Several horses having been killed it became necessary to remove them to bank before the bodies of the men could be brought up. About six o'clock the first portion, being about six in number were brought to the surface and immediately sent to their different dwellings. In another hour, the remainder had been brought up and carried to the railway where they were placed in trucks and thus conveyed up the line, stopping at Colliers' Row, Penrheol and Georgetown for the purpose of leaving the bodies at their different homes.
>
> The following incident respecting the poor and trying circumstances of one of the deceased men who lived at Abercanaid, is very affecting. He had a family of six children, two of whom, had, unfortunately through an accident in the works been deprived of a limb each, and they were obliged to shift as well as they could by the assistance of a wooden leg, in their underground labour. The father and one of the sons were killed in the explosion.

Despite the vigilance of the inspectors and improved legislation conditions improved only marginally towards the end of the nineteenth century. The total number of fatal accidents altered little but the causes of those accidents changed. Roof falls continued to exact the greatest toll and while explosions fortunately became a thing of the past fatalities caused by mechanised underground haulages began a rapid increase.

With only one exception the first fifty years of the story of coal mining in the area is dominated by the iron companies. That one exception when analysed in terms of employment or coal production is insignificant but is important in that it was the first concern in South Wales to supply the London Market with steam coal. In 1828 Robert Thomas leased land at

Waunwyllt Abercanaid on a yearly tenancy from the Earl of Plymouth. At first only the householders of Merthyr and Cardiff were supplied but soon the quality of coal attracted the attention of men like George Insole who was prepared to sell it more widely. In 1831 Insole supplied 3,000 tons of this coal to sellers in London and already this 'Myrther Coal' had gained a reputation with steam ship companies. Sometime in the mid-thirties after the death of her husband, Lucy Thomas aided by her son William, took a lease on the neighbouring Graig property, paying royalties of 1/3d on every ton of coal worked. This Graig Pit, known locally as Pit y Witw was conveniently situated on the canal bank at Abercanaid and was visited by John Nixon in 1840 whilst he was preparing a report on the Dowlais Mineral Property for the Marquis of Bute. 'On arriving at Graig Colliery, Mr. Nixon found himself in the midst of the idyllic period of the coal trade. Mrs. Thomas—she may be called the mother of the coal trade—was held to be carrying on a very good business. She sat in her office, a wooden hut near the pit's mouth, and traded for cash, placing in a basket over her head the moneys which she received for her coal'.[22] Nixon however, was unable to secure any coal because she already had markets for all the coal she was able to produce.

Other men who were to dominate the South Wales coal trade in the latter years of the nineteenth century had their origins in the Merthyr area. Thomas, son of Morgan Joseph, a native of Cyfarthfa opened a level at Danyderi near Merthyr Vale in 1842 in partnership with Samuel Thomas who supplied coal to the Plymouth Works. Thomas Joseph was an able engineer who later opened the Dunraven Collieries in the Rhondda while Samuel Thomas, father of D. A. Thomas (later Lord Rhondda) sunk pits at Bwllfa (Aberdare) and Clydach Vale in 1878 thereby laying the foundation of the great Cambrian Combine.[23] W. T. Lewis (later Lord Merthyr), who was born at Abercanaid House in 1837, was articled at the age of thirteen to his father who was engineer at the Plymouth Collieries. In 1855 he became assistant to W. T. Clarke, Agent to the Marquis of Bute and soon began to speculate in the Rhondda. In 1870 he acquired two collieries in the lower Rhondda which were to form the nucleus of the Lewis Merthyr Collieries, probably the most formidable mining concern in Britain.

Table 3

Coal raised in the Parish of Merthyr Tydfil, year ending December, 1861.

Dowlais Iron Company	265,874 tons
Plymouth Iron Company	250,000 tons
Cyfarthfa Iron Company	240,000 tons
Graig Coal Company (Abercanaid)	24,000 tons
Graig Troedyrhiw (Dan y Deri)	5,000 tons
Perthygleision Colliery (Aberfan)	4,000 tons
Cefn Glas Colliery (near Pontygwaith)	1,000 tons

From the late 1850s onward a gradual change came over the character of coal mining in the Taff and Taff-Bargoed Valleys. Both the Dowlais and Plymouth Iron Companies had sent coal for Admiralty Trials in the late '40s but Dowlais in particular found difficulty in supplying the needs of the iron-works so no consideration was given to the sale coal trade at that time. In 1859, however, when Plymouth was already exporting 200,000 tons annually, Dowlais bought the Penydarren lease and began to expand coal output with the opening of a colliery at Fochriw in the early 1860s. Cyfarthfa too saw that the profits to be made from the export of steam coal could no longer be ignored and joined its neighbours in the trade with the sinking of Castle Pit at Troedyrhiw in 1866. As the seams at the top end of the valley became exhausted so the companies were forced to sink deeper and more costly shafts further south. Dowlais concentrated its efforts in the Fochriw area, Taff-Bargoed and Bargoed Valleys with pits at Tunnel, Fochriw and Bedlinog.

The opening of new and deeper mines like Bedlinog posed many problems. Began in 1874 and 580 yards deep, coal was not produced from the two pits until the early 1880's and only then at an expenditure of £131,000. While the Bedlinog pits were sunk to the rich steam coal seams the relatively shallow Nantwen pit nearby, was opened in 1883 to increase the bituminous coal supplies to the Dowlais Works.[24]

In the Taff Valley itself, Cyfarthfa, besides sinking Castle Pit, expanded workings at Gethin and Cwm whilst Plymouth continued to produce coal from extensive workings at Graig and Dyffryn; in 1883 Plymouth even re-opened their Upper Abercanaid Colliery which had been closed for over twenty years.[25]

This colliery could boast in 1890 of the only electrically driven underground haulage in Britain, installed to maintain production from the Seven Feet, Nine Feet, Six Feet and Gellideg Seams of coal which were worked at the colliery.

Finally, further down the valley at Merthyr Vale and Treharris were to be sunk pits which were the deepest and most productive of the day.

Compared with the sinking of the early balance pits at the top end of the valley these seemed almost impossible ventures. At Merthyr Vale the first of the valuable steam coal seams, the Four Feet, lay at 426 yards, at Deep Navigation 692 yards and the other seams considerably deeper.

Despite the fact that the necessary capital was available and mining technology had advanced considerably since he had first been so impressed with the qualities of the coal in the Merthyr Valley, John Nixon was to find that the coal was not easily won. He was not a man to be easily daunted, having experienced and overcome difficulties with mining operations in the Aberdare Valley, but the sinkings at Ynysowen (later Merthyr Vale) were to be perhaps his greatest trial.

The story of the sinking which began in August 1869 is one of great courage and endurance. For just over five years the sinkers had to contend

Plate 44a: SOUTH DUFFRYN COLLIERY about 1890
(By permission of Merthyr Borough Council)

with the hardships and dangers offered by a succession of strata which held a great deal of water. To begin with, suspended side walls of timber were used to overcome the running silt but little ground had been won before the whole structure collapsed. Eventually, Nixon secured a supply of old Barlow rails from the Great Western Railway and together with cast iron tubbing these were used to sink the pits through the treacherous strata.

The diary of the sinking tells of sudden inrushes of water, hairbreadth escapes and weeks of inactivity as a result of flooded shafts. Although

Plate 44b: CASTLE PIT, TROEDYRHIW, 1895
(By permission of Merthyr Borough Council)

accidents were caused by stonefall from the shafts side or improper use of explosives, it was the inevitable water which caused most havoc. An entry for 21 June, 1873 recalls an unfortunate incident:

> All went on well up till 4.00 p.m. when a piece of shuttering blew out. The men got out all right . . . They came to bank and took down the half stage and while putting in the piece of sheeting a second piece blew out and caught William Morris a sinker and knocked him down the pit among the water, this happened at 7.20 p.m. I went down myself at 7.55 p.m. and found that the poor fellow could not be got out till the water was stopped.

Not unnaturally, such conditions caused problems in sustaining a workforce, and strikes held up work in 1871 and 74. Not all stoppages, however, stemmed from physical or financial disadvantage as an entry from 25 November, 1872 explains, 'It was 3 o'clock before they got into the pit through Joseph Randel leaving his work and going up to the new public and getting tite.'

Plate 45a: MERTHYR VALE COLLIERY about 1880
(By permission of Clive Thomas)

Plate 45b: MERTHYR VALE COLLIERY about 1905
(By permission of Clive Thomas)

Once the difficulties of sinking had been overcome the colliery rapidly became one of the largest and most successful in the coalfield. John Nixon, himself an innovative mining engineer, did much to make Merthyr Vale together with Deep Duffryn and Navigation Collieries in the Aberdare Valley a formidable combination. Merthyr Vale was notable for a number of interesting features, one being Nixon's own patent ventilator which consisted of three large exhausting pistons capable of drawing 400,000 sq. feet of air per minute from the workings. Experiments were undertaken by Colonel Grey and Major Grey involving the use of large gas discharges from the coal seams. The 'blowers' as they were called were piped to the pit-top where the gas was used to heat boilers, reputedly saving one hundred tons of coal weekly. The No. 1 Pit winding engine was also of interest in that it was originally built for Her Majesty's Warship Gibraltar but subsequently purchased and adapted for Merthyr Vale by John Nixon.

From the 1881 men and boys producing 536,631 tons of coal in 1892, the colliery grew rapidly in size so that by 1907 the 3,439 employed produced 852,418 tons of coal.[26] But as well as being a highly productive colliery it also had a good safety record. In 1907 for example it suffered one death for every 860 men employed while in comparison the Dowlais collieries suffered one death for every 575.

Deep Navigation Colliery, Treharris, still a successful highly productive enterprise, enjoyed a somewhat chequered early history. Began in 1873 and known as Harris' Navigation Pits, after Mr. F. W. Harris, Chairman of the company, the two shafts were producing coal by 1881. An adventurous undertaking by any standards, the shafts were 760 yards in depth, far deeper at that time than any other in the coalfield. The venture was however, dogged by financial difficulties for several years until it was purchased in 1893 by the Ocean Coal Company Ltd. In 1897 596,000 tons of much sought after steam coal were raised at the colliery which then employed 2,500 men and boys. The Ocean Coal Company did much to aid production and modernise the colliery. Plant was mechanised where possible and in 1916 the welfare of the miners was given consideration with the building of a pit head baths. One of the first baths in the coalfield, they were constructed after representatives of the Ocean Coal Company had visited pit head baths on the continent.

Although outside the administrative boundaries of our area, mention must be made here of a third deep sinking at Abercynon. Here, in 1890, the Dowlais Iron Company began the sinking of two pits to be called the Dowlais—Cardiff Colliery. As at Merthyr Vale the sinkers had to contend with heavy water feeders, some issuing as much as 21,000 gallons per hour. In 1892 in fact, sinking was suspended completely for 15 months whilst a large Hawthorn Davy pumping engine was erected. By 1896 however, once again, man's endeavours had overcome great difficulties and the pits were completed the 740 yards to the Nine Feet Seam.[27]

The period from 1870 to the outbreak of the First World War was one of

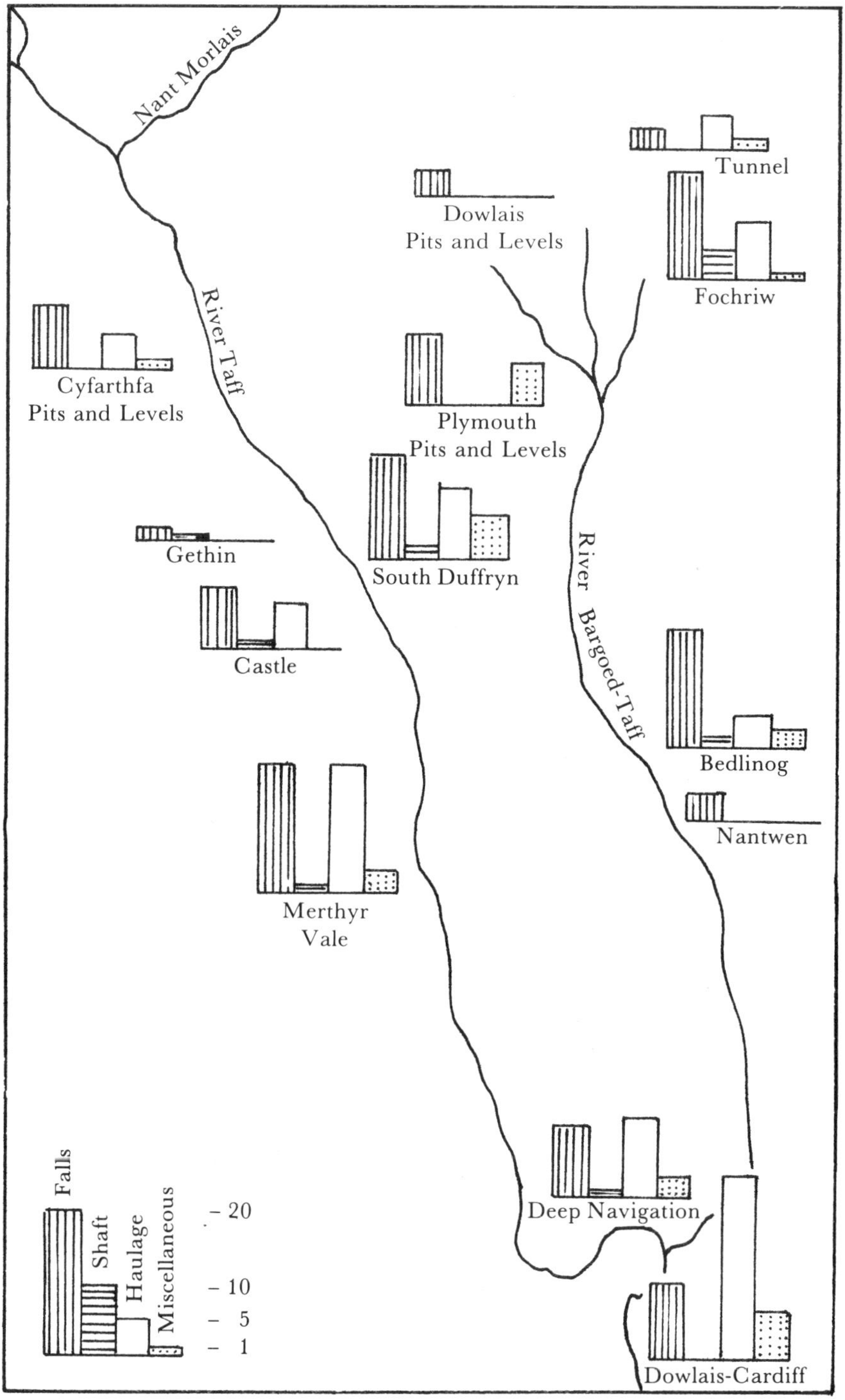

Fig. 71a: Fatal Accidents: Merthyr Collieries 1905-1914

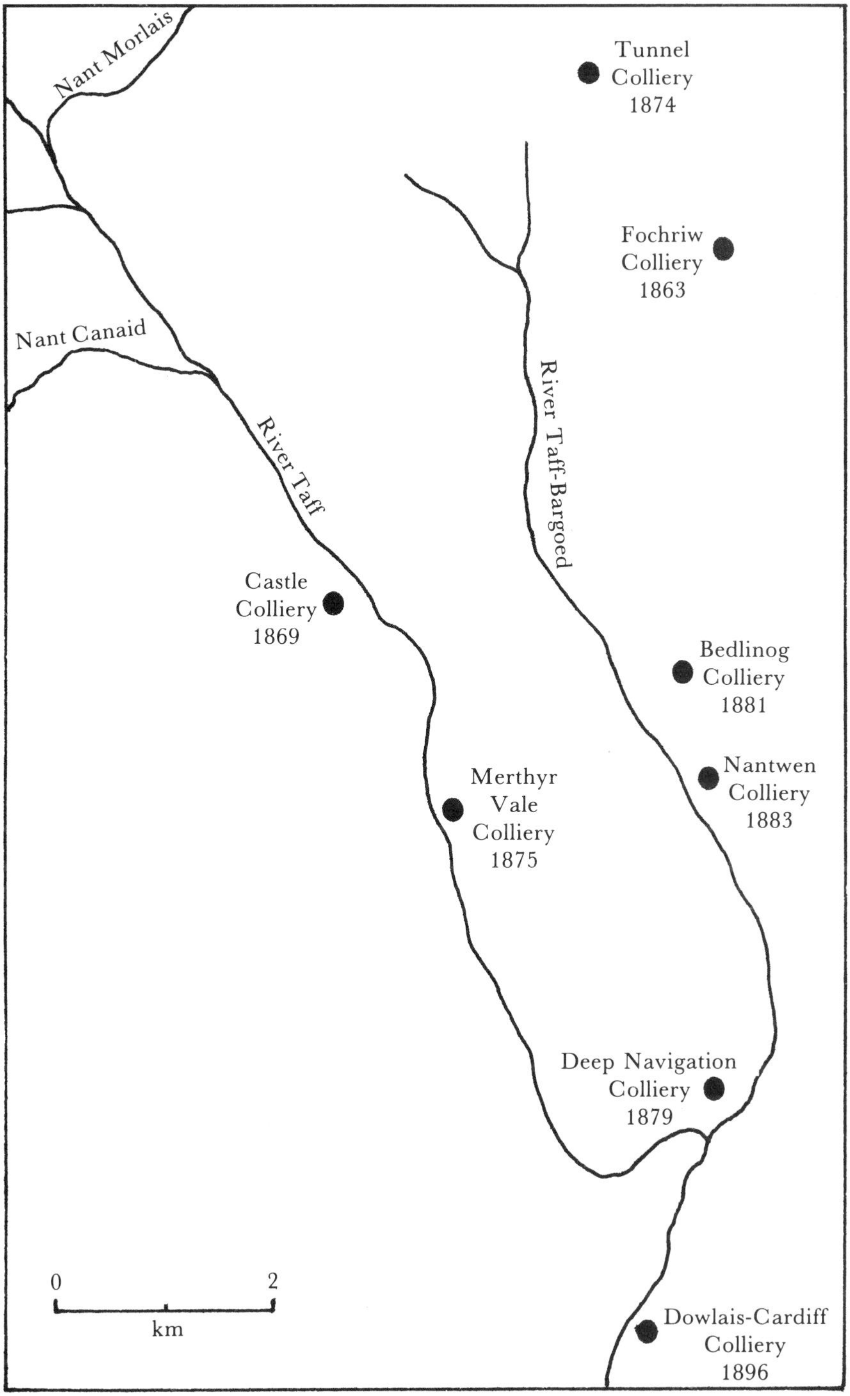

Fig. 71b: Collieries opened 1860-1900

Plate 46a: DOWLAIS IRON COMPANY'S BEDLINOG COLLIERY about 1905
(By permission of Clive Thomas)

Plate 46b: DEEP NAVIGATION COLLIERY, TREHARRIS, 1981
(By permission of Clive Thomas)

rapid expansion as far as the coal industry in the Merthyr Area and the rest of South Wales was concerned. But despite the achievements and the relative prosperity engendered by the new undertakings, the years were not without strife and bitterness. Whereas in the previous decades the Merthyr colliers had depended on the iron trade, by the 1870s, with more and more coal going for 'sale' purposes, other factors began to play their parts in deciding wages. Before 1870, strikes involving colliers were usually confined to the mines of one or other of the iron companies and wages were usually the motivating factor. After 1870 however, fluctuations in the 'sale coal' markets and attempts at combination resulted in conflict and confrontation between owners and men.

During 1874 contractions in the coal trade resulted in two substantial wage reductions but a further 10% reduction the following year forced the men belonging to the Amalgamated Association of Miners to stop work rather than submit. Men at Cyfarthfa who initially accepted the reduction were expelled from the union showing that the workers were determined to fight. The five month stoppage which ensued was concluded by the men accepting a 12½% reduction and a new method of fixing wages. The new sliding scale which fixed wages according to the price of coal was to prove a bone of contention throughout the coming years. Although looked upon favourably by the employers Keir Hardie was later to comment that under it the conditions of the miners had gone from bad to worse. The strike of 1875 had disastrous consequences not only for miners and their families, but also saw the demise of the Amalgamated Association of Miners. Unionism was not to revive in our area until the early 1880s with the formation of the Aberdare and Merthyr Miners Association. In 1882 David Morgan (Dai o'r Nant), who had been employed at the age of seven in the Cyfarthfa Mines, became agent and his splendid efforts inspired fellow unionists in the coming years.[28]

Already by the 1890s many of the workers' leaders had become disillusioned by the workings of the sliding scale. Wage rates fell steadily between 1891 and 1893 and by 1898 the miners throughout the coalfield decided to bring the sliding scale to an end. The powerful South Wales Coal Owners Association Ltd. led by Sir W. T. Lewis refused to negotiate however, and a long and bitter lock-out ensued. Keir Hardie, writing for the 'Labour Leader' on the night of Monday, 25 June, 1898 painted a grim picture. 'The soup kitchens are the principal means of relief. I regret to hear that the soup kitchens in some districts are in danger of being closed for lack of funds. The Taff runs through the valley which is enclosed by high mountains all round. In this grand amphitheatre is Troedyrhiw, and behind the village is the stoneyard. Today, 1,045 men are at work. They are paid 1s. per day and 2d for each child. The old men are kept for herding off the children, whilst the young and the strong are at work earning their shilling. In the Merthyr district there are 18,000 children being fed every day at a cost of five farthings a head.'[29]

By the end of August, lacking the necessary financial support, the miners and their families were at the end of their tether, and once again they were forced to return on the owners conditions. Despite failing to reach its objectives the strike of 1898 was important in that it resulted in a regeneration of interest in unionism and the formation of the South Wales Miners Federation. The new century brought a new wave of prosperity for the collieries in the Merthyr Area. The price of coal improved and with it wages. Although there were further bitter strikes in 1912 and 1915 it was a period of success with substantial numbers of workmen employed and large tonnages of coal produced.

Table 4

Colliery	*1911*		*1918*	
	No. Employed	*Tonnage*	*No. Employed*	*Tonnage*
Dowlais Collieries	8,246	1,132,826	6,723	1,353,067
Cyfarthfa Collieries	3,381	484,435	2,559	342,902
Plymouth Collieries	2,400	567,985	2,000	354,191
Merthyr Vale Colliery	3,421	610,849	2,745	441,968
Deep Navigation Colliery	1,913	321,282	1,946	307,238

The 1920s saw the rapid decline of the coal industry in the Merthyr Area. Depletion of the most profitable coal seams and decline in demand for coal generally resulted in the closing of many local collieries. The Fochriw, Tunnel, Cwmbargoed and Bedlinog Collieries belonging to G.K.N. closed in 1923/24.[30] Although the Cyfarthfa leases expired in 1924 Cwm and Gethin continued towards the end of the decade and Castle Pit at Troedyrhiw was linked to the old Plymouth Iron Company's South Duffryn Colliery, which continued to work up to the Second World War. Only the deeper and more modern collieries at Merthyr Vale, Treharris and Abercynon were able to survive the traumas of the twenties and thirties and remain today our most tangible links with Merthyr's lost industrial greatness.

References

[1] Williams G., *Glamorgan County History*, p. 322, Glamorgan County History Trust.
[2] Raistrick A., *Industrial Archaeology*, p. 70-71, Paladin 1973.
[3] Williams G., *Glamorgan County History*, p. 48.
[4] West E., *Woollen Mills of Wales*, p. 19-25, Celtic Educational 1974.
[5] Wilkins C., *The History of Merthyr Tydfil*, p. 76, Merthyr Tydfil 1908.
[6] Rees W., *Industry Before the Industrial Revolution*, p. 252-258, University of Wales Press 1968.

[7] Morgan Rees D., *Mines, Mills and Furnaces*, p. 54-55, H.M.S.O. 1969.
[8] Manatoux P., *The Industrial Revolution in the Eighteenth Century*, University Paperbacks 1964.
[9] Manatoux P., op. cit p. 293.
[10] For more comprehensive accounts of Dowlais Ironworks see: Elsas M., *The Dowlais Iron Company Letters*, 1960; Owen J. A. O., *A Short History of the Dowlais Ironworks*, Merthyr Tydfil Borough Council 1972.
[11] Taylor M. S., *The Crawshays of Cyfarthfa Castle*, p. 156, R. Hale 1967.
[12] Owen J. A. O., *Merthyr Historian Vol. 2*, p. 34, Merthyr Tydfil Historical Society 1978.
[13] For more comprehensive accounts of Cyfarthfa Ironworks see: Addis J. P., *The Crawshay Dynasty*, U.W.P. 1957; Taylor M. S., *The Crawshays of Cyfarthfa Castle*, R. Hale 1967.
[14] Taylor M. S., *Glamorgan Historian Vol. 5*, The Plymouth Ironworks, Stewart Williams 1968.
[15] Taylor M. S., *Glamorgan Historian Vol. 3*, The Penydarren Ironworks, Stewart Williams 1966.
[16] Williams G., *Glamorgan County History*, p. 364, Glamorgan County History Trust.
[17] Morris J. H. and Williams L. J., *The South Wales Coal Industry 1841-1875*, p. 50, U.W.P. 1958.
[18] Pedler F., *History of the Hamlet of Gellideg*, p. 95.
[19] Morris J. H. and Williams L. J., op. cit., p. 71.
[20] Ridd T., *Glamorgan Historian Vol. 3*, Truck, Trappers and Trammers, Stewart Williams 1966.
[21] Evans E. W., *The Miners of South Wales*, P. 54, U.W.P. 1961.
[22] Vincent H., *The Life of John Nixon*, p. 108, John Murray 1900.
[23] Phillips E., *A History of the Pioneers of the South Wales Coalfield*, p. 136.
[24] Owen J. A. O., *A Short History of the Dowlais Ironworks*, p. 58, Merthyr B.C.
[25] Bailey T. J., *Journal of Institute of Mining Engineers*, 1892.
[26] Merthyr Vale Colliery, Official Returns for 1892 and 1907.
[27] Owen J. A. O., op. cit., p. 50.
[28] Evans E. W., op. cit., p. 138.
[29] Page Arnot R., *South Wales Miners*, p. 63, George Allen & Unwin 1967.
[30] Owen J. A. O., *Merthyr Historian Vol. 2*, p. 42, Merthyr Tydfil Historical Society 1978.

In addition the following works were consulted:

1. *The Story of Merthyr Tydfil*, Merthyr Teachers 1932.
2. *The Early History of the Old South Wales Ironworks, 1760-1840*, J. Lloyd 1906.
3. *The South Wales Coal Industry*, C. Wilkins 1888.
4. *A Guide to Merthyr Tydfil*, T. E. Clarke 1848.
5. *Merthyr, Rhondda and the Valleys*, A. Trystan Edwards 1958.
6. *Industrial Archaeology of Wales*, D. Morgan-Rees 1975.

The Inter-War Years

by A. MORGAN M.A.

The Depression Years

The years between the two world wars saw Merthyr fall into great economic difficulty out of which there seemed little or no chance of it emerging. The statistics tell only a small amount but they nevertheless graphically convey Merthyr's economic distress. In 1921 six thousand people were registered as unemployed, in 1931 this had risen to thirteen thousand and by 1935 six out of every ten men living in the Borough were without jobs—in Dowlais it was *eight* of ten who were jobless. Furthermore, between 1921 and 1939 an average of *over a thousand* people left Merthyr *every* year.

The reasons for leaving were obvious. For the majority of its population life in Merthyr had never been easy as far as making ends meet was concerned but now poverty began to reach desperate levels. This was brought about by a combination of long-term weaknesses in Merthyr's economic structure and world wide economic difficulties throughout the inter war years.

Merthyr's economic weakness stemmed from the fact that it was one of Britain's oldest industrial communities and it had not developed in a planned, stable fashion. Merthyr's industrial set up was, in fact, highly unsuited for any long term economic development. It was based entirely on outdated structures, as J. England states in his article in *Merthyr Politics*, (ed.) Glanmor Williams, 'Merthyr at the beginning of the century was living on borrowed time'.

The reasons which produced this situation are clear. The twin pillars of the town's industrial strength were in decline. The local ore deposits were, by 1900, proving increasingly inadequate in both quantity and quality. Two tons of ore from Spain were brought into the area for every one produced there. The coal industry was also in similar difficulties, especially in the northern half of the Borough around Dowlais and Penydarren. Many of the mines were small and old fashioned, and their deposits of coal were wearing thin and difficult to obtain. In addition road and rail communications, vital to economic development, were very good from Merthyr to Cardiff but to the new centres of economic growth, the South-East and Midlands of England, they were poor and this was one of the main reasons why newer forms of industry were almost completely absent from the area.

Unemployment was no stranger to Merthyr; it had reached very high levels at certain times throughout the nineteenth century but there were definite indications by 1914 that the situation was reaching increasingly serious levels. In 1891 part of the huge Dowlais Steel works was moved to Cardiff; in 1910 the Cyfarthfa works were closed down. The town thus faced an uncertain future when the outbreak of World War 1 breathed new life into the area's failing economy due to the huge and consistent demand for coal and steel needed to keep the war effort operating. But nothing was done to improve the town's basic weakness, i.e. it had all its economic eggs in two baskets and those baskets were in danger of toppling over.

This became clear after the end of war in November, 1918. Demand for coal and steel now dropped sharply and a severe slump hit Merthyr; three thousand steel workers at Dowlais were given a month's notice and, although withdrawn, this was an ominous foretaste of the terrible times to come. Merthyr's outdated economy was in no shape to cope with twentieth century developments but, ironically, a few of these gave this sick set-up temporary and false appearances of recovery. Coal stocks were replenished after the three-month lock-out of British miners in 1921; a miners strike in the U.S.A. in 1922 led to a greatly increased demand for Welsh coal and when in 1924, French troops occupied the great German coalfield, the Ruhr, there was another very sharp increase in demand. At this time two and a half million tons of coal were mined per year in the Borough and this provided employment for fourteen thousand miners. By 1931 over 6,000 of these would have lost their jobs and over 4,000 steelworkers thrown out of work in the same time.

The series of staggering economic blows which were to bring the town to its knees began in 1925 when the Chancellor of the Exchequer, Winston Churchill, took the decision to put Britain back onto the Gold standard. Explained simply this system valued a state's currency in relation to the value of gold. At this time the effect of this was to make almost all British raw materials and goods more expensive—demand dropped sharply.

A year later the General Strike ended quickly and suddenly but the miners dispute, which had caused it, lasted for six months. The people of Merthyr seem to have faced this long dispute with much the same spirit of endurance as did the rest of the coalfield but the effects of the stoppage on the town's economy was crippling. The local coal industry was left battered and impoverished. The dispute had begun over the coal owners' demands for cuts in pay and longer hours by their workers, but the owners now sought even more drastic means of saving money. Small, unproductive mines were a natural target and the mines north of Merthyr Vale were nearly all of this type. Thus there was a spate of closures of local collieries between 1926-31. The pits in the southern end of the Borough at Merthyr Vale and Treharris were in a much better condition, but the use of new machinery meant that fewer men were needed to work in these pits than previously.

Worldwide economic difficulties in the late nineteen twenties led to a slump in demand for steel. This hit Merthyr very hard. In 1928 Cyfarthfa, which had revived during World War 1 was completely dismantled. In October 1930, the main section of the Dowlais steelworks was closed and three thousand men lost their jobs. The works kept going on a small scale until 1936 when it closed completely. These events shattered Dowlais, the town existed because of the steel works—its closure was like a death sentence, a person with a job became a rarity.

The problem of unemployment was made even worse by the fact that once a person lost a job there was virtually no chance of finding another within miles and also because once the main industries sacked thousands of workers a chain-reaction set in.

Shops and pubs which once thrived closed down. The town's Third Division (South) football team, short of money and playing before dwindling crowds, fell well below the standard needed to keep going in the League. They lost their place at the end of the 1929 season having conceded 135 goals (still a record). The whole town seemed to be slowly wasting away.

Many people who lost jobs in cafes, pubs and shops were girls and women. Although it was a commonly held belief that 'a woman's place was in the home' around 3,500 women were employed in Merthyr in 1931. Within a short time after this, many had lost their jobs and the last hope a family had of at least bringing home a little money was now gone. Large numbers of young girls had been employed as maids in the homes of Merthyr's well off but the rich also sensed Merthyr's decline and many moved away. The result was that the main options open to the town's youth on leaving school at fourteen was unemployment or move away.

There was little relief available to offset the cruel effects of unemployment. Even when they had been working Merthyr people had not enjoyed a reasonable level of wages since around the end of World War 1, e.g. in 1930 a miner averaged wages of about £2.00 per week. Wages were not high throughout the South Wales valleys, indeed some Merthyr people who found work some miles away discovered that, after travelling expenses, they were actually better off if they were receiving unemployment benefit. This benefit was not large; the 1928 rate was £1 3s. 0d. (£1.15) for a married man and 2/- (10p) for each of his children not in work. In the 1930's the rate of benefit was calculated by looking at all the possible sources of money a person might have. This process was known as the Means Test and it was hated by many of those subjected to it. Most found it a humiliating and distressing experience.

Besides this the amount paid was proving insufficient to meet the basic

Plate 47a: 'NIXON'S ASH GANG', MERTHYR VALE COLLIERY, 1926 *(By permission of Clive Thomas)*

Plate 47b: TAFF MERTHYR COLLIERY, 1981
(By permission of Clive Thomas)

needs of a family unit, i.e. decent food, warmth and clothing. This gives an indication of how poor most working peoples pay was, but they were reluctant to complain because the job they held was a very scarce commodity for which there would be no shortage of outside takers.

The results of this lack of basic needs were grimly predictable. In 1928 a writer for *The Times* newspaper reported on the plight of the unemployed in South Wales: 'as the months go by first boots and clothing wear out and then bedclothes and cooking utensils . . . men and women are starving; not starving outright, but gradually wasting away through lack of nourishment'. This picture of gloom and despair was accurate and the results of insufficient warmth and nourishment soon became apparent. The diseases that flourish from such circumstances began to show themselves increasingly: the number of women in the 15-35 age group suffering from tuberculosis was more than double the rate in the rest of England and Wales (outside a few equally depressed areas in the North-East). Near enough to one in every five children died before their fifth birthday, young men aged before their time, the old suffered chronically and in 1935 the condition of Merthyr's school children was vividly portrayed in a report by the town's Health Officer, Dr. Stephens. This report stated firmly that the disease caused by lack of nourishment (malnutrition) was alarmingly prevalent; a bone disease caused by lack of nourishment, rickets, was rampant and tuberculosis, diphtheria and other potential killer sicknesses, while on the decline almost everywhere else in the country, were still very prevalent in Merthyr. The report concluded that bad housing and lack of good food were the main reasons for this deplorable situation.

The effect of the depression on the appearance of the town was also alarming. A major reason was that some money given to the unemployed and their families had to be found by the local council. With so many townspeople out of work this proved an impossible burden for Merthyr's council. In 1923-33 the amount paid was more than the *whole* of the council's services had cost in 1919. To raise this money the council had to continually raise the rates on property—by 1937 they were the highest in Britain. But because of the depression the value of property plummeted. It was a vicious circle. The council had, therefore, to beg the government for money. Some grants were given, but these were not large. All of these grants were, in turn, spent on public assistance and the council had little money to spare on other services.

With the town on its knees what were the political reactions of the local population? Merthyr had been a stronghold of liberal politics in the late nineteenth and early twentieth centuries. In those times it formed a single constituency with Aberdare, and sent two members to Parliament at each election. In the 1900 contest a socialist, James Keir Hardie, came second and thus became the first Labour member ever sent to Parliament. Since that time support for the Independent Labour Party had grown substantially. It was not difficult to see why—wages, housing conditions and living standards in general were very poor for most of Merthyr's population and it was little wonder that many began to feel sympathetic towards a social, economic and political system which suggested a better alternative to their present condition. In the 1919 election Merthyr (now a one member constituency) returned Dick Wallhead, the Independent Labour Party candidate, by a comfortable margin. However, his visits to Merthyr were infrequent and due to this and other influential reasons the once flourishing I.L.P. organisation in Merthyr fell into decline throughout the 1920s. At the same time a split occured betwen the I.L.P. and the rest of the groups who made up the Labour party over how much of its identity and right to criticise official policy the I.L.P. should be prepared to give up. This resulted in the I.L.P. officially leaving the Labour Party organisation in 1932 and some of the earliest tests of how much support each group enjoyed came in Merthyr in two elections, a by-election caused by Wallhead's death in 1934, and a contest as part of the General Election of 1935.

For the 1934 election the Labour Party picked an extremely strong candidate, S. O. Davies. He was a convinced socialist, a brilliant speaker and as miners agent for Dowlais he had become one of the best known trades unionists in South Wales. His powerful campaign earned him an easy victory over his four opponents. He polled 18,000 plus, J. Victor Evans (Liberal) followed him with just over 10,000 votes and a long way behind came J. Campbell-Stephens (I.L.P.) with 3,509, then one of the leading figures in the British Communist party, Wal Hannington, with a little over 3,400 votes. In the 1935 contest there were only two candidates, S. O. Davies and a very well known and respected socialist, Claude Stanfield, who stood for the I.L.P. He ran a very strong campaign and won over 11,000 votes, but once again S. O. Davies came out on top with over 20,000. These elections indicate several clear political attitudes of Merthyr people in those desperate times for their town.

1. The Liberal party, which had enjoyed such great support in the town a few decades earlier, was now in clear decline. To many it seemed to have neither understanding nor answers to the problems of the day.

2. Another dominant force in the town's politics, the I.L.P., was unable to mount a significant enough challenge to the official Labour Party and its strong trade union links. This was a signal that it too would enter a period of irreversible decline.

3. The revolutionary alternatives offered by the Communist party were also rejected by most of the town's electorate. Despite the dire predicament many people found themselves in, they possibly felt Communism too much of a gamble to pledge themselves to—'a shot in the dark', while the still powerful, if declining, influence of religion and the Labour party propaganda that communism could only be achieved through violence and bloodshed also robbed the Communist part of much support.

4. There was a very broad commitment for the brand of *parliamentary socialism* identified with people such as Aneurin Bevan, M.P. for nearby Ebbw Vale, and S. O. Davies himself. This was a belief that improvement and change would be brought about by the Labour party winning power through elections and using its' power to bring about improvements for the working people of Britain and to end such things as inequality, unemployment and privilege.
5. The Conservative Party, although the most powerful party in Britain at this time, did not even bother to put up a candidate at either of these elections.

Of course politics is not simply about elections. It involves many other areas of activity also. Political organisations, political arguments had long been a feature of Merthyr and the depression caused an intensification of this. The Communist Party was particularly active in organising and representing the grievances of the unemployed, all the left-wing groups in the area united in fighting the system of Means Testing and resisting other policies which threatened to bring economic death that little bit nearer. All put forward detailed plans for attracting new industry to the area. Most people looked to the political left for hope but a few joined the extreme right-wing Blackshirts, inspired by Mussolini and Hitler's activities. They were led in Merthyr by an ex-Communist, ex-wrestler, Arthur Eyles. They staged several demonstrations and marches and were involved in some minor brawls with local Communist groups. But they never held any appeal for most Merthyr people and their presence was short lived.

As months of unemployment and poverty turned into years, as the town becoming increasingly shabby and run down, as thousands went on leaving, we can understand why those who stayed must have felt increasingly helpless against the seemingly insoluble forces working against them. However, this is not to say that they accepted their condition without question or protest. There were Merthyr contingents on all the Hunger Marches in which people walked from South Wales to London to protest at their plight. When some men tried to take the jobs of miners who were on strike large numbers of people in Dowlais demonstrated against them (the Taff—Merthyr dispute, 1935).

Some men, mainly Communists, took their beliefs and struggle from Merthyr to the Spanish Civil War where they fought against the Fascist rebellion led by Franco. The unemployed in the town gave notice that they were going to at least defend their admittedly very low standard of living when, (after new regulations introduced by Government in 1935 effectively cut the amount of benefit many people received), a large demonstration erupted in to angry disorder and the windows of the Unemployment Assistance Board offices at Iscoed House, Pontmorlais, were smashed—one of many such incidents up and down the country in protest at the new regulations which were hastily withdrawn.

One organ of government and authority which most Merthyr people still seemed to support was the Monarchy. In 1935 George V and his Queen celebrated twenty-five years on the throne by instituting national celebrations. These were taken up in Merthyr with the same great enthusiasm as elsewhere although it must be said that no matter what the cause people in Britain at this time deserved an opportunity to at least briefly relax and enjoy themselves. Most people in Merthyr saw it as a chance to forget for a short time their hunger, poverty and unemployment. Further evidence of support for the Monarchy came in 1936 when a visit by Edward, Prince of Wales, to the area received rapturous welcome. As the prince gazed on the closed shops, empty and derelict, and the idle shell of the once great works at Dowlais which his parents had visited in triumphant style through the great Coal Arch just twenty five years earlier he uttered sincerely 'Something must be done'—possibly one of the great understatements of modern history.

It is time to examine now what was actually 'done' to help the area. New industry was completely put off moving to the area because of the necessary but nevertheless extremely high rates, because of the whole run down appearance of the area, because of inadequate communications and because they feared people who had been without work for so long would prove lazy and inefficient (this last fear proved totally unfounded when industry did eventually move back into the area). Therefore any action to help would have to come from the Government.

At this time the country was in the hands of the coalition known as the National Government. Although it had been formed as a result of many Labour members led by their leader, MacDonald, joining forces with Conservatives and Liberals in 1931 by 1935 the government was very much dominated by the Conservative Party and the Prime Minister was the party leader, Stanley Baldwin. It had never seemed to understand the economic crisis which had afflicted Britain and offered little hope of solving it, seeming to think that only time and patience would solve a situation that no government had real control of. This offered little to the areas worst hit by the crisis, of which Merthyr was one of the main examples.

This is not to say the government did nothing. It knew full well that Britain's economic structure had for far too long been based on a huge over-dependence on the older industries of coal, steel, textiles and heavy engineering. It knew, too, that there was a need for newer forms of industry such as consumer goods (e.g. radios, motor cars, household appliances), chemicals and light engineering to be expanded. There was a steady growth in these industries, especially after 1935, *but the growth took place well away from the depressed areas of heavy industry such as Merthyr.*

Thousands of Merthyr people went to live and work in areas such as Slough, Welwyn Garden, Birmingham and Coventry where these new industries were developing. Thousands of others went to Canada and Australia. After 1935 there was a steady improvement in the economic state of both Britain and the rest of the industrial world. *What singles out Merthyr and a few other areas is that at this time of general improvement their situation threatened to get worse because their whole economic foundation had collapsed in ruins.*

The Government did accept that because of these exceptional circumstances it should try and give special help to the areas concerned. Thus it attempted a series of measures, none of which were to prove highly successful. These included:

1. *Persuasion*: A circular was issued by the Board of Trade in 1934 asking firms if they would contemplate establishing branches in the depressed areas. 5,829 circulars were sent out; 1,313 firms replied to these—12 said they would establish branches.
2. *Distressed Area Status*: Given to a few badly hit areas such as Merthyr. It provided them with special assistance but this was often on a relatively small scale and the title distressed areas painted a picture which many industrialists found too gloomy to bother establishing bases there.
3. *Trading Estates*: Established by government acts. The nearest one to Merthyr was at Treforest (in the days before widespread ownership of cars a lot further away than it seems now) and although this did provide some jobs it was just a drop in the ocean.
4. *Royal Commission*: Set up by the Government to investigate Merthyr's problems. It sat in 1935 and speakers called by it painted a vivid picture of the gloom and despair of the town. The Mayor outlined the terrible living standards experienced by not only the unemployed but most of the town's working people as well. He also outlined plans to bring more work to the area which included such suggestions as moving part of the large Woolwich Arsenal plant to Merthyr. The Commission rejected these and in its Report recommended that Merthyr lose its County Borough status so that the burden of finding money to supply unemployment benefit could be lightened. This was of little help to a town facing catastrophe.

The Commission seemed to have caught the same ideas as the Government which appointed it. The depression was caused by uncontrollable forces and only patience would see it through. To people pinched by hunger, short of money and out of work patience is, however, often in short supply. The town's M.P. reacted very sharply to Government policy. In 1935 he asked the Prime Minister, 'Does the Right Honourable Gentleman know that the conviction is spreading in South Wales today that this Government deliberately abandoned it to its poverty and destruction? . . . We are not accepting quietly the destruction of the coalfield and the crucifixion of a little nation'.

Another example of government policies having little success was the *Special Area* scheme in which encouragement and assistance was offered to firms to set up plant in these depressed areas. It brought a little success, between 1932 and 1938 235 factories were built in Special Areas but in the same period over 2,000 were built in the Midlands and Greater London—*none* was built around Merthyr.

The growing menace of Germany began to increase armaments production in Britain after 1937 and this brought a little relief to local unemployment figures as the demand for steel and coal increased and a new works at Ebbw Vale was opened in 1938. But Merthyr's industrial structure was so shattered that there was no chance of either the coal or steel plants re-opening. The town remained down and only the pawn shops flourished.

Another stage in Merthyr's economic doom seemed to come with the Report on the Location of Industry published by the Parliamentary Political and Economic planning unit in March 1939. At this time, with much of the country economically healthier than ever before, no new industry showed any sign of coming to the area and unemployment stood at over 7,000 while hundreds left the town *every month*. The Report on Merthyr's plight concluded that 'the sole justification for a large town on this site has been the abundance of profitable coal and iron deposits, and no detached person would be likely to favour going to live at such a spot after the minerals have ceased to make it worthwhile'. *The Report then recommended that the town be completely abandoned and that its population be moved in full to the coast or to the Usk Valley*.

Merthyr seemed on its knees and ready to be counted out in its long fight with economic misfortune. But then that supreme element of destruction, war, ironically brought fresh life to the economic corpse. After World War II began in September 1939, Merthyr re-emerged as an industrial centre for the following reasons:

1. Its remote, hilly situation was a great handicap to peacetime economic development but in war this would be very useful in protecting factories from air-raids.
2. It had large areas on which industrial development could take place immediately.
3. A large pool of readily available male and female labour.
4. War would create a vastly increased demand for steel and coal.

The results were that by 1941 male unemployment had fallen to just over 1,000 and many women found work in the newly opened factories. After years on the dole many people were at work again. Days spent aimlessly on street corners or pool halls, desperately trying to live off a pittance and knowing what starvation was, were now gone for many. The town began to stir to new life again. But many sensed that the war had created beneficial and freak conditions, what did the future hold when it was finally over?

At first the outlook seemed bleak. Munitions factories closed as the demand for steel and coal dropped. Large numbers came home from armed service in search of jobs. By mid 1946 Merthyr was once again a place of high unemployment, 7,000 were out of work—hundreds more began to leave to look for better times elsewhere. But there had been a change in the political approach to economic problems. The ideas of men such as Aneurin Bevan who felt the state should *own* certain vital industries were now far more widely accepted. Along with this the ideas of the Liberal economist, J. M. Keynes, which put forward the view that Government should be involved deeply in the economy and should itself spend *to deliberately create* employment were now seen as prophetic. In the 1945 election a Labour government had been returned and they quickly set about putting both sets of ideas into practice.

Fortunately, measures such as the Distribution of Industry Act (1945) and the Town and Country Act (1947) brought a series of new firms and opportunities to the area. These included Teddington, O.P., Ceramics, Thorns, Hoovers and Lines Brothers. There was a solid economic base on which to build long-term industrial strength and in 1951 unemployment was at its lowest level for thirty years.

But as profoundly a shattering experience as the depression is something from which recovery in other senses takes more time. The town began to recover its confidence—the soccer team reformed and established a reputation as Britain's best non-league side. The rugby club revived, shops re-opened and new businesses came to the town. Activities such as greyhound racing, pigeon fancying and, the sport which thrives on hard times, boxing, maintained their popularity of the depression years but now they were leisure time hobbies, not the centre of a workless existence.

Despite all this, the depression left a bitter, haunting legacy. Because the town had been virtually bankrupt no real schemes of house building, no social improvements such as school and hospital building and no development of any great degree had taken place between the wars. Much of the town was, therefore, blighted with inadequate and inferior housing and equally poor community and social facilities. Furthermore when redevelopment did take place in the nineteen fifties and sixties it was largely in the hands of men who had been boys and youths in Merthyr at the peak of the depression. This cruel, desperate experience seems to have inculcated in them a loathing of nearly everything which represented Merthyr's past. The result was on the one hand very necessary social improvements but on the other hand some unnecessary schemes which have destroyed much of Merthyr's important historic heritage.

Since 1951 Merthyr has undergone great physical change and varied fortunes. Many of the firms who came to the town after the war have since closed up and left but another has expanded greatly. Depopulation continues, particularly among the young, (e.g. out of my school class of 37 eleven years ago only 5 now live or work in Merthyr) but the problem is very much less serious than pre-war years.

Overall, the town now has a stability and strength which suggests that those in the 1930s who wrote the town off as dying will have an extremely long wait before they bury the corpse. The birth of Merthyr as an industrial society had been turbulent, violent and tough. Gradually, factors such as the growth of non-conformity, the spread of education and the growth of working class organisation had produced a more stable community in which the worst degradation, crime and vice of the middle of the nineteenth century all but disappeared although Merthyr remained a hard society (e.g. in 1975 there were 188 convictions for drunkenness, in 1910 there were 1,070). But all the time a more responsible sense of community was developing and despite the extreme hardship of the depression it says much for this that Merthyr did not return to its violent, racy ways but instead always maintained dignity in spite of its pitiable condition. From their bitter experiences Merthyr's people built up a strength of spirit, a strength of community and a belief in humanity which provided *them* with resistance and resilience against even the starkest economic hardships which left a whole decade indelibly and vividly etched in the minds of Merthyr's population. Those who stayed through those dark days and the thousands who left remember that period, with just cause, as simply the Hungry Thirties.

The Economic Development Since 1939

by G. HOPKINS M.A., M.Litt.

The disastrous years of economic depression which characterised the 1930s were brought to an end by the onset of the even darker days of the Second World War. However, for the country as a whole and for Merthyr Tydfil in particular war represented a period of economic recovery. True, the recovery had begun a few years earlier after central government had initiated a policy of limited but active intervention in regional economic development. As a result of the Special Areas Acts of 1934, 1936 and 1937, Merthyr Tydfil had acquired a nucleus of manufacturing industry by the outbreak of war. In 1939 four new firms were operating, namely I.C.I., Kayser Bondor, Hall Telephones and Welsh Products Ltd.; these were, of course, in addition to the Dowlais Foundary. Yet these new factories provided work for only 900 people; the town still had a total of 4,000 unemployed.

Nevertheless, the war strengthened the economy of Merthyr Tydfil by reducing the numbers of unemployed. New and expanded works provided additional opportunities for employment; labour was directed to work by government and military conscription absorbed some unemployed as well as the employed. Wartime factories established in the town included those owned by Unilever and Rotax. The building of the ordnance works at Hirwaun and the expansion of the Trading Estate at Treforest meant that some of Merthyr Tydfil's labour force found work outside the borough. This reduction in the numbers of unemployed was the more remarkable as it took place when, for the first time, women were employed on a relatively large scale.

However, the ending of the hostilities in 1945 threatened a return to the bad years of the 1930s. The rapid curtailment of the need for munitions coupled with the demobilisation of service personnel led to the closure of factories at the very time when the labour supply was suddenly expanded. Unemployment rose again, reaching 6,000 in January 1946. By now, however, the economic situation in Merthyr Tydfil, as in other valleys of the coalfield had changed significantly. Heavy industry which had dominated the town for nearly two centuries no longer held sway. The basic iron and steel industries had ceased to be a factor for some time, of course, but coal mining, too, had been on the decline. While in 1939 mining had accounted for 30% of the labour force, by 1951 this percentage had fallen to 22.3%.

In 1939 only seven pits were operating in the borough although two more existed in the neighbouring Cwm Bargoed. Of all these collieries, only the Deep Navigation mine at Treharris, the Merthyr Vale Pits and the Taff Merthyr Colliery at Trelewis employed more than 1,000 men. The Castle, South Duffryn and Gethin collieries at Troedyrhiw and Abercanaid respectively were maintained only for pumping and ventilation. The remaining collieries were Bedlinog Drift, Lucy Thomas No. 4 and Brug Drifts. It is noticeable that mining was concentrated in the south of the valley. Throughout the war these mines continued in production though in 1947, the year of nationalisation, the Castle and Gethin Pits, and Brug Drift were closed. Further closures resulted in the 1950s from increasing competition from other fuels. Thus Lucy Thomas No. 4 ceased operations in 1955 and Bedlinog Drift in the following year. In each case the labour force had been reduced continually since 1948. However, to compensate for these losses, a new drift mine was opened at Trelewis in 1954 and this colliery has proved to be the most profitable in the coalfield. In 1971 it had the largest production, the highest output per manshift and the second smallest labour force. There have been no further closures since 1956 but each of the four older pits now employs fewer men than it did a decade ago. Indeed the labour force of the pits in what is now the District of Merthyr Tydfil has fallen from just over 6,000 to about 2,500 in 1977. To some extent this reflects increased mechanisation in the mines but another factor has been the problem of obtaining recruits for the industry, for the time when son followed father into the pit in South Wales is long passed.

The main markets now served by the pits in the District are the electricity generating stations and the phurnacite plant at Mountain Ash. It seems that the future of these collieries is reasonably secure for during the 1960s, £2 million was spent on modernising Merthyr Vale pit and about £500,000 on each of Taff Merthyr and Deep Navigation. Currently plans for further development include a concentration scheme involving these three collieries. The cost of the scheme exceeds £9 million, part of which will cover the deepening of both shafts at Taff Merthyr.

Besides deep and drift mining, Merthyr Tydfil also possesses opencast workings. In 1951 Glyn Mil private site was opened and a year later it was producing coal at a rate of 80,000 tons a year and employing 54 workers. The output was small compared with the roughly 400,000 tons produced by the Deep Navigation pit in the same year. More important in terms of

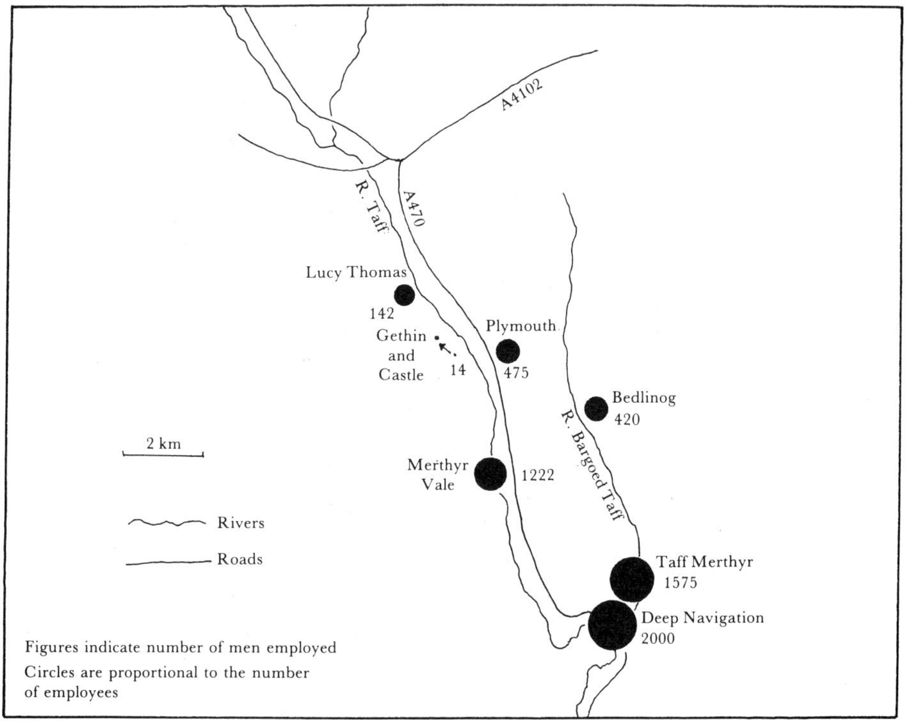

Fig. 72a: Collieries 1939

output and labour force are the workings operated by private firms under contract to the N.C.B. The sites occupy an area extending from Rhymney towards Dowlais to the south of the A4060 and the A465(T) roads. The workings are referred to as the Royal Arms Group which includes the Dowlais Top, Pantywain and Cae Harris sub-areas.

Preparation of the site began in November 1958 and the first coal was produced in April of the following year when 76 men were employed; by 1968 the labour force had increased to 232. The contracted target output was raised from 1.17 million tons initially to 3.4 million tons in 1975. Work was completed in August of that year. In the September work began on the Trecatty site with a target output of 0.9 million tons. The labour force of 127 comes almost entirely from Merthyr Tydfil.

The coal produced is transported by road to a disposal point at Cwm Bargoed where 30 men are employed. Road is also the method of transporting the coal to markets which are largely coke ovens and power stations although some coal finds its way to the household market. Nevertheless, opencast operations have a relatively short life and output from the present site will cease long before production comes to an end at the deep mines.

Mining in the town brought economic benefits but it also brought

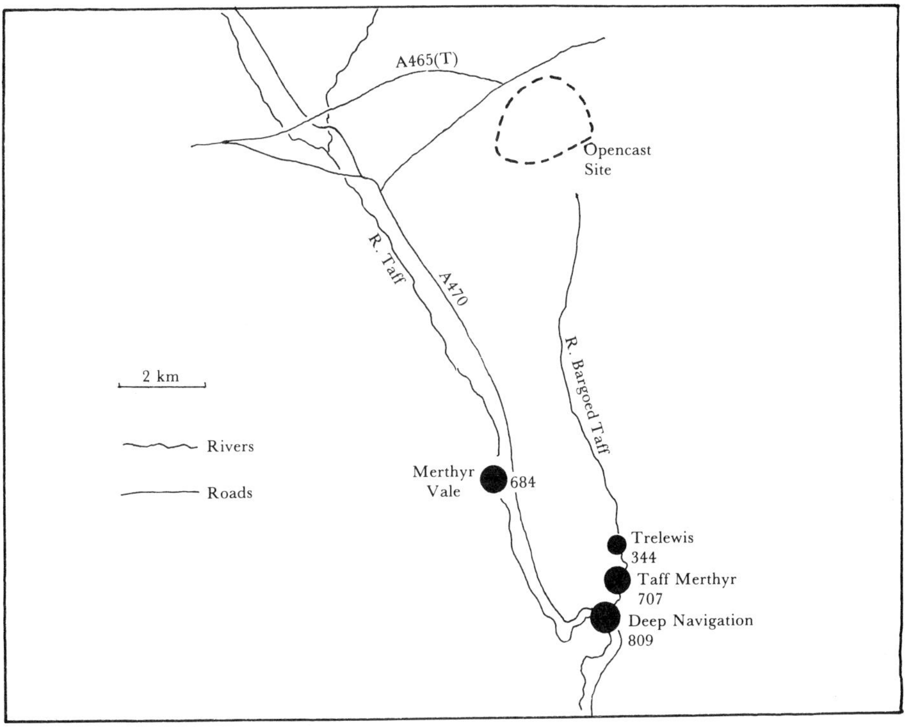

Fig. 72b: Collieries 1977

disasters. The greatest calamity occurred on 21 October, 1966, a day of deep sorrow in Aberfan. On a misty autumn morning, 143 children and adults died beneath a flood of colliery waste which slumped onto the valley floor from the neighbouring hillside. Those who died were in the village junior school and sixteen neighbouring houses, which were all nearly submerged beneath the slurry.

This tragedy highlights the legacy of decades of industrial exploitation which is revealed now in a highly derelict environment. In 1973 the Planning Department of the Borough recognised 3,203 acres of dereliction which formed nearly 20% of the total area of the town. Much of the dereliction occurs in the northern part of the District where heavy industry has had its longest history. The extent of dereliction listed varies from a quarry half an acre in size in Trelewis to the vast opencast workings at Trecatty covering 293 acres.

Not only are such areas visually unattractive but they take up land which could be used for other purposes. Thus in 1972 the County Borough of Merthyr Tydfil joined the Monmouthshire Derelict Land Reclamation Joint Committee to undertake improvements in the environment. The degree of dereliction is such that the task of reclamation will extend over a number of

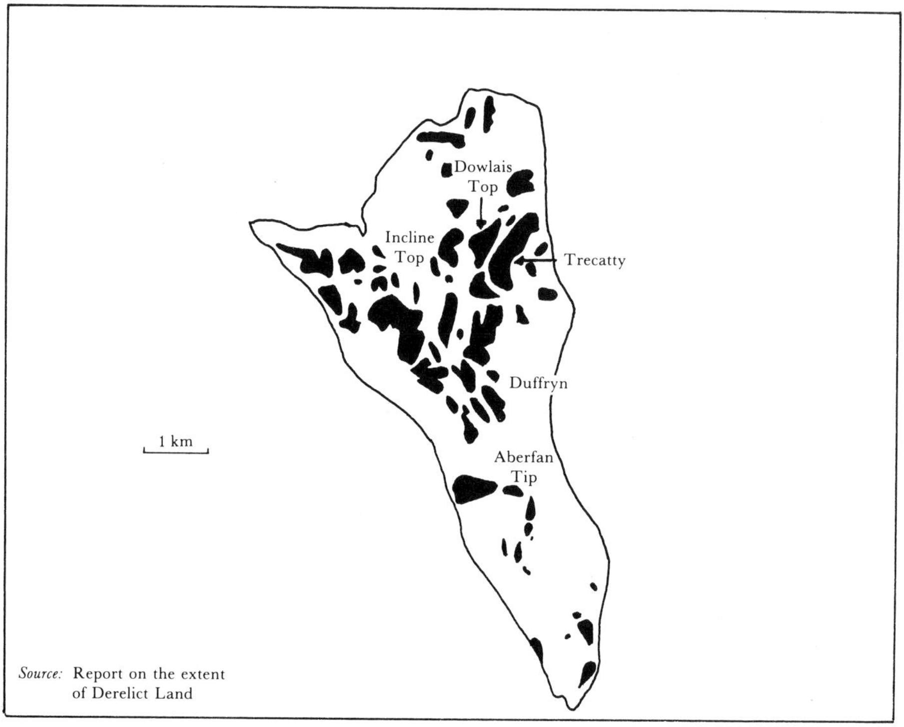

Fig. 73a: Derelict Land 1973

years. However, a start has been made. The Aberfan tip was one of the first to be removed and the site has now been landscaped. Other smaller areas already treated include Nant y Gwenith tip, Cyfarthfa tip, Trebeddau, Dowlais Top and the Cae Harris site.

The use to which such land is put after reclamation varies. Some areas will revert to farm land, some will be made available for amenity and recreational purposes and some to urban development. Yet others will provide much needed space for industrial sites. Some reclamation has already been undertaken, for by 1977 the Duffryn complex, north of Troedyrhiw, had been reformed, much of its tip waste having been transported across the main road to raise the level of Dix's Field. The latter is now available as a site for factories and the first buildings have been erected.

Factories are the symbol of hope in Merthyr Tydfil for, if mining has been on the decline, manufacturing industry has experienced a period of major growth since the Second World War. Again the Borough's experience was little different from that of the rest of South Wales for with the return of the Labour Party to power in 1945, a strengthening of government action to control the economy was to be expected. A succession of Acts concerned with economic development was passed, commencing with the Distribution

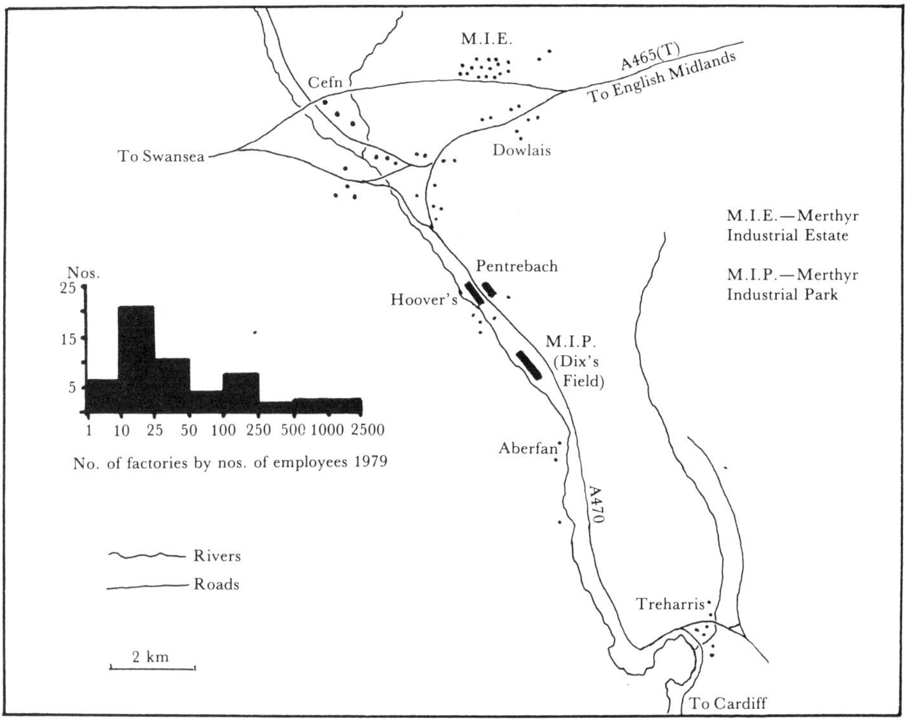

Fig. 73b: Location of Factories

of Industry Act of 1945. Other important Acts in the postwar period were the Town and Country Planning Act of 1947, the Distribution of Industry Act of 1950, the 1958 Distribution of Industry (Finance) Act, the 1960 and 1963 Local Employment Acts, the 1966 Industrial Development Act and the Industry Act of 1972. In brief, much government action in the economic field has sought to encourage the dispersion of industrial and service activities to the problem regions of the country, including South Wales. One way in which it attempted to achieve its aims was to control the location of industry by limiting the issue of industrial development certificates to firms wishing to set up large factories where economic conditions were relatively good. Additionally, to encourage development in less prosperous areas, the government has provided numerous financial incentives such as building advance factories, giving grants and loans for the installation of plant and making payments towards labour costs in manufacturing industry and providing taxation allowances.

This carrot and stick policy had a measure of success in Merthyr Tydfil as can be seen in the following figures which relate to the number of factories established or to major extensions undertaken. 'Industry' includes manufacturing establishments and such service activities as warehousing, plant hiring and motor coach services.

Number of new industries or extensions by five year periods

Pre 1939	4	1960-64	8
1945-49	8	1965-69	22
1950-54	5	1970-74	17
1955-59	0	1975-76	2

Source: Merthyr Tydfil Planning Office.

Among the larger firms which came to Merthyr Tydfil in the postwar period were Teddington Aircraft Controls, Cefn Coed (1945), Hoover Ltd. (1945), B.S.A. (1951), Lines Bros. (1951), and Thorn Electrical Industries (1951). Many of the firms, often small, have settled on the Merthyr Tydfil Industrial Estate which the Borough set up in 1966 in the north of the town on the site of the old I.C.I. works. This is a particularly favourable location in the town for it lies adjacent to the Heads of the Valleys road which, with other improvements completed by 1976, provides rapid transport to the Midlands of England and to Swansea via the Neath Valley. In contrast to the old heavy industries, which dealt with a narrow range of products, the new factories turn out a variety of manufactures often small in size and light in weight.

However, this picture of success has its dark side too, for some firms have ceased operating over the same period. The first important works to close was B.S.A. in 1958; this works had employed about 500 people. Export Packing, another firm on the Dowlais Estate, also shut its doors in the same year, putting 200 more people out of work. To some extent this set-back followed a reduction in defence expenditure, but the cyclical nature of the economy led to further closures in later years. Thus in 1962, I.C.I. closed

Plate 48a: AERIAL VIEW OF HOOVER's PENTREBACH FACTORY, 1974
(By permission of Hoover Ltd.)

Plate 48b: MANUFACTURE OF AUTOMATIC WASHING MACHINES AT THE HOOVER FACTORY *(By permission of Hoover Ltd.)*

their plant at Dowlais and Standard Box shut its factory. In 1971 Cold Precision Forgings Ltd. ceased operations while the collapse of Rolls Royce in the same year resulted in the closure of Teddington's which meant that 700 workers had to find new employment; in 1976 Ballito on the Dowlais Estate was another factory to close. Less severe but no less serious for the individuals concerned was short time working introduced by Hoovers in the early 1960s and the laying off of 300 at Teddington's following the cancellation of the TSR 2 aircraft project in 1965. In contrast, it was announced in January 1977 that a £10 million extension to the Hoover works was to be built by the Welsh Development Agency. Additionally financial assistance was to be given to equip the factory under the provisions of the Industry Act 1972. It was hoped that 3,000 new jobs would be created in a 500,000 sq. feet factory to be completed by the summer 1979. However, the worsening economic climate of 1979 and 1980, coupled with the new Conservative government's actions to reduce inflation, dashed such hopes. In 1980 a decision was taken to leave the new factory empty. Additionally the firm shed 1,400 workers out of a total of 3,000 during the period 1979-1980.

A disadvantage common to nearly all factories which have been 'directed' to Merthyr Tydfil and other areas is that they are often branch works of companies the head quarters of which are located elsewhere in the country.

Plate 49a: TRIANG TOYS FACTORY, CYFARTHFA, 1969 (Demolished early 1981)
(By permission of Clive Thomas)

Plate 49b: THORNS ELECTRICAL INDUSTRIES CYFARTHFA FACTORY, 1969
(By permission of Clive Thomas)

Kayser Bondor, for example, derives its main raw materials from its main factory at Baldock in Hertfordshire. At times of economic crisis it is these subsidiary works which are often closed or put on short time. Merthyr Tydfil as a site for a subsidiary works possessed disadvantages particularly with regard to transport costs which, admittedly, were more serious before the building of the Heads of the Valleys road. Nevertheless, an entrepreneur considering the site for a new factory has to balance such disadvantages against the financial inducements offered by the government. The latter, indeed, may not be so competitive since the inclusion of South Glamorgan in the Intermediate category of areas qualifying for government aid. It has been claimed that there is relatively little advantage for firms to settle in Special Development Areas, such as Merthyr Tydfil, rather than in Development or Intermediate Areas. The lowland of south-eastern Wales, clearly, provides greater benefits socially and economically than valley sites such as Merthyr Tydfil. Shopping and entertainment facilities are much more available in the larger towns of Cardiff and Newport and the transport system is incomparably better. While Merthyr Tydfil is on a branch line, Cardiff and Newport are served by the main railway to London. With the completion of the M4 westwards nearly to Bridgend at the end of 1977, the Vale area again possesses a superior road connection with the rest of the country.

Clearly, the conomic situation in the Intermediate areas of South Wales is not satisfactory but their ability to attract firms is considerably greater than that of Merthyr Tydfil. Admittedly a large percentage of the growth in employment in the larger towns has been in the service sector but it is this very area of employment that occupies an important role in the employment structure of Merthyr Tydfil itself.

Even in the 1930s service occupations ranked high in employment terms for, of course, this was a period when there was little other source of work, except for mining. Agriculture offered no opportunity for large scale employment and, with the disappearance of the steel works, manufacturing industry was in no position to absorb the unemployed. In 1939 manufacturing industries accounted for only about 10% of the labour force while mining and service industries each took about 45% of the total. By 1960, when manufacturing had established itself in the town and accounted for 43% of the employed, service industries represented 32% of the work force. The major change over this period, of course, had been the decline in mining. In 1970 out of the total employment in primary, secondary and service industries, the latter accounted for 51% but by 1974 the percentage had fallen to 36. While the fluctuations in these figures are quite large, the important feature is that service industries have long held a notable place in Merthyr Tydfil. However, when compared with data for other areas (1974, Mid Glamorgan, services = 45.5%, Wales 63%, England and Wales 62%), the figures show that Merthyr Tydfil has not reached the levels for the country as a whole.

A survey undertaken in 1973 produced a more detailed picture of the employment structure.

Employment Structure, Merthyr Tydfil, 1973

	Numbers	%
Mining/quarrying	2,203	9.8
Manufacturing	12,642	56.0
Retailing	1,671	7.4
Services	2,820	12.4
Recreation	355	1.6
Office Work	2,886	12.8
	22,577	100

Source: Merthyr Tydfil Planning Office.

Much of the employment in the tertiary sector of the economy is concentrated in the central area of the town but there is some dispersion of activities, particularly in the case of retailing. As the demand for food is greater than that for other goods, suburban areas are able to support a number of food shops. On the other hand, shops selling clothes, furniture, electrical goods, etc. require a larger market and a location which is easily accessible, so that they tend to be sited in the town centre. Again a feature of

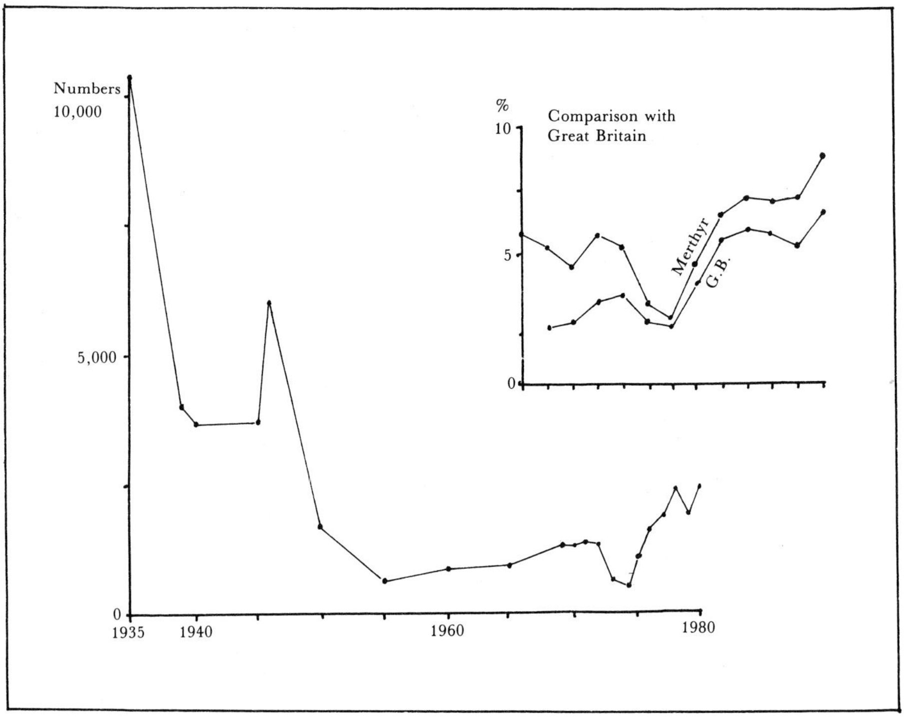

Fig. 74a: Unemployment in Merthyr Tydfil

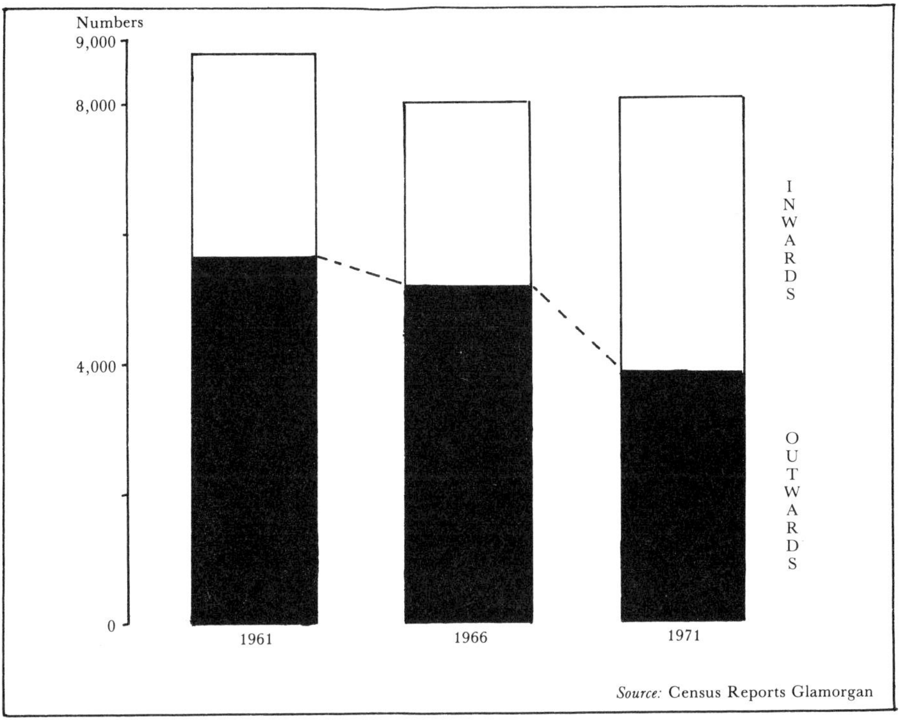

Fig. 74b: Journey to Work

the central area is that it contains larger shops which have a big turnover. It is a fact, also, that Merthyr Tydfil is not a major shopping centre for much of its trade is concerned with convenience goods. The latter may be defined as products in frequent demand, such as food, newspapers, etc. Larger shopping centres have a higher percentage of their trade in durable goods, e.g. television sets and washing machines.

However, the provision of services is rarely a static phenomenon and Merthyr Tydfil has witnessed considerable changes since the 1960s. Central Merthyr has been transformed by the construction of a new shopping precinct while in suburban areas such as the Gurnos Estate, Dowlais and Penydarren, small retail units have been built or are planned. Work is complete too, on the construction of a large superstore covering 50,000 square feet to the east of Dowlais. Other developments have included the building of a motel on the Heads of the Valleys road and a community centre and swimming pool at Aberfan. In 1975 a leisure centre was opened at Rhydycar while a new District Hospital has been completed on the Gurnos estate.

Of all the service occupations, the one which has experienced the greatest expansion is administration, resulting from increased government and commercial activity. Such development is reflected in the building of offices in the town, as can be seen in the following table.

Merthyr Tydfil Detached Office Floorspace
(1,000 square feet)

	Commercial Offices	*Central Gov. Offices*	*Local Gov. Offices*	*Total Gov. Offices*	*Grand Total*
1967	82	57	44	101	184
1968	94	57	46	103	197
1969	127	56	46	102	229
1974 (est.)	172	103	99	202	374
% Change 1967-1974	110.9	55.3	122.2	99.1	103.8

The completion of a new Magistrate and Crown Court in the town centre has added a further 62,000 square feet to these figures. Clearly Merthyr Tydfil's urban fabric is taking on a new appearance.

Fluctuations in the economic fortunes of Merthyr Tydfil, as outlined earlier, are emphasised, obviously, by the varying levels of unemployment in the town. The pattern which characterised the war period has already been considered. Since 1950 the numbers of unemployed have always been below 2,000 and consequently the variations in these numbers have been small compared with those of the period from 1920 to 1950. Despite this improvement, Merthyr Tydfil's recovery from the economic depression of the pre-war years has been less successful than that of many areas. A comparison of the town's unemployment with that of Great Britain shows that the rates of unemployment for the District have been consistently higher. Nevertheless, if such figures are used as an index of economic performance, Merthyr Tydfil's progress has been rather better than that in adjacent valleys of Mid Glamorgan.

During the 1970s certain changes in unemployment levels were sufficiently marked to justify some comment. Between 1971 and 1973 unemployment fell dramatically but the rapid rise in world oil prices in 1973 and 1974 plunged the economy into deep trouble. Consequently unemployment in Merthyr Tydfil climbed steeply again. This general pattern masks certain detailed features which need to be considered. Throughout the period from 1939 the number of males out of work has exceeded that of females, usually by a large margin. This is in keeping with the fact that roughly twice as many males as females are in employment. Nevertheless, the growth in unemployment in the female sector is faster than that in the male sector. Of greater concern is the even faster rate of increase in the number of youths unemployed. It was because of these deteriorating economic conditions that the government introduced in 1976 its 'job creation' programme which, at least, kept a number of the young from inflating the dole queue.

Related to the question of unemployment are activity rates, defined as the proportion of the population of working age who are part of the labour force.

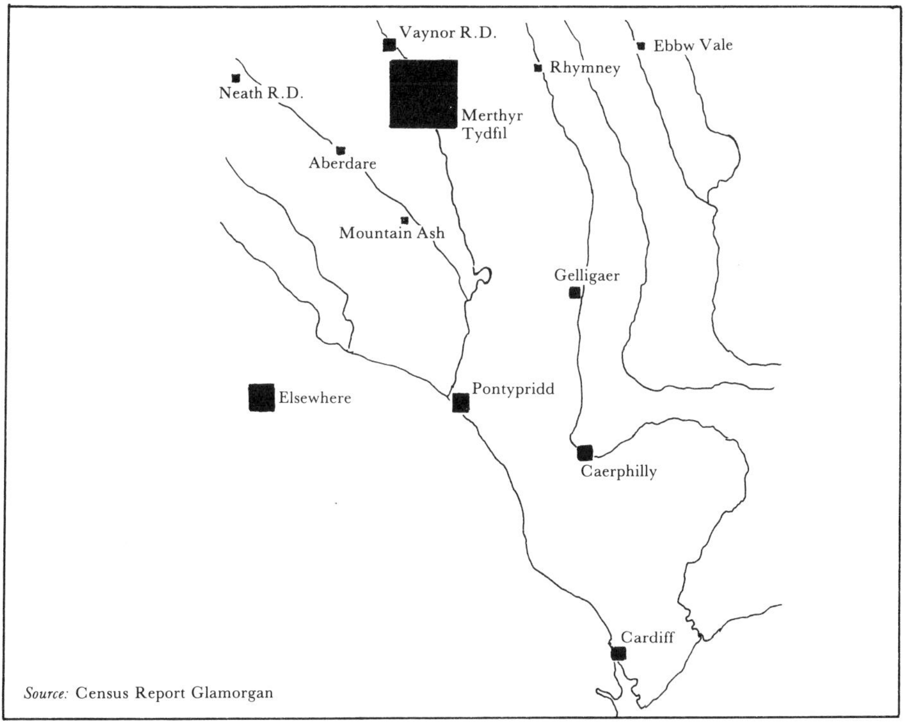

Fig. 75a: Daily Journey to Work Outward Movement 1971

It is clear from statistics that there has been an increase in the activity rates over the five year period but that, also in most cases, the percentages for Merthyr Tydfil are lower than those for England and Wales. This may reflect the relatively large numbers of disabled people in the town.

The restricted opportunity for work in the town forces many people to seek employment elsewhere and hence to undertake a journey to work every day. This daily migration, both outward and inward, is recorded in census reports and interesting patterns are revealed in the relevant statistics. In general terms, between a quarter and one sixth of the working population of Merthyr Tydfil are employed outside the town, but over the last quarter of a century this proportion of the population has been declining. Additionally the numbers involved in the diurnal flow have decreased by about one third, from over 6,000 in 1951 to just under 4,000 in 1971.

In each of the four censuses since 1951 the geographical county of Glamorgan attracted more workers than other areas, a not surprising fact in view of the developed nature of the county. The numbers involved decreased from 4,884 in 1951 to 2,550 in 1971. Breconshire was ahead of Monmouthshire and other parts of the country. In more detail, the Rural District of Vaynor and Penderyn had always been an important magnet for workers because of the Teddington works at Cefn Coed. The old Gelligaer Urban

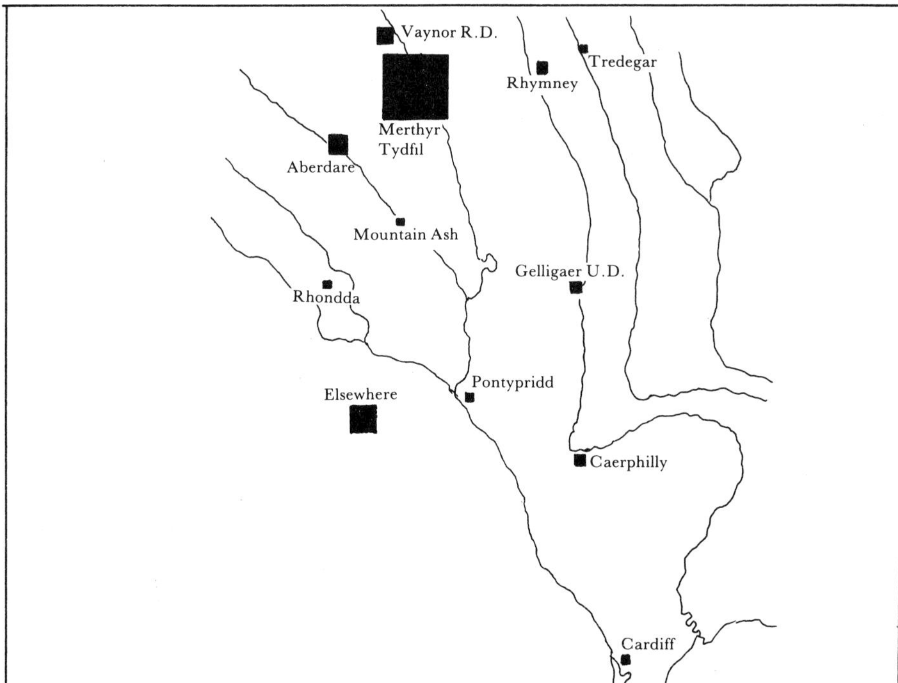

Source: Census Report Glamorgan

Fig. 75b: Daily Journey to Work Inward Movement 1971

District was also notable but between 1961 and 1971 its labour force originating in Merthyr Tydfil fell from 830 to 360. Neath Rural District (Hirwaun Industrial Estate) also declined considerably over the same period but the City of Cardiff, while attracting fewer workers in 1971, had improved its relative position compared with other centres of employment. Possibly the increasing importance of service industries in the Capital has given added employment opportunities to people to travel to work. By 1971, too, Pontypridd (Treforest Industrial Estate) had risen to first place as an outlying centre of employment. It was the only town which increased its labour force from the Borough at each of the censuses. Other towns which took smaller numbers of workers were Aberdare, Mountain Ash, Ebbw Vale and Caerphilly. Between 1961 and 1971 Caerphilly rose from ninth to fifth place in the list of important towns, possibly as a result of the industrial developments which have taken place in that former urban district.

There is an equivalent daily inflow of workers into Merthyr Tydfil and, generally, the pattern of this migration is the opposite of that for the outward movement of labour. Indeed, while the movement from the town has been decreasing, the inward migration has been increasing, to such an extent that in 1971 the journey to work was greater to Merthyr Tydfil than from it—4,150 workers compared with 3,920. It is possible that the post 1950 expansion of manufacturing industry in the town not only absorbed more of its labour force and reduced the journey to work but attracted workers from other towns as well. During this period Vaynor and Penderyn has supplied more workers than any other individual centre while Aberdare and Gelligaer have also been important; in fact these three areas in 1971 accounted for more than half of the inward journey to work. In that year, too, other relatively important centres were Rhymney, Caerphilly, Tredegar, Rhondda and Cardiff.

It may seem strange that while there are apparent job vacancies in Merthyr Tydfil, represented by workers travelling to the town, a large number of residents work outside the District. However, an important factor influencing the pattern of movement is the type of employment available. The limited number of professional people living in the District suggests that in this type of employment at least there are vacancies for people resident in other towns. A survey in 1977 of teachers in secondary and further education establishments revealed that 170 travelled into Merthyr Tydfil to work; this number represents about 45% of the teaching force in those sectors of the education service. Clearly, they form only a small part of the daily inflow of workers but they do illustrate the general point that vacancies exist in specific jobs.

Over the last two hundred years major changes have occurred in the economic base of the town. Now, of course, Merthyr Tydfil is largely dependent on manufacturing and service industries. However, it is questionable whether the present situation is satisfactory. The size of Hoover's works and its planned expansion may mean that the District will be overdependent on one industry. Again, the employment structure indicates that economically Merthyr Tydfil is moving only slowly towards an advanced stage of development. Primary industry has declined considerably but manufacturing is still the dominant employer. Yet even in this sector, progress is slow for high technology industry is notable only by its absence. Furthermore, while service industries dominate the employment pattern of England and Wales, in Merthyr Tydfil they are declining relatively. The District has benefited little from government transfer of office jobs from south-eastern England. The large establishments that have been transferred have gone to the coastal towns of Swansea, Newport and Cardiff. It is clear that if Merthyr Tydfil is to make swifter progress economically, it will need to receive more aid from central government. But Merthyr Tydfil is but one of many similar areas in need of such help.

Bibliography

The Story of Merthyr Tydfil, N.U.T. 1932

The Changing Economic Geography of Merthyr Tydfil, D. G. R. Belshaw.

The Contemporary Economic Problems in Merthyr Tydfil, B. M. Brunt.

An Analysis of Industrial Change within the County Borough of Merthyr Tydfil, E. Willis.

Coal in East Wales, N.C.B. pamphlet.
South Wales Area Annual Reports, N.C.B.
N.C.B. Opencast Division Office, Aberaman for data on opencast activities.
Colliery Guardian, Colliery Yearbook and Guide to the Coalfields.
List of Mines, H.M.S.O.
Preparing and Planning the South Wales Coalfield for the 1980s, C. J. Davies. Proceedings of the South Wales Institute of Engineers, Vol. XC1, Nov. 1976.
Supplementary Report on the Extent of Derelict Land, 1973. Monmouthshire Derelict Land Reclamation Joint Committee.
Aberfan and the Teachers, N.U.T. booklet.
Mid Glamorgan Industrial Directories, 1978, 1979, and 1980.
Merthyr Tydfil Planning Department for information on industry, commerce and employment.
Western Mail 11 January, 1977, '£10m. go ahead for Hoover'.
Western Mail 19 June, 1980, 'Hoover Extension'.
Western Mail 19 August, 1980, 'Hoover Extension'.
Report on the Census of Distribution and Other Services, H.M.S.O.
Census Reports: *Glamorgan* 1951, 1961, 1971; *Workplace and Transport Tables*, H.M.S.O. 1950, 1961, 1971; *Sample Census of Population—Workplace and Transport Tables*, H.M.S.O. 1966.

The Development of Transport

by E. WILLIS B.A.

Improvements in the technology of transporting goods and people have been both a spur and a response to industrial advances. Changes have taken place at a steadily accelerating pace since the 1750s and Merthyr Tydfil has been at the vanguard of the process of technological advance from this early period. Merthyr was always the first of the areas in Britain to be served by any of the new and relatively embryonic transport systems of the day. Until the beginning of the relative decline in the importance of Merthyr from the 1860s onwards, the rest of South Wales and indeed at times, the rest of the world has tended to follow Merthyr's lead. Unfortunately, the penalty for innovation and pioneering in any form of technology tends to be early obsolescence and associated decline as improved methods and techniques are developed and supersede the old. Just as this concept applies to Merthyr's former industrial dominance in iron and steel so it applies equally to Merthyr's transport system. The vestiges of most of Merthyr's formally advanced and comprehensive transport infrastructure are now at best neglected and at worst completely derelict and obliterated. From being the centre of a vortex of ruthless competition between different railway and canal companies, Merthyr's transport system has steadily stagnated to that of a dead end single track railway and an indifferent road network.

It is perhaps a sad feature of Merthyr Tydfil, that the town can look back on many past glories but the corporately planned future seems to hold little but mundanity and conformity. The realisation of the importance of preserving what is left of Merthyr's past is vital if the vitality and individuality of the past is to be retained and nurtured by succeeding generations. This philosophy applies particularly to Merthyr's transport heritage, the significance of which stretches back to the early period of industrialisation in the mid-eighteenth century. At this period, the early entrepreneurial efforts of producing iron on a comparatively large scale basis succeeded in spite of rather than because of the transport facilities available. Indeed, the initial

Plate 50a: GLAMORGAN CANAL AT YNYSFACH, MERTHYR TYDFIL
(By permission of Clive Thomas)

expansion took place because little transport was involved in the production process.[1] The wood, iron ore and limestone were all available locally. Problems arose when the iron had to be distributed to the rest of Britain. This involved a slow, expensive and inefficient journey to the coast by pack-horse along roads little changed for seventeen hundred years. The lack of adequate transport facilities not only handicapped expansion of the industry but also handicapped any expansion in the population of Merthyr. Prior to 1750 the Merthyr area was essentially self sufficient. The growth of the early iron works meant that feeding, clothing and generally supplying the growing population became an acute problem. In 1787, coke smelting began to replace the charcoal smelting of the iron ore, but without the improvement in transport facilities the Iron Masters were incapable of fully benefiting from the associated technological advance. Thus, impetus was generated for the construction of the first canal in Wales to link Merthyr with Cardiff. The Glamorgan Canal started in 1790.[2] The first section from Cardiff to Abercynon was completed in four years. But the canal builders faced their first major obstacle in the section from Abercynon to Cefn Glas where the River Taff cuts through a deep gorge in an outcrop of Pennant Sandstone. This stretch of the Taff Valley is a recurring problem for civil engineers to the present day. In the 1790s there was a considerable prize to be gained in reaching Merthyr and with the aid of 16 locks, including the then deepest in the world, the canal reached Quaker's Yard and thence continued to Merthyr for completion in 1798.

Plate 50b: BRIDGE OVER PENYDARREN TRAMROAD, NEAR PONTYGWAITH
(By permission of Clive Thomas)

As was perhaps normal in this period when business expertise tended to be based very much on raw and abrasive individual enterprise the building of the canal on the fringes of technology was fraught with difficulties. Even when it was completed the personality clashes of the iron masters created

Plate 50c: STONE SLEEPERS ON PENYDARREN TRAMROAD, NEAR PONTYGWAITH
(By permission of D. Packer)

further problems which the anachronistic legal system compounded. Problems over access rights, prompted the owners of the Dowlais, Penydarren and Plymouth Ironworks to amalgamate and build a tramroad to a canal basin at Abercynon. Tramroads were not a particularly new innovation and had been used for a number of years to handle materials within the ironworks, using horses to pull the trams. The greater length of this tramroad was a new development but the most significant technological development took place in 1804, when in response to a wager between Crawshay and another master Homfray, the Penydarren Works engineer Trevithick constructed the first steam engine to run on rails.

In the event, Trevithick's engine fulfilled the demands of the wager, but Crawshay attempted to avoid payment on a technical point. Perhaps the most notable thing about this important innovation was its complete lack of initial impact. As so often happens the potential of a new technological advance is not immediately recognised especially when the back-up technology is not available. In this case the cast iron track was not able to withstand the pounding of the locomotive wheels and broke up in a number of places. Trevithick's locomotive after developing a fault was towed back by horses on the return trip, the wheels removed and once more re-employed as a works stationary engine. Possibly the manner in which the trial had taken place, for a wager, tended to cloud its potential and Trevithick went on to develop locomotives for their entertainment and novelty value rather than for their practical usefulness. It was not for almost a further quarter of a century that the technological potential of the railway locomotive was developed more fully by Robert Stephenson.

However, the technological advance of the canal and the tramroad improved the growth potential of the Merthyr industry. In terms of efficiency one horse could pull a 24-ton barge or a 10-ton tram, compared to a 2-ton load by road. The locational advantage of Merthyr for the production of iron could therefore be better exploited and traffic on the canal increased with the burgeoning of the iron industry. By 1830 the canal became increasingly congested as the movement of coal and iron ore was added to the basic traffic of bar iron.[3] The carriage of iron ore was an important innovation. The early iron industry in Merthyr was dependent on the black band ore found within the coal measures.[4] The difficulty and expense of mining these thin seams of ore resulted in a move to import iron ore from Northern Spain, once cheaper transport facilities became available with the completion of the Glamorgan Canal and the dock basin at Cardiff. The establishment of the trade with Northern Spain resulted in the movement of Spanish migrants to work in Merthyr to add to the flow of migrants to Merthyr from rural Wales, other parts of England (notably Cornwall) and Ireland.

The mushroom growth of Merthyr from 7,705 in 1801 to 17,404 in 1821,[5] once more posed problems of transporting sufficient supplies to meet the needs of the population. This gave impetus to a further road building programme, notably the completion of the Merthyr to Abergavenny road in 1824 to ease access to the Welsh borderland and London. The lucrative Merthyr market was thus opened up to a wider area leading to a steady increase in carrier's traffic using covered wagons. Transport costs by road were still high, however, and in the 1820s it cost 11d. to send a letter to London while the fare to Bristol by coach was £1. Ownership of a horse or carriage was still very much a preserve of the uppermost strata of society in Merthyr and the lack of any cheap form of transport meant that the mass of the population had to walk everywhere. This influenced the pattern of settlement whereby the lack of mobility, and absence of any planning regulations, resulted in a dense concentration of housing near to the main work centres. This meant that Merthyr as we know it today developed as a number of relatively autonomous villages clustered around the ironworks, for example Dowlais, Pentrebach, Penydarren, Georgetown and Merthyr Tydfil itself. This separate identity is still maintained today, in a more diluted form, and it is often surprising to an outsider that what appears to be an area of continuous urban development has so many different facets with a separate social structure, strong rivalries and even different Welsh dialects, in districts which may only be a mile apart.

The continued growth of Merthyr gradually resulted in the coalescing of these various villages and as the iron industry continued to grow so the congestion of the Glamorgan Canal grew.[6] Cargoes started to pile up at the docks creating dissatisfaction amongst the iron masters, even though the excessive profits of the Canal company resulted in rebates being given so that for up to three months in the year, there was no charge for the transport of materials. The situation had worsened since the development of railways created a large new market for iron rails made in Merthyr. The trade relationships established with these new customers led in 1834 to John Guest (whose company was suffering most from the canal congestion) commissioning Brunel to build a railway from Merthyr to Cardiff. The Taff Vale Railway Company was floated and work started. Again the major obstacle was the incline between Abercynon and Quaker's Yard. Abercynon was reached in 1840 and Merthyr in 1842.

Initially a stationary engine was used to drag trucks up the Abercynon incline. This was replaced by the construction of an incline with the steep gradient of 1 in 19 in 1864, which still tended to limit the capacity of the line with the traction power available at that time. This stretch of railway is still in use today and its steepness can be gauged on the approach to Abercynon Station. Initially the railway and the canal companies existed alongside one another. The increase in industrial traffic however, prompted by the boom in demand generated an almost frantic expansion of the rail network in Britain. From 1860 onwards the canal gradually fell into disrepair as the Taff Vale and other railway companies captured more and more traffic. The first section from Cyfarthfa to Merthyr closed in 1865 and successive sections in 1898, and 1915. In 1952 following the collapse of parts of the canal bank the canal was effectively abandoned and filled in with only one or two short residual sections now remaining.

The improved access provided by the Taff Vale railways and the increased specialisation of the Merthyr iron industry in the production of rails created suitable conditions for the peak of the iron boom in Merthyr. Merthyr was termed the iron capital of the world in 1850,[7] but it is perhaps important to consider that the relative position of Merthyr both in the South Wales and British economy declined from this date onwards. However, Merthyr was still a prized target for the highly competitive railway companies of that era. The traffic generating potential of the town was jealously viewed by railway companies like the Great Western Railway, Rhymney, Brecon and Merthyr and London and North Western all of whom from 1850 onward sought to break the monopoly position of the Taff Vale. The two decades following saw a succession of new railways constructed to serve Merthyr in a complex interlocking saga of intensive rivalries and self interested co-operation between companies who on numerous occasions tottered on the fringes of bankruptcy. The Great Western was the first rival to the Taff Vale, which by 1857 was prospering to such a degree that the initial single track was doubled to cope with the traffic. In the same decade the GWR started to develop its main east-west network through Newport, Cardiff, Neath and Swansea by a parallel route running northwards, in order to tap more easily the traffic now being generated by the expansion of the South Wales coalfield and the continued expansion of the iron and steel industry. The route through Pontypool, Crumlin, Quaker's Yard, Aberdare, Hirwaun, Glyn Neath and Neath was against the grain of the relief and the line featured some spectacular viaducts and bridges to span the succession of narrow valleys. Most notable of these was the Crumlin steel viaduct and the stone viaduct at Pontllanfraith. However, financial constraints meant that the viaducts spanning the Taff at Quaker's Yard were less substantial stone and timber structures, which created many difficulties in later years. The initial impact of the Great Western line was, however, limited due to its mixed gauge, partly broad (7 feet 0¼ inch) and partly standard (4 feet 8½ inches). The greater potential of the broad gauge visualised by Brunel, was only adopted by the Great Western, its rivals opting for the greater economy and tradition of the standard gauge. By 1865, the Great Western finally sacrificed its pride and adopted the standard gauge. This combined with the construction of a link from Hirwaun to Merthyr improved the access of Merthyr to East and West Wales via the GWR's 'mid-valley' line.

By the 1860s the most frantic railway building activity was concentrated to the north and east of Merthyr. The relief obstacles facing the Taff Vale and GWR builders were considerable but even they tended to pale against the problems posed by the railway route across the Brecon Beacons, and from Merthyr to Abergavenny crossing the Heads of the Valleys and the gorge from Brynmawr to Abergavenny.

Both the Brecon and Merthyr Railways and the London and North Western hoped to attract considerable traffic by providing a direct link from South Wales to the important, rapidly growing areas like the West Midlands and Lancashire, and more specifically the seaports on the Mersey. There much of the similarity ended. The LNWR was a powerful, wealthy railway company with considerable capital resource whilst the B & M was a small company with little resources surviving very much on its wits and by cutting as many engineering corners as possible. Both companies after considerable setbacks completed the miles from Brecon to Merthyr by 1868, and Abergavenny to Merthyr by 1879. A circuitous route had to be taken from Dowlais via Cefn Coed and Cyfarthfa to a terminus near the Taff Vale Station, now Merthyr High Street. The journey was eight miles by rail but only three miles as the crow flies. One of the notable features of the route, still standing, is the gracefully arched stone viaduct at Cefn Coed.

Continued economic expansion stimulated further railway construction in the 1870s and 1880s as companies jostled for a larger share of the growing trade. The GWR and Rhymney Railway joined forces to build a new route along the Taff Valleys from Quaker's Yard to Merthyr via Aberfan and Abercanaid, whilst the Rhymney railway built a new link via Nelson and

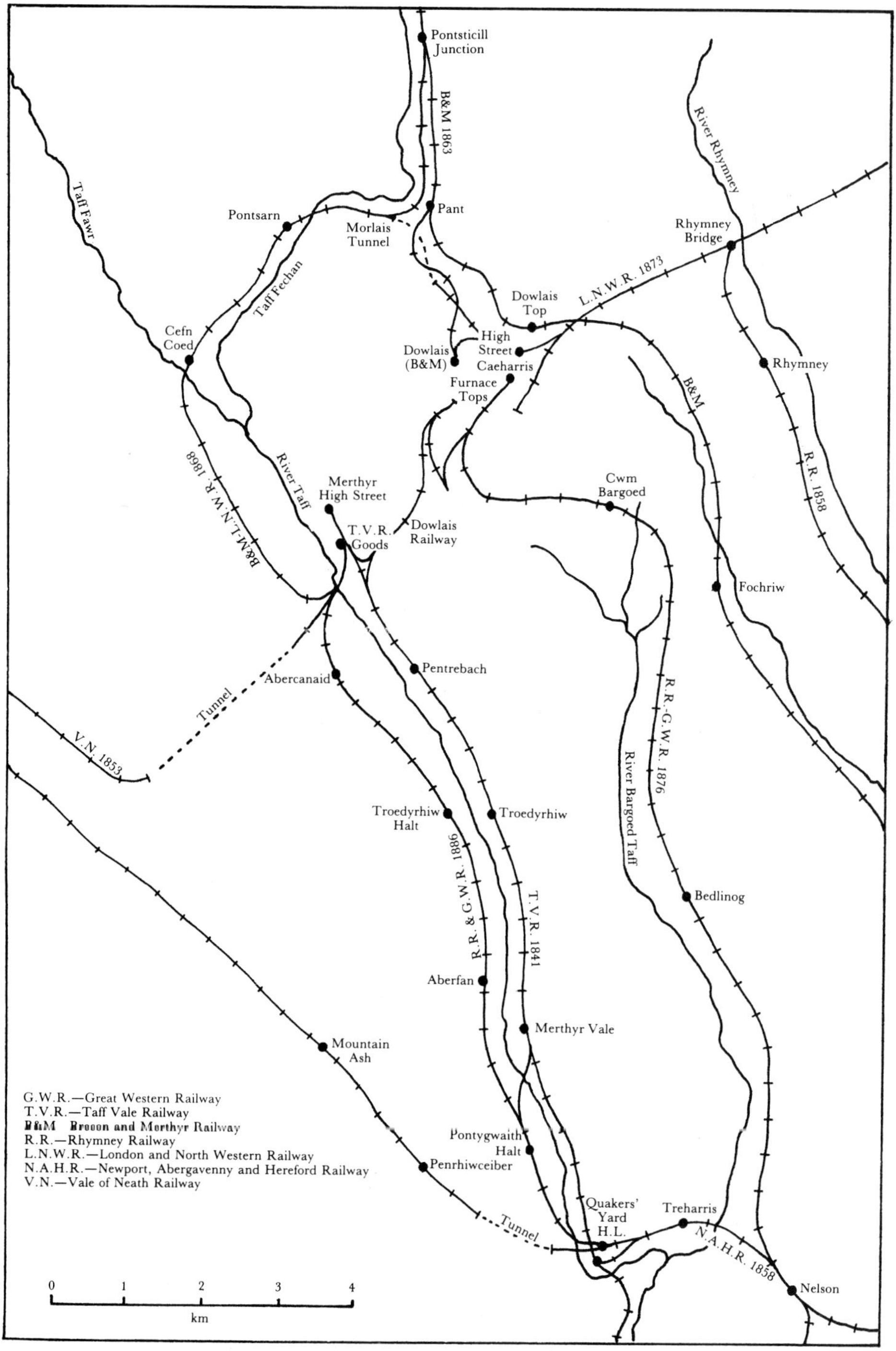

Fig. 76: Merthyr Area: Development of Railway System

Llancaiach primarily to serve the Dowlais works.

As a result by 1890 Merthyr had a dense network of railways with a wide choice of duplicated services. The railways were primarily freight carriers, but passenger services were also available from Merthyr to Cardiff via the Taff Vale; Merthyr to Cardiff via Quaker's Yard and the Rhymney Valley; Merthyr to Hirwaun and Swansea; Merthyr to Brecon and thence to Aberystwyth, Hereford, Shrewsbury; Merthyr to Abergavenny and thence to Hereford, Birmingham, Chester; Merthyr to Llantrisant via the Taff Vale to Treforest; Dowlais Cae Harris to Cardiff via Bargoed and the Rhymney Valley; Dowlais to Brecon and Abergavenny; Dowlais to Newport via the Sirhowy Valley.

Thus new horizons were opened up for people to travel and improved living standards, combined with gradual increases in holidays and cheapening rail fares led to greater passenger traffic. Shopping trips to Cardiff, Pontypridd Market and Abergavenny Market, became popular and day trips to Barry and Swansea and the Mumbles became a reality for working people. The greater provision and competition of rail transport facilities both stimulated industrial growth and provided a much greater range of goods for local shops in Merthyr. It also became feasible to commute longer distances to work allowing people wider job opportunities.

The improved mobility provided by the railways was not matched by local transport, however. Most people were still unable to afford their own carriages or horses, whilst the local horse-drawn buses were still expensive and slow. The local distribution of goods by horse and cart was also slow, cumbersome and expensive. The lack of local transport meant that the majority of new houses were still terraced, since this allowed high population densities to be accommodated—within easy access of the main sources of employment. The corner shop was also important due to the lack of transport and a wide range of goods were available on almost every street corner. Similarly schools, chapels, churches, community halls and public houses were all provided within easy walking distance of the dense concentrations of houses. Thus the street was the basis for the provision of goods and services rather than an estate or a town.

By 1898 the population of Merthyr had reached 60,000 and the cheapest fare from Merthyr to Dowlais by horse drawn tram was 6d., which was beyond the pocket of the vast majority of the population. Thus a considerable potential existed for a cheap form of public transport. At the end of the twentieth century, technological advances in the production and use of electricity let to the growth of electric tramways. Considerable investment was needed to lay the tram tracks and the resulting system was very inflexible. However, the tramways had low operating costs once built and for the first time lowered the price of local public transport to a level acceptable to most people. The first tramway from Cefn to Dowlais was opened in 1901 and was immediately a great success.[8]

The development of the tramways tended to reinforce the established

Plate 51a: HORSE DRAWN BUS ON TROEDYRHIW SQUARE

Plate 51b: MERTHYR TYDFIL CORPORATION BUS NO. 1
(By permission of Merthyr Borough Council)

settlement patterns. Housing within the Merthyr Borough tended to be concentrated either near local railway stations or within easy access to the tram routes, the only exception was housing clustered around the ironworks and coal mines. However, the tramways allowed a wider choice of housing location, less densely constructed. Thus in places like Cefn Coed more spacious houses with larger gardens were developed.

The pre-eminence of the tramway for local transport was short lived, however. The development of the petrol engine advanced rapidly especially with the stimulus of the World War I and by the early 1920s motor buses were becoming increasingly popular in Merthyr. In 1924 Merthyr Corporation bought its first bus and the comfort of passengers was further improved with the development of pneumatic tyres.

The motor bus was considerably more flexible than the tram and a much more diffuse network of services could be operated. The use of the first diesel engine bus in Merthyr in 1933 and the increased size of buses further cheapened bus transport costs. The tramways could not withstand the competition and in 1939 the last tramway in Merthyr was closed, when the track had become in need of renewal.

The bus also became increasingly competitive with the rail network. Particularly popular in the 1920s and 1930s were charabanc and later motor coach outings. This brought Merthyr people for the first time within easy access to areas like the Gower, West Wales and many other destinations not linked by the railways to Merthyr.

Thus in the 1930s bus travel had increasingly attracted traffic away from the railways. However, during this period we were entering the era of cheap motoring. Mass production techniques had been developed in Britain to produce relatively cheap cars which were within the price range of an increasing percentage of those still employed in Merthyr.

The increased car ownership necessitated a widespread road building and road widening programme in the Merthyr area. This was not so much the building of dual carriageways but rather the metalling of unsurfaced roads and the widening of roads to allow two lorries or buses to pass each other without colliding.

World War II temporarily halted the growth of motor traffic with petrol rationing, and people were urged to travel as little as possible. The war, however, like World War I, gave a tremendous stimulus to technological advance and by the end of the war considerable achievements had been made in motor engineering (particularly with heavy goods vehicles), which had important implications for the post war industrial structure of Merthyr.

Acknowledging the immense hardship and waste of the depression years, successive post war Governments were committed to the concept of redeveloping the industrial base of Merthyr from being highly dependent on iron and steel and coal to a much more diversified structure, with a wide range of manufacturing industries.[9] However, the railways tended to be unsuited for the distribution of many of the goods produced at these new

Plate 52a: TRAIN ON RHYMNEY LINE NEAR JUNCTION WITH L.N.W.R. AND B.M. JOINT LINE NORTH OF ABERCANAID *(By permission of Merthyr Borough Council)*

Plate 52b: DIESEL MULTIPLE UNITS NEAR MERTHYR VALE, 1968 *(By permission of Clive Thomas)*

factories which were often low weight/high value goods intended for a wide range of destinations. Thus firms like Hoovers, OP Chocolates, Kayser Bondor and Thorns became almost totally dependent on road distribution. However, road access from Merthyr to the rest of Britain was very poor.[10] Lorries had to use congested, narrow roads with numerous steep gradients. There was no bridge linking South Wales to S.W. England and most traffic for South England had to travel via Gloucester. This position remained unchanged for most of the 1940s and 1950s creating a significant disadvantage for industries located in Merthyr.

At the same time the railways had begun to run down rapidly with the loss of traffic to cars, lorries and buses. In the 1950s the Merthyr to Abergavenny and Merthyr to Taffs Well via Aberfan routes were closed and all the other lines serving Merthyr started to lose money.

The 'you've never had it so good era' of the 1950s led to a dramatic increase of car ownership as unemployment levels in Merthyr reached all time lows of around 2.5%. Formerly quiet terraced streets became blocked by parked cars and roads around Merthyr became increasingly congested.

Areas like Merthyr were very much starved of road building resources until the early 1960s when the Heads of the Valley road was built linking Merthyr with Abergavenny. However, even this road was built at minimum cost with only three lanes, and no link was provided between Abergavenny and the Ross Spur section linking to the M5 which was then being constructed.

At the same time as the new road was being constructed, however, Merthyr suffered from an almost unpredented number of cuts in its rail services following the Beeching Report, on reshaping Britain's railways.

Between 1961 and 1963 the Merthyr to Hirwaun and Swansea; Merthyr to Brecon; Dowlais to Cardiff; and Dowlais to Newport and Merthyr to Llantrisant services were all abandoned, leaving Merthyr with a sole surviving hourly passenger service to Cardiff along the original Taff Vale line.

Since the 1960s a number of road improvements have occurred to reduce considerably journey times to the Midlands and South East England, with the completion of the Severn Bridge and M4, and the M5/Ross Spur, and perhaps most significant the A470 dual carriageway from Cardiff to Abercynon. However, immediate road links in the Merthyr area remain relatively poor. The Heads of the Valleys road remains a highly dangerous stretch of road, whilst the dual carriageway link between Abercynon and Merthyr on the A470 has not been completed. Again the steep narrow sided valley between Abercynon and Merthyr Vale remains a major civil engineering obstacle. Completion of this link will immensely improve Merthyr's accessibility to the rest of South Wales and allow for Merthyr to develop as a growth point for the northern part of the coalfield, as a balance to the pull of Cardiff.

Greater car ownership and flexible public transport has dramatically altered the landscape of Merthyr. Greater personal mobility has led to the development of large new housing estates, both private and council, in areas like Swansea Road, Gurnos, Heolgerrig and Pant. The corner shop has tended to decline and it appears that in turn the town centre of Merthyr and Dowlais will suffer as the growth of peripheral hypermarkets occurs.

People's mobility has increased enormously since the early periods of the industrial revolution and at a time when holidays in Spain and Majorca are the norm it is sobering to consider that a day trip to Pontsarn was considered a major expedition as recently as the 1930s. The greater mobility of people also has significance in the social structure of Merthyr, which is still regarded as a relatively tightly knit community. It seems likely that the community spirit will be retained if only because of the dense housing patterns inherited from the late nineteenth century, and hopefully Merthyr will avoid the lack of soul prevalent in the dormitory suburbs or large council estates of towns and cities which do not have their roots in the nineteenth century.

It is difficult to predict what is likely to happen to the transport infrastructure of Merthyr in the future. The uncertainties of the provision of cheap energy supplies may lead to a reduction in the level of mobility and rates of car ownership that society has got used to in the 1970s. Thus pressure for road space may be reduced and it may be difficult to justify new road building programmes. So the final dual carriageway link between Abercynon and Merthyr may not be built unless pressure is maintained for its completion. Decreased dependence on the car may lead to increased usage of public transport if wage costs can be contained. However, there is unlikely to be a return to the days when Merthyr was the railway centre of North Glamorgan or the periods when Merthyr was always first to benefit from any new advance in the technology of transport.

References

[1] Rees J. F., *The Industrial Revolution and After*, p. 107, British Association Handbook, Cardiff.

[2] *The Merthyr Historian*, chapter 6, Starling Press, 1976.

[3] Lloyd J., *Old South Wales Ironworks (1760-1840)*, p. 64, 1906.

[4] Moore L. R., *The South Wales Coalfield*; Trueman A. E., *Coalfields of Great Britain*, p. 101, 1954.

[5] Hodges T. M., *The Peopling of the Hinter Land and the Port of Cardiff*, (1801-1914) in Minchinton W. E., *'Industrial South Wales 1750-1914*, p. 5, Cass 1969.

[6] Morgan Rees D., *Industrial Archaeology of Wales*, p. 191, David & Charles, 1975.

[7] Wilkins C., *The History of Merthyr Tydfil*, p. 247, 1908.

[8] Williams S., *Vintage Buses and Trams in South Wales*, Ch. 10, Stewart Williams, 1975.

[9] Willis E., *An Analysis of Industrial Change within the Borough of Merthyr Tydfil*, Part A, Merthyr Library, 1971.

[10] Willis E., op. cit., Ch. 7.

[11] Beeching, *The Reshaping of Britain's Railways*, British Rail Board, 1963.

Social and Cultural History

IV

Population

by GARETH HOPKINS

The economic changes which have been discussed in earlier chapters affected considerably the numbers and nature of the population of the town. By the time that reasonably accurate figures had become available through the Census of Population Report for 1801, Merthyr Tydfil had emerged as the largest town in Wales. Its inhabitants numbered 7,705 compared with the 6,821 in Swansea, then the second largest town in the Principality. During the nineteenth century the population continued to grow although by 1871 those of Cardiff, Swansea and Rhondda had increased more rapidly, causing Merthyr Tydfil to lose its position as the most populous town.

It was in 1901 that the population reached its peak of 80,000; thereafter in successive censuses the number of inhabitants fell, so that in 1971 the population was just over 55,000. However, the reorganization of local government in 1974 increased the area of Merthyr Tydfil by the addition of Vaynor and Bedlinog as new wards. Consequently, the estimate of the population of the District in 1975 was 60,000.

Clearly the degree of change in the number of inhabitants has varied in time. In absolute terms, the nineteenth century can be divided into three periods, the first of which lasted from 1801 until 1851. During this period the population increased rapidly by some 38,000 but the second period from 1851 until 1881 was relatively stable, for the population rose by only 2,500. It included a decade (1871-1881) when, because of boundary changes, the town suffered a technical decline in population. The final period, extending until 1911, saw another rapid growth in population, this time totalling 32,000. Since then the population trend has been falling, slowly until 1921, but then more quickly until 1939. Following another stable period of eleven years, the decline has accelerated slightly recently. In relative terms, of course, the significant years were again those of the early ninteenth century

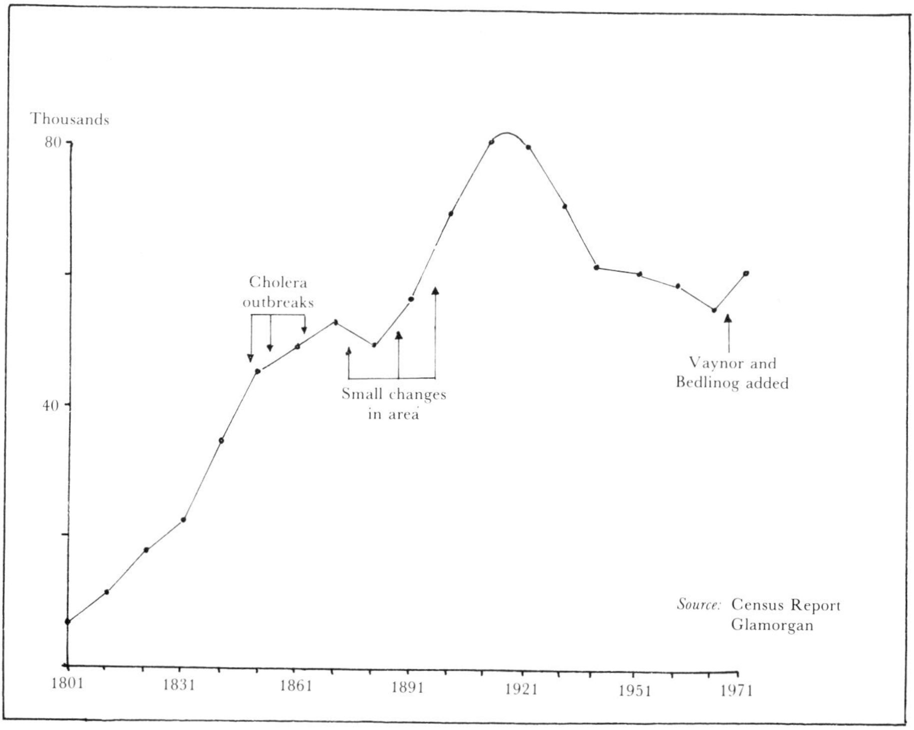

Fig. 77: Changes in the size of the population

when increases of over 5% were recorded in three of the decades. As is to be expected, the relative growth at the end of the century was much smaller for not only was the actual increase less but the base population was also considerably larger. (Fig. 77)

At the beginning of the nineteenth century the small population was concentrated at Dowlais, Cyfarthfa, Penydarren, Plymouth and the town's centre (Fig. 78). Such nuclei were associated obviously with the growth of the iron works over the previous forty years. This concentration had become more noticeable by the 1830's though there existed, as in the past, a scattered and sparse rural population in the surrounding valley. Cefncoed y Cymmer, then, of course, not part of the future town, also stood out as a small centre of concentration.

By 1911 the previously separated nuclei had merged to form a substantial urban area in the northern part of the Borough while mining villages in the south of the valley had appeared to form the settlements of Troedyrhiw, Merthyr Vale and Treharris (Fig. 79). This pattern clearly remains to the present, though with the decline in the number of inhabitants the density of population has been reduced. This decline in population has been irregular, however. Percentage changes in those wards which have experienced decline since 1911 vary from 18% in Cyfarthfa to 59% in the Town ward. Other

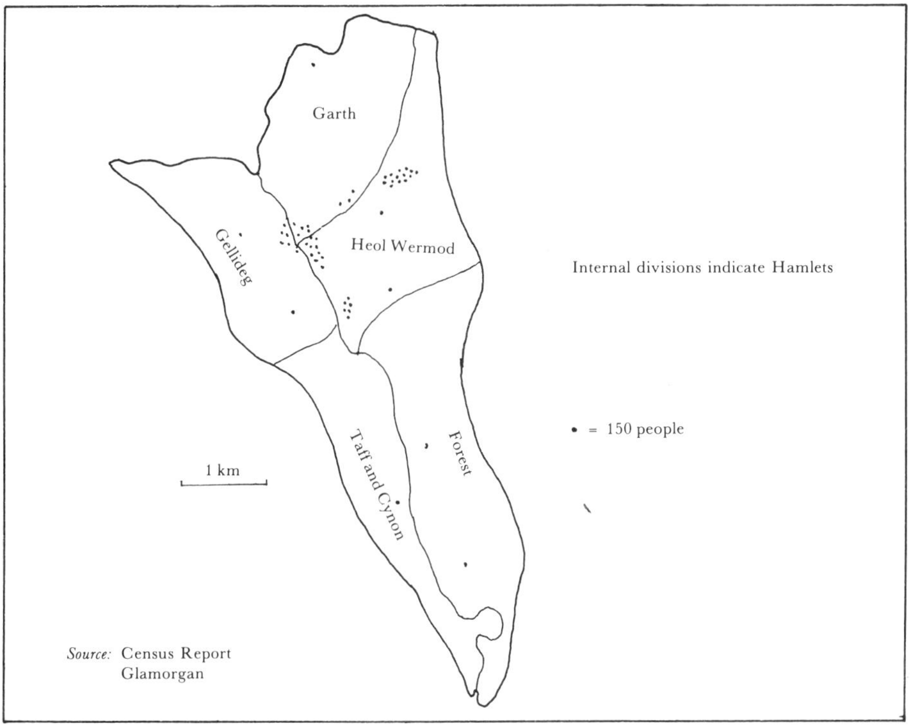

Fig. 78: Distribution of population 1801

areas which experienced heavy losses of population are Dowlais (47%) and Penydarren (45%) (Fig. 80). However, in the cases of Town ward, Penydarren and Dowlais the changes have been caused partly by urban renewal whereby older houses have been demolished in the last decade or so. Equally the growth of population in Park ward has resulted from the building of large residential estates in that area in the same period. To some extent the latter development is to be explained by the transfer of people from the areas which have undergone urban renewal. Nevertheless, the general decline in the number of inhabitants in Merthyr Tydfil has probably affected most wards. Merthyr Vale, however, witnessed a growth in the number of inhabitants between 1961 and 1971, the first intercensal rise since 1901.

The changes which characterized Merthyr Tydfil's population over the last two hundred years can be explained largely by the natural increase in population and by migration. Until the industrialization of the town, the slow growth in population was caused mainly by the excess of births over deaths, but since the beginning of the nineteenth century migration has assumed a more important role. The expansion of the iron industry in the town provided an opportunity for employment which was taken up by immigrants from a wide area of England as well as Wales. Similarly the

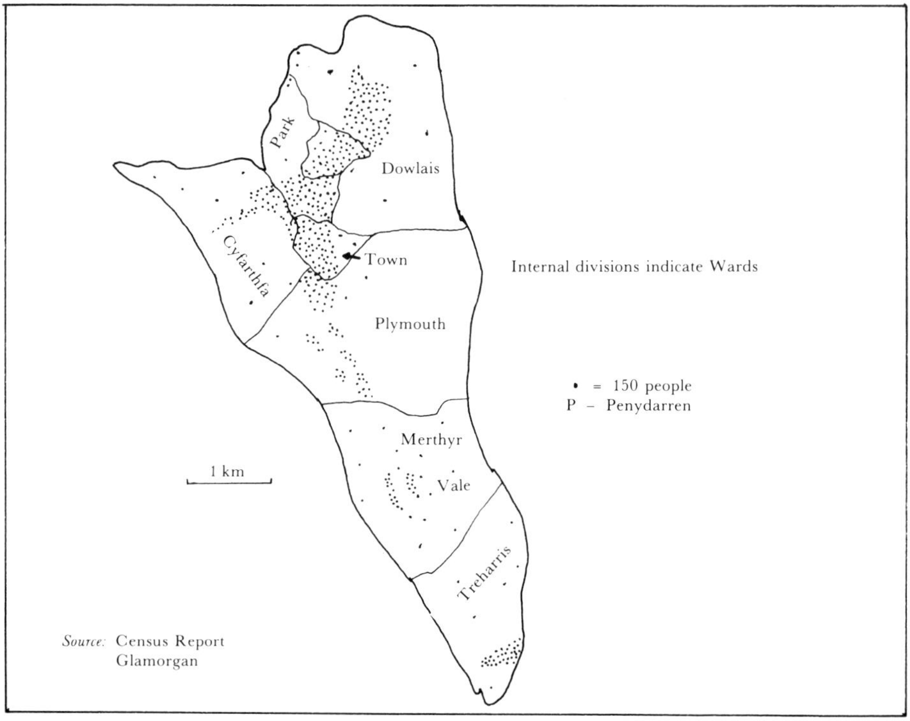

Fig. 79: Distribution of population 1911

development of the steel industry and especially that of coal mining after 1875 added an extra attraction for immigrants which helped swell the town's population. The following figures show generally the influence of both factors.

Registration District of Merthyr Tydfil No. 588.
(includes Aberdare, Gelligaer and Vaynor)

	1881		*1891*		
Population	101,441		117,205	Actual growth	16,764
1881-1891 Births	37,302	Deaths	24,328	Excess of Births over Deaths	12,924
				Net increase by immigration	3,840

Source: Census of Population Reports

To some degree the period of low growth in the third quarter of the nineteenth century was caused by the high death rate induced by the cholera epidemics between 1849 and 1861. Again, towards the end of the century the

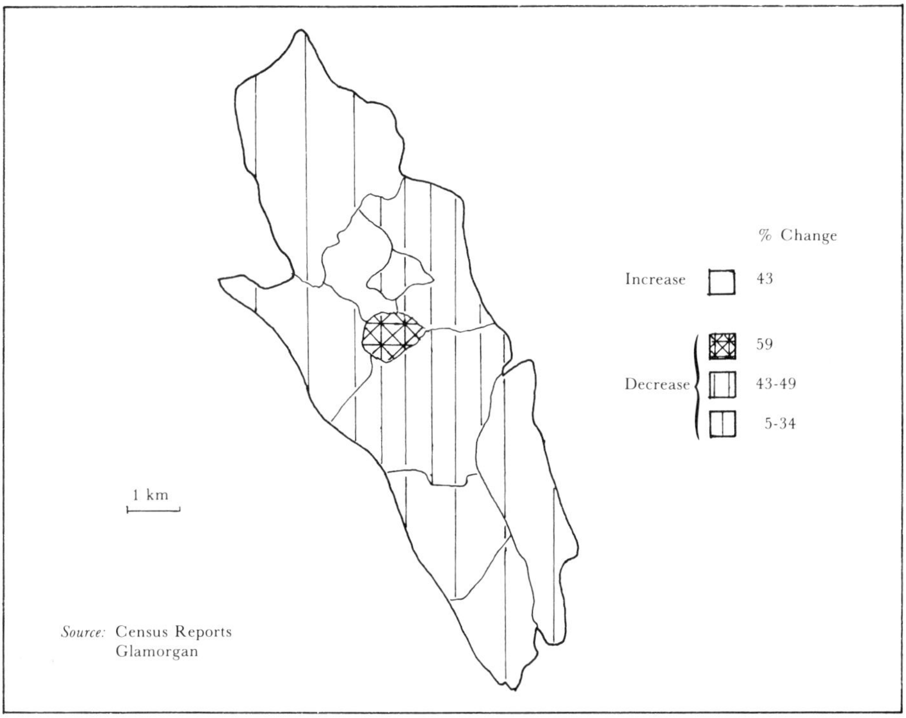

Fig. 80: Changes in the distribution of population 1911-1973

demand for labour could be satisfied partly by the already sizeable population in the town so that immigration would not necessarily be as important as in the earlier phase of expansion (see Fig. 77). Nevertheless, during the twentieth century the decline in the numbers of inhabitants is attributable wholly to migration. Between 1911 and 1921 the population decreased by 884 and yet there was a natural increase of 9,578; thus emigration accounted for the net loss of 10,472. This trend is continuing as the following statistics illustrate.

Merthyr Tydfil County Borough

	1941		*1977*
Population	64,220		61,400
Excess of Births over Deaths		5,473	
Decrease in population		2,820	
Net loss by emigration		8,293	

Source: Registrar General's Statistical Review of England and Wales, Part 11. (Annual).

Fig. 81: Birth places of residents 1891

The influx of migrants in the first half of the nineteenth century is reflected in the birth places of residents according to the 1861 Census.

Registration District of Merthyr Tydfil No. 582 (includes Aberdare and Gelligaer)

Place of Birth of Residents 1861

Wales	78,036	Wales of which	78,036	
England	6,543			
Ireland	5,256	Glamorgan	48,839	
Scotland	15	Brecknock	8,308	
Colonies	55	Carmarthenshire	7,243	
Foreign	193	Monmouthshire	5,635	29,197
		Pembrokeshire	4,551	
		Elsewhere	3,460	

Source: Census of Population, 1861

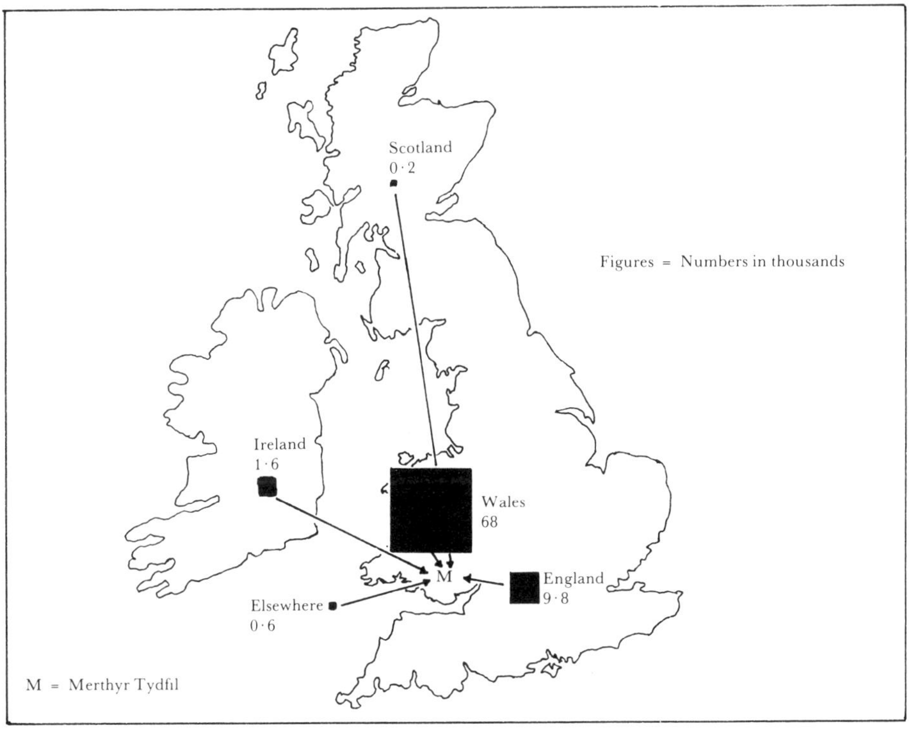

Fig. 82: Birth places of residents 1921

Clearly, most residents hailed from Wales and the majority of these came from Glamorgan. Obviously an unknown proportion of those who were born in Glamorgan originated in the Registration District of Merthyr Tydfil itself, so that it is not possible to deduce precisely the origin of immigrants from such data. Nevertheless it is significant that nearly 30,000 of the inhabitants were born in other counties of Wales. It is noticeable, too, that greater numbers of people came from neighbouring rather than other counties. Further, although the immigrants from the other countries of the United Kingdom formed a relatively small percentage, nearly 5,000 out of the total of 12,000 were born in adjacent counties of south western England and the west Midlands.

This pattern of the origin of the population is one related to distance and, consequently conditioned by the transport system of the time. By 1861 the railway network had began to extend across the country but it was only relatively extensive in South Wales. Central and North Wales were as yet poorly served by the railway. Links with distant parts of England were equally restricted. Movement to South Wales in general and to Merthyr Tydfil in particular was, therefore, not easy and whether people moved or not depended partly on the local economic conditions. Thus the dire situation in Ireland following the potato famines of 1845, 1846 and 1847 could explain the rather numerous Irish element in the population. As can be seen in the table above the Irish were, as a group, not much smaller than the English.

More detailed statistics are available for 1901 although again no distinction is made between those who were born in Merthyr Tydfil and those who came from other parts of Glamorgan. However, the basic pattern is rather similar to that of 1861 in that, generally the nearer counties of Wales and England supplied a large percentage of the total number of immigrants. Indeed, nearly 20,000 of the total population originated in such counties. The composition of the population in 1901, of course, reflects partly the rapid growth of the town in the late nineteenth century.

By 1921, when the town had ceased to grow, the same general pattern prevailed (see Fig. 82). At this stage the Welsh born element still dominated the population, forming 84% of the total compared with 86% in 1901. The English born had increased form 8% to 12% of the total, but those from Ireland had decreased absolutely and relatively, from 3.6% to 2%. During the succeeding half century, emigration and the reduction in immigration has affected this composition. Thus, a very high percentage of the residents in 1971 were born in Wales. It is clear, also, that aliens and colonial immigrants have never formed a large element in the town. However, there tends to be some degree of concentration in their distribution, for the four wards of Park, Town, Penydarren and Cyfarthfa accounted for over 63% of the total overseas immigrants in that year.

Merthyr Tydfil Urban District and County Borough

Place of Birth of Residents

	1901		*1921*		*1971*	
	Numbers	%	*Numbers*	%	*Numbers*	%
Wales	59,758	86·3	67,680	84·4	50,569	92·8
England	6,137	8·8	9,824	12·2	2,963	5·4
Ireland	2,541	3·6	1,626	2·0	302	0·5
Scotland	170	0·2	160	0·1	148	0·2
Colonies	97	0·1	100	0·1	130	0·2
Foreign	525	0·7	534	0·6	379	0·6

Mere statistics, however, give little colour to the picture. Thus the 0·5% of the 1971 population who were listed as being born in Ireland might suggest that the Irish were insignificant in the town. However, the 302 Irish and the descendants of immigrants recorded in earlier censuses make their mark if only because many of them are Catholics. Hence the existence of a Catholic comprehensive school in Merthyr Tydfil, one of only three in the County of Mid Glamorgan. The Irish are scattered in the District but a concentration exists in Penydarren and Dowlais. Equally notable are those of Spanish descent. These, largely of Basque origin, came to Merthyr Tydfil in the

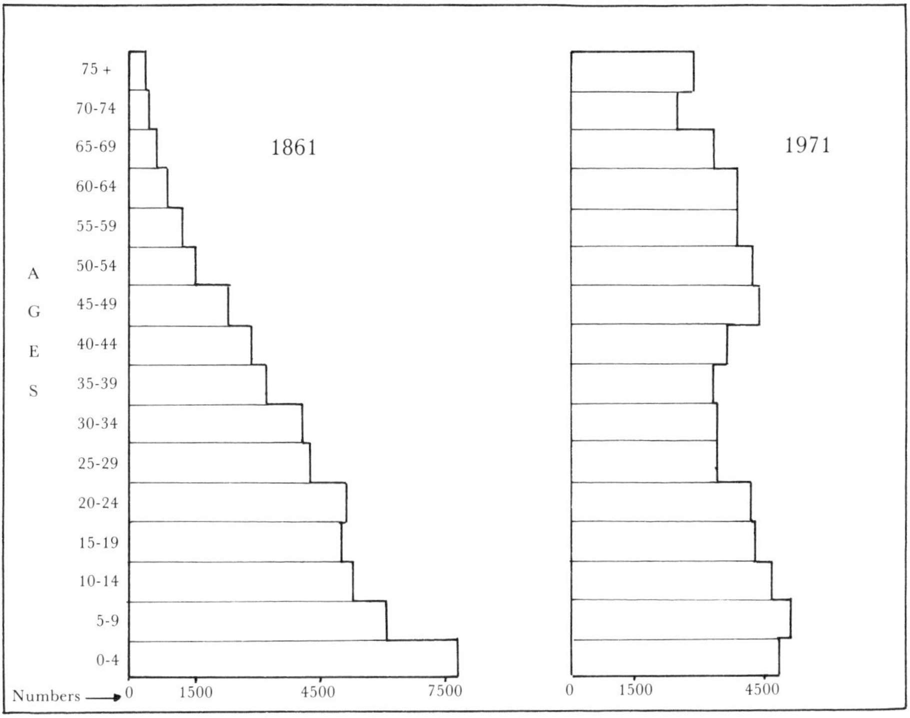

Fig. 83: Age structure of the population

1890's after the Dowlais Works began to import iron ore from northern Spain. It was natural for the early immigrant to settle near the works so that, again, Dowlais is where many still live. Their presence is suggested in the name of Alfonso Street, known locally as Spanish Row. Some of the older generation still wear clothing more typical of the traditional Spanish scene than of the local style. Again, at home Spanish is sometimes spoken though not as frequently as in the past. Over the years intermarriage with local people has reduced the numbers of those able to speak the language and diluted the Spanish characteristic of former immigrant families.

Migration of people induces changes in the population of any town. By 1861 when the first wave of immigrants had swollen Merthyr Tydfil's population, the age structure of the residents had assumed the characteristics of the model of an underdeveloped country (Fig. 83). In the middle of the nineteenth century Merthyr Tydfil was a new town. The recently arrived migrants were young and fertile so that the pyramidal age structure for 1861 conforms to the model with a high percentage of the population occurring in the lower age groups. Few old people were represented for the incidence of disease, a limited medical service and a high death rate ensured that life expectancy was low. During this century the outflow of people has reversed the situation for the younger section of the community has dominated the movement of people, as can be seen in the following figures.

Migration Patterns 1961 – 1966

	Emigration Ages		*Immigration Ages*	
	5-44 years	*45-65 years*	*5-44 years*	*45-65 years*
Males	1,600	290	820	220
Females	1,470	430	930	220
Sub total	3,070	720	1,750	440
Total		3,790		2,190

Consequently the age structure in the third quarter of the twentieth century is rather different from that in the nineteenth century. No longer is there a regular decline in the numbers in the different age groups. Obviously the difference in the two graphs is not that marked, as age pyramids reflect not only the effect of migrations but also that of the past incidence of death and birth rates. A reduction in the death rate over the last century has helped to increase relatively the number of people in the older age groups. Equally the fall in the birth rate over the last decade has tended to reduce the numbers in the younger age groups. The result of these developments is a higher

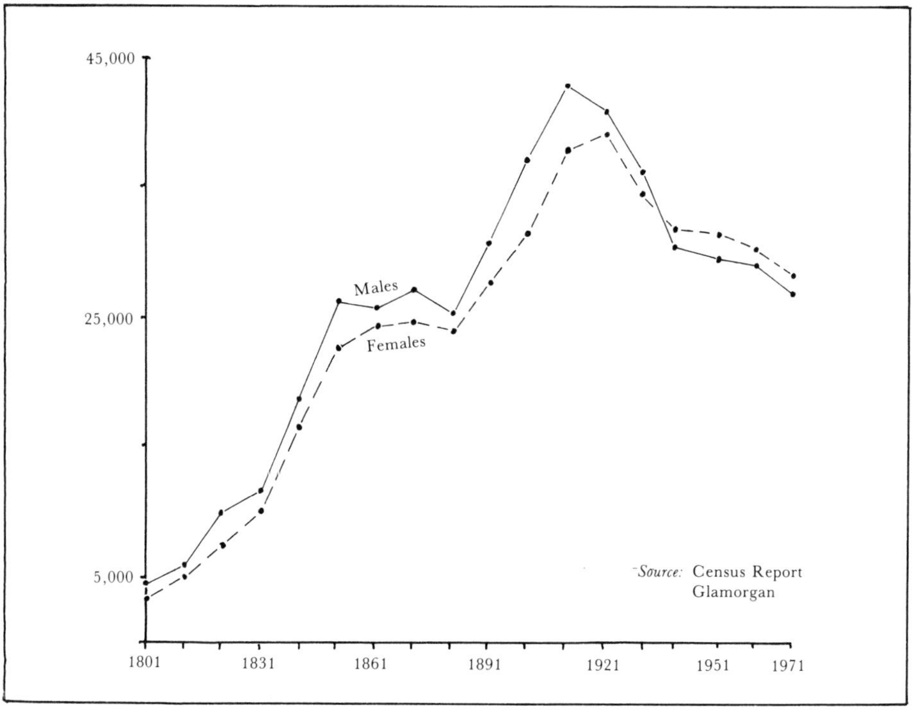

Fig. 84: Male and female composition of the population

average age level. Now an ageing population creates some economic and social problems. First, as the younger element is reduced, the labour force becomes smaller. Secondly, one element of the 'burden of dependency' gets larger as those above the age of retirement increase in number.

Another aspect of population structure is the sex ratio which can be defined as the number of females per thousand males. In the case of Merthyr Tydfil there is a close relationship between this ratio and the economic fortunes of the valley. The new town of the early nineteenth century attracted not only the young migrant but especially the male. Thus as early as 1811, the census revealed that there were only 885 females for every thousand males. Ten years later the figure had fallen to 822 but by 1861 when the first wave of migration had ceased and families had become established, the ratio had climbed to 942. However, the second phase of immigration introduced more males, for by 1901 the ratio had slipped again to 869 to 1,000. It rose irregularly to 957 in 1931 but by 1951 the number of females exceeded the number of males by 1,047 to 1,000. The ratio has continued to exceed 1,000 ever since and in 1971 it stood at 1,053 to 1,000. Clearly this reversal of the pattern parallels the change in economic fortunes and the decline in the total population although there is a time lag between change and the rise in the female element of the ratio.

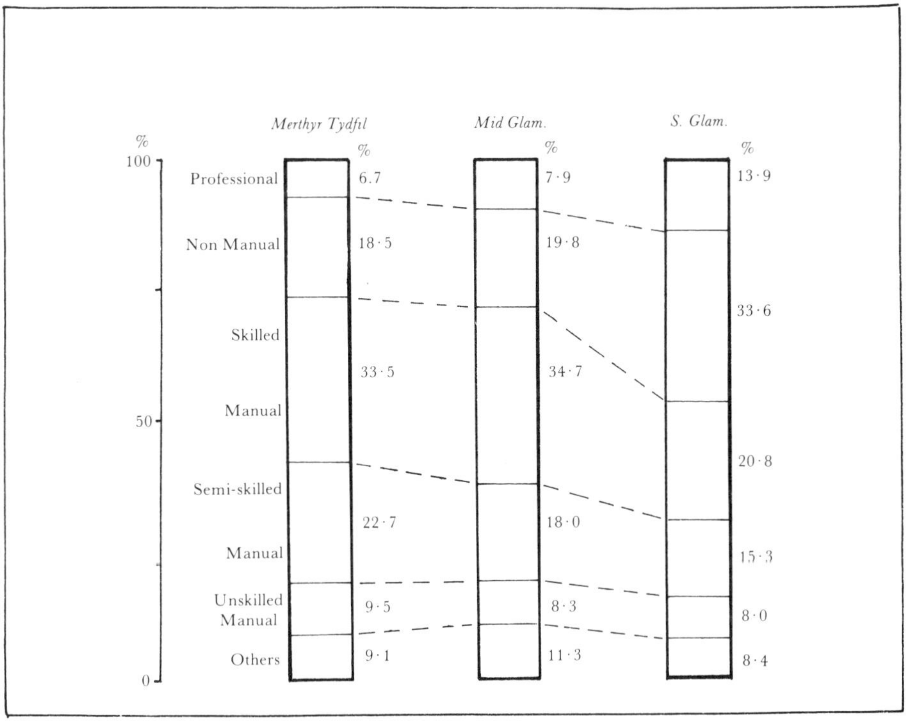

Fig. 85: Socio-Economic Groups

A knowledge of the economic history of South Wales would suggest that the socio-economic structure of Merthyr Tydfil's population is not well balanced (Fig. 85). Indeed, the 1971 Census showed that the professional and managerial group accounted for just under 7% of the total and that non-manual workers barely exceeded 25%. Again, the percentage represented by the semi-skilled (22·7%) was higher than that of any other district in the County and was nearly double that of South Glamorgan (12·6%). It is not surprising, then, that income levels are low. In 1973, the average gross weekly earnings of full time male adults in the industrial valleys of South Wales was £38, compared with £39·5 for Wales as a whole. The figure for women in the same year was £21·8, which equalled that for the average for women in Wales.

Such relatively low increases are but one indication of the disparate wealth of Merthyr Tydfil's population compared with that for other areas. In 1971, 70% of the District's housing stock had been built before 1914. This may explain why Merthyr Tydfil had the second highest rate of overcrowding in the County (6·3% of all households compared with 6·5% for Rhymney District). The quality of the housing, on average, was also low and again is to be explained by the age of the houses. This can be seen in the following data.

Merthyr Tydfil Borough

	Household lacking or sharing					
	Hot water		*Fixed Bath*		*Inside W.C.*	
	Nos.	*%*	*Nos.*	*%*	*Nos.*	*%*
Merthyr Tydfil	3,594	17·2	6,073	29·0	7,375	32·2
Mid Glamorgan	23,656	13·7	37,388	21·6	51,352	29·7
Wales	87,960	9·8	133,210	14·6	183,800	20·4

If there is one aspect of the population that emphasizes the influx of migrants into Merthyr Tydfil then that is the decline in the Welsh language. Before the period of industrialization the language of the people was Welsh but, with the increase in population, the percentage of the total able to speak the language fell (Fig. 86). When, in 1911, the Census first recorded the language spoken by the population, 50% of Merthyr Tydfil's inhabitants could speak Welsh. Succeeding censuses have revealed a continuous and almost steady decline in this percentage until in 1971 the figure reached 12·9%. The reason for this decline was obviously the arrival of large numbers of English speakers at Merthyr Tydfil. Additionally, social and legal processes contrived to dissuade many Welsh speakers from using their native tongue. However, it has been argued that the immigration of Welsh speakers from other parts of Wales helped to maintain the percentage at a higher level than would have been the case if the immigrants had come mainly from England.

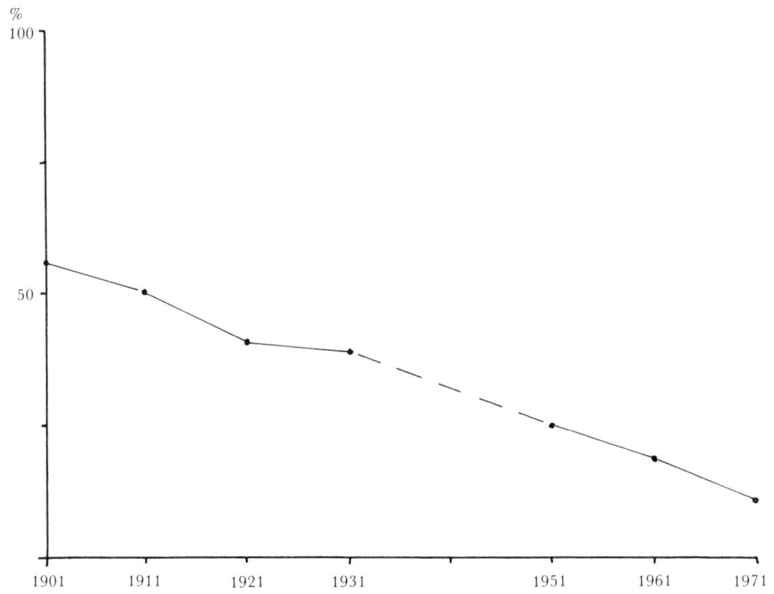

Fig. 86: Percentage of population (over 3 years) able to speak Welsh

Over the last few years concern has been felt in many quarters about this decline in the ability to speak Welsh and this has found expression in the demand for government to arrest this deterioration. The old borough authority had no official policy on the teaching of Welsh in schools before 1972. Indeed there was little public demand for the provision of such education. Except for the long standing inclusion of Welsh in the curriculum of the former grammar schools, it was left to the headteachers of primary and secondary modern schools to decide whether Welsh should be given a place in the list of subjects taught in their schools. However, in September 1972 a Welsh primary school was opened at Gellifaelog; a growing demand for education through the medium of the Welsh language led to the formation of another Welsh primary school at Treharris in January 1976. In September 1974 the Mid Glamorgan Education Authority appointed an Adviser in Welsh to further the development of bilingual education in the County; his area of responsibility, obviously, covers Merthyr Tydfil District. Again, the introduction of the Certificate of Secondary Education examination helped to widen the teaching of Welsh in secondary schools. Every year since 1970 the number of candidates entered for public examinations in Welsh has increased so that the 145 candidates in 1975 were more than twice as numerous as the 64 in 1964. These statistics include students in the Vaynor and Penderyn Comprehensive which was administered by the Breconshire Authority until April 1974. In 1975 the number of candidates had fallen to 105.

A revival in interest in the Welsh language is noticeable, too, in the number of students registered for adult classes in the language. In 1974 the figure was 144, in 1975 it was 157 but in 1976 only 109; the decline in the last year may reflect an increase in tuition fees which was introduced in 1976.

Whether such developments will be sufficient to arrest the decline in spoken Welsh is difficult to judge at the moment. The major factor appears to be the opening of Welsh primary schools, for if the younger Welsh speakers are insufficient to replace the loss occurring in the older age groups, the chances of success are slight. In January 1977 only 19 children attended the Welsh primary schools. The 1981 Census should reveal interesting results.

It is appropriate as a conclusion to compare the developments in Merthyr Tydfil with those occurring elsewhere in the country so that the trends may be put in perspective. As is to be expected, neighbouring valleys in the coalfield experienced similar population changes, though, generally, as many of them developed through the exploitation of coal, the changes in the nineteenth century took place a little later. The problems affecting the mining industry produced, again, the familiar emigration picture and a declining and increasingly older population. In the Vale country adjoining the coast, however, a contrasting pattern evolved. Here the industrial and commercial base supported a population which continued to increase in the twentieth century. To a degree, therefore, Merthyr Tydfil can be used to represent the demographic patterns of the declining, old industrial areas of Britain.

References

Office of Population Censuses and Surveys
Census Reports – Counties of Glamorgan, Monmouthshire and
Brecon – various. H.M.S.O.

Registrar General's Statistical Review of England and Wales, Part 11, Civil Tables, Population. Annual. H.M.S.O.

Mid Glamorgan Planning Office,
Structure Plan, Population. 1975.

National Register of U.K. Statistics of Population.

Merthyr Tydfil Borough Council
Structure Plan Report on the Survey of Population, 1974

Symposium of the Royal Society of Health held at Merthyr Tydfil 1968
'Redevelopment of a Welsh Industrial Town'

Report of the Sanitary Conditions of Merthyr Tydfil (1854-1873), Dr. Dyke.
Economic Vol. 10. 1930, page 277
B. Thomas, Migration of Labour into the Glamorgan Coalfield.
Digest of Welsh Statistics – annual H.M.S.O.
Mid Glamorgan Education Authority,
Merthyr Tydfil Technical College for information on adult evening classes in Welsh.
Mid Glamorgan Education Authority,
Merthyr Tydfil District Office for data on Welsh schools and examination candidates in Welsh.

Health

by J. GROSS

Conditions in the 1850's

The growth of Merthyr during the first half of the 19th century was phenomenal. From an estimated 500 inhabitants in 1759, it reached 7,700 in 1801 and 46,000 in 1851. This growth was caused by the immense expansion of the four principal ironworks, namely Cyfarthfa, Dowlais, Penydarren and Plymouth Works. Connected with the works was an extensive transport system employing many people, namely tramroads, the Glamorganshire Canal and later the railways. People flocked in a continuous stream to Merthyr from all parts of Wales, from England and Ireland and later even from abroad.

Yet right up to 1850 no proper civic authority existed as in older established towns of similar size. There was no elected council, no appointed official to look after paving, lighting or sanitation. The only local organization was the parish, so that Merthyr really resembled an enormous village. This lack of any civic organization resulted in a complete absence of any plan for housing, the lay out of streets and squares, the forming of sewers and the provision of an adequate water supply. In consequence the living conditions of the population were appalling and hardly to be imagined today.

Whilst built solidly enough of stone, the houses were constructed without any system or regard to the disposition of neighbouring property. In order to save space, houses were packed together in close courts and narrow alleys. Many were built back to back, many people lived in cellars. A large number of houses consisted of two rooms only, and were very small. Many of them did not exceed 8ft by 10ft or 12ft. In these two roomed houses, there were generally three beds in the upper or sleeping apartment, occupied by five or six persons. Other houses had a kitchen, pantry and sleeping room on the ground floor and two sleeping rooms above. Many people kept pigs and chickens in small back gardens close to their houses.

Plate 53a: BETHEL STREET AND THE ENTRANCE TO BETHEL COURT, GEORGETOWN, 25/8/71

The houses were, with few exceptions, unprovided with toilets or accommodation of any kind for the disposal of excrement or refuse, save what the street or river afforded. There was a total lack of sewers or drainage. All slops or refuse were thrown into the streets, most of which were not properly formed. In wet weather, they were often impassable for mud.

'The crowning evil' says one report of the time, 'under which the inhabitants of Merthyr Tydfil labour as regards their social and sanitary conditions, is the utter want of provision for the supply of water.' This was so in spite of the comparatively high average rainfall in Merthyr and the surrounding hills. The water in the principal streams was diverted to and used by the ironworks. Furthermore, the whole surface of the mountains surrounding the town was carefully drained and the water collected in large ponds or reservoirs for exclusive use in the ironworks. After passing through the works, the water was fouled and unsuitable for domestic purposes. The inhabitants had to rely for their water supply for drinking and cooking either on private wells or on natural springs or waterspouts. In winter there could be as few as six or eight such spouts, some as far as a mile distant from the houses. In summer their number could be reduced to three. At these spouts, 50, 80, even 100 people could be seen waiting their turn. Some had to wait 6, 8 or even 10 hours at a time. They were known to wait up the whole night.

Plate 53b: WEST LANE, GEORGETOWN, 25/8/71

As a consequence of these deplorable conditions the health of the inhabitants suffered. In the period 1845-1855 the death rate was 33 per 1000 inhabitants, about twice as high as todays. Out of 1000 children born, over 180 died in their first year, over fifteen times as many as today. The average age at death of the people of Merthyr in 1851 was calculated to be 17½

Plate 54: Dr. T. J. DYKE (from a painting of 1894)

years, in 1976 it was 71 years. The main causes of death and illness were frequent epidemics. The most dreaded were the cholera epidemics. The first occurred in 1832/33 and claimed 160 victims. The worst was in 1849, when 1432 people died. Two more outbreaks killed 424 people in 1854 and 119 in 1866. Among the diseases which most frequently carried off young children were pneumonia, bronchitis, dysentery, tuberculosis, scarlet fever and small pox. Among the adult population occurred indigestion (often fatal in those days) tuberculosis, inflammation of the lungs, fever in its various forms and dysentery. In spite of the high death rate the population grew steadily fed by the constant inflow of 'rosy cheeked young adults' from other areas.

The care of the sick was in the hands of a number of doctors. They treated for a fee patients who could afford to pay. The majority of the working population and their families were in case of illness treated by Works

Surgeons employed by the iron works. The workers paid approximately 4d per £ of earning for medical assistance, sickness benefit and education of their children. The Merthyr Board of Guardians, established in 1836, was responsible for the sick poor. They appointed their own Medical Officers. There were no hospitals in Merthyr in 1850. Sir John Guest had subscribed to the Swansea Infirmary since 1820, thereby obtaining the right to nominate patients for treatment.

Merthyr was not alone in the lack of sanitary amenities caused by the rapid population growth during the Industrial Revolution. Many large towns, Manchester, Liverpool, parts of London were in a similar plight. Slowly the conscience of the country was aroused. A number of enquiries were conducted into the state of health, particularly the health of towns. Among them was an enquiry into the 'Sanatory Conditions of Merthyr Tydfil' conducted by Sir H.T. De La Beche in 1844. As a result of this and many similar reports a Public Health Act was passed in 1848. This made it possible to set up Local Boards of Health in towns and localities where there was no organisation to provide water, sewers and other sanitary facilities. Upon the initiative of Dr. T.J. Dyke, a well known medical practitioner of Merthyr, a public meeting was held in Merthyr, which petitioned the General Board of Health to hold a public enquiry and to establish a Local Board of Health. The enquiry was held in May 1849 and conducted by Mr. T.W. Rammell. He published a famous report, upon which most of our knowledge of the sanitary conditions of the town at the time is based. As a result, the Local Board of Health was established in 1850. Its main powers and duties were to carry out essential drainage, to lay down a sewerage system and to provide an adequate supply of piped water.

Origins of the Water Supply and Sewerage System

It was not until 1858 that the work for supplying water finally started. The water was taken from the river Taf Fechan at a point near Dolygaer and conveyed by pipe to Penybryn in Merthyr. Here storage tanks and filter beds were constructed and the water supplied to various parts of Merthyr and Penydarren. A small steam engine pumped the water to a service reservoir at the top of Dowlais, from where Dowlais and Pant were supplied. The first water reached Merthyr in 1861 and was initially available from eleven standpipes. From then on the supply of water to houses in Merthyr and Dowlais proceeded quickly and most had running water installed within a few years. At the same time an impounding reservoir was built at Dolygaer. It was completed in 1862 and was called the Pentwyn Reservoir or Dolygaer Lake. It now forms the northern part of the Taf Fechan Reservoir at Pontsticill, above the bridge near Dolygaer. It supplied unfiltered water to the ironworks for many years.

The construction of the sewers was even more delayed. A comprehensive scheme was designed by the surveyor, Mr. Samuel Harpur, in 1864. By

Plate 55: TAF FECHAN RESERVOIR

1868 55 miles of sewers were constructed and the houses of nearly half the population connected with them. At that time the untreated sewage was let into the river Taf near Troedyrhiw, until a new sewage treatment system could be brought into operation. Merthyr Tydfil was the first place in the whole country to use a method called 'The Downward Intermittent Filtration', which had been developed in the laboratory only. It was installed on land situated near Troedyrhiw. In this system, four plots of land of five acres each were provided with pipes buried about 6ft deep. The sewage was directed to each plot for a period of six hours, then switched to the next plot and so on. It was then left for 18 hours to filter through trenches to the pipes below and eventually left the plots as clear water. The plots were planted with vegetables and grass and gave high yields of excellent produce. By 1875 nearly all the properties in Merthyr and Dowlais were properly drained by connection to the main sewers.

In 1878 the Merthyr Tydfil Corporation and the Aberdare Council formed a Joint Farms Management Committee, which administered the sewage farms at Troedyrhiw and another one developed in Abercynon. The Farms Committee operated till 1972.

Dr. T.J. Dyke

Once an ample supply of water was available and a good system of drainage and sewage disposal completed, the health of the population improved immensely. One person among all others who laboured to bring about these advances was the revered Dr. Thomas Jones Dyke, one of the most prominent and respected citizens of Merthyr in the second half of the nineteenth century.

He was born in Merthyr in 1816. He was apprenticed to D. Davies and E. Davies, surgeons to the Cyfarthfa Iron Works in 1831. In 1834 he went to London where he qualified as an apothecary and became a member of the Royal College of Surgeons. In 1866 he was elected a Fellow of the College. In 1839 he returned to Merthyr and began practice as a doctor. In 1842 he took a cottage in Bridge Street, called the Hollies. (The name is now used for the Health Centre in Merthyr built in 1972). Dr. Dyke lived there for 52 years. He became in turn district parish surgeon and district surgeon to the Dowlais Iron Company. In 1848, and 1849 he gave two important lectures on the causes of unhealthiness of towns and of Merthyr Tydfil, which lectures led to the public enquiry held by T.W. Rammell. This enquiry held in 1849 led to the establishment of the Merthyr Board of Health in 1850, the first public authority concerned with the health of the whole population of Merthyr. (The Board of Guardians set up in 1836 was only concerned with the health of the destitute poor). During the cholera epidemic of 1849 Dr. Dyke was in charge of one of nine districts into which the town had been divided during the epidemic. He contracted the disease himself and was ill for six weeks.

On the 5th October 1865 he was appointed the first permanent Medical Officer of Health for the Merthyr Board of Health, an appointment which he held until his death in 1900. During this period he presented annual reports about the state of health of Merthyr which are models of their kind in interest and lucidity. In 1877 he was one of the founders of the Children's Hospital in Bridge Street and acted as its honorary surgeon. He gave a number of papers to professional societies. Of particular interest is a paper given in 1885 to the British Medical Association Meeting in Cardiff, on the 'Sanitary History of Merthyr Tydfil'. On this occasion, Dr. Drysdale from London, paid him the following tribute: 'A man who could reduce the death rate from 33 to 23 (per 1000 inhabitants) and the cases of phthisis (tuberculosis) from 38 to 18, should occupy a far higher position even than the emperor, who found Rome of bricks and left it of marble'.

Dr. Dyke's public services were recognised in 1876 and 1877, when he was appointed High Constable of Caerphilly Higher. He was made a Justice of the Peace in 1886. He died in 1900 and is buried in Cefn Coed cemetery.

Health and sanitary conditions of Merthyr in the second half of the 19th century

The most feared and dreadful epidemics in the middle of the 19th century were the cholera epidemics. Fortunately they led to a number of Acts of Parliament in the field of sanitation, which brought about substantial improvements. The first epidemic of 1832 claimed 160 victims. In 1849 the second epidemic occurred. Nine cholera districts were formed by the Board of Guardians, with a medical officer in charge of each. He was assisted by one or two lay visitors. A temporary building was erected in the Brecon Road area as a House of Refuge for the healthy members of families in which cases of cholera occurred. The present cemetery in Pant was opened in 1849 for victims of the cholera, as the existing burial grounds were insufficient. 1432 people died in this second, the most terrible of all the outbreaks. The third epidemic reached the United Kingdom in 1853. As it threatened to spread to Merthyr, a temporary Officer of Health was appointed in November 1853. He was Dr. William Kay from Bristol. His report was published in May 1854 and showed that the conditions of the health of Merthyr had hardly if at all improved since Rammell's report in 1849. The epidemic reached Merthyr in September 1854 and claimed 424 victims. Ten medical districts were formed by the Board of Guardians for their area, with a medical officer in charge of each. The Board of Health created nine divisions in its smaller area at the same time. The Guardians erected a permanent, brick built House of Refuge in the Tydfil Wells area, which could house 100 people. It survived well into the 20th century.

The fourth epidemic occurred in 1866 and lasted eleven weeks. 119 people lost their lives. More effective measures were taken. The Board of Health employed extra inspectors who had to disinfect all houses where the disease

Plate 56: ST. TYDFIL'S HOSPITAL *(Photograph by Robert Haines)*

occurred. Particular attention was paid to the treatment of the effluent of the new sewer near the southern boundary of the Taff Vale railway station. 'Directions to cottagers' were issued and a night dispensary established at the Union Workhouse. The House of Refuge in Tydfils Well was furnished as a temporary cholera hospital by the Board of Health and the Workhouse made a place of refuge for healthy members of families attacked by cholera.

But cholera was only one of the infectious diseases which afflicted the people of Merthyr in the third quarter of the century. Dr. Dyke, who had been appointed Medical Officer of Health to the local Board of Health in October 1865, stated in this first report published in 1866, that typhus occurred in all but four years in the period 1850-1866, small pox occurred in six years in that period, measles in six and scarlet fever in five. In one and the same year, 1865, four epidemics occurred simultaneously; typhus, scarlet fever, small pox and measles. Improvement was slow. Typhus epidemics occurred again in 1866 and 1869, relapsing fever in 1871, and a particularly severe outbreak of small pox in 1871/72, claiming 368 deaths.

Slowly institutions for the treatment of infectious diseases came into being. There was a fever ward in the Infirmary of the Workhouse built in 1853, where sick destitute poor could obtain treatment. The Sanitary Act of 1866 made it possible for the Merthyr Board of Health to convert the House of Refuge in Tydfil's Well into a Fever Hospital in 1869, when a severe outbreak of Typhus occurred. It was fitted out to accommodate 20-30 patients with a sister in charge. At the same time a new wooden Fever Hospital was built in Pant, for 32 patients. These fever hospitals were only occupied when epidemics of infectious diseases occurred.

Progress was steady, if slow. In his account for 1872, Dr. Dyke summed up the preceding 27 years as follows:

'In the eleven years 1845-55, before any works of Sanitary Improvement were begun, the death rate was 33.2 per 1000.

During the following six years 1856-61, works of paving, inspection and removal of nuisances were carried out, and the death rate fell to 28.0 per 1000.

In a further period of four years, 1862-1865 the water supply was introduced and the main drainage formed. This brought about a reduction of the death rate to 26.2 per 1000. In the following seven years 1866-1872 the drainage of houses was being effected and the death rate fell to 25.7 per 1000.'

By 1875 the average age at death had risen to 25, whereas in 1850 it had been 17½ years. By 1879 Merthyr was comparatively free from measles, scarlet fever and diphtheria. Finally in his report of 1890 Dr. Dyke could say: 'In the last 25 years Merthyr Tydfil has been brought into the sacred circle of "Healthy Towns".'

Merthyr Hospitals 1870-1948

By 1870, two separate authorities were providing hospitals: the Board of Guardians administered the Infirmary, where the destitute poor people of Merthyr obtained treatment for all types of illness, and the Merthyr Board of Health who maintained two fever hospitals in Tydfil's Well and Pant. In the late 70s we find another group of hospitals of a type long established in London and other large towns, namely the voluntary hospitals. They were called voluntary because they were maintained entirely by charitable gifts and voluntary contributions. The patients were not required to make any payment for their treatment to either the hospital or the doctors. The doctors either gave their services free or received a honorarium from hospital funds. One of the voluntary hospitals was the children's hospital in Bridge Street. It started in 1877 and Dr. Dyke was one of its chief promoters and acted as honorary surgeon. In 1860 Mrs. C.T. Clark, wife of one of the Trustees of the Dowlais Iron Company founded a hospital in Dowlais which closed in 1882. Eventually, the Merthyr General Hospital was founded. It owes a great deal to the energetic zeal of W.T. Lewis, who later became Sir W.T. Lewis and eventually Lord Merthyr. He persuaded the Marquess of Bute to contribute a substantial amount. The remainder of the funds required were raised by public subscription. The hospital was opened in 1888. It consisted of two wards for 10 patients each and a children's ward, transferred from Bridge Street children's hospital. The latter was closed. All beds in the General Hospital were supported by voluntary subscriptions; several beds were maintained by the workers of the ironworks and collieries of the area. In 1897 an accident ward was endowed by Lord Merthyr, whose

Plate 57: MERTHYR GENERAL HOSPITAL FROM THOMASTOWN PARK, May 1976

statue stands in front of the hospital. Treatment was in the hands of the medical practitioners of Merthyr, many of whom were highly qualified specialists. They admitted and treated their own patients, although outside consultants were called in from time to time. No patients suffering from infectious diseases were admitted. They were sent to the fever hospitals of the Local Board of Health or the fever ward in the Infirmary.

Two surgical wards were added in 1922, housed in wooden buildings. From 1923 until 1947 Annual Fetes were held each Whitsun in Cyfarthfa Park, which raised considerable funds. Another substantial proportion of the funds came from workmen's contributions, deducted from their weekly wages.

In 1930, the Lord Buckland Memorial Building was erected. The funds were provided by the Executors of the late Lord Buckland in his memory. It provided accommodation for outpatients, an operating theatre, X-ray departments and ophthalmic wards. After this building had been opened, there were 118 beds in the General Hospital. The hospital then was one of the most modern in South Wales.

The functions of the Merthyr Board of Health were taken over in 1894 by the Urban District Council of Merthyr Tydfil, and this became the Merthyr Borough Council in 1905. These councils thus took over the administration of the fever hospitals in Tydfil's Well and Pant. In 1902, during an outbreak of small pox, a Small Pox hospital was erected near the site of the present Mardy Hospital. It was a corrugated iron building and held 18 beds.

In 1906 a new large Isolation Hospital was built and called the Mardy Isolation Hospital. It stands in 4½ acres of grounds and consists of a number of separate pavilions. It was opened on 23.3.1907 by Keir Hardy, the Junior Member of Parliament for Merthyr. The Medical Officer of Health of the Merthyr Council was the doctor in charge of the hospital. There was a matron, sisters and nurses. Patients suffering from infectious diseases such as typhus, diphtheria, scarlet fever were treated there, as were tuberculosis patients. In 1920 an outpatients clinic for venereal diseases was opened and used until 1961. Vegetables and fruit were grown in a garden in the hospital grounds and chickens, ducks, geese and pigs kept.

With the opening of the Mardy Hospital the fever hospitals in Brecon Road and Pant became superfluous. The Pant hospital, a wooden structure, was destroyed by fire on order of the Council. The Brecon Road hospital ceased to be used as a hospital. It became a school canteen and was later used for stores.

The small pox hospital in Mardy was too close to the new isolation hospital and was bodily moved to a site in Mountain Hare. It was intermittently used for small pox patients until 1928, when it was severely damaged in a gale. The patients were transferred to the Mardy Hospital until 1931, when a Small Pox Hospital was established in Fedwhir near Aberdare in conjunction with four other local authorities. It ceased to be used as a small pox hospital in 1934.

The Board of Guardians steadily extended and improved the Infirmary. A syphilitic ward seems to have been built in 1882. In 1895 a new Isolation Ward was provided. A new infirmary building was added in 1897. A children's ward was built in 1906. Further extensions were erected in 1909, which provided new accommodation for nurses, a new maternity block and a new syphilitic ward for men. In 1920, a resident medical officer was appointed. In that year, conditions for nurses were improved and a separate nursery for children under one year provided. At that time, the total number of beds was 300 and the Infirmary was the largest hospital in Merthyr. The conditions in the Infirmary, and especially in the Maternity Ward improved so much that private, fee paying patients sought admission and this was arranged from 1922.

In 1930 the Board of Guardians ceased to exist and the Infirmary was taken over by the Merthyr Corporation. In that year Consultants were appointed to the Infirmary for the first time. These included an Orthopaedic Surgeon and a Consulting Obstetrician and Gynaecologist.

The Board of Guardians built another hospital in the Merthyr area. This was the Pontsarn Sanatorium for tuberculosis patients. It was built in 1913 and could accommodate 50 patients. In 1914 it was leased to the King Edward VII Welsh National Memorial Association, who eventually bought it in 1923.

Plate 58: PONTSARN SANATORIUM AFTER CONVERSION INTO FLATS

Health and Sanitary Conditions in the first half of the 20th century

By the 1880's the area of Merthyr had expanded to such an extent, that an additional water supply became necessary. Thus a new reservoir, the Lower Neuadd Reservoir was built in 1884. At 1412 ft above sea level it was high enough to supply water directly by gravitation to the Garth storage reservoir (1250 ft above sea level) and a new 12" main was laid first to independent filterbeds and then to Garth. Thus Dowlais, Pant and other higher areas could be now supplied directly. The steam engine which up to now had pumped water from Penybryn to Dowlais could be dispensed with. A smaller main took the water from Garth to Treharris and Quakers Yard.

In 1895 the Upper Neuadd Reservoir was built and opened in 1902. The watersupply now reached Bedlinog and Abercynon. New filterbeds were installed at the two new reservoirs and a new High Level Aqueduct took the water from the Upper Neuadd Reservoir to Garth and thence to a new service reservoir at Pengarnddu, which supplied Cwmbargoed, Merthyr Vale and Treharris.

Further supplies were required by 1910 not only for Merthyr but also for the local authorities in the Rhymney Valley, Pontypridd and even Barry. A new reservoir was started, the Taf Fechan Reservoir in Pontsticill. Work was delayed during the war 1914-18 and after the war several local

Plate 59: TAF FECHAN RESERVOIR, PONTSTICILL
(Photograph by Robert Haines)

authorities joined to form the Taf Fechan Water Supply Board. This took over all existing works of supply of the constituent authorities. The distribution of the water from certain points of supply however remained the responsibility of each authority. The authorities included Merthyr Tydfil Corporation, the Rhymney Valley Water Board, the Pontypridd and Rhondda Joint Water Board, Llantrisant and Llantwit Fadre Rural District Council and Aberdare Urban District Council. Water was also to be supplied to Barry. The Taf Fechan Reservoir in Pontsticill was completed in 1927 and included the old Pentwyn Reservoir. The water supply increased from 5.3 million gallons a day in 1927 to 10 millions in 1949.

Throughout the 20th century the health of the population continued to improve, due to a large measure to the progress made in medical science and the development of preventive measures carried out mainly by the local health authorities. Merthyr, whilst advancing steadily, lagged for a long time behind the progress made in England and Wales as a whole. Dr. J. Thomas, the Medical Officer for Health, stated in his report for 1901, that the deathrate from measles, scarlet fever, whooping cough, diphtheria, enteric fever and diarrhoea and small pox was half as high again in Merthyr as the average for England and Wales. Infant mortality, that is the number of deaths of children under one year old, at 261 per 1000 births in Merthyr compared unfavourably with the England and Wales average of 151. The reason for these poor results in Merthyr he blames on the ignorance displayed by the mothers in the rearing of children, poor housing conditions and the reluctance of parents to have their children suffering from measles removed to isolation hospitals.

Some improvements in the housing conditions were made possible by the Housing of the Working Classes Act 1890. This introduced two important measures: in the first place it allowed local authorities to clear areas with insanitary property and in Merthyr large parts in the Cyfarthfa Ward were so cleared. Secondly, local authorities were empowered to build single family houses. The first council houses to be erected in Merthyr were 100 houses in Urban Street and Council Street in Penydarren, which were completed in 1904. Yet much overcrowding and faulty construction remained. There were still back to back houses, dwellings in cellars, under and over houses, houses erected with high ground in the rear. 286 houses were investigated in 1901 and showed a death rate twice as high as the rest of the district.

In 1906 and 1907 important legislation to improve the health of school-children was passed. In 1906 Local Authorities were empowered to provide school meals for necessitous children and in Merthyr school canteens were opened in the old fever hospital in Brecon Road and in Dowlais. In 1907 a school medical service was established and all children in local authority schools had to be inspected. School Medical Officers and School Nurses were appointed in 1909 and a school clinic opened in Glebeland Place, in 1911.

By 1911 the incidence of infectious diseases had decreased, but tuberculosis was still prevalent. The National Insurance Act of 1911 provided financial assistance for the treatment of tuberculosis. The King Edward VII Welsh National Memorial Association was given powers to carry out the relevant provisions of the act in Wales. Thus they undertook to finance tuberculosis beds in the Mardy Hospital, set up a chest clinic in Church Street, Merthyr and leased the Pontsarn Sanatorium from the Board of Guardians in 1914 and bought it in 1923. Another important step in the fight against tuberculosis was taken in 1909, when the Merthyr Council arranged for the examination of cows for tubercle bacilli.

In 1913 the death rate in Merthyr (13.4 per 1000) was for the first time lower than that of England and Wales (13.7). Infant Mortality, whilst the lowest on record in Merthyr at 126 per 1000 births, was still higher than that of England and Wales of 103. Improvements occurred, when two Infant Welfare Centres were opened in 1916 and another two in 1920. They were situated in different parts of the borough. By 1927 the infant mortality rate of Merthyr with 103 deaths had reached the average of England and Wales of 1913. But that rate had fallen by 1927 to 69.

With the passing of the Local Government Act of 1929, the Boards of Guardians were abolished and the Merthyr Council became responsible for the education, maternity and child welfare, the blind and mentally deficient of all the inhabitants of the borough.

In 1933, Dr. Stephens, the new Medical Officer of Health, could report that nearly 2/3 of all expectant mothers attended antenatal clinics and that all abnormal cases were seen by a specialist and entered St. Tydfil's Lodge. The infant mortality rate at 73 per 1000 births was now the lowest on record and compared favourably with that of 108 Boroughs and Great Towns (69 per 1000), having regard to the distressing economic conditions.

Ten years later, in the report for 1944, Dr. Stephens could point to the astonishing decline in the infant mortality rate from 261 in 1901 to 64 in 1944 in Merthyr, although still higher than the average for England and Wales (46). The deaths of mothers in childbirth per 1000, which had been 9.7 in 1928, had fallen to 2.6 in 1944. The reason for these improvements, he said, were better ante-natal supervision with subsequent anticipation of obstetrical difficulties, greater facility for institutional delivery and employment of consultants. Out of 1086 births, 823 had confinements either at Tydfil's Lodge or Gwaunfarren Maternity Home.

With regard to infectious diseases he could say that the days of cholera, typhus and certain other infectious diseases had gone, but they still had to deal with some killing diseases like diphtheria. There was improvement even here, as as recently as 1921, 20 persons died for every 100 cases of diphtheria, but in 1944 less than one per hundred. The deaths from tuberculosis too were constantly falling. Merthyr was the first local authority in England and Wales to have all school children X-rayed by the Miniature Mobile X-Ray plant.

In 1946, six health visitors were employed to assist with the care of mothers and young children and at school medical clinics. Eleven Municipal Midwives were appointed to help with home confinements. Specialist services were provided for children in respect of orthopaedic, ophthalmic, ear, nose, throat, heart and rheumatic diseases. District Nurses were available in the six districts arranged in the Borough for this purpose. Ambulances were kept at Tydfil's Lodge, the Mardy Hospital, the Merthyr General Hospital, the police, the Ocean Colliery and Merthyr Vale Colliery.

The National Health Service Act 1946 and the period of its operation 1948-1974

Following the famous Beveridge Report of 1942, the National Health Service Act of 1946 was passed, which introduced a comprehensive free health service for every man, woman and child in the country. It created three distinct health services: The hospital services; the family practitioners' services; and health services provided by the local health authorities.

The hospital services were carried out by the Minister of Health, to whom all existing hospitals were transferred. The services were administered in Wales by the Welsh Regional Hospital Board, which supervised a number of Local Hospital Management Committees. For Merthyr this was the Merthyr and Aberdare Hospital Management Committee. This Committee took over the Merthyr General Hospital, Tydfil's Lodge, now renamed St. Tydfil's Hospital, the Mardy Isolation Hospital, Pontsarn Chest Hospital, Fedwhir Hospital, Gwaunfarren Maternity Hospital and Sandbrook House, Merthyr. It also took over the Chest Clinic in Courtland Terrace.

The Local Health Authority, namely the Merthyr Tydfil Borough Council, became responsible for certain health services of a preventive rather than curative nature. They included the care of mothers and young children, midwifery, health visiting and home nursing, vaccination and immunisation, ambulance services and home help. Local Authorities were empowered to set up Health Centres, where medical, dental and pharmaceutical practitioners could have their surgeries, as well as clinics dealing with certain specialities for outpatients. Such Health Centres were not set up in Merthyr until 1972.

The third group of services were those provided by general medical practitioners, dentists, pharmacists and opticians, whose activities were administered by local Executive Councils. One such council was set up in Merthyr. The members of these councils included representatives of the local health authority and of the various groups of practitioners mentioned.

After the introduction of the new health service, a uniform system of administration was introduced in all the hospitals. Thus similar systems of remuneration of all grades of staff, of accounting and stores control were

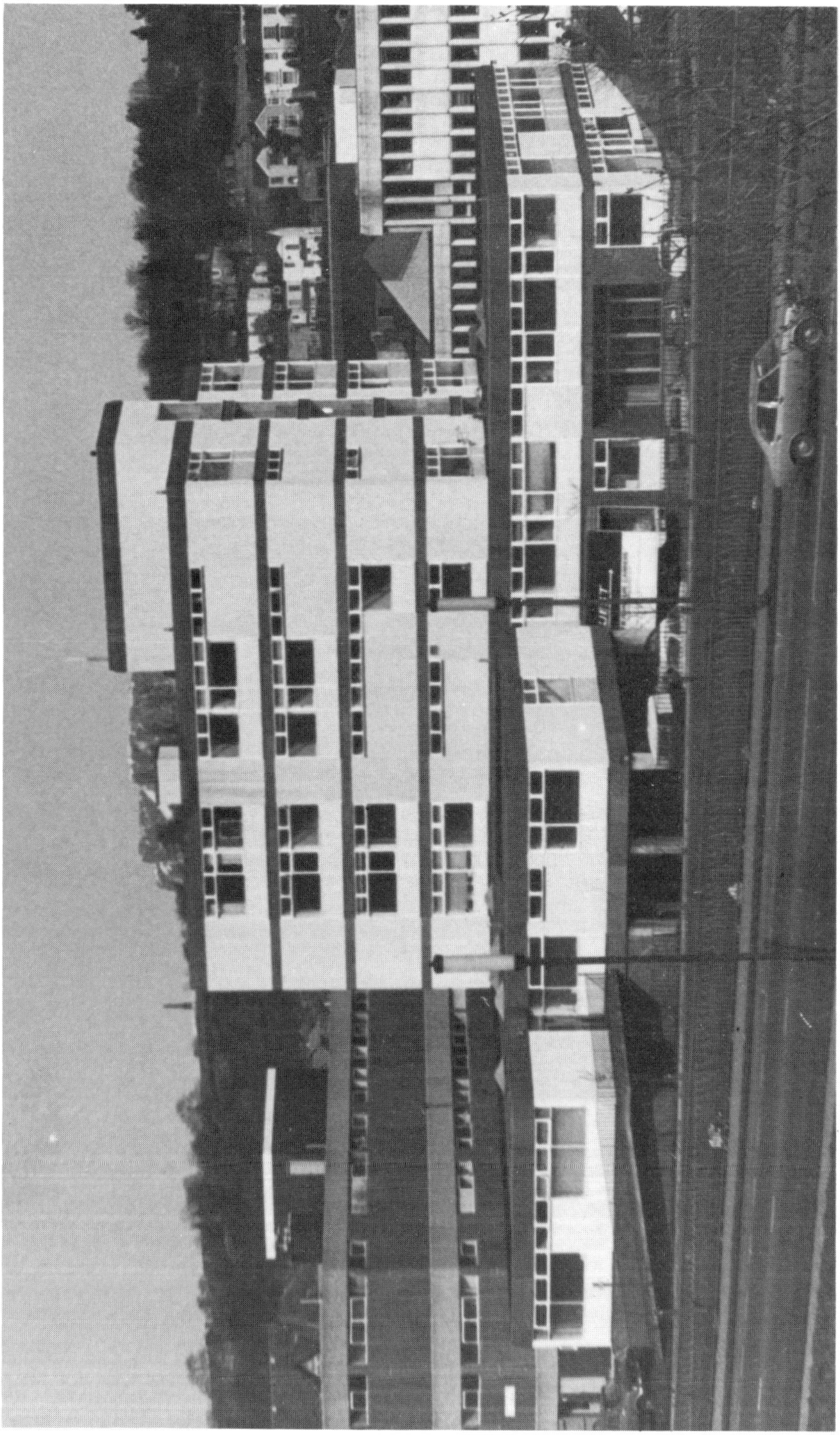

Plate 60: 'THE HOLLIES' HEALTH CENTRE, MERTHYR TYDFIL, 1976

being used. Another even more important measure taken was that the hospitals became 'Consultant Hospitals.' This meant that the Senior Hospital Medical Staff decided on the admission and treatment of patients and that all beds were allocated to them.

In 1948 the size of the hospitals in Merthyr can be compared by the number of beds in each. St. Tydfil's Hospital was by far the largest with 607 beds, Merthyr General Hospital had 120 beds, Mardy 120. Pontsarn Sanatorium was much smaller with 40 beds, Gwaunfarren Maternity Hospital had 21 beds, Sandbrook House 20, Fedwhir 72.

By 1955 a large number of specialist treatments were provided by the Merthyr and Aberdare Hospital Management Committee in their various hospitals. They were listed as follows: Anaesthetics, Dermatology, Diseases of the chest, ear, nose and throat. General Medicine, General Surgery, Gynaecology and Obstetrics. Infectious diseases. Neurology, Ophthamology. Oral Surgery and Dentistry. Orthopaedic Surgery. Paediatrics. Pathology. Psychiatry. Urological Surgery. Venereal Diseases.

Training for nurses had been provided in the Merthyr Hospitals for many years. In the report for 1953 of the Merthyr and Aberdare Management Committee details were given as follows: The Merthyr General Hospital provided a complete Training School for State Registered Nurses. Fever training for nurses was being provided at the Mardy Isolation Hospital. St. Tydfil's Hospital had a training school for State Enrolled Assistant Nurses and a three months Preliminary Training Course ran at Gwaelodygarth, Merthyr.

Important new departments were opened in St. Tydfil's Hospital in 1953. They were a Group Pathological Laboratory, an Orthopaedic Department and Outpatient Department. These included a Physiotherapy Department and a Hydrotherapy Department. The hydrotherapy bath installed there was the first in Wales. In 1958 a new Accident and Emergency Department was provided as a result of extensive alterations of existing premises. These new facilities led to a vast expansion of the outpatients work in St. Tydfil's Hospital.

Pontsarn Sanatorium closed in 1960. Sandbrook House was also closed as a hospital in that year and was from then on used as a home for elderly women.

A new maternity unit was opened in St. Tydfil's Hospital in 1957. It cost £45,000 and contained 40 beds including a premature baby unit. A review of the period 1949-1964 shows that whilst the total number of beds since the inception of the National Health Service had fallen by 25%, yet 70% more patients were admitted and discharged.

At outpatient clinics, four times as many new patients were seen in 1964 than in 1949 and total attendance increased five fold. The number of different clinics in various specialities too rose substantially, namely three and a half times.

During the Aberfan disaster in October 1966 an accident centre was set up in St. Tydfil's Hospital and manned day and night. A rescue centre and rescue stations were set up in Aberfan, with teams of nurses from hospitals in the group in attendance.

In 1968 the decision was taken to build a new hospital in the Gurnos. It covers a site of 32 acres. The first phase of 362 beds was opened in 1978 by H.R.H. Prince Charles.

We must now turn to the services provided by the Merthyr Tydfil Borough Council after the introduction of the National Health Service. In 1955 Pentrebach House was adopted as a Residential Home for elderly men. In 1956 vaccination against Poliomyelitis was offered for the first time. In 1963 a Training Centre for Subnormal children and adults was opened in Pentrebach.

In November 1965 Dr. A. M. Williams succeeded Dr. Stephens as Medical Officer of Health. In the report for that year, Dr. Williams paid tribute to Dr. Stephens and described the advances made in public health, in Merthyr during the last 33 years. There was a spectacular drop in the number of deaths of infants under one year, which was 16.4 per 1000 birth in 1965. This was for the first time lower than the national average of 19.0. The average age at death in 1952 was 63.6 years, whereas hundred years ago it was 17½ years.

Much of Dr. Stephens' work was devoted to the treatment of infectious diseases in general and diphtheria in particular. In the report for 1933 Dr. Stephens stated, that 243 children suffered from diphtheria, of whom 20 died. By 1938 of 153 notified cases only six died. Dr. Stephens' immunisation campaign did much to eradicate the disease in Merthyr Tydfil. The last recorded death was in 1945, and no case had been reported in the last 15 years. The number of deaths from tuberculosis also fell conspicuously. There had been 71 in 1933 and only 11 in 1965. As a consequence of the decrease in numbers affected, the Pontsarn Sanatorium could be closed in 1960.

In 1968 we learn that seven clinics operated in the area. A new building to house ambulances was opened in 1970 in Merthyr. In that year the deaths from tuberculosis fell to three and the Mass Miniature Radiography Service, introduced in 1944, could be withdrawn. The long awaited Health Centres, for which provision had been made in the National Health Act of 1946, were finally provided in 1972. There were two opened at the same time, one in Merthyr, The Hollies, and one in Dowlais.

In 1975, the population of Merthyr was 60,000. The death rate in the Merthyr and Cynon Valley Health District was 14.8 per 1000, as compared to 11.8 for England and Wales. Infant Mortality in the Merthyr and Cynon Valley district was 12 per 1000 births, much lower than the rate for England and Wales of 16 per 1000. In that year 70% of all deaths in the area of the Mid Glamorgan Health Authority occurred at the age of 70 years or more, and of these 40% occurred at 75 years of age or more.

Reorganisations of 1974

Three Acts of Parliament came into force simultaneously on 1 April 1974 and substantially changed the management of many services concerning the health of the people of Merthyr.

Merthyr Tydfil lost its status as a County Borough and became a district, forming part of the new County of Mid-Glamorgan. Merthyr retained the responsibility for housing, slum clearance, parks and open spaces, baths, cemeteries and crematoria. A new department for environmental health became responsible for refuse collection, food safety, hygiene and slaughter houses. Mid-Glamorgan County Council became responsible for education.

The supply and distribution of water and the provision of public sewers became the responsibility of the Welsh National Water Development Authority. This authority thus took over the Taf Fechan reservoirs and filterbeds, storage reservoirs and pipe lines. They also took over all sewers including the new trunk sewer to Abercynon, as well as the old sewage treatment farms at Troedyrhiw and Abercynon. They will also be responsible for a new sewage treatment plant for the Merthyr area presently under construction in Cilfynydd.

The National Health Services were also reorganized, although the main principles laid down in 1948 remained unaltered. The Welsh Office were made responsible for the overall control for the whole of Wales. Eight area health authorities were set up whose territories correspond to the new counties in Wales. Merthyr thus comes under the Mid-Glamorgan Health Area. Further sub-divisions are health districts. Merthyr falls within the Merthyr and Cynon Valley Health District. The Area Health Authorities are responsible for the overall control of hospitals, the family practitioner services, community health services and the ambulance service. The Health Districts are in charge of the day to day management of the hospitals in each district, the Health Centres and Clinics. Community Health Councils were set up in each district to afford the inhabitants of the district access and information concerning all health services in their district.

References

Board of Guardians. Merthyr Union. Minutes 1836-1930.

Merthyr Tydfil Board of Health. Minutes 1850-1894.

Merthyr Tydfil Urban District Council Minutes 1895-1905.

Merthyr Tydfil Borough Council Minutes 1905-1974.

Reports by the Medical Officers of Health for Merthyr 1854-1970.

Report on the Sanatory Conditions of Merthyr Tydfil by Sir H.T. De La Beche 1845.

Report into the sewerage, drainage and supply of water, and the sanitary condition of the inhabitants of the town of Merthyr Tydfil by T.W. Rammell 1850.

Public Records Office Box MH 13/125.

The Sanitary History of Merthyr Tydfil by T.J.Dyke. British Medical Journal 1885 p.192.

The Merthyr Waterworks by T.F. Harvey, 1899. (Proceedings of the Inc. Association of Municipal & County Engineers 1899/1900).

The Taf Fechan Supply Board. By A.C.Quininborough 1962.

The Merthyr Sewage Farms by T.F. Harvey. Proceedings of the Royal Sanitary Institute 1908. p.648.

The Sewage Question by C.N. Bazalgette. Proceedings of the Institution of Civil Engineers Vol. 48 1876/77, pp 105-250.

Annual Reports and Minutes of the Executive Board of the Merthyr General Hospital. Incomplete.

Notes on the Merthyr General Hospital, kindly supplied by Miss D.R. Grassick.

Annual Reports of the Merthyr and Aberdare Hospital Management Committee 1948-1971.

Notes on the history of the hospitals in Merthyr Tydfil, kindly supplied by the Merthyr and Cynon Valley Health District.

Description of the opening ceremony of the Merthyr General Hospital, Merthyr Express 6.10.1888.

Obituary of T.J.Dyke: Merthyr Express 27.1.1900 and South Wales Daily News 22.1.1900.

Merthyr Tydfil, the Politics of Survival. By I. G. Jones, Llafur, Vol.2. No. 1, 1976.

The Role of Dr. Dyke in the Public Health Administration of Merthyr Tydfil 1865-1892 (Unpublished Swansea University MA Thesis 1968). By B.A. Frampton.

The Hospitals 1900-1948, by Brian Abel Smith, Heinemann 1964.

English Public Health 1834-1939 by W.M. Frazer. Balliere, Tyndall and Cox, 1950.

Water Supply, Sewerage and Hospitals in Merthyr Tydfil 1850-1974 by Joseph Gross, *Merthyr Historian*, Volume Two, 1978.

Education

by JOHN FLETCHER

Merthyr Tydfil has a long proud record in the field of education. It is a story of initiative, inventiveness and determined action, sometimes in the face of daunting adversity.

The veil of time parted briefly in the middle of the seventeenth century to reveal a glimpse of the educational scene during Commonwealth times. Nathaniel Jones, rector of Merthyr Tydfil, found it necessary to set down his story of harassment by local dissenters and reported:

> 'They have taken away timber, stone and the seats out of the Church, and they have putt in school-masters, whose boys have demolished so much lead, yt will not be made up with four or five pounds, and if it be not made up the steeple is like to fall.'

This brief passage indicates the importance placed on education, that it was considered appropriate for boys only and that vandalism is not limited to twentieth century society.

Education remained a responsibility of religion for many years to follow. Reference to schools in the district reappeared in the early eighteenth century. Records of the Society for Promoting Christian Knowledge for the period 1699 to 1737, indicate that the village of Merthyr Tydfil possessed no less than three schools, more than all other Glamorgan centres.

In 1731, Griffith Jones, vicar of Llanddowror, suggested a novel approach to mass education. He was moved to bring the Bible to the common people but first he had to tackle the problem of illiteracy. His solution was to send out itinerant school masters to many parts of Wales to teach both children and adults to read in the vernacular. The teacher would gather his class together at a suitable centre and teach children by day and adults in the evening until a measure of success was achieved. Three such groups or circulating schools were established in the district in 1738; one at Blaen Glais in

Vaynor, another at a second farm in Vaynor and the third in the village of Merthyr itself. A total of 163 young people were taught by day and two or three times as many adults in the evenings.

Year by year, the schools moved around the district, stopping at such places as Pantcad Ivor, Taf Fechan, Abercar, Cefn Coed, Pontsticill, Groes Cilsanws, Pontrhyn, Duffryn, Ty Taldon, Pandy and in the hamlets of Forest and Heolwermod.

In a letter dated 4 February 1752, the Minister at Merthyr, Anthony Martin, asked Griffith Jones to allow the itinerant teacher, known only by his initials D.T., to stay on in the district. The appeal appeared to be successful, since there were two further schools set up the following year. However, a further plea was not successful; local inhabitants had to wait until 1756 for a school to be re-established.

Griffith Jones died in 1761 and the circulating schools eventually disappeared. His achievement had been remarkable. It has been estimated that over a period of twenty-four years more than 150,000 children and adults had been taught to read. No doubt, there were many grateful people in this district.

When the results of new educational initiatives reached the area, it had already suffered a traumatic transformation from peaceful agriculture to bustling industry. This time it was the Sunday school which took the strain of the educational burden. This institution had been established by Robert Raikes in Gloucester and Thomas Charles in north Wales. Raikes has been personally credited with visiting Merthyr at the invitation of Robert Crawshay to found a Sunday school in Georgetown. Later this merged with the Sunday schools of the English and Welsh Wesleyan chapels.

The Welsh chapel with its earthen floor became a schoolroom on Sundays at 9 am and 2 pm. The class, boys only, formed up inside a chalked square, with the tutor and his assistant at its head. A monitor, armed with a cane, patrolled the perimeter to maintain discipline.

By 1815, there were nine Sunday schools in operation. Such was the pace of population growth that new places of worship were opening their doors at the rate of one per year, and there were Sunday schools associated with most of them. When the Commission of Inquiry into the State of Education in Wales visited Merthyr in 1847, there was a total of 36 Sunday schools in Merthyr and a further six in Cefn Coed. The Dowlais Iron Company supported the two Church schools in that district but all the rest relied on subscriptions and collections.

The Commission found that there were 6,902 scholars attending Sunday schools, more than one-third of them being over fifteen years of age. About twenty per cent of the scholars also attended day school. Attendance was very regular – about 96 per cent, but only 28 per cent of the scholars were 'able to read the Scriptures'. The emphasis, as in the circulating schools, was on the teaching of reading. There was no instruction in writing or arithmetic. Ten of the schools were conducted in the Welsh language, eleven in the English language whilst the remaining schools favoured a bilingual approach. Some advanced classes concentrated on 'teacher training'.

The Sunday school remained an influential educational agent for much of the last century. In its care many thousands of Merthyr's workpeople and their children were taught to read in English or in Welsh.

Paralleling the growth of the Sunday school was the development of private schools; there were just four establishments in 1815 but forty-five were listed in 1845. The 1847 Commission found 2,301 children of the 'labouring classes' attending private schools. They were for the most part, dame schools, giving instruction to small numbers of children at the home of the teacher, in exchange for school pence. There were a few larger establishments, like Mr. Butler's in Dowlais, Mr. Christmas's in Pontmorlais and Mr. Kernick's in Cae-pant-tywyll. These also provided evening instruction for adults. They were all conducted in English.

For those who could afford more than the school pence, there was a selection of superior private schools. One of the earliest such schools destined to gain a notable reputation was founded by Taliesin Williams, son of Iolo Morgannwg. He came from a teaching position in Neath to found the Merthyr 'Grammar' school, initially based in Caedraw, but later moving to the Glebeland. Taliesin Williams was responsible for the education of such famous sons of the town as Penry Williams, the artist, John Petherick, African explorer and Charles Herbert James, destined to be Member of Parliament for Merthyr.

Later in the century, a quality private school was established in 1857 by Evan Williams, a Glasgow MA. After several temporary premises were used, a school was built in Courtland Terrace under the name 'Tydfil School'. Boarders were taken on for £23. 2. 0d. per annum whilst day scholars were charged £5 for English or commercial classes or six guineas for French, classics or mathematics. Evan Williams also made a major contribution to science education by arranging Science and Art classes. Unfortunately, in the summer of 1873, he went to London to arrange classes for the following session, became ill and died shortly afterwards, at the early age of forty-four.

The 1847 Commission, whilst being rather unimpressed by the private schools catering for the working class, were singularly complimentary about the Ironworks schools at Dowlais. Sir John and Lady Charlotte Guest had produced a remarkable educational scheme, in some ways similar to contemporary Prussian schools. There had been a school associated with the works as early as 1828 but in 1844, new premises, designed by Sir Charles Barry, architect of the Houses of Parliament, were opened. The boys' school was staffed by a master Mathew Hurst, and an assistant, both of whom had been among the first trained teachers to emerge from Battersea training college. The girls' school was also in the care of trained personnel.

Commissioner Lingen described the upper school as 'by far the best provided school-room which I have seen in Wales'. The schools were supported by stoppages from the workers' wages and by payment of school-pence. The curriculum of the upper school included, besides the three Rs, history, geography, Scripture, music, drawing, chemistry and algebra. Because of the quality of the education given, parents were in no great haste to remove their children, consequently boys were *required* to leave at fourteen, but could continue their studies through a further education scheme.

Soon there were schools and evening classes associated with the other ironworks. The Cyfarthfa ironworks' school opened in 1848 and by 1852 there were schools supported by the Plymouth and Penydarren works.

Two National (Church of England) schools were reported by the 1847 Commission, the boys' school dating from 1816 and the girls' from 1839. A further National school opened in Georgetown in 1850, on the site of the Kirkhouse Hall. Later similar schools were set up in Pentrebach and Troedyrhiw. The non-conformists were also active, establishing British schools. In 1867 Lady Charlotte Schrieber laid the foundation stone for Abermorlais British school on a cinder tip. Additional British schools were opened in Penydarren and Troedyrhiw. Local Roman Catholics provided schools in Georgetown and Dowlais. In 1865 there was also a Ragged school in operation in the town.

Contributions to educational advancement also came from other organisations. In December 1807, sixty local people met to found the Cyfarthfa Philosophical Society, subscribing a guinea each to purchase scientific equipment, including an astronomical telescope. The society's first president was Rhys Howell whose father had farmed at Blaen Glaes, location of a circulating school seventy years earlier. Meetings were held at the Dynevor Arms, Georgetown. The society eventually merged with the Merthyr Library, founded by Thomas Stephens, chemist and literateur. Charles Wilkins was its Librarian.

There was also an early Mechanics Institute in the town, founded in 1830. In 1851 it was reported to have 134 members and a library of 1,382 volumes. The institute also had a newsroom and provided twelve lectures a year for a quarterly subscription of one shilling and sixpence. Sir John Guest was the first president of a Literary and Scientific society founded in 1834. He also set up a workmen's library in Dowlais in 1845.

A survey in 1851 showed that Merthyr was the only town in south Wales with a Young Men's Mutual Improvement Society. It had a membership of 96 with 50 students attending classes. In 1856 Charles Herbert James addressed them on the subject 'Are our laws and customs in this country just towards women?'

In 1857, Merthyr's position as a major centre of the iron industry was recognised when it was chosen as the meeting place for the South Wales Institute of Engineers. At the inaugural meeting at the Castle Hotel, William Menelaus, chief engineer at Dowlais, was elected president and Edward Williams, son of Taliesin Williams, grandson of Iolo Morganwg, became secretary.

Thus Merthyr Tydfil arrived at the critical year of education advance 1870, with a substantial voluntary educational structure – Sunday schools and dame schools, works schools and private schools, church schools and 'chapel' schools, together with a veritable cluster of scientific, philosophical, literary and cultural organisations whose objectives, at least in part, were educational.

The aim of the 1870 Education Act was to fill the gaps in the existing voluntary system. Rate money, raised by a locally elected school board, was to be used to extend elementary education. Merthyr responded with alacrity to the call. In 1871, the eleven members of the Merthyr School Board set out to assess the work that they had to carry out. To this end, a census of children eligible for elementary education was taken. It was found that there were 2,735 children between the ages of three and five and 8,831 children between five and thirteen. Ten per cent of the total was deducted for the children of the middle classes, whom the Board assumed would be privately educated, leaving, it was calculated, 10,434 children to accommodate. There existed provision for 6,654 pupils, so that the Board had to face the urgent demand to place an additional 3,780 pupils.

The Board proposed that extension should be made to the Dowlais schools and that new schools should be erected in Penydarren, Merthyr, Twynyrodyn and Cyfarthfa; the fast-growing village of Troedyrhiw would also require a new school. A useful start was made when the nonconformists handed over the British schools at Abermorlais, Penydarren and Troedyrhiw on 1 November 1871. A year later a mixed infants' school was opened in temporary premises in Abercanaid. In 1874 a new board school was opened in Penydarren whilst the following year R.T. Crawshay handed over the Cyfarthfa Works school to the Board. New schools were erected in Twynyrodyn and Caedraw in 1875.

In 1876 the Troedyrhiw school was extended and a new infants' school constructed. By the end of the period of office of the third board – they were elected triennially – a new school had been built in Abercanaid and schools opened in rented premises in Heolgerrig and Clwydyfagwyr. The rapid growth of population around the new mines at Merthyr Vale and Treharris, was responsible for the opening of board schools in these districts. By 1883, the Board had become the agent for educating about half the school population of the district, some 4,779 children. The Dowlais Iron Company with its complex of schools catered for 2,642 pupils whilst there were 1,029 children attending the Roman Catholic schools and 933 the St. David's and Pentrebach National schools.

During the lifetime of the first school board, in 1873, the members had taken an extraordinary and farsighted decision when they saw fit to appoint a full-time teacher of science to the board's schools, later claimed to be the first such appointment in the Kingdom. A detailed twenty-three point argument entitled 'Report on the Right to appoint a teacher in Science and Art', noted the silence of the 1870 Act on technical education and set out to justify science classes in the elementary schools, concluding 'there is no class of workmen who in certain processes of their daily occupations, more need this sort of educational training than those engaged in the manufacture of iron'.

Soon the Science and Art committee of the Board were organising classes for older pupils, evening students and pupil teachers. Throughout the remaining decades of the last century, there was a steady expansion in technical education. A laboratory was set up in Penydarren and an increasing number of part-time teachers appointed. The first call for a technical college came at this time.

The Board also took steps to help those adults who had missed out on elementary education and young people who had left school inadequately prepared. Evening continuation classes were organised throughout the district in the late 'eighties, where the emphasis was on basic education. In the 'nineties, the educational and social needs of women were the Board's concern when it set up a number of evening institutes.

In the meanwhile, the need for some form of secondary education had become apparent to the far-sighted Board. Schools called advanced elementary or higher grade had been established in the north of England in the 'seventies. True to form, the Merthyr Board had considered setting them up as early as 1875. By 1880, interest had intensified when a meeting of parents and others at the Temperance Hall resulted in a memorial on the subject being presented to the Board.

Later that year, the Aberdare Commission visited Merthyr as part of its quest for evidence on the state of intermediate and higher education in Wales. The Commission was told that the demand for secondary education in Merthyr had been so strong that in 1876 a company had been formed to establish the Merthyr Proprietary School. Penydarren House had been rented for the purpose and it was turned into a school to house boarders and day pupils, with tuition fees ranging from six pounds to twelve pounds a year. T.C. Fawcett, MA was appointed headmaster. The proprietors included W.H. Daniel, chairman of the School Board. The school operated for twelve years, closing in 1888 through lack of funds.

Among the far-reaching recommendations of the Aberdare Report was one calling for the introduction of higher grade schools in Wales. In 1882, this move was sanctioned in a circular to boards in the industrialised areas, from A.J. Mundella, vice-president of the Council in Gladstone's second ministry.

Merthyr's board needed no coaxing. The assiduous clerk to the Board, Edwin Stephens, prepared a detailed study on higher grade schools. The Board decided to set aside the Caedraw school to accommodate three hundred boys and girls. A fee of ninepence a week was to be charged, compared with twopence a week for elementary education. Fears were expressed that this fee would prevent working class children from participating in this more advanced form of education, so the Board established twenty scholarships to add to the nine offered by private individuals.

Interest in Dowlais led the Board to set up an advanced school in rooms adjoining Gwernllwyn Chapel. G.T. Clark of the Dowlais Iron Company agreed to pay the rent for two years and to provide desks, cleaning, fuel and light. W.A. Potter, BA of Bradford was appointed head at Caedraw, whilst the Dowlais school had George Fleming, MA of Galashiels as its head teacher.

From the beginning, Caedraw Higher Grade school was desperately overcrowded, with classes spilling over into adjacent vestries and temporary buildings. There were no specialist rooms or laboratories and after a time there was pressure for the schools to revert to their elementary purpose and for the advanced school to be moved to a new site. A location was found near Pontmorlais Circus but declared unsuitable. Then the Board's activities in this direction ground to a halt with the announcement in 1900 of the Cockerton Judgement which disallowed certain expenditure on higher grade and evening school work.

The rapid expansion in the education service had highlighted the need to prepare large numbers of teachers for the local schools. By 1883, for example, in addition to eight headmasters, sixteen headmistresses, two certificated male assistants, three certificated female assistants, eight uncertificated male assistants, and twenty-seven uncertificated female assistants, there were fifty pupil teachers and fifty monitors employed by the Board.

The headteachers had charge of thirty pupils, the assistants for standard IV upwards forty pupils whilst those teaching lower standards fifty pupils apiece; pupil teachers had thirty pupils to a class. The role of the monitors was to help throughout the school.

The pupil teachers, pursuing a four-year preparatory course, attended classes on two evenings a week and one Saturday morning, studying a variety of subjects including school management. In 1889 these classes were centralised at Abermorlais school. During school hours, the pupil teachers' heads were expected to instruct them in reading, writing, penmanship and spelling.

In 1894 the system was improved when day classes were arranged for pupil teachers at Morlais Hall, at the foot of the British Tip, in the care of T.H. Kemp, D. George and Mrs. J.E. Jenkins. By 1900 no fewer than 188 students were attending the Pupil Teachers' Centre, including some from the voluntary schools and the Vaynor Board. In that year, there were 423 teachers employed by the Merthyr Board, including 119 pupil teachers. Morlais Hall by then was bursting at the seams.

Although the Higher Grade school was providing some post-elementary education, there was a growing demand for a school that would prepare pupils for entry to the developing university colleges, a school intermediate between elementary and university education. The Aberdare Report had called for these in 1880 but it was 1889 before the Welsh Intermediate Education Act passed through Parliament. Merthyr immediately offered the Caedraw school to the recently elected Glamorgan County Council, for use as an intermediate school. However, Glamorgan, Monmouthshire, Cardiff and Swansea had jointly agreed to keep higher grade schools as a separate entity.

A building costing £2,700 and a freehold site were needed but efforts to raise sufficient donations for an intermediate school failed. To the rescue, however, came the Technical Instruction Act which had passed through Parliament almost simultaneously with the Welsh Intermediate Education Act. This enabled the Council to raise a penny rate for technical education. A further unexpected source of funds was the Local Taxation Act of 1890 which allowed certain duties on beer and spirits, soon to be known as 'whisky money' to be used for technical or intermediate education.

Thus financed from a variety of sources, Merthyr Intermediate School was opened on 12 October 1896 with 35 boys and 17 girls in attendance. The headmaster was Charles Owen MA. With the development of the Central Welsh Board, it became possible to submit candidates for Junior, Senior, Higher and Honours certificates. There were also technical and commercial examinations available. The school got off to a good start; in the summer of 1900, its pupils took three of the first five places in the competition for County exhibitions. In 1909 the school gained more CWB certificates than any other in Glamorgan.

However, success tended to be concentrated in a narrow range of academic subjects. It was not until 1911 that a pupil was to offer all science subjects. When A.J. Perman took over as head in 1904, he proposed that after three years of general education a pupil should have a choice between a classical education leading to university or a profession, and a commercial or technical education.

Following the 1902 Education Act, the Merthyr School Board was dissolved, control of education passing firstly to the Glamorgan County Council and eventually returning to the County Borough Council after 1908. At this time, St. David's National School in the town centre was closed. It was also planned to rehouse the overcrowded Caedraw Higher Grade school in a temporary building across the river in Rhydycar, prior to a new building being constructed in Twynyrodyn.

During the early years of this century however, there was a movement against the extension of higher grade schools, on the grounds that they were likely to perpetuate rigid class divisions. The NUT president, Mr. Pickles, addressing a meeting in Zoar Chapel in 1907 advocated instead the founding of Municipal Secondary schools. The idea was enthusiastically received in Merthyr.

The intermediate school was already becoming overcrowded and in addition the Pupil Teachers' Centre had had to move to Zoar vestry. Consequently, the Council decided to review the provision of secondary education in Merthyr. It was proposed to utilise Cyfarthfa Castle as municipal secondary schools for 200 boys and 300 girls, with a technical school to be built in the Park. The Caedraw school would then close and the activities of the Pupil Teacher Centre be abandoned in favour of the Bursar System, whereby the teachers-to-be would attend secondary school.

Major structural alterations were instituted to convert Cyfarthfa Castle into a boys' and a girls' school, which would be free of fees. It was found that it was impossible to include a technical school in the plan, but it was hoped to provide facilities for technical instruction. The schools opened in 1913.

Whilst the years before the first World War saw a stress on the development of secondary education, further education also raced ahead, spurred on by the prosperity of the expanded population of Edwardian Merthyr. There were for example, in 1908, nearly three thousand students attending technical and evening continuation classes at fifteen centres throughout the new County Borough. In 1908, also, steps were taken to appoint the first full time organiser of evening classes. The need for a technical college, first recognised during the lifetime of the school board, remained unsatisfied.

The early years of the county borough also saw a rapid extension in primary school provision, since the population was growing by one thousand a year. Pantglas girls' and infants' schools were opened in 1908, Penydarren infants' opened in 1909 for 400 children and the same year a start was made on a new infants' school for Dowlais. Extensive additions were made to Pant, Clwydyfagwr, Merthyr Vale, Treharris and Twynyrodyn schools. In 1909 the boys of the town area were housed in temporary buildings in Pontmorlais, following the closure of St. David's National school. Such was the increase in the number of children to be educated that there were relief schoolrooms in many parts of the borough.

In 1909 the Quakers' Yard truant school became known as an industrial school, with Merthyr being responsible for fifteen of the seventy-five beds in the institution. The County school also changed its title – to the Intermediate and Technical school. The county borough on taking over responsibility for the school, paid for repairs and improvements and utilised its powers to provide scholarships, bursaries and allowances so that there were as many free places as possible. For example, in 1911 there were about fifty per cent free places. Those not granted a free place had to pay £3 a year.

At the end of the first World War, the Cyfarthfa and the Intermediate schools were very crowded and, acknowledging the distribution of the borough's population, the council sought a site for a new secondary school at the lower end of the valley. It was decided to erect a temporary structure at Quakers Yard. Thirteen army huts were purchased for £1,300 on Salisbury Plain and re-erected by unemployed ex-servicemen. Despite a worsening economic situation, the school was ready for occupation in January 1922.

From 1933 the four schools, the Intermediate, Quakers' Yard and the two Cyfarthfa schools operated in a system which provided a relatively high proportion of selective secondary places. The Education Committee had also shown a quick response to the Hadow Report which had recommended 'modern' schools or classes for senior children who were not attending the selective schools. The Depression which prevented the authority from erecting new schools for this purpose, also produced surplus elementary accommodation, brought about by the steady exodus from the borough.

The Queen's Road schools became boys' and girls' modern schools from 1 January 1934. The Town and Dowlais schools were re-organised from January 1936, Troedyrhiw from 1939 and Pantglas from 1940. The outbreak of war prevented re-organisation in Treharris.

Despite a number of attempts, Merthyr had remained for some years the only Welsh county borough without a technical school. However, moves were made to establish technical institutes in various districts within the South Wales coalfield, financed by a levy of one penny per ton on coal. Quakers Yard was chosen as a suitable site for a mining institute and a building was erected alongside the secondary school and opened in February 1929. The building was extended in 1936 and the following year a junior technical school was opened.

The level of unemployment among young people in the 'twenties caused a juvenile instruction centre to be opened in 1928. It was first housed in a building alongside the Town Hall but later moved to specially constructed premises at the rear of the YMCA. Its initial grant was for fifteen weeks; it remained operative for fifteen years. It was later supplemented by the Home Training Centre located at the Gwaelodygarth Settlement, aimed at preparing girls for work in domestic service. This settlement and the one at Dowlais carried out stirling work both socially and educationally during this grim period.

In the light of the 1944 Education Act, development plans were prepared for education in post-war Merthyr Tydfil. One of the most significant proposals for secondary education was to group future secondary schools in pairs, a grammar school and a non-grammar school, on the same site. However, a lack of suitable sites made implementation difficult. A site in Troedyrhiw was approved to replace the Quakers Yard Grammar and Technical school – a merger having taken place in 1955.

The merger had come about because the technical institute at Quakers Yard had been replaced by the newly constructed Merthyr Tydfil College of further education. The latter had been started in 1950 with the construction of a workshop block at Ynysfach. The main block was begun in 1952 and officially opened by Mr. S.O. Davies, MP in December 1955. Further blocks were added in 1964, 1966 and 1977, whilst the old county school also was turned over to technical education on becoming vacant.

This had occurred due to a change in the climate of opinion as to selection for secondary education. It was agreed to replace all secondary schools with comprehensive schools. The Afon Taf High School was opened in September 1967 and selection abandoned in the lower valley. The same year, a new era of Roman Catholic education was initiated with the opening of Bishop Hedley High school, servicing not only Merthyr but also adjoining districts in the Heads of the Valleys area.

It was decided that all secondary pupils would attend comprehensive schools from September 1970. Although the County Grammar school and several secondary modern schools had been replaced by Pen-y-dre High school, which was completed in 1973, Cyfarthfa High school had to come into being using the existing schools in Georgetown and the Cyfarthfa Castle, pending construction of a new school at Caer-mari-dwn in Thomastown.

The final years of the County Borough saw educational development in several directions. New primary schools were erected; nursery education was extended and an outdoor pursuit centre established at Dolygaer in 1971. Purpose-built youth centres were erected at Pen-y-dre in 1967 and at Afan Taf in 1971.

On the 1 April 1974, control of the technical college, the comprehensive schools, the special school, the primary schools, the youth centres, the outdoor pursuit centre and the various services for education, passed to the new county of Mid Glamorgan, of which Merthyr Tydfil, enlarged by the addition of Vaynor and Bedlinog, was one of six districts. Merthyr Tydfil presented to the infant county a proud tradition of progress and innovation in education, born out of a profound recognition of the value of education to the spiritual and physical well-being of its people.

Bibliography

Theses

J. Fletcher, 'A Study of the Development of Further Education in Merthyr Tydfil', Unpublished M.Ed. dissertation, University of Wales (1972).

A.W. Howells, 'Secondary Education in Merthyr Tydfil from 1881', Unpublished M.Ed. dissertation, University of Wales (1972).

Printed Source

J. Fletcher, *A Technical Triumph: One Hundred Years of Public Further Education in Merthyr Tydfil 1873-1973,* Merthyr Tydfil Corporation (1975).

Reports

Merthyr School Board. Triennial Reports 1871-1903.
Merthyr Tydfil Urban District Council – Minutes.
Merthyr Tydfil Borough Council – Minutes.
Merthyr Tydfil County Borough Council – Minutes.

Eminent Men and Women

by GWYNNETH E. EVANS

Stephen Owen Davies, MP, BA (Econ)

Affectionately known as 'S.O.' Stephen Owen Davies was born in 39 John Street, Abercwmboi, Aberdare, in 1886, into a mining family whose father was victimised for agitating for miners' rights.

By the age of twelve he had left Cap Goch School, Abercwmboi to become a miner in Mountain Ash Colliery – and an early rebel.

Never having the benefit of Secondary Education, he matriculated through evening-class studies after his day's work in the mine.

He prepared for the Ministry by studying Greek and Hebrew, but his unorthodoxy in Christianity denied him acceptance at Brecon Memorial College.

He turned to economics and obtained his BA (Econ) degree at University College, Cardiff.

Returning to mining at the Great Mountain Colliery, Tumble, Carmarthenshire, though having secured a Colliery Manager's Certificate, he refused the status, preferring to remain with the workers as a Mining Engineer, fighting the private ownership of the mines.

In 1918, 'S.O.' became a Miners' Agent and lived with his first wife, the former Madge Eley, whom he had met at University, and their three daughters at Gwent House, Dowlais.

He became a member of the Executive Committee of the South Wales Miners' Federation and subsequently , its Vice-President.

In the late 1920s, so many of his district's miners became unemployed, 'S.O.' refused to accept his full salary as Miners' Agent.

In 1934, the widowed S.O. married Sophora, the daughter of David Daniel Davies, Miners' Leader for Gwauncaegurwen and a member of Glamorgan County Council for approximately thirty-six years. Miss Davies was a former English teacher at Quakers Yard Grammar School. The family now moved to 'Haddington', The Grove, Merthyr.

In June 1934, S.O. became the Labour Member of Parliament for Merthyr Tydfil. He won his first election, a four-cornered contest with Communist, Liberal and ILP, by a vast majority.

Annual salary for MP's in his early Parliamentary days was a meagre £400. With three daughters from his first marriage and a son, Alun, born in 1935, from his second, S.O. found it impossible to maintain a home in Merthyr and London, so in 1937 the family moved to London, where it remained until wartime bombing drove it back to 'Gwynfryn', Park Terrace, Merthyr, in 1940. A second son, David, was born in 1943.

A source of pride to S.O. was the winning of a ballot for a Parliamentary Bill, for which he chose 'The Better Government of Wales' – the forerunner of 'Self-Government for Wales'. The Bill was outvoted because of the Government's refusal to sponsor it since it was not in its current plan.

Always inspired by opposition, S.O. considered his 1970 election his most interesting. The Labour Party would not sponsor him as an official candidate – ostensibly on grounds of age – but in effect on grounds of his being too left-wing and the number of ambitious candidates seeking Parliamentary seats. Characteristically S.O. campaigned as an Independent Labour candidate and regained his seat with a majority of more than 7,000 the official Labour Party conceding defeat early in the count.

At his death on 25 February 1972, Stephen Owen Davies had completed thirty-eight years' Parliamentary service to Merthyr. Aspiring Minister of Religion, a tenacious rebel and Parliamentarian, he had worked for seventy-four of his eighty-six years, the majority being dedicated to public service.

Lady Charlotte Guest

Born Lady Charlotte Bertie, in 1812, to the English Ninth Earl of Lindsay, and raised a socialite, Lady Charlotte became the second wife of widowed ironmaster John Josiah Guest in 1833. With a husband forty-eight years her senior, she came to live in Dowlais.

Youth and enthusiasm for living helped her quickly to identify with the totally new Welsh industrial environment.

In spite of bearing ten children, Charlotte found time to assist her husband in his business transactions, working as his secretary, writing his innumerable letters and their copies in longhand and keeping his business records.

After her husband became a Member of Parliament an even busier life was shared between Dowlais and London.

She enthusiastically supported her husband's endeavours to improve social and educational opportunities for the community created by the Dowlais ironworks.

Dowlais Parish Church, the old Dowlais Central Schools and the Guest Memorial Library became public testimonies to the couple's generosity.

Further evidence of Lady Charlotte's affinity with Welsh life was her industrious study of the Welsh language. Such became her proficiency that her translation into English of the old Welsh romantic stories, the 'Mabinogion', published in 1849, still figures prominently in English classical literature.

Created Sir John Josiah Guest, Lady Charlotte's husband died in 1852 and soon afterwards she left Dowlais, though continued to visit the area into old age.

As her eldest son, Ivor, approached University age, Lady Charlotte had engaged a tutor for him. He was Charles Schreiber. In 1855 she married Schrieber, who also became a Member of Parliament. Under the terms of her late husband's will, remarriage meant the forfeiture of any power in the iron industry, which she had previously enjoyed, and the sole legal guardianship of her children. Consequently, though they still continued, her visits to Dowlais became less frequent.

In 1867, as Lady Charlotte Schreiber, she laid the foundation stone of the former British Schools, subsequently renamed Abermorlais Schools.

Though still referred to locally as Lady Charlotte Guest, benefactress and translator of the 'Mabinogion', her fame as Lady Charlotte Schreiber is also recognised for bequests of china to the Victoria and Albert Museum, and fans and playing cards to the British Museum.

Penry Williams

In 1800, in a small cottage in Ynysfach, behind where Merthyr Tydfil's Technical College now stands, Penry Williams was born to the family of a housepainter.

The flourishing local ironworks and the Merthyr Riots of 1816 provided the striking artistic genius he showed with its opportunity.

Serving an apprenticeship to a local printer, Penry Williams' genius at the age of sixteen was recognised by ironmaster William Crawshay through his pictures of Ynysfach and the 1816 Riots.

Together, Mr. William Crawshay, Sir John Guest and Sir Joseph Bailey sent the young artist to study at the Royal Academy of Art under Sir Thomas Lawrence.

At 22 years of age, he travelled to Rome to study the art of the Italian masters.

Quiet in personality, Penry Williams became famous for pictures of Italian peasantry. All his work was produced with such thorough preparatory sketches finely drawn and his finished work was so colourful, he soon earned undisputed success.

His representation of a religious procession seen near Naples and called 'Festa of the Madonna del Arco' is considered his masterpiece; 'General View of the Iron Works at Merthyr Tydfil' (1820) and 'Swansea Town and

Bay' (1825) and three drawings made for the daughter of William Crawshay II – 'Cyfarthfa Works Furnaces', 'View from Cyfarthfa Castle' and 'Pont-y-Capel' – all dated 1820, are among his most famous works.

Living most of his life in Rome, he made occasional visits to Britain and on one visit was in Merthyr Tydfil during the Riots of 1831.

He died in Rome in 1885, having attracted by his genius throughout his lifetime, such illustrious visitors as Sir Walter Scott (1832) and the Prince of Wales (1853).

His deaf mute brother had also shown artistic genius, but an early death robbed him of his opportunity.

Though an Italian domicile, it must not be forgotten that the acclaimed artistic genius, Penry Williams, was born and spent the first sixteen years of his life in Merthyr Tydfil.

James Keir Hardie

Politician and journalist James Keir Hardie was born on 15th August, 1856, at Legbrannock, near Holytown, Lanarkshire.

Impoverished conditions saw him working at seven years, his education restricted to evening parental tuition.

A six-month lock-out of Clyde shipworkers made Hardie's weekly 4/6d. as a rivet-heater the family's sole income.

At twenty he was a skilled miner and experienced quarryman.

Following his own and two younger brothers' boycott at No. 4 Quarter Pit, Hardie made his reputation as an agitator feared by colliery managers.

In 1879 he became a Miners' Agent in Scotland, in 1884 National Secretary and an active Liberal Party member.

Having formed an Ayrshire Miners' Union in 1886, he became its Organising Secretary. By 1887 he was Secretary of the newly-formed Scottish Miners' Federation and involved in the adoption of a resolution recognising the urgent need for a Labour Party in the House of Commons.

Failing adoption by the Mid-Lanark Liberal Association in 1888, Hardie stood unsuccessfully as the first ever Parliamentary Independent Labour candidate.

An ardent advocate for Scottish Home Rule, in 1892, four years after the formation of the Scottish Parliamentary Labour Party, Hardie succeeded as Independent Member for West Ham, making his first Commons speech on 7th February, 1893.

In 1900, while unsuccessfully contesting Preston, Hardie was adopted Merthyr's candidate. Desperate to retain the Labour seat, local campaigners ensured his return as Junior Member for Merthyr Tydfil.

A firm advocate of the Co-operative Movement, in 1901 he put down the first complete Socialist declaration in the House, calling for common ownership of land and capital and equal opportunity for every citizen

He held the Merthyr Tydfil seat in 1906.

In the January and December General Elections of 1910 he again held Merthyr, representing the town until he died on 26th September, 1915.

During the miners' strike which originated in Rhondda, he attacked the Home Secretary and War Minister for having sent the Military into Tonypandy and Aberaman.

He was a Boer War anti-militarist and immediately before the 1914-1918 War he was still urging the downfall of class rule, the peaceful rule of the people and warning against conscription.

During the Dowlais Ironworks dispute for quality of pay among identical firms and recognition of Trade Unionism, Hardie pressurized the Government on the Fair Wages Clause, causing Guest, Keen and Nettlefolds to concede the employees' demands in order to retain their foreign contracts.

His last recorded Parliamentary speech opposed the relaxation of educational by-laws during the 1914-1918 War to allow employment of children under twelve in agriculture. He saw their education curtailment as the provision of cheap labour rather than the release of men for war-service.

Lay Preacher, anti-militarist, supporter of Women's Rights, anti-monarchist and pioneer of Socialism, Hardie strove for the abolition of class, improved conditions for the workers and for action on the needs of Wales.

To his death, Hardie's rigid motivation was 'Loyalty to the Working Class'.

Dr. Joseph Parry

Joseph Parry was born in Chapel Row, Georgetown, on 21 May 1841, to Daniel Parry (Pembrokeshire) and Elisabeth Bett (Carmarthenshire), a relative of Merthyr's Member of Parliament Henry Richard. He was the seventh of eight children.

At nine he worked as a pit-boy in Pwll Robbling, joining his father in Cyfarthfa Ironworks puddling mill at twelve.

When he was thirteen the family sailed from Cardiff to join Daniel Parry, already in Danville, Pennsylvania.

Working in the rolling mills there, he studied music under Merthyr's John Abel Jones and Rhymney's J.M. Price.

His musicianship emerged through the eisteddfod, first at a Danville Eisteddfod with his composition 'A Temperance Vocal March'.

Public funds provided a term's study at Normal College, Genesse, New York State, in 1861. Appointments as church organist launched his professional career.

Successfully he submitted for the 1863 Swansea National Eisteddfod, using the nom-de-plume 'Bachgen Bach o Ferthyr, Erioed, Erioed', again winning all the prizes at the Llandudno National Eisteddfod in 1864.

Attending the adjudication at the 1865 Aberystwyth 'National', he found his entries had never arrived, among them the famous 'Ar Don o Flaen Gwyntoedd'.

His competitive career ended with the success of his cantata 'The Prodigal Son' in Chester in 1866.

The Aberystwyth Eisteddfod Committee offered him a year's general tuition under Dr. Evan Davies, Swansea, followed by a year at the Royal Academy. A dependent wife and child caused him to refuse.

But American friends provided the necessary financial aid. In August 1868, Joseph brought his family to Britain and pursued three years' study at the Academy – composition under Sterndal Bennett, vocal under Manuel Garcia, organ under Dr. Stegall. He won the bronze medal for composition, followed by the highly prized silver medal, presented by Mrs. Gladstone.

Obtaining his 'Mus.Bac.' from the Academy and his Doctorate in Music in 1878, using a hundred strong Aberdare choir for the required performance of his oratorio 'Jerusalem', he is believed to be the first Welshman to obtain these degrees.

Joseph had returned to America after taking his Mus.Bac., but permanently returned to Wales in 1874, as Professor of Music at University College of Wales, Aberystwyth.

In 1880 he opened a school of music in Swansea, accepting the Chair of Music at Cardiff University College of Wales in 1888.

His compositions number over 400 hymn tunes, including the famous 'Aberystwyth', 300 anthems, chorales, glees, choruses and orchestral works, 26 complete works, nine of them operas.

Among his best-known works are his famous opera 'Blodwen', oratorios 'Emmanuel' and 'Saul of Tarsus', and 'The Maid of Cefn Ydfa'. His last, unfinished work was 'Iesu o Nazareth'.

In 1888 Joseph published the first of an intended series of books in Welsh on 'The Theory of Music' for young musicians, also editing a national collection of Welsh songs in six volumes, published in 1893, called 'Cambrian Minstrelsie'.

Post-operative complications caused his death on 17 February 1903. He was buried where he then lived in Penarth.

Henry Seymour Berry – Lord Buckland of Bwlch

Henry Seymour Berry – Baron Buckland of Bwlch, William Ewart Berry – Baron Camrose of Long Cross, and James Gomer – Sir Gomer Berry, Bart, were the sons of Alderman John Mathias Berry, JP, of Gwaelodygarth, Merthyr Tydfil, a devoted public servant and Mayor of the town in 1912 when the King and Queen first visited it.

Lord Camrose and Sir Gomer Berry became successful London newspaper proprietors, but their eldest brother, Henry Seymour, remained in Merthyr for the greater part of his life, becoming a great influence later on British business life.

Born in 1877, Lord Buckland was educated at Abermorlais School and the Higher Grade, intending to become a teacher. Though he commenced training for this career, he soon entered his father's business as an auctioneer and estate agent. His rapid grasp of the business soon made him a partner and when his father retired, he became the business head.

At the outbreak of World War I Henry Seymour volunteered for military service. When Lord Rhondda received an invitation to become a Cabinet Minister, he chose Henry Seymour to take over his business responsibilities. Berry's brilliant business acumen indirectly contributed valuable service to Britain in a time of emergency by freeing Lord Rhondda for his Cabinet duties. This brilliance was later recognised by Lloyd George at the Conference of the Freedom of Merthyr Tydfil on Henry Seymour Berry.

When peace was restored, Berry's wartime reputation brought countrywide industrial controllers in search of his services and the directorship of more than eighty public and other companies.

His chief concern was iron, steel and coal. His foresight brought about the amalgamation and reorganisation of many businesses and eventually he became director and chairman of Guest, Keen and Nettlefolds, in which capacity he ensured the greatest possible employment for the men and boys of the Merthyr Borough.

In spite of his consuming business commitments, he devoted every effort to public good. His contributions to Merthyr Tydfil were the building of the Gwaunfarren Swimming Baths for the boys and girls of the town, two new wards at the General Hospital – the Buckland and Berry Wards – and the provision of financial aid for college and university education for the local youth, as well as anonymous monetary aid for the distressed.

In 1923 Merthyr Town Council recognised Lord Buckland's public service by making him the third Honorary Freeman of the Borough.

To celebrate this honour a fete was organised in Cyfarthfa Park to raise funds for the General Hospital, with Lord Buckland as President.

In 1923 he left his home at Gwaelodygarth for his new estate in the Usk valley at Bwlch.

In 1926 King George V conferred upon him a Barony of the United Kingdom and from his new estate's name he became known as Lord Buckland of Bwlch.

His interest in Merthyr was not diminished by his removal from the town. To prevent dereliction of the mines and to provide employment for Merthyr miners, he bought Plymouth Collieries.

His sudden death in 1928 due to a riding accident at Bwlch aroused national dismay. Thousands whom he had served contributed financially for the addition of the Buckland Wing at Merthyr General Hospital as a memorial to a man, the loss of whose business genius and public service spirit was greatly felt in the adversities which followed. Goscombe John's

(RA) statue outside the Public Library became a further perpetuation of his memory.

Though only fifty-two when he died, he left a record of business brilliance, of service to his town and country and of an overwhelming concern for and generosity towards his fellowmen, particularly those of the town of his birth.

He has no grave. His body was cremated and the ashes returned for scattering on his estate.

Jack Jones

Born in Tai Harri Blawd, behind the Theatre Royal, Jack was the ninth surviving of fifteen children born to David and Sarah Jones.

Often missing from St. David's School to run his mother's errands, he was virtually self-educated.

At twelve he worked at the coalface and by the 1898 strike was a member of the Miners' Union.

Serving with the Army in South Africa at the end of the Boer War he deserted, but was recaptured and sent to India's North West Frontier.

His marriage in 1908 to Laura Gremes of Builth Wells was nearly broken by a gambling fever, but it survived for thirty-nine years.

As an Army Reservist he was called up at the outbreak of World War I and after one day's training served in France and the Retreat from Mons. For attempting to save a wounded colleague at Ypres he was mentioned in despatches. Finally invalided out of active service, Jack became a Recruiting Officer in Merthyr.

Post-war disillusionment drove him to Communism. As Miners' Secretary-Representative in Blaengarw he was expelled from the Party for indulgence in cultural activities and in 1923 joined the Labour Party.

In Blaengarw he wrote 'Dad's Double' which won him £3 in a Manchester one-act play-writing competition.

Vociferous exhortation of Miners' Leaders from 1926-1928 prompted an invitation from Lloyd George to become a Liberal Staff-Speaker and an unsuccessful attempt to become Liberal MP for Neath. By 1930 the Liberals had dismissed him. He was unemployed.

His attempts to earn enough to keep his family as a platform speaker for Mosley's Party and as a salesman failed. He had to rely on Public Assistance.

The urge to write became increasingly powerful though far from successful until the publication of his novel 'Rhondda Roundabout' in 1934.

'Black Parade' appeared in 1935 and through his play 'Land of My Fathers' (1937) he discovered his opportunity on radio as writer, actor and reader.

'Bidden to the Feast' (1938) was adapted for theatrical production and by 1939 he was commissioned to write the film script for 'Proud Valley', starring Paul Robeson, with himself in a minor role.

Broken health, the deaths of his son Lawrence from war wounds in 1942, shortly afterwards, his mother, his wife in 1946 and in 1948 his son David caused lost confidence and loneliness.

The award of the CBE for service to the community and literary achievement strengthened him somewhat.

One of his best works was the first of an autobiographical trilogy, 'Unfinished Journey'. This was followed between 1946 and 1951 by the other two volumes – 'Me and Mine' and 'Give Me Back My Heart', plus three novels – 'Off to Philadelphia in the Morning', 'Some Trust in Chariots' and 'River Out of Eden'.

At 65 he collapsed in Philadelphia while promoting Moral Rearmanent in America, it being some time before he recovered sufficiently to return home.

By 1954 he wrote chiefly press articles and radio scripts.

His second marriage to widowed Cardiff library-assistant Gladys Morgan brought him the peace and comfort for which he longed.

Abundant experience produced an undisciplined verbosity in his literary rebellion against the conditions of his fellowmen, but in February 1970, he received a £700 Arts Council award for his contribution to Welsh Literature.

Jack Jones died on 7 May 1970.

Rose Mary Crawshay

At eighteen, Rose Mary Yeates married Robert Thompson Crawshay at St. Peter's Church, Coversham, on 15 May 1846.

A gifted organiser, the new mistress of Cyfarthfa Castle soon corrected domestic laxity and waste. Surplus vegetables provided soup and for thirty-three years, thirty tickets for free soup were issued three times weekly to the needy.

Among material and cultural benefits for Robert's employees and their families, she personally advanced and maintained heated, free libraries in Merthyr and Cefn Coed, which opened seven days a week, and free literary and musical entertainment for the workers in a room at Cyfarthfa Ironworks.

She gave birth to William (1847), Rose Harriet (1848), Henrietta Louise (1851), Robert (1855) and Richard Frederick (1859).

In January 1860, her husband became completely deaf following a stroke, and though she did all she could to help him, his persistent obsession with his health widened the rift which had opened with his interest in local girls. Rose spent increasing periods discussing philosophy, literature and women's rights with London friends and visiting libraries and museums in London, and studying painting and sculpture in Rome.

Very concerned about the unemployment of governesses, declaring domestic work should not be considered degrading, she financed an agency for their employment as lady helps, personally administering it until 1880, after which it developed into a registry for governesses and ordinary servants.

The practical Rose chose her friends for their stimulus and originality, one being oil-seller Thomas Norbury, a widely-read, self-taught astronomer, whose gravestone she ultimately provided in Vaynor churchyard in 1872.

Her very advanced beliefs included cremation, euthanasia, women's rights (though not for her daughters) and the approaching disappearance of the division between the idle rich and workers.

She was prepared to be cremated in one of the works' furnaces. Only after cremation was permitted in Britain did she cancel a £200 payment to ensure the removal of her body to Dresden, where cremation had earlier been legalised.

She became the only woman in the eleven member first Merthyr School Board in 1871. Her talent and culture attracted to Cyfarthfa Castle such illustrious visitors as Emerson, Charles Darwin, Herbert Spencer, Robert Owen, Dean Stanley, Sir Henry Irving and Robert Browning.

The currently existent Rose Mary Crawshay Prize for English Literature was founded by Rose in 1882 with a personal endowment of £2,000. This annual award is made to any female of any nationality for literary work, preferably on Byron, Shelley and Keats. In 1892 she also endowed three Art prizes for work connected with these poets.

Until 1878, Robert Crawshay excluded his wife from his will, but finally bequeathed her his carriages, saddle horses, with furniture and harnesses, plus £1,000, before he died in 1879.

After Robert's death Rose moved to Cathedine, near Llangorse Lake, where she died on 2 June 1907. She was cremated in Golders Green.

Religion

by Rev. NOEL GIBBARD

Saint Tudful was the daughter of a native prince of Brychan. According to tradition she was martyred at Merthyr, and the parish church which dates from the fourteenth century, was dedicated to her memory. It was part of the one church in the West, with the Pope as its supreme head. Nothing happened to break the unity of this Church until Henvry VIII broke with Rome. Even then the people of Wales accepted quietly the system imposed upon them by Henry, and never experienced any profound spiritual upheaval. Edward VI made further reform possible, and his system was finalised by Elizabeth I. It was represented by the Crown, the Bishop and the Book of Common Prayer.

During Elizabeth's reign an attempt was made in many districts to provide more places of worship for the people. The parishioners of Merthyr built a chapel near Troed-y-rhiw, but before the middle of the seventeenth century it was a dwelling place. However the parish church in the town safeguarded the middle way of Elizabeth, which avoided the extremes of Roman Catholicism on the one hand, and the extremes of Puritanism on the other. The Catholics wanted to keep the link with Rome, but the Queen demanded an oath of allegiance from her subjects, and made herself 'Supreme Governor' of the church in England.

According to Anglican thought, all parishioners belonged to the church, and the order was perpetuated by baptizing all children. The church was thought of in territorial terms. It was also a natural unit of civil administration. The Vestry was responsible for arranging the elements of the Lord's Supper, the church building, and matters like the condition of the poor. All men were involved directly, or indirectly, in the life of the church and the parish. Tithes and church rates were expected from the people, whatever they thought of the new Anglican set up. Eventually these payments led to bitter struggles between Anglicans and Nonconformists.

The Puritans emerged during the early years of Elizabeth's reign. By the second decade of her rule, they were a formidable influence in the land. They thought that the Queen had stopped short of what was truly Scriptural. They wanted to continue with the work of reformation, some advocating reform from within, and others urging separation from the Anglican church. During his life, John Penry held both views in turn, changing from Presbyterianism, which represented change from within, to Separatism.

It is impossible to give an exact date to the beginning of Puritan activity in Merthyr. Although 1620 has been suggested, there is no documentary evidence to support this date. Most probably it commenced before Cromwell came to power, but it was during his rule that the work was really established. During that period there was no bishop, king, or Book of Common Prayer, and the Puritans enjoyed a liberty denied them by Elizabeth and the early Stuarts. Being able to worship openly, they used the parish church as their centre. They emphasised however that the congregation was a company of believers, called out of the world, and gathered together to worship God.

The Puritans became a thorn in the flesh for Nathan Jones (1603-63), the Rector of Merthyr, who in spite of his opposition to reform, retained his position under Cromwell. The Rector bears witness to puritan activity in Merthyr. According to him an all out attempt was made to disrupt the work of the minister and the church. Horses were taken into the church during the wedding of one of the Puritan preachers. Three of the church bells were sold, and the boys in the school did much damage to the lead. The reformers behaved most rudely during the sermon; interrupting the minister, and would even pull him out of the pulpit. The minister was refused tithe money, which made it very difficult for him to sustain his wife and seven children. Sometimes when he was preaching a puritan would preach outside under the yew tree. Jones says that some of these were 'lay preachers', and belonged to 'all tribes and traders.' That is, they were not ordained men, but having the gift of exposition they would comment on a passage of Scripture.

A deliberate spoiling policy was adopted. But all Puritans were not the same, and not all would agree on the methods to achieve their ends. The Quakers thrived on interrupting meetings, but others were not so militant. It is quite possible also that others with no real puritan interest, took advantage of the situation to further their own ends. Nathan Jones himself disliked the Puritans, and would be rather biased in his opinion. This does not in any way cast doubt on Jones' reliability, but it does suggest that he could be prone to exaggeration. If there was a negative element to this work, the positive contribution was the emphasis on preaching in a period when it was sadly lacking, and the serious attempt to grapple with the nature of the church.

The most prominent leader was Jenkin Jones of Llanddety, a Baptist, but who was for open communion between Baptists and Independents. He cast his pastoral eye over the people of Llanigon, Breckonshire, and Merthyr Tydfil. One of his supporters was Captain Henry Williams, who 'knew only the Welch toung.' He was an Independent, and like Jones was for open communion. Both refused to be paid out of tithe money. Other names mentioned at this time are Edward Jenkins, an Independent, and Howell Lewis, Blaencanaid, a Baptist.

With the return of the King in 1660, and with him the bishop, and the Book of Common Prayer, the Puritans were in difficulties again. The Act of Uniformity (1662); the Conventicle Act (1664), and the Five Mile Act (1665) made it illegal for them to worship according to their conscience. They had to conform, or go into hiding. In the Merthyr district the Puritans found a home at Blaencanaid, a farmhouse on the mountain between Merthyr and Aberdare. But they worshipped in other houses too. In 1669, Captain Henry Williams is referred to as the leader of the Puritans, who had conventicles in the houses of Howell Rees, and Phillip and Joanne John Morgan. In 1672, the Captain had a licence to preach in the house of Howell Rees, according to an order drawn up that year, but the privilege was almost immediately withdrawn.

George Fox must have inspired the Quakers during his visit to Merthyr and Quaker's Yard. They are mentioned in 1661, and in 1669 they met in the houses of Jenkin Thomas, Henry Thomas and Lewis Becke. In spite of their early success, their work did not last, neither in Merthyr nor Quaker's Yard, although there were occasional meetings in the latter place during the eighteenth century, including some in the open air.

One of Jenkin Jones' co-workers in Wales was Vavasor Powell, the greatest of the itinerant preachers. When he arrived in Merthyr (1668) he preached to a large congregation in the churchyard. He took as his text Jeremiah chapter 17, verses 7 and 8, and he described the blessed man. During the service the vicar of Merthyr reported his presence to the magistrates in Cardiff. Soldiers were sent to arrest Powell, and take him to Cardiff goal. The case was taken to Cowbridge, where Powell defended himself with much ability. The main charge against him was that he was an unordained minister. Powell not only refuted this charge, but also revealed the false charges that were brought against him, especially the claim that he had soldiers with him on his preaching tours. On 30 October 1668 he was committed to remain in Cardiff goal, until further arrangements were made to continue with the case. The trial was re started on 8 November, but was again postponed until 13 January 1669, when a writ was obtained to move the trial to London. There he was committeed to prison, where he remained from 24 March 1669 until his death 27 August 1670.

During the period of persecution (1660-1688), the Puritans were like birds in a cage chirping. They could not be silenced, but they were not free. The Act of Toleration (1689) changed their position. It gave them the right to build chapels, and to worship in them, if they and the ministers were licensed. The Dissenters in Merthyr grasped the opportunity, and built a chapel at Cwm-y-glo in 1690. They could settle down now, and concentrate on matters of doctrine and church government. In doing so they tended to be introspective and carnal, losing the missionary zeal of previous days.

As the eighteenth century progressed, two forces clashed on the religious field. On the one side rationalism appealed to the mind, and on the other side enthusiasm appealed to the heart. The majority of the people were superficially religious, and the intellectual arguments of the rationalists did not appeal to them. During the Methodist Revival spiritual forces were released which gripped the hearts of men and women, and moved them to their innermost being. A profound lasting change took place in the life of the nation. Wales was never to be the same again.

Howell Harris was the only Methodist leader who had a fairly close connection with Merthyr. During the early period of the revival he visited the district twice. On 28 March 1739 he visited Vaynor and Cwm-y-glo. His contact was the Rev James Davies, minister of Cwm-y-glo, a Dissenter who deeply sympathised with the Methodists, although later in his ministry he leaned heavily to the Arian persuasion, which was frowned upon by orthodox Methodists and Dissenters. James Davies had invited the Revivalist to Merthyr in a letter dated 13 January 1739, in which he said:

> 'I haste and invite you unfeignedly (if it be not very averse to your inclination) to spend an hour one day again at Rhiw'rychen, another at Gwaelod y Garth, where before at Merthyr whether they will hear or whether they will forbear. If you comply, I will gratefully acknowledge it cordially with a fullness of blessing and your best reward. If so, if it can be near Candlemas, but not that day nor the two before: nay, choose your time, excepting those three days. For I desire to be present and help with warm wishes. Further, if it can be, that you may begin about the hours of 10 or 11.'

Most probably, Harris was too busy to answer the invitation. James Davies wrote to him again on the 3 March, urging the Revivalist to come to Vaynor, Merthyr, Aberdare, and Llanwinio, and informing him that he could stay two nights at Merthyr. Davies was able to report that 'our friends' at Ynystaf had frequent meetings, and that he himself had 'a large and comfortable meeting there.' Harris responded almost immediately to this letter, and arrived at Merthyr 28 March 1739. On 8 April 1740, Harris was at Llangynidr and Merthyr Tydfil. Even towards the end of his days on 17 December 1766, he was at Twyn Waun, near Merthyr Tydfil.

John Wesley had connections with the district, as he would travel from Pontsticill to Gelligaer, and from Penderyn to Cardiff. He also knew Thomas Price, Rector of Merthyr.

The congregation at Cwm-y-glo was divided theologically. One section left in 1747 to build a chapel at Cefn Coed, which eventually became Unitarian. They were ministered to by Richard Rees of Gwernllwyn Uchaf (1707-49), who was educated at Carmarthen Academy. He was the author

Plate 61: HEN DY CWRDD CHAPEL, CEFN COED
(Photograph by Robert Haines)

of a few hymns, and was well known in unorthodox circles. He was one of the key figures in the development of Unitarian theology at Cefn Coed. The tradition was strengthened in the district by the witness of the General

Baptists, led by Henry Evans, but the work was short lived, and their chapel was sold to the Particular Baptists who championed the Calvinistic tradition.

But if the Arminians-Unitarians lost the support of the General Baptists, they were fortunate to have the muse on their side. Sion Llewelyn (1690-1776) was a member at Cwm-y-glo, and left with the Arminians in 1747. Under the influence of the ministers, Roger Williams and Richard Rees, he was convinced of the truth of the Arminian doctrine. In his poetry he condemned Calvinistic doctrine, and exhorted his readers to enthrone reason as the only rule of belief and conduct. His work was widely read, and it is said that it was more influential than the sermons of Richard Rees. His grandson William Harri (Gwilym Garwdyle, 1763-1844), continued the poetic tradition, but he was a better craftsman than his grandfather. Some of his religious compositions won prizes at meetings held by a philosophical society at the Crown, Merthyr, which reveals his sympathy with the radical ideas of his day.

Apart from the cause at Cefn Coed, Arminian tendencies were still found at Ynysgau, where the other section from Cwm-y-glo built a chapel in 1749. Therefore when T.B. Evans, a champion of orthodoxy, came there in 1811, a clash was inevitable. It started in 1812, and soon the matter of trust deed and ownership of the chapel led to a legal case. The Unitarians were brought closer together, and when Mr Wright the Unitarian missionary visited South Wales in 1816, he came to Merthyr twice during his tour. This visit was encouraged by Edward Williams (Iolo Morganwg), whose son Taliesin also supported the cause at Merthyr. During 1820 the Unitarians were appealing for financial help to complete their chapel at Twynrodyn, and it must have been successful because the chapel was opened in 1821. The building served them until 1903, when they moved to Thomas Street.

The first minister at Twynrodyn was David Rees, M.D., but his stay was rather a stormy one. There were tensions between him and the congregation, and he absented himself for a while in Scotland. In 1825, Charles Lloyd, a prominent Unitarian, settled in Merthyr to try and re-establish the work there, but with little success. Yet Lloyd claimed that the most intelligent and influential people supported the cause, which must have been a source of joy for him, as the movement appealed mainly to the mind. The situation improved under the ministry of David John, and the able leadership of Morgan Williams. It was a great asset to the cause also to have visits from Thomas Evans (Thomas Glyn Cothi, 1764-1833), who ministered at Aberdare from 1811/13-33.

All denominations took advantage of the influx of people into the rapidly growing town of Merthyr. At the turn of the eighteenth century, Merthyr was the largest town in South Wales. Many of the newcomers were from rural, Welsh, nonconformist areas, and gave a new lease of life to the cause of nonconformity in Merthyr. This happened in spite of the immorality and degradation associated with the place. Parents in West Wales would warn their children not to go to Merthyr, because whatever they would find there, they would be sure to lose their religion. It was thought of as the Gehenna of Wales. Even morally neutral habits were frowned upon by the rural inhabitants. When David Williams of Troedrhiw dalar, Breckonshire, returned from Merthyr he brought with him a kettle and a teapot. His parents could not understand how their son could have adopted such a worldly habit as tea drinking.

The character of the nonconformist in this new industrial society was forged in the heat of hard work. Daniel Davies, the blind Baptist preacher, lived in Merthyr for a while at the beginning of the nineteenth century. The inhabitants took advantage of his father's good nature, and never paid their debts. He was forced to look for other work, which he had for three shillings a day. Daniel himself started work at the Dowlais Iron Works when he was eleven years old, and earned four shillings a week. He later worked for a dyer, who had originally come from Liverpool. In such circumstances the newcomers were glad of a spiritual home.

Ynysgau was the only chapel in Merthyr until 1788. But the coming of so many people from outside soon changed this situation. The Baptists were greatly indebted to the people of Hengoed. The local leaders of Calvinistic Methodism, Josiah Prosser and Josiah Davies, were from Merthyr, Breckonshire, and Caio, Carmarthenshire respectively. The Congregationalists that met in the Crown Inn (1794), included people from Carmarthen, Breckon, Monmouth and other parts of Glamorgan. At least two of the deacons were from outside the county.

Nonconformity was firmly established in Merthyr during the end of the eighteenth and the beginning of the nineteenth century. The Baptists built Zion in 1788, and Ebenezer in 1794, and the General Baptists had a chapel which they sold to the Particular Baptists in 1813. The Calvinistic Methodists had a place of their own in Pontmorlais in 1793. Congregationalists managed to build Zoar in 1798, and Bethesda in 1807. Lastly the Wesleyans built their chapel in 1796. All but one of these centres were Welsh speaking, and the English Wesleyans worked closely with their brethren the Welsh Wesleyans. Apart from the chapels there were other places registered for worship, and the majority of these also were Welsh causes. Between 1789 and 1850, at least 38 places of worship were licensed in Merthyr, Dowlais, and Penydarren. In Merthyr itself the Baptists and Independents had 10 each; the Calvinistic Methodists 3; the Latter Day Saints 3, and the Wesleyans 1.

During the period 1786 to 1837, 3,524 children were baptized by the Ynysgau ministers. This was an average of 70 per year, kept up for fifty years. The population of Merthyr in 1801 was 7,705, with 1,404 inhabited houses. There was an increase of 4,000 between 1801 and 1811, and during that period Ynysgau would have baptized 700 children. Membership figures could be staggering. During a ministry of thirty years, the Rev Methusalem Jones received 3,000 members into fellowship at Bethesda. This was an average of a 100 per year. The Baptists and Congregationalists continued to be the strongest denominations throughout the century. In Merthyr itself the Baptists had about 1,1500 members in 1865, and the Congregationalists about 1,400.

New causes had to be pioneered in surrounding districts. The Baptists built three or four chapels before 1850, but the real expansion took place between 1850 and 1900, when they erected at least 12 places of worship from Dowlais to Merthyr Vale. The Congregationalists built just one chapel in Merthyr during 1850-1890, but this does not mean that they had been idle. Even before 1850 they had opened 9 new chapels in nearby districts. As a result of such work they could boast about 4,000 members in 1890. But the hearers and the children must be taken into account too. Bethania, Dowlais, had 649 members in 1890, but had 600 children, and 400 hearers, that is those who attended but were not members. Dowlais clearly illustrates the firm grip that nonconformity could have on a people. During the first half of the century 11 Nonconformist chapels were built there, and 12 during the second half of the century. These 23 chapels were built during a period of 87 years, which meant that a chapel was erected every four years.

Gradually the English cause gained ground. The Wesleyans and the Baptists were the first to provide for this section of the community. The Baptist cause was nurtured in its infancy by David Jones, the historian, who was that time a printer in Merthyr. Gradually there was a change of attitude towards the Welsh language. The vast majority of members were Welsh speaking, but many of the leaders of nonconformity came to believe that the Welsh language would die out. Therefore a special effort should be made to establish English causes. This was true of David Rees, Capel Als, Llanelli, one of the preachers at the opening of Market Square English Congregational Church in 1841. However the Welsh churches in Merthyr were rather aloof, and did not give much support to this venture by the English and the Scots, although the ministers were co-operative. Another unusual feature of this cause was the influence of the Free Masons on its formation. Some of the founders belonged to that order, and gained the support of the Loyal Cambrian Lodge for the laying of the foundation of the church. It suggests also the social status of the members. Most of the members of the other churches belonged to the working class, and would not join the Free Masons. Market Square became the mother church of Ivor, Dowlais and Troed-y-rhiw.

Although the English Baptists had started their work early in the nineteenth century, it was not until 1840 that real advance was made. In that year the old cause at Bethel moved to High Street, but even then it took the Baptists some time to spread their influence. Between 1856 and 1913 they established 7 English causes in Merthyr and district. The Calvinistic Methodists did not build Hope until 1875.

The Anglicans laboured under many difficulties. The parish was a cumbersome unit to deal with. In this respect, the nonconformists with their close knit, localised fellowships had a great advantage. It was not until 1827 that the people of Dowlais were given a church of their own. It was provided by John Guest, an employer, and English speaking. This was typical of Anglicanism, in spite of the fact that an occasional incumbent learnt the Welsh language. As a result of this situation, the Anglican Church could not appeal to the mass of the people.

One further result of growth and bad conditions was that many left to look for a paradise elsewhere. A good number went to America, and came into contact with new religious sects. There is no doubt that the most colourful was the Latter Day Saints. Dan Jones, a native of Caerwys, Fflintshire, crossed the Atlantic and became acquainted with Joseph Smith, the leader of the movement. Jones returned to Merthyr to champion the work which was under the care of an Englishman, William Henshaw. But Dan Jones was Welsh speaking, and a good amount of the movement's literature was published in that language. He preached with power and fervour, and under his leadership the Saints gained phenomenal success during the early years of the movement. After a five year period, 1843-48, they had over a thousand members in Merthyr, Twynrodyn, Dowlais and Penydarren. In 1857, they worshipped in the Cymreigyddion Hall, Mill Street; Railway Inn, Plymouth Street, and Alfred's Arms, Georgetown.

The Saints had new ideas which attracted people, especially their apocalyptic emphasis, and their belief in miraculous healing. The dynamic preaching of Dan Jones won admirers and adherents. They had a true missionary zeal. But some of their claims were fantastic, and some of their practices dubious. Joseph Smith had the gift of reading some mysterious gold plates, no one had ever seen, and explained them in the *Book of Mormon*. He had a further vision in 1843, and introduced polygamy into the movement. This practice was denounced in 1890. The people grew tired of their tactics, as they would disrupt any meeting that could be detrimental to their cause.

Many colours were woven into the pattern of religious life. Conservatism, evangelical zeal, radicalism, and apocalyptic frenzy were found in the same town. The more radical of the Nonconformists, especially the Unitarians, made a substantial contribution to local government. The Unitarians were more wealthy than the other denominations, as is borne out by the occupations of some of the leaders, Richard Jenkins, farmer; Joseph Coffin, tanner; George Kirkhouse, agent, and Christopher James, merchant, who became one of the richest men in Merthyr. These men with their supporters, dominated the Vestry during the period 1822-26, and were staunch supporters of reform. Another of their members, Morgan Williams, became a Chartist leader. Charles H. James, nephew of Christopher James, was a zealous liberal, who supported Henry Richard in 1868, and was elected Member of Parliament in 1880. Some of these public leaders received part of their education with Unitarian schoolmasters, such as Taliesin Williams in Merthyr, and John James at Gellionnen, Pontardawe.

Nonconformity was one of the main influences that moulded the shape of politics in Merthyr. The radicalism of the Unitarians changed into the liberalism of Henry Richard, which in turn gave way to the socialism of Keir Hardie. But it was a slow process, especially from the ideas of Richard to those of Hardie. Liberalism had gained such a strong hold on Merthyr, that the denominations thought it was the only power that could release the people from the grip of the Anglican Tory party. At their annual meeting in Merthyr in 1874, the Congregationalists were urged to face up to their political responsibilities. It was true that no specific political party was mentioned in the proposal, but really there was no need for such a reference, because the chairman of the public meeting held during the week was Henry Richard. When a vote of thanks was proposed to the Member of Parliament, the whole congregation sprang to its feet as one man to applaud him.

Keir Hardie was elected as a Member of Parliament for Merthyr in 1900. He and his followers championed the idea of Christian socialism, although it was labelled by their opponents as atheism. Already in 1897 the characteristics of their movement were displayed in a meeting at Merthyr, where the Union Jack and the Red Flag were hoisted side by side, and when a male voice choir sang a Psalm tune and the Crusaders. Hardie claimed that society based on self interest was unjust, and that the Church had made a grave mistake in supporting such a system. Liberalism had failed to solve the economic and industrial problems of the country. The great need Hardie argued, was to base society on the Christian socialism of the Sermon of the Mount. That is, abstract doctrine should be buried, and practical Christianity revived.

Hardie was careful to explain that he was not attacking religion, but only the misuse of it, especially the hypocrisy of the Christian leaders, some of whom he would name on the platform or in the press. The world had to be redeemed from sin, poverty and war. The only way to do this was by service and sacrifice. It is by serving our fellow man that we serve God. Such a work must be done within and without the Church, and Hardie concludes, 'And the only Christian today worthy of the name is the man or woman, whether in the Church or out of it; who is sacrificing life and leisure for the uplifting and ennobling of the race.' His socialism won adherents in the churches, but it also opened the way for many socialists to leave their places of worship. For some Christianity and Socialism were allies, but for others they were enemies. Some of those who left, still retained their religious convictions, but were very critical of the Church as an institution. The late Mr. S.O. Davies continued this tradition.

In spite of the criticism levelled at Christian doctrine, the Nonconformists continued to claim that the basis of the Christian religion was revealed truth. Whenever such an emphasis was attacked, they would willingly enter the field of battle to uphold the content of the faith. When the theological battles raged fiercely early in the nineteenth century, two of the Merthyr ministers entered the fray on the side of orthodoxy. David Saunders, Baptist, and Samuel Evans, Congregationalist, defended the deity of Christ and the doctrine of the Trinity. Saunders entered into a friendly argument with David Davis of Castell Hywel regarding the person of Christ. Evans preached a sermon on the Trinity in Zoar, which was published. The work gained the support of Saunders, and the opposition of the Unitarians in Merthyr.

Such a work demanded the discipline of the mind, and it was not the ministers only that engaged in it. The congregations could be well versed in the intricacies of theology. However other aspects of life were considered. Daniel Jones came to Bethesda Chapel in 1840, and he was one of the first ministers in Wales to introduce cultural and competitive meetings into the chapel. Many of the members did not like this at first, but slowly it was accepted, and other ministers followed suit. Meetings were held in individual chapels, but a group of churches or Sunday Schools would also come together, to sing, recite, and be catechised.

Attention was given to weightier matters. The Sunday Schools provided the children with religious knowledge, but before this work could be done effectively they had to be taught to read. Very often the percentage of those who could read in a Sunday School, was higher than the percentage of children attending a day school. That is for many of the children Sunday was their only school day. Bethesda chapel held its Sunday School for a while at 9 o'clock in the morning, and it included a class to learn Welsh grammar. At the same chapel there was a Bible Study, prayer meeting and a music practice, that is, apart form the regular Sunday services.

The people at Dowlais were up before 9 o'clock even on a Sunday morning. They gathered at Hermon to study the Calvinistic Methodist's Confession of Faith, and that at 8 o'clock in the morning. A number of people from different chapels formed a study group during the revival of 1859-60. The first teacher was William Griffith of Bethesda. In turn they studied Butler's *Analogy,* and a handbook of Welsh grammar. They also arranged Bible Studies on a Monday morning for those working the night shift. These men welcomed the hard work of study, and also the emotional experiences of the revival. These revivals broke out in Merthyr in 1803, 1805, 1829, 1859, and 1904. As a result of these extraordinary visits of the Spirit of God, the worship of the people became more intense and meaningful; more members excercised their gifts in public, and they expressed a deeper concern for the conversation of others. One result of the 1904 awakening was the formation of pentecostal groups in Merthyr and Dowlais.

Some of the meetings could be attractive socially. In spite of the fact that tea drinking was frowned upon at the beginning of the century, the tea meeting was popular in the chapels around 1845-1850. In 1844, 4,000 people gathered at Zoar to enjoy such an event. They were there to meet each other, and to use the occasion as a means of reducing the debt on the chapel. The meeting realised £140. This was a substantial sum, considering the nature of the meeting, and that the members belonged mainly to the working class. It was not only on special occasions that the members faced up to their financial responsibilities. In 1890 the annual collection of the chapels worked out at about £1 per head. In a few cases it was much higher. Market Square Congregational Church had 147 members, and the collection for 1890 amounted to £647.

The excess of drinking in such a populous place as Merthyr disturbed many of the inhabitants. The churches however were slow in grappling with the problem. Many of the leaders thought that the best policy was that of moderation. When the temperance work started in Merthyr in October 1836, not a single minister supported it, and out of eighteen churches only three were willing to open their doors to a total abstinence meeting. Slowly however the movement gained ground, and the Rev Joshua Thomas of Adulam gave his support to it. More chapels opened their doors, and an annual festival was arranged which became popular and influential. Once the work was established Bands of Hope were organised where the children would be warned of the evils of drink, and urged to sign the pledge. The majority of these meetings were held in chapel vestries, and continued well into the present century. But there were signs of waning at the turn of the century. Dowlais had only three temperance societies in 1911. Of these, two were very weak, although the third had 301 members. These temperance societies made good use of music in their meetings. Dowlais was one of the first places in the country to form a temperance choir, which pioneered the way for a variety of choirs, and the Gymanfa Ganu.

At the end of the nineteenth century Merthyr could boast strong nonconformist churches. There was an increase of membership immediately after the 1904 revival, followed by a slight decease, but the numbers soon rose a little, and in some chapels continued to do so until the early thirties. In other places there were suggestions of a decline before this period. The economic situation of the country brought the people together in some places of worship, as it did in Dowlais, where the people of Pen-y-wern built their vestry during the strike of 1926. But in other places the difficult circumstances drove the people from the chapels. The war of 1939 quickened the process.

This general pattern can be illustrated from some Baptist statistics:

1868	1918	1939
12 chapels inc. 3 Eng.	21 chapels inc. 9 Eng.	21 chapels inc. 9 Eng.
Members		
3,000	4,000	3,000

But the decline was more marked during the period 1939-75, especially in the Welsh churches. In 1975 there were II Welsh Baptist chapels in the Baptist Union, but six of these held bilingual services, and quite often services in English only. The vast majority were willing to have occasional English services. As far as membership was concerned the number was 500, while the same eleven chapels had 1,700 members in 1939. Detailed figures have been kept for Caersalem, Dowlais. From the beginning of the cause until 1900, the membership fluctuated from about 230 to about 360, but in the present century it was only during 1904-1907 that the number exceeded 300. At the beginning of the war in 1939 it was 216; in 1940, 190, and in 1975 it was down to 85.

But there is room for some optimism. A number of churches and chapels are holding their ground. One or two are making headway in the new housing estates. It is true that chapels are being demolished, and that numbers are decreasing quickly, but it is possible that as the present pattern is crumbling, a new one will soon emerge.

Bibliography

Thomas Richards, *The Puritan Movement in Wales* (1920).
Thomas Richards, *Religious Developments, 1654-1662* (1923).
Thomas Richards, *Wales under the Penal Code* (1925).
'Notes on the Parish Register of Merthyr Tydvil, 1703-1763', *Y Cymmrodor*, vol. XXXV, 1925.
A good number of chapel histories are available. Those used include:
J. Ronald Williams and Gwyneth Williams, *History of Caersalem, Dowlais* (Llandysul, 1967).
R. Griffith, *Hanes Zoar, Merthyr* (Merthyr Tydfil, 1869).
Jacob Jones, *Hanes Bethesda, Merthyr Tydfil* (Merthyr Tydfil, 1907).
D. Cunllo Davies, *Hanes Eglwys Hermon,* Dowlais (Bala, 1905).
Denominational Histories:
Thomas Rees and John Thomas, *Hanes Eglwysi Annibynnol Cymru,* 4 vols. (Liverpool, 1871-75); John Thomas, vol. 5 (Dolgellau, 1891).
Joshua Thomas, *Hanes y Bedyddwyr,* ed. B. Davies (Pontypridd, 1885).
T. Mardy Rees, *The Quakers in Wales*
John Hughes, *Hanes Methodistiaeth Cymru* (Wrexham, 1851-56).
A. H. Williams, *Welsh Wesleyan Methodism, 1800-50.*

(a) The history of the Anglican Church

by Rev. D. S. LEE

Rector of Merthyr

Prior to 1920 the Anglican Church in Merthyr Tydfil was part of the Established Church of England. As such it had an influence upon the life of the town out of proportion ot its numerical strength, partly because of its privileged legal position and partly because it was the Church of the ruling class. Since 1920 the Anglican Church has been called the Church in Wales, an independent province with its own government and Archbishop of Wales. Although its legal privileges were removed at disestablishment, and also much of its ancient wealth, it has retained an influence on the community. By comparison with other Churches, especially the Free Churches this influence has increased. This is partly due to the decline in the Free Churches, especially to the decline of Free Church Ministers. The Church in Wales has maintained a relatively strong parochial system with a clergyman resident in every parish, and this has strengthened the position of the Anglican Church very much.

The Rector of Merthyr Tydfil, George Martin Maber, died in 1843, and so did not live to see the realisation of his plans for a new Church and Church School in Merthyr Tydfil. He was succeeded by James Colquhoun Campbell. Campbell was a Scot who had been Vicar of Roath, a small country parish outside Cardiff. On coming to Merthyr he learnt to speak Welsh and immediately concerned himself with the development of a Church School and a new Church for the English congregation. Both these were opened on a site outside the centre of the old town, the present site of the Public Library and St. David's Hall. The new St. David's Church and School were opened by 1847. Campbell's ministry in the town was much respected, and Wilkes speaks with great appreciation of it in his History. Campbell left to become Bishop of Bangor in 1859.

Campbell was succeeded by John Griffith, who was Vicar of Aberdare. He had been the founder of St. Elvan's Church Aberdare, and there were those who thought that by the time he came to Merthyr he was past his prime. It is true that during his incumbency there were no major developments in Church life, although it seems likely that St. Tydfil's Well Church, Quar, was opened during this time. But this is to misunderstand the situation. The fact was that Griffith's ministry coincided with a period of industrial depression and social suffering. Griffith identified himself with many efforts and campaigns to alleviate the condition of the working classes. Another of his contributions to the life of the town was his willingness to work with the Free Churches and his support for the Evangelical tradition in the Anglican Church. In both these respects he incurred the disapproval of Church authorities and did not get the disapproval of Church authorities and did not get the preferment which he might have expected, in virtue of the importance of his parish, and the recognition of his predecessor, Bishop Campbell. He died in office in 1885.

Daniel Lewis was instituted as Rector of Merthyr Tydfil on 30th August 1885. He was a very different character from his predecessor, and proved to be a controversial Rector. It was a time of the urban development of the town, and he proved to be a difficult opponent for the civic authorities, especially with such things as the widening of roads around the Parish Church of St. Tydfil. He was said to be more of a barrister than a clergyman, and it is a fact that his litigations delayed the development of the centre of the town. During his time the Parish Church of St. Tydfil was rebuilt and was opened in 1897, a fine new building to the design of Pearson, a very famous and fashionable architect. Lewis was notorious for introducing High Church practices in St. David's Church, and in his declining years the Church was badly neglected both pastorally and structurally. In 1914 the National School closed, because it became too small for the town. The fact that it was replaced by Board Schools rather than by another Church School was due to the Rector's poor relationships with local authorities, and the particular way in which the School had been founded, which meant that there was no capital fund to be used by the Church to found a new Church School. There was a dispute between the Rector and the local council about the title of the property of the National School which was not settled in his time. He died in office in 1920.

John Richards Pugh was instituted as Rector on 13th January 1921 and began a vigorous ministry of reconstruction of Church life both pastorally and structurally. In 1926 St. David's Church was repaired and improved at great cost. In 1935 he obtained a judgement in the High Court which settled the dispute about the site of the National School. The public Library had been built on the site of the teacher's house and girls' school. The boys' school was vested in the Rector and Churchwardens and Trustees of an educational foundation, and they gained absolute control. The old school was enlarged and modernised and re-opened as St. David's Hall in November 1938. Pugh left to become Vicar of Carmarthen in 1942, having done much to restore Church life in the town, and having been deeply involved in the problems of the depression in the same sort of way as Griffith had fifty years before.

Pugh was succeeded by T.M. Hughes who left to become Vicar of Cardiff after four years. He was succeeded in 1946 by Canon Alban Lloyd Jones. Both these Rectors worked in times of great difficulty in the war and immediate post war period, and little change is noted in the development of Church life, although they were deeply respected. Hughes became assistant Bishop of Llandaff in 1961, and now lives in retirement in Cardiff.

Gwyn Lewis became Rector in 1957 and during his incumbency the Parish Church of St. Tydfil was closed for parochial worship, because of the decline in the congregation. There are those who hold that it never succeeded in maintaining Church life after rebuilding 'it was altogether too grand for the simple folk of Merthyr' (Bishop Glyn Simon). Since its closure it has found a useful role as a Chapel of Rest, and remains an imposing architectural feature at the entrance to the town. It is still vested in the Representative Body and is administered by an Authority on which the Church and the local Council are represented. Gwyn Lewis left to become Rector of Litton Cheney in 1969.

The present Rector, David Stanley Lee, was instituted on 20th April 1970. His incumbency has been the time of great change in the life of the Church in the town. In 1972 the parish was united with the Parish of Cyfarthfa to form the Rectorial Benefice of Merthyr Tydfil and Cyfarthfa. Thus the whole town centre and the estates of Gurnos, Gellideg, Heolgerrig, Twynyrodyn, and Keir Hardy have come under one parochial authority. Also in 1972 St. David's Hall was refurbished and re-opened as a flourishing parish and community centre. During this time the two curates on the Parish became engaged in the political life of the town, and both gained positions of power in their respective parties, a fact which has caused some controversy in Church circles. In 1976 one of the curates, Bill Morgan, left to become Priest-in-Charge of Penydarren, and the other, Gareth Foster, was appointed Vicar in the Rectorial Benefice. In 1977 St. David's Church was repaired and redecorated, and the North Aisle was converted into an exhibition centre called the Dewi Gallery, in an attempt to make better use of the building and to involve it with the wider life of the community.

(b) The Hebrew Community

by B. HAMILTON

From enquiries which I have made it would seem that Jews originally came to Merthyr Tydfil in the early part of the last century, and I have had evidence of seeing a Marriage Certificate in which a Jew who was a sweet merchant married in 1833.

At that time it would appear that there was a Synagogue built somewhere in the area of Bethesda Street and Brecon Road, but now there is no evidence of this whatsoever.

In 1852 another Synagogue was built. This Synagogue was built at the back of the present Temperance Hall, the walls of which are still in evidence, and is now used as a garage by the Merthyr Tydfil Post Office.

The present Synagogue was built in 1872 and is therefore well over 100 years old.

In 1860 when the Jewish Community started to enlarge they purchased a piece of land in Cefn Coed as a Jewish Cemetery. Prior to that Jewish burials had taken place in Swansea, but the first burial in Cefn Coed took place in 1870.

At that time there was a Minister by the name of The Reverend Simmonds who left Merthyr Tydfil to go to a larger Jewish Community in Penzance, but in recent years the community have completely disappeared.

He was followed by the Reverend Abelson who ministered to Merthyr Tydfil from 1870 to 1901 and after that there came the Reverend Bloom whose sons were well known Doctors in the Town and a well known Chemist and whose grandson is a Professor in the Cardiff University. Reverend Bloom ministered from 1901 to 1939.

The Jewish Community seemed to have grown from 1870 to 1901, but from 1901 until 1905 there started to be a large build up due entirely to the Pogroms in Russia. At that time there came about 200 to 300 families, all of whom lived in various parts of Merthyr Tydfil and Dowlais, and in fact there were Jews living in every village from Treharris to Dowlais. In Pentrebach there was a Shoemaker, in other villages there were shop keepers and peddlers.

The influx between 1901 and 1905 was due to refugees who sought work at the Dowlais Steel Works and Local Collieries. It was well established that the men in the Steelworks would work a 36 hour shift, night and day, in order to save sufficient money to emigrate to America and Canada. There were so many Jews living in Dowlais that it was decided to have a small Synagogue, which was a room under the Oddfellows Hall and this existed from 1905 to 1910. During that period the majority of these refugees had saved sufficient money, together with the help of the London Jewish Board of Guardians, to emigrate.

During the 1914-1918 war many came to visit their old homes and a number of them came to see my late parents.

The Local establishement seemed to have reached its apex in 1921 and from 1921 to the present date the Community greatly declined. The older families died out and the younger families moved to larger towns where there were greater facilities for education and for Universities, with the result that now there are no more than 5 or 6 families living in Merthyr.

The present Synagogue in accordance with Jewish Custom is built on the top of a Hill, the location being at Church Street, Merthyr Tydfil and it is lit by old Gas Lamps. The Synagogue is very rarely used now, and is only opened on High Festivals.

One of the Ministers was The Reverend Raffalividtch who was in Merthyr Tydfil during the period of 1901 to 1905 and he worked to assist poor Jewish people who had come as Refugees from abroad. When he left Merthyr he became Chief Rabbi at Brazil and at the end of his office in Brazil he returned to live in Israel.

The next time the Merthyr Tydfil Synagogue was completely full was in 1940, when many refugees came from London. Furthermore the Local Jewish Community adopted a number of children from families who escaped from the Hitler Regime, and they at the end of the war went to America and London. One was killed whilst serving in the Air Force.

In conclusion I wish to point out that the original founders were mostly shop keepers, but in later years there developed in the local Community a large number of professional men namely Doctors, Lawyers, Chemists and School teachers.

The present outlook in 1977 is very dismal, as the Community is fast declining.

It is right to point out that the local Jews always participated in all local Charities, and for Charities in Israel. Furthermore, they participated in the activities which took place in the town and at one time the Chairman of the Chamber of Trade was a Jew. All Jews are always ready to be of benefit and help to any deserving cause of the Community in which they dwell. They are constantly reminded of the words of Jeremiah the Prophet who spoke to the Exiles in Babylon after the destruction of the First Temple in Jerusalem when he advised them to pray for the peace and welfare of the Community in which they dwelt, for therein lies their own peace and welfare.

This sums up the Jews as excellent citizens who always participate in all activities and movements in the towns in which they dwell.

(c) The Church of Jesus Christ of Latter-Day Saints

by Dr. MORGAN EVANS

The history of the 'Mormons' in Merthyr Tydfil falls into three periods. The first began in 1840, when John Needham, a priest from North Wales, was sent to Monmouthshire to labour and he baptised several Welsh people in the winter of that year. The work continued to spread in South Wales and William Henshaw and others began active missionary operations and formed the Penydarren branch on March 26th, 1843; they later formed a 'Conference' or District which included branches in Aberdare, Beaufort, Merthyr Tydfil, Rhymney and Tredegar. Growth was rapid and The Merthyr Tydfil Conference was organised on 6th April, 1844. Captain Dan Jones, a Welsh speaking Missouri riverboat owner, was District President immediately after the general conference of the British Mission held in Manchester on 16th April, 1845. Sixty days later he was publishing a pamphlet in Welsh. He also reported the district as consisting of 28 branches, with 687 members, 378 of whom had been baptised in the interim; furthermore, he had lately baptised the only two remaining non-Latter Day Saints from an active Baptist Church. On 15th March, 1847 he reported at conference in Merthyr Tydfil, 102 baptisms for two months, total membership 900. In December of the same year he was publishing the 'Welsh Star', with a circulation of 12,000 per month. He also published another periodical, the Welsh 'Udgorn Seion'. On 6th January, 1849 at the Welsh General Conference, he reported 2000 present of a total membership of 3,603; the latter rose to 4,645 by the end of the year. When he sailed for home not long after, he took with him 249 Latter-Day Saints who formed the Welsh settlement which comprised the Salt Lake City 15th and 16th Wards. In August, 1852 he came on a second mission and returned in 1856 with 703 emigrating saints. Such then was the first period with its rapid conversion and emigration.

By the end of the nineteenth century, missionary activity slowed down but new work led to the first baptisms after many years in 1930. In ensuing years, the Merthyr Tydfil branch was led by local men usually, but they relied heavily on American missionaries. Generally a tightly knit social life was followed which was a consequence of the Church's teachings, particularly those relating to abstention from alcohol and stimulants, to the ideals of strong family ties and of marrying within the Church, and to the fellowship of ones fellows in the Church. However this does not mean that it was an exclusive life, because it is a proselyting church, and as such would be a failure if members did not awaken interest in their friends and associates. During the depression a wooden meeting house was erected in Penyard and served well. This was dedicated by Heber J. Grant, who was then leader of the Church. This era came to an end with the erection in 1963 of the large and beautiful building in Georgetown. Notably this contains an organ donated by the Salt Lake City Chamber of Trade to David O McKay, then President of the Church to commemorate his mother's birth in Clwydyfagwr.

From then the congregation grew, emigration virtually ceased, and the local leadership grew in strength until January 1975, when Bruce R. McConkie, a member of the Quorum of Twelve Apostles was sent to organise South Wales on a Stake (roughly, a small archdiocese) basis with the Stake Headquarters at Merthyr Tydfil. The Church in Wales is now autonomous and responsible directly to the General Authorities. In late 1975 the Stake purchased a nursery in Ynysfach to use as a site to encourage the Church's out-of-work to labour and not feel dependent and thus restore dignity and the importance of work; this was the first Church welfare project in Europe.

None of the ecclesiastical officers is paid, but each does his church work in his spare time as well as making a living.

(d) Roman Catholicism

by J. F. LANE, M.A.
Headmaster Bishop Hedley High School

There are few records of the Pre-Reformation Catholic Church in the Merthyr area. In the 15th Century, the 'humble priest' of Merthyr Tydfil was sufficiently prosperous to be able to extend his patronage to Guto'r Glyn, one of the few outstanding Welsh poets of the 15th Century.[1] A century later, Lewis ap Richard, in his will of 1521, left £20 to repair the bells of Merthyr Tydfil Church,[2] and one pound to re-gild the statue of St. Tydfil there.[3]

Where Merthyr is concerned, little is known of the years that follow. Although Catholicism remained alive in areas such as Abergavenny and Llanarth, there are no natives of Merthyr named in the Recusant Lists of the Penal Days. There is an unsubstantiated theory that one Lawrence Hughes, an Irish rebel – fleeing, we may presume, from the aftermath of Vinegar Hill – arrived in Merthyr in 1798, and found no fellow-Catholics there.[4] The Propaganda, or report, of the Western District for 1813 tells us that 'in Wales were very few Catholics',[5] and makes no mention of Merthyr.

Although the iron industry of Merthyr suffered in the economic depression that followed the Napoleonic Wars, the fame it had achieved during those wars drew a wave of immigrants to the area, seeking an escape from agricultural and industrial decline elsewhere. It was this population explosion, which more than doubled the population of the area in the twenty years to 1831 and was to do so again in the following twenty years, that led first to the revival, and then to the rapid growth, of Roman Catholicism in Merthyr Tydfil. For among the flood of workers, skilled and unskilled, seeking work and life for their families in Merthyr, came a trickle of Irish Catholics, peasants seeking relief from the grinding poverty and religious repression of their homeland.

The parish registers of Abergavenny, which recorded Merthyr Catholics until 1836, show very few non-Welsh before 1820; Irish names first appear in 1820, and within twenty years the names of Irish outnumber those of native Roman Catholics.[6] On September 5th, 1824, Mass was offered in Merthyr, almost certainly for the first time since the Reformation, by Father Edward Richards, the Franciscan Recollect Provincial stationed at Abergavenny.[7] Father Richards found about 300 Catholics in Merthyr[8], as he rode across the Valleys, saying Mass as far afield as Maesteg. The need of these Irish Catholics for the pastoral care of a priest was recognised, and, in November, 1827, Father Patrick Portal, a Waterford man, was sent to Merthyr by Bishop Collingridge. In his work, he was befriended and helped by the Jones family of Llanarth. The vast majority of his flock was very poor, and he found 'this mission is one of the most severe and disagreeable I have even ever heard of . . . the poor people are indeed extremely good and kind', but most of them could not afford to support their priest; many, he wrote, had not been to 'their duties' for between three and ten years.[9] Father Portal hired a large room in Merthyr at a rent of £14 per year; he also used the club-room of the Inn at Old Rhymney, and he heard Confessions until midnight at these places, alternatively on Fridays and Saturdays. He could not have carried on without constant financial help from Bishop Collingridge, and some idea of the crushing burden of his task is found in one sad sentence of a letter to his Bishop in 1829, 'Nothing here but hardship when out, and solitude at home'.[10]

That the Old Faith had not died out completely is illustrated by the fact that Father Portal, who spoke no Welsh, used the services of a Mr. Lewis, a Welsh speaker from Nantyglo, who, after Mass on Sundays, would explain the Faith in Welsh, and crowds of Welsh-speaking people came to hear him; Mr. Lewis had a son, Peter, who was ordained in March, 1843, became a Monsignor, and died at Nazareth House, Cardiff, on 24th October, 1902.[11]

Father Portal left Merthyr in 1831, and the Catholics of the area were without a resident priest until the appointment of Father James Carroll, in 1836. Father Carroll began the first Parish Registers of Merthyr on January 28th, 1836. The 1838 Propaganda records 940 Catholics in Merthyr, compared with 900 in Cardiff and 3005 in Wales as a whole. The speed of the growth of the Catholic population is shown by the fact that, in the years 1836 to 1841, Father Carroll carried out 273 infant Baptisms. An analysis of these early registers[12] is interesting, as they show a rapid growth of intermarriage between Irish and non-Irish, and also the slower growth of non-Irish Catholics. Based purely on the author's personal interpretation of the 'Irishness' of surnames, we find:—

Year	*Both Parents Irish*	*One Parent Irish*	*Neither Parent Irish*	*Total*
1836	35	13	3	51
1837	20	7	1	28
1838	13	7	—	20
1839	36	10	3	51*
1840	34	21	1	56**
1841	43	18	6	67

*This total includes two illegitimate children where no father's name was given, and the mother's name was not Irish.

**On August 30th, 1840, the first Spanish name appears in the Register.

The figures for 1837 and 1838, compared with the years immediately before and after, give some idea of the ravages of the cholera epidemic among the poorest class. Father Carroll was to become a local legend in his own life time. His Parish included Rhymney and Pontlottyn, and he laboured untiringly, refusing offers of moves to other and easier parishes. IN 1846, he was given four cottages in Dowlais, which was the area where most of the

Irish then lived, and on the site there, where the present St. Illtyd's Church now stands, he built the first permanent Roman Catholic Church; the Ordo of 1847 refers to its opening 'in this long-destitute mission'.[13] Barely had he achieved this, when he died of cholera on 19th June, 1847; he is believed to have been buried in his Church, though his grave has never been found there, and Wilkins, twenty years later, referred to him as 'a martyr to his zeal'.[14] Father Carroll's life forged strong links in the chain that is the history of Irish Catholicism in Merthyr, and the greatest tribute paid to his work was the inspiration it gave to John Parker to write his 'Iron in the Valleys'.

During the twenty years from 1841 to 1861, while the population of the British Isles as a whole rose from 26.7 million to 28.9 million, the population of Ireland fell from 8.2 million to 5.8 million.[15] Although most of these starving Irish millions went to the New World, many came to South Wales, and the trickle that had begun in the 1820's, became a steady flow of Irish Catholics to Merthyr after the Famine of 1845-46. As a result of this growth, on March 16th, 1859, the Catholic Parish of Merthyr, which had been based on Dowlais since Father Carroll's time, was divided into the two parishes of St. Mary's, Merthyr, and St. Illtyd's, Dowlais.[16] The combined Baptism Registers of these two parishes illustrate the growth of Catholicism during this period, with 970 live infant baptisms during the three years 1859-1861:—[17]

	Merthyr	*Dowlais*	*Total*
1859	95	223	318
1860	200	153	353
1861	150	149	299

In 1861 a separate Parish was created in Rhymney, and the Benedictine priests of Merthyr and Dowlais concentrated their pastoral efforts on the ever-increasing Catholics of the Merthyr area, from Cefn Coed southwards to Cilfynydd Common, and including many adjacent villages. Already, efforts had begun to provide Catholic schools where Catholic children could be educated in their Faith, as well as in the small range of basic subjects which in those days comprised the normal curriculum. The poverty of the Catholic population, which made the work of the priests so difficult and yet so rewarding, is attested by a letter in 'The Nation', which refers to 'two thousand Irish of the poorest class'' in Merthyr, where ''there is no school', nor funds to provide it, so that, to help them build a school, the Catholics of the area 'are compelled to appeal to the charity of Irish Catholics elsewhere'.[18] Already, by 1851, there were 60 pupils and 1 teacher at Dowlais and 100 pupils and 2 teachers at Merthyr.[19] By 1858, a Catholic school was firmly established in Dowlais, and by 1867 in Merthyr.[20]

Roman Catholicism was now thoroughly rooted in Merthyr, its numbers growing as more Irish came in the 1850's, and, later in the century, increased again by Spanish ironworkers, and its members gradually became accepted by, and so became an integral part of, Merthyr Tydfil. The present St. Mary's Church was opened in 1894, and, from 1908, served St. Benedict's, Merthyr Vale, until, in 1919, the separate Parish of St. Benedict's was created to cater for Catholics in the Lower Valley.[21] St. Illtyd's Church, Dowlais, was expanded by additional building in 1920.[22]

The Benedictines left the area in 1930, when the Parishes came into the care of the secular priests of the Archdiocese of Cardiff. By 1969, the combined Catholic population of Merthyr and Dowlais Parishes was 6117,[23] and, in June, 1970, St. Aloysius' Parish was created by dividing the two older parishes into three; the first Mass in the new St. Aloysius Church was said by Father P. Maher on the 18th June, 1977, Mass having previously been said at St. Aloysius School.

By the late 1950's, the Catholic Schools in Merthyr and Dowlais were old, and educationally were sadly out-of-date in terms of buildings and facilities. Father, later Canon, Timothy O'Leary, who had become Parish Priest of Merthyr in 1956, built a new school, St. Mary's, Caedraw, in 1962; he was the driving force behind the opening of Bishop Hedley Comprehensive School in 1967, when St. Mary's became a Primary School; and he built a new Primary School, St. Aloysius, Gurnos, in 1968. A record to be proud of, that gives Canon O'Leary an honoured place in the history of Roman Catholicism in Merthyr Tydfil. In 1972, Father Paul Chigey opened a new St. Illtyd's Primary School in Dowlais.

At the time of writing, there are 6880 Catholics, four Parishes, three modern Catholic Primary Schools, and a purpose-built Catholic Comprehensive School, in Merthyr Tydfil, and all owing their existence, in the last analysis, to those destitute Irish immigrants of a century-and-a-half ago, who brought with them little but the Faith that their descendants, both proudly and humbly acknowledge.

References

1 Glamorgan County History, Cardiff 1971, Vol.3, p.152.
2 Ibid, pp.330-331.
3 'The Welsh Church from Conquest to Reformation', G.Williams, Cardiff 1962, p.458.
4 'History of St. Illtyd's, Dowlais' – a MS history circulated in the Parish in the 1940's.
5 'Annals of the Catholic Hierarchy, 1585-1876' W.M. Brady, Rome 1877, London 1883, pp.307-308.
6 'Transactions of the Catholic Record Society', Vol.27, 1927, No.III, p.110.
7 Ibid, p.208.
8 'Review of Catholicism in Wales in 1827' Rev. J.M. Cronin, St. Peter's Magazine, Feb. 1928, Vol.8, No.2. p.39
9 Ibid, p.40.
10 Ibid, p.40.

[11] Annals of Nazareth House, Cardiff; obituary 'Western Mail', 25th October, 1902.
[12] Parish Registers of Merthyr, now at St. Illtyd's, Dowlais, and quoted with the permission of Rev. Fr. P. Chidgey, Parish Priest.
[13] Cardiff Archdiocesan Archives.
[14] 'A History of Merthyr Tydfil', C. Wilkins, 1867 edition, p.291; Wilkins mistakenly gives the date of Fr. Carroll's death as 1849; in the 1908 edition, p.519, he is referred to as a 'victim of his humanity'.
[15] National Census Figures.
[16] Dowlais Parish Register, entry for March 16th, 1859.
[17] Parish Registers of Merthyr and Dowlais, now held in those Parishes, and quoted with the permission of Very Rev. Canon T. O'Leary, Parish Priest of Merthyr, and Rev. Fr. P. Chidgey, Parish Priest of Dowlais.
[18] Letter in 'The Nation', October, 1859.
[19] MS History of St. Illtyd's Dowlais, op.cit.; 'A History of Merthyr Tydfil', C. Wilkins, 1908 edition, p.519.
[20] 'The Origins and Subsequent Development of Roman Catholic Education in the Heads of the Valleys Region', J.S. Williams, Chapters 1 & 2. This unpublished University of Wales M.Ed. thesis contains a full account of the history of Catholic Education in Merthyr Tydfil.
[21] Cardiff Archdiocesan Archives.
[22] 'History of St. Illtyd's Dowlais', op.cit.
[23] Cardiff Archdiocesan Year Book, 1970.

(e) The Salvation Army

by V. JONES

On a February day in the year 1878 Kate Watts and Harriet Parkin, two young evangelists, arrived in Merthyr for the purpose of establishing a branch of a new religious organisation, known as the Christian Mission.

The movement, founded by the Rev. William Booth in the East end of London, had already spread to various parts of the country and the unorthodox methods of the missioners aroused much curiosity. Large crowds were attracted to the Sunday meetings held in the old Drill Hall, and also to week-night services in premises known as 'The British Workman' situated near St. Tydfil's Parish Church; the movement became known locally as 'The Savers'.

The two lady evangelists were succeeded by Mrs. Sayers and Miss Smith who rendered valuable service in consolidating the good work of their predecessors; meanwhile the Founder summoned the evangelists in charge of the several branches of the Mission to a special conference in London when they were informed of momentous changes to be made in the style and structure of the organisation. The principal changes provided for the re-organisation of the Mission on a quasi-military basis, to be known as 'The Salvation Army', under the direction of the Founder, who was accorded the title of 'General'. Each Mission Station would function as a Corps, the evangelist-in-charge taking the rank of 'Captain'.

The first male evangelist appointed to Merthyr was John Roberts, who arrived in the town on 7 August, 1879 following a fruitful period of service in Hastings. By this time the administrative changes referred to had become effective and *Captain* John Roberts arrived as the Commanding Officer of the Merthyr Tydfil Corps (No. 34) of the Salvation Army. He was a remarkable personality and became a high-ranking Officer. From the time of his first appointment as an evangelist by the founder he kept a journal recording his experiences, and the booklet 'John Roberts—Evangelist' edited by Ethel B. Rohu (daughter) contains the following extract concerning her father's arrival in Merthyr:

> 'I arrived at Merthyr Tydfil very late on Friday, August 8th, 1879, but approximately a hundred of our own people were awaiting me at the station. There were reclaimed drunkards, Sabbath-breakers, whoremongers, infidels, blasphemers, sinners of the deepest dye. Some were black, some were white; some wore a good coat, some were collarless. One had a wooden leg and another no fingers. Some spoke Welsh, some English, and others a mixture of both.'
>
> 'What!' I asked myself, 'can these be believers?' When we formed a ring and they began to testify I was re-assured. These were—many of them—well-known characters, their former reputation was remembered and the change in their lives was convincing. As we processioned through the town, many onlookers must have been inwardly echoing my own ejaculation, 'What hath God wrought!'

Captain Roberts' period in Merthyr was a landmark in the history of the Corps. The rapid development of the organisation necessitated the appointment of additional whole-time officers, and Roberts had been authorised by the Founder to recommend any suitable members of the Merthyr Corps for appointment as officers.

The formation of bands as an aid to evangelism was not envisaged by the Founder at the outset, but as the movement spread the use of musical instruments by individuals and small groups at various centres had proved to be effective. In this connection the efforts of the Fry family of Salisbury proved to be epoch making. Charles Fry, a local business man and choirmaster, with his three sons constituted a brass instrumental group who started this trend. The stirring story of their first appearance in the market place in Salisbury, and subsequently at Councils conducted by the Founder in various parts of the country is contained in 'Play the Music, Play' (Brindley Boon).

In March 1880 an order appeared in the *War Cry* which foreshadowed the formation of Brass Bands and it would seem that enthusiasm for the new development soon reached Merthyr; evidence of this is provided in the photograph of the original band which hangs in the present bandroom. The first bandmaster was Mr. Israel Price (Senior) who in later years would recall with amusement the difficulty encountered by the pioneer bandsmen in deciphering musical symbols and endeavouring to make a 'joyful sound' on a weird collection of instruments, some of which were obtained from local pawnshops.

The Merthyr Corps formed many sections including the Songsters Brigade started in 1908, the Home League founded in the 1914/1918 war, the Silver Threads Fellowship for senior citizens and a thriving Young Peoples' Corps.

The corps first used to meet in a part of the former Market Block known as The Old Theatre. Sadly in 1878 a fire destroyed all equipment there and they then met in shop premises in Glebeland Street until they moved to larger premises in Penry Street.

In 1904 Morlais Baptist Chapel moved to new buildings in The Walk and the Corps took possession of the former chapel in Glebeland Street till 1925. A flood in the Morlais Brook undermined the foundations of this building and caused another evacuation.

Still the Corps held together in the following years despite many difficulties. The kindness of several local churches must be mentioned here for they provided accommodation for the Corps on many occasions. More relatively permanent bases were Salem Church, in Newcastle Street, and premises in Dynevor Street where services were held on Sundays and weekdays respectively.

It was in 1937 that the present Citadel at the top of Glebeland Street (now the new Law Courts) was opened by the British Commissioner Charles Rich where the good work continues while not forgetting the past 100 years.

'Great the heritage they left us, Great the conquests to be won.'

Appendix

Place Names

ABER CANAID. *Aber* = mouth of a river, *Canaid* = clear: Mouth of the Canaid.

ABERFAN. *Aber* = mouth of river: The mouth of the Fan. This is a tributary of the Taf.

ABERMORLAIS. *Aber* = mouth of river: Mouth of the Morlais. This is the spot where the Morlais joins the Taf. See Dowlais

BALCA. *Balc* = baulk, break in a furrow: unploughed strips.

BEGWNS. Corrupt form of Beacons.

BEDLINOG. Corrupted from Bedd-Llwynog: Fox's grave.

BEDD Y GWYDDEL. *Bedd* = grave, *Gwyddel* = Irishman: The grave of the Irishman. See Pre-history chapter. One old manuscript says that it marks the site of a battle which Nefydd, grandson of Brychan, fought against the Irish Picts, after the massacre of his relatives.

BLAEN BARGOED. *Blaen* = source: Source of the Bargoed, or *Bargod* = border.

BLAEN CANAID. *Blaen* = source: Source of the Canaid.

BLAEN CWM. Top of the valley.

BRYN CAERAU. *Caerau* = fortresses: Hill of the fortresses.

BLAEN DOWLAIS. *Blaen* = extremity, source: The source of the Dowlais Brook. The brook which now flows under Dowlais Works, and is a tributary of the Morlais, has its source in these parts. Some people believe that this brook was called Dowlais, and that later this name was given to the industrial village that sprang up.

BLAEN GARTH. *Garth* = (i) promontory, headland, hill: The beginning of the hill or headland; (ii) enclosure, field: The beginning of the field.

BLAEN MORLAIS. Source of the Morlais.

BÔN-Y-MAEN. *Bôn* = base, *maen* = stone or rock: The base of the rock.

BRYN RHEDYN. *Rhedyn* = fern: Fern Hill.

BONT NEWYDD. New Bridge.

BUARTH GLAS. The green fold.

BUARTH WEUNYDD. *Bu* = cattle, *garth* = enclosure, *weunydd* = moor: The moor cattle fold.

BRANDY BRIDGE. *Ebran* = fodder, provender, *tŷ* = house: Fodder house.

BRYN Y BADELL. *Bryn* = hill, *padell* = pan: The Pan Hill.

BRYN Y GWYDDEL. The Hill of the Irishman.

BRYN GWYN. *Gwyn* = white, pleasant: The white or pleasant hill.

BRYN CAE OWEN. *Bryn* = hill, *Cae* = field: The hill of Owen's field.

BRYNIAU. Hills.

BUNKER'S HILL WOOD. There is no certainty about the derivation of his name. We know that certain local iron-masters had to provide material for the British forces during the American War of Independence. At the battle of Bunker's Hill our forces were victorious, so the name might have been given to commemorate the event.

CAE PANT TYWYLL. *Cae* = field, *pant* = hollow, *tywyll* = dark: The field of the dark hollow.

CARN BUARTH MAEN. *Carn* = cairn, *maen* = stone, *buarth* = fold: The cairn of the stone fold.

CARN Y FRWYDR. *Brwydr* = battle: The cairn of the battle. A skirmish is said to have taken place here between the forces of Rhys ap Tewdwr and Iestyn ap Gwrgant, before the Battle of Hirwaun Common.

CAEDRAW, *Cae* = field, *draw* = yonder, beyond: The yonder field, i.e., the field beyond the village.

CADAIR IFOR. *Cadair* = chair, encampment: Ifor's Chair. Local tradition associates this name with Ifor Bach.

CAE HARRIS. *Cae* = field: Harris's field.

CAERACCA. *Rhaca* = rake: Rake field.

CARN CASTELL Y MEIBION. *Carn* = cairn, *meibion* = sons: The cairn of the sons' castle.

CARN TYLE HIR. *Tyle (Tyla)* = slope, hill, *hir* = long: The cairn of the long slope or hill.

CAE MARI DWN. Mary Dunne's field.

CAPEL Y FAN. The chapel on Cefn Fan.

CAPEL Y FFOREST. The Forest chapel.

CEFN COED-Y-CYMMER. Wooded ridge at the river confluence.

CEFN Y FAN. (i) *Cefn* = ridge: The Fan peak; (ii) The ridge of the peak.

CEFN FFORDD. *Cefn* = ridge, *ffordd* = road, way: The ridgeway or highway.

CEFN FFOREST. Forest Ridge.

CEFN PENNAR. *Pen-ar* = end of the arable land: The ridge at the end of the arable land.

CEFN PWLL DWR. *Pwll* = pool, *dwr* = water: The ridge of the water pool.

CEFN YSTRAD. *Cefn* = ridge, way; *ystrad* = valley, dale: The ridge or way overlooking the valley.

CILFACH. Retreat or nook.

CILSANWS. *Cil* = retreat. *Sannos* = daughter of Brychan Brycheiniog.

CLWYD Y FAGWYR. *Clwyd* = gate, *magwyr* = wall built without mortar: The gate in the dry-stone wall.

COED CAE. *Coed* = wood, *cae* = field: Woody field.

COED MEURIG. Meurig's Wood.

CNWC. Hillock.

COURT HOUSE. This was formerly called Y Cwrt. It is one of the oldest houses in the district and some people believe that it was built during the fourteenth century. In later times it was the home of the squire. It was in the possession of Ifor Bach's descendants until 1717.

CWM-NANT-Y-COED. *Cwm* = valley, *nant* = stream, *coed* = wood: The stream of the wooded valley.

CYFARTHFA. *Cyfarth* = barking, *fa* = place: Barking place. The place where the quarry stood at bay with the hounds barking around.

CRAIG PEN DDEU CAE. *Craig* = rock, *pen* = head, *ddeu* = two: The rock at the top of the two fields.

CRAIG Y PWLL. The rock pool.

CWM BARGOED. Bargod valley. Border valley.

CWM GOLEU. *Goleu* = bright, light: The bright or light valley.

CWM DIFLAS. *Diflas* = insipid, disagreeable. The disagreeable valley.

CWM PEN COED CAE. The valley at the top of the wooded field.

CWM COTHI. Cothi Valley.

CIL HAUL. *Cil* = retreat, *haul* = sun: The sun's retreat, the place where the sunlight does not shine.

CRAIG BERTH LWYD. Grey bush rock.

CRAIG YR EFAIL. Smithy rock.

CWM CAPEL. *Cwm* = valley, *capel* = chapel: The chapel valley. A chapel in earlier times was built to enable those who lived too far from the parish church to attend a religious service.

CWM DU. *Du* = black: Black valley.

CWM FELIN. *Melin* = mill: The Mill valley. This name takes us back to the time when farmers ground their corn in local mills.

CWM Y GLO. *Glo* = coal: Coal valley. See Religious History chapter.

CWM WAUN NEWYDD. *Gwaun* = meadow, *newydd* = new: The valley of the new meadow.

CWM CANOL. *Cwm* = valley, *canol* = middle: Middle valley.

CWM RHYD Y BEDD. *Bedd* = grave, *rhyd* = ford: The valley of the ford of the grave. Local tradition says that Ifor Bach was killed in this district and buried near this ford.

DOWLAIS. *Dow* = an early form of 'du' meaning black or dark; *lais, glais* = stream.

DAN Y DERI. Under the oaks.

DISGWYLFA. *Disgwyl* = to look, to watch; *fa* = place: Look-out place.

DAN Y GRAIG. Under the rock.

DARREN Y CELYN. Holly ridge.

DYFFRYN. Valley.

EDWARDSVILLE. Named after Mr. Edmund Edwards a property owner.

FFOS Y FRAN. *Ffos* = ditch, *bran* = crow: The crow's ditch.

GARN LAS. *Glas* = blue, green: The green cairn.

GARDDINOS. *Gardd* = garden, *un* = one, *nos* = night: One-night garden. This is another name for Trecatty, and recalls the old Welsh custom of claiming a plot of waste land by enclosing it and erecting a rude hut thereon during one night. A condition of ownership was that smoke had to be issuing from the chimney before daybreak. Many people, therefore, simply built a fire-place and a chimney in the night.

GARTH. Hill, headland, enclosure. See Madoc's Castle.

GALON UCHAF. *Cae* = field, *lon* = lane, *uchaf* = upper: Field of the upper lane.

GARN. *Carn* = Cairn.

GARW. Rough, rocky.

GARTH FAWR. *Garth* = hill, *mawr* = big: The great hill.

GELLIDEG. *Celli* = grove, *teg* = fair: Fair Grove.

GELLIFAELOG. *Celli* = grove: Maelog's Grove. Maelog was an old Welsh saint of princely family, who had, so tradition says, a hermitage in this part of Morlais Valley. He wandered to monasteries in many parts of the country and died in Brittany, where many places are named after him.

GEORGETOWN. This district was named after George Crawshay, grandson of the first William Crawshay.

GILFACH YR ENCIL. *Gilfach* and *encil* = retreat: The retreat of retreats.

GILFACH CYNON. *Cilfach* = retreat: Cynon's Retreat. It is said that Cynon was a son of Rhys ap Tewdwr, and served under his father at the battle of Hirwaun Common. Their forces were defeated and Cynon fled, finding refuge for a time in this district.

GLEBELAND. Land owned by the church authorities.

GLYN DYRYS. *Dyrys* = intricate, tangled: The intricate valley.

GLYN MIL. *Glyn* = valley, *mil* = animals: Animals' valley.

GOITRE COED. Homestead in the wood. '*Coed*' was added later when the original meaning of Goitre had been lost.

GRAIG GETHIN. *Cethin* = hard, severe, dark: The dark, forbidding rock.

Y GRAIG. The Rock.

GURNOS. This word is probably a diminutive form of curn = peak or cairn: Little peak.

GWAELOD Y GARTH. *Gwaelod* = bottom, *garth* = hill: Bottom of the hill.

GRAWEN. (i) *Garw Waen* = rough meadow; (ii) *Crawen* = crust.

GRAIG CWM. *Craig* = rock: The rock in the valley.

GWERN LLWYN. *Gwern* = alder, swamp, *llwyn* = grove: Alder grove. There are two districts in Dowlais with this name, Gwernllwyn *Uchaf* and Gwernllwyn *Fach*.

GWAUNFARREN. *Gwaun* = meadow, *farren* = warren: Warren meadow.

GOITRE (COED-TREF). *Coed* = wood, *tref* = dwelling, homestead: The dwelling in the wood.

HAFOD TANGLWYS(T). *Hafod* = summer residence: The summer residence of Tanglwyst. Tanglwyst was Tydfil's sister. See notes on Hendre Fawr.

HEN DAFARN. The old inn.

HENDRE FAWR. *Hen* = old, *tref* = homestead, *mawr* = large: The large old homestead. In early times it was usual for the well-to-do to have two residences, one for the summer and the other for the winter. This was the winter residence.

LLWYN CELYN. *Llwyn* = grove, bush, *celyn* = holly: Holly grove, holly bush.

LLWYN Y GWCW. *Cwcw* = cuckoo: Cuckoo grove.

LLECH FAEN BICA. *Llech* = slab, *maen* = stone, *pica* = pointed: The pointed slab.

LLWYN YR EOS. Nightingale grove.

LLWYN MOELGOCH. *Llwyn* = grove, *moel* = bare, *coch* = red: The grove at the top of the red, bare hill. Local tradition says that one Moelgoch was a warrior who hid here from his enemies, hence Moelgoch's Grove.

LOCK Y WAUN. Lock meadow. This was the name of one of the locks on the old Glamorganshire Canal.

MADOC'S CASTLE. Madoc ap Hywel was a descendant of Ifor Bach, and some old records state that he was the first of this family to take up permanent residence in this district. He is said to have built a castle on the site of the present Garth Farm, but no trace now remains.

MAEN BRYCH. *Maen* = stone, *brych* = mottled: The mottled stone.

MAES Y GOLLEN. Hazel field.

MELIN CAIACH. Caiach Mill.

MELIN CANAID. *Melin* = mill: The Canaid Mill.

MERTHYR TYDFIL is associated with Tydfil (Tudful), a Christian princess, who was put to a cruel death in 420 or 480 A.D. The Welsh word *Merthyr* comes from the Latin *martyrium*, which means among others: (i) the place where a martyr is buried, and (ii) a church dedicated to a saint. It is in these senses that we have to translate the *Merthyr* in Merthyr Tydfil, which means the burial place of Tydfil, and the church dedicated to Saint Tydfil (Tudful).

MARDY. *Maer* = steward, *tŷ* = house: Steward's house. As this is one of the oldest houses in the district, it probably had, in earlier times, some connection with the Court Estate.

MORLAIS. *Mawr* = great, *glais* = stream: Great stream.

MYNYDD ABERDÂR. *Mynydd* = mountain: Aberdare Mountain.

MYNYDD Y CAPEL. Chapel Mountain.

MYNYDD GETHIN. The dark, or ugly, mountain.

MYNYDD GOITRE COED. Goitre Coed Mountain.

NANT ABERFAN. Aberfan stream.

NANT COTHI. The Cothi stream.

NANT CWM DU. The stream of the black valley.

NANT GRAIG. The valley of the rock.

NANT GWALL. *Gwall* = fault: The valley of the fault (geological).

NANT WERN LAS. *Gwern* = swamp: The stream of the green swamp.

NANT Y FFIN. *Ffin* = boundary: the boundary stream.

NANT YR ODYN. *Odyn* = kiln: The kiln stream.

NANT DDU FACH. The small black stream.

NANT LLWYN YR EOS. The stream of the nightingale grove.

NANT MAFON. Raspberry stream.

NANT CANAID. *Nant* = stream, valley: The Canaid stream.

NANT CWM PANT BACH. The stream in the small hollow valley.

NANT CWM GLO. The coal valley stream.

NANT FFRWD. *Ffrwd* = stream: The valley of the stream.

NANT GAU. (i) *Cau* = hollow: The valley of the hollow; (ii) *Cau* = enclosed: The enclosed valley.

NANT Y GWENITH. *Gwenith* = wheat: Wheat Brook.

NANT TOR GWYN. *Nant* = stream, *tor* = prominence, *gwyn* = white: Steam of the white prominence. This is the name given to the Morlais near its source in the Twynau Gwynion.

NEWFOUNDLAND. At one time this district, with Pontmorlais, formed the valley of the Morlais. In course of time the brook was culverted over, and refuse from the Penydarren Works tipped thereon. This new land subsequently built upon was called Newfoundland.

NIXONVILLE. This is named after John Nixon, one of the first men to realise the value of steam coal. At a great financial risk, he sank the coal pits at Merthyr Vale. See chapter on Coal Trade.

NANT WEN. The white or pure stream.

NANT Y FEDW. Birch stream.

NANT Y MAEN. Stone stream.

OCHR Y MYNYDD. *Ochr* = side: The mountain side.

PAN DŶ. *Pan* = fulling, *tŷ* = house: Fulling house. This was the mill to which the old farmers and weavers took their woollen cloth after weaving, to be properly shrunk and cleaned.

PANT. Hollow.

PANT CADIFOR. Cadifor's Hollow. The name has been split up in other ways to prove an association with Ifor Bach. Thus, as Cad means battle, some people say it means the hollow where Ifor Bach was engaged in battle, but these tales have no proof in fact.

PANT GERDDINEN. *Cerddinen* = mountain ash: Mountain ash hollow.

PANT Y FFIN. *Ffin* = boundary, border: Boundary hollow. There is a spring here, the waters of which are supposed to be good for sore eyes.

PANT YSGALLOG. *Ysgallog* = full of thistles: Thistle dingle.

PANT ANNAS. *Annas* = Agnes: Agnes's hollow.

PANT GLAS. The green, or verdant, hollow.

PANT YR HEN GEFNFFORDD. *Cefnffordd* = highway: The hollow of the old highway.

PEDWRAN FACH. Pedwran is perhaps a corruption of *pedryfan* = a square. The houses were arranged in a square courtyard; hence, the little square.

PEN YARD. *Pen* = top. Top of the yard. The yard referred to was connected with the Penydarren Iron Works.

PEN-YR HEOL-FERTHYR. *Heol* = road. Top of the Merthyr Road. Two hundred years ago this was the chief approach to Merthyr from the outside world.

PEN CAE. *Pen* = top, *cae* = field: Top of the field.

PEN COED CAE. *Coed* = wood: Top of the wooded field.

PEN DDEU CAE. Top of the two fields.

PEN RHIW PORTHMON. *Porthmon* = drover: Top of the drover's hill. This place-name recalls the time when the district was pastoral and the farmers sent their flocks to fairs and markets to be sold.

PERTHI GLEISION. The green or verdant bushes.

*PEN BWLCHA. Top of the gaps or passes.

PEN LOCKS. Top of the locks.

PEN Y GRAIG. Top of the rock.

PEN TWYN BERTH LWYD. Top of the grey bush hill.

PEN TWYN DEINTYR. *Deintur* = tenter: Top of the tenter hill. The tenter is a machine for stretching cloth, which is attached to hooks. We still speak of tenter hooks. Here the cloth made in the factory near by was washed and stretched after washing. The name recalls the time when there were many such factories in the district.

PEN CAE BACH. Top of the small field.

PEN DDEU CAE FACH. Top of the two small fields.

PEN Y LAN. *Glan* = bank: Top of the bank.

PEN RHIW'R ONNEN. *Rhiw* = slope, *onnen* = ash: Top of the ash slope.

PENTRE BACH. *Pentre* – village: Small village. It was given this name in the early days of the iron industry, when the Plymouth works were flourishing, to distinguish it from Merthyr, which was called Y Pentre.

PEN WAUN PWLL GWELLT. *Gwellt* = reeds: Top of the reedy pool moor.

PEN Y GARN DDU. *Pen* = top, *carn* = cairn, *du* = black: Top of the black cairn.

PEN Y WERN. *Gwern* = swamp: Top of the swamp.

PEN Y WAUN FAWR. *Gwaun* = moor, *mawr* = great: Top of the big moor.

PEN Y BRYN. *Pen* = head, *bryn* = hill: Top of the hill.
PEN Y DARREN. This was originally the name of an old farmhouse, which gave its name to the district around. *Tarren* = wild rough land in midst of good land. Therefore 'top of piece of wild land'.
PEN YR HEOL GERRIG. *Heol* = road, *cerrig* = stones: Top of the stony road.
PEN LLWYN DERI. *Deri* = oak: Top of the oak grove.
PEN COED CAE. *Pen* = top, *coed* = wood, *cae* = field: Top of the wooded fields.
PEN CAE MAWR. Top of the big field.
PEN Y GARN. Top of the cairn.
PEN YR YNYS. *Ynys* = island, water-meadow: Top of the water-meadow.
PIT WELLT. *Gwellt* = straw, grass, sward: Grassy pit.
PLAS. Palace, mansion, place.
PLAS Y COED. *Plas* = hall. The hall in the wood. (Mansion)
PLYMOUTH. This name was given to the works in 1763 because the land was leased from the Earl of Plymouth, who had inherited it by marriage from a descendant of Ifor Bach. In later times the name has been given to one of the borough wards.
PONT MORLAIS. *Pont* = bridge: Morlais Bridge.
PONTSTICILL. The bridge of the stile. An older name was Y Garn (Cairn).
PONT Y CAFNAU. *Pont* = bridge, *cafn* = trough: Bridge of troughs.
PONT Y DDERWEN. Oak Bridge.
PONT Y GWAITH. This place name is linked with one of the earliest iron-works in the district.
PONT Y GWAITH. The work's bridge. This refers to a bridge which led to the old iron-works.
PONT RHUN. Rhun's Bridge.
PONT SARN. *Pont* = bridge, *sarn* = causeway: The bridge of the causeway. An older form is Pont-y-Sarn-Hir, the bridge of the long causeway. This was where the Roman road leading from the fort at Penydarren to the Gaer (Brecon) crossed the Taf Fechan.
PONT SQUIRE. Squire's bridge.
PWLL GLAS. *Glas* = blue: Blue pool.
PWLL MAWN. *Mawn* = peat: The peat pit or bog.
PWLL WAT. *Pwll* = pool: Wat's Pool. Watkin George was an engineer at the Cyfarthfa Works. He designed the Iron Bridge which was constructed in 1800.
PWLL YR HWYAID. *Pwll* = pool, *hwyaid* = ducks: Ducks' pool.
QUAKERS' YARD. This was one of the first Quaker meeting places in Wales. A plot of land was given to them in 1667, as a burial ground. See Rhyd y Grug.
QUAR. Quarry.
RHYD Y CERRIG LLWYD. The ford of grey stones.
RHYD Y GRUG. Heather ford. This was the old name for Quakers' Yard.
RHYD Y CAR. *Rhyd* = ford, *car* = cart, carriage: The ford for carts.
TAI BACH. Small houses.
TAI HARRI BLAWD. *Tai* = houses, *blawd* = meal: Harry the Meal's houses.
TAI MAWR. *Tai* = houses, *mawr* = big: Big Houses. See Religious History Chapter.
TAI'R ONNEN. Ash houses.
TAI'R EFAIL. *Tai* = houses, *gefail* = smithy: Smithy houses.
TARREN Y GIGFRAN. The Raven's wild ground.

THOMAS TOWN. So called after Dr. Thomas, who became the owner of the Court Estate.
TIR COOK. Cook's land. Cook was one of the first English iron-masters to settle in the parish.
TIR ISAF. Lower land.
TIR LAN. Bank land.
TON Y FFALD. (i) *Ton* = broken land, meadow, *ffald* = fold: The meadow of the fold; (ii) *Ton* = sward: Sward fold.
TREBEDDAU. *Tref* = homestead, *beddau* = graves: Homestead of graves.
TRE CAE. *Tref* = town, homestead, *cae* = field: Homestead field.
TRE CATTY. Kate's homestead.
TREFECHAN. Small town, note Taf Fechan.
TRELEWIS. Named after William Lewis of Llwyngolau farm.
TREHARRIS. Harris's town. A Mr. Harris sank the Navigation Pits here and the village that grew up was named after him.
TROED Y RHIW. *Troed* = foot, *rhiw* = hill, slope: Foot of the hill.
TWYN BRYN BYCHAN. The knoll on the small hillock.
TWYN GWERSYLLFA. *Twyn* = hill, *gwersyllfa* = encampment: The encampment hill.
TWYNAU GWYNION. *Twyn* = hill, *gwyn* = white: White Hills. These are composed largely of limestone, hence the *white.*
TWYN Y WAUN. The hill of the meadow or moor.
TWYN-YR-ODYN. *Twyn* = hillock, *odyn* = kiln: The hillock of the kiln.
TWYN SYCH. *Sych* = dry: Dry hillock.
TYLA HAIDD. *Tyla (tyle)* = slope, mound, hill, *haidd* = barley: Barley slope or hill.
TŶ'R NYTH. Nest House.
TŶ YN Y COED CAE. (i) *Tŷ* = house: The house in the wooded field; (ii) *Tyddyn y Coed Cae* = Small farm in wooded field.
TWYN Y GARREG. Rock hillock. This was the original name of Treharris.
TŶ'N CAE. The homestead in the field.
TŶ LLWYD. Grey house.
TŶ LLWYN. Grove house.
TŶ NEWYDD. New house.
VAYNOR. *Maenor* = manor: Possibly *Y Maenor Wynno* = Manor House of Gwynno.
WAUN WYLLT. *Gwaun* = meadow, moor; *gwyllt* = wild: The wild meadow.
WERN LAS. Green swamp. *Gwern* = wet ground.
WILLIAM'S TOWN. This district is named after Willam Crawshay, brother of George Crawshay, whose name appears in Georgetown.
WINCH FAWR. Big Winch.
YNYS FACH. The little water meadow. Some famous furnaces were built here by the Crawshays in 1801.
YNYS GAU. *Ynys* = water-meadow, *cau* = enclosed: The enclosed water-meadow.
YNYS Y GORED. *Cored* = weir: The water meadow of the weir.
YNYS HIR. The long water-meadow.
YNYS OWEN. This is the old name for Merthyr Vale. (i) Owen's water meadow. Old stories associate the place with Owen Glyndwr; (ii) *Owen (ywen)* = yew: Yew water-meadow.
YSGUBOR NEWYDD. *Ysgubor* = barn, *newydd* = new: New barn.

Pre-Publication Subscribers

Printed here are the names of individuals and agencies who generously ordered copies of this book prior to publication and so helped the project to completion.

The Editorial Board acknowledges with sincere thanks these advance orders without which the publication would not have been possible.

VICTOR JONES
Chairman Editorial Board

E A Abraham
A E M Adams
K Adams Morgan
R Adler
J Alford
Mr & Mrs W Allman
G Andrew-Reid
P Atkinson
M Attwood
D D Aubrey
M Aylward
P D Ayres
K J Ball
H Balleisen
S Bann
G Barber
K Barbero
A Barnard
S Barnard
G J Barrett
P A Bater
R Benjamin
D H C Bennett
J Bennett
Joyce Bennett
J H Bennett
M Bennett
R Bennett
Mr & Mrs J M Berridge
A Best
A J Bevan
L E Bevan
M R & M R G Bevan
J A Beynon
E Bigham
P Billings
R Bishop
D Blackmore
B & J Blair
J Blunt
M Blunt
Mr & Mrs F Booth
N Bowden
C A Bowen
D M Bowen
P Bowen
S Bowen
P Bracegirdle
F J Bradley
N J Brill
I Brown
J Bryant
E H Bullock
N P Burke
A Burns
A Bush
R Bush
S Bush
M Butcher
F Butler
M Byard
D Campbell
R R Campbell
Mr & Mrs I Carbin
R Carbin
B M Carston
J & K Caswell
Keith Caswell
J A Caudle
J M Caudle
G H Chamberla
N M Chamberl
M Chambers
R Chandler
M A Chappell
D E Chennells
P Chidgey
Mr & Mrs G C
J Cleary
L Clee
V Clement
J Clifford
C Cole
M Cole
M Collins
S Collins
A H Collinson
J Cook

V Cooke
Coombs
E Coombs
Cootes
Corke
Coughlin
A Criddle
n Crimmings
e Crimmings
Crimmings
ry Crimmings
chael Crimmings
rowe
uff
Daley
Daniel
Daniel
J Daniel
aniels
nne Dauncy
C Davies
H Davies
Davies
Davies
C & M A Davies
E Davies
H G Davies
L Davies
P Davies
S Davies
Davies
M Davies
R Davies
Davies
L Davies
Davies
M Davies
on Davies
et Davies
avies
I Davies
& Mrs J B Davies
Davies
elwyn Davies
J Davies
isie Davies
Davies
rk Davies
Ll. Davies
& I Davies
ureen Davies
V Davies
& Mrs N Davies
Davies
N B Davies
P Davies
P A Davies
P W Davies
Rachel Davies
Richard Davies
Royston Davies
Ronald Davies
Shirley Davies
Sylvia Davies
S O Davies
T Davies
V Davies
V E Davies
V & V Davies
W & B Davies
H J Dawkins
L S L Deas
M Deasy
M Delaney
M E Dennis
R Denyer
M Dewland
A Doolan
A P Downey
G Durston
J Edwards
Hugh Edwards
Julia Edwards
V Edwards
W E Edwards
J & D Elias
B Elliott
I Ellis
V Ellis
A Estabanez
A Evans
Mr & Mrs A Evans
A J Evans
A V Evans
B Evans
C Evans
Mr & Mrs C Evans
C W Evans
D Evans
Mr & Mrs D Evans
D H Evans
D K Evans
D N Evans
Elizabeth Evans
Emlyn Evans
E R Evans
Mr & Mrs G Evans
G Evans
Geraint Evans
Glenise Evans
Glenys Evans
G L Evans
G M Evans
I B Evans
Janice Evans
Judith Evans
J Evans
J & L Evans
J O Evans
K Evans
L Evans
Mr & Mrs L Evans
M & S Evans
N A Evans
Roy Evans
Ruth Evans
T Evans
T C Evans
T I Evans
V Evans
W B Evans
G M Everitt
J Everson
M Farrar
E Farrell
J P Fearn
P J Fearn
J Felton
D Flye
Thelma Flye
D S Foley
Mr & Mrs E Foley
C Fontaine
J Ford
L Ford
N Ford
A Foster
D Foster
Gareth Foster
Mr & Mrs A Francis-Williams
D M Francis
David Francis
E Frederick
P French
Mr & Mrs J Fry
Mr & Mrs M Fry
P Fullalove
H Fuller
Mr & Mrs A E Galleozzie
J Garland
L J George
D Gerlach
D R Gethin
Dr G Gethin
J Glencross
Mr & Mrs P C Glencross
S Goggin
A Gough
C Gough
D S Gough
R & S Gray
B Griffiths
B E Griffiths
B L Griffiths
D G Griffiths
G Griffiths
M Griffiths
P Griffiths
R Griffiths
R & B Griffiths
W J Griffiths
E Grint
J Gross
J Guard
K Gunter
L Gunter
L D Gunter
M Gunter
N K Gunter
M S Gwynne
S Haines
J Hagerty
I Hales
K Hall
B Hallisey
N Hamer
P C Hancock
I Handley
D Handy
A F Harrhy
E Harrhy
G Harwood
M J Harris
Myrddin Harris
R Hatton
D Haverson
V Hawkins
E Hayes
C, I & P Haynes
J Head
S & M Hedges
L C Hickey
S Hier
T S Heir

A Hill
V Hill
D Hinks
F Holley
C Hooper
Mr & Mrs G A Hooper
R Hooper
C Hopkins
G Hopkins
I R Hopkins
K S Hopkins
N & J Horne
M M Horvath
J Hourihan
Judith Howard
A Howells
B Howells
D Howells
R Howells
J Howes
C Hughes
G A Hughes
G T Hughes
S A Hughes
V Hughes
W & M Hughes
P Hunt
M Hurley
E Ikin
Alvin Isaac
J Isaac
M Iverson
A James
David T James
Derek James
G H James
G H James
H James
J James
K James
L James
L P James
P James
S James
S T R James
W D James
Sian Jarman
Susan Jarman
Mr & Mrs D L Jarrett
A Jenkins
M Jenkins
M E Jenkins
M J Jenkins
M N Jenkins
N Jennings
R John
V Jonathan
Adrian Jones
Ann Jones
A E Jones
B Jones
Barrie Jones
B W Jones
C Jones
C A Jones
Mr & Mrs C T Jones
Mr & Mrs D Jones
Daryl Jones
D Jones
D C W Jones
Mr & Mrs D E F Jones
D L Jones
Don Jones
D S Jones
D & S Jones
David T Jones
D W Jones
E Jones
Enid Jones
Erastus Jones
Eveline Jones
E J Jones
E W Jones
G Jones
Gareth Jones
Glyn Jones
Gwilym Jones
Gwyn Jones
H Jones
H G Jones
Iain Jones
Idris Jones
J B Jones
J Jones
Janet Jones
Mr & Mrs L J Jones
J M Jones
Joan Jones
Karen Jones
Kevin Jones
K G Jones
K J Jones
K, K & K Jones
L Jones
Lynette Jones
M Jones
Mary Jones
Margaret Jones
Marian Jones
M A Jones
M E Jones
M I Jones
M J Jones
M K Jones
P Jones
Paula Jones
P A Jones
P W Jones
R Jones
R & L Jones
S Jones
S L Jones
S S Jones
T Jones
Mr & Mrs T Eyton Jones
Tudor Jones
V Jones
W Jones
W J Jones
W T Jones
C Judge
H & S Kalami
J C Karn
R Keen
E Y Kidgell
R G King
E Kinsey
J Knight
C & M Knibbs
M Krol
B Lawrence
D S Lee
E O Leese
S Legge
Allison Lewis
A Lewis
Ann Lewis
Barbara Lewis
Brychan Lewis
C E Lewis
C & N Lewis
D Lewis
D M Lewis
E Lewis
E E Lewis
Mr & Mrs G Lewis
G Lewis
G & C Lewis
I M Lewis
J A Lewis
M Lewis
M L Lewis
M M Lewis
M P Lewis
P Lewis
P A Lewis
P M Lewis
R Lewis
R D Lewis
T Lewis
W J Lewis
W M Lewis
W R Lewis
J R Leyshon
G Leyshon
P Leyshon
D S Littlewood
C Llewellyn
G Llewellyn
E P Lloyd
F Lloyd
G L Lloyd
H Lloyd
M & L Lloyd
M Lloyd
T Long
K Lowry
Gareth Lynne
Geraint Lynne
G B McAleer
Mr & Mrs D McCarthy
S M McNally
J Maddock
P Maher
Mr & Mrs J D Mahoney
N Manley
M Mansfield
F March
B Martin
T & L Martin
Mr & Mrs W Ma Jones
E Martin Jones
Mr & Mrs R May
C A Mazey
G D J Mazey
P & S Mazumdar
M P Meadows
S Mee
N M Meredith
R Miles
R Mills
T Minoli

A Mitchell
H Mitchell
P Mitchell
D Moakes
B Mochan
A Moore
C Morgan
C A Morgan
D Morgan
D E Morgan
D W Morgan
E C Morgan
E L Morgan
G Morgan
G J Morgan
G W Morgan
H Morgan
H E Morgan
I Morgan
J E Morgan
K Morgan
M Morgan
Mair Morgan
M E Morgan
N Morgan
N L Morgan
R Morgan
Rhian Morgan
Rosemary Morgan
R T Morgan
S Morgan
W Morgan
William Morgan
W S Morgan
O Morgans
B J Morris
M Morris
E M Morse
J Murray
R Murray
K Neill
D Newman
S Newman
N Nolan
A Norman
Mr & Mrs D A Northover
Mr & Mrs G O'Connell
E M O'Driscoll
J O'Driscoll
Gavin O'Hanlon
K O'Shea
M T O'Sullivan
D I J Oakley
G W A Oates
Mr & Mrs K Oates
C J Oliver
A Owen
G Owen
J Owen
M Owen
M M Owen
S Owens
V Owens
P Packer
A R Parry
C Parry
G Parry
I Parry
J M Payne
Mr & Mrs T Pearsey
D Pearson
R Pendry
L Perkins
A Peters
A Phillips
C M Phillips
G Phillips
H Phillips
J Phillips
M & G Phillips
P Phillips
M Pierce
C Pope
A D Powell
C Powell
Claire Powell
D Powell
E Powell
J Powell
J N & J A Powell
O Powell
R G Powell
A J Power
M Pratt
D J Preece
C R Preston
C Price
C M Price
M Price
T Price
W S Price
Mr & Mrs J
Price Thomas
R Probert
A Prosser
D Prosser
M Prosser
E Protheroe
Mr & Mrs W S
Protheroe
M Prowle
C L Pugh
N Pugh
R I Pugh
J R Pugsley
E Quirk
G Rafferty
H J Ras
S A Rasbridge
W T Rasbridge
Annette Rawden
H Raynes
G A Reed
L Reed
Rosemary Reed
Russell Reed
A M Rees
C Rees
D Rees
G Rees
Grahame Rees
G T Rees
H Rees
H G Rees
I Glyn Rees
Islwyn G Rees
K D Rees
M Rees
P Rees
A C Reynolds
L Rhydderch
B P Richards
E Richards
H P & L Richards
M Richards
C Richardson
J Richardson
A Roberts
C Roberts
D Roberts
Dean Roberts
Emrys Roberts
Mrs E. Roberts
G Roberts
G W Roberts
I Roberts
M Roberts
T W Roberts
Z Roberts
S M Robinson
M A Rosser
P Rosser
B Rowe
A M Rowlands
K Salter
L Samuel
E Sankey
R Santos
Mrs Sarll
A Scott Thomas
D J Scully
S Scully
S J Scully
V C Selby
Mr & Mrs T E Seldon
R Selway
J R Sellwood
L N Sharp
R H Sims
D Singer
J & G Smallwood
A Smith
D A Smith
E M Smith
G Smith
Geraint Smith
Gillian Smith
H Smith
C Snook
J Spurle
D Stafford
F B Stanfield
M & E Star
P & J Star
Mr & Mrs C Steadman
G Steadman
Roy Stephens
C Strange
V Strange
A Sullivan
D Sullivan
E Sullivan
J L Sullivan
L Sullivan
Michael Sullivan
M Sullivan
P D Sweet
M Tasker
R Taylor
Rosemary Taylor
E Tedstone
A Thomas
A D Thomas
A G Thomas
A W Thomas
B R Thomas

C Thomas
Clive Thomas
Craig Thomas
C D Thomas
Mr & Mrs D C Thomas
D F Thomas
Mr & Mrs D G Thomas
D W Thomas
E Thomas
G Thomas
Gareth Thomas
Gaynor Thomas
G G Thomas
G K Thomas
H & S Thomas
Mr & Mrs I Thomas
I M Thomas
J Thomas
Jill Thomas
Joan Thomas
Mr & Mrs K Thomas
Kitty Thomas
L Thomas
M Thomas
Margaret Thomas
Marlene Thomas
N Thomas
O M Thomas
R L Thomas
R M Thomas
R V Thomas
Mr & Mrs R Thomas
S Thomas
U A Thomas
W Thomas
W A Thomas
W & S Thomas
J I Timbrell
C J Tinsley
E A Tonge
I Trailor
C Trewartha
B Tucker
R Tucker
W D Tudor
W Tuthill
C Type
C Vaughan
F Vaughan
P Vaughan
R Vaughan
S J Vowles
E Wall
Mr & Mrs R J Wallen
M S Walsh
T B Walsh
A Walters
D Ll. Walters
J Walters
Havard Walters
J Warburton
R Ward
A Watkins
A S Watkins
Mr & Mrs D Watkins
D Watkins
E & E Watkins
G Watkins
Mr & Mrs H Watkins
H Watkins
M Watkins
N Watkins
N A Watkins
Mr & Mrs G Webb
R & L Weekes
M & L Wheeler
S Wheeler
H G Whitehead
D Wiggins
M Wilding
R O Wilding
T Wilding
A Wilson
J Wilson
A Williams
B Williams
B & A Williams
C Williams
C R Williams
D G Williams
Eluned Williams
Eironwen Williams
Ethel Williams
F Williams
G M Williams
H Williams
H L Williams
I V Williams
J Williams
Janice Williams
Jean Williams
J A Williams
J J Williams
K Williams
L Williams
Mari Williams
Muriel Williams
M E Williams
N M Williams
P Williams
P G Williams
P L Williams
R L Williams
R M Williams
R V Williams
S W Williams
T H Williams
W Williams
W J Williams
J Wilson
I & L Wiltshire
W Wyn
S Yeo

Merthyr Tydfil Borough Council
Merthyr Tydfil Borough Library
Merthyr Tydfil Historical Society
Mid Glamorgan County Council
Mid Glamorgan Community Services Agency, Treharris
Mid Glamorgan County Library
National Union of Teachers
Simbec Research Laboratories

Cynon Valley District Education Office

Aberaman Primary School
Abercynon Infants School
Abernant Primary School
Abertaf Primary School
Caegarw Primary School
Capcoch Primary School
Cwmbach Infants School
Cwmdar Primary School
Glenboi Primary School
Glynhafod Junior School
Gwernifro Junior School
Hirwaun Junior School
Penderyn Primary School
Pengeulan Primary School
Penrhiwceiber Junior School
Rhigos Primary School
Town Church in Wales Junior School
Town Church in Wales Infants School
Ynysboeth Junior School
Ysgol Gynradd Gymraeg, Aberdâr
Ysgol Maesgwyn
Aberdare Boys' Comprehensive School
Aberdare Girls' Comprehensive School
Blaengwawr Comprehensive School
Mountain Ash Upper Comprehensive School
Abertaf Lower Comprehensive School
Aberdare College of Further Education

Merthyr Tydfil District Education Office

Gurnos Nursery School
Trefechan Nursery School
Treharris Nursery School
Ynysowen Nursery School

Abercanaid Primary School
Bedlinog Junior School
Bedlinog Infants School
Brecon Road Infants School
Caedraw Primary School
Cyfarthfa Junior School
Dowlais Infants School
Edwardsville Junior School
Edwardsville Infant School
Gellideg Junior School
Gellideg Infants School
Gellifaelog Junior School
Gellifaelog Infants School
Goetre Junior School
Goetre Infants School
Graig Bedlinog Infants School
Gwaunfarren Primary School
Gwernllwyn Junior School
Heolgerrig Primary School
Mount Pleasant Primary School
Pant Primary School
Pentrebach Infants School
Trelewis Primary School
Troedyrhiw Junior School
Troedyrhiw Infants School
Twynyrodyn Junior School
Ysgol Rhyd y Grug
Ynysowen Junior School
Ynysowen Infants School
Ysgol y Graig Junior
Ysgol y Graig Infants
Ysgol Santes Tudful
St Illtyd's RC Primary School
St Aloysius RC Primary School
St Mary's RC Primary School

Bishop Hedley RC High School
Afon Taf High School
Cyfarthfa High (Upper) School
Cyfarthfa High (Lower) School
Pen y Dre High School
Vaynor and Penderyn Comprehensive School
Greenfield Special School
Merthyr Tydfil Technical College

Taff Ely District Education Office

Abercerdin Primary School
Brynnau Primary School
Cefn Primary School
Cilfynydd Primary School
Coed-pen-maen Primary School
Coed-y-lan Primary School
Coed-yr-esgob Primary School
Craig-yr-hesg Primary School
Creigiau Primary School

Cwm-lai Junior School
Dolau Primary School
Ffynnon-taf Primary School
Graig-y-wion Primary School
Gwaelod-y-garth Primary School
Gwauncelyn Junior School
Gwaunmeisgyn Junior School
Hawthorn Primary School
Hendreforgan Junior School
Hendreforgan Infants School
Heol-y-celyn Primary School
Llanharan Primary School
Llanhari Primary School
Llanilltud Faerdref Junior School
Llwyn-crwn Primary School
Maes-y-bryn Primary School
Maes-y-coed Primary School
Parclewis Primary School
Pentyrch Primary School
Penygawsi Primary School
Pont Sion Norton Primary School
Pont-y-clun Primary School
St Michael's RC Primary School
Tonyrefail Primary School
Tonysguboriau Primary School
Trefforest Junior School
Tref-y-rhyg Primary School
Trehopcyn Primary School
Trerobart Primary School
Y. G. G. Garth Olwg
Y. G. G. Llantrisant
Y. G. G. Pont Sion Norton
Y. G. G. Tonyrefail
Bryn Celynnog Comprehensive School
Coed-y-lan Comprehensive School
Hawthorn Comprehensive School
Newman RC Comprehensive School
Tonyrefail Comprehensive School
Y Pant Comprehensive School

Rhymney Valley District Education Office

Plas y Felin Junior School

Teachers' Centre

Ogwr Teachers' Centre
Rhondda Educational Centre
Cynon Valley Teachers' Centre
Merthyr Tydfil Teachers' Centre
Rhymney Valley Teachers' Centre
Taff Ely Teachers' Centre

Index